Clinical Assessment and Diagnosis in Social Work Practice

Clinical Assessment and Diagnosis in Social Work Practice

Second Edition

JACQUELINE CORCORAN

JOSEPH WALSH

OXFORD
UNIVERSITY PRESS

2010

OXFORD
UNIVERSITY PRESS

Oxford University Press, Inc., publishes works that further
Oxford University's objective of excellence
in research, scholarship, and education.

Oxford   New York
Auckland   Cape Town   Dar es Salaam   Hong Kong   Karachi
Kuala Lumpur   Madrid   Melbourne   Mexico City   Nairobi
New Delhi   Shanghai   Taipei   Toronto

With offices in
Argentina   Austria   Brazil   Chile   Czech   Republic France   Greece
Guatemala   Hungary   Italy   Japan   Poland   Portugal   Singapore
South Korea   Switzerland   Thailand   Turkey   Ukraine   Vietnam

Library of Congress Cataloging-in-Publication Data
Corcoran, Jacqueline.
Clinical assessment and diagnosis in social work practice /
Jacqueline Corcoran, Joseph Walsh. — 2nd ed.
p.   ;   cm.
Includes bibliographical references and index.
ISBN 978-0-19-539886-1
1. Mental illness—Classification.   2. Mental illness—Diagnosis.
3. Diagnostic and statistical manual of mental disorders.   4. Psychiatric social
work.   5. Social service.   I. Walsh, Joseph (Joseph F.)   II. Title.
[DNLM: 1. Diagnostic and statistical manual of mental disorders. 2. Social Work,
Psychiatric—methods. 3. Mental Disorders—classification. 4. Mental
Disorders—diagnosis. WM 30.5 C793c 2010]
RC455.2.C4C72 2010
616.89′075—dc22
2009037721

9   8   7   6

To my parents, Myra and Patrick Corcoran
                    —Jacqueline

To Ruth and Gus Simpson, for their kindness and
support over so many years
                    —Joe

ACKNOWLEDGMENTS

We wish to acknowledge the valuable help of several students and professionals who offered case studies and assisted with other material in chapters: Jennifer Crowell, Vicki Cash Graff, Marty Ford, Angela Gannon, Catherine Johnson, Liat Katz, Sarah Koch, Susan Munford, Susan Parrott, Benjamin Smith, Silvana Starowlansky-Kaufman, Candace Strother, and Amy Waldbillig. Thank you particularly to Jessica Jagger, whom we credit with the revision of the measures appendices for each of the chapters. Jennifer Shadik was instrumental in revising the adult anxiety measures. Further, we are very appreciative to Christine Bates for her diligence in completing reference lists. Finally, we extend our thanks to Patrick Corcoran for his painstaking proofreading efforts and hard work.

CONTENTS

Clinical Assessment and Diagnosis in Social Work Practice

1   Introduction

Social workers in clinical settings need to demonstrate facility with client diagnosis. The *Diagnostic and Statistical Manual of Mental Disorders* (*DSM*) is the preeminent diagnostic classification system among clinical practitioners in this country. Knowledge of the *DSM* is critical so that social workers can be conversant with other mental health professionals and are eligible to receive reimbursement for services they deliver. The challenge for a social work book on mental, emotional, and behavior disorders is to teach social workers competence and critical thinking in the diagnostic process, while also considering diagnosis in a way that is consistent with social work values and principles. These values include a strengths-based orientation, concern for the worth and dignity of individuals, and an appreciation for the environmental context of individual behavior.

To meet these challenges, this book will integrate several perspectives:

- The *DSM*
- A critique of the *DSM*
- The risk and resilience biopsychosocial framework
- Evidence-based practice
- Measurement tools for assessment and evaluation
- A life-span approach

Here we discuss in general terms how these perspectives affect social work diagnosis and how they are integrated into the book.

The *DSM*

The *DSM* catalogs, codes, and describes the various mental disorders recognized by the American Psychiatric Association (APA). The manual was first published in 1952 and has undergone continual revisions during the past 50 years. The latest version is *DSM-IV-TR* (text revision), published in 2000 (APA, 2000). The *DSM-V* should be published in the next few years, although a release date has not been announced as of this writing.

Much of the terminology from the *DSM* has been adopted by mental health professionals from all fields as a common language with which to discuss disorders. Chapter 2 provides much more information on the history of the *DSM*. Other chapters cover many of the mental, behavioral, and emotional disorders found in the *DSM*. The disorders that were selected for inclusion are those that social workers may encounter in their employment or field settings.

Critique of the *DSM*

Despite the widespread use of the *DSM*, critiques have emerged from social work and related professions. These are covered in more detail in Chapter 2. They include the *DSM*'s lack of emphasis on environmental influences on human behavior (Kutchins & Kirk, 1997). Social work considers the reciprocal impact of people and their environments in assessing human behavior. From this perspective, problems in social functioning might result from stressful life transitions, relationship difficulties, or environmental unresponsiveness. None of these situations needs to assume the presence or absence of "normal" or "abnormal" personal characteristics. In this volume we offer a critique of the diagnosis for each disorder, usually applying to the *DSM* diagnosis.

Risk and Resilience Biopsychosocial Framework

In response to the critique that the *DSM* tends to view mental disorders as arising from pathology inherent to the individual, *Clinical Assessment and Diagnosis in Social Work Practice* draws on the *risk and resilience biopsychosocial framework*. Risk and resilience considers the balance of risk and protective processes at the biological, psychological, and social levels that interact to determine an individual's propensity toward *resilience*, or the ability to function adaptively and achieve positive outcomes despite stressful life events. The strengths perspective underlies the concept of "resilience" in that resilient people not only are able to survive and endure but also can triumph over difficult life circumstances.

Risks, on the other hand, can be understood as hazards or problems at the biological, psychological, or social levels that may lead to poor adaptation (Bogenschneider, 1996). *Protective factors* may counterbalance or buffer against risk (Pollard, Hawkins, & Arthur, 1999; Werner, 2000), promoting successful adjustment in the face of risk (Dekovic, 1999). Risk and protective factors are sometimes the converse of each other. For instance, at the individual level, difficult temperament is a risk factor, and easy temperament is a protective factor. Indeed, researchers have found many pairs of risk and protective factors that are negatively correlated with each other (Jessor, Van Den Bos, Vanderryn, Costa, & Turbin, 1997).

The biopsychosocial emphasis expands the focus beyond the individual to a recognition of systemic factors that can create and ameliorate problems. The nature of systems is that the factors within and between them have influence on each other. For instance, the presence of a certain risk or protective factor may increase the likelihood of other risk and protective factors. Wachs (2000) provides the example of how an aversive parenting style with poor monitoring increases children's risk for socializing with deviant peers. If parents are overwhelmed by many environmental stressors, such as unemployment, lack of transportation and medical care, and living in an unsafe neighborhood, their ability to provide consistent warmth and nurturance may be compromised. This phenomenon also operates for protective factors. For example, adolescents whose parents provide emotional support and structure the environment with consistent rules and monitoring tend to group with peers who share similar family backgrounds (Steinberg, 2001). Supportive parenting will, in turn, affect the characteristics of the child in that, through receiving it, he or she learns to regulate emotional processes and develop cognitive and social competence (Wachs, 2000). Systemic influences also play themselves out from the perspective of a child's characteristics. A child who has resilient qualities, such as social skills, effective coping strategies, intelligence, and self-esteem, is more likely to attract high-quality caregiving, and attachment patterns formed in infancy tend to persist into other relationships across the life span.

Although precise mechanisms of action are not specified, data have begun to accumulate about the number of risk factors that are required to overwhelm a system and result in negative outcomes (e.g., Fraser, Richman, & Galinsky, 1999; Kalil & Kunz, 1999). The cumulative results of different studies seem to indicate that four or more risk factors represent a threat to adaptation (Kalil & Kunz, 1999; Runyan et al., 1998; Rutter, Maugham, Mortimore, & Ouston, 1979). However, risk does not proceed in a linear fashion, and all risk factors are not weighted equally (Greenberg, Speltz,

DeKlyen, & Jones, 2001). Furthermore, the amount of risk has a stronger relation to variation in problem behavior than the amount of protection has (Dekovic, 1999).

The chapters in this book delineate the unique risk and protective factors that have been identified from the research for both the initial onset of a particular disorder, as well as an individual's adjustment or recovery from that disorder. This second edition provides updated information on all these influences. Some of the risk and protective factors discussed in each chapter are not specific to that particular disorder; in other words, certain risk and protective factors play a role in multiple disorders. In a prevention and intervention sense, these common risk factors occurring across multiple domains are good targets for reduction or amelioration, and these protective factors are good targets for enhancement.

Case examples illustrate how the risk and resilience biopsychosocial framework can be used for assessment, goal formulation, and intervention planning. The focus is the micro (individual and family) level of practice.

Evidence-Based Practice and Measurement

Evidence-based practice (EBP) began in medicine in the early 1990s (Sackett et al., 1997) and was defined as the integration of the best available research knowledge with clinical expertise and consumer values. In other words, evidence-based treatment is a process of using research knowledge to make decisions about intervening with particular clients. The process of gathering the available research knowledge involves formulating specific questions, locating the relevant studies, assessing their credibility, and integrating credible results with findings from previous studies (Sackett et al., 1997). In the current environment, however, the term "evidence-based" has come to mean that there is an empirical basis to treatments and services (Zlotnik, 2007). The process of clinical decision making according to EBP is therefore distinguished from the product, which involves compilations of the research evidence (Proctor, 2007). In this book, we provide compilations of the evidence for best treatment for each disorder. We will mainly rely upon systematic reviews and meta-analyses for our evidence basis. These will be briefly defined here, although more information is available in Littel, Corcoran, and Pillai (2008).

A *systematic review* aims to comprehensively locate and synthesize the research that bears on a particular question, using organized, transparent, and replicable procedures at each step in the process (Littel et al., 2008). *Meta-analysis* is a set of statistical methods for combining quantitative results from multiple studies to produce an overall summary of empirical knowledge on a given topic. Results of the original studies are converted to one or more common metrics, called effect sizes, which reveal the strength or magnitude of the relationships between variables. In meta-analysis, effect sizes are calculated for each study, weighted by sample size, and then averaged to produce an overall effect. The most commonly discussed effect size in this book will be the *standardized mean difference* (SMD), also known as *Cohen's d* (Cohen, 1988), which is the mean difference divided by the pooled standard deviation of the two groups. For the SMD, a negligible effect ranges from 0.0 to 0.2; a small effect ranges between 0.2 and 0.5; a medium effect ranges from 0.5 to 0.8; and a large effect is greater than 0.8 (Cohen, 1988).

Whenever possible, we relied on Cochrane Collaboration systematic reviews for treatment evidence for our mental health disorders. The Cochrane Collaboration is an international, nonprofit organization devoted to high-caliber systematic reviews on health and mental health care (see http://www.cochrane.org). Other published systematic reviews and meta-analyses are discussed in this volume in the absence of Cochrane reviews, although the criteria for their inclusion were use of conventional and up-to-date meta-analytic techniques.

Another part of evidence-based practice involves using evidence to assess people for the presence of mental disorders and to determine that they are responding in the desired way to intervention. For this second component of evidence-based practice, information on measurement tools for particular disorders is presented in each chapter. Social workers can use these measures as appropriate to assess the effects of their practice. This book emphasizes client self-report measures and ones that do not involve specialized training on the part of the social worker.

A Life-Span Approach

This book is organized according to a life-span approach, which means that disorders typically appearing in childhood and adolescence are discussed first, followed by those with an onset in adulthood, and then those that begin in older age. Despite the assignment of disorders to different phases of the life span, each chapter shows how the particular disorder is manifested across the life span, with accompanying assessment and intervention considerations.

The section on childhood includes autism, mental retardation, oppositional defiant disorder, attention-deficit/hyperactivity disorder, posttraumatic stress disorder, and anxiety disorders. Most of these disorders begin in childhood. However, conduct disorder may begin either in childhood or in the adolescent years. (It is discussed along with oppositional defiant disorder because the symptoms of these two disorders, as well as the research, overlap considerably.) Posttraumatic stress disorder and anxiety disorders are included in the childhood section. Although anxiety disorders can occur at any stage of the life span, we balance our discussion in these two chapters on how the disorder presents in both childhood and adulthood, with assessment and intervention considerations specific to particular developmental stages.

The section on disorders in adolescence refers to disorders with typical onset in adolescence: eating disorders, depression, substance use disorders, and sexual disorders (pedophilia). We recognize that onset is not always in adolescence for these disorders, and there is much discussion in each of these chapters on presentation in adulthood.

Disorders in adulthood include bipolar disorder, schizophrenia and other psychotic disorders, and personality disorders (borderline and antisocial personality disorders). While there is increasing evidence that bipolar disorder often appears in childhood and adolescence, we consider it as primarily a disorder of adulthood, where the majority of research has been focused. Disorders associated with older adulthood include the dementias.

Disorders chosen for inclusion in this book had to meet the following criteria:

- They are disorders that clinical social workers may encounter, irrespective of clinical setting.
- They have sufficient research backing them to warrant discussion. For instance, reactive attachment disorder and intermittent explosive disorders were not included because of the lack of research information on them.
- They do not contribute to discrimination or oppression. For instance, gender identity disorder is a *DSM* diagnosis, but social work is committed to the rights of transgendered, as well as lesbian and gay, populations. We briefly discuss this "disorder" in the book only to illustrate this point.

Format of the Book

The second chapter provides a historical overview of the *DSM*, its principles and components, and critiques of the *DSM* and its biological basis. Each of the subsequent chapters on the mental, emotional, and behavior disorders includes the following:

- A summary description of the particular mental disorder, including its prevalence, course, and common comorbid disorders
- Assessment factors, including relevant measurement instruments
- The risk and protective factors for both the onset and course of the particular disorder
- Evidence-based interventions
- A critique of the diagnosis from the social work perspective
- A case study and illustration of the multiaxial diagnostic system, with a suggested treatment plan

Our goal in developing this format was to guide you through the assessment and intervention process with various mental, emotional, and behavior disorders that may occur throughout the life span. You will gain in-depth knowledge about important aspects of these disorders and the social work roles connected with them. Most important, you will learn about diagnosis and disorders in a way that is consistent with social work principles and values.

References

American Psychiatric Association. (2000). *Diagnostic and statistical manual of mental disorders* (4th ed., text rev.). Washington, DC: Author.

Bogenschneider, K. (1996). An ecological risk/protective theory for building prevention programs, policies, and community capacity to support youth. *Family Relations: Journal of Applied Family & Child Studies, 45,* 127–138.

Cohen, J. (1988). *Statistical power analysis for the behavioral sciences* (2nd ed.). Hillsdale, NJ: Erlbaum.

Dekovic, M. (1999). Risk and protective factors in the development of problem behavior during adolescence. *Journal of Youth & Adolescence, 28,* 667–685.

Fraser, M., Richman, J., & Galinsky, M. (1999). Risk, protection, and resilience: Toward a conceptual framework of social work practice. *Social Work Research, 23,* 131–143.

Greenberg, M., Speltz, M., DeKlyen, M., & Jones, K. (2001). Correlates of clinic referral for early conduct problems: Variable- and person-oriented approaches. *Development & Psychopathology, 13,* 255–276.

Jessor, R., Van Den Bos, J., Vanderryn, J., Costa, F. M., & Turbin, M. S. (1997). Protective factors in adolescent problem behavior: Moderator effects and developmental change. In G. A. Marlatt & G. R. Van Den Bos (Eds.), *Addictive behaviors: Readings on etiology, prevention, and treatment* (pp. 239–264). Washington, DC: American Psychological Association.

Kalil, A., & Kuntz, J. (1999). First births among unmarried adolescent girls: Risk and protective factors. *Social Work Research, 23,* 197–208.

Kutchins, H., & Kirk, S. A. (1997). *Making us crazy. DSM: The psychiatric bible and the creation of mental disorders.* New York: Free Press.

Littel, J., Corcoran, J., & Pillai, V. (2008). *Systematic reviews and meta-analysis.* New York: Oxford University Press.

Pollard, J., Hawkins, D., & Arthur, M. (1999). Risk and protection: Are both necessary to understand diverse behavioral outcomes in adolescence? *Social Work Research, 23,* 145–158.

Proctor, EK. (2007). Implementing evidence-based practice in social work education: Principles, strategies, and partnerships. *Research on social work practice, 17*(5), 583–591.

Runyan, D. K., Hunter, W. M., Scololar, R. R., Amaya-Jackson, L., English, D., Landsverk, J., et al. (1998). Children who prosper in unfavorable environments: The relationship to social capital. *Pediatrics, 101*(1), 12–19.

Rutter, M., Maugham, N., Mortimore, P., & Ouston, J. (1979). *Fifteen thousand hours.* Cambridge, MA: Harvard University Press.

Sackett, D.L., Richardson, W.S., Rosenberg, W., & Haynes, R.B. (1997). *Evidence-Based Medicine—How to Practice and Teach EBM.* New York: Churchill Livingstone.

Steinberg, L. (2001). We know some things: Parent–adolescent relationships in retrospect and prospect. *Journal of Research on Adolescence, 11*, 1–19.

Wachs, T. (2000). *Necessary but not sufficient*. Washington, DC: American Psychiatric Association.

Werner, E. (2000). Protective factors and individual resilience. In J. Shonkoff & S. Meisels (Eds.), *Handbook of early childhood intervention* (2nd ed., pp. 115–132). New York: Cambridge University Press.

Zlotnik, J. (2007). Evidence-based practice and social work education: A view from Washington. *Research on social work practice, 17*(5), 625–629.

2 Social Work and the *DSM*

Person-in-Environment Versus the Medical Model

This book is based on the *Diagnostic and Statistical Manual of Mental Disorders* (*DSM*) (APA, 2000) classification system because it is the standard resource for clinical diagnosis in this country and has been for more than 50 years. The purpose of the *DSM* is to "provide clear descriptions of diagnostic categories in order to enable clinicians and investigators to diagnose, communicate about, study, and treat people with various mental disorders" (APA, 2000, p. xi). It is important to recognize, however, that the *DSM* represents a medical perspective, only one of many possible perspectives on human behavior. There has always been tension between the social work profession's person-in-environment perspective and the requirement in many settings that social workers use the *DSM* to "diagnose" mental, emotional, or behavioral disorders in clients. The purpose of this chapter is to explore this uneasy relationship of social work with the *DSM*. As an introduction to the process, the concept of *disorder* will be reviewed.

The Concept of "Disorder"

There is no single definition of normalcy in any discipline. Many of the human service professions, all of which have their own unique value and knowledge bases, develop formal standards for evaluating and classifying the behavior of clients as *normal* or *abnormal*, *healthy* or *unhealthy*, *rational* or *irrational*. Since its beginnings, the profession of social work has made efforts to put forth such classification systems (one of which will be described later in the chapter), but at the same time it has always been uncomfortable with the act of labeling behavior.

The current definition of *mental disorder* utilized by the American Psychiatric Association (2000) is a "significant behavioral or psychological syndrome or pattern that occurs in an individual and that is associated with present distress (e.g., a painful symptom) or disability (i.e., impairment in one or more important areas of functioning) or with significantly increased risk of suffering death, pain, disability, or an important loss of freedom" (p. x). The syndrome or pattern "must not be an expectable and culturally sanctioned response to a particular event." Whatever its cause, "it must currently be considered a manifestation of behavioral, psychological, or biological dysfunction in the individual." This medical definition used in the *DSM-IV-TR* thus focuses on underlying disturbances within the person and is sometimes referred to as the *disease model* of abnormality. Neither deviant behavior nor conflicts between an individual and society are to be considered disorders unless they are symptomatic of problems within the individual. This implies that the abnormal person must experience changes within the self (rather than create environmental change) in order to be considered normal, or healthy, again.

The profession of social work is characterized by the consideration of *systems* and the reciprocal impact of persons and their environments (the psychosocial perspective) on human behavior (Andreae, 1996). Social workers tend not to classify individuals as abnormal, or disordered, but consider the *person-in-environment (PIE)* as an ongoing transactional process that facilitates or blocks one's ability to experience satisfactory social functioning. The quality of a person's social functioning is related to the biological, psychological, and social factors in his or her life. Three types of PIE situations likely to produce problems in social functioning include stressful life transitions, relationship difficulties, and environmental unresponsiveness (Gitterman, 2009). All of these are transactional and do not emphasize the presence or absence of "normal" personal characteristics.

Social work interventions may thus focus on the person *or* on the environment. Still, clinical social workers specialize in work with client populations at the "micro" level of the PIE spectrum. Practitioner and scholar Eda Goldstein (2007) defines *clinical social work practice* as the application of social work theory and methods to the treatment and prevention of psychosocial dysfunction, disability, or impairment, including emotional and mental disorders, in individuals, families, and groups. She adds that it is based on an application of human development theories within a psychosocial context. The fact that this definition includes references to emotional and mental disorders highlights the tension noted earlier between the philosophy of the profession and the focus of many direct practitioners.

Classifying Mental, Emotional, and Behavioral Disorders

The first edition of the *DSM* reflected the influence of two previous works that had been widely used in the United States during the prior 30 years (APA, 1952). Each of these volumes was the result of efforts to develop a uniform nomenclature of disease. First, the American Medico-Psychological Association and National Council for Mental Hygiene collaborated to produce a standard reference manual in 1918 (initially titled the *Statistical Manual for the Use of Institutions for the Insane*). It included 22 categories of mental illness and reflected this country's primary focus on psychiatric hospitals and severe forms of mental illness. In addition, the New York Academy of Medicine published the *Standard Classified Nomenclature of Disease* in 1933 that, although focused on medical diseases, made great strides in developing a uniform terminology.

The *Statistical Manual*, responsibility for which was eventually assumed by the American Psychiatric Association, was used until World War II. During the war, observations of relatively mild mental disorders among soldiers uncovered the manual's limitations. Psychiatrists began to treat problems such as personality disturbances, psychosomatic disorders, and stress reactions. The *Statistical Manual* was not helpful for diagnosing these cases, and the Armed Forces and Veteran's Administration actually developed their own supplemental nomenclatures. In 1948, with the war over, the APA initiated new action for the standardization of diagnosis (Grob, 1991). The need for change was felt most strongly by practitioners in clinics and private practice, reflecting the gradual movement of psychiatry out of the institutions and into the communities. The result was publication of the first edition of the *DSM* in 1952.

Since its beginning the *DSM* has relied on symptom clusters, or *categories*, as the basis for diagnosis. An accurate diagnosis is important because it implies that certain interventions should be used to "treat" the problems inherent in the diagnosis. There are other ways that the process could be advanced, however. For example, clients could be classified on the basis of *dimensions* of behavioral characteristics (Millon, 2004). From this perspective human behavior is seen as occurring on a continuum, from normal through problematic. For example, rather than diagnosing "major depression," a client could be assessed as having a certain score for "negative affectivity" along a continuum of "normal" to "problematic." Thus, a client might not be diagnosed as having a certain disorder, but with exhibiting certain characteristics to a problematic degree. Dimensions may refer to the severity of defined sets of symptoms, individual traits, or underlying vulnerabilities. A dimensional system would probably result in fewer categories of disorder and reflect the reality that similar behaviors may serve different functions across individuals. In acknowledgment of the dimensional approach, we have included measurement instruments in this book that can be used for each disorder. We will have more to say about dimensional approaches to diagnosis later in this chapter.

The Relationship Between Social Work and the *DSM*

Social workers account for more than half of the mental health workforce in the United States (Whitaker, 2009). All social workers in direct practice need to diagnose clients, to make judgments upon which to base professional actions for which they will be held accountable. It is our view that the *DSM* has benefits *and* limitations with respect to clinical social work practice. The *DSM* classification system is a product of the psychiatric profession and as such does not fully represent the knowledge base or values of the social work profession. Still, it is extensively used by social workers (and many other human service professionals) nationwide for the following reasons (Brubeck, 1999; Kirk, 2005; Miller, 2002):

- Worldwide, the medical profession is preeminent in setting standards for mental health practice. Thus, social workers, along with members of other professions, are often expected by agency directors to use the *DSM* in their work.
- Accurate clinical diagnosis is considered necessary for selecting appropriate interventions.
- Competent use of the *DSM* helps social workers claim expertise similar to that of the other professions.
- Practitioners from various disciplines can converse in a common language about mental, emotional, and behavioral disorders of social functioning.
- The *DSM* perspective is incorporated into professional training programs offered by members of a variety of human service professions.
- Portions of state social worker licensing exams require knowledge of the *DSM*.

Throughout the remainder of this chapter the manual will be examined with regard to both its utility and limitations.

The Evolution of the *DSM* Since 1952

Because the "medical" perspective may sometimes be at odds with social work's "person-in-environment" perspective, it is important for social workers to understand the evolution of the manual (Beutler & Malik, 2002; Eriksen & Kress, 2005; Kutchins & Kirk, 1997). Social workers can see how some diagnostic categories have social as well as medical and psychological origins. They can also get a sense about the relative validity of the various diagnostic categories.

DSM-I

The first edition of the *DSM* (APA, 1952) was constructed by a small committee of APA members who prepared drafts of the material and sent them to members of the APA and other related organizations for feedback and suggestions. The final product included 106 diagnoses, each of which had descriptive criteria limited to several sentences or a short paragraph. The manual had a psychodynamic orientation, reflected in the wide use of the term *reaction*, as in "schizophrenic reaction" or "anxiety reaction." It included many new diagnoses specifically intended for use with outpatient populations.

DSM-I's two major categories included (*a*) disorders caused by or associated with impairment of brain tissue function, and (*b*) disorders of psychogenic origin without clearly defined physical cause or structural change in the brain. The former category included acute and chronic brain disorders resulting from such conditions as infection, dementia, circulatory disturbance, and intoxication. The latter category included problems resulting from a more general inability to make successful adjustments to life demands. It included psychotic disorders (such as manic depression, paranoia, schizophrenia), autonomic and visceral disorders, psychoneurotic disorders (anxiety, dissociative, conversion, phobic, obsessive-compulsive, and depressive reactions), personality disorders, and situational personality disturbances.

DSM-II

The *DSM* was revised for the first time in 1968, following three years of preparation. The APA's decision to do so was justified by its desire to bring American nomenclature into closer alignment with that of the *International Classification of Diseases*, the worldwide system for medical and psychiatric diagnosis that was updated and published that same year. Still, the *DSM-II* was not so much a major revision as an effort to reflect current psychiatric practice. The Committee wanted to record what it "judges to be generally agreed upon by well-informed psychiatrists today" (APA, 1968, p. viii). Its process of construction was similar to that of *DSM-I*. Following its adoption by APA leadership, it attracted little attention from the general public. Psychiatry at that time was far less a social force than it was to become during the next 10 years.

The *DSM-II* included 182 diagnoses, occupying 10 classes of disorder described in less than 40 pages, as follows:

- Mental retardation
- Psychotic organic brain syndromes (such as dementia, infection, and cerebral)

- Nonpsychotic organic brain syndromes (epilepsy, intoxication, circulatory)
- Psychoses not attributed to physical conditions (schizophrenia, major affective disorders)
- Neuroses
- Personality disorders
- Psychophysiology (somatic) disorders
- Transient situational disturbances
- Behavior disorders of childhood and adolescence
- Conditions without manifest psychiatric disorder

The term *reaction* was eliminated from the manual, but the *neurosis* descriptor was retained for some categories, indicating an ongoing psycho-dynamic influence.

Through *DSM-II* there was no serious effort on the part of psychiatry to justify its classifications on the basis of scientific evidence. The manual was empirically weak with regard to validity and reliability (Kirk & Kutchins, 1992). Nevertheless, it was popular among clinical practitioners and far more useful to them than it was to researchers.

After the publication of *DSM-II*, a conflict erupted within psychiatry over whether homosexuality should be classified as a mental illness (Kutchins & Kirk, 1997). While generally considered to be a disorder up to that time, it first appeared as a separate diagnostic category in *DSM-II*. The gay rights movement had become powerful by the early 1970s, however, and protests were directed against the APA for its perceived stigmatization of those persons. The psychiatry profession was divided about the issue, and the conflict reached a resolution only in 1974 when a vote of the APA membership (note how far the APA had to go to live up to any claims of science) resulted in homosexuality being deleted from further editions of the manual. Still, as a kind of compromise measure, it was retained in subsequent printings of *DSM-II* as "sexual orientation disturbance" and in *DSM-III* as "ego dystonic homosexuality." The diagnoses were intended for use only with persons who were uncomfortable with their homosexuality and wanted to live as hetero-sexuals. This episode provides a good example of the "politics" of mental illness. Such a debate is currently raging with regard to the diagnosis of gender identity disorder (Langer & Martin, 2004) (see Chapter 11).

DSM-III

The publication of the *DSM-III* in 1980 represented a major turning point in the field of psychiatry. This third edition represented a clear effort by psychiatry to portray itself as an empirical scientific enterprise. It promoted a nontheoretical approach to diagnosis, a five-axis diagnostic system, and behaviorally defined criteria for diagnosing disorders. For the first time the

DSM included an official definition of "mental disorder"(presented earlier in this chapter). It included 265 disorders, and for each of them information was presented about diagnostic features, coding information, associated features, age at onset, course, impairment, complications, predisposing factors, prevalence, and sex ratio. It was a much larger manual than its spiral-bound predecessors were. Disorders were classified into 17 categories, usually by shared phenomenological features, although there was some inconsistency in this process. For example, there were two chapters devoted to "not elsewhere classified" groups of disorders, and the infancy, child, and adolescent disorders were all classified together.

The development of *DSM-III* was far more intensive, and involved many more participants, than development of the earlier editions. It was put forth as a scientific document, based on research findings. Even so, the APA recognized that supporting these claims was difficult. In addition to literature reviews and field trials, criteria for the inclusion of many disorders were based on whether they were used with relative frequency, whether interested professionals offered positive comments about it, and whether it was useful with outpatient populations. This final criterion indicates the psychiatry profession's desire to continue moving away from its roots in the public mental hospitals.

The multiaxial system of diagnoses (see Exhibit 2.1) introduced in *DSM-III* is still in use, of course, although in amended form. Its justifications were a desire to make the process of diagnosis more thorough and individualized and to recognize the medical and psychosocial factors that contribute to the process of diagnosis.

One rationale for differentiating Axis I, which covers clinical or mental disorders and other conditions that may be a focus of clinical attention, from Axis II, which covered personality disorders, mental retardation, and other developmental disorders, was the perceived etiology of the disorders. Transient disorders, those for which a client would be more likely seeking intervention, were placed on Axis I and more "constitutional"conditions on Axis II. Other

Exhibit 2.1		
The *DSM* Classification of Mental Disorders		
Axis I	Clinical or mental disorders	
	Other conditions that may be a focus of clinical attention	
Axis II	Personality disorders	
	Mental retardation	
Axis III	General medical conditions	
Axis IV	Psychosocial and environmental problems	
Axis V	Global assessment of functioning	

Source: Adapted from the American Psychiatric Association (2000).

rationales for differentiating Axes I and II were their formal structure (psychological versus organic components) and their temporal stability (those on Axis II were presumed to be either long term or permanent) (APA, 1980). The division was also intended to highlight the personality disorders that had become of great interest to psychiatrists, even though they had been included in previous editions. Over the years, however, critics have found less conceptual support for the distinction between the axes (Cooper, 2004).

Axes IV and V, which bring attention to environmental influences on a client's functioning, should be of great interest to social workers. No method was presented to systematically identify and record these factors on Axis IV, however. It was left to the practitioner to briefly describe the stressor and rate its severity on a scale of 1 to 7 between "none" and "catastrophic." This approach changed over subsequent editions. Further, there was confusion over whether the identified stressors were intended to represent a *cause* or a *consequence* of the Axis I disorder (Brubeck, 1999). To regard the stressors as a consequence of a disorder contradicted social work's interest in person–situation interactions as contributing to the development of problems in living; social workers are thus more likely to consider stressors as causes of disorders. Axis V, the *global assessment of functioning (GAF)*, also broadened the scope of diagnosis as the practitioner was asked to summarize the level of a client's social, occupational, and leisure functioning on a scale between 1 (superior) and 7 (grossly impaired).

Another innovation of the *DSM-III* that was conceptually appealing to the social work profession was the introduction of *V-codes*, "conditions attributable to a mental disorder that are a focus of attention or treatment" (APA, 1980, p. 331). They include *relational* problems and thus represent the only coding category for problems that are recognized to exist outside the individual. V-codes include interpersonal issues that complicate the treatment of another disorder or arise as a result of it. Listed on Axis I when they will be a major focus of the intervention, they include the following:

- Problem related to a general mental disorder or general medical condition (a client's main difficulty is related to interaction with a relative or significant other who has a mental disorder or physical disease)
- Parent–child relational problem (symptoms or negative effects on functioning are associated with how a parent and child interact)
- Partner relational problem (symptoms or negative effects on functioning are associated with way a client and spouse/partner interact)
- Sibling relational problem
- Relational problem not otherwise specified (e.g., with a neighbor or coworker)

The V-codes also include problems related to abuse or neglect, including the physical abuse of child or adult, sexual abuse of a child or adult, and neglect of a child.

DSM-III reflected a major expansion of psychiatric "turf" in the United States. Unlike other editions of the manual, it became a target of criticism from some social workers and other mental health professionals for its perceived lack of validity and reliability. Its authors defended against these criticisms by presenting it as a work in progress (Kutchins & Kirk, 1997).

DSM-III-R

The APA justified the publication of *DSM-III-R* (1987), the "R" standing for "revised," because of the lengthy time lag between *DSM-III* and the projected publication date of *DSM-IV* (approximately 5 years away). The editors stated that accumulated research findings indicated a need for revisions in the descriptions and criteria for some disorders and a clarification or updating of information about others. All diagnoses were reviewed for consistency, clarity, and conceptual accuracy by appointed committees. The participants were initially asked to limit their criticisms and input to improving existing descriptions of disorders, but many new disorders were eventually included. No new reliability studies were conducted, however, to substantiate evidence for the existence of these disorders.

The new manual reflected more than minor adjustments. There were 292 mental disorders included in the product. The manual introduced the *hierarchical exclusionary rules*, which were estimated to affect 60% of diagnoses (Clark, Watson, & Reynolds, 1995). That is, a diagnosis was to be excluded from consideration if it was judged to occur during the course of a coexisting disorder that had a higher position in the hierarchy. For example, a person with schizophrenia who developed depression would not be given the latter diagnosis, because many symptoms of depression are implicit in the former diagnosis. Axes I and II now permitted *specifiers* of the severity of a disorder (mild, moderate, and severe). On Axis IV (psychosocial stressors) *DSM-III-R* provided separate scales for children and adolescents and adults. It also offered 11 types of psychosocial stressors to choose from. These were now to be coded on a 1 (none) to 6 (catastrophic) scale and described as predominantly *acute* (less than 6 months) or *enduring*. Axis V was now to be coded along a continuum from 0 to 100, with anchor descriptors at every 10 points. Two scores were now required, reflecting the client's GAF at present and his or her highest level during the past year. These changes did seem to enhance the thoroughness of a client's clinical description.

Much controversy emerged, however, about the proposed inclusion of three new diagnoses. All of them were strongly criticized by feminist groups (and others) for alleged gender biases (Figert, 1995; Lerman, 1996). The proposed sexual disorder of *paraphilic rapism* received strong objections because it appeared to make the act of rape, or more specifically repeated rape, a disorder, and thus an act for which perpetrators might conceivably not be held legally accountable. *Premenstrual dysphoric disorder* described a type of depression experienced by women during menstruation. This diagnosis might stigmatize women as mentally unstable during their menstrual cycles. *Masochistic personality disorder*, characterized by a recurrent need to experience interpersonal suffering, might label women who have difficulty separating from abusers as disordered. There was clearly a concern among the general public that psychiatry was again about to pathologize behavior that had been previously conceptualized as either normal or criminal. In the end, the editors of *DSM-III-R* did not include any of these three diagnoses in the text, but they were put into an appendix as conditions that merited further study.

DSM-IV

The *DSM-IV* was published in 1994 and, like the second and third editions, it represented a major effort to update the state of diagnostic knowledge in the United States. The editors also continued to work toward terminological and coding consistency with the *International Statistical Classification of Diseases and Related Health Problems (ICD)*. The massive effort was conducted with a 16-member task force and 13 work groups, each consisting of 50 to 100 persons who had expertise in particular topic areas. The editors claimed that the manual benefited from the "substantial increase in research on diagnosis" and that "most diagnoses now have an empirical literature or available data sets that are relevant to decisions" related to manual revisions (APA, 1994, p. xviii). Preparations for the new manual included 150 reviews of the published literature, reanalysis of 50 data sets already collected, and 12 issue-focused field trials to test diagnostic options. New diagnoses were included only if there was research support, although categories already scheduled to be included in the 10th edition of the *ICD* were given priority. An effort was also made to simplify the wording of diagnostic criteria to make the manual more user-friendly for practitioners.

The final product included approximately 340 mental disorders classified into 16 types, which continued the APA's practice of adding disorders to each edition of the *DSM*. Most other changes were minor. The term *rule out* was replaced by *provisional* on Axes I and II. Of interest to social workers, Axis IV was revised to include nine factors representing psychosocial and environmental problems, and the severity codes were deleted. An even more significant change was the inclusion of clinical significance criteria in almost half the diagnostic criteria sets, requiring that symptoms not merely be present but cause clinically significant distress or impairment in important areas of the client's functioning (Spitzer & Wakefield, 1999). While these criteria were not empirically based, they represented an attempt to make diagnostic criteria stricter. This change was favored by many social workers in that a person did not have a disorder if he or she merely exhibited symptoms, but only if those symptoms created distress in an environmental context.

DSM-IV-TR

This "text revision" of the *DSM-IV* that appeared in 2000 was presented, like the 1987 revision, as a compromise between those who felt that the manual is updated too often to facilitate research and those who wanted access to the most up-to-date information about mental disorders (First & Pincus, 2002). The editors reported that with *DSM-V* not due until 2010 (or later) there would be at least 16 years between editions, too great a gap to accommodate accumulating knowledge about mental disorders. The purpose of the 3-year text revision project was to ensure that the descriptive information about disorders was up to date, correct any errors or ambiguities from *DSM-IV*, and reflect changes in *ICD* coding, required by the United States government for the reporting of health care statistics. The manual included no changes in diagnoses, diagnostic criteria, or organizational structure.

Examples of diagnostic categories where the wording was clarified include pervasive developmental disorder not otherwise specified, the tic disorders, the paraphilias, and polysubstance dependence. Coding changes were made for the cognitive disorders and several others. Instructions for using Axis V, the global assessment of functioning, were clarified. The "current" score was articulated as referring to "the past week," and practitioners were advised to use the lower of two rating scores when there were differences in the quality of a client's functioning among the social, occupational, and leisure domains. *DSM-IV-TR* was not a significant change from its predecessor with respect to clinical usage.

DSM-V

The next edition of the *DSM* will probably be published within the next 4 years. While there are many preliminary reports available from various task groups about changes being considered for the manual, it is too early to say how diagnostic categories and criteria may be different. It is certain, however, that the *DSM-V* will continue with the five-axis classification system (Kupfer, First, & Regier, 2002). During each chapter in this book that addresses a diagnostic category we will consider some of the adjustments that have been proposed.

Now that the nature of the *DSM* has been described, we can review how clinical practitioners currently use it. Exhibit 2.2 below includes a summary of instructions for the use of the *DSM-IV-TR* (APA, 2000).

Exhibit 2.2

Procedures for Completing a *DSM* Diagnosis

General Guidelines

a. Sufficiently investigate the presenting symptoms to ensure that they are genuine
b. List diagnosis first that is most responsible for the current evaluation
c. When uncertain if a diagnosis is correct, use the "provisional" qualifier
d. When appropriate, use the following severity criteria. They are required for mood, substance abuse, mental retardation, conduct disorder, but can be used for any Axis I or II diagnosis

  1. Mild—minimum criteria
  2. Moderate intermediate; between mild and severe
  3. Severe—many more symptoms than minimum criteria; some are especially severe; social functioning is especially compromised
  4. In partial remission—the client previously met full criteria; some symptoms remain, but there are too few to fulfill criteria currently
  5. In full remission—the client has been symptom-free for a period of time that seems clinically relevant
  6. Prior history—the client appears to have recovered, but the clinician feels it is important to mention it

Hierarchic Principles

a. Disorders due to a general medical condition (such as panic attacks due to hypoglycemia) and substance-induced disorders (psychotic episode during an amphetamine binge) preempt a diagnosis of any other disorder that could produce the same symptoms
b. When a more pervasive disorder has essential or associated symptoms that are defining symptoms of a less pervasive disorder, the more pervasive disorder is diagnosed if its diagnostic criteria are met. For example, if dysthymia is present when schizophrenia is present, then only schizophrenia should be diagnosed. If oppositional defiant and conduct disorders are both present, use the conduct disorder diagnosis.

Axis II (Personality Disorders, Mental Retardation)

If the personality disorder is the most important reason for the client's seeking evaluation, add the "principal diagnosis" term.

Axis III (General Medical Conditions)

a. These may have a direct bearing on client's Axis I diagnoses (especially true of cognitive disorders)
b. In other cases, physical illness may affect (or be affected by) management of Axis I or II diagnosis.
c. Note the source of the information, such as "according to the client" or "confirmed in chart by a physician."

Axis IV (Psychosocial and Environmental Problems)

a. The duration of the problem is only intended to include the past year.
b. These can be coded on Axis I when they are a focus of evaluation or treatment.
c. A positive stressor may be included if it has caused problems for client.
d. More than one may be listed. These may include:

1. Primary support group (death of or illness in a relative; divorce or separation; remarriage of parent; abuse; conflicts with relatives)
2. Economic (poverty, debt, credit problems, inadequate welfare or child support)
3. Social environment (loss or death of friend, acculturation problems, racial or sexual discrimination, retirement, living alone)
4. Access to health care services (inadequate health services, insufficient health insurance, no transportation for health services)
5. Educational (academic problems, conflicts with classmates or teachers, illiteracy, poor school environment)
6. Interaction with the legal or criminal systems (arrest, incarceration, suing or being sued, victim of a crime)
7. Occupational (stressful work conditions, changing jobs, unemployment)
8. Housing problems (homelessness, poor housing, dangerous neighborhood)
9. Other psychosocial stressors (conflicts with human service professionals, exposure to war, natural disasters or catastrophes)

Axis V (Global Assessment of Functioning)
a. These rating are based on the clinician's judgment.
b. Scores reflect the client's overall occupational, psychological, and social functioning (not physical limitations or environmental problems) on a continuum of mental health and illness.
c. Two scores are included: one reflecting the client's current GAF (the past week), and another reflecting the client's highest level during the past year.
d. Scores range from 0 to 100, for example:

Axis 90–100: Superior functioning in a wide range of activities
0–10: Persistent danger of severely hurting self or others, persistent inability to maintain minimal personal hygiene, or serious suicidal acts with clear expectation of death.

Source: Adapted from the American Psychiatric Association (2000).

Criticisms of the DSM

The American Psychiatric Association has always maintained that the *DSM* is not a perfect classification system and that it is a work in continuous process. The editors assert that each edition represents an improvement on the previous one because it incorporates the most complete knowledge available at the time about the nature of mental disorders. Still, the manual has been critiqued as fundamentally flawed by members of the social work and other professions. The most important criticisms for clinical social work practitioners are described here.

The DSM *promotes reductionistic thinking about people.* It tends to minimize the complexity of the human condition, although to be fair this would likely be true of any diagnostic manual. A danger of this reductionism is that many social workers come to perceive client behaviors only in terms of available

DSM categories (Miller, 2002). Likewise, the process of diagnosis may be biased by the social worker's awareness of a client's prior diagnoses in cases where previous records exist. The editors of the *DSM* (APA, 2000) attempt to dispel this notion, stating in an introduction that the manual is "meant to serve as guidelines to be informed by clinical judgment and is not meant to be used in a cookbook fashion" (p. xxiii).

It promotes an arbitrary medical model for thinking about human problems. Disorders are conceptualized as residing *within* clients. Many authors have criticized the tendency of psychiatry to overstate the case for biological causation of some mental disorders (such as attention-deficit/hyperactivity disorder, depression, bipolar disorder, and schizophrenia), and with it, to overemphasize biological rather than psychosocial interventions (Healy, 2002; Valenstein, 1998). Some nosologists actually look forward to a day when the diagnostic categories are organized with respect to neurological sources of the disorders (Hyman, 2007). Others point out, however, that distinctions between biological and psychological causal influences on mental functioning are artificial, that there are still no solid biological markers for any of the disorders, and that the available evidence contradicts any monocausal theory of pathology (Millon, 2004). As noted earlier, social work considers the reciprocal interactions between the person, including developmental, biological, and psychological influences, and the environment, including the immediate social environment and wider social and cultural influences.

The DSM *views clients in isolation.* It does not comprehensively address interpersonal problems and the roles played by systems in the emergence of problem conditions. Some have argued that "relational disorders" should be considered for addition to the manual, and that many of these can be derived from existing V-codes (First, 2005a). This is not likely in the near future, however, because such disorders must necessarily be conceptualized differently from the APA's current view of disorders as residing within individuals (First, 2005b). Still, such a development would satisfy a major criticism of feminist theorists, who give primacy to many problems in living as relational rather than psychological in nature (Derry, 2004). While the V-codes allow practitioners to articulate relational issues, these are not reimbursable by insurance companies and are thus not accorded the same legitimacy as other diagnoses. Axis IV is also helpful in overcoming this individualistic bias, but neither does it receive great emphasis from practitioners compared to the issues recorded on Axes I and II. It is possible, of course, for social workers to bring greater visibility to Axis IV by advocating more strongly for its use in assessments and treatment planning.

The DSM *makes no provisions for recording client strengths.* It is conceivable that a multiaxial classification system might devote one or more axes to strengths. The manner in which the *DSM* has evolved even leads some professionals to believe that disorders are probably more numerous than is acknowledged at the present time. For example, in his otherwise useful text *DSM-IV Made Easy* (1995), Morrison writes, "The fact that the manual omits a disorder doesn't mean it doesn't exist. With each new edition of the *DSM*, the number of listed mental disorders has increased . . . . The conclusions should be obvious: there are probably still more conditions out there, waiting to be discovered" (p. 9). This orientation to human behavior is hardly strengths oriented.

Strengths-oriented practice implies that social workers should assess all clients in light of their capacities, talents, competencies, possibilities, visions, values, and hopes (Saleebey, 2006). This perspective emphasizes human resilience, or the skills, abilities, knowledge, and insight that people accumulate over time as they struggle to surmount adversity and meet life challenges. It refers to the ability of clients to persist in spite of their difficulties. Among the major principles of strengths practice are the following: All people have strengths, problems can be a source of challenge and opportunity, and practitioners can never know the "upper levels" of clients' growth potentials.

The DSM is organized for use in determining a diagnosis prior to intervention. Social workers, in contrast, regard the assessment process as ongoing throughout intervention, with new hypotheses being tested as new information emerges. While a practitioner can always change a client's *DSM* diagnosis, the manual suggests that a decision about diagnosis should be made early in the clinical process, so that appropriate interventions can be selected.

This criticism points to a related issue: that there is little research investigating how clinical practitioners use the *DSM*. It is widely recommended that multiple sources should be used in arriving at a *DSM* diagnosis, and the extent to which practitioners base their diagnoses with specific reference to the criteria versus other methods is not known (First & Westin, 2006). Some practitioners, especially those with more experience, may base their diagnoses on internalized prototypes (i.e., a current client's similarity to previous clients with the same presenting problems). Interestingly, the first two editions of the *DSM*, out of date for 40 years now, included paragraph-long prototypes to serve as guides to diagnosis. To encourage more consistency in how diagnoses are made, First and Westin (2006) make two suggestions: category-specific severity criteria based on the number of symptoms a client demonstrates, and the inclusion of empirically validated prototypes with each set of criteria.

There is an abundance of unclassifiable "boundary cases" (those that do not meet all required symptom criteria) and an acknowledged comorbidity (commonly shared disorders) and heterogeneity (within-groups variability) in DSM diagnosis. Overlapping boundary problems are evident, for example, with the disruptive behavior disorders (attention-deficit/hyperactivity disorder, oppositional defiant disorder, and conduct disorder) and bipolar disorder in children. Further, the not otherwise specified (NOS) categories included with many disorders lack diagnostic specificity due to their absence of clear criteria. This is not a minor issue because there are a high proportion of NOS diagnoses in the mood, dissociative, and personality disorder categories (Kirk, 2005). In fact, NOS is the most common diagnosis in the eating disorders category. This complicates the process of diagnosis but perhaps more seriously the process of determining intervention strategies, since people who have the same diagnosis are presumed to benefit from similar interventions. These problems have been dealt with in part by adding new subtypes of disorders, but these tend to demonstrate poor validity and reliability. The introduction of *severity* qualifiers in *DSM-III-R* represented another effort to add descriptive specificity to many disorders. Many theorists believe that this problem could be avoided by moving from a "categorical" diagnostic system (a person either has or does not have a disorder) to a dimensional one, in which is a person is given an ordinal rating with regard to having symptoms along a continuum from "normal" to "disordered" (Kraemer, Shrout, & Rubio-Stipec, 2007).

Regarding comorbidity, the APA encourages the recording of more than one diagnosis on an axis when the assessment justifies doing so. Nonetheless, research indicates that while 52% to 91% of clients merit several diagnoses, practitioners infrequently recorded them (Eaton, 2005). Social workers (and others) may resist doing so at times in an effort to minimize the perceived stigmatizing aspects of diagnosis. Several strategies for dealing with the comorbidity and boundary problems with the *DSM* have been offered. The chapters of the manual could be reorganized to include diagnostic categories based on symptom similarity or the degree to which they are correlated with each other (Watson & Clark, 2006). For example, the diagnoses of generalized anxiety disorder and depression could be featured together since they are often comorbid. Additionally, the "internalizing" (depression, eating disorders) and "externalizing" (behavior disorders) could be separated out.

At this point it is important to elaborate on the ways in which a dimensional classification system might represent an improvement on the current diagnostic system, by suggesting a continuum of social functioning rather than an "either/or" position. This approach is already present in the *DSM-IV-TR* in some ways. Mental retardation, for example, is diagnosed according to severity (borderline, mild, moderate, severe, and profound) with the understanding that, for example, persons with mild mental retardation will experience fewer problems in social functioning than those with more severe retardation. The severity criteria that are in place for some disorders represent a kind of dimensionality. For example, major depression is specified as mild, moderate, or severe depending on the number of symptoms and quality of social functioning that the person exhibits. Further, Axis V is intended to describe a person's overall level of social functioning on a continuous scale of 0 to 100.

Several examples are presented here about how such dimensionality could be implemented. Clark (2005) suggests that Axis I could be devoted to categorical diagnoses, while Axis II could include dimensional ratings of personality styles that may serve as risk or protective influences on the Axis I conditions. Some research has indicated that persons could be assessed for their possession of temperamental qualities, including negative affectivity, positive affectivity, and disinhibition. Ratings of these temperaments, if based on empirical evidence, might help the clinician to identify pertinent risk and protective influences for the Axis I conditions and to suggest a differential selection of intervention strategies. As another example, Widiger and Samuel (2005) argue for the use of a five-factor model of personality in which clients are rated along 30 subscales that underlie their five factors (see Chapter 13 for an extended discussion of this point). These authors admit that the use of their five-factor model would be problematic for practitioners, who would find it simpler to report a single diagnosis compared to 30 subscale scores, even though such a process might increase the validity of the diagnostic process. Millon (2004) argues that the organization of Axes I and II have become inadequate, even though he was a proponent of that system in the 1970s. He asserts that a three-axis system would be more comprehensive, summarizing problems as related to simple reactions (suggesting the role of environmental conditions), complex syndromes (a person–environment interaction), and inherent personality patterns.

The DSM *has become a major moneymaking enterprise for the American Psychiatric Association.* All professional associations, including the National Association of Social Workers, must be concerned with their finances and devise a variety of ways to raise money. Some outsiders, however, remark on the great income-generating potential of each edition of the *DSM* and feel that the APA's frequent updating of the manual has as much to do with revenues as with scientific advances. Publication of the manual is always accompanied by the publication of supplementary books (case study texts and handbooks for differential diagnosis, as examples), and professional development seminars on the use of the manual also draw sizeable enrollments (Kutchins & Kirk, 1997).

The expanded classification of disorders in the DSM also furthers the purposes of pharmaceutical companies. As more constellations of behaviors are considered mental disorders, they become reimbursable and treatable through medication (Weber, 2006). The drug companies benefit financially as more reimbursable disorders are discovered. The influence of pharmaceutical companies on the practice of psychiatry is not always recognized. For instance, drug companies sponsor research on medications, block unfavorable results from publication, fund psychiatric conferences and continuing education programs, and are major advertisers for psychiatric journals (Angell, 2004).

While many of the proposals described above are in response to the *DSM*'s limitations, they still are inadequate for fully embracing the person-in-environment perspective of the social work profession. The current format of the *DSM* is likely to continue for many more years as the primary resource for the formal classification of mental, emotional, and behavioral disorders. While social workers should advocate for *DSM* revisions or other classification systems that are compatible with its value base, they can productively work within the *DSM* framework to help clients with many serious problems in living. Before closing this chapter we present one example of an alternative classification system that was developed by members of the social work profession.

The Person-in-Environment Classification System

In 1981 the California chapter of the National Association of Social Workers (NASW) initiated an effort to enhance social work's professional identity and value base by developing a new classification system for problems in living. The *person-in-environment (PIE)* classification system was developed to describe, classify, and code social functioning problems of the adult clients of social workers (Karls & O'Keefe, 2008). The purposes of PIE were similar to some of the purposes of the *DSM*: to clarify the practice domain of social work, provide a basis for gathering data to measure service needs, promote clearer communication among social workers, and promote common descriptions of client situations to facilitate intervention.

The PIE system was developed and field-tested between 1981 and 1984 (with efforts to establish interrater reliability and content validity), but due to funding problems the project was dropped and NASW has not endorsed further work on it. Although the PIE is not currently in use, it serves as a reminder that social workers can participate in the development of classification systems that attend more thoroughly than the *DSM* to the biopsychosocial components of human functioning. It remains an example of an alternative method for formulating diagnosis, one that is consistent with the perspective of the social work profession.

The PIE (see Exhibit 2.3) is intended to balance client problems and strengths and does not endorse any particular theory of human development. It comprises four factors, including *social functioning* problems, *environmental* problems, *mental health* problems, and *physical health* problems. It addresses two major criticisms of the *DSM* in "social functioning" factor, including relational problems in the first two sections and dimensionality (severity) in the third. The system also includes a means of noting client strengths in the Factor 1 section "ability to cope with the problem."

One positive development in social work's pursuit of a holistic perspective on problems in living is NASW's participation in the field testing of a manual that will help health care professionals learn the World Health Organization's *International classification of functioning, disability, and health* (O'Neill, 2004). This coding framework, first published in 2001 but not yet in widespread use, provides a means for professionals to look beyond

Exhibit 2.3

The Person-in-Environment Classification System

Factor I: Social Functioning Problems

A. Social role in which each problem is identified

1. Family (parent, spouse, child, sibling, other, significant other)
2. Other interpersonal (lover, friend, neighbor, member, other)
3. Occupational (worker/paid, worker/home, worker/volunteer, student, other)

B. Type of problem in social role

1. Power
2. Ambivalence
3. Responsibility
4. Dependency
5. Loss
6. Isolation
7. Victimization
8. Mixed
9. Other

C. Severity of problem

1. No problem
2. Low severity
3. Moderate severity
4. High severity
5. Very high severity
6. Catastrophic

D. Duration of problem

1. More than 5 years
2. One to 5 years
3. Six months to 1 year
4. Two to 4 weeks
5. Two weeks or less

E. Ability of client to cope with problem

1. Outstanding coping skills
2. Above average
3. Adequate
4. Somewhat inadequate
5. Inadequate
6. No coping skills

(continued)

Exhibit 2.3

(Continued)

Factor II: Environmental Problems

A. Social system where each problem is identified

   1. Economic/basic needs
   2. Education/training
   3. Judicial/legal
   4. Health, safety, social services
   5. Voluntary association
   6. Affectional support

B. Specific type of problem within each social system
C. Severity of problem
D. Duration of problem

Factor III: Mental Health Problem

A. Clinical syndromes (Axis I of *DSM*)
B. Personality disorders or mental retardation (Axis II of *DSM*)

Factor IV: Physical Health Problem

A. Disease diagnosed by a physician (Axis III of *DSM*)
B. Other health problems reported by client and others

health care diagnosis and record clients' levels of functioning and disability. The code is based on a biopsychosocial approach and incorporates person-in-environment, ecological, and strengths models of practice.

Conclusion

Clinical social workers need to understand and be able to use the *DSM* for the diagnosis of their clients in mental health agencies. The manual is well established as the standard document for diagnosis in the United States and is used by practitioners from many professions. It enhances the assessment process in many ways but is also at odds with the social work profession's philosophy of person-in-environment transactions as determining the quality of a client's social functioning. By appreciating the *DSM*'s limitations, social workers are more likely to bring to the assessment process other aspects of a client's situation, including strengths, resources, and environmental influences on functioning. They will also maintain awareness that the *DSM* is not representative of "truth" but offers one system of classification among many possible systems.

References

American Psychiatric Association. (1952). *Diagnostic and statistical manual of mental disorders*. Washington, DC: Author.

American Psychiatric Association. (1968). *Diagnostic and statistical manual of mental disorders* (2nd ed., text rev.). Washington, DC: Author.

American Psychiatric Association. (1980). *Diagnostic and statistical manual of mental disorders* (3rd ed.). Washington, DC: Author.

American Psychiatric Association. (1987). *Diagnostic and statistical manual of mental disorders* (3rd ed., rev.). Washington, DC: Author.

American Psychiatric Association. (1994). *Diagnostic and statistical manual of mental disorders* (4th ed.). Washington, DC: Author.

American Psychiatric Association. (2000). *Diagnostic and statistical manual of mental disorders* (4th ed., text rev.). Washington, DC: Author.

Andreae, D. (1996). Systems theory and social work treatment. In F. J. Turner (Ed.), *Social work treatment* (4th ed., pp. 601–616). New York: Free Press.

Angell, M. (2004). *The truth about the drug companies: How they deceive us and what to do about it.* New York: Random House.

Beutler, M. E., & Malik, M. L. (2002). *Rethinking the DSM: A psychological perspective.* Washington, DC: American Psychological Association.

Brubeck, M. (1999). Social work and the *DSM*. In F. J. Turner (Ed.), *Adult psychopathology* (2nd ed., pp. 121–135). New York: Free Press.

Clark, A. (2005). Temperament as a unifying basis for personality and psychopathology. *Journal of Abnormal Psychology, 114*(4), 505–521.

Clark, L. A., Watson, D., & Reynolds, S. (1995). Diagnosis and classification of psychopathology: Challenges to the current system and future directions. *Annual Review of Psychology, 46,* 121–154.

Cooper, R. (2004). What is wrong with the DSM? *History of Psychiatry, 15*(57, Pt1), 5–25.

Derry, P. S. (2004). A kaleidoscope of perspectives. *Psychology of Women Quarterly, 28*(3), 267–268.

Eaton, W. W. (Ed.) (2005). *Medical and psychiatric comorbidity over the course of life.* Washington, DC: American Psychiatric Press.

Eriksen, K., & Kress, V. E. (2005). *Beyond the DSM story: Ethical quagmires, challenges, and best practices.* Thousand Oaks, CA: Sage.

Figert, A. E. (1995). The three faces of PMS: The professional, gendered, and scientific structuring of a psychiatric disorder. *Social Problems, 42*(1), 56–73.

First, M. B. (2005a). Clinical utility: A prerequisite for adoption of a dimensional approach in DSM. *Journal of Abnormal Psychology, 114*(4), 560–564.

First, M. B. (2005b). Relational processes in the DSM revision process: Comment on the special section. *Journal of Family Psychology, 20*(3), 356–358.

First, M. B., & Pincus, H. A. (2002). The DSM-IV text revision: Rationale and potential impact on clinical practice. *Psychiatric Services, 53*(3), 288–292.

First, M. B., & Westin, D. (2006). Classification for clinical practice: How to make ICD and DSM better able to serve clinicians. *International Review of Psychiatry, 19*(5), 473–481.

Gitterman, A. (2009). The life model. In A. R. Roberts (Ed.), *Social workers' desk reference* (2nd ed., pp. 231–235).

Goldstein, E. G., (2007). Social work education and clinical learning: Yesterday, today, and tomorrow. *Clinical Social Work Journal, 35*(1), 15–23.

Grob, G. N. (1991). *From asylum to community: Mental health policy in modern America.* Princeton, NJ: Princeton University Press.

Healy, D. (2002). *The creation of psychopharmacology.* Cambridge, MA: Harvard University Press.

Hyman, S. E. (2007). Can neuroscience be integrated into the DSM-V? *Neuroscience, 8,* 725–732.

Karls, J. M., & O'Keefe, M. (2008). *Person-in-environment system manual* (2nd ed.). Washington, DC: National Association of Social Workers Press.

Kirk, S. A. (Ed.). (2005). *Mental disorders in the social environment: Critical perspectives.* New York: Columbia University Press.

Kirk, S. A., & Kutchins, H. (1992). *The selling of DSM: The rhetoric of science in psychiatry.* Hawthorne, NY: Aldine de Gruyter.

Kraemer, H. C., Shrout, P. E., & Rubio-Stipec, M. (2007). Developing the diagnostic and statistical manual V: What will "statistical" mean in DSM-V? *Social Psychiatry and Psychiatric Epidemiology, 42,* 259–267.

Kupfer, D. J., First, M. B., & Regier, D. A. (2002). *A research agenda for DSM-V.* Washington, DC: American Psychiatric Association

Kutchins, H., & Kirk, S. A. (1997). *Making us crazy. DSM: The psychiatric bible and the creation of mental disorders.* New York: Free Press.

Langer, S. J., & Martin, J. I. (2004). How dresses can make you mentally ill: Examining gender identity disorder in children. *Child & Adolescent Social Work Journal, 21*(1), 5–23.

Lerman, H. (1996). *Pigeonholing women's misery: A history and critical analysis of the psychodiagnosis of women in the twentieth century.* New York: Basic.

Miller, J. (2002). Social workers as diagnosticians. In K. J. Bentley (Ed.), *Social work practice in mental health: Contemporary roles, tasks, and techniques* (pp. 43–72). Pacific Grove, CA: Brooks/Cole.

Millon, T. (2004). Biological explanations of psychopathology, the DSM, and essential necessities for advancement of diagnostic classification: An essay review. *Journal of Psychotherapy Integration, 14*(1), 106–119.

Morrison, J. (1995). DSM-IV made easy: The clinician's guide to diagnosis. New York: Guilford.

O'Neill, J. V. (2004). New diagnosis framework: NASW involved in setting codes for functioning. *NASW News, 49*(1), 9.

Saleeby, D. (Ed.). (2006). *The strengths perspective in social work practice* (2nd ed.). White Plains, NY: Longman.

Spitzer, R. L., & Wakefield, J. C. (1999). DSM-IV diagnostic criteria for clinical significance: Does it help solve the false positives problem? *American Journal of Psychiatry, 156,* 1856–1864.

Valenstein, E. (1998). *Blaming the brain: The truth about drugs and mental health.* New York: Free Press.

Watson, D. & Clark, L. A. (2006). Clinical diagnosis at the crossroads. *Clinical Psychology Science and Practice, 13,* 210–215.

Weber, L. J. (2006). *Profits before people? Ethical standards and the marketing of prescription drugs*. Bloomington: Indiana University Press.

Whitaker, T. (2009). *Workforce trends affecting the profession 2009*. Washington, DC: National Association of Social Workers Press

Widiger, T. A., & Samuel, D. B. (2005). Diagnostic categories or dimensions? A question for the Diagnostic and Statistical Manual of Mental Disorders–Fifth edition. *Journal of Abnormal Psychology, 114*(4), 494–504.

Disorders With Onset in Childhood

3 Intellectual Disabilities

The term *mental retardation* is becoming obsolete among consumers, family members, advocacy groups, and the mental health professions. It is gradually being replaced by the term *intellectual disability*, which is correctly perceived as more value neutral and scientifically accurate in the context of other disorders of childhood and adolescence. Still, the *DSM-IV-TR* uses the older terminology, and it is unclear whether this will change in *DSM-V*. Despite the use of the American Psychiatric Association (APA) nomenclature, we will employ the term *intellectual disability* except when referring to existing DSM nomenclature, because it is becoming widely accepted and adopted as the better and less perjorative term.

Intellectual disability is a complex diagnosis that takes into account both a person's intelligence quotient (IQ) and quality of interactions with his or her environment. The diagnosis was once based solely on IQ, but this has changed over the years; the current definition relies on one's level of adaptive functioning as much as IQ. The two most widely accepted diagnostic criteria for intellectual disability are those presented by the American Association of Intellectual and Developmental Disabilities (AAIDD) and the *Diagnostic and Statistical Manual of Mental Disorders* (*DSM IV-TR*) (APA, 2000).

The AAIDD (formerly known as the American Association on Mental Retardation) is the major international organization in the intellectual disability field. It was established in 1876 and has been defining intellectual disability since 1921. As an advocacy body, AAIDD points out that intellectual disability is not something a person *has* or *is*, nor is it truly a medical or mental disorder. Rather, it is characterized by both limitations in intellectual functioning and adaptive skills that are shaped by the person's environmental supports. The AAIDD (2009) presents the following five assumptions as essential to the diagnosis of intellectual disability:

1. Limitations in present functioning must be considered within the context of community environments typical of the individual's age, peers, and culture.
2. Valid assessment considers cultural and linguistic diversity, as well as differences in communication, sensory, motor, and behavioral factors.
3. Within an individual, limitations often coexist with strengths.
4. An important purpose of describing limitations is to develop a profile of needed supports.
5. With appropriate personalized supports over a sustained period, the life functioning of the person with intellectual disability generally will improve.

The diagnostic category of intellectual disability in the *DSM-IV-TR* (APA, 2000) essentially follows AAIDD guidelines but is more specific. With an onset before the age of 18, the diagnosis is listed and subclassified according to its severity under Axis II in the multiaxial scale. The classifications include *mild* (IQ level ranges from 50–55 to approximately 70), *moderate* (35–40 to 50–55), *severe* (20–25 to 35–40), and *profound* (below 20 or 25), as well as *severity unspecified*. The etiology, if known (e.g., lead poisoning, Down syndrome), is coded on Axis III. A "borderline intellectual functioning" V-code may be used on Axis II if a person's IQ level is around 70 (APA, 2000). The *DSM-IV-TR* does speculate as to what deficits and what achievements people at each severity level may acquire, and it is impossible to accurately gauge the capabilities of an individual without knowledge of his or her attitudes, strengths, and support systems.

Like the AAIDD, the *DSM-IV-TR* specifies that a person diagnosed with mental retardation (the *DSM* term) must have concurrent deficits in adaptive functioning in at least two of the following areas: self-care, communication, home living, social/interpersonal skills, use of community resources, self-direction, functional academic skills, work, leisure, health, and safety. Adaptive skills vary most widely in those diagnosed with mild mental retardation (Arvidsson, Granlund, & Thyberg, 2008).

Although the term *developmental disability* is often used interchangeably with *mental retardation*, especially in reference to services or entitlement, it is a legal concept rather than a medical category (Szymanski & King, 1999). Developmental disabilities involve a broad spectrum of disorders, including intellectual disability, the autism spectrum disorders, and epilepsy, although intellectual disability is the most common of these. All of these disorders refer to mental or physical impairments that manifest before a person is 22 years of age and generally begin in early childhood.

In the *DSM-IV-TR*, several other diagnostic classifications, including learning disorders and pervasive developmental disorders (PDDs) (e.g., autistic disorder, Asperger disorder), share some degree of cognitive or adaptive functioning impairment; however, they can be differentiated from intellectual disability. Learning disorders are characterized by below-average academic functioning in a particular academic area. Although a PDD is often comorbid with intellectual disability, criteria related to social interaction distinguish it from intellectual disability. In PDD, impairments exist in reciprocal social interaction and the development of communication skills (see Chapter 4). In both learning disorders and the PDDs, the person need not necessarily show impairment in general intellectual development or in other domains of adaptive functioning.

Prevalence

The prevalence of intellectual disability in the United States is estimated at 1%–3% of the general population (Yeargin-Allsopp, Boyle, Braun, & Trevathan, 2008). The majority (about 85%–90%) of diagnosed persons have mild intellectual disability; 10% have moderate intellectual disability; 3%–4% have severe intellectual disability; and 1%–2% have profound intellectual disability.

It is difficult to estimate the prevalence of intellectual disability outside the United States. Keeping in mind that the diagnosis includes criteria of IQ and functional ability, its prevalence differs cross-culturally, in that some societies are more accepting of persons with limited intelligence and are better able to find functional social roles for them (Skinner & Weisner, 2007).

Although intellectual disability is diagnosed across lines of racial, ethnic, educational, social, and economic backgrounds, some trends exist related to diversity. More boys than girls are affected, and mild intellectual disability is more prevalent in lower socioeconomic groups and in African Americans than among Caucasian or Hispanic persons.

Comorbidity

Approximately 34% of persons with intellectual disability have a comorbid disorder (Bhaumik, Tyrer, McGrother, & Ganghadran, 2008). The most common of these are the disruptive behavior disorders (20%) and autism spectrum disorders (9%). Smaller percentages of comorbid disorders include the feeding and eating disorders, tic disorders, and elimination disorders. Other comorbid disorders include schizophrenia (rarely), mood disorders, and anxiety disorders (such as posttraumatic stress disorder and obsessive-compulsive disorder).

Physiological disorders are also frequently associated with intellectual disability. The greater the severity of the disability, the higher the prevalence of associated disorders. Fifteen percent to 30% of people diagnosed with severe or profound intellectual disability have seizure disorders (Matthews, Weston, Baxter, Felce, & Kerr, 2008), 20%–30% have motor-related disorders such as cerebral palsy (Chadwick & Jolliffe, 2009), and 10%–20% have sensory impairments such as hearing and vision loss (Kerr, 2006).

Comorbid psychiatric disorders affect one's capacity for social adjustment and quality of life. Particularly detrimental are behavioral problems; as inappropriate behavior increases, so does the risk of compromising employment and residential opportunities. Unfortunately, practitioners who treat people with a dual diagnosis of intellectual disability and a mental illness tend to emphasize the individual's intellectual disability diagnosis and underemphasize the mental illness (Saeed, Ouellette-Kuntz, Stuart, & Burge, 2003). Thus, the individual may not receive adequate intervention. See Appendix II at the end of this chapter for measures assessing comorbid mental, emotional, and behavior problems.

Assessment

The goals of the assessment process with persons who may have intellectual disability should include determining diagnoses, strengths and abilities, general support needs, and possible physiological interventions. The subsequent treatment plan should maximize independence, taking into account the individual and family's needs and desires.

Assessment should begin with a comprehensive physical examination to specify the physical symptoms and their possible etiology. Formal testing for cognitive development and adaptive functioning should follow. In addition, interdisciplinary teams comprised of specialists in various areas should evaluate individuals for their other ancillary support needs. These elements of assessment are discussed in more detail in the following sections.

Physical Examination

Because children with intellectual disabilities generally reach their developmental milestones (e.g., walking and talking) later than the general population, the pediatrician is often one of the first professionals to suggest further testing. Initially, if a diagnosis of intellectual disability is suspected, a comprehensive physical exam and a medical, family, developmental, health, social, and educational history should be taken to discover any possible organic causes of symptoms. Some disorders that can cause intellectual disability symptoms are treatable, such as the enzyme deficiency phenylk-etonuria (PKU) and hyperthyroidism. However, in a significant percentage of cases—between one-quarter and one-third—no brain abnormality or etiology can be found (The Arc, 2004).

Depending on initial findings, laboratory tests may include a chromo-somal analysis; appropriate brain imaging tests; an electroencephalogram; tests for urinary amino acids, blood organic acids, and lead level; and bio-chemical tests for inborn errors of metabolism. The necessity for these tests must be balanced with the person's tolerance of the procedures involved.

Cognitive Assessment

For both diagnostic and educational purposes, testing should be completed to assess the individual's intellectual functioning and learning abilities. Some of the standard tests utilized are the Stanford-Binet Intelligence Scale, the Kaufmann Assessment Battery for children, and the Weschler Intelligence Scales (there are separate tests for children and adults). For infants, the Bayley Scales of Infant Development are used to assess language, personal and social, motor, and pro-blem-solving skills (Bayley, 1993). In the choice of testing instruments as well as in the interpretation of the results, the person's sociocultural background and native language should be taken into account to ensure the validity of results (APA, 2000).

Adaptive Functioning Assessment

Because intellectual disability is a product of the interaction between the individual and his or her environment, it is critically important to examine the individual's level of support and adaptive functioning level. A recent literature review indicates that categories of adaptive functioning for persons with intellectual disability include technology (including computers), rela-tionship support, attitudes of acceptance from others, and the availability of formal services for habilation (Verdonschot, deWitte, Reichrath, Buntinx, & Curfs, 2008). The social worker can play a key role in this assessment. The first step in this process is comprehensively interviewing the individual and his or her parents or other caregivers to assess the person's daily living, commu-nication, social, and behavioral skill levels. Guidelines for the interview include the following (Cederborg, La Rooy, & Lamb, 2008):

- Interviews should be conducted in the natural environment: home, school, or community residence.
- Most often, reassurance, support, and concrete and clear communication will yield needed information.
- The person's understanding of the disability, the reasons for referral, unique strengths and resources, ability to relate, expression of affect, and attention span should be assessed.

- People with intellectual disability may deny their disability, as they want to present themselves in the best light possible.
- Open-ended questions should be relied on as much as possible, as people with intellectual disability may not provide accurate information to leading questions (wanting to please the interviewer) or to closed-ended questions that require a yes or no response (they may be likely to respond with the choice that has been presented last).

When people evidence poor communication skills, the social worker will have to increasingly rely on caregivers for information, as well as behavioral observation. Measurement instruments can also assess adaptive functioning. (See Appendix I at the end of this chapter for a sample of these.) It should be noted that all scales lack some accuracy in depicting an individual's actual skill level because they rely on subjective informant reporting. Scales should therefore be supplemented with historical data, clinical interviews, and direct observation. Finally, the level of support the individual is currently receiving and the support required to achieve maximum independence should be assessed.

Multidisciplinary Teams

A multidisciplinary team is required to address the comprehensive needs of people with intellectual disability (Sturmey, 2007). Psychologists are needed to perform cognitive assessments, developmental pediatricians and clinical geneticists complete physical diagnostic evaluations, and psychiatrists and behavioral psychologists assess the psychological and behavioral abilities of the individual. Other members of an interdisciplinary team helpful for diagnosing the individual's comprehensive needs are speech and language therapists, physical therapists, educational specialists, school social workers, occupational specialists (for adults), recreational therapists, social workers in child protective services (intellectual disability is represented among both parents and children in that system), and workers from home-based skills-training programs, behavioral support agencies, residential programs, and mental health settings.

Some developmental disorders clinics are available for comprehensive assessments. The Association of University Centers on Disabilities (2004) is a national resource for consumer-focused facilities that provide training programs to agencies in the developmental disabilities field and technical assistance to individuals, families, and advocates.

Following assessment, individualized support plans must be written up with the client's participation. These plans have a variety of names depending on the support agency: individualized education plans (IEPs) for children in school, individualized support plans (ISPs) or individual treatment plans (ITPs) for adults in residential or vocational support settings, or consumer service plans (CSPs) for case coordination services. These plans are usually required by the regulatory and funding agencies that oversee support agencies. They typically include the individual's personalized long-term goals and measurable short-term objectives, and they delineate the support services the individual will receive to accomplish the goals and objectives. The plans typically have a time frame for reassessing the individual's progress and revising the plan accordingly.

▇▇▇▇ Risk and Protective Mechanisms for the Onset of Intellectual Disability

Determining the causes of early-onset intellectual disability is one of the great unsolved problems of health care (Ropers, 2008). That is, its causes are not known in a significant percentage of cases (25%–33%). In about 35% of people diagnosed with intellectual disability, a genetic cause is found, and in fewer than 10%, a malformation syndrome of unknown origin may be identified. The most common genetic cause of intellectual disability is Down syndrome, an abnormality in the development of chromosome 21. In addition to Down syndrome, other major causes of intellectual disability are fetal alcohol syndrome and fragile X (a gene abnormality on the X chromosome).

Categories of risk for intellectual disability include genetic conditions, problems during pregnancy, problems at birth, problems after birth, and poverty and cultural deprivation. These are reviewed by The Arc (2004). (See Exhibit 3.1.)

Genetic conditions result from abnormalities of inherited genes, problems when certain genes combine, or other errors in genes caused during pregnancy by such events as infections and exposure to X-rays (Ropers, 2008). Most research to date has focused on the X chromosome, but this has recently expanded. At least 500 genetic diseases have been associated with intellectual disability. Chromosomal disorders, such as Down syndrome, are in this category and include structural changes in chromosomes or when there are too few or too many chromosomes. The fact that boys are overrepresented in intellectual disability diagnoses is due to particular sex-related disorders of which the most prevalent is fragile X syndrome.

Certain maternal behaviors during pregnancy may increase the risk for intellectual disability (Collier & Hogue, 2007). These include excessive alcohol intake in the first 12 weeks of pregnancy, prenatal drug use, cigarette smoking, and malnutrition. A pregnant woman's exposure to contaminants or illnesses, such as rubella and syphilis, may also pose risk for the developing child. In addition, if a woman has HIV, she may pass it to her child, causing possible neurological damage.

Risk mechanisms at birth most commonly include prematurity and low birth weight. Risks after birth include childhood diseases (such as whooping cough,

Exhibit 3.1

Risk and Protective Mechanisms for the Onset of Intellectual Disability

Risk	Protective
Biological	
Prenatal illnesses and conditions	Regular prenatal care
Maternal behaviors during pregnancy	Prenatal screening and genetic counseling, if
(drugs, alcohol, tobacco, diet)	needed
Birth defects	Routine newborn developmental screenings.
Genetic (chromosomal)	Childhood immunizations against such
abnormalities	diseases as measles and Hib
	Specific treatment of an underlying condition
Childhood illnesses and trauma	Proper diet for pregnant woman and child
Male gender	
Social	
Lower socioeconomic status	Dissemination of educational information by
African American heritage	community organizations on preventable
Environmental conditions, such as	aspects of mental retardation
exposure to lead	Government programs to provide for the
	nutritional needs of young children
	Early intervention and education
	Child safety seat laws

chickenpox, measles, and Hib disease), a blow to the head or near drowning, and exposure to lead, mercury, or other environmental toxins. Poverty is a risk factor for intellectual disability because of its association with malnutrition, disease, inadequate prenatal and medical care, and environmental health hazards (Birdsong & Parish, 2008). Extreme deprivation of nurturance and of social, linguistic, and other stimulation may also contribute to intellectual disability. African American children are more likely to be diagnosed than Caucasian individuals, and while the reasons for this are unknown, they may be due to the overrepresentation of African Americans among those living in poverty (Neely-Barnes & Marcenko, 2004).

Several protective influences may offset the identified risks for intellectual disability (The Arc, 2004). These include regular prenatal care, childhood immunizations, and routine developmental screenings. Good prenatal care involves regular visits to a physician, ultrasounds, and education by the physician about appropriate behavioral changes, such as smoking and drinking cessation and dietary needs. Education about the importance of folic acid supplementation in pregnancy can also prevent neural tube defects that can cause intellectual disability. Pediatric human immunodeficiency virus (HIV) infection can be reduced by the pregnant mother's treatment with zidovudine (AZT). Removal of lead from the environment and other preventive interventions, such as child safety seats and bicycle helmets, reduce the risk of brain damage.

There is growing evidence that consistent exposure to highly responsive parenting styles throughout the early childhood period provides a variety of important child benefits in terms of language, cognitive, social, and emotional development. Maternal responsivity refers to a growth-producing relationship consisting of such caregiver characteristics as warmth, nurturance, stability, predictability, and contingent responsiveness (Spiker, Boyce, & Boyce, 2002). This is a construct of central importance to the development of children with intellectual disability just as it is for typically developing children. A systematic review of the literature revealed that studies have focused on four aspects of responsivity: contingent responding, emotional-affective support, joint attention with the child, and language input that is matched to the child receptive language level (Warren & Brady, 2007).

Specific treatment of an underlying condition, if known, can prevent or minimize brain injuries that result in intellectual disability (Chew, Takanohashi, & Bell, 2006). Examples of such preventive measures include changing the diet for a child diagnosed with PKU (a genetic condition affecting food metabolism) and inserting a shunt in the case of hydrocephalus (excess fluid in the brain).

Recovery and Adjustment

The course and continued eligibility for the intellectual disability diagnosis are contingent on continuous reevaluation of the individual's adaptive skills and the level of support required to achieve these skills. Although IQ may remain unchanged, the person's adaptive functioning and quality of life can improve, perhaps to the point where the individual no longer meets criteria for intellectual disability (Martin, 2007). Adaptive skills can be enhanced by the availability of environmental supports, such as individualized habilitative, educational, medical, residential, and other supportive services. The quality and expectations of support givers and the amount of empowerment opportunities given to an individual can also be key environmental factors in achieving higher levels of adaptive functioning.

Another influence on the course of intellectual disability is the naturally occurring psychosocial supports by community members and family members that can enrich individuals' lives and provide the resources needed to enhance adaptive functioning (Skinner & Weisner, 2007). In particular, family support is critical, and without a repertoire of effective coping strategies, parents are unable to give adequate support to their child with intellectual disability. In one study, Taanila, Syrjala, Kokkonen, and Jarvelin (2002) found the following positive coping strategies used by parents: obtaining information about intellectual disability and their child's specific co-occurring issues, having a realistic and accepting attitude about the diagnosis, enlisting cooperation among family members, possessing solid social network support, and openly expressing feelings and affection. Family therapy may be one method used to develop support and coping skills. The Arc (formerly the Association for Retarded Citizens), comprising a national organization as well as local and state chapters, is also available for family members. Originally formed by parents of children with intellectual disability 50 years ago, The Arc provides both service delivery and advocacy functions.

Family atmosphere is another predictor of the course of intellectual disability, as evidenced by studies of expressed emotion (Hastings & Lloyd, 2007). Expressed emotion (EE) is a measure of the affective relationship between two people characterized by criticism, hostility, and emotionally overinvolved attitudes. Outside of the field of intellectual disability there has been much interest in EE as a family characteristic that explains variance in the severity and course of several psychiatric disorders, including schizophrenia and bipolar disorder. It is important to emphasize, however, that EE may be an expected feature of the experience of caring for someone under stressful circumstances, and it is not something for which families should be blamed. Only 11 published studies have been done of EE in families of children and adults with intellectual disabilities, but their pooled findings support that there is evidence of high EE in some families of persons with intellectual disability. Thus, some behavior problems in children and adults with intellectual disability may be related to high EE in parents.

Adaptive skill level may be based not only on support received but also on health status and psychological functioning. Biomedical causes of intellectual disability may continue to manifest problems for the individual in terms of abilities and, ultimately, life span. However, even biomedical conditions encompass a heterogeneous course that cannot be entirely predicted. Regular physical exams should be received as a protective measure to rule out any physical problems and to manage those that are present. See Exhibit 3.2.

Individual life stressors, such as interpersonal loss or rejection, environmental stressors, transitional phases, parenting and social support problems, illness or disability, and stigmatization because of physical or intellectual problems, also act as risk influences (Rush & Frances, 2000). Another risk present for those diagnosed with intellectual disability is their vulnerability to sexual or physical abuse or to being taken advantage of financially. A research review concluded that, while studies are not extensive, persons with intellectual disability are more at risk for sexual and physical abuse than "normal"children, and more at risk than certain other disadvantaged populations (Horner-Johnson & Drum, 2006). People with intellectual disability are also vulnerable to more subtle dangers, such as limited opportunities for development, because those around them have lowered expectations for people diagnosed with intellectual disability. Furthermore, predictable life stressors can have a stronger impact on people diagnosed with intellectual disability and trigger

Exhibit 3.2

Risk and Protective Influences for the Course of Intellectual Disability

Risk	Protective
Biological	
Co-occurring physiological disorders (such as epilepsy, cerebral palsy)	Medications to combat symptoms from mental retardation or co-occurring disorders Regular physical exams
Psychological	
Presence of aggression, self-injury, mood disorders, or other psychiatric conditions Presence of autistic disorder and other pervasive developmental disorders	Person's strengths and attitude Communication skills
Social	
Life stressors	Individual and family have adequate coping strategies
Lack of adequate support system Lack of familial support and resources Vulnerability to abuse Stigma	Educational supports and interventions that utilize principles of empowerment, normalization, and independence Skills training in independent living and job skills

behavioral problems. Older adults with intellectual disability do not experience significantly different health problems compared to others, although there is a higher risk of Alzheimer disease in those with Down syndrome (Torr & Davis, 2007).

At the same time, an individual's own strengths and attitude can be a protective factor for the course of intellectual disability, because it is through such strengths that an individual has the motivation to learn, develop, and grow his or her own talents, despite any limitations presented by a diagnosis of intellectual disability.

Intervention

Psychosocial

Persons with intellectual disability often have difficulty meeting their health care and psychosocial needs (Balogh, Ouellette-Kuntz, Bourne, Lunsky, & Colantonio, 2008). They have historically exhibited poorer health and had more difficulty finding, getting access to, and paying for health and habilitation services. Public support for intellectual disability in the United States grew from $2.3 billion in 1955 to $82.6 billion in 2004, and the federal government emerged during this period as the principal provider of such support (Braddock, 2007). Despite this growth in financial support, many inequities persist in the distribution of financial resources and services across states and communities. Tens of thousands of people with intellectual disability continue to live in institutions and nursing homes. Waiting lists and aging caregivers are growing rapidly, and family support and supported employment programs receive limited funding. Research and training support have declined in comparison to the growing financial commitments for services and income maintenance. The forces shaping intellectual disability policy making are diverse. Emerging demographic and sociocultural trends directly affecting the intellectual disability field include aging, changing labor markets, immigration, families, federalism, and culture (Fujiura & Parish, 2007).

Federal legislation—for example, the Individuals with Disabilities Education Act (IDEA)—entitles children with intellectual disability from ages 3 to 21 years to free testing and appropriate individualized education and skills training within school systems. Most states have also established early intervention programs (EIPs) for children under age 3. Special education programs within school systems include the provision for an individualized education plan (IEP) that acts as a protective mechanism when implemented properly. Comprehensive IEPs include objectives that are individualized, measurable, and achievable; address appropriate class placement and support services; and are created with input from the student, teachers, support staff, and the student's family members. Despite mandates, the cost of such services can be astronomical, and many parents, school systems, and municipalities cannot afford to provide them (Rush & Frances, 2000).

Most programs currently involved in the habilitation and treatment of persons with intellectual disability are grounded in self-determination, community integration, person-centered planning, strengths-based approaches, and normalization. This last term refers to making conditions normal for the person with intellectual disability rather than making the person "normal." The goals of these support organizations (residential, educational, vocational, and recreational) are to empower and educate individuals with intellectual disability so that they can live the most meaningful and independent lives in their own communities as possible. Toward this end, Dykens (2006) advocates for a "positive psychology" for people with intellectual disability, with a greater intervention focus on promoting positive internal states, including happiness, contentment, and hope.

It is difficult to describe globally effective treatment strategies because protocols are based on the treatment of particular manifestations of intellectual disability, one's demonstrated adaptive functioning level, evident strengths, the supports needed, and the specific goals the person wants to achieve. With the additional caveat that intervention strategies will not be effective for each individual, some general approaches have been found effective, such as the following (Balogh, et al., 2008; Rush & Frances, 2000):

1. Enlist the cooperation and support of the person diagnosed with an intellectual disability and his or her family so they are invested and part of the treatment approach.
2. Treat the underlying condition, if known, to prevent or minimize brain injury that results in intellectual disability.
3. Diagnose and treat the comorbid physical conditions, such as hypothyroidism, congenital cataracts, or heart defects in children with Down syndrome and seizures in people with tuberous sclerosis.
4. Provide education and supportive therapies (such as physical, occupational, and language therapies).
5. Provide needed supports, such as child care specific to children with disabilities, residential support, behavioral training, support systems in school, day support, vocational support, and respite support.
6. Ensure continuity of care and easy and timely access to services to ensure that all of the individual's needs are coordinated.
7. Psychosocial stressors should be minimized, as they can lead to higher levels of impairment and behavioral problems due to frustration.
8. Select an individually tailored residential arrangement in the least restrictive setting possible.
9. Treat the symptoms of mental illnesses and the problem behaviors that often accompany a diagnosis of intellectual disability. Internalizing symptoms and social maladjustment tend to be more amenable to intervention than externally destructive behaviors.

For psychosocial intervention for behavior problems and co-occurring psychiatric disorders, first-line treatments are client and family education, social skills development, applied behavior analysis, and environmental management (Gustafsson et al., 2009). Cognitive-behavioral therapy is also recommended as a first-line treatment for some co-occurring mental disorders, including major depressive disorder, posttraumatic stress disorder, and obsessive-compulsive disorder. While each of these types of intervention lays claim to effectiveness, such support was found to be weak in a recent systematic review (Gustafsson et al., 2009).

Applied behavior analysis involves delineating sequences of behaviors, such as self-care and communication, into their constituent parts, managing stimulus and reinforcement conditions, and gradually fading prompts and reinforcements for the behavior. Teaching skills to parents and teachers in behavioral methods, using accelerating differential reinforcement procedures, and teaching social and communication skills to clients can be used across different severity levels of intellectual disability (Rush & Frances, 2000). Managing the environment refers to alteration of conditions that might trigger behavior problems: activities required (e.g., restructuring a job to make it easier), physical conditions (e.g., noise, temperature, lighting, crowding), and social conditions (e.g., changes in social grouping or enrichment through social stimulation).

Although most of the writing on psychotherapy is anecdotal, consensus in the field is that individuals with mild intellectual disability can benefit from individual, family, and group therapy if necessary language skills are in place and approaches are modified as appropriate (Taylor, Lindsay, & Willner, 2008). Most of the time, a concrete, skills-oriented approach is taken. For example, teaching how to handle peer pressure is critical so the individual can protect himself or herself against exploitation and behaviors that can be inappropriate or cause harm. One important goal is the development of a positive self-image and an understanding of limitations as a "lack of talent" in certain domains that is counterbalanced by knowledge of unique strengths and talents. Contextual interventions are also key aspects of intervention. For instance, a way to build self-esteem may be changing a frustrating classroom experience or job that does not fit with the client's abilities.

Persons with intellectual disability who are involved in habilitation programs are usually encouraged, when able, to participate in job training programs toward permanent employment, commensurate with their abilities. This is often successful, and there is consistent evidence of positive change in the levels of autonomy and perceived locus of control enjoyed by persons with intellectual disability in competitive employment (Jahoda, Kemp, Riddell, & Banks, 2008). Even if workplace tasks are repetitive or boring, requiring little autonomous thought or action, earning money affords greater choices in other life domains, and the social status of employees confers a greater sense of control. The sense of autonomy achieved by workers with intellectual disability seems dependent on environmental factors, however, including the stability of their home situations. One discouraging finding of these studies is that, even though persons with intellectual disability can integrate well into their workplaces, the relationships they form are generally not reciprocal and remain limited to those settings.

The development and expansion of community services for persons with intellectual disability has been successful in providing opportunities for such clients to enter the workforce. The ability of persons to work, however, is hindered by a shortage of professionals who can provide direct support in the workplace (Hewitt & Lawson, 2007). A workforce with the knowledge, skills, and attitudes needed to maintain the previous successes, and assure increased access to supports for people to the lives they want in the homes and communities, will require the active involvement of policy makers throughout the service system.

Regarding family intervention, the needs of the family vary, depending on when the diagnosis is made and the developmental stage of the child. Parents of young children who have just been diagnosed need education about the child's condition, an opportunity to express feelings of loss and anger, and information and referral about services and early intervention. The Arc can be an important source of information for family members.

Parents of older children need guidance and support in managing their children's behaviors and in generalizing to the home gains made in school interventions. At the same time, a focus on the child's strengths and abilities and the development of a positive self-image must be maintained. Parents may also need assistance and advocacy relevant to receipt of educational supports provided under federal and local laws. Families with adolescents need help in adjusting to the youth's sexuality and increasing independence from the family. Depending on the culture of the family, parents of adults with intellectual disability may need help to find appropriate out-of-home community placements and to appropriately separate from their children emotionally.

Parents may require resources and support if their children are still living in the home. Most research on the families of persons with intellectual disability has tended to focus on how members can support one another, rather than looking outside the family for more institutional supports (Turnbull, Summers, Lee, & Kyzar, 2007). Further, the literature has historically been dominated by focusing on the importance of the mother–child relationship, rather than a more systemic family perspective. Thus, there is a need for more intervention studies that take into account the resources and limits of the person's family of origin.

To summarize, for treatment approaches to be effective, they must be individualized, involve the individual and his or her family, and look for the presence of psychosocial strengths that can support the person's development. These treatment approaches are most effective when they exist within a framework of a normalizing community-based setting.

Medication

Medications can ameliorate some of the problematic behavioral symptoms that may arise from intellectual disability or its co-occurring disorders. The problem of physical aggression is probably the most common reason why medications are prescribed (Antonacci, Manuel, & Davis, 2008). The source of a person's aggression may include a poor attention span, impulsivity, memory impairment, seizures, allergies, social and communication limitations, sensory impairments, comorbid disorders such as anxiety and depression, and frustrating living conditions.

The antipsychotic medications are prescribed most often for persons with intellectual disability, followed by the anticonvulsants, antidepressants, lithium, and anxiolytic drugs. There is modest evidence that these medications have a significant effect on aggression. The antipsychotic drug risperidone reduces states of high aggression in persons with intellectual disability (Thaddeus, Ulzen & Powers, 2008), the mood stabilizers (lithium and the antiepilepsy drugs) help to reduce behavior management problems (Deb et al., 2008), antidepressant medications (especially the selective serotonin reuptake inhibitors) reduce aggressive behavior (Sohanpal et al., 2007), and amphetamine helps reduce agitation in persons with a dual diagnosis of intellectual disability and attention-deficit/hyperactivity disorder (Thompson, Maltezos, Paliokosta, & Xenitides, 2009).

Because of abuses encountered with the use of medication in people with intellectual disability, the following guidelines are recommended (Rush & Frances, 2000):

1. Medication should be one part of an overall plan that addresses all relevant aspects of the person and his or her environment.
2. The person's functional status should not be diminished as a result of the medication.
3. The person should receive the lowest effective dose possible, and dose reductions should be periodically attempted.
4. The possibility of adverse effects should be continually assessed.
5. The medication should lead to the desired outcome; otherwise there is no need to continue with that particular medication.

Medications are not as effective as psychosocial interventions in helping persons with intellectual disability to achieve their optimal functional levels, so we now turn to a consideration of the latter interventions.

Treatment and Special Populations

No differences in intervention have been suggested relative to the special populations of persons with intellectual disability. Indicators of level of adaptive functioning will of course differ depending on the client's environment, which includes the cultural environment.

Critique of the Diagnosis

At present, the APA, the AAIDD, and the World Health Organization each maintain separate definitions of the disorder. While these distinctions are subtle, they embody differences in philosophical orientation with implications for treatment, insurance coverage, and the self-concept of persons with intellectual disability and their families. For example, the APA, in an effort to provide a more empirical basis for the diagnosis and to allow for greater comparability between individuals, has mainly tied the diagnosis to scores on standardized tests. This emphasis places intellectual disability more firmly within a medical model. Critics of these tests claim that they do not measure innate intellectual ability, but rather the degree of fit between the individual and the class cultural norms of the White, middle-class U.S. educational system. However, the *DSM* criteria also stipulate that concurrent adaptive impairments must be present in at least two domains. This can be viewed as an effort to mitigate the focus on IQ by providing a more comprehensive parameter of intellectual disability.

The AAIDD, which often functions in an advocacy capacity, has tried to make the diagnosis less stigmatizing and more politically palatable to both persons with intellectual disability and the public at large, most obviously by adopting a new term for the disorder. The efforts of the AAIDD are transforming the concept of intellectual disability from an inherent trait or defect to a disability, arising from the interaction of the individual and his or her environment. As such, it can be ameliorated with appropriate supports, lending greater hope to persons with intellectual disability and their families.

Case Study

Ms. Rochelle Hunt is a 41-year-old African American woman who was diagnosed in her childhood with an intellectual disability. During her school years, she was in special education services, and a variety of IQ tests taken over time consistently placed her in the "mild" range of *DSM*-diagnosed mental retardation (about 65). She had been a pleasant, likeable, and persistent young woman, but her adaptive functioning was considered poor because of her ongoing reliance on family emotional support and reluctance to take steps toward independent living, even when encouraged by her own family, which had included two parents and an older sister.

Ms. Hunt first entered into case management services through her county's Mental Retardation Services Department 11.5 years ago, when she was pregnant. At that time, she came to the county government center for help. Her father had asked her to leave his house (her mother had passed away 10 years earlier), where she had been living, because he disapproved of her having a baby out of wedlock. Since then, Ms. Hunt has received services intermittently, returning of her own accord when she needed additional help. She had initially required intensive services because of poor independent living skills, but gradually she became able to manage her life in a small apartment. Ms. Hunt tended to get involved with people who might take advantage of her cognitive impairments because she hated to be alone.

Throughout the years, Ms. Hunt has been involved in an on-again, off-again relationship with her daughter's father, who has struck her multiple times. Ms. Hunt's daughter was diagnosed with mild mental retardation (the *DSM* term) and has been receiving case management services from the same case manager as Ms. Hunt. Although Ms. Hunt's daughter (now age 11) experienced some protective influences against having an intellectual disability (developmental screenings, immunizations, and regular physical examinations), she had a genetic risk and many environmental risk factors, such as the absence of appropriate cognitive and psychosocial stimulation, which precipitated her diagnosis.

Most recently, Ms. Hunt sought help because she lost her hotel service job (because of not showing up for work on some days) and was being evicted from her apartment. Ms. Hunt had left food out in her kitchen, which led to an insect problem. The landlord was forced to respond because others tenants were complaining. The landlord also reported an incident in which either Ms. Hunt or her boyfriend had defecated over her back porch. In addition, Ms. Hunt's neighbors had complained to the landlord that frequent yelling and what sounded like physical altercations could be heard between Ms. Hunt and her boyfriend.

These two areas of diminished adaptive functioning (home living and work), combined with her IQ and the onset of symptoms before age 18, supported her ongoing diagnosis. Because Ms. Hunt had come into services as an adult and there were no records of her developmental milestones, it is not clear what risk mechanisms for an intellectual disability she had experienced. Ms. Hunt did possess certain risks for the course of her disorder, however. She had suffered a number of stressors, such as eviction from her apartment, losing her job, raising her daughter, and dealing with domestic violence. Ms. Hunt's support system was not always adequate to her needs. On occasion, Ms. Hunt decided that she could do things on her own without any support and would refuse services. Ms. Hunt's father had developed serous kidney problems, and her sister became emotionally cut off from the family at an early age, which prevented them from responding to Ms. Hunt's support needs. Several times throughout the years, Ms. Hunt had sought vocational support services from the county agency. Because of inadequate funds, the agency was unable to serve her, and her name remained on a waiting list. Another possible risk for Ms. Hunt was that she had not had a physical exam in the past 2.5 years. She explained that she had not known how to access and use her health benefits.

Protective influences for the course of Ms. Hunt's intellectual disability included self-confidence that she could do things relatively independently and the fact that she was able to take care of her daughter. In addition, Ms. Hunt's religious beliefs and the emotional support she received from her church congregation were protective. Ms. Hunt's self-confidence was enhanced by her belief that God was taking care of her, and the church provided her with some friendships and recreational opportunities.

A multidisciplinary team was assembled to assess Ms. Hunt and develop a treatment plan. The team consisted of a vocational support provider, a case manager, a representative from the local office of the national advocacy group (The Arc), and Ms. Hunt herself. As an example of the assessment process, the case manager helped Ms. Hunt acquire a primary care doctor and assisted her in sorting out health insurance and transportation issues. The subsequent physical examination indicated that Ms. Hunt had hypertension. She was provided with education about diet and exercise and was given medication to manage her condition.

The team assessed her goals, her strengths, and the support she would require to accomplish those goals. Ms. Hunt came up with the goals of dating a different boyfriend, getting a new affordable place to live, finding and maintaining employment, and participating in more recreational activities. She stated that her ultimate goal was to own her own home. As for Ms. Hunt's strengths, the team determined that she was able to do most things in her life independently (shop, take care of her daughter, perform activities of daily living). She was confident, had the support of the agency, had a steady income (Social Security and SSI), and had a fulfilling spiritual life.

The following multiaxial diagnosis was made:

Axis I: 309.24 Adjustment Disorder with Anxiety

Ms. Hunt said her "nerves" were bothering her after the eviction notice and being fired, and she was having a hard time sleeping.

Axis II: 317. Mild Mental Retardation
Axis III: Hypertension
Axis IV: Occupational problems (loss of job)

Housing problems (eviction from apartment) Problems with primary support group (domestic violence by boyfriend)

Axis V: GAF: 60

The team concluded that Ms. Hunt needed professional assistance in finding a job and an apartment, education about the dynamics of domestic violence, financial counseling, and assistance in making a Section 8 housing application. Each representative from the various agencies and departments (vocational services, The Arc representative, case management services) stated what support that agency could offer and proposed it to Ms. Hunt.

Each department or agency then developed an individualized support plan with Ms. Hunt that addressed supports she would need to achieve her goals for that particular part of her life (i.e., vocational, case management, recreational). The case manager coordinated the services to ensure that the various intervention steps were consistent in addressing Ms. Hunt's goals.

Interventions

The treatment strategy for Ms. Hunt was grounded in self-determination and person-centered planning. Ms. Hunt was involved in every step of the treatment planning process—she was asked about her goals and her desired level of support, and she was involved in the writing of the plan itself. When she brought up the domestic violence situation, the treatment team respected that it was her choice to remain with her boyfriend. The team did not make value statements or rescue her from the situation and counseled her on her options. Still, Ms. Hunt was informed that if her daughter was harmed by the situation in her home, the team social worker might be obligated to call child protective services.

The social worker further ensured that each plan had long-term goals and measurable short-term objectives. The plans also included a list of support services that were needed to achieve the goals and objectives. An example of a long-term goal was as follows: "Ms. Hunt will gain meaningful and steady employment." An accompanying objective stated, "Ms. Hunt will pick up three job applications per week from neighborhood stores, with 80% success, within 3 months of the writing of this plan." Eighty percent effectiveness referred to the fact that after 3 months Ms. Hunt would pick up three applications per week for 80% of the weeks to be considered successful with that objective. Another objective was, "Ms. Hunt will attend a Section 8 housing informational meeting within 1 month from now." There were many such goals and objectives written. The team agreed to meet again in 3 months to assess Ms. Hunt's progress.

At the follow-up meeting Ms. Hunt proudly announced that she was able to get Section 8 housing assistance. She attended the Section 8 informational meeting, and her social worker helped her fill out the appropriate forms. With the further assistance of her social worker, Ms. Hunt called several apartments and was waiting to hear back from them. She also reported that she had been getting some job applications (she had not quite met that particular objective because she rarely sought applications three times in a week). Her job coach helped her fill out the applications and prepare for interviews, and Ms. Hunt had two interviews scheduled for the following week in an elementary school cafeteria. She was excited about working in a school. She noted that she was still with her boyfriend but was talking with him about going to counseling sessions at the county's mental health clinic. The team congratulated her for the work she had done, reassessed her goals and support needs, and set a date to evaluate Ms. Hunt's progress in another 3 months.

References

American Association on Intellectual and Developmental Disabilities (AAIDD). (2009). *Definition of intellectual disability*. Retrieved April 23, 2009, from http://www.aamr.org/FYI.

American Psychiatric Association. (2000). *Diagnostic and statistical manual of mental disorders* (4th ed., text rev.). Washington, DC: Author.

Antonacci, D. J., Manuel, C., & Davis, E. (2008). Diagnosis and treatment of aggression in individuals with developmental disabilities. *Psychiatric Quarterly, 79*(3), 225–247.

The Arc. (2004). *Introduction to mental retardation*. Retrieved on June 29, 2004, from http://www.thearc.org/faqs/mrqu.html.

Arvidsson, P., Granlund, M., & Thyberg, M. (2008). Factors related to self-rated participation in adolescents and adults with mild intellectual disability: A systematic literature review. *Journal of Applied Research in Intellectual Disabilities, 21*(3), 277–291.

Association of University Centers on Disabilities. (2004). *About AUCD.* Retrieved June 1, 2005, from http://www.aucd.org/aucd_about.htm.

Balogh, R., Ouellette-Kuntz, H., Bourne, L., Lunsky, Y., & Colantonio, A. (2008). Organising health care services for persons with an intellectual disability. *Cochrane Database of Systematic Reviews, 4,* Art. No.: CD007492. DOI: 10.1002/14651858. CD007492.

Bayley, N. (1993). *Bayley scales of infant development* (2nd ed.). San Antonio, TX: Psychological Corporation.

Bhaumik, S., Tyrer, F. C., McGrother, C., & Ganghadaran, S. K. (2008). Psychiatric service use and psychiatric disorders in adults with intellectual disability. *Journal of Intellectual Disability Research, 52*(11), 986–995.

Birdsong, S., & Parish, S. L. (2008). The Healthy Families Act: Vital support for families of people with developmental disabilities. *Intellectual and Developmental Disabilities, 46*(4), 319–321.

Braddock, D. (2007) Washington rises: Public financial support for intellectual disability in the United States, 1955–2004. *Mental Retardation and Developmental Disabilities Research Reviews, 13,* 169–177.

Cederborg, A. C., La Rooy, D., & Lamb, M. E. (2008). Repeated interviews with children who have intellectual disabilities. *Journal of Applied Research in Intellectual Disabilities, 21*(2), 103–113.

Chadwick, D. D., & Jolliffe, J. (2009). A descriptive investigation of dysphagia in adults with intellectual disabilities. *Journal of Intellectual Disability Research, 53*(1), 29–43.

Chew, L. J., Takanohashi, A., & Bell, B. (2006). Microglia and inflammation: Impact on developmental brain injuries. *Mental Retardation and Developmental Disabilities Research Reviews, 12*(2), 105–112.

Collier, A., & Hogue, C. J. R. (2007). Modifiable risk factors for low birth weight and their effect on cerebral palsy and mental retardation. *Maternal & Child Health Journal, 11*(1), 65–71.

Deb, S., Chaplin, R. S., Sohanpal, S., Unwin, G., Soni, R., & Lenotre, L. (2008). The effectiveness of mood stabilizers and antiepileptic medication for the management of behaviour problems in adults with intellectual disability: A systematic review. *Journal of Intellectual Disability Research, 52*(2), 107–113.

Dykens, E. M., (2006). Toward a positive psychology of mental retardation. *American Journal of Orthopsychiatry, 77*(2), 185–193.

Fujiurai, G. T., & Parish, S. L. (2007). Emerging policy challenges in intellectual dis-abilities. *Mental Retardation and Developmental Disabilities Research Reviews 13,* 188–194.

Gustafsson, C., Ojehagen, A., Hansson, L., Sandlund, M., Nystrom, M., Glad, J., Cruce, G., Jonsson, A. K., & Fredriksson, M. (2009). Effects of psychosocial interventions for people with intellectual disabilities and mental health problems. *Research on Social Work Practice, 19*(3), 281–290.

Hewitt, A., & Lawson, S. (2007). The direct support workforce in community supports to individuals with developmental disabilities: Issues, implications, and promising practices. *Mental Retardation and Developmental Disabilities Research Reviews, 13,* 178–187.

Hastings, R. P., & Lloyd, T. (2007). Expressed emotion in families of children and adults with intellectual disabilities. *Mental Retardation and Developmental Disabilities Research Reviews, 13,* 339–345.

Horner-Johnson, W., & Drum, C. E. (2006). Prevalence of maltreatment of people with intellectual disabilities: A review of recently published research. *Mental Retardation and Developmental Disabilities Research Reviews, 12,* 57–69.

Jahoda, A., Kemp, J., Riddell, S., & Banks, P. (2008). Feelings about work: A review of the socio-emotional impact of supported employment on people with intellectual disabilities. *Journal of Applied Research in Intellectual Disabilities, 21,* 1–18

Kerr, M. (2006). Improving the general health of people with intellectual disabilities. *Directions in Psychiatry, 26*(4), 235–240.

Martin, E. D. (2007). Adaptation to disability: Perspectives of persons with disabilities. In M. E. Davis (Ed.), *Principles and practices of case management in rehabilitation counseling* (2nd ed., pp. 71–82). Springfield, IL: Charles C. Thomas.

Matthews, T., Weston, N., Baxter, H., Felce, D., & Kerr, M. (2008). A general practice-based prevalence study of epilepsy among adults with intellectual disabilities and of its association with psychiatric disorder, behavior disturbance and career stress. *Journal of Intellectual Disability Research, 52*(2), 163–173.

Neely-Barnes, S., & Marcenko, M. (2004). Predicting impact of childhood disability on families: Results from the 1995 National Health Interview Survey Disability Supplement. *Mental Retardation, 42*(4) 284–293.

Ropers, H. H. (2008). Genetics of intellectual disability. *Current Opinion in Genetics and Development, 18,* 241–250.

Rush, A. J., & Frances, A. (Eds.). (2000). Expert consensus guideline series: Treatment of psychiatric and behavioral problems in mental retardation. *American Journal on Mental Retardation, 105,* 159–228.

Saeed, H., Ouellette-Kuntz, H., Stuart, H., & Burge, P. (2003). Length of stay for psychiatric inpatient services: A comparison of admissions of people with and without developmental disabilities. *Journal of Behavioral Health Services & Research, 30,* 406–418.

Skinner, D., & Weisner, T. S. (2007). Sociocultural studies of families of children with intellectual disabilities. *Mental Retardation and Developmental Disabilities Research Reviews, 13,* 302–312.

Sohanpal, S. K., Deb, S., Thomas, C., Soni, R., Lenotre, L., & Unwin, G. (2007). The effectiveness of antidepressant medication in the management of behaviour problems in adults with intellectual disabilities: A systematic review. *Journal of Intellectual Disability Research, 51*(10), 750–765.

Spiker, D., Boyce, G., & Boyce, L. (2002). Parent-child interactions when young children have disabilities. *Mental Retardation and Developmental Disabilities Research Reviews, 25,* 35–70.

Sturmey, P. (2007). Psychosocial and mental status assessment. In J. W. Jacobson, J. A. Mulick, & J. Rojahn (Eds.), *Handbook of intellectual and developmental disabilities* (pp. 295–315). New York: Springer.

Szymanski, L., & King, B. H. (1999). Practice parameters for the assessment and treatment of children, adolescents, and adults with mental retardation and comorbid mental disorders. *Journal of the American Academy of Child & Adolescent Psychiatry, Vol 38*(12,Suppl), 5S-31S.

Taanila, A., Syrjala, L., Kokkonen, J., & Jarvelin, M. R. (2002). Coping of parents with physically and/or intellectually disabled children. *Child: Care, Health, & Development, 28*(1), 73–86.

Taylor, J. L., Lindsay, W. R., & Willner, P. (2008). CBT for people with intellectual disabilities: Emerging evidence, cognitive ability and IQ effects. *Behavioural and Cognitive Psychotherapy, 36*(6). 723–733.

Thaddeus, P., Ulzen, E., & Powers, R. E. (2008). A review of empirical evidence of somatic treatment options for the MI/DD Population. *Psychiatric Quarterly, 79,* 265–273.

Thomson, A., Maltezos, S., Paliokosta, E., & Xenitidis, K. (2009). Amfetamine for attention deficit hyperactivity disorder in people with intellectual disabilities. *Cochrane Database of Systematic Reviews, 1,* Art. No.: CD007009. DOI: 10.1002/14651858.CD007009.pub2.

Torr, J., & Davis, R. (2007). Ageing and mental health problems in people with intellectual disability. *Current Opinion in Psychiatry, 20*(5), 467–471.

Turnbull, A. P., Summers, J. A., Lee, S. H., & Kyzar, K. (2007). Conceptualization and measurement of family outcomes associated with families of individuals with intellectual disabilities. *Mental Retardation and Developmental Disabilities Research Reviews, 13,* 346–356.

Verdonschot, M. M. L., deWitte, L. P., Reichrath, E., Buntinx, W. H. E., & Curfs, L. M. G. (2008). Impact of environmental factors on community participation of persons with intellectual disability: A systematic review. *Journal of Intellectual Disability Resaerch, 53*(1), 54–64.

Warren, S. F., & Brady, N. C. (2007). The role of maternal responsivity in the development of children with intellectual disabilities. *Mental Retardation and Developmental Disabilities Research Reviews, 13,* 330–338.

Yeargin-Allsopp, M., Boyle, C., Braun, K., & Trevathan, E. (2008). The epidemiology of developmental disabilities. In P. J. Accardo (Ed.), *Caput and Accardo's neurodevelopmental disabilities in infancy and childhood, Vol. 1: Neurodevelopmental diagnosis and treatment* (pp. 61–104). Baltimore: Brookes.

Appendix I: Measures of Adaptive Behavior

Information on psychometric properties was obtained from Handen (2007).

Adaptive Behavior Scale—Residential and Community, 2nd ed. (ABS-RC:2)

AAMR Adaptive Behavior Scale—School, 2nd ed. (ABS-S:2) (Lambert, Nihira, & Leland, 1993)

- Assesses the ability of persons from ages 3 to 21 who are intellectually disabled, emotionally maladjusted, or developmentally disabled to cope with the natural and social demands of their environment. There are two forms for this scale: one for school and the other for residential and community settings.

- May be completed by parents, teachers, nurses, and institutional aides, as well as psychologists, social workers, and speech and language professionals.
- Items are scored "yes/no" or "select which statement best applies."
- Part 1 is designed to evaluate coping skills considered important to personal independence and responsibility in daily living and is grouped into nine behavior domains (independent functioning, physical development, economic activity, language development, numbers and time, prevocational/vocational activity, self-direction, responsibility, and socialization).
- Part 2 measures personality and behavior disorders and is grouped into seven domains (social behavior, conformity, trustworthiness, stereotyped and hyperactive behavior, self-abusive behavior, social engagement, and disturbing interpersonal behavior).
- The ABS-S assesses the same domains, except domestic ability and inappropriate body exposure.

Reliability: Adaptive Behavior Fulld Scales—School Version
- Internal consistency for all scores exceeds .90.
- Split-half reliability for ages 8–9 was .91.
- Test-retest reliability for ages 6–13 was .66 (same interviewer 2–4 weeks apart).
- Interrater reliability for ages 6–18 years was .74 (two interviewers).

Reliability: Problem Behavior Scales—School Version
- Split-half reliability for ages 8–9 was .94.
- Test-retest reliability for ages 6–13 was .83 (same interview 2–4 weeks apart).
- Interrater reliability for ages 6–8 was .57 (two interviewers).

Validity: Adaptive Behavior Full Scales—School Version
- Adaptive behaviors were significantly correlated with age 0–18 (.41), indicating construct validity.
- Adaptive behaviors were positively correlated with IQ (.41–.72), indicating criterion validity. Correlations ranged from high for heterogeneous groups of handicapped children to low for nonhandicapped adults.
- Positive correlations with other adaptive behaviors scales (.53–.61), indicating criterion validity.

Appendix II: Measures for Emotional, Behavioral, and Mental Problems for Persons With Intellectual Disability

Aberrant Behavior Checklist (ABC) (Aman & Singh, 1986; Brown, Aman, & Havercamp, 2002)

- A symptom checklist for assessing problem behaviors of children and adults (ages 6–21) with mental retardation, including moderate to severe intellectual disability, in different settings: at home, in residential facilities, and in work training centers.

- May be completed by parents, special educators, psychologists, direct caregivers, nurses, and others with knowledge of the person being assessed.
- The ABC–Residential version includes 58 items rated on a 4-point scale divided into five subscales: irritability/agitation, lethargy/social withdrawal, stereotypic behavior, hyperactivity/noncompliance, and inappropriate speech.
- The ABC–Community version contains the same item content except that home, school, and workplace are listed as the relevant settings.

Reliability

- Across studies, internal consistency for subscales ranged from .76 to .94.
- Interrater reliability ranged from .39 to .67 for staff providers; parent–teacher agreement ranged from .39 to .45.
- Test-retest reliability ranged from .55 to. 83 for care providers and .50 to .67 for teacher ratings.

Validity

It established convergent and divergent validity with the Behavior Problems Inventory (Rojahn, Aman, Matson, & Mayville, 2003).

Behavioral and Emotional Rating Scale (BERS) (Epstein & Sharma, 1998)

- A 52-item scale administered on a 4-point Likert scale
- Includes five subscales: interpersonal strength, family involvement, intrapersonal strength, school functioning, and affective strength
- Completed by teachers, parents, counselors, or others knowledgeable about the child in approximately 10 minutes
- Focuses on the child's strengths

Reliability

- Internal consistency is strong: All alpha coefficients for subscales were above .80, and half were above .90.
- Interrater and test-retest reliability were evaluated in two separate studies in which teachers or teachers' aides rated individuals with emotional and behavioral disturbance; the results showed stability over time and consistency between raters, with all correlations over .80 and half over .90.

Validity

Convergent validity has been examined in two studies: Correlations between the BERS Subscales and total score from the Walker McConnell

Scale of Social Competence and School Adjustment–Adolescent Version were moderate to high (.50 to .75). Correlations between the BERS and the five competence scales, the broad-band dimensions, and the total problem score of the teacher report of the Child Behavior Checklist were moderate to high (.39–.72).

Reiss Scales for Children's Dual Diagnosis (Reiss & Valenti-Hein, 1994)

- Designed as a children's version (ages 4–21) of the Reiss Screen for Maladaptive Behavior
- The 60-item instrument that produces scores on a total score, 10 psychometric scales (anger/self-control, anxiety disorder, attention deficit, autism, conduct disorder, depression, poor self-esteem, psychosis, somatoform behavior, and withdrawn/isolated), and 10 rare behavior problems (crying spells, enuresis/encopresis, hallucinations, involuntary motor movements, lies, obese, pica, sets fires, sexual problem, and verbally abusive)
- The scale may be completed by caretakers, teachers, parents, and others who know the child.

Reliability
Internal consistency was .92 for the total score and an average of .75 for the psychometric scales.

Validity
Factor analysis supports the construct validity of the instrument.

Reiss Screen for Maladaptive Behavior (Reiss, 1988)

- Screens for mental health problems in adolescents and adults with intellectual disability
- Uses caretaker, teacher, work supervisor, or parent ratings of behavior and symptoms for persons with intellectual disability age 16 and older
- Raters indicate the extent to which each of 36 defined symptoms of psychiatric disorder is "no problem," "a problem,"or "a major problem."
- Five-item scales produce scores for aggressive behavior, autism, psychosis, paranoia, depression (behavioral signs), depression (physical signs), dependent personality disorder, and avoidant disorder; in addition, "special maladaptive behavior" items assess drug/alcohol, sexual problems, stealing, self-injury, overactivity, and suicidal tendencies.

- Screens for psychiatric disorder in three different ways (severity of challenging behavior, diagnosis, and rare but significant symptoms such as suicidal behavior)
- Takes 10 minutes to complete

Reliability
- Good interrater reliability, modest to good test-retest reliability, and good internal consistency with a random sample of 60 adults with moderate to profound intellectual disability living in an institutional setting; however, the autism, depression (physical signs), and depression (physical signs–revised) scales showed only marginal or unacceptable degrees of reliability (Sturmey, Burcham, & Perkins, 1995).
- Reliability is adequate for internal consistency, ranging from .57 to .84, and for interrater reliability, ranging from .61 to .84 for a series of research samples (Prout, 1993).
- Internal reliability for six of eight clinical scales and the total score is fairly high, ranging from .73 to .84, with the exceptions of the autism and depression (physical) scales, which were .58 and .54, respectively (Johns & McDaniel, 1998).

Validity
- Modest to good concurrent validity with the Psychopathology Inventory for Mentally Retarded Adults, the Aberrant Behavior Checklist, and patterns of service use (Sturmey & Bertman, 1994).
- Criterion validity was established for the scales by showing that the subjects with a dual diagnosis scored highest on the scales that were most relevant to their specific mental health diagnosis in a diverse sample of 306 adolescents and adults with intellectual disability (Havercamp & Reiss, 1997).

References for Intellectual Disability Measures

Aman, M., & Singh, N. (1986). *Aberrant behavior checklist: Manual.* East Aurora, NY: Slosson.

Brown, E., Aman, M., & Havercamp, S. (2002). Factor analysis and norms for parent ratings on the Aberrant Behavior Checklist–Community for young people in special education. *Research in Developmental Disabilities, 23,* 45–60.

Epstein, M. H., & Sharma, J. (1998). *Behavioral and emotional rating scale: A strength-based approach to assessment.* Austin, TX: PRO-ED.

Havercamp, S. M., & Reiss, S. (1997). The Reiss screen for maladaptive behavior: Confirmatory factor analysis. *Behaviour and Research Therapy, 35*(10), 967–971.

Johns, M., & McDaniel, W. (1998). Areas of convergence and discordance between the MMPI-168 and the Reiss Screen for Maladaptive Behavior in mentally retarded clients. *Journal of Clinical Psychology, 54*(4), 529–535.

Lambert, N., Nihira, K., & Leland, H. (1993). *AMR adaptive behavior scale–residential and community* (2nd ed.) (ABS-RC:2). *Examiner's manual.* Lutz, FL: PAR.

Prout, H. T. (1993). Assessing psychopathology in persons with mental retardation: A review of the Reiss Scales. *Journal of School Psychology, 31*, 535–540.

Reiss, S. (1988). *The Reiss Screen for Maladaptive Behavior test manual.* Worthington, OH: IDS.

Reiss, S., & Valenti-Hein, D. (1994). Development of a psychopathology rating scale for children with mental retardation. *Journal of Consulting and Clinical Psychology, 62*, 28–33.

Rojahn, J., Aman, M., Matson, J., & Mayville, E. (2003). The Aberrant Behavior Checklist and the Behavior Problems Inventory: Convergent and divergent validity. *Research in Developmental Disabilities, 24*, 391–404.

Sturmey, P., & Bertman, L. J. (1994). Validity of the Reiss Screen for Maladaptive Behavior. *American Journal on Mental Retardation, 99*(2), 201–206.

Sturmey, P., Burcham, K., & Perkins, T. S. (1995). The Reiss Screen for Maladaptive Behaviour: Its reliability and internal consistencies. *Journal of Intellectual Disability Research, 39*, 191–195.

4   Pervasive Developmental Disorders

WITH AMY WOOLEY

The *pervasive developmental disorders* (PDDs) are among the disorders first evident in childhood and adolescence. The American Psychiatric Association (APA) has delineated five types of PDDs in the *Diagnostic and Statistical Manual of Mental Disorders* (*DSM-IV-TR*) (APA, 2000). These disorders are characterized by "severe and pervasive impairment in several areas of development: reciprocal social interaction, communication skills, or the presence of stereotyped behavior, interests, and activities" (p. 65). *Autism* is the best known of these disorders, and it is characterized by severe impairments in all three areas noted above.

In the past several decades researchers have noted that three of the PDDs (autistic disorder, Asperger disorder, and pervasive developmental disorder—not otherwise specified) may in fact represent different disability levels of the same core disorder, and these have come to be known as the *autism spectrum disorders* (*ASDs*). However, we will retain the nomenclature of the *DSM-IV-TR* and refer to these as PDDs (APA, 2000).

Autism is a PDD with an early childhood onset. It is characterized by marked abnormal development in social interaction and communication and a stereotypical, repetitive range of ritualized behaviors such as rocking, toe walking, flapping, clapping, whirling, and an obsessive desire for sameness. The disorder was first identified in the literature by Leo Kanner in 1943

(Smith, Magyar, & Arnold-Saritepe, 2002). Its *DSM-IV-TR* criteria include 12 symptoms divided among three categories, including social interaction, communication/play/imagination, and limitations of interests and behaviors (APA, 2000). Still, there is a great variability in possible symptoms among persons with autism. Relatively few such persons (10%–40%) display any particular behavioral marker, regardless of the diagnostic system being used (APA, 2000). No common neural or cognitive deficits, behavior patterns, or life courses have been found among persons with the disorder; nor is there a typical response to behavioral or drug intervention.

Despite differences in individual presentation, the impairments in social relatedness underlie and define autism (Peliosa & Lund, 2001). These include a lack of awareness of the feelings of others, an impaired capacity to imitate and express emotion, and the absence of capacity for social and symbolic play. Even in infancy children with autism may lack reciprocal social engagement and are unable to maintain eye contact with another person. As the child grows older, these social disabilities persist, as indicated by difficulty in forming friendships, showing empathy, and understanding rules and expectations that are a part of daily social interaction.

Communication deficits in persons with autism include nonverbal communication (seen in 50% of clients), echolalia (repetition of words or phrases), abnormal prosody (atypical speech rhythm, stress, intonation, and loudness), and pronoun reversal (for instance, the person refers to "you" as him or herself, and the other person as "me"). These impairments are most pronounced in the pragmatic or social aspects of language (Akshoomoff, 2006). Persons with autism may present irrelevant details, inappropriately perseverate on a topic, suddenly shift to a new topic, and ignore others' attempts to initiate conversation. Deficits also involve language comprehension; speech is interpreted in overly concrete and literal ways. In fact, persons with autism have more difficulty understanding language than they do learning the structures necessary to produce language. Thus, half the autistic population does not develop speech, and a majority fails to use speech functionally (Peliosa & Lund, 2001). Persons with autism do, however, often possess characteristic "pockets" of ability, such as memorization, visual and spatial skills, and attention to details.

The characteristics of autism are spread across two other PDDs, Asperger disorder and pervasive developmental disorder—not otherwise specified (PDD-NOS), without clear lines of demarcation among them (Akshoomoff, 2006). The core symptoms of autism are less severe in these other two diagnostic categories, and Asperger disorder and PDD-NOS are sometimes referred to as "high functioning" autism.

In *Asperger disorder*, early development (both cognition and language) is apparently normal, but the child often has unusual interests that are pursued with great intensity (Holter, 2004). The child's approaches to peers and new adults may be unusual or idiosyncratic, but attachment patterns to family members are well established. Social deficits become more prominent as the child enters preschool and is exposed to peers. The current criteria for Asperger disorder emphasize impairments in social interaction and non-verbal communication similar to those found in autism, but without the unusual behaviors and environmental responsiveness. Referral for assessment is usually later than in cases of suspected autism (Smith, Magyar, & Arnold-Saritepe, 2002).

The term *pervasive developmental disorder—not otherwise specified* (PDD-NOS), sometimes termed atypical PDD or atypical autism, encompasses sub-threshold autism cases where, for example, there is marked impairment in social interaction, communication, or stereotyped behavior patterns or interests, but the full features of autism or another defined PDD are not met (Koyama, Tachimor, Osada, & Kurita, 2006). This category represents the highest level of functioning within the spectrum. While deficits in social and other skills have been noted, these problems are less severe than in classical autism. Pervasive developmental disorder—not otherwise specified is more commonly seen than autism (Towbin, 2005).

Prevalence

The reported incidence of PDDs has increased at a remarkably high rate across the world in the past 20 years. The causes of this increase include changing diagnostic criteria, service eligibility regulations, knowledge about intervention, political advocacy, and the increase in diagnosis of very young children (Shaattuck & Grosse, 2007). The Centers for Disease Control and Prevention found that the prevalence of PDDs was 6.6 per 1,000 children in the United States (Rice, 2007). The number of students aged 6–21 years identified in the PDD reporting category in U.S. special education grew between 1994 and 2005 from 18,540 to 165,552, with 109,869 being in the 6–11 age group (Safran, 2008). To put this into context, the PDDs are more common in childbood than cerebral palsy, hearing loss, vision impairment, and diabetes, but less so than intellectual disabilities (Yeargin-Alsopp et al., 2003). Some researchers argue that subthreshold symptoms of PDD are even more prevalent, with one study finding that 2.7% of all 7–9 year olds exhibited such symptoms (Posserud, Lundervold, & Gillberg, 2006).

Comorbidity

Persons with PDD have an increased risk for certain other psychiatric problems due to its broadly debilitating features, cognitive impairment, the frequent presence of medical disorders, and problematic life experiences related to having PDD (Solomon, Ono, Timmer, & Goodlin-Jones, 2008).

Exhibit 4.1

Common Co-Occurring Disorders With Pervasive Developmental Disorders

Comorbid Disorder	Prevalence and Features
Intellectual disability	Severe or profound in 50% of persons with PDD, mild to moderate in 30%, and within the normal IQ range in 20%
Seizure disorders	Present by early adulthood in 25% to 30% of persons with PDD
Depression	Rates of 4.4% to 57.6% in persons with PDD; this comorbid disorder is most often found in adults.
Anxiety (agoraphobia, separation anxiety, specific phobias, and obsessive-compulsive disorder)	Present in 7% to 84% of persons with PDD
Attention-deficit/hyperactivity disorder	Present in 21% to 72% of persons with PDD
Oppositional defiant disorder	Present in 50%–60% of children with PDD
Tic disorders	Present in 7%–29% of persons with PDD

IQ, intelligence quotient; PDD, pervasive developmental disorder.

Source: Aman & Langworthy, 2000; Bernard et al., 2002; de Bruin, Ferdinand, Meester, de Nijs, & Verheij, 2007; JAACAP, 1999; Leyfer et al., 2006; Schopler, 2001; Tsakanikos et al., 2006.

Estimates of the frequency of comorbid disorders in persons with PDD vary widely, with some as high as 81% (de Bruin, Ferdinand, Meester, de Nijs, & Verheij, 2007). This is because the majority of studies rely on clinical rather than epidemiological samples as well as different sample selection processes, ages of participants, methods of inquiry, and diagnostic measures used. Furthermore, as noted earlier, the features of PDD can make the diagnosis of other psychiatric disorders difficult. Exhibit 4.1 lists common comorbid disorders that have been established for the PDDs.

Course

Studies on the course of PDD show variable results depending on the severity of the condition, but all of the spectrum disorders are associated with poor outcomes regarding quality of social functioning. In one longitudinal study of 120 persons with autism, 78% had severe social and perceptual disturbances in adulthood and only four persons were living independently (Billstedt, Gillberg, & Gillberg, 2005). Another study by the same authors of 105 persons with autism in adulthood revealed that while a large majority continued to display the disturbances noted above, one-third to one-half demonstrated improvements in self-care skills, explosive and stereotypical behavior, and emotional responsiveness (Billstedt, Gillberg, & Gillberg 2007). A third study of the course of autism by McGovern and Sigman (2005) supported these findings, but it emphasized again that better outcomes were associated with persons who had milder forms of the disorder. Barnhill (2007) studied the course of Asperger disorder into adulthood and found that persons continued to experience impairments in employment, perception, social isolation, motor skills, and mood, with depression being a common feature.

Assessment

Early diagnosis of the autism spectrum disorders is important so that intervention can begin as soon as possible, when it is most effective. Autism does not appear any later than the age of 3 years and is usually diagnosed by the age of 4 years (Smith et al., 2002). The other spectrum disorders may not be diagnosed until several years later because their associated symptoms may not be as prominent. Delays in diagnosis may be due to a dearth of knowledge about PDDs (even among primary health care physicians) and a lack of easily applied screening tools (Matson, Nebel-Schwan, & Matson, 2007). Practice guidelines adopted by the American Academy of Pediatrics call for pediatricians to examine for signs of PDDs in babies and toddlers (Smith et al., 2002).

The assessment of persons with a PDD requires careful attention to environmental influences that precipitate or maintain the problem behaviors (Ozonoff, Goodlin-Jones, & Solomon, 2007). This ensures that the system around the child, including caregivers, parents, and teachers, changes to promote lasting change in the child. Social workers should never diagnose a PDD by themselves, because the process is complex, involves medical knowledge, and requires interprofessional collaboration. A comprehensive assessment should include input from the fields of psychiatry, medicine, psychology, social work, speech/language/communication therapy, occupational therapy, and physical therapy. It is essential to involve parents and, as appropriate, other family members in the assessment process, to set the stage for long-term collaborative relationships and help parents become better-informed advocates for their child.

While biochemical tests may someday distinguish at least some of the conditions within the autistic spectrum, identification at present is made through behavioral symptoms. Still, no single behavior or even set of behaviors unequivocally denotes a PDD (Jordan, 2001). Symptom patterns occur in different areas of functioning, which is why assessment involves professionals from different areas of expertise.

In diagnosing PDDs, other disorders must also be considered. Exhibit 4.2 addresses some disorders that share characteristics with PDDs that must be ruled out before a diagnosis is made.

Exhibit 4.2

Differential Diagnosis of Pervasive Developmental Disorders

Differential Diagnosis	Distinctions Between Diagnoses
Intellectual disability	Persons with PDD show specific impairments in reciprocal attention, imitation, and symbolic play.
Developmental language disorders	Children with PDD show more pervasive verbal communication difficulties, nonverbal communication impairment, and social difficulties.
Schizophrenia	Schizophrenia is rare in childhood; usually a period of normal development precedes the appearance of hallucinations and delusions.
Stereotypic movement disorders	These disorders involve odd and repetitive motor mannerisms and mental retardation. The diagnosis is not made if the individual has a PDD.
Schizoid personality disorder	The person suffers from isolation but is able to relate to others in some situations
Reactive attachment disorder	The person has a history of severe neglect; the social deficits typically remit with a more responsive environment.

PDD, pervasive developmental disorder.

Source: Aman & Langworthy, 2000; Bernard et al., 2002; JAACAP, 1999; Matson & Nebel-Schwalm, 2006; Schopler, 2001.

Psychiatric and Medical Assessment

Psychiatric and medical assessments focus on gathering historical information regarding the child's social relatedness and development of language, communication, and motor skills. Medical information must be gathered about the mother's pregnancy, labor, and delivery, and the child's early neonatal course. Parents should be asked when they first had concerns about their child and the nature of these concerns. Medical history and neurological exams (including an electroencephalogram [EEG] or magnetic resonance image [MRI]) should look for evidence of possible seizures, sensory deficits such as hearing or visual impairment, or other medical conditions. The family history should be reviewed for the presence of other developmental disorders.

Another critical aspect of the assessment is the child's physical examination, which involves identifying treatable medical conditions that sometimes produce symptoms suggestive of a PDD. Visual and audiological examinations should be performed if there are concerns about possible sensory problems. The family may report frequent ear infections, but in some cases chronic ear infections are recognized late because of the language delay related to PDDs. Lead levels should also be checked, if the child has had exposure. The physical examination should further assess for any inherited medical conditions. For example, the presence of small body deformities may suggest the need for genetic screening for inherited metabolic disorders. Other metabolic causes of developmental delays include fragile X syndrome, which is the most common cause of genetically inherited intellectual disability (National Fragile X Foundation, 2003). Its symptoms of hyperactivity are similar to those of PDD. Tuberous sclerosis is another relevant genetic condition, in which small substances form and calcify on the child's brain surfaces (Tuberous Sclerosis Association, 2003). Its effects range from mild to serious, but it can cause epilepsy, developmental delays, and autistic-like behavior. Unlike PDD, these other disorders can be identified medically, and thus the PDD diagnosis may be supported or ruled out.

Psychological Assessment

The development of standardized tests to assess PDD, particularly in young children, is a topic of considerable interest in the research community, and the number of available scales has grown exponentially (Matson, Nebel-Schwaim, & Matson, 2006). The general consensus is that scaling methods are the core means of establishing an accurate diagnosis. A selection of these instruments is included at the end of this chapter.

Psychologists are often in the best position to assess the child's intellectual ability and learning styles, and to develop plans for modifying behavior. Assessment of the child's cognitive ability helps to establish his or her overall levels of function. (Such tests are required in many states to determine eligibility for some services.) When possible, separate estimates of verbal and nonverbal IQ should be obtained. Persons with autism typically perform better on nonverbal and visual-spatial tasks than verbal tasks. In addition, assessment of the client's adaptive skills is essential to document the possible presence of any associated intellectual disability.

Speech and Language Assessment

The speech and language therapist assesses the child's understanding of all aspects of language and communication, reviewing grammatical level, semantic knowledge, pragmatic ability, and language learning style (Tager-Flusberg & Caronna, 2007). This information is vital for planning a program for the child to learn communication and for his or her future educational placement.

Social Work Assessment

The social worker's examination includes observation of the child in structured and unstructured settings. Observations of the child interacting with parents and siblings provide important information about the child, the levels of stress experienced by the family in response to the child's symptoms, and the effectiveness of parental interventions. Information on family support and stress is important. Studies have demonstrated that the family stress associated with having a child with a PDD is greater than having a child diagnosed with an intellectual disability, Down syndrome, or chronic physical illness (Gabriels, Hill, Pierce, Rogers, & Wehner, 2001). This includes a high divorce rate (Sobsey, 2004).

The social worker should also assess the child's developmental level, as well as symptoms in the areas of social interaction, communication/play, restricted and unusual interests, and any unusual behaviors (e.g., excessive hand washing). The social worker should note the presence of specific problem behaviors that may interfere with intervention programs, such as aggression, self-injury, and other behavioral oddities. The social worker should further examine the child's prior response to any educational programs or behavioral interventions. This information may be ascertained from previous evaluations for educational and other services, information from standard rating scales and symptom checklists, and narrative reports of teachers and care providers.

Other Assessments

Occupational and physical therapy assessments may be indicated for children with a suspected PDD, particularly if sensitivity to the environment is excessive or dulled or if motor skill development is impaired. Some diagnostic centers can include even wider assessments. A music therapy assessment, for example, can determine the child's ability to participate in and form relationships through structured musical activities.

In summary, the goal of an assessment of a PDD is not merely to determine whether a child has the disorder but also to gain some idea of the child's potential and to offer guidance on forms of education and treatment that are likely to be beneficial.

Risk and Protective Mechanisms

Onset

The research suggests that PDDs are genetic, neurobiological disorders (Maimberg & Vaeth, 2006). There is no association of PDDs with any psychological or social influences, including parenting styles. Approximately 60% to 70% of persons with PDDs manifest distinct neurological abnormalities and various levels of intellectual disability. Although brain abnormalities exist in a majority of diagnosed individuals, 30% to 40% of the population of persons

Exhibit 4.3

Risk and Protective Mechanisms for the Onset of Pervasive Developmental Disorders

Risk	Protective
Biological	Female
Genetic loading	Later-born child
Brain abnormalities	Younger age of parents
High levels of serotonin	
Male gender	
First-born child	
Older age of parents (mother 35+, father 40+)	

with PDDs possess an anatomically intact central nervous system (Peliosa & Lund, 2001). Thus, PDDs have many etiologies, including the following:

- Genetic conditions (see "Heredity" section)
- Viral infections (such as congenital rubella, a type of intellectual disability that results from infection during pregnancy)
- Metabolic conditions (such as abnormalities of purine synthesis, the amino acid that energizes many physical reactions)
- Congenital anomaly syndromes (such as Williams syndrome, a genetic disability characterized by outgoing behavior and intellectual and developmental deficits)

None of the identified etiologies are invariably associated with PDD, however, and knowledge of these causes has not clarified the neuropsychological basis of the disorder.

Exhibit 4.3 lists the risk and protective mechanisms for the onset of the pervasive developmental disorders.

Brain Development

Several brain abnormalities have been identified in persons with PDD, but it is unclear which of them are specific to the disorders. The most consistent findings point to disruptions in the limbic system and the cerebellum and its circuits (Holter, 2004). Structural and functional brain imaging studies have also indicated that PDD may be associated with enlarged overall brain size and decreased size and activity in specific areas of the brain. One of these areas may be the *midsagittal* area of the cerebellum, thought to be involved in the sequencing of motor activities. Another is the lower *hippocampus* (in the midbrain), which is associated with complex learning processes. A third area is the *amygdala* (located in the temporal lobe), which is believed to contribute to the recognition of faces and emotional expression. A final area is the *brain stem*, in a section associated with attention.

With regard to deficits in brain functioning, PDD has been conceptualized in a variety of ways (Tager-Flusberg, Joseph, & Folstein, 2001). It may be a disorder of *central coherence* in which the person is unable to holistically process information and develops a bias toward part-oriented processing. It may be a disorder of *executive function* in which the person is not able to process bits of information or regulate behavior, and thus is inclined toward rigid, repetitive behaviors and impoverished social interaction. It may be a deficit in *social cognition* in that the internal mental states of other people are not understood. Today, however, most research on brain deficits in autism focuses on *language and communication*, involving the difficulties in using and comprehending words and their meanings.

Neurotransmitters

Children with PDD may have an overgrowth of neurons in some areas of the brain, coupled with an underdeveloped organization of neurons into specialized systems. These findings have not been consistently replicated across studies, however, and therefore must be viewed with caution (Southgate & Hamilton, 2008). Research also indicates that children with PDD may have high levels of the neurotransmitter serotonin in the midbrain and brain stem (Lam, Aman, & Arnold, 2006). Genes that promote serotonin may thus facilitate the multiple neuron interactions that are prerequisites for developing PDD. Again, any conclusions about these processes are speculative at this time.

Heredity

In twin studies, the concordance rate for PDD in identical twins ranges from 36% to 91% (Veenstra-Vanderweele & Cook, 2003). In other family studies, up to 90% of siblings are diagnosed with one of the PDDs (Matson, Nebel-Schwalm, & Matson, 2006). Parents of individuals with PDD perform worse than controls on measures of executive function and subtle measures of their ability to apprehend the mental states of significant others (Baker & Crnic, 2009).

The research suggests that different genes and the variety of ways they can be manifested contribute to different symptoms of PDD (Smith et al., 2002). In addition, there are probably several genes that must interact with each other to cause the characteristics of the disorders; PDD involves perhaps 3–10 or more genes altogether, with 2–4 genes that must interact to produce symptoms (Liu, Paterson, & Scatmari, 2008). Thus, in genetic studies, one would expect to find evidence for genes at more than one locus. To date, there is some evidence for three loci: chromosomes 7q, 13q, and 15q, each of which may make distinct contributions to the disorder's symptoms (Happe & Ronald, 2008). In the search for causes, researchers have come to appreciate the great complexity of the genetic interactions that appear to produce PDD (Veenstra-Vanderweele & Cook, 2003).

Prenatal and Perinatal Complications

Some children with PDD have experienced identifiable prenatal or perinatal (immediately after birth) events that are linked to the disorders (Maimberg & Vaeth, 2006). Perinatal factors include low birth weight, and prenatal factors include bleeding during pregnancy and use of medications in pregnancy (Gardener, Spiegelman, & Buka (2009). In the latter, specific medications were not pinpointed for risk. Firstborns also have a higher risk of autism, may be related to a firstborn's greater ingestion of maternal toxins in utero, or to the hygiene hypothesis, which suggests that firstborns are exposed to fewer infections from other children early in childhood and thus are more likely to develop autoimmune toxins that affect brain development (Niehus & Lord, 2006). A higher risk of PDD has been seen among children of older parents (mothers aged 35 years or older, and fathers aged 40 and older) (Reichenberg et al., 2006). Parental age may be associated with age-specific genetic and chromosomal damage in the parents or the effects of environmental toxins over time.

Recovery and Adjustment

While there is no recovery from the PDDs, certain factors contribute to a more positive adjustment. Early diagnosis is important so that intervention can begin as soon as possible, when it is most likely to have a positive impact on the core features of the disorders (Rogers & Vismara, 2008). Unfortunately, diagnosis is often delayed. Researchers at the Center for Disease Control found that children with PDDs were initially evaluated at a mean age of 48 months, but they were not diagnosed until 61 months (with no differences by gender or SES) (Wiggins & Cather, 2006). Most practitioners (70%) did not use a diagnostic screening instrument in the process, and 24% of children were not diagnosed until after entering school. Often neurologists and developmental pediatricians are responsible for diagnosing PDDs, with primary pediatricians playing only a small role in diagnosis (12% of the time) (Harrington et al., 2006). Some of the reasons cited by Harrington, Rosen, Garnecho, and Patrick (2006) to explain the low rate of pediatrician contribution to diagnosis include the inability of the physician to feel equipped to do so, time constraints on conducting screens, and fear of labeling a child prematurely.

Other than the timing of intervention, risk and protective influences for the course of PDD are related to age of onset, the person's IQ, and the presence of co-occurring medical disorders, female gender (Billstadt et al., 2005; Billstadt et al., 2007), the severity of the disorder (McGovern & Sigman, 2005), aggression, and self-injury. The acquisition of nonverbal communication and functional play skills has been linked to subsequent gains in language skills for persons with PDD, and the acquisition of intelligible speech capacity by the age of 5 years acts as a protective influence. Children with higher IQs (over

60) are more responsive to intervention; IQ scores usually stabilize after 5 years and correlate with later academic and work achievement.

Child aggression and self-injury, such as head banging, finger biting or hand biting, head slapping, and hair pulling, compromise home and community placements (Dominick, Davis, Lainhart, Tager-Flusberg, & Folstein, 2007). Aggressive behaviors are typically due to the following reasons:

- Cognitive and emotional impairments, which lead to impulsivity, low frustration tolerance, poor emotional and behavioral regulation, and difficulties with coping skills
- Deficits in functional communication
- Difficulty negotiating change
- Learned behaviors to escape or avoid undesirable tasks or situations, gain access to tangible items or activities, or gain access to attention from others
- Misreading the nonverbal cues of others
- Seizures or other biological factors

Exhibit 4.4

Risk and Protective Influences for the Course of Pervasive Developmental Disorders

Risk	Protective
Biological	
Earlier age of onset (before 24 months)	Later age of onset (after 24 months)
Severity of the condition (including cognitive and emotional impairments)	
Co-occurring mental disorders	
Female gender	
Psychological	
Aggression and self-injury	Nonaggressive
Unintelligible speech	Intelligible speech
IQ under 60	IQ over 60
	Early nonverbal communication and functional play skills
Social	
Family	
Poor parent–child interactions	Quality parent–child interactions
Services	
Late detection	Early detection
Lack of services available	Early intensive, behavioral intervention

IQ, intelligence quotient.

Another protective mechanism identified for the course of the disorder is the quality of parents' interactions with their children, which may affect the development of children's language skills over time. In a literature review, Altiere and von Kluge (2009) found that moderate levels of family cohesion and adaptability are associated with higher levels of positive coping for all members, and that the more coping strategies a family implements, the greater their satisfaction with family functioning.

Exhibit 4.4 presents a summary of the mechanisms that affect the course of PDD.

Interventions

Psychosocial

The range of psychosocial interventions should include special education, family support, behavioral management, and social skills training for persons with higher functioning PDD. Social workers can facilitate many of these interventions, and they can also serve as the central point of intervention, that is, the case manager that coordinates the care being provided by psychiatry, medicine, psychology, and other disciplines that may be involved. Following a discussion of each of the aforementioned interventions, treatments will be explored for adolescents and adults.

Special Education
Federal law 94-142 mandates the provision of an appropriate educational plan for all children with PDDs in the United States (Holter, 2004). As part of this educational plan, ancillary services are often required, including speech or language therapy, occupational therapy, and physical therapy. Sustained, continuous programming is more effective than episodic programming; summer programming may also be needed because children with autism often regress in the absence of such services.

Social workers in school settings should be prepared to consult and collaborate with teachers and other school personnel and have working knowledge of state as well as federal laws and policies related to services (Holter, 2004). School social workers can help families understand the laws, help them determine their child's educational needs, and advocate for their children (Rogers & Vismara, 2008).

Behavioral Management
Behavioral management (also called applied behavior analysis and behavior modification) involves the examination of the antecedents of a problem behavior (the event or situation that precedes the behavior) and its consequences (the event or situation that follows the behavior). Any avoidable antecedents for a

problem behavior are removed and desirable behaviors are broken down into their component parts. Positive reinforcement is then provided for their performance. The program developed by Lovaas was the first of the structured behavioral modification programs (Lovaas, 1987, 2003), but others have followed. Seida et al. (2009) conducted a review of the meta-analyses and systematic reviews that have been conducted for autism interventions. Support was provided for behavioral management in terms of improvements in adaptive, cognitive, and language skills, as well as reductions in problem behavior.

Rogers and Vismara (2008) conducted a review of the last 10 years of research on autism interventions according to the American Psychological Association's Task Force 12 Criteria (Chambless & Hollon, 1998). None were concluded to be "well-established" (meaning that the interventions are represented by treatment manuals and either two independent well-designed control/comparison group studies indicating the benefit of an intervention over placebo or alternative treatment, or that it is at least as effective as another well-established treatment). The intensive behavioral treatment program developed and tested by Lovaas (1987, 2003), involving one-on-one assistance 40 hours a week for 2 or more years, garnered the categorization of a "probably efficacious" intervention. This means that the test of the intervention involves either of the following: two methodologically sound group studies by the same investigator showing the experimental intervention to be better than placebo or an alternative treatment, or at least three single-subject studies that compare the intervention to another intervention (Chambless et al., 1998).

Parental Support

As discussed, many parents of children with PDDs feel guilt, sorrow, anger, and stress, and siblings may also be affected in these ways (Solomon et al., 2008). The family, in almost every case, must adjust to the needs of the child's disability. Therefore, the social worker must provide support for families and refer them to appropriate groups and organizations for information and support.

We have already explored behavioral management interventions in the previous section. Although the literature commonly urges parental participation in such programs (Rogers & Vismara, 2008), a Cochrane Collaboration review indicated that only two randomized, controlled studies have been conducted of parent-mediated training, and they could not be synthesized because of methodological differences (Diggle & McConachie, 2002). A more recent systematic review of parent-implemented early intervention for PDD has been undertaken by McConachieand Diggle (2007), with 12 studies located. The authors concluded that randomized and controlled studies of parent training resulted in improved child communication skills for the treatment groups. Parent training also resulted in enhanced maternal knowledge of autism, maternal communication style, and parent–child interaction, and reduced maternal depression. However, the studies were analyzed through a vote count method rather than meta-analyzing the results of studies across common domains.

In Rogers and Vismara's (2008) review, the intervention known as pivotal response training (PRT) earned the categorization of "probably efficacious." A type of behavior management taught to parents, PRT focuses on "pivotal" aspects of the child's functioning: motivation, self-management (to be more independent and less reliant on prompts), initiation (to initiate interactions), and the ability to respond to multiple cues (to select cues that are relevant in a given situation) (Koegel, Kern Kogel, & Carter, 1999). It is distinguished from other behavioral approaches by taking advantage of naturally occurring teaching situations and consequences offered to children. Pivotal response training was rated as probably efficacious (Rogers & Vismara, 2008), based primarily on single-subject studies, although a recent larger-scale study was done on a diverse sample (Baker-Ericzén, Stahmer, & Burns, 2007).

Social Skills Training

Social skills interventions are widely recommended and typically provided to persons with PDDs because social reciprocity deficits are a core feature of the disorders. These programs can take a variety of forms, but most of them incorporate modeling, coaching, social problem solving, behavior rehearsal, feedback, and reinforcement strategies (Bellini & Peters, 2008). However, only two studies (Ozonoff & Miller, 1995; Solomon et al., 2004) used a comparative group design that controls for the effects of maturation and time over the course of treatment.

Adolescents and Adults

For adolescents, interventions should emphasize the acquisition of adaptive and vocational skills to prepare the individual for independent living. Sexual development in adolescence brings with it some potential behavioral problems, which may be addressed using sexual education and behavioral techniques (Holter, 2004).

Because public school responsibility ends when a person reaches age 22, the identification of community resources and support for adults in planning for long-term care is critical. Options include independent (or more likely, semi-independent), living at home with parents (sometimes funded by Supplemental Security Income [SSI] and Social Security Disability Insurance [SSA]), foster homes, supervised group living, and institutions (for those who need intensive, constant supervision) (NIMH, 2007). In many states adults with PDDs are not eligible for services that provide supported employment and residential living arrangements unless they also have an intellectual disability.

Medication

The symptoms of PDD that respond to *medications* do not represent the basic deficits in social interaction and communication. Rather, drug intervention may help with aggression, self-injury, inattention, and stereotyped movements, and these improvements may help the individual become more amendable to education and other interventions (des Portes, Hagerman, & Hendren, 2003). What follows is a review of medications used to treat these symptoms.

For the client's anxiety, selective serotonin reuptake inhibitor (SSRI) drugs may be helpful (Leskovec, Rowles, & Findlay, 2008), although behavior programs, desensitization, structure, and steps to minimize stressful situations should be used as first-line interventions.

General attention in children with PDD may be improved through the use of stimulants and other medications, but controlled studies are limited and adverse affects may outweigh benefits in some cases (Oswald & Sonenklar, 2007). The response for children with PDD for the stimulants is generally lesser than with non-PDD youth with attention-deficit/hyperactivity disorder (Aman & Langworthy, 2000). Empirical evidence for significant reductions in hyperactive symptoms is strongest for the antipsychotic drugs (particularly Risperidal), psychostimulants, and naltrexone, an opiate antagonist that is most often used to treat alcohol dependence. For children with PDD who have co-occurring attention-deficit/hyperactivity disorder, the psychostimulant medications produce a positive response rate of 50% to 60%. Some evidence of the benefits of risperidone in irritability (including aggression, deliberate self-injury, and temper tantrums), repetition, and social withdrawal were apparent (Jesner, Aref-Adib, & Coren, 2007), but long-term studies have yet to determine the range of possible risks. Weight gain is a noticeable side effect, even at the short term.

For reducing aggression, antipsychotic medications, including risperidone, may be effective, often without inducing severe adverse reactions (Jesner, Aref-Adib, & Coren, 2007). This medication has been shown to improve self-injury, aggression, and agitation in 70% of children and adolescents, compared to a placebo rate of 11.5%. Other antipsychotics, such as olanzapine and clozapine, have also been recommended for treating aggression. In addition, naltrexone has been posited to block opiods that may be released during self-injurious repetitive behaviors.

Complementary and Alternative Medicines

In a constant search for ways to help their children, parents may try various *complementary and alternative medicines* (*CAMs*). The National Center for Complementary and Alternative Medicine groups these therapies into four domains: mind–body medicine, biologically based practices, manipulative and body-based practices, and energy medicine. The most commonly used CAM treatments for PDD fall into the categories of biologically based and manipulative and body-based practices. Approximately half of families of children with PDD use a biologically based therapy (e.g., dietary supplements), 30% use a mind–body therapy (e.g., music therapy), and 25% use a manipulation or body-based method (e.g., auditory integration) (Hanson et al., 2007). Hanson et al. (2007) reported that 41% of respondents endorsed benefit with dietary and nutritional treatments, whereas Wong and Smith (2006) found that 75% of respondents thought their treatments were helpful. Several of these CAM interventions will be briefly discussed here because Cochrane Collaboration reviews have been conducted on them.

Music Therapy

Because people with PDDs have difficulties with communication, music therapy is sometimes used to facilitate communication and expression of feelings. Three small experimental studies have examined the short-term effect of brief music therapy interventions for autistic children (Gold, Wigram, & Elefant, 2006). Music therapy was shown to be superior to placebo with respect to verbal and gestural communicative skills, but it was uncertain whether there were effects on behavioral outcomes.

Sound Therapies

Auditory integration therapy and other sound therapies were formulated to counteract the abnormal sound sensitivity in individuals with autism and improve concentration (Levy & Hyman, 2008). Unfortunately, results of most of the studies could not be synthesized because of methodological problems, but for the two studies that could be meta-analyzed, results were positive.

Special Diets

A high-use complementary intervention for PDDs is gluten and/or casein exclusion (e.g., wheat, oat, rye, barley, milk) diets. Current evidence for efficacy of these diets is poor, however (Millwood, Ferriter, Calver, & Connell-Jones, 2008). Secretin is a gastrointestinal hormone, but there is no evidence that it is effective, and as such it should not currently be recommended as a treatment for autism (Williams, Wray, & Wheeler, 2005). The use of vitamin B_6 for improving the behavior of individuals with autism also cannot currently be supported (Nye & Brice, 2005). In general, the recommendations of these systematic reviews is that large-scale, randomized controlled trials are needed, given the appeal of these interventions to families.

There is also a lack of generalizability to people and settings external to the treatment environment (Rao, Beidel, & Murray, 2008). Many of the studies are also relatively short term in nature, without follow-up over time. This is a particular concern given the chronicity of the PDDs (Schopler, 2001).

Social Diversity

Both epidemiological and clinic-based studies indicate that PDDs occur more often in males than females, with ratio estimates ranging from 2.5:1 to 4:1

(Carter et al., 2007). Females tend to be more severely affected by the disorder because of a greater likelihood of intellectual disability. Despite this tendency, females are diagnosed later as having PDDs. This suggests the possibility of disparate clinical practices in terms of referral and screening, as well as gender bias in expectations of behavior that is considered normal in boys and girls (Shattuck et al., 2009).

In earlier reports, families of high socioeconomic status (SES) were over-represented in cases of autism. This finding was apparently due to selection bias in that high SES parents were more likely to seek treatment. Now it is generally believed that autism is represented in all social classes and races (Shattuck & Grosse, 2007). More generally, children of ethnic minority groups, from low socioeconomic groups, and those living in nonurban areas receive fewer services and receive them at a later age than their counterparts (Thomas, Ellis, McLauren, Daniels, & Morrissey, 2007). These disparities in diagnosis and intervention may result from clinician behaviors and differences in families' help-seeking behaviors, advocacy efforts, and support for services.

Additionally, interventions have targeted Caucasian youth, but culture may play an important role in how well programs work with children from ethnic minorities (Rogers & Vismara, 2008). Many potential cultural issues must be taken into account: Language and socioeconomic barriers exist, as do different expectations about appropriate child behavior, namely independence, parental authority, and the role of extended family and kin in child care. Further, different perceptions of the causes of PDDs and the stigma attached to mental disorders may impact receipt of services. Efforts to provide programming that is sensitive to cultural and socioeconomic factors, as well as training for researchers and service providers, are critical (Rogers & Vismara, 2008).

Critique of the Diagnosis

Autistic disorder first appeared as a formal diagnosis in *DSM-III* (APA, 1980). Interestingly, it was initially formulated as an Axis II disorder but was moved to Axis I in *DSM-IV*. A high rate of false-positive cases (meaning more people are diagnosed than truly warrant the diagnosis) has been identified using the *DSM* criteria, indicating their low validity and reliability (Peliosa & Lund, 2001). For this reason, the three disorders of autism, Asperger disorder, and PDD-NOS have come to be considered as a single classification along a continuum of more to less severe. Until the past 10 years or so, however, research efforts have been focused almost exclusively on autism. The advent of formal definitions in *DSM-IV* and *ICD-10* of the other PDDs has stimulated much additional research, and it is likely that the definitions of these conditions will be further refined. What remains to be determined is whether the spectrum disorders represent the same disorder or distinct abnormalities. This is a critical issue for many reasons, one of which is the need to identify interventions that are specifically targeted to each diagnosis.

Case Study

Jacob was a 2.5-year-old Latino boy, who lived with his mother and father in an urban neighborhood. Jacob's father supported the family financially, while his mother stayed at home and served as Jacob's primary caregiver. Suspecting autism, the family's pediatrician had suggested that Jacob undergo a formal assessment at a clinic specializing in services to children and adults with autism.

The initial assessment for the child was administered in the home under the assumption that a child will feel most comfortable in his or her natural environment. During the interview, Jacob's parents reported that he engaged in several inappropriate behaviors, including excessive mouthing of objects, inappropriate toy use (such as trying to throw or bounce stationary objects) and excessive tantrums. His parents handled his tantrums by trying to console him. Jacob's parents also stated that he did not communicate appropriately and had difficulty following through on requests. As a result, they tended to complete tasks for him. Jacob had severe deficits in social skills. He preferred to be alone rather than interact with peers or adults. He also refused to eat many foods and would often exhibit tantrums when new foods were introduced. His parents inadvertently reinforced this behavior by providing him with only preferred foods such as cookies and pudding.

While interviewing Jacob's parents, the social worker also observed his behaviors and the parent–child interactions. Jacob lacked both verbal and nonverbal communication skills. He did not make any speech sounds, point to desired objects, or shake his head in response to questions or requests. Additionally, Jacob did not make eye contact, and he had deficits in imitation and fine motor skills. Lastly, Jacob did not show any affection toward either parent.

Jacob had a very predictable daily routine. He stayed home with his mother, watched excessive amounts of a particular television show, and engaged in frequent self-stimulating behaviors (i.e., hand flapping and twirling). His inappropriate behaviors were not interrupted, and he was often permitted to hand flap or spin car wheels for several minutes at a time. Very few demands were placed on him at home, and the frequency of unexpected events (such as grocery shopping) was minimized due to his tantrum behavior.

Multiaxial Diagnosis

Axis I. 299.00 Autistic Disorder: The first criterion involves qualitative impairment in social interaction, for which Jacob manifested all the symptoms. The second criterion involves qualitative impairments in communication, for which he also demonstrated all symptoms. He further met criteria for having restricted repetitive and stereotyped patterns of behavior, interests, and activities. The delays occurred prior to age 3, and he did not meet criteria for Rett disorder or childhood disintegrative disorder.

Axis II. V71.09 No diagnosis: Testing did not reveal a low enough IQ to suggest the presence of intellectual disability.

Axis III. None: Unlike many other children with autism, Jacob did not have any comorbid medical conditions.

Axis IV. None GAF. 30: Jacob's severe impairments included many areas of functioning, including communication, social functioning, and feeding.

Risk and Protective Influences

Jacob's male gender was his only observable risk influence for the onset of autism. He may have had a genetic propensity for autism and brain abnormalities, but these could only be indirectly assessed through his behaviors. Jacob did have several important risk influences for the course of autism. He had a low IQ, demonstrated aggressive behaviors, and had no functional communication.

While these factors were discouraging, Jacob had some protective social influences. His autism was detected early and his parents enrolled him into an early, intensive behavioral intervention that included 10 hours of applied behavioral analysis (ABA) per week. His parents were also quite involved in the intervention process and did not support Jacob's isolative behaviors; instead they engaged in parallel play with him.

Goal Formulation and Treatment Planning

Because of the severity of Jacob's disorder, both his pediatrician and the early interventionist believed it was necessary to begin ABA therapy, occupational and sensory integration therapy, speech therapy, and physical therapy immediately after he was diagnosed. The family and social worker agreed that the most important behaviors to address were those that set Jacob apart developmentally from other children. His parents believed that his lack of communication was hindering him in other developmental areas, most clearly that of socialization.

It was important to validate the parents' feelings, but at the same time, it would be detrimental to give them false hope. Jacob made no speech sounds, and there was a possibility that he could never expressively converse without some type of communication system.

The social worker helped Jacob's parents to understand that it is often difficult to pinpoint the needs of a nonverbal child; therefore, addressing difficulties relating to all five of the developmental domains would be necessary. Agreed-upon initial treatment goals involved the basic areas of feeding and learning readiness skills.

Interventions

Feeding goals included a shaping procedure to increase the tolerance of non-preferred foods and transitioning from a bottle to a cup. Learning readiness skills included simple one-step commands (i.e., sit down, stand up, come here), appropriate sitting (attending to tasks with no tantrums or self-stimulatory behaviors), object manipulation, gross motor imitation, and eye contact.

After mastering the goals with the primary therapist, Jacob needed to be able to generalize to other individuals. The social worker would teach Jacob's parents to apply the techniques described above to the home setting. The parents were linked to the agency's ongoing support group and to the Autism Association of America for ongoing resources as well.

References

Altiere, M. J., & von Kluge, S. (2009). Family functioning and coping behaviors in parents of children with autism. *Journal of Child and Family Studies, 18*(1), 83–92.

Aman, M., & Langworthy, K. (2000). Pharmacology for hyperactivity in children with autism and other pervasive developmental disorders. *Journal of Autism and Developmental Disorders, 30*(5), 451–459.

American Psychiatric Association. (2000). *Diagnostic and statistical manual of mental disorders* (4th ed., text rev.). Washington, DC: Author.

American Psychiatric Association. (1980). *Diagnostic and statistical manual of mental disorders* (3rd ed.). Washington, DC: Author.

Akshoomoff, N. (2006). Autism spectrum disorders: Introduction. *Child Neuropsychology, 12*, 245–246.

Baker, J. K., & Crnic, K. A. (2009). Thinking about feelings: Emotion focus in the parenting of children with early developmental risk. *Journal of Intellectual Disability, 53*(5), 450–462.

Baker-Ericzén, M. J., Stahmer, A. C., & Burns, A. (2007). Child demographics associated with outcomes in a community-based pivotal response training program. *Journal of Positive Behavior Interventions, 9*(1), 52–60.

Barnhill, G. (2007). Outcomes in adults with Asperger syndrome. *Focus on Autism and Other Developmental Disabilities, 22*(2), 116–126.

Bellini, S., & Peters, J. K. (2008). Social skills training for Youth with autism spectrum disorders. *Child and Adolescent Psychiatric Clinics of North America, 17*(4), 857–873.

Bernard, L., Young, A. H., Pearson, J., Geddes, J., & O'Brien, G. (2002). Systematic review of the use of atypical antipsychotics in autism. *Journal of Psychopharmacology, 16*(1), 93–101.

Billstedt, E., Gillberg, C., & Gillberg, C. (2005). Autism after adolescence: Population-based 13- to 22-year follow-up study of 120 individuals with autism diagnosed in childhood. *Journal of Autism and Developmental Disorders, 35*(3), 351–360.

Billstedt, E., Gillberg, C., & Gillberg, C. (2007). Autism in adults: Symptom patterns and early childhood predictors. Use of the DISCO in a community sample followed from childhood. *Journal of Child Psychology and Psychiatry, 48*(11), 1102–1110.

Chambless, D. L., & Hollon, S. D. (1998), Defining empirically supported therapies. *Journal of Consulting and Clinical Psychology, 66*(1), 7–18.

Correll, C. U., Penzner, J. B., Lenez, T., Auther, A., Smith, C. W., Malhotra, A. K., Kane, J. M., & Cornblatt, B. A. (2007). Early identification and high-risk strategies for bipolar disorder. *Bipolar Disorders, 9*, 324–338.

De Bruin, E. I., Ferdinand, R. F., Meester, S., de Nijs, P. F. A., & Verheij, F. (2007). *Journal of Autism and Developmental Disorders, 37*, 877–886.

Des Portes, V., Hagerman, R. J., & Hendren, R. L. (2003). Pharmacotherapy. In S. Ozonoff, S. J. Rogers, & R. L. Hendren (Eds.), *Autism spectrum disorders: A research review for practitioners* (pp. 161–186). Washington, DC: American Psychiatric Association.

Diggle, T. T. J., & McConachie, H. H. R. (2002). Parent-mediated early intervention for young children with autism spectrum disorder. *Cochrane Database of Systematic Reviews*, Issue 2. Art. No.: CD003496. DOI: 10.1002/14651858.CD003496.

Dominick, K. C., Davis, N. O., Lainhart, J., Tager-Flusberg, H., & Folstein, S. (2007). Atypical behaviors in children with autism and children with a history of language impairment. *Research in Developmental Disabilities, 28*(2), 145–162.

Gabriels, R. L., Hill, D., Pierce, R., Rogers, S., & Wehner, B. (2001). Predictors of treatment outcome in young children with autism. *Autism: The International Journal of Research and Practice, 5*(4), 407–429.

Gardener, H., Spiegelman, D., & Buka, S. L. (2009). Prenatal risk factors for autism: Comprehensive meta-analysis. *British Journal of Psychiatry, 195*, 7–14.

Gold, C., Wigram, T., & Elefant, C. (2006). Music therapy for autistic spectrum disorder. *Cochrane Database of Systematic Reviews*, 2. Art. No.: CD004381. DOI: 10.1002/14651858.CD004381.pub2.

Hanson, E., Kalish, L. A., Bunce, E., Curtis, C., McDaniel, S., Ware, J., & Petry, J. (2007) Use of complementary and alternative medicine among children diagnosed with autism spectrum disorder. *Journal of Autism and Developmental Disorders, 37*(4), 628–636.

Happe, F., & Ronald, A. (2008). The "fractionable autism triad": A review of evidence from behavioural, genetic, cognitive and neural research. *Neuropsychology Review, 18*(4), 287–304.

Harrington, J., Rosen, L., Garnecho, A, & Patrick, P. (2006). Parental perceptions and use of complementary and alternative medicine practices for children with autistic spectrum disorders in private practice. *Journal of Developmental and Behavioral Pediatrics, 27*(2 Suppl), S156–61.

Holter, M. (2004). Autistic spectrum disorders: Assessment and intervention. In P. Allen-Meares & M. Fraser (Eds.), *Intervention with children and adolescents: An interdisciplinary perspective* (pp. 205–228). Washington, DC: NASW Press.

Jesner, O. S., Aref-Adib, M., & Coren, E. (2007) Risperidone for autism spectrum disorder. *Cochrane Database of Systematic Reviews 2007*, 1, Art. No.: CD005040. DOI: 10.1002/14651858.CD005040.pub2.

Jordan, R. (2001). Multidisciplinary work for children with autism. *Educational and Child Psychology, 18*(2), 5–14.

Kanner, L. (1943). Autistic disturbances of affective content. *Nervous Child, 2*, 217–250.

Koegel, R. L., Kern Koegel, L., & Carter, C. M. (1999). Pivotal teaching interactions for children with autism. *School Psychology Review, 28*(4), 576–594.

Koyama, T., Tachimor, H., Osada, H., & Kurita, H. (2006). Cognitive and symptom profiles in high-functioning pervasive developmental disorder not otherwise specified and Attention-Deficit/Hyperactivity Disorder. *Journal of Autism and Developmental Disorders, 36*(3), 373–380.

Lam, K. S. L., Aman, M. G., & Arnold, L. E. (2006). Neurochemical correlates of autistic disorder: A review of the literature. *Research in Developmental Disabilities, 27*(3), 254–289.

Leskovec, T. J., Rowles, B. M., & Findlay, R. L. (2008). Pharmacological treatment options for autism spectrum disorders in children and adolescence. *Harvard Review of Psychiatry, 16*(2), 97–112.

Levy, S. E., & Hyman, S. L. (2008) Complementary and alternative medicine treatments for Children with autism spectrum disorders. *Child and Adolescent Psychiatric Clinics of North America, 17*(4), 803–820.

Leyfer, O. T., Folstein, S. E., Bacalman, S., Davis, N. O., Dinh, E., Morgan, J., Tager-Flusberg, H., & Lainhart, J. E. (2006). Comorbid psychiatric disorders in children with autism: Interview development and rates of disorders. *Journal of Autism and Developmental Disorders, 36*, 849–861.

Liu, X., Paterson, A. D., & Szatmari, P. (2008). Genome-wide linkage analyses of quantitative and categorical autism subphenotypes. *Biological Psychiatry, 64*(7), 561–570.

Lovaas, O. I. (2003). *Teaching individuals with developmental delays: Basic intervention techniques.* Austin, TX: PRO-ED.

Lovaas, O.I. (1987). Behavioral treatment and normal education and intellectual functioning in young autistic children. *Journal of Consulting and Clinical Psychology, 55*(1), 3–9.

Magda, C., Schopler, E., Cueva, J. E., & Hallin, A. (1996). Treatment of autistic disorder. *Journal of the American Academy of Child and Adolescent Psychiatry, 35*(2), 134–143.

Matson, J. L., Nebel-Schwaim, M., & Matson, M. L. (2007). A review of methodological issues in the differential diagnosis of autism spectrum disorders in children. *Research in Autism Spectrum Disorders, 1*(1), 38–54.

McConachie, H., & Diggle, T. (2007). Parent implemented early intervention for young children with autism spectrum disorder: A systematic review. *Journal of Evaluation in Clinical Practice, 13*(1), 120–129.

McGovern, C. W., & Sigman, M. (2005). Continuity and change from early childhood to adolescence in autism. *Journal of Child Psychology and Psychiatry, 46*(4), 401–408.

Millward, C., Ferriter, M., Calver, S. J., & Connell-Jones, G. G. (2008). Gluten- and casein-free diets for autistic spectrum disorder. *Cochrane Database of Systematic Reviews* Issue 2. Art. No.: CD003498. DOI: 10.1002/14651858.CD003498.pub3.

National Institute of Mental Health (2007). *Autism spectrum disorders: Pervasive developmental disorders*. Washington, DC: National Institute of Health.

Niehus, R., & Lord, C. (2006). Early medical history of children with autism spectrum disorders. *Journal of Developmental & Behavioral Pediatrics, 27*(Suppl. 2), S120–S127.

Nye, C., & Brice, A. (2005). Combined vitamin B6-magnesium treatment in autism spectrum disorder. *Cochrane Database of Systematic Reviews* 2005, Issue 4. Art. No.: CD003497. DOI: 10.1002/14651858.CD003497.pub2.

Oswald, D. P., & Sonenklar, N. A. (2007). Medication use among children with autism-spectrum disorders. *Journal of Child and Adolescent Psychopharmacology, 17*(3), 348–355.

Ozonoff, S., Goodlin-Jones, B. L., & Solomon, M. (2007). Autism spectrum disorders. In E. J. Marsh & R. A. Barkley (Eds.), *Assessment of childhood disorders* (4th ed., pp. 487–525). New York: Guilford.

Ozonoff, S., & Miller, J. (1995) Teaching theory of mind: A new approach to social skills training for individuals with autism. *Journal of Autism and Developmental Disorders, 25*(4), 415–433.

Peliosa, L., & Lund, S. (2001). A selective overview of issues on classification, causation, and early intensive behavioral intervention for autism. *Behavior Modification, 25*(5), 678–697.

Posserud, M. B., Lundervold, A. J., & Gillberg, C. (2006). Autistic features in a total population of 7-9 year old children assessed by the ASSQ (Autism Spectrum Screening Questionnaire). *Journal of Child Psychology and Psychiatry, 47*(2), 167–175.

Rao, P. A., Beidel, D. C., & Murray, M. J. (2008). Social skills interventions for children with Asperber's Disease or high-functining autism: A review and recommendations. *Journal of Autism and Developmental Disabilities, 38*, 353–361.

Reichenberg, A., Gross, R., Weiser, M., Bresnahan, M., Silverman, J., Harlap, S., Rabinowitz, J., Shulman, C., Malaspina, D., Lubin, G., Knobler, H. Y., Davidson, M., & Susser, E. (2006). Advancing paternal age and autism. *Archives of General Psychiatry, 63*(9), 1026–1032.

Rice, C. (2007). Prevalence of —Autism Spectrum Disorders — Autism and Developmental Disabilities monitoring network, six sites, United States, 2000. □*Morbidity and Mortality Weekly Report, 56*(SS-1,; 1–11).

Rogers, S. J., & Vismara, L. A. (2008). Evidence-based comprehensive treatments for early autism. *Journal of Clinical Child and Adolescent Psychology, 37*(1), 8–38.

Safran, S. P. (2008). Why youngsters with autistic spectrum disorders remain underrepresented in special education. *Remedial and Special Education, 29*(2), 90–95.

Schopler, E. (2001). Treatment for autism: From science to pseudo-science or anti-science. In E. Schopler, N. Yirmiya, C. Shulman, & L. M. Marcus (eds.), *The research basis for autism intervention* (pp. 9–24). New York: Kluwer Academic/Plenum Publishers.

Seida, J. K., Ospina, M. B., Karkhaneh, M., Hartling, L., Smith, V., & Clark, B. (2009) Systematic reviews of psychosocial interventions for autism: An umbrella review. *Developmental Medicine & Child Neurology, 51*(2), 95–104.

Shattuck, P. T., Durkin, M., Maenner, M,, Newschaffer, C., Mandell D. S,. Wiggins, L, Lee, L. C., Rice, C., Giarelli, E., Kirby, R., Baio, J, Pinto-Martin, J, & Cuniff, C.

(2009). Timing of identification among children with an autism spectrum disorder: findings from a population-based surveillance study. *Journal of the American Academy of Child and Adolescent Psychiatry, 48*(5), 474–483.

Shattuck, P. T., & Grosse, S. D. (2007). Issues related to the diagnosis and treatment of autism spectrum disorders. *Mental Retardation and Developmental Disabilities, 13,* 129–135.

Smith, T., Magyar, C., & Arnold-Saritepe, A. (2002). *Autism spectrum disorder.* New York: John Wiley & Sons, Inc.

Sobsey, D. (2004). Marital stability and marital satisfaction in families of children with disabilities: Chicken or egg? *Developmental Disabilities Bulletin, 32*(1), 62–83.

Solomon, M., Goodlin-Jones, B. L., & Anders, T. F. (2004) A social adjustment enhancement intervention for high functioning autism, Asperger's syndrome, and pervasive developmental disorder NOS. *Journal of Autism and Developmental Disorders, 34*(6), 649–668.

Solomon, M., Ono, M., Timmer, S., & Goodin-Jones, B. (2008). The effectiveness of parent-child interaction therapy for families of children on the autism spectrum. *Journal of Autism and Developmental Disabilities, 38,* 1767–1776.

Southgate, V., & de C. Hamilton, A. F. (2008). Unbroken mirrors: Challenging a theory of autism. *Trends in Cognitive Sciences, 12*(6), 225–229.

Tager-Flusberg, H., & Caronna, E. (2007). Language disorders: Autism and other pervasive developmental disorders. *Pediatric Clinics of North America, 54*(3), 469–481.

Tager-Flusberg, H., Joseph, R., & Folstein, S. (2001). Current directions on research on autism. *Mental Retardation and Developmental Disabilities Research, 7*(1), 21–29.

Thomas, K. C., Ellis, A. R., McLaurin, C., Daniels, J., & Morrissey, J. P. (2007). Access to care for autism-related services. *Journal of Autism and Developmental Disorders, 37* (10), 1902–1912.

Towbin, K. E. (2005). Pervasive developmental disorder not otherwise specified. In F. R. Volkmar, R. Paul, A. Klin, & D. Cohen (Eds.), *Handbook of autism and pervasive developmental disorders, Vol. 1: Diagnosis, development, neurobiology, and behavior* (3rd ed., pp. 184–191). New York: Wiley.

Tsakanikos, E., Costello, H., Holt, G., Bouras, N., Sturmey, P., & Newton, T. (2006). Psychopathology in adults with autism and intellectual disability. *Journal of Autism and Developmental Disorders, 36,* 1123–1129.

Tuberous Sclerosis Association. (n.d.). *Tuberous sclerosis.* Retrieved November 17, 2003, from http://www.tuberous-sclerosis.org/publications/tsc.shtml.

Veenstra-Vanderweele, J., & Cook, E. H. (2003). Genetics of childhood disorders: XLVI. Autism, part 5: Genetics of autism. *Journal of the Academy of Child and Adolescent Psychiatry, 42*(1), 116–119.

Wiggins, J. B. & Cather, S. (2006). Examination of the time between first evaluation and first autistic spectrum disorder diagnosis: A population-based sample. *Journal of Developmental & Behavioral Pediatrics, 27*(2), 79–95.

Williams, K. J., Wray, J. J. Wheeler, D. M. (2005). Intravenous secretin for autism spectrum disorder. *Cochrane Database of Systematic Reviews,* Issue 3. Art. No.: CD003495. DOI: 10.1002/14651858.CD003495.pub2.

Wong, H. H. L., & Smith, R. G. (2006). Patterns of complementary and alternative medical therapy use in children diagnosed with autism spectrum disorders. *Journal of Autism and Developmental Disorders, 36*(7), 901–909.

Yeargin-Allsopp, M,, Rice, C,, Karapurkar, T., Doernberg, N,, Boyle, C,, & Murphy, C. (2003) Prevalence of autism in a U. S. metropolitan area. *The Journal of the American Medical Association.* 289(1), 49–55

Appendix I: Pervasive Developmental Disorders

The revision for this edition was obtained from Ozonoff, Goodin-Jones, and Solomon (2007).

Autism Screening Questionnaire (ASQ) (Berument, Rutter, Lord, Pickles, & Bailey, 1999)

Description
- Commonly used and accepted parental questionnaire for autism
- Takes less than 10 minutes to complete
- According to Ozonoff et al. (2007), ASQ has excellent psychometric properties.
- The 40-item screening measure, which was developed from the Autism Diagnostic Interview Revised (ADI-R) for use by the primary caregiver, focuses on three areas of functioning:

  o Reciprocal social interaction
  o Language and communication
  o Repetitive and stereotyped behaviors

Reliability
Based on the ADI-R, this instrument is thought to have good reliability.

Validity
The ASQ has been found to have good discriminative validity separating pervasive developmental disorders from non-PDDs at all IQ levels; the cut-off of 15 was most effective.

Autism Social Skills Profile (Bellini & Hopf, 2007)

Description
- A comprehensive measure of social functioning in children and adolescents with PDDs
- A 49-item, 4-point Likert scale that can be completed in 15–20 minutes

- Can be completed by a parent, teacher, or other adult who is familiar with the child's social behaviors
- Contains the three subscales of social reciprocity, social participation/avoidance, and detrimental social behaviors.

Reliability

- Cronbach's alpha scores ranged from .926 to .940; these were slightly lower (.848) for persons with mental retardation or severe language deficits.
- Test-retest reliability was .904 for a total sample ($n = 254$).

Validity

- Content validity was established through the use of a panel of experts in scale construction.
- Concurrent validity was established by comparing mean scores with scores of another survey that measured whether the person had at least one friend; this correlation was statistically significant.

Children's Social Behavior Questionnaire (CSBQ) (Luteijn, Jackson, Volkmar, & Minderaa, 1998; Luteijn, Luteijn, Jackson, Volkmar, & Minderaa, 2000)

Description

- Ninety-six-item questionnaire designed to examine behavioral problems in children with mild variants of PDD.
- Evaluates five categories of behaviors:

  1. Acting-out
  2. Social contact problems
  3. Social insight problems
  4. Anxious/rigid behaviors
  5. Stereotypical behaviors

Reliability

Interrater reliability between parents of the same child was satisfactory. Test-retest reliability (4-week) was also satisfactory. Internal consistency was satisfactorily high.

Validity

- The five subscales of the CSBQ yield high correlations with the Autism Behavior Checklist and the Autism Behavior Checklist.
- Discriminant analyses have indicated that only about 27% of children diagnosed with PDD-NOS can be correctly classified on the basis of the

CSBQ, with almost 29% misclassified as autistic and 24% misclassified as having attention-deficit/hyperactivity disorder.
• Correlations between CSBQ scales and *DSM-IV* criteria for PDD were reportedly weaker than expected.

Modified Checklist for Autism in Toddlers (M-CHAT) (Dumont-Mathieu & Fein, 2005)

Description
• Twenty-three-item parent checklist
• Designed to screen for autism at the 24-month well-child check
• Sensitivity of .87 and specificity of .99 according to Ozonoff, Goodin-Jones, and Solomon (2007).

References for Autism Measures

Bellini, S., & Hopf, A. (2007). The development of the Autism Social Skills Profile: A preliminary analysis of psychometric properties. *Focus on Autism and Other Developmental Disabilities, 22*(2), 80–87.

Berument, S., Rutter, M., Lord, C., Pickles, A., & Bailey, A. (1999). Autism screening questionnaire: Diagnostic validity. *British Journal of Psychiatry, 175,* 444–451.

Dumont-Mathieu, T. & Fein, D. (2005). Screening for autism in young children: The Modified Checklist for Autism in Toddlers (M-CHAT) and other measures. *Mental Retardation and Developmental Disabilities Research Reviews, 31,* 253–262.

Luteijn, E., Jackson, A., Volkmar, F., & Minderaa, R. (1998). The development of the children's social behavior questionnaire: Preliminary data. *Journal of Autism and Developmental Disorders, 28,* 559–565.

Luteijn, E., Luteijn, F., Jackson, S., Volkmar, F., & Minderaa, R. (2000). The children's social behavior questionnaire for milder variants of PDD problems: Evaluation of the psychometric characteristics. *Journal of Autism and Developmental Disorders, 30,* 317–330.

Ozonoff, S., Goodin-Jones, B. L., and Solomon, M. (2007). Autism spectrum disorders. In E. J. Mash & R. A. Barkley (Eds.), *Assessment of childhood disorders* (pp. 487–525). New York: Guilford.

5   Oppositional Defiant Disorder and Conduct Disorder

Although oppositional defiant disorder (ODD) and conduct disorder (CD) are empirically shown to be separate disorders (Loeber, Burke, Lagey, Winters, & Zera, 2000), they are discussed together in this chapter because they overlap considerably. They both feature anger, defiance, rebellion, lying, and school problems (Biederman, et al., 1996; Loeber et al., 2000). The distinction between them is that children with ODD do not seriously violate the basic rights of others. On the other hand, CD includes aggression toward people or animals, destruction of property, or a pattern of theft or deceit (American Psychiatric Association, 2000).

Another reason for discussing both disorders together is that ODD is often a developmental antecedent to CD. Almost all children with CD have had an earlier ODD diagnosis (Kronenberger & Meyer, 2001), and about a quarter of youth with ODD eventually develop more serious behavioral problems in the form of CD (Hinshaw & Anderson, 1996). In turn, CD is a risk factor for antisocial personality disorder in adulthood (Kronenberger & Meyer, 2001).

Yet ODD and CD are different diagnoses. Oppositional defiant disorder is characterized by a pattern of negativistic, hostile, and defiant behaviors toward authority figures, such as parents and teachers. At least four of the following behaviors must be present (APA, 2000). The child often:

- Loses his or her temper
- Argues with adults
- Actively defies or refuses to comply with adults' requests or rules
- Deliberately annoys people
- Blames others for his or her mistakes or misbehavior
- Is touchy or easily annoyed by others
- Is angry and resentful
- Is spiteful or vindictive

These behaviors persist for at least 6 months and occur more frequently than is typically observed in children of a comparable age and developmental level. Oppositional defiant disorder is usually evident before age 8 and not later than early adolescence.

Conduct disorder also involves an entrenched pattern of behavior, but in this diagnosis the basic rights of others or major age-appropriate societal norms or rules are violated (APA, 2000). This pattern involves four categories of behaviors:

- Aggressive conduct either causing or threatening harm to people or animals
- Nonaggressive conduct leading to property loss or damage
- Deceitfulness or theft
- Serious violations of rules

At least three of these behaviors need to have been present in the past year, with at least one behavior demonstrated in the past 6 months. The *DSM-IV* acknowledges that these behaviors may be a reaction to the immediate social context, such as living in a high-crime area, and thus would not be symptoms of CD. It is often difficult to discriminate, however, between the child's internal dysfunction and reactions to social contexts (Loeber et al., 2000).

Because so many types of offender acts are symptomatic of CD, we must selectively present information from the literature in this chapter (see also Loeber et al., 2000). Keep in mind, however, that to warrant a diagnosis of CD, an individual must be engaged in a pattern of behavior over time that consistently violates the rights of others and societal norms.

The *DSM-IV* includes subtypes of CD based on age of onset and the number and intensity of symptoms. These include childhood-onset CD, in which at least one criterion is present before age 10, and adolescent-onset CD, in which no criterion emerges before the age of 10.

Prevalence of ODD and CD

Oppositional defiant disorder, which also includes some symptoms of attention-deficit/hyperactivity disorder and CD, is more common than either CD or antisocial personality disorder, with a lifetime prevalence rate of 10.2% in the U.S. population when adults were surveyed retrospectively about their symptoms (Nock, Kazdin, Hiripi, & Kessler, 2007). For preschoolers, estimates for the rates of ODD range between 4% and 16.8% (Egger & Angold, 2006). In population studies, rates of CD range between 1% and 10% (APA, 2000).

For ODD, the rate of diagnosis for males is 11.2% and for females is 9.2%. Oppositional defiant disorder is more prevalent for males than females at all ages, but the rate is not statistically significant (Nock et al., 2007). The persistence of ODD is related to being male. Males also have a higher rate of CD than females (12% compared to 7.1%) (APA, 2000).

Comorbidity

Conduct disorder poses an enhanced risk for many other mental, emotional, and behavioral disorders (Loeber et al., 2000). The more severe the CD symptoms, the higher the risk of other disorders (Nock, Kazdin, Hiripi, & Kessler, 2006). In the majority of cases, CD occurs before mood disorders and substance use disorders, whereas impulse control disorders precede CD. Attention-deficit/hyperactivity disorder is common in children with ODD and CD. Anxiety disorders show no particular temporal relationship with CD. For girls, depression is comorbid with CD more commonly than it is with boys and often precedes CD (Ehrensaft, 2005).

Course

Over 40% of those with ODD end up developing CD (Egger & Angold, 2006). Antisocial personality disorder in adulthood is a possibility for males with conduct problems as youth at about a 25% rate (Lemery & Doelger, 2005) whereas borderline personality disorder may be a risk for girls with antisocial behavior (Ehrensaft, 2005).

The course of the disorders might be different, depending on the age of onset. Childhood-onset type, as opposed to adolescent onset, results in more severe and chronic problems that persist into adulthood (Moffit, Caspi, Harrington, & Milne, 2002) and sometimes leads to antisocial personality disorder (Goldstein, Grant, Ruan, Smith, & Saha, 2006). In a longitudinal study conducted in New Zealand, with participants followed until age 26, the childhood-onset group had the most severe personality, mental health, substance use, financial, and work problems (Moffitt et al., 2002). They also produced more children and exhibited higher rates of drug-related and violent crime, including violence against women and children.

This is not to say that adolescent-onset ODD and CD are benign. The adolescent-onset group still showed problems with impulsivity, mental health, finances, substance dependence, and property offenses. These youth as adults expressed little hope for their future and indeed suffered significant impairment.

As adults, the group of young men in the study who had childhood but not adolescent ODD or CD presented as low-level chronic offenders with accompanying anxiety, depression, and social isolation. They had problems with work and finances, and few were college educated. Only 15% of these 87 individuals had no adjustment problems. Therefore, it appears that even those who had recovered from the disorder were impaired in critical ways.

A recently published British study was the first of its kind in reporting the 40-year outcomes of population-based (not clinically referred) adults who had been reported by teachers as having externalizing problems as adolescents (Colman et al., 2009). Those with severe externalizing problems had poorer social and economic outcomes in terms of early parenting, divorce, leaving school early, and manual employment. These negative outcomes also extended to those with milder externalizing behaviors.

Assessment of ODD and CD

Assessment for ODD and CD requires a multimethod approach for several reasons (Fonagy & Kurtz, 2005). Youths may act differently depending on the setting (the *DSM* criteria for CD require behavior problems in more than one setting). Moreover, self-reports by children tend to be unreliable. Children downplay their own symptoms, especially hyperactivity, attention problems, and oppositional behavior (Loeber et al., 2000). Symptom reports from parents and teachers are usually preferable, although even these two sources may have biases. Loeber et al. (2000) reported in their literature review that teachers were more accurate than mothers in identifying child symptoms of hyperactivity and inattentiveness, and parents were better informers of their children's oppositional behavior. At the same time, depressed mothers (and mothers of conduct-disordered children are at risk of depression) may attribute more negative behaviors to their children than are reported by mothers with no mental health problems (Najman et al., 2000).

Valid and reliable self-report scales designed to assess ODD and CD are available for use with parents and teachers after the child has reached a certain age (see Appendix). In addition to collecting information on child behavior, social workers can seek information on relevant biopsychosocial risk and protective factors (highlighted in the next section).

Here are some additional guidelines for making *DSM* diagnoses (APA, 2000):

- Because transient oppositional behavior is common in preschool children and adolescents, caution should be exercised in diagnosing ODD during these developmental periods.

- Oppositional behaviors in children and adolescents should be distinguished from the disruptive behavior resulting from inattention and impulsivity that is associated with attention-deficit/hyperactivity disorder (Carlson, Tamm, & Gaub, 1997).
- A diagnosis of ODD or CD should not be made when the symptomatic behavior is *protective* for a child living in an impoverished, high-crime community.
- ODD should be distinguished from a failure to follow directions that is the result of impaired language comprehension due to hearing loss or a learning disability.
- In cases in which both CD and ODD are present, only CD should be diagnosed.
- When ODD or CD is diagnosed, a child and family relational problem (which would appear as a V-code) should not be included because the ODD or CD diagnosis includes conflict.
- A less severe diagnosis should be considered initially—either an adjustment disorder with disturbance of conduct in response to an identifiable stressor or the V-code for "child or adolescent antisocial behavior."
- Conduct disorder should be diagnosed in adults older than 18 only if the criteria for antisocial personality disorder are not met.

Risk and Protective Factors for ODD and CD

Extensive research has been conducted on risk factors for CD. Not as much work centers on ODD, but both disorders share similar risk factors and may have a common underlying genetic basis (Burke, Loeber, & Birmaher, 2002). Carlson, Tamm, and Hogan (1999) conducted a literature review to determine whether CD and ODD should be considered separately with regard to risk and protective factors. In some risk domains, the ODD groups were similar to the CD groups. In others, the ODD groups did not experience as many risk factors as the CD groups, but they were still at greater risk than control groups. Risk and protective factors, therefore, are discussed here for both disorders.

Onset

In this section, we will elaborate on some of the risk and protective influences detailed in Exhibit 5.1. These include genetics, some of the psychological characteristics that put youth at risk for ODD and CD, and the social factors that influence the occurrence of these disorders.

Exhibit 5.1

Risk and Protective Factors for ODD and CD

Risk Factors	Protective Factors
Biological Factors	
Heritability	
Maternal smoking and drinking during pregnancy[a]	Mother nicotine-free and alcohol-free during pregnancy
Difficult temperament	Behavioral inhibition (e.g., anxiety and shyness)
Low autonomic nervous system reactivity	
Male gender	Female gender
Psychological Factors	
Hyperactivity[b]	
Early aggression	
Lack of guilt	
Lack of empathy	
Low harm avoidance	
High stress and poor coping (for girls)	
Negative attribution bias (external locus of control)	
Social Factors	
Family composition	
Large family size (4 or more)[c]	Smaller family size (less than 4)
Single parenthood	Two-parent home
Inconsistent parental figures	Consistent parental figures
	Family stability
	Stable couple relationship
	Social support for parents
Family functioning	
Family instability	
Parental conflict, including discord, separation, and family violence	
Parent–child Relationship	
Poor parent–child attachment	Early parent–child attachment, particularly for males
Parental rejection of the child	Parental acceptance
Lack of supervision	
Lack of involvement in child's activities	
Inconsistent use of discipline	Consistent and effective discipline strategies[d]
Failure to use positive change strategies	
Excessive use of corporal punishment	

Physical and sexual abuse

Parental psychopathology

Parental depression, substance abuse, antisocial
    personality disorder, or other psychiatric disorders[e]

Criminal offending in parents

Peers

Low social cognition	Social skills
Peer rejection	Acceptance by and feelings of closeness peers
Social withdrawal	
Delinquent peer relationships	Positive peer relationships
Negative attribution bias	

Academic/School

Low IQ	High IQ
Poor academic performance	Good academic performance
Verbal deficits	Verbal skills

Community

Low socioeconomic status, particularly in urban areas	Living in rural areas
	Middle to upper socioeconomic status
Community violence and crime	Neighborhood cohesion
Religious involvement[f]	

[a] Disney et al. (2008)

[b] Cote, Tremblay, Nagin, Zoccolillo, & Vitaro (2002).

[c] Werner (2000).

[d] Steinberg (2001).

[e] APA (2000).

[f] Johnson, Jang, Li, & Larson (2000); Johnson, Jang, Larson, & Li (2001).

IQ, intelligence quotient.

Sources: Burke et al. (2002), Hill (2002), Holmes et al. (2001).

Biological Influences
Genetics

Genetics may account for 50% or more of the variance in CD (Gelhorn et al., 2006). However, heritability is also sensitive to environmental circumstances (Legrand, Keyes, McGue, Iacono, & Krueger, 2008). Additionally, children with a greater predisposition to CD are more likely to encounter environments that foster antisocial behavior (Loeber et al., 2000). That is, they may be raised by ineffective (and sometimes abusive) parents with histories of antisocial behavior, psychopathology, and substance abuse problems.

Additionally, the likelihood of persons with particular characteristics selectively partnering and producing children is substantial for antisocial behavior (Ehrensaft, 2005). One can see how both genetic and environmental risk can be compounded in these circumstances.

Psychological Influences

The dominant personality profile for child-onset type is impulsivity, low verbal intelligence quotient (IQ), and a lack of emotional regulation, coupled with higher rates of family problems. The problems with emotional regulation result in impulsive and reactively aggressive behaviors. Another psychological factor conferring risk for the development of ODD and CD involves hyperactivity (Frick, 2006). We will elaborate on other psychological deficits, including IQ, impaired verbal skills, and a related characteristic to these: poor social problem-solving functioning.

Intelligence and Language-Based Verbal Skills

Low IQ is a risk factor for antisocial behavior, over and above the effects of socioeconomic status and race. Wachs (2000) cites evidence that youths with IQ scores one standard deviation lower than normal (approximately 85) have three times the risk for developing CDs. However, Hogan (1999) claimed, from a review of 27 studies controlling for attention-deficit/hyperactivity disorder, that the relationship of CD with IQ failed to reach significance. In addition, high intelligence does not necessarily protect against conduct problems. High verbal IQ has been related to boys' "growing out of" CD only when a parent did not have antisocial personality disorder (Lahey, Loeber, Burke, & Rathouz, 2002).

Extensive documentation of the relationship between deficits in verbal ability and conduct problems is available, but the reasons for the link are not well understood (Hill, 2002). One hypothesis is that children who are unable to reason verbally may use aggression to manage social dilemmas. Poor verbal abilities may also make it harder for children to identify emotions in themselves and others. If children cannot reflect on their emotional states, they may react in physical or aggressive ways rather than by talking about their feelings, seeking comfort, or engaging in problem-solving activities.

Social Cognitive Problem Solving

Related to the poor ability to reason verbally are deficits in cognitive processing that are associated with conduct problems. Cognitive processing refers to the way people perceive and code their experiences (Kazdin, 2001). Youths who are aggressive tend to display the following distortions in the way they perceive and code their social experiences (Dodge, 1986):

- An inability to produce a variety of strategies to manage interpersonal problems
- Difficulty in figuring out ways to achieve a particular desired outcome
- Difficulty with identifying the consequences of a particular action and its effects on others
- A tendency to attribute hostile motivations to the actions of others
- Misunderstanding how others feel

The combination of perceived threat and limited options for managing social situations makes antisocial youths more likely to respond with aggression rather than other problem-solving strategies.

Social Influences
Abuse

As noted in Exhibit 5.1, family factors are highly implicated in the development of CD. We will expand upon abuse in the family here, which is associated with youth behavior problems. The use of physical discipline (not just abuse) correlates with child aggression for Caucasian children, although not for African American children (Pettit, Bates, Dodge, Bates, & Pettit, 2004). Historical factors of slavery, such as the norm of physical punishment, and the current threat of oppression and societal punishment may lead African American families to view physically harsh discipline as an acceptable part of a positive parent–child relationship, sometimes necessary to prevent economic and social failure for a child growing up in an unforgiving society.

Genetic risk may interact with maltreatment when it occurs. A large-scale twin study recently established that maltreatment along with the presence of genetic risk increases the rate of conduct problems by almost one-quarter (24%), whereas maltreatment without such risk increases the rate of conduct problems by 2% (Jaffee et al., 2005).

Peer Relationships

Children diagnosed with CD often experience rejection by peers for their aggression and poor social skills (Holmes, Slaughter, & Kashani, 2001). Because of their impulsivity and attention problems, these children disrupt other children's activities, and as a consequence other children become annoyed and rejecting (Miller-Johnson, Coie, Maumary-Gremaud, & Bierman, 2002). Peers may also unwittingly reinforce aggression by acquiescing to a child's demands and demonstrations of force. Peers may alternately respond with aggression in kind, confirming the child's negative view of others and contributing to continuing aggression in future encounters (Holmes et al., 2001; Morrison, Macdonald, & Leblanc, 2000).

For adolescent-onset CD, deviant peer relationships are a major pathway (Frick, 2006). In adolescence, the rate of ODD in females increases to that of boys', most likely because of girls' involvement with antisocial boyfriends (Burke et al., 2002; Moffit, Caspi, Rutter, & Silva, 2001).

Neighborhood and Socioeconomic Factors

Living in poor and disadvantaged communities poses substantial risks for antisocial behavior in children. Such risks include poverty, unemployment, community disorganization, availability of drugs, the presence of adults involved in crime, community violence, and racial prejudice (Hankin, Abela, Auberbach, McWhinnie, & Skitch, 2005; Hill, 2002; Loeber et al., 2000). Positive family processes, such as parents' positive marital functioning and parenting abilities, can override the effects of social disadvantage (Hill, 2002). However, even in the presence of protective factors, living in public housing poses a substantial risk for antisocial behavior (Wikström & Loeber, 2000).

Parenting abilities are often challenged by the many stressors that attend living in a low socioeconomic environment, including unemployment, underemployment, the lack of safe child care, the lack of transportation, inadequate housing, and exposure to crime. These stressors may not only negatively affect parenting but also inhibit access to treatment resources. Impaired parenting abilities elicit further behavior problems in youth (Burke et al., 2002).

A recent study demonstrates how environmental context may shape genetic factors (Legrand et al., 2008). For males residing in urban areas, heritable factors explained a majority of the variance, but for males in rural areas, environmental effects played a larger role in the development of CD. To explain these findings, it could be that stronger community norms operate in smaller towns or that parents might be able to more easily monitor their adolescents' behaviors in rural areas.

Recovery and Adjustment

The number of risk influences present in a child's life appears to affect the persistence of antisocial behavior. In one study, 2% of youth who had no childhood risk influences showed persistent delinquency in adolescence, compared with 71% of youth who had risk influences in five different areas of life (Frick, 2006). The risk and protective factors for recovery and subsequent adjustment involve many child factors, but social factors, such as the family, peers, and socioeconomic status, are also important. Exhibit 5.2 indicates that many of the recovery and adjustment influences are similar to the onset factors listed in Exhibit 5.1.

Risk and Protective Factors for Recovery and Adjustment of Oppositional Defiant and Conduct Disorder

Risk Factors	Protective Factors
Biological Factors	
Early onset	
Low autonomic nervous system reactivity	
Male gender	Female gender
Low verbal intelligence	
Psychological Factors	
ADHD	Lack of comorbid ADHD
Lack of guilt	Remorse
Lack of empathy	Ability to show empathy
Low harm avoidance	Harm avoidance
Lack of emotional expression	Ability to express feelings
Social Factors	
Family	
Being born to a teenage mother	Being born to an adult mother
Presence of an antisocial biological parent	Biological parents are prosocial
Community	
Low socioeconomic status	Middle to upper socioeconomic status
Delinquent peers	Prosocial peers

ADHD, attention-deficit/hyperactivity disorder.

Sources: Frick, 2006; Goldstein et al., 2006; Lahey et al. 2000; Loeber et al., 2000; Moffitt et al., 2002, Nock et al., 2007.

Interventions

Psychosocial

Family Interventions

Family factors seem to be a critical variable in the formation of conduct problems. Therefore, treatments often have a family emphasis. For younger children, parent training has been researched extensively, and for teenagers, several "multi-dimensional" models that combine theoretical perspectives have been developed.

Parent Training

Parent training is based on operant behavioral theory in which reinforcement plays a key role in determining future behavior. In this model, parents are taught various skills, including:

- Specifying goals for behavioral change
- Tracking target behaviors
- Positively reinforcing prosocial conduct through the use of attention, praise, and point systems
- Employing alternative discipline methods, such as withdrawal of attention, time out from reinforcement, imposition of costs on inappropriate behavior, and removal of privileges

This educational material is generally presented through a variety of formats, including didactic instruction, interactive discussion, modeling, role play, and feedback. These elements are presented in several empirically supported training manuals and programs (Eyberg, Nelsen, & Boggs, 2008): *The Parent Management Training Oregon Model* (ages 3–12) (Patterson & Gullion, 1968); *Helping the Noncompliant Child* (ages 3–8) (Forehand & McMahon, 1981); *Parent–Child Interaction Therapy* (ages 2–7) (Brinkmeyer & Eyberg, 2003); *The Incredible Years* (ages 2–8) (Webster-Stratton, 2001); and the *Positive Parenting Program* (called Triple P) (preschool through adolescence) (Sanders, 1999).

Two quantitative reviews have been conducted on parent training programs. McCart, Priester, Davies, and Azen (2006) focused on the outcome of child aggression. Locating 30 studies, the authors found a small- to medium-sized overall effect (.47) for reducing child aggression and a small effect size for its impact on parental distress (.33). Sufficient information was not available to conduct a follow-up effect size.

In the other review, using only randomized, controlled studies that compared a parenting program to either a wait list control or to another treatment, Dretzke et al. (2009) located 57 trials. Their meta-analysis of the studies indicated an overall medium effect of intervention according to parent reports (SMD = 0.67) and a small to medium effect according to independent observations (SMD = 0.44). However, the authors were unable to determine the differential effectiveness of parenting programs compared to one another.

Although effect sizes for parent training on conduct problems are higher than those for other child mental health problems, the demands of learning and implementing parent skill procedures in the home may overwhelm some parents. They may attend sessions sporadically, drop out of treatment, or fail to practice the skills they learn (Fonagy & Kurtz, 2005). A recent meta-analysis of the parent training research examined predictors associated with both outcome and dropout (Reyno & McGrath, 2006). A good outcome was defined as parent participation in treatment, measurable improvements, and maintenance of gains. For predictors of outcome, low family income had a strong association with poor outcomes, and barriers to treatment, such as transportation and lack of child care, had a moderate association. Key family factors for compromised outcome involved adverse parenting, younger maternal age, and, most importantly, maternal psychopathology.

Multidimensional Family Models for Adolescents

Most of the family models that have developed with adolescents have been in response to their contact with other systems, namely the juvenile justice system. In an overall examination of family interventions for adolescents with conduct problems, Woolfenden, Williams, and Peat (2001) found eight trials. Although parent- and family-focused treatment reduced time spent by youth in residential treatment and other institutional settings, incarceration and arrest rates were not affected. Further, no significant differences between parent/family interventions and other types of treatment emerged on psychosocial outcomes, such as family functioning and youth behavior. Therefore, the impact of family involved treatment seems to offer certain benefits and cost savings, since residential treatment is an expensive alternative; however, the benefits are limited to only certain domains.

Multisystemic Therapy   Multisystemic therapy has been developed specifically for adolescents in the juvenile justice system. Drawing on family systems theory and Bronfenbrenner's (1979) ecological model as the theoretical basis, multisystemic therapy (MST) views the juvenile offender as embedded in a context of multiple and interrelated systems (Henggeler, Schoenwald, Borduin, Rowland, & Cunningham, 1998). The child's own intrapersonal system (i.e., cognitive ability, social skills), the parent–child system, the family system, the school system, peers, and the neighborhood system are targeted for intervention.

Multisystemic therapy also draws on several other models. It shares with the family preservation model the central aim of retaining the adolescent in the home. The client's ability to generalize new behaviors is key, and thus treatment is usually delivered in the home or a community setting. Multisystemic therapy also takes an individualized approach in recognizing participants' strengths and limitations. In contrast to the family preservation model, however, MST is applied through the use of manualized treatment. Although MST includes family systems interventions (structural and strategic), it also focuses on nonsystemic interventions derived from cognitive-behavioral therapy, such as parent training, social skills training, problem-solving training, and behavior therapy.

Multisystemic treatment has been extensively studied with approximately 800 families participating in the intervention (Henggeler, Schoenwald, Rowland, & Cunningham, 2002). Several prominent national organizations—including the National Institute of Mental Health, the National Institute on Drug Abuse, the Center for Substance Abuse Prevention, and the Office of Juvenile Justice and Delinquency Prevention—promote MST as a model community program because of its strong empirical support (Henggeler et al., 2002). However, a more recent, systematic analysis of the data indicates that treatment outcomes are not as strong as previously reported (Littell, Popa, & Forsythe, 2005). Indeed, among the various outcome measures across studies, none showed significant differences from "treatment as usual." Because training and supervision in the MST model are costly, agency personnel need to be aware of these most recent findings.

Functional Family Therapy   Functional family therapy (FFT), which has also been applied with juvenile offenders, integrates systems, cognitive, and behavioral theories (Alexander & Parsons, 1982). From this perspective, juvenile offending and other clinical problems are conceptualized from the standpoint of the functions they serve for the family system and its members. The goal of FFT is to alter maladaptive interaction and communication patterns so that more direct means of fulfilling these functions can develop (Alexander & Parsons, 1982). Functional family therapy combines knowledge about parent–child interactions and social learning, along with knowledge about the individual cognitive styles that influence juvenile offending. The model has also been referred to as behavioral-systems family therapy (Gordon, Arbuthnot, Gustafson, & McGreen, 1988).

Relatively few outcome studies have evaluated FFT. Although a recent literature review highly supported FFT as an efficacious treatment (Waldron & Turner, 2008), a systematic review being conducted should tell us more about the benefits of this treatment (Littell, Bjørndal, Winsvold, & Hammerstrøm, 2008).

Treatment Foster Care   Treatment foster care programs serve children and youth who are at risk for being placed in institutional or other restrictive, non-home settings due to their emotional, behavioral, medical, or developmental problems. Often these children face a series of progressively more restrictive placements. One type of treatment foster care, multidimensional treatment foster care (MTFC; Chamberlain & Smith, 2003), is targeted specifically for youth with severe and chronic delinquent behavior. It is a community-based program originally developed as an alternative to institutional-, residential-, and group-care placements. Youth are placed one per foster home for 6 to 9 months and given intensive support and treatment in the foster home setting. The foster parents receive a 20-hr preservice training conducted by experienced foster parents and learn to implement a daily token reinforcement system that involves frequent positive reinforcement and clear and consistent limits. During treatment, the foster parents report point levels daily by telephone to program supervisors and meet weekly with supervisors for support and supervision (Eyberg et al., 2008).

Youth in MTFC meet at least weekly with individual therapists who provide support and advocacy and work with the youth on problem-solving skills, anger expression, social skills development, and educational or vocational planning. They also meet once or twice a week (2 to 6 hr per week) with behavioral support specialists trained in applied behavior analysis who focus on teaching and reinforcing prosocial behaviors during intensive one-on-one interactions in the community (e.g., restaurants, sports teams). Moreover, youth have regular appointments with a consulting psychiatrist for medication management. At the same time youth are in MTFC treatment, the biological parents (or other after-care resource) receive intensive parent management training. This training is designed to assist in the reintegration of youth back into their homes and communities after treatment.

A recent Cochrane Collaboration review on treatment foster care located only five studies that met inclusion criteria (Macdonald & Turner, 2008). Although results favored treatment foster care, studies typically did not assess similar outcome measures, and therefore, quantitative synthesis was difficult. The authors concluded that treatment foster care may be a successful alternative to more costly higher levels of care, such as residential treatment, and may help young people avoid some of the deleterious outcomes for children with CD (Macdonald & Turner, 2008). However, the authors also warn that the evidence is not as robust as the claims that have been made.

Individual Interventions

Although relationship-based and psychodynamic interventions are often applied in clinical work with children and adolescents with ODD and CD, they have not been studied in relation to this population. Instead, cognitive-behavioral therapy (CBT) has been a focus of research and will be discussed here.

Cognitive-behavioral therapy involves a large body of present-focused intervention. It may include anger management, assertiveness training, cognitive restructuring, relaxation, social problem solving, or social skills development as interventions. Thus, a wide range of interventions are offered under the rubric of CBT.

A recent meta-analysis examined the effectiveness of CBT overall for youth aggression (McCart et al., 2006). The small mean effect size of .35 was significant, but it was smaller than parent training intervention (.47) for the age range of children (6–12 years) for which both interventions were offered. Cognitive-behavioral therapy continued to demonstrate a small positive effect over time at follow-up (.31). McCart et al. (2006) found that CBT was more effective for older youth, who have attained the cognitive ability to achieve formal operations.

Wilson and Lipsey (2007) conducted a meta-analysis of CBT targeting youth anger in the school setting, including both published and nonpublished reports. They found that the effect of anger interventions varied according to the target population. In 249 school-based studies that used aggressive and disruptive behavior as an outcome, selected/indicated programs (those involving youth who had been referred for problems) were most effective, although the overall effect size was small (.29). Universal programs (those applied to whole student populations) showed an even smaller effect (.21). Cognitive-behavioral therapy delivered in alternative high schools and special education classes for behavioral problems had a negligible effect. Surprisingly, comprehensive and multimodal interventions that combined special parent and teacher training with student interventions were not shown to be effective. The implication of this study for school social workers is that offering CBT to youth in schools is more effective when it is presented to those who have been referred for anger problems in mainstreamed school settings.

One of the most common types of cognitive-behavioral treatments with this population, social problem-solving programs/social information processing programs (e.g., Dodge & Coie, 1987), targets the previously described deficits that youth with antisocial problems often show in the context of peer relations and solving social problems. These programs are assumed to assist such youth both in managing their anger (by interpreting cues differently and having strategies to manage their anger more effectively) and in developing needed social skills.

Wilson and Lipsey (2006) examined the effectiveness of a specific type of these programs—social information processing—implemented in the school setting for youth identified with anger and behavior problems. Social information processing involves training children in at least one of a number of thinking processes. These steps include encoding and then interpreting situational and internal cues, setting goals, determining possible responses, and role playing the behavioral responses. The meta-analysis of 47 studies, most of them involving group treatment, examined social information processing programs that were implemented with students who were selected, or indicated as already having behavioral problems. The overall effect for these interventions was statistically significant, yet low at .26.

Another systematic review concentrated on school-based secondary prevention of violence; that is, interventions targeted at children identified as aggressive or at risk of being aggressive (Mytton, DiGuiseppi, Gough, Taylor, & Logan, 2006). In all, the interventions produced moderately beneficial effects, as measured by teacher ratings, behavioral observations, or school discipline reports. Even more importantly, the effects found were maintained at 12-month follow-up. The most effective types of programs were those focusing on improving relationships with others and building social skills. These findings seem to emphasize the importance of helping youth with antisocial problems develop these skills.

For adolescents, multidimensional cognitive-behavioral treatments have also been developed. These include *aggression replacement training* (Goldstein & Glick, 1987), which combines social skills training, anger control, and moral reasoning training and has been used with institutionalized adolescents. The intervention has shown to have a high benefit–cost ratio (Aos, Phipps, Barnoski, & Lieb, 2001). However, Lipsey, Landenberger, and Wilson (2007), in a review of 58 studies of adolescent and adult offenders who received treatment while they were on probation, found that commercial packages, such as aggression replacement training (Goldstein, Glick, & Gibbs, 1998), showed no statistically significant benefits over other programs. However, implementation of the intervention was a key moderator. When programs were implemented as they had been designed, better outcomes were produced. Like the other meta-analyses of CBT, small effects were found for CBT with this population, but this translated into a 25% reduction in reoffending (Lipsey et al., 2007).

Crucial elements of CBT were also identified. Anger control and interpersonal problem solving were important elements, whereas victim impact and behavior modification were not (Lipsey et al., 2007. This replicates the other studies that showed the importance of these skills. Social workers in direct practice and program planning for such youth, therefore, need to know the value of anger control and interpersonal problem solving for this population.

One other systematic review examined the impact of CBT for antisocial adolescents in another specific setting, that of residential treatment (Armelius & Andreassen, 2007), where youth with CD are overrepresented. Effect sizes again were small, yet positive, indicating CBT showed advantages over control conditions for recidivism.

Medication

Several classes of medication have been researched for their impact on children and adolescents with disruptive disorders and co-occurring conditions, including the stimulants, selective norepinephrine reuptake inhibitors, antipsychotics, mood stabilizers, and alpha-2 agonists. Other classes of medication, such as antidepressants and beta-blockers, have either not been studied sufficiently or show little evidence of effectiveness (Pappadopulos et al., 2006).

In one meta-analysis of 14 studies exploring the effectiveness of pharmacotherapy for the disruptive behavioral disorders, Ipser and Stein (2007) found a strong overall treatment response in terms of reducing aggression. However, the medication benefits were accompanied by the possibility of side effects that may differ with each category of medication (Pappadopulos et al., 2006).

Stimulants

Stimulants are the most widely prescribed medication for youth (see Chapter 6). Two meta-analyses have indicated the effectiveness of stimulants in reducing aggression in youth with conduct problems (Ipser & Stein, 2007; Pappadopulos et al., 2006). They are particularly effective for children with comorbid attention-deficit/hyperactivity disorder and aggression.

SNRIs

Pappadopulos et al. (2006) explored the effectiveness of atomoxetine (Strattera), a nonstimulant attention-deficit/hyperactivity disorder intervention categorized as a selective norepinephrine reuptake inhibitor (SNRI). Only a small effect size (0.18) was shown for reducing maladaptive aggression. Patterns of prescription in a study of 905 juvenile patients, however, showed that atomoxetine is prescribed more commonly than stimulants when attention-deficit/hyper-activity disorder is comorbid with conduct disturbances and externalizing behavior (Christman, Fermo, & Markowitz, 2004). This may be due to concerns about unwanted side effects from stimulants or substance abuse. Note that the use of stimulants in youth is not associated with the development of substance use disorders, although youth who already have such problems may not be candidates for the stimulants (see Chapter 6).

Antipsychotics

Both typical and atypical antipsychotic medications have been studied in relation to antisocial problems in youth. Of these, the atypical medications are increasingly prescribed for children and adolescent psychiatric problems (Pappadopulos et al., 2002). In youth with conduct problems, the atypical antipsychotics have effectively curbed aggression (Ipser & Stein, 2007; Pappadopulos et al., 2006). Risperidone (Risperdal) is the most thoroughly studied, and it has been shown to substantially reduce aggression in youth with CD and below-average IQ (Aman, Binder, & Turgay, 2004). Health risks due to the use of atypical antipsychotics may be significant, however, and may include cardiac rhythm concerns, weight gain, and type II diabetes (Schur et al., 2003).

The older (typical) antipsychotic agents, particularly haloperidol and thioridazine, have also produced large effect sizes for the treatment of aggression (Pappadopulos et al., 2006). There is significant documentation, however, that these medications may produce symptoms of movement disorders in children and adolescents; therefore, they are prescribed infrequently (Connor, Fletcher, & Wood, 2001).

Mood Stabilizers

The mood stabilizers are another category of psychotropic medication found to be effective by Pappadopulos and her colleagues (2006). Lithium was the most beneficial of these, although only a small to medium effect was obtained. However, lithium requires a therapeutic dose to achieve benefits, which involves several weeks of treatment. Side effects, including nausea and vomiting, diminished muscle coordination, fatigue, weight gain, and cognitive dulling, coupled with the requirement of frequent blood monitoring, hinder the use of this medication for young people, however (Bassarath, 2003).

Alpha-2 Agonists

The final category of medication that may be effective for CD and aggression, alpha-2 agonists, are increasingly being used in combination with stimulants. The alpha-2 agonists are sometimes used as alternatives to the stimulant drugs, but they can also be used to extend or enhance the effects of the stimulants (Arnsten, Scahill, & Findling, 2007). Pappadopulos and her associates (2006) found a moderate mean effect size for aggression (0.5) across two studies using alpha-2 agonists; one with clonidine (Catapres), and the other with guanficine. Noted side effects for the alpha-2 agonists include dizziness and drowsiness, but these can balance out the effects of stimulant treatment when they are used together.

Social Diversity

Ethnicity and Poverty

African American children (after controlling for poverty) are more likely than Caucasian children to be diagnosed with disruptive and conduct-related problems (Nguyen, Huang, Arganza, & Liao, 2007). In the Nguyen study (N = 1200 youth), although disruptive behavioral diagnoses were more common among African American youth, their externalizing symptoms on the parent-rated Child Behavior Checklist (CBCL) were not elevated. This discrepancy could be due to the inconsistency between clinician-derived diagnosis and parents' report on the CBCL; parents might not view their children's behavior as disruptive, although clinicians might view this differently.

Many minority ethnic groups are overrepresented in poverty, and, as discussed, the conditions of poverty, such as unsafe and crime-ridden neighborhoods, may increase the risk of ODD and CD. Further, peer influences are significant, and deviance and crime may be an orientation of certain youth in these neighborhoods when other opportunities are not seen as available.

A notable exception to the study of the impact of programs on minorities is a meta-analysis of 305 studies conducted by Wilson, Lipsey, and Soydan (2003). These researchers found that programs for juvenile offenders were equally effective for minority youths as they were for Caucasian youths. Unfortunately, these programs, in general, had only a small (though statistically significant) impact on delinquency. The salient issue for effectiveness was not the type of program but how successfully the programs were implemented.

Gender

As mentioned, rates of ODD are comparable in males and females, although CD is more common in males. At the same time, symptoms of CD vary by gender. Male youth engage in more confrontational and aggressive behavior and have a higher rate of criminal offending than females (Lahey et al., 2000), while females manifest indirect or relational aggression, such as the exclusion of others; threats of withdrawal from relationships; efforts to alienate, ostracize, or defame others; and rumor spreading (Ledingham, 1999; Loeber et al., 2000). Because these behaviors are not listed in the *DSM* as criteria for CD, some have suggested that the diagnostic criteria should be modified for females (Loeber et al., 2000).

Although ODD is prevalent for both boys and girls with no significant difference, the number of females in treatment outcome studies is low. None of the parent training or cognitive-behavioral studies in the McCart et al. (2006) meta-analysis included a predominantly female sample (McCart et al., 2006), and most studies in a review of school-based secondary violence prevention involved only boys (Mytton et al., 2006). Clearly there is a need for research into gender-specific treatment outcomes, particularly as consequences for females (and their offspring) may be problematic.

In a review of longitudinal studies, girls with adolescent CD were over five times more likely than others to have entered a cohabiting relationship by age 21, many of these with deviant men. These relationships tended to cause further problems for the females; by their early 20s, almost half of them had suffered some form of physical violence at the hands of a partner (Maughan & Rutter, 2001).

Although a history of conduct problems predicts earlier sexual involvement for both boys and girls, the consequences of sexual behavior are more serious for girls because they may become pregnant and drop out of school (Ledingham, 1999). The problem of assertive matching with deviant males means that both genetic and environmental risks are increased for any children born in such relationships.

Case Study

Janine is a 12-year-old African American female in foster care. Janine is an attractive, well-developed young lady who is outspoken and athletic. She enjoys playing basketball and other sports and listening to music.[1]

Janine entered the foster care system at age 10, when she reported that her biological uncle was sexually abusing her and her brother. Janine is the oldest of five; all the children have the same mother but different biological fathers. Janine states that her uncle drinks a lot and that he was drunk when he sexually abused her. At the time of removal, Janine and her siblings were living with their grandmother, uncle, and biological mother. They resided in a housing project in an area known for high crime, drug trafficking, and gang violence. Janine was responsible for making the call to child protective services (CPS) to report her uncle's abusive behaviors. When family members discovered that she had initiated the call, they refused to speak with her.

Although Janine's biological mother lived in the home, Janine's grandmother was her primary caregiver. Her mother was a teenager at Janine's birth, so her grandmother had assumed a lot of the responsibility for Janine's care from the beginning. Janine's grandmother described her as an overactive, hard-to-control child.

During the past 2 years, Janine has lived in five separate foster homes. Each time she has been removed because of outbursts that begin as verbal tirades and then progress to hitting. She has also stolen money from various foster parents.

In addition, she has reportedly stolen from her classmates at school (money, clothes). More recently, she was caught stealing from the convenience store across the street. Janine at times has rationalized her stealing, stating that if people didn't want her to take their things, then they shouldn't leave them out where she could get at them.

Janine has lived in her current foster home, which is located in a working-class neighborhood, for 6 months. Her foster mother is African American, unmarried, and employed full time. Janine appears to have become attached to her foster mother. However, her foster mother says that Janine often argues with her and has, on occasion, become violent. Janine's foster mother is willing to keep her if Janine's aggression and lying can be controlled. According to her foster mother, teachers, and social workers, Janine often lies to avoid doing things (e.g., "I've already done it" when asked to do chores or tasks at school) or to get out of trouble (e.g., blaming others for starting physical altercations she initiated). Janine's foster mother is worried that because she has to work until dinnertime, she is unable to supervise Janine adequately during the frequent times Janine has been suspended from school.

Janine's CPS worker reported that if Janine is asked to leave her current foster home, she will be sent to a residential placement. Janine has begged her caseworker and foster mother not to send her away. Janine's brother, Kyle, attends a therapeutic day treatment center and is in the process of being returned to his biological father's home. Janine has questioned her caseworker about returning to her own biological father. However, her father has now married another woman, who has children of her own. He and his wife are reluctant to have Janine come into their home and potentially disrupt their lives and set a bad example for the other children.

Recently, Janine's CPS worker referred her to a therapeutic day treatment center after she was expelled from public school for violent outbursts, fights with peers, and poor academic performance. The poor school performance seems partially attributable to frequent suspensions, but Janine also seems to have difficulty with concentrating and focusing on her work, according to teacher reports relayed to the foster mother. Her foster mother has also noted similar qualities when Janine attempts homework.

Multiaxial Diagnosis

The following diagnosis was given at the intake interview for the day treatment program. Janine, the foster mother, and the CPS caseworker provided information necessary for the diagnosis.

Axis I:312.89 Conduct Disorder Unspecified Onset, Mild Severity V61.21 Sexual Abuse

314.01 Attention-Deficit/Hyperactivity Disorder, Predominantly Inattentive Type (see Chapter 6 for more information on ADHD)

Axis II: V71.09 No diagnosis

Axis III: None

Axis IV: Problems with primary support group (sexual abuse, removal from the home, foster care, inadequate discipline); educational problems (academic failure, discord with teachers and classmates); problems related to the social environment (lack of friendships)

Axis V: Global Assessment of Functioning: 51

The first required criterion for CD is that disruptive behaviors must be present for at least a year. Furthermore, the client must exhibit at least three of the behaviors listed for CD in the *DSM*, with at least one occurring within the past 6 months. Janine's conduct problems became apparent 2 years ago and have persisted during that time frame. It is possible, based on Janine's grandmother's description of Janine as an overactive, out-of-control child, that Janine met criteria for CD in early childhood. However, the grandmother's report might have been tainted in an attempt to discredit Janine for the sexual abuse allegations. Therefore, the age of onset is unknown (unspecified onset). Janine exhibited four of the listed behaviors, and each of these occurred within the past 6 months. The first two behaviors are threatening or bullying others and starting fights. Janine often initiates fights both at home and at school, with her foster mother, with peers, and with teachers. Although the majority of her fights have been verbal, some of them have extended to physical violence. Two other behaviors listed under conduct disorder that Janine displays involve theft without confrontation and frequent lying. The severity specifier "mild" is given because Janine barely meets the conduct problems criteria with only four symptoms, and the impact on other people is "intermediate" (i.e., most of the fighting she displays involves verbal argument).

The second required criterion for a CD diagnosis is that the behaviors must seriously impair academic and social functioning. Janine's academic record is poor (several failing grades), and over the past school year she has often been absent because of frequent fights. In the social realm, Janine has failed to remain in a foster home for any length of time because of these behaviors. Moreover, Janine admits that she does not have friends.

The *DSM* cautions that when conduct behaviors are protective against a dangerous environment, such as in a low-income, high-crime, overcrowded urban area, then the diagnosis of CD should not be given. Since foster care, Janine has been living in safe neighborhoods, but before that time, she lived in a dangerous area. Conduct problems, if they existed prior to the current 2-year period, might have served a protective function in such a neighborhood. However, in the past 2 years, she has had no need to rely on such behaviors to maintain her safety.

When examining other diagnoses that may better encapsulate her symptoms, it must be noted that Janine also meets the criteria for ODD. She often loses her temper, argues with adults, refuses to follow adult rules, blames others for misbehavior, is touchy or easily annoyed by others, and is angry and resentful. Thus, Janine meets six of the behaviors listed under ODD, whereas only four are required to make the diagnosis. However, Janine's behaviors meet the diagnosis for CD, leading one to rule out ODD on the basis of the *DSM*'s guidelines.

In addition to ODD, adjustment disorder is a possibility. The criteria for adjustment disorder with disturbance of conduct require that the client's behaviors surface within 3 months of a stressor and impair social and academic performance. Other criteria for adjustment disorder are that the behaviors cannot be attributed to bereavement and the behaviors can last no longer than 6 months. Janine's case history is notable for sexual abuse and foster care placement. Janine acted out aggressively almost immediately after being placed into foster care, leading one to the conclusion that her behaviors were a reaction to severe life stressors. Furthermore, her reactions have impaired her school performance and relationships. Although her symptoms have persisted for longer than 6 months, one can argue that the stressors involved have been ongoing. Janine faces continual rejection from her family of origin because of their reaction to her allegations of sexual abuse; they make only sporadic attempts to comply with the CPS case plan for reunification. Being forced to live in foster care is another chronic stressor. Hence, a diagnosis of adjustment disorder with disturbance of conduct could be justified, although most clinicians would probably concur with a diagnosis of CD.

Sexual abuse has also been listed under Axis I because Janine is still facing the aftermath of abuse by her uncle. However, this diagnosis has been placed second. It is the aggressive and acting-out behaviors that have received more attention, requiring her to attend a day treatment program.

Because of Janine's sexual and physical abuse history, another diagnosis to possibly explore is posttraumatic stress disorder.

- Criterion A for posttraumatic stress disorder could be justified by Janine's exposure to traumatic events. The second part of Criterion A is that the child's response is expressed in disorganized or agitated behavior. It could be argued that her aggression represents agitated behavior.
- Criterion B involves reexperiencing of the trauma. However, Janine denies thinking about the sexual abuse or having dreams related to it. She also denies flashbacks and does not appear to experience psychological distress or physiological reactivity to any particular cues associated with the abuse.
- Criterion C, involving avoidance and numbing, could be reflected in Janine's avoidance of thoughts, feelings, or conversations associated with the trauma. She says she cannot remember important aspects of the sexual abuse, although it is unclear whether her stating so is a posttraumatic symptom or reflects embarrassment, oppositionality, or irritation at having to repeat her story. Janine does display a restricted range of affect, in that anger and aggression seem to be her primary feelings.

- Criterion D, involving arousal symptoms, could also be involved in Janine's case. She has frequent bouts of irritation and anger, she has difficulty concentrating, and her seeing threat in other people's actions could be interpreted as hypervigilance.

Although Janine seems to meet several of the criteria related to posttraumatic stress disorder, the reexperiencing component does not seem to be present, and so she does not receive this diagnosis.

The justification of the attention-deficit/hyperactivity disorder diagnosis in Janine's case is taken up in Chapter 6. The rationale for the GAF score of 51 (the low end of "moderate" symptoms) is as follows: Janine has no friends, her academic performance is poor, she has been expelled from school, and she has recently stolen from a convenience store; she has also had difficulty maintaining a stable placement because of her behavior.

Janine's risk and protective factor assessment is displayed in Exhibit 5.3. Goal and intervention planning have been placed within the context of this assessment.

Exhibit 5.3

Janine's Risk and Protective Factors Assessment

Risk	Protective	Goals
Biological Factors		
Maternal smoking during pregnancy: *Janine's mother smoked during her pregnancy.*		Sexuality education and pregnancy prevention. (Janine is at risk for early sexual involvement and becoming involved with antisocial males.)
Psychological Factors		
Early aggression: *Janine's grandmother said that Janine has always been overactive and "hard to control."*	*Positive coping mechanisms include listening to music when she feels "mad," as it has a calming effect, and playing basketball.*	Help Janine examine sexual abuse experience and its aftermath in a graduated fashion, accompanied by the development of coping skills, such as cognitive restructuring and developing appropriate attributions (she was not responsible for abuse, but she is responsible for her actions now). Possibly use a system of rewards, such
High stress and poor coping: *Janine has suffered from a number of highly stressful life events, including sexual abuse, rejection from her biological family, the absence of her biological father, and placement in a number of different foster homes. Her coping methods*	*Janine was able to stop the abuse from happening by initiating a call to Child Protective Services.*	

include externalizing behaviors; she avoids talking about the abuse and does not have friends. Negative attribution bias: *Janine blames the physical fights on others' provocation; she sees her stealing as justified in that "if people didn't want me to take their stuff, they shouldn't leave it out."*

as time playing basketball or other physical activity in therapy sessions after she has spent time processing the abuse.

Social Factors

Family

Large family size: Janine is *one of five children in her biological family.*

Smaller family size: *Janine is the only child in her foster home.*

Work toward getting an effective discipline strategy in the home, as well as increasing positive interactions and providing empathy for Janine's feelings.

Single parenthood: *Janine's foster mother is a single* parent; while her biological mother is also a single parent, *Janine's grandmother was also available in the home as a parent figure.* Inconsistent parental figures: *Since she has been removed from her home, Janine has been in several foster placements.*

Social support for parents: *Janine's foster mother has informal (family, friends) and formal (CPS) supports.*

Poor parent–child attachment: *The quality of infant–child attachment is unknown, but a risk is that Janine's mother was a teenager when she was born, and her grandmother assumed a lot of the caregiving.*

Janine will attend a day treatment program so that treatment and structure will be provided on a consistent basis.

Have an aggressive plan in place to involve Janine's biological mother and grandmother in belief and support of Janine; if unworkable, then develop a permanency plan for placement.

Parental rejection of the child: *Not only Janine's mother, but her whole biological family has rejected her.*

(continued)

Exhibit 5.3

(Continued)

Risk	Protective	Goals
Lack of supervision: *Foster mother works until dinnertime, so she is unable to supervise Janine the frequent times she has been suspended from school.*		
Inconsistent use of discipline: *Foster mother has found Janine's aggression and noncompliance difficult to manage.*		
Sexual abuse: *Janine was sexually abused by her mother's brother for 2 years.*		
Peers		
Low social cognition		*As above, attribution retraining, increase perspective taking; develop social problem-solving skills and other social skills.*
Peer rejection		
Social withdrawal: *Janine has few social skills and lacks friends; she sees others as initiating and provoking negative interactions.*		
Academic/School		
Poor academic performance: *Janine is failing several classes.*	*Janine has refrained from grouping with other delinquent peers.*	Involve in extracurricular activities, such as basketball and other sports.
		Work on maintaining foster care placement, so she can remain at current school. Refer for testing for IQ and learning disabilities.
Community		
With her biological family, Janine lived in a low-income urban area afflicted with violence and crime.	Janine attends the Baptist Church with her foster mother.	
	In her current foster home, Janine lives in a working-class neighborhood.	

CPS, child protective services; IQ, intelligence quotient.

Critique of the Diagnosis

According to the *DSM-IV*, excessive and continuing displays of aggressive behavior can be considered a mental disorder and formally labeled as conduct disorder (CD). As one reviews Janine's case, it is clear that she meets the criteria for CD. However, a social work practitioner must question the validity of applying a *DSM-IV* diagnosis to Janine.

Although Janine displays many of the behaviors listed under CD, it is imperative to explore other motivations behind her aggressive behaviors. As stated in the case history, Janine has been a victim of sexual abuse and over the past 2 years has been rejected by five different foster homes. In their critique of the *DSM-IV*, Kutchins and Kirk (1997) emphasize the importance of distinguishing between behavior as a dysfunction within a person and behavior as a reaction to life stressors. Although it is possible that Janine's behavior signifies a dysfunction within Janine, it is more probable that Janine is reacting negatively to her circumstances. It is unfair to expect a child to react appropriately after being sexually abused, rejected by parents, and forced to live in numerous unstable environments—all within the context of poverty. As one examines Janine's situation, it seems likely that her behaviors can be attributed to the stressors in her life. This case will also be continued in Chapter 6.

The *DSM* view of disorders is that they evolve from individual dysfunction. Indeed, the *DSM-IV-TR* states, "Consistent with the *DSM-IV* definition of mental disorder, the Conduct Disorder diagnosis should be applied only when the behavior in question is symptomatic of an underlying dysfunction within the individual and not simply a reaction to the immediate social context" (p. 96). However, the literature on ODD/CD identifies coercive family factors and other social environment variables as key to the development of these disorders. The *DSM* definition is therefore not in line with what has been empirically validated as contributing to these disorders.

References

Alexander, J., & Parsons, B. V. (1982). *Functional family therapy*. Monterey, CA: Brooks/Cole.

Aman, M. G., Binder, C., & Turgay, A. (2004). Risperidone effects in the presence/absence of psychostimulant medicine in children with ADHD, other disruptive behavior disorders, and subaverage IQ. *Journal of Child and Adolescent Psychopharmacology, 14*(2), 243–254.

American Psychiatric Association. (2000). *Diagnostic and statistical manual of mental disorders* (4th ed., text rev.). Washington, DC: Author.

Aos, S., Phipps, P., Barnoski, R., & Lieb, R. (2001). *The comparative costs and benefits of programs to reduce crime*. Olympia: Washington State Institute for Public Policy.

Armelius, B. A., & Andreassen, T. H. (2007). *Cognitive-behavioral treatment for antisocial behavior in youth in residential treatment*. Retrieved January, 8, 2009, from The

Campbell Collaboration Web site: http://www.campbellcollaboration.org/campbell_library/index.php.

Arnsten, A.F., Scahill, L., & Findling, R.L. (2007). Alpha2-Adrenergic receptor agonists for the treatment of attention deficit/hyperactivity disorder: Emerging concepts from new data. *Journal of Adolescent Psychopharmacology, 17 (4)*, 393–406.

Bassarath, L. (2003). Medication strategies in childhood aggression: A review. *Canadian Journal of Psychiatry. Revue Canadienne De Psychiatrie, 48*(6), 367–373.

Biederman, J., Farone, S., Milberger, S., Jetton, J., Chen, L., Mick, R., et al. (1996). Is childhood oppositional defiant disorder a precursor to adolescent conduct disorder? Findings from a four year follow-up study of children with ADHD. *Journal of the American Academy of Child and Adolescent Psychiatry, 35*, 1193–1204.

Brinkmeyer, M. Y., & Eyberg, S. M. (2003). Parent-child interaction therapy for oppositional children. In A. E. Kazdin & J. R. Weisz (Eds.), *Evidenced-based psychotherapies for children and adolescents* (pp. 204–223). New York: Guilford.

Bronfenbrenner, U. (1979). *The ecology of human development: Experiments by nature and design.* Cambridge, MA: Harvard University Press.

Burke, J., Loeber, R., & Birmaher, B. (2002). Oppositional defiant disorder and conduct disorder: A review of the past 10 years, part II. *Journal of the American Academy of Child and Adolescent Psychiatry, 41*, 1275–1294.

Carlson, C. L., Tamm, L., & Gaub, M. (1997). Gender differences in children with ADHD, ODD, co-occurring ADHD/ODD identified in a school population. *Journal of the American Academy of Child and Adolescent Psychiatry, 36*(12), 1706–1714.

Carlson, C., Tamm, L., & Hogan, A. (1999). The child with oppositional defiant disorder and conduct disorder in the family. In H. Quay & A. Hogan (Eds.), *Handbook of disruptive behavior disorders* (pp. 337–352). New York: Kluwer Academic/Plenum.

Chamberlain, P., & Smith, D. K. (2003) Antisocial behavior in children and adolescents: The Oregon multidimensional treatment foster care model. In A. E. Kazdin, & J. R. Weisz (Eds.), *Evidence-based psychotherapies for children and adolescents* (pp. 282–300). New York: Guilford Press.

Christman, A. K., Fermo, J. D., & Markowitz, J. S. (2004). Atomoxetine, a novel treatment for attention-deficit/hyperactivity disorder. *Pharmacotherapy, 24*(8), 1020–1036.

Colman, I., Murray, J., Abbott, R. A., Maughan, B., Kuh, D., Croudace, T. J., & Jones, P. B. (2009). Outcomes of conduct problems in adolescence: 40 year follow-up of national cohort. *British Medical Journal, 8*, 338: a2981. doi: 10.1136/bmj.a2981.

Connor, D. F., Fletcher, K. E., & Wood, J. S. (2001). Neurolepticrelated dyskinesias in children and adolescents. *Journal of Clinical Psychiatry, 62*(12), 967–974.

Cote, S., Tremblay, R., Nagin, D., Zoccolillo, M., & Vitaro, F. (2002). Childhood behavioral profiles leading to adolescent conduct disorder: Risk trajectories for boys and girls. *Journal of the American Academy of Child and Adolescent Psychiatry, 41*, 1086–1095.

Disney, E. R., Iacono, W., McGue, M., Tully, E., & Legrand, L. (2008). Strengthening the case: Prenatal alcohol exposure is associated with increased risk for conduct disorder. *Pediatrics, 122*(6), e1225–e1230.

Dodge, K. (1986). A social information processing model of social competence in children. In M. Perlmutter (Ed.), *The Minnesota Symposium on Child Psychology* (Vol. 18, pp. 77–125). Hillsdale, NJ: Erlbaum.

Dodge, K., & Coie, J. (1987). Social information factors in reactive and proactive children's aggression in children's peer groups. *Journal of Personality and Social Psychology, 53*, 1146–1158.

Dretzke, J., Davenport, C., Frew, E., Barlow, J., Stewart-Brown, S., Bayliss, S., Taylor, R., Sandercock, J., & Hyde, C. (2009). The clinical effectiveness of different parenting programmes for children with conduct problems: A systematic review of randomised controlled trials. *Child and Adolescent Psychiatry and Mental Health, 3*(1), 7.

Egger, H., & Angold, A. (2006). Common emotional and behavioral disorders in preschool children: presentation, nosology, and epidemiology. *Journal of Child Psychology & Psychiatry, 47*(3/4), 313–337.

Ehrensaft, M. K. (2005). Interpersonal relationships and sex differences in the development of conduct problems. *Clinical Child and Family Psychology Review, 8*(1), 39–63.

Eyberg, S. M., Nelson, M. M., & Boggs, S. R. (2008). Evidence-based psychosocial treatments for children and adolescents with disruptive behavior. *Journal of Clinical Child and Adolescent Psychology, 37*(1), 215–237.

Fonagy, P., & Kurtz, Z. (2005). Disturbance of conduct. In P. Fonagy, M. Target, D. Cottrell, J. Phillips, & Z. Kurtz (Eds.), *What works for whom? A critical review of treatments for children and adolescents* (2nd ed.). New York: Guilford.

Forehand, R. L., & McMahon, R. J. (1981). *Helping the noncompliant child: A clinician's guide to parent training*. New York: Guilford.

Frick, P. J. (2006). Developmental pathways to conduct disorder. *Child and Adolescent Psychiatric Clinics of North America, 15*(2), 311–331.

Gelhorn, H., Stallings, M., Young, S., Corley, R., Rhee, S. H., Christian, H., & Hewitt, J. (2006).Common and specific genetic influences on aggressive and nonaggressive conduct disorder domains. *Journal of the American Academy of Child and Adolescent Psychiatry, 45 (5)*, 570–577.

Goldstein, A., & Glick, B. (1987). *Aggression replacement training*. Champaign, IL: Research Press.

Goldstein, A. P., Glick, B., & Gibbs, J. C. (1998). *Aggression replacement training: A comprehensive intervention for aggressive youth* (rev. ed.). Champaign, IL: Research Press.

Goldstein, R. B., Grant, B. F., Ruan, W. J., Smith, S. M., & Saha, T. D. (2006). Anstisocial personality disorder with childhood vs. adolescence-onset conduct disorder: Results from the national epidemiologic survey on alcohol and related conditions. *Journal of Nervous and Mental Disease, 194*(9), 667–675.

Gordon, D. A., Arbuthnot, J., Gustafson, K. E., & McGreen, P. (1988). Home-based behavioral-systems family therapy with disadvantaged juvenile delinquents. *American Journal of Family Therapy, 16*, 243–255.

Hankin, B. L., Abela, J. R., Auerbach, R. P., McWhinnie, C. M., & Skitch, S. A. (2005). *Development of behavioral problems over the life course: A vulnerability and stress perspective*. In B. L. Hankin, J. R. Abela, & R. Z. John, *Development of psychopathology: A vulnerability-stress perspective* (pp. 385–416). Thousand Oaks, CA: Sage.

Henggeler, S. W., Schoenwald, S. K., Borduin, C., Rowland, M., & Cunningham, P. B. (1998). *Multisystemic treatment of antisocial behavior in children and adolescents*. New York: Guilford.

Henggeler, S., Schoenwald, S., Rowland, M., & Cunningham, P. (2002). *Serious emotional disturbance in children and adolescence: Multisystemic therapy*. New York: Guilford.

Hill, J. (2002). Biological, psychological and social processes in conduct disorders. *Journal of Child Psychology and Psychiatry, 43*(1), 133–164.

Hinshaw, S., & Anderson, C. (1996). Conduct and oppositional defiant disorders. In E. Mash & R. Barkley (Eds.), *Child psychopathology* (pp. 113–149). New York: Guilford.

Hogan, A. E. (1999). Cognitive functioning in children with oppositional defiant disorder. In H. C. Quay & A. E. Hogan (Eds.), *Handbook of disruptive behavior disorders* (pp. 317–335). New York: Kluwer.

Holmes, S. E, Slaughter, J. R., & Kashani, J. (2001) Risk factors in childhood that lead to the development of conduct disorder and antisocial personality disorder. *Child Psychiatry & Human Development, 31*, 183–193.

Ipser, J., & Stein, D. J. (2007). Systematic review of pharmacotherapy of disruptive behavior disorders in children and adolescents. *Psychopharmacology, 191*, 127–140.

Jaffee, S. R, Caspi, A., Moffitt, T. E., Dodge, K. A., Rutter, M, Taylor, A, Tully, L A. (2005). Nature × nurture: Genetic vulnerabilities interact with physical maltreatment to promote conduct problems. *Development and Psychopathology, 17*(1) 67–84.

Johnson, B. R., Jang, S. J., Larson, D., & Li, S. D. (2001). Does adolescent religious commitment matter? A reexamination of the effects of religiosity on delinquency. *Journal of Research in Crime and Delinquency, 38*, 22–43.

Johnson, B. R., Jang, S. J., Li, S. D., & Larson, D. (2000). The "invisible institution" and black youth crime: The church as an agency of local social control. *Journal of Youth and Adolescence, 29*, 479–498.

Kazdin, A. (2001). Treatment of conduct disorders. In J. Hill & B. Maughan (Eds.), *Conduct disorders in childhood and adolescence* (pp. 408–448). New York: Cambridge University Press.

Kronenberger, W. S., & Meyer, R. G. (2001). *The child clinician's handbook* (2nd ed.). Needham Heights, MA: Allyn & Bacon.

Kutchins, H. & Kirk, S. A. (1997). Making us crazy. *DSM: The psychiatric bible and the creation of mental disorders*. New York: Free Press.

Lahey, B., Miller, T., Schawb-Stone, M., Goodman, S., Waldman, I., Canino, G., et al. (2000). Age and gender differences in oppositional behavior and conduct problems: A cross sectional household study of middle childhood and adolescence. *Journal of Abnormal Psychology, 109*, 488–503.

Lahey, B. B., Loeber, R., Burke, J., & Rathouz, P. J. (2002). Adolescent outcomes of childhood conduct disorder among clinic-referred boys: Predictors of improvement. *Journal of Abnormal Child Psychology, 30*(4), 333–349.

Ledingham, J. (1999). Children and adolescents with oppositional defiant disorder and conduct disorder in the community: Experiences at school and with peers. In H. Quay & A. Hogan (Eds.), *Handbook of disruptive behavior disorders* (pp. 353–370). New York: Kluwer Academic/Plenum.

Legrand, L. N., Keyes, M., McGue, M., Iacono, W. G., & Krueger, R. F. (2008). Rural environments reduce the genetic influence on adolescent substance use and rule-breaking behavior. *Psychological Medicine, 38*, 1341–1350.

Lemery, K. S., & Doelger, L. (2005). Genetic vulnerabilities to the development of psychopathology. In B. L. Hankin & J. R. Z. Abela (Eds.), *Development of psychopathology: A vulnerability-stress perspective* (pp. 161–198). Thousand Oaks, CA: Sage.

Lipsey, M. W., Landenberger, N. A., & Wilson, S. J. (2007). *Effects of cognitive-behavioral programs for criminal offenders*. Retrieved January, 8, 2009, from The Campbell Collaboration Web site: http://www.campbellcollaboration.org/campbell_library/index.php.

Littell, J. H., Bjørndal, A., Winsvold, A., & Hammerstrøm, K. (2008). *Functional family therapy for families of youth (ages 11–18) with behaviour problems*. Retrieved January, 8, 2009 from The Campbell Collaboration Web site: http://www.campbellcollaboration. org/campbell_library/index.php.

Littell, J. H., Popa, M., & Forsythe. B. (2005). Multisystemic therapy for social, emotional, and behavioral problems in youth aged 10–17 (Cochrane Review). In *The Cochrane Library*, Issue 3. Art. No. CD004797.Chichester, England: John Wiley & Sons.

Loeber, R., Burke, J. D., Lagey, B. B., Winters, A., & Zera, M. (2000). Oppositional defiant and conduct disorder: A review of the past 10 years, part I. *Journal of the American Academy of Child and Adolescent Psychiatry, 39*(12), 1468–1484.

MacDonald, G. M., & Turner, W. (2008). Treatment foster care for improving outcomes in children and young people (Cochrane Review). *The Cochrane Library*, (1), Art. No.: CD005649.

Maughan, B., & Rutter, M. (2001). Antisocial children grown up. In J. Hill & B. Maughan (Eds.), *Conduct disorders in childhood and adolescence* (pp. 507–552). New York: Cambridge University Press.

McCart, M. R., Priester, P. E., Davies, W. H., & Azen, R. (2006). Differential effectiveness of behavioral parent-training and cognitive-behavioral therapy for antisocial youth: A meta-analysis. *Journal of Abnormal Child Psychology, 34*(4), 527–543.

Miller-Johnson, S., Coie, J. D., Maumary-Gremaud, A., & Bierman, K. (2002). Peer rejection and aggression and early starter models of conduct disorder. *Journal of Abnormal Child Psychology, 30*(3), 217–231.

Moffitt, T., Caspi, A., Harrington, H., & Milne, B. (2002). Males on the life-course-persistent and adolescence-limited antisocial pathways: Follow-up at age 26 years. *Development and Psychopathology, 14*, 179–207.

Moffitt, T., Caspi, A., Rutter, M., & Silva, P. (2001). *Sex differences in antisocial behavior: Conduct disorder, delinquency, and violence in the Dunedin longitudinal study*. Cambridge, England: Cambridge University Press.

Morrison, M., Macdonald, G., & Leblanc, T. (2000) Identifying conduct problems in young children: Developmental pathways and risk factors. *International Social Work, 43*(4), 467–480.

Mytton, J., DiGuiseppi, C., Gough, D., Taylor, R., & Logan, S. (2006). School-based secondary prevention programmes for preventing violence. *The Cochrane Database of Systematic Reviews*, (3), CD004606.

Najman, J., Williams, G., Nikles, J., Spence, S., Bor, W., O'Callaghan, M., et al. (2000). Mothers' mental illness and child behavior problems: Cause-effect association or observation bias? *Journal of the American Academy of Child and Adolescent Psychiatry, 39*(5), 592–602.

Nguyen, L., Huang, L. N., Arganza, G. F., & Liao, Q. (2007). The influence of race and ethnicity on psychiatric diagnoses and clinical characteristics of children and adolescents in children's services. *Cultural Diversity and Ethnic Minority Psychology, 13*(1), 18–25.

Nock, M. K., Kazdin, A. E., Hiripi, E., & Kessler, R. C. (2006). Prevalence, subtypes, and correlates of DSM-IV conduct disorder in the National Comorbidity Survey Replication. *Psychological Medicine, 36*(5), 699–710.

Nock, M. K., Kazdin, A. E., Hiripi, E., & Kessler, R. C. (2007). Lifetime prevalence, correlates, and persistence of oppositional defiant disorder: Results from the National Comorbidity Survey Replication. *Journal of Child Psychology and Psychiatry, 48*(7), 703–713.

Pappadopulos, E., Jensen, P. S., Schur, S. B., MacIntyre, J. C., 2nd, Ketner, S., & Van Orden, K., et al. (2002). "Real world" atypical antipsychotic prescribing practices in public child and adolescent inpatient settings. *Schizophrenia Bulletin, 28*(1), 111–121.

Pappadopulos, E., Woolston, S., Chait, A., Perkins, M., Connor, D. F., & Jensen, P. S. (2006). Pharmacotherapy of aggression in children and adolescents: Efficacy and effect size. *Journal of Canadian Academy of Child and Adolescent Psychiatry, 15*(1), 27–36.

Patterson, G., & Guillon, M. (1968). *Living with children: New methods for parents and teachers.* Champagne, IL: Research Press.

Pettit, G. S., Bates, J. E., Dodge, K. A., Bates J. E., & Pettit G. S. (2004). Ethnic differences in the link between physical discipline and later adolescent externalizing behaviors. *Journal of Child Psychology and Psychiatry and Allied Disciplines, 45*(4), 801–812.

Reyno, S. M., & McGrath, P. J. (2006). Predictors of parent training efficacy for child externalizing behavior problem—a meta-analytic review. *Journal of Child Psychology and Psychiatry, 47*(1), 99–111.

Sanders, M. R. (1999). Triple p-positive parenting program: Towards an empirically validated multilevel parenting and family support strategy for the prevention of behavior and emotional problems in children. *Clinical Child and Family Psychology Review, 2*, 71–90.

Schur, S. B., Sikich, L., Findling, R. L., Malone, R. P., Crismon, M. L., & Derivan, A. et al. (2003). Treatment recommendations for the use of antipsychotics for aggressive youth (TRAAY). Part I: A review. *Journal of the American Academy of Child and Adolescent Psychiatry, 42*(2), 132–144.

Steinberg, L. (2001). We know some things: Parent-adolescent relationships in retrospect and prospect. *Journal of Research on Adolescence, 11*, 1–19.

Wachs, T. (2000). *Necessary but not sufficient.* Washington, DC: American Psychological Association.

Waldron, H. B., & Turner, C. W. (2008). Evidence based psychosocial treatments for adolescent substance abuse. *Journal of Clinical Child & Adolescent Psychology, 37*(1), 238–261.

Webster-Stratton, C. (1981; revised 2001). *Incredible years parents and children training series.* Retrieved November 7, 2003, from http://www.incredibleyears.com.

Werner, E. (2000). Protective factors and individual resilience. In J. Shonoff & S. Meisels (Eds.), *Handbook of early childhood intervention* (2nd ed., pp. 115–133). Cambridge, England: Cambridge University Press.

Wikström, P. O., & Loeber, R. (2000). Do disadvantaged neighborhoods cause well-adjusted children to become adolescent delinquents? *Criminology, 38,* 1109–1142.

Wilson, S. J., & Lipsey, M. W. (2006). The effectiveness of school-based social information processing programs: Part I: Universal programs. *Campbell Collaboration Systematic Reviews* 2006:5. DOI 10.4073/CST.2006.5.

Wilson, S. J., & Lipsey, M. W. (2007). School based interventions for aggressive and disruptive behavior: Update of a meta-analysis. *American Journal of Preventive Medicine, 33*(2S), S130–S143.

Wilson, S., Lipsey, M., & Soydan, H. (2003). Are mainstream programs for juvenile delinquency less effective with minority youth than majority youth? A meta- analysis of outcomes research. *Research on Social Work Practice, 13,* 3–26.

Woolfenden, S. R., Williams, K., & Peat, J. K. (2001). Family and parenting interventions in children and adolescents with conduct disorder and delinquency aged 10–17. *Cochrane Database of Systematic Reviews, 2, Art. No.: CD003015.*

Appendix: Measures for Conduct Disorder/ Oppositional Defiant Disorder

Revisions for this edition have been drawn from Frick and McMahon (2008).

Youth Self-Report (Achenbach, 1991; Achenbach & Rescorla, 2000, 2001)

Description
- Assesses 11–18 year olds' self-reports of their problems and competencies for the last 6 months.
- Designed as part of a multi-informant Achenbach System of Empirically Based Assessment (ASEBA), using also the parent-informed Child Behavior Checklist and the teacher-informed Teacher Report Form. Items are parallel to CBCL and TRF.

  o Norms for YSR and CBCL are representative of the 48 contiguous U.S. states for SES, gender, ethnicity, religion, and urban/suburban/rural.
  o For diagnosis, internal consistency and test-retest reliability are rated as excellent, and interrater reliability is adequate.
  o Content validity is rated as good, and construct validity and validity generalization are excellent.

- Three-response format (0/ "not true," 1/ "somewhat" or "sometimes true," 2/ "very true" or "often true")
- Seventeen competence items include the following:

  1. Activities
  2. Social
  3. Mean of youth's self-report of academic performance

- One hundred and three problem items include the following:

  1. Thought problems
  2. Attention problems
  3. Self-destructive/identity problems (only for boys)

Internalizing
  4. Withdrawn
  5. Somatic complaints
  6. Anxious/depressed

Externalizing
  7. Delinquent behavior
  8. Aggressive behavior

Reliability
- One-week test-retest reliabilities: mean .76 for competence scores and mean .72 for problems scores
- Six-month test-retest reliability: mean of .69 for problem scores
- Seven-month test-retest reliabilities: mean of .50 for competence scales and .49 for problem scales

Validity
Discriminates between referred and nonreferred youth.

Eyberg Child Behavior Inventory (ECBI) (Eyberg, 1992)

Description
- A parent-completed, 36-item, behavior rating scale developed to assess disruptive behaviors in children ages 2–16 years
- Two scales:

  1. Intensity ("never"/1 to "always"/7): how often the behaviors currently occur
  2. Problem ("yes"/"no"): identifies the specific behaviors that are currently problems

- Takes 10 minutes to complete

Reliability
- Interparent agreement was .86 for Intensity and .79 for Problem scales.
- Internal consistency was .98 for both Intensity and Problem scales for nonreferred pediatric clinic sample and for pediatric clinic adolescents.
- Test-retest reliability was .86 for Intensity and .88 for Problem scales over 3 weeks, .80 for Intensity and .85 for Problem scales over 3 months, and .75 for Intensity and .75 for Problem scales.

Validity
- Valid across ethnic groups (Collett, Ohan, & Myers, 2003)
- Scores were correlated with observational measures of parent–child interactions.
- Problem (.67) and Intensity (.75) scores were correlated with Externalizing scale of the Child Behavior Checklist and with Internalizing scale (Problem = .48; Intensity = .41).
- Problem (.62) and Intensity (.59) scores correlated with Parenting Stress Index child domain scores and with parent domain scores (Problem = .62; Intensity = .59).
- When comparing preschool disruptive children and a comparison group without such problems and adolescents who were disruptive versus adolescents who were not, mean Intensity and Problem scores differentiated between groups.
- The scale appears to be sensitive to treatment change in young children.

Child Behavior Checklist (CBCL) (Achenbach & Rescorla, 2000, 2001)

Description
- Scale, along with YSR, is rated as adequate for clinical utility and highly recommended by Hunsley and Mash (2008).
- Parent-report checklist assessing child (ages 4–18) functioning with response set ("0" not true/ "2" very or often true) in last 6 months
- Written at fifth-grade reading level and requires 20 minutes to complete
- A briefer version available for 2–3 year olds
- Assesses two primary areas:

  1. Social competence (20 items): amount and quality of child's participation in extracurricular activities, school functioning, jobs, chores, friendships, and other activities
  2. Behavior problems (118 behaviors): eight syndromes under two broad groupings: *Internalizing* (withdrawn, somatic complaints, anxious/ depressed) and *Externalizing* (delinquent behavior, aggressive behavior, social problems, thought problems, attention problems, sex problems)

Reliability
- One-week test-retest reliability ranged from .70 to .95.
- One-year test-retest reliability was a mean correlation of .62 for competence scales and .75 for problem scales.
- Two-year test-retest reliability was a mean correlation of .56 for competence scales and .71 for problem scales.

Validity
- Correlations between Child Behavior Checklist and Connors Parent Questionnaire ranged from .59 to .86, with total problem scores correlating .82.
- Correlations between Child Behavior Checklist and Quay-Peterson Revised Behavior Problem Checklist ranged from .59 to .88, with total problem scores correlating .81.
- Discriminates between clinic and nonclinic children
- Sensitive to treatment effects

Behavior Assesment System for Children, 2nd Edition (BASC-2) (Reynolds & Kamphaus, 2004)

Description
- Teacher and parent versions are very similar; child report asks less about behavior assessment and more about child's attitudes.
- Norms are excellent; samples between 3400 and 4800 children/ adolescents in 375 U.S. and Canadian locations

Reliability
- Internal consistency is rated as excellent.
- Test-retest reliability is rated as excellent.
- Interrater reliability is adequate.

Validity
Construct validity is good.

Child Symptom Inventory for DSM-IV (CSI-IV) (Gadow & Sprafkin, 1998)

Description
- Designed specifically to match the content of DSM-IV for conduct problems among other DSM disorders for children ages 5–12 years
- Parent (97-items) and teacher (77-items) versions
- Spanish version available
- Takes 10 minutes to complete

Reliability
- Internal consistency, interrater reliability, and test-retest reliability are adequate.

Validity
Construct validity is good.

References for ODD/CD Measures

Achenbach, T. M. (1991). *Manual for the Child Behavior Checklist/4-18 and 1991 profile*. Burlington: University of Vermont Department of Psychiatry.

Achenbach, T. M., & Rescorla, L. A. (2001). *Manual for the ASEBA school-age forms and profiles*. Burlington: University of Vermont Research Center for Children, Youth, & Families.

Achenbach, T. M., & Rescorla, L. A. (2000). *Manual for the ASEBA preschool forms & profiles*. Burlington: University of Vermont, Department of Psychiatry.

Collett, B., Ohan, J., & Myers, K. (2003). Ten-year review of rating scales. VI: Scales assessing externalizing behaviors. *Journal of the American Academy of Child and Adolescent Psychiatry, 42*, 1143–1171.

Eyberg, S. (1992). Assessing therapy outcome with preschool children: Progress and problems. *Journal of Clinical Child Psychology, 21*, 306–311.

Frick, P., & McMahon, R. (2008). Child and adolescent conduct problems. In J. Hunsley & E. Mash (Eds.), *A guide to assessments that work* (pp. 41–66). New York: Oxford University Press.

Gadow, K. D., & Sprafkin, J. (1998). *CSI-4 screening manual*. Stony Brook, NY: Checkmate Plus.

Hunsley, J., & Mash, E. J. (Eds.). (2008). *A guide to assessments that work*. New York: Oxford University Press.

Reynolds, C. R., & Kamphaus, R. W. (2004). *Behavior Assessment System for Children -2 (BASC-2)*. Bloomington, MN: Pearson Assessments

6 Attention-Deficit/Hyperactivity Disorder

Attention-deficit/hyperactivity disorder (ADHD) is characterized by a persistent pattern (6 months or more) of *inattention* and/or *hyperactivity* and *impulsive behavior* that is more frequent and severe than what is typically observed in others at a comparable developmental level (American Psychiatric Association, 2000). Children with ADHD show a lack of self-control and ability to sustain direction. They are distractible, do not often finish what they start, and are irritable and impatient, often interrupting and pestering others. Adults with the disorder are usually not hyperactive but are impatient, restless, and moody. They have difficulty managing their time and priorities.

The *DSM* delineates three subtypes of ADHD, depending on which symptoms predominate: the *hyperactive/impulsive*, *inattentive*, and *combined* types. Younger children are more likely to be diagnosed with the hyperactive/impulsive type, and not as much research has been conducted with the primarily inattentive type (Root & Resnick, 2003). To be diagnosed, the child must have demonstrated symptoms before the age of 7.

Attention-deficit/hyperactivity disorder is considered to be one of the disruptive behavior disorders (along with conduct disorder and oppositional defiant disorder), and the *DSM* diagnosis is made on the basis of behavioral symptoms. The most recent conceptualization of ADHD is that it involves a cognitive or neuropsychological impairment that is manifested in terms of self-regulation, behavior inhibition, and self-control (Barkley, 2006).

Prevalence of ADHD

The United States Center for Disease Control (CDC) reports a prevalence of 7.8% among children aged 4–17 (Centers for Disease Control and Prevention, 2005). The lifetime prevalence rate of ADHD in adults is 8.1% (Kessler, Berglund, Demler, Jin, & Walters, 2005).

Attention-deficit/hyperactivity disorder is more prominent among boys by approximately a 2.5:1 ratio (CDC, 2005), and more research has been done on boys (Rucklidge & Tannock, 2001). Boys may have a greater genetic liability for the disorder (Derks, Dolan, Hudziak, Neale, & Boomsma, 2007), and their disruptive behavior more often comes to the attention of professionals.

Comorbidity

Reviews have indicated that about 45% of persons with ADHD may have at least one comorbid disorder (Barkley, Fischer, Smallish, & Fletcher, 2004; Langstroem, 2002), but in the largest study of ADHD to date, the Multi-Modal Treatment Study of Children with Attention Deficit Hyperactivity Disorder (discussed in the section "Intervention"), only 31.8% of the participants had a diagnosis of ADHD alone (Jensen et al., 2007). The most frequent co-occurring diagnosis is another of the disruptive disorders (ODD or CD), rates of which range considerably in studies (25%–75%) (see Wolraich, Bickman, Lambert, Simmons, & Doffing, 2005 for a review). In the MTA study, almost a third (29.5%) were diagnosed with ADHD and either ODD or CD. Comorbid ODD puts a child at risk for continued ODD and depression in early adulthood (Biederman, Petty, Dolan et al., 2008). Comorbid CD puts a child at risk for substance use disorders, bipolar disorder, and smoking in early adulthood.

Substantial comorbidity also exists between ADHD and the mood disorders (0%–72%) (Carlson & Meyer, 2009), anxiety disorders (25%), and the learning disorders (25%–70%) (Tannock & Brown, 2009).

Course

The majority of youth (two-thirds) who are diagnosed with ADHD in childhood will continue to meet criteria into adolescence (Mannuzza & Klein, 1999; Wolraich, Wibbelsman, et al., 2005). Despite the substantial persistence of ADHD in adolescence and its serious consequences, most studies on ADHD treatment outcome research have been conducted on children (Barkley et al.,

2004). Adolescents are less likely than children to receive mental health services and are often noncompliant with those services.

About a third (36%) of childhood cases continue into adulthood with 8.1% of adults meeting diagnostic criterion, according to the National Co-Morbidity Replication Study (Kessler et al., 2005). A meta-analysis of prevalence studies of adult ADHD (N = 6 studies) found a pooled rate of 2.5% (Simon, Czobor, Bálint, Mészáros, & Bitter, 2009). Although this rate was lower than the Kessler et al. (2005) finding, the authors believed that the difficulty of applying *DSM* criteria for ADHD to adults resulted in an underestimation of rates.

Adults with ADHD tend to have more problems in the work and social arenas. In a study following children with ADHD into young adulthood, a third (32%) had failed to complete high school and far fewer were in college compared to the "normal" control group (Barkley et al., 2004). In addition, young adults with hyperactivity had fewer friends and had more difficulty keeping friends. Sexual risk taking, in terms of number of partners and unprotected sex, was also indicated. Moreover, adults with ADHD show impaired work performance, and this effect is particularly evident among blue-collar workers (Kessler, Adler, et al., 2005). People with ADHD have more car accidents, citations, and speeding tickets than people without ADHD, although they do not perceive themselves as poor drivers (Knouse, Bagwell, Barkley, & Murphy, 2005).

Assessment

This section considers the salient diagnostic issues regarding ADHD at each developmental stage, beginning with preschool children and ending at adulthood. Attention-deficit/hyperactivity disorder generally begins before the age of 4 or 5. Although earlier assessment can inform intervention that might minimize later problems, difficulties abound in diagnosing ADHD in preschool-age children (Shepard, Carter, & Cohen, 2000). For instance, valid and reliable instruments for assessing ADHD are lacking. Caution must also be exercised in diagnosing ADHD in preschool because the child may be reacting to a difficult environment, displaying anxiety symptoms, or experiencing other problems with emotional regulation. As a result, most children are not diagnosed until elementary school.

Assessment at the school-age stage, recognizing that no definitive biological or neurological test establishes the diagnosis, includes several components (Root & Resnick, 2003):

- A physical examination and a review of health records
- Interviews with the child, parents, teachers, and any other significant persons.

Problems related to trauma, stress, depression, and anxiety should be ruled out.

It must be noted that children tend to underreport their symptoms (Pelham, Fabiano, & Massetti, 2005). In addition, teachers are usually the first people (followed by parents) to suggest that children be evaluated for ADHD (Sax & Kautz, 2003), and their judgments of child symptoms tend to be valid (Mannuzza, Klein, & Moulton, 2002).

- Rating scales completed by parents and teachers can also provide useful information. (See the Appendix at the end of the chapter for a list of instruments.)
- Behavioral observations of the child and of parent–child interactions

The social worker can advise parents about the assessment process. He or she may find that many parents, suspecting ADHD in their children, have brought their children to their primary care providers, who then diagnosed the child with ADHD and prescribed medication. However, a national survey has indicated that the majority of primary care physicians do not use *DSM* criteria to diagnose ADHD (Chan, Hopkins, Perrin, Herrerias, & Homer, 2005), and one-fifth to one-third do not routinely incorporate teacher and school information into the evaluation process.

The social worker can assume primary responsibility for certain aspects of the assessment (clinical interviews with the child and parent, assessing parent–child interactions, interviewing teachers, and administering measures). Other aspects of the assessment require referrals for medical and psychological evaluation. Social workers should also be familiar with the child study process in the school districts in which they work. (Information is typically available on state education Web sites.)

Regarding diagnosis in adults, the following components are involved (American Academy of Child and Adolescent Psychiatry, 2002):

- Completion of a screening instrument for assessing *DSM-IV* ADHD in adults, the Adult ADHD Self-Report Scale (Kessler, Adler, et al., 2005) available at http://www.med.nyu.edu/psych/assets/adhdscreen18.pdf
- A clinical interview, with discussion of ADHD symptoms present in childhood
- History taking of drug and alcohol use, because ADHD can be comorbid with substance abuse and dependence
- Information from collateral sources (parents, significant others), who may be more accurate reporters of symptoms
- A medical history and physical examination to rule out physical conditions
- The completion of rating scales, such as the Brown Attention-Deficit Disorder Scale for Adults (Brown, 1996) and the Conners Adult Attention Rating Scale (Conners et al., 1999)

Risk and Protective Factors

Onset

Several theories have arisen regarding the nature of ADHD, but a prominent one is that it is an inherited neuropsychological disorder, involving executive functioning of the brain (Johnson, Wiersema, & Kuntsi, 2009). Credence is given to the fact that ADHD is due more to child individual influences rather than environmental risk (Ford, Goodman, & Meltzer, 2004). Risk and protective factors for the onset of ADHD are listed in Exhibit 6.1, and in the following section, some of the risk and protective factors are further elaborated.

Genetics

Having a parent with ADHD places a child at risk for ADHD. In a review of 20 twin studies, the heritability of ADHD was estimated at 76% (Faraone et al., 2005). Similarily, another review indicated heritability estimates between 70% to 90% (Polderman et al., 2007). The precise genetic mechanisms that contribute to the onset of ADHD are not known, but dopamine transmitter and receptor genes, as well as several serotonin transporter and

Exhibit 6.1	
Risk and Protective Factors for the Onset of Attention-Deficit/ Hyperactivity Disorder	
Risk	Protective
Biological	
Genetic predisposition	No genetic predisposition
Maternal smoking, alcohol and drug use during pregnancy	Mother does not smoke or use substances during pregnancy
Complications during pregnancy and delivery	Complication-free pregnancy and delivery
Preterm delivery	
Lead exposure	No lead exposure
Male gender	Female gender
Social	
Family	
Lack of an attachment bond, coupled with low maternal social support	High levels of maternal social support and a strong mother–child attachment bond
Low socioeconomic status	High socioeconomic status

Sources: Bhutta, Cleves, Casey, Cradock, & Anand, 2002; Kahn, Khoury, Nichols, & Lanphear, 2003; Linnett et al., 2003.

receptor genes, have been linked to the disorder (Faraone & Khan, 2006; Levy, Hay, & Bennett, 2006). As noted earlier, ADHD is more prevalent in boys (CDC, 2005), and they may have a greater genetic liability for the disorder (Derks et al., 2007).

Along with neurobiological risks for the development of the disorder, there are also protective factors related to the development of the prefrontal cortex (certain gene systems and response inhibition, or the capacity to inhibit impulsive behaviors) that may help children, in the face of environmental stressors, to avoid ADHD (Nigg, Nikolas, Friderici, Park, & Zucker, 2007). Of note is that genetics are not the only biological mechanism by which children may develop ADHD. Prenatal and perinatal risk factors are also significant and are listed in Exhibit 6.1.

Family Influences

Some researchers posit that attachment patterns and family interactions may contribute to the onset of ADHD. Severe early deprivation, as often occurs in institutional rearing, may be one way this occurs. A recently published study indicated that institutional rearing was associated with elevated inattention and overactivity into early adolescence even when a child had been adopted at an earlier stage (Stevens et al., 2008).

In another study, hostile family interactions when the child was 2 years old predicted child ADHD at age 7 (Jacobvitz, Hazen, Curran, & Hichtens, 2004). For boys, enmeshed family patterns at age 2 were associated with ADHD symptoms at age 11. One question is whether symptoms of ADHD were already present in toddlers, contributing to the family hostility and enmeshment patterns described.

In a third study, family adversity was related to ADHD symptoms independent of conduct problems, suggesting that family and social risk influences may be a cause as well as a consequence of ADHD (Counts, Nigg, Stawicki, Rappley, & von Eye, 2005). It is also likely that certain risk factors, such as family adversity, affect children with a genetic vulnerability to develop ADHD (Laucht et al. 2007).

Recovery and Adjustment

Exhibit 6.2 summarizes the risk and protective factors for the course of ADHD. We will elaborate only on the social influences, as the psychological risks resemble those presented for the onset of the disorder.

Social Influences
Family Factors

Any parental or family difficulties that contribute to inconsistent, coercive, or decreased efforts at managing the child's behavior may increase problem

Exhibit 6.2

Risk and Protective Factors for the Course of Attention-Deficit/ Hyperactivity Disorder

Risk	Protective
Psychological	
Comorbid oppositional defiant disorder or conduct disorder[a]	No comorbid diagnosis or a comorbid anxiety disorder
More severe ADHD[b]	Less severe ADHD
Social	
Family	
Parent with ADHD	Parents do not have ADHD
Coercive and inconsistent parenting	Effective child management strategies
Single-parent home	Two-parent home

[a] Biederman, Petty, et al. (2008).
[b] Barkley, Murphy, O'Connell, Anderson, & Connor (2006); Kessler et al. (2005).
ADHD, attention-deficit/hyperactivity disorder.

behaviors in the child with ADHD (Weiss & Hechtman, 1993). Family adversity, particularly marital conflict, is associated with ADHD (Counts et al., 2005). It is unclear whether these factors contribute to or are a consequence of child ADHD. Parental expressed emotion may moderate the genetic effect associated with ADHD (Sonuga-Burke et al., (2008). Specifically, maternal warmth may protect against ADHD becoming severe or from conduct disorder developing. On the other hand, maternal depression predicts worse improvement outcome (Owens et al., 2003). These findings are not surprising given that distressed individuals often lack the motivation or organization to complete effortful tasks that require ongoing work, such as the consistent implementation of behavioral management techniques.

Another factor identified in families involves household composition. A two-parent home may be a protective influence because two parents are more likely to successfully manage the stress related to having a child with ADHD (Cuffe et al., 2001). A child's living in a single-parent home contributed to worse outcomes for parent-involved treatment (Corcoran & Datallo, 2006). At the same time, having a child with ADHD puts a strain on marriages. Wymbs et al. (2008) found that parents with a child with ADHD were more likely to divorce than parents without a child with ADHD.

Pervasive child problems in the way of daily negative interactions and behavioral management difficulties demand considerable parental resources

(Coghill et al., 2008). These demands often result in failure, fatigue, demoralization, isolation, strained marital relationships, and neglect or overindulgence of siblings (Whalen & Henker, 1999). For these reasons, the social worker's empathic understanding and support of parents can facilitate constructive family interactions.

Socioeconomic Status

People in poverty tend to be less successful than their non-poor counterparts in terms of ADHD improvement when undergoing treatment (Jensen et al., 2007). This may be due to lack of access to health care and managing the stressors of poverty in which child ADHD symptoms play a lower priority.

Intervention

The evidence for treatment of ADHD mainly centers around one type of psychosocial treatment—behavioral therapy—and medication. Within these somewhat limited options, there is some controversy about which should be the first-line treatment (Pelham & Fabiano, 2008), which will be discussed further in the section on medication.

Psychosocial Interventions

Behaviorally based interventions at the family and school levels have received empirical support in the literature (Pelham & Fabiano, 2008) and will therefore be a focus here. Despite the use of cognitive-behavioral therapy, particularly social skills training, with youth with ADHD, such interventions do not seem to be effective (Pelham & Fabiano, 2008) and will not be explored further for this reason.

Family Interventions

As described previously, parenting practices can play a large role in determining the outcome of ADHD for a child. Because of problems children have with listening and following through with directions, interactions between children and their caregivers may easily turn coercive. Such parent–child exchanges are, in turn, linked to the development of conduct problems (Patterson, 1982, 1986; Patterson, DeBaryshe, & Ramsey, 1989).

The empirical literature on family intervention for ADHD focuses on parent training, which was initially developed to address conduct problems (see Chapter 5). Children learn prosocial behavior (e.g., following directions, completing homework, doing household chores, getting along with siblings) by positive reinforcement through praise, token economies, and rewards.

Parents are taught to respond to children's negative behaviors by ignoring or punishing the child so that he or she will have to suffer negative consequences (e.g., time out from reinforcement, the loss of points and privileges, or work duty) for engaging in the behavior. Parents are taught these principles through didactic instruction, behavioral rehearsal, modeling, and role plays.

Parent training is a brief treatment model with about 12 sessions in either individual or group formats. The strategies learned must be enacted consistently long after treatment is over so that the child does not revert to previous undesirable behaviors. Along with behaviorally based skill-building, psychoeducation is typically offered for parents of children with ADHD so that parents gain knowledge about ADHD, its treatment, and how to manage parental stress.

Because children with ADHD have problems with schoolwork, other interventions for parents include structuring the home environment (so that the child has a quiet, uncluttered place to work relatively free of distractions, perhaps with a parent sitting nearby), regular teacher verification of satisfactory homework completion, and a home-based reinforcement system featuring regular school–home note exchanges (DuPaul & Power, 2000). In such a system, the teacher evaluates the child once per day (0 = work harder, 1 = OK, 2 = good job!) on selected target behaviors (such as completion of work, attention to instruction, and speaking at appropriate times). Parents review the teacher rating and provide incentives for goal attainment and punishment for failing to make agreed-upon changes (DuPaul & Power, 2000).

A meta-analysis was conducted on parent-involved treatment of ADHD, and all 16 of the experimental or quasi-experimental studies involved parent training (Corcoran & Dattalo, 2006). Compared to control and comparison conditions, parent-involved treatment of ADHD had a low to moderate effect on ADHD and externalizing symptoms. It must be recognized that some of the control conditions involved viable treatments, such as medication and child treatment; therefore, the fact that parent-involved treatment produced overall gains above and beyond these control treatments is noteworthy. Parent-involved treatment had an even greater effect on child internalizing symptoms and family functioning. Child social skills, on the other hand, were not affected by family treatment, despite the thrust of many programs on improving such skills. This echoes the finding that social skills programs, except for a specialized day camp summer program (see Pelham & Fabiano, 2008), typically are not helpful for improving ADHD deficits in this area.

School Interventions

School-based services for children with ADHD rest on a foundation provided by several federal laws. The way each law addresses the educational needs of children with ADHD is briefly described next, referencing the work of DuPaul and Power (2000), Root and Resnick (2003), and Tannock and Brown (2000). Section 504 of the 1973 Rehabilitation Act prohibits schools from discriminating against people with handicaps. The Individuals with Disabilities Education Act (IDEA) of 1990 (the reauthorization of the Education for All Handicapped Children Act, PL 94-142) includes several relevant provisions for persons with ADHD. It qualifies children with ADHD for special education services under the disability category (such as a learning disability or the category of "other health impairment") when symptoms affect alertness, which, in turn, limits school performance. It also provides free and appropriate public education for children with ADHD and a multidisciplinary evaluation process toward the development of an individualized educational plan. The Americans with Disabilities Act (ADA) ensures that reasonable accommodations must be made for individuals who have a substantial limitation of a major life activity, such as learning. Social workers, as well as parents of children with ADHD, can find more information about these laws and their enactment at state departments of education. If it is necessary for parents to seek legal services for better enforcement of the laws, they should be referred to local bar associations, which have listings of attorneys who specialize in these cases (Root & Resnick, 2003).

The types of interventions required by a student with ADHD to perform well in school depend on multiple factors: the settings where the impairment is occurring; the level of functional impairment; the resources available in the home, school, and community; the motivation of the student to change; the presence of comorbid psychiatric conditions; and the child's prior response to educational, behavioral, or pharmacological interventions (DuPaul & Power, 2000). Children and adolescent students with ADHD are typically placed in general education classrooms, which is appropriate as long as modifications are implemented effectively by the general education teacher. Indeed, mixed findings have been indicated for the use of special education with students with ADHD.

A meta-analysis of 63 studies of school-based interventions indicated that contingency management programs and academic interventions were more effective than cognitive-behavioral interventions for affecting the classroom behavior of children with ADHD (DuPaul & Eckert, 1997). However, academic performance was more difficult to change through intervention. DuPaul and Power (2000) have suggested the following modifications to instruction:

- Repeating instructions frequently
- Presenting information in color
- Remaining on one topic for only a brief time
- Presenting material quickly
- Providing frequent breaks

- Representing time limits in concrete ways, such as the use of a timer on the child's desk
- Requiring an active motor response from the child, such as pressing a button
- Giving the child frequent opportunities to receive feedback for performance
- Giving a menu of possible assignments, such as completing a worksheet, doing problems on the computer, or practicing problems with a classmate
- (For adolescents and young adults) providing instruction in note-taking, study, and test-taking skills

Management of behavior in the classroom involves providing brief, firm reprimands immediately following an undesired behavior and making sure that verbal praise is given at least three times as often as reprimands. However, praise may not sufficiently galvanize children with ADHD, who may suffer impairments in motivation (Barkley, 2006). As a result, tokens, which can be exchanged for rewards, can be more effective because they represent concrete, external sources of motivation (DuPaul & Power, 2000). Tokens can also be used for "response cost" strategies, in which they are withdrawn from a child's "account" for unacceptable behavior. The social worker may also play the role of mentor or identify a mentor within the school system. This person spends a great deal of one-on-one time with the child through the school day. The purposes of mentoring are to develop a relationship of support and trust with the child, design an organizational system so that the child can track materials and assignments, negotiate behavioral contracts, monitor academic performance (with frequent input from teachers), and help teachers structure classroom interventions (DuPaul & Power, 2000).

Medication

Types of Medication

The primary psychostimulant drugs are methylphenidate, the amphetamines (including dextroamphetamine and methamphetamine, which are more potent substances), and pemoline. They are classified (except for pemoline) as Schedule II drugs by the Drug Enforcement Agency because of their abuse potential. Schedule II is the most restrictive classification for medications, prohibiting both their prescription by phone and the writing of refills. In this country the majority of children (71%) with ADHD take methylphenidate, because it is effective, has been available the longest (since 1958), and has been tested most thoroughly (NIH, 2000).

Schachter, Pham, King, Langford, and Moher (2001) conducted a meta-analysis of the randomized, controlled trials in the English-language published literature of short-acting methylphenidate with youth under age 18. Sixty-two trials were included, involving 2,897 participants. The impact of medication compared to placebo was 0.78 for teacher-report (a large effect size) and 0.54 for parent report (a moderate effect size).

Limitations were apparent in studies. Trials were short (on average 3 weeks); many studies had methodological problems, and there was an indication of publication bias, meaning that the focus on published studies may conceal the fact that unpublished studies may contradict these findings. Adverse side effects were also reported. For example, decreased appetite was common according to both parent and teacher reports and was statistically significant compared to placebo.

Although the stimulants have traditionally been the drug of first choice in treating ADHD, alternatives are sometimes necessary due to side effects or lack of positive impact. See Daughton and Kratochvil (2009) for more information on stimulants and other medications prescribed for ADHD, their dosages, and advantages and disadvantages. Some typical alternatives are bupropion (Wellbutrin) and atomoxetine (Strattera), a selective norepinephrine reuptake inhibitor. Atomoxetine has been studied extensively since the last edition of this book. The Integrated Data Exploratory Analysis (IDEA) study in which data from six randomized controlled trials were pooled indicated that about equal numbers of youth responded (were much improved) as did not respond to atomoxetine (Newcorn, Sutton, Weiss, & Sumner, 2009). Youth who improved showed at least a minimal response at week 4. Therefore, the recommendation is to either augment or switch medications at this point if there is no improvement.

Concerns Related to Medication Prescription for Children

Although pharmacological intervention is certainly less expensive than psychosocial interventions, there are concerns with the use of medication for children and adolescents. First, the fact that a stimulant improves attention in those who take it is not diagnostic, as most people, if given stimulants, show better focus and concentration (DeGrandpre, 1999).

Second, medication for children under 5 years of age is rarely indicated because the main reason to use medications is to help school-age children perform better in school (Shepard et al., 2000). Therefore, the primary use for stimulants with preschool children is behavior control, which might be aptly managed through structuring the environment with improved parenting skills. In addition, it has been hypothesized that the prefrontal cortex, the brain area that is the primary site of action of psychostimulants, is not fully mature at this young age. Other organ systems that are active in the breakdown and secretion of psychostimulants are also immature (Shepard et al., 2000).

Third, stimulant treatment does not appear to alter the adolescent or adult outcome of ADHD, despite well-established therapeutic gains in childhood when it is taken (Brown et al., 2007). Fourth, some people experience intolerable adverse reactions to medication. In the MTA study, which will be reported in the following section, a majority of participants (64%) experienced a mild side effect, and a proportion (14%) suffered moderate-to-severe side effects (MTA, 1999). Another concern is the negative effect of stimulant treatment on growth (see Faraone, Biederman, Morley, & Spencer, 2008, for a review). Fifth, for nonstimulant medications, short-term safety data are lacking, and there is a lack of long-term evidence that medication is safe when taken over a number of years.

Sixth, a concern specific to adolescents is that they will be at increased risk for substance use as they become habituated to using medication to regulate their behavior. However, a meta-analysis examining the association between medication use and substance abuse in adolescence and adulthood found that children who took medication were at lower risk for substance abuse than those who had not (Faraone & Wilens, 2003; Wilens, Faraone, Biederman, & Gunawardene, 2003). An additional safeguard against abuse is provided through the use of longer-acting medications, such as extended-release methylphenidate (e.g., Concerta). With these drugs, the medication need be given only once daily by the parents and not taken to school, where it could be given away or sold. Furthermore, the active ingredient in this extended-release caplet is in the form of a paste, which cannot be ground up or snorted (NIH, 2000).

Multimodal Treatment Study of Children with ADHD (MTA)

The MTA Cooperative Study is the largest study to date on the treatment of ADHD in youth. At four sites throughout the United States, children (N = 479) were randomized to four groups:

1. Medication, which was delivered in an intensive and carefully monitored fashion
2. Behavior therapy, which was offered both in the home and at the school.
3. Combined medication and behavior therapy
4. Community control in which families were free to receive treatment from providers in the community

Treatment was continued for a 14-month period. At the end of this time, the combined treatment (medication and behavior therapy) performed better than behavior therapy alone in reducing ADHD symptoms, although not significantly better than medication alone (Swanson et al., 2008). Children in the combination group were taking a 20% lower dose than those in the medication group. This suggests that the addition of behavior therapy allowed children to take a lower dose and still have the same benefits (Swanson et al., 2008).

At 24 months, the medication groups still maintained an advantage over the behavior therapy and community control groups, though to a lesser extent. At a 36-month follow-up, any advantages of medication had disappeared. There was a protective effect for behavior therapy against early substance use. Weight and height were diminished in children now aged 11–13 who had taken medication. It is not known whether they would catch up by early adulthood in terms of their growth.

Some of the dissipation of the positive effects of medication was due to the fact that medication was being provided according to community standards; that is, it was no longer necessary to closely monitor and adjust dosages. Indeed, a study using a large claims database from U.S. managed health care organizations showed that the titration of dosage in usual practice is less than at recommended levels, suggesting that children are not receiving optimal treatment (Olfson, Marcus, & Wan, 2009).

Some evidence indicates that certain comorbid disorders could be targeted by particular components of ADHD intervention. In the MTA study, children with oppositional defiant disorder or conduct disorder continued to be impaired, but this group tended to improve when medication was one part of the total intervention (Jensen et al., 2007). In contrast, children with comorbid ADHD and anxiety responded best to interventions that included behavior therapy. In fact, for children with comorbid anxiety disorders, behavioral treatment alone yielded comparable effects to medication alone and combined treatment on *both* ADHD and anxiety symptoms.

The findings from the MTA study do not provide clear guidelines on treatment and do not resolve the controversies about appropriate treatment. The American Academy of Child and Adolescent Psychiatry recommend medication as a first-line treatment, while psychologists typically suggest behavioral interventions (Pelham & Fabiano, 2008). Indeed, authors of the MTA study disagree among themselves about appropriate treatment—whether behavioral treatment or medication should be offered as treatment (Vedantam, 2009).

Medication for Adults

A meta-analysis was recently conducted on medications for adult ADHD (Peterson, McDonagh, & Fu, 2008). Twenty-two studies were located, and the shorter-acting stimulants (namely methylphenate) were found to produce benefits over other medications. Further, they were the only medication to reduce ADHD symptoms in adults with substance use disorders. The results of Peterson et al. (2008) confirm an earlier meta-analysis of only methylphenidate for adult ADHD, which comprised six studies (Faraone, Spencer, Aleardi, Pagano, & Biederman, 2004). There were some limitations because of nonindependence of comparison groups, but effectiveness was demonstrated with higher doses showing more benefits. An implication is that if adults do not experience adverse events, then they should receive a full therapeutic dose of methylphenidate.

If stimulants either do not work for certain adults or are associated with adverse effects, then antidepressants have been recommended. A systematic review of these medications was conducted with only eight randomized controlled studies meeting criteria (Verbeeck, Tuinier, & Beckkering, 2009). The majority of these studies involved bupropion (Wellbutrin) ($n = 5$) and when these studies were pooled, a beneficial effect for bupropion was found compared to placebo.

Social Diversity

Ethnicity

Although the incidence of ADHD is similar to rates found in Caucasian populations, fewer African Americans are diagnosed and treated (Bailey & Owens, 2005). Some barriers may relate to the health care system, involving the lack of culturally competent health care providers, racial stereotyping by professionals, and the failure of clinicians to evaluate the child in multiple settings before diagnosis. Barriers are parental lack of education about symptoms, treatment, and the consequences of untreated ADHD.

Few population prevalence studies of ADHD have been done with the Hispanic population. One estimate by the National Center for Health Statistics reported a prevalence of 3.3% in Hispanics and 6.5% in Caucasians (Bloom & Dey, 2006). The incidence of ADHD may truly be lower in Hispanic children, but underdiagnosis may also explain the differential rates (Rothe, 2005). Other explanations for differences in these rates include language barriers that interfere with the ability to report ADHD symptoms, the family's degree of acculturation (less acculturated parents may not recognize symptoms of ADHD), or different developmental expectations by Latina parents, or physician bias that may cause dismissal of concerns regarding symptoms in the Hispanic population.

Gender

As mentioned, ADHD is more prevalent in boys (CDC, 2005), and more research has been done on boys (Rucklidge & Tannock, 2001), but the validity of the *DSM* criteria for females has also been challenged (Ohan & Johnston, 2005). Fewer girls tend to be diagnosed with the disorder even controlling for the fact that the disruptive behavior of boys may more often bring them to the attention of treatment providers. Females have a lower base level of inattentiveness and hyperactivity than their male counterparts, and thus they have to deviate much further from girls without symptoms in order to be diagnosed (Arnold, 1996). As a result, discussion has centered on appropriate diagnostic criteria for females, so that girls are appropriately identified for services (Ohan & Johnston, 2005).

A recent study on females with ADHD compared them 5 years after they had been diagnosed to girls their ages without ADHD (Hinshaw, Owens, Sami, & Fargeon, 2006). Those with ADHD had significantly more impairment across all the symptom domains, including externalizing, internalizing, substance use disorders, eating problems, peer relations, and academic performance. Girls diagnosed with ADHD in childhood seem at particular risk for anxiety and depression by the time they reach adolescence (Biederman, Ball, et al., 2008; Owens, Hinshaw, Lee, & Lahey, 2009). They are also more at risk for future diagnosis of conduct disorder in adolescence (Monteaux, Faraone, Gross, & Biederman, 2007). These researchers also found that the girls with ADHD had more maltreatment (mostly sexual abuse and neglect) when they were younger than the comparison girls (Briscoe-Smith & Hinshaw, 2006). It is uncertain whether the abuse was a causal factor in the ADHD. These findings indicate the seriousness of ADHD symptoms in girls and the importance of proper diagnosis and treatment. At the same time, girls did better than boys in the MTA study over the 36-month period in which they were followed after undergoing intervention for 14 months (Jensen et al., 2007). This is encouraging as girls may perform at least as well as boys when they receive treatment.

Critique

Attention-deficit hyperactivity disorder is considered an inherited neuro-psychological disorder, but substantive supporting evidence is lacking (Johnson, Wiersema, & Kuntsi, 2009). Attention-deficit hyperactivity disorder is currently defined by its behavioral symptoms rather than any particular biological marker. Social influences, such as attachment patterns, parental stress, and poverty, and other biological contributing factors, such as maternal smoking, may be underrecognized.

We must also not underestimate the tremendous profit reaped by drug companies and their influence on prescribing rates, which in some communities are alarmingly high. For instance, it is not widely known that drug companies fund such groups as Children and Adults with Attention Deficit Disorder, where the use of medication is promulgated (DeGrandpre, 1999).

Another problem is that psychopharmacological intervention is often handled by primary care physicians rather than by psychiatrists. The general practitioner commonly sees the parent and child and may make a diagnosis and provide a prescription largely based on parent complaints. As discussed, teacher reports are critical, as is a comprehensive assessment.

A further problem with the diagnosis of ADHD involves the validity of the criteria for females and for adults. As mentioned, fewer girls tend to be diagnosed with ADHD, even controlling for referral bias, because females as a group have a lower base level of inattentiveness and hyperactivity than their male counterparts. Therefore, they have to deviate much further from girls without symptoms in order to be diagnosed (Arnold, 1996). As a result, discussion has been generated on appropriate diagnostic criteria for females.

Finally, adults are now being diagnosed with ADHD at higher rates, but the diagnostic criteria center on the behaviors of children. There have been some attempts to make the criteria more relevant for adults. For instance, for the symptom "often runs about or climbs excessively in situations in which it is inappropriate," a note states that for adolescents or adults, this may be translated into subjective feelings of restlessness (APA, 2000, p. 92). Still, the criteria for adults must not only be made uniformly relevant but also be validated empirically. Related to adult diagnosis particularly is a debate about the age of onset criterion (age 7) (Faraone, Biederman, et al., 2006). Often adults interviewed retrospectively about their childhood are not able to recall the age of onset of their symptoms.

Case Example

This case was begun in Chapter 5 (Oppositional Defiant Disorder and Conduct Disorder) and is continued here. See Chapter 5 for details of the case and the other diagnoses that were given. We focus here only on the diagnosis of attention-deficit/hyperactivity disorder, inattentive type.

To make this diagnosis, several assessment components had to be addressed. Janine had a physical examination, which indicated no physical ailment that would account for symptoms. Janine's foster mother and her teacher at the public school completed their respective versions of the Conners Rating Scales. The teacher version showed higher rates of attention problems and hyperactivity for Janine than the parental version. As you will recall, teacher reports of ADHD have more credence.

At the day treatment program, Janine went through a series of tests for intelligence and learning disabilities. Her intelligence quotient (IQ) was found to be slightly below average, marked by verbal deficits. No learning disabilities were detected.

The child protective services (CPS) worker accessed school records and found that Janine's grades had been poor throughout her school career. Little is known about Janine's developmental history because of the lack of cooperation by her mother and grandmother. Janine's mother did reveal that all three boys living in her home are on Ritalin, which was prescribed by a general physician. Kyle, Janine's brother who was also removed from the home, has been diagnosed with ADHD as well. The shared diagnosis among siblings might indicate a possible genetic link; however, these children have all faced similar early caregiving difficulties and low socioeconomic status, which may contribute to the development of ADHD.

When examining the diagnostic criteria for ADHD, one important consideration is whether inattention symptoms, such as "often does not seem to listen when spoken to directly" and "often does not follow through on instructions and fails to finish schoolwork or chores," are attributed to oppositionality or to inattention/impulsivity-hyperactivity. The clinician determined that Janine's behaviors were influenced by both these traits, which was confirmed by the rating scales. Other inattention symptoms Janine displayed include the following: often has difficulty sustaining attention in tasks; often has difficulty organizing tasks and activities; often avoids, dislikes, or is reluctant to engage in tasks that require sustained mental effort; is often easily distracted by extraneous stimuli; and is often forgetful in daily activities. Note that the inattention criterion requires six symptoms and Janine possibly meets seven.

Janine demonstrates a single hyperactivity symptom: often fidgets with hands or feet or squirms in seat. She has two symptoms of impulsivity: often blurts out answers before questions have been completed; and often interrupts or intrudes on others. For hyperactivity and impulsivity symptoms, the client should meet at least six; therefore, Janine does not appear to be hyper-active-impulsive.

See Exhibits 6.3 and 6.4 for the risk and protective factors assessment for both the onset and course of ADHD for Janine. Germane goals have already been discussed in Chapter 5.

Exhibit 6.3

Case Example: Janine's Risk and Protective Factors Assessment for Onset of Attention-Deficit/Hyperactivity Disorder

Risk	Protective
Biological	
Genetic predisposition is possible because Janine's brothers have been diagnosed with attention-deficit/hyperactivity disorder. *Janine's mother smoked during pregnancy.*	*Other than smoking, Janine's mother denied the use of alcohol and drugs during pregnancy.*
Social	
Family	
Lack of an attachment bond coupled with low maternal social support. *The attachment bond Janine has with her mother might have been compromised. Janine's mother was a teenager when she had Janine, and grandmother did a lot of the caretaking throughout the years, as Janine's mother moved in and out of the home. At this point, the attachment has been damaged because both Janine's grandmother and her mother have cut off contact from her.*	
Low socioeconomic status: *Janine's biological family lives well below the poverty line.*	

Case Example: Janine's Risk and Protective Factors Assessment for the Course of Attention-Deficit/Hyperactivity Disorder

Risk	Protective
Psychological	
Comorbid conduct disorder	
Social	
Family	
Coercive and inconsistent parenting: The different foster homes in which Janine was placed have had difficulty managing Janine's behaviors to the point where she had to leave these homes.	*Effective child management strategies: Janine's current foster mother is working to get effective discipline methods in place.*
Single-parent home: *Janine's foster mother is a single parent.*	

References

American Academy of Child and Adolescent Psychiatry. (2002). Practice parameter for the use of stimulant medications in the treatment of children, adolescents, and adults. *Journal of the American Academy of Child and Adolescent Psychiatry, 41* (Suppl.), 26S–49S.

American Psychiatric Association. (2000). *Diagnostic and statistical manual of mental disorders* (4th ed., text rev.). Washington, DC: Author.

Arnold, L. (1996). Sex differences in ADHD. *Journal of Abnormal Child Psychology, 24,* 555–569.

Bailey, R. K., & Owens, D. L. (2005). Overcoming challenges in the diagnosis and treatment of attention-deficit/hyperactivity disorder in African Americans. *Journal of the National Medical Association, 97*(10), 5S–0S.

Barkley, R. A. (2006). *Attention deficit hyperactivity disorder: A handbook for diagnosis and treatment* (3rd ed.). New York: Guilford.

Barkley, R. A., Fischer, M., Smallish, L., & Fletcher, K. (2004). Young adult follow- up of hyperactive children: Antisocial activities and drug use. *Journal of Child Psychology and Psychiatry, 45*(2), 195–211

Barkley, R. A., Murphy, K. R., O'Connell, T., Anderson, D., & Connor, D. F. (2006). Effects of two doses of alcohol on simulator driving performance in adults with attention-deficit/hyperactivity disorder. *Neuropsychology, 20*(1), 77–87.

Bhutta, A., Cleves, M., Casey, P., Cradock, M., & Anand, K. (2002). Cognitive and behavioral outcomes of school-aged children who were born preterm: A meta-analysis. *Journal of the American Medical Association, 288,* 728–737.

Biederman, J., Ball, S. W., Monuteaux, M. C., Mick, E., Spencer, T. J., McCreary, M., Cote, M., & Faraone, S. V. (2008). New insight into the comorbidity between

ADHD and major depression in adolescent and young adult females. *Journal of the American Academy of Child and Adolescent Psychiatry, 47*(4), 426–434.

Biederman, J., Petty, C. R., Dolan, C., Hughes, S., Mick, E., Monuteaux, M. C., & Faraone, S. V. (2008). The long-term longitudinal course of oppositional defiant disorder and conduct disorder in ADHD boys: Findings from a controlled 10-year prospective longitudinal follow-up study. *Psychological Medicine, 38,* 1027–1036.

Bloom, B., & Dey, A. N. (2006). Summary health statistics for U.S. children: National Health Interview Survey, 2004. *Vital Health Statistics, 10*(227), 1–85.

Briscoe-Smith, A. M., & Hinshaw, S. P. (2006). Linkages between child abuse and attention-deficit/hyperactivity disorder in girls: Behavioral and social correlates. *Child Abuse and Neglect, 30*(11), 1239–1255.

Brown, R. T., Antonuccio, D. O., Dupaul, G. J., Fristad, M. A., King, C. A., Leslie, L. K., McCormick, G. S., Pelham, W. E., Piacentini, J. C., & Vitiello, B. (2007). *Childhood mental health disorders: Evidence-base and contextual factors for psychosocial, psychopharmacological, and combined interventions.* Washington, DC: American Psychological Association.

Brown, T. (1996). *Brown Attention Deficit Disorder Scales: Manual.* San Antonio, TX: Psychological Corporation.

Carlson, G., & Meyer, S. (2009). ADHD with mood disorders. In T. Brown (Ed.), *ADHD comorbidities* (pp. 97–130). Washington, DC. American Psychiatric Association.

Centers for Disease Control and Prevention. (2005). Mental health in the United States. Prevalence of diagnosis and medication treatment for attention-deficit/ hyperactivity disorder. United States, 2003. *Morbidity and Mortality Weekly Report, 54,* 842–847.

Chan, E., Hopkins, M. R., Perrin, J. M., Herrerias, C., & Homer, C. J. (2005). Diagnostic practices for attention deficit hyperactivity disorder: A national survey of primary care physicians. *Ambulatory Pediatrics, 5*(4), 201–208.

Coghill, D., Soutullo, C., d'Aubuisson, C., Preuss, U., Lindback, T., Silverberg, M., & Buitelaar, J. (2008). Impact of attention-deficit/hyperactivity disorder on the patient and family: Results from a European survey. *Child and Adolescent Psychiatry and Mental Health, 2*(1), 31.

Conners, C. K., Erhardt, D., & Sparrow, M. A. (1999) *Conners Adult ADHD Rating Scales (CAARS).* New York: Multihealth Systems, Inc.

Corcoran, J., & Dattalo, P. (2006). Parent involvement in treatment for ADHD: A meta-analysis of the published studies. *Research on Social Work Practice, 16*(6), 561–570.

Counts, C. A., Nigg, J. T., Stawicki, J. A., Rappley, M. D., & von Eye, A. (2005). Family adversity in DMS-IV ADHD combined and inattentive subtypes and associated disruptive behavior problems. *Journal of the American Academy a of Child and Adolescent Psychiatry, 44*(7), 690–698.

Cuffe, S. P, McKeown, R. E., Jackson, K. L., Addy, C. L., Abramson, R., & Garrison, C. Z. (2001). Prevalence of attention-deficit/hyperactivity disorder in a community sample of older adolescents. *Journal of the American Academy of Child and Adolescent Psychiatry, 40*(9), 1037–1044.

Daughton, J. M., & Kratochvil, C. J. (2009). Review of ADHD pharmacotherapies: Advantages, disadvantages, and clinical pearls. *Journal of the American Academy of Child and Adolescent Psychiatry, 48*(3), 240–248.

DeGrandpre, R. (1999). *Ritalin nation: Rapid fire culture and the transformation of human consciousness.* New York: Norton.

Derks, E. M., Dolan, C. V., Hudziak, J. J., Neale, M. C., & Boomsma, D. I. (2007). Assessment and etiology of attention deficit hyperactivity disorder and oppositional defiant disorder in boys and girls. *Behavior Genetics, 37*(4), 559–566.

DuPaul, G. J., & Eckert, T. (1997). The effects of school-based interventions for attention deficit hyperactivity disorder: A meta-analysis. *School Psychology Review, 26,* 5–27.

DuPaul, G. J., & Power, T. J. (2000). Educational interventions for students with attention-deficit disorders. In T. Brown (Ed.), *Attention-deficit disorders and comorbidities in children, adolescents, and adults* (pp. 607–634). Washington, DC: American Psychiatric Press.

Faraone, S., & Wilens, T. (2003). Does stimulant treatment lead to substance use disorders? *Journal of Clinical Psychology, 64,* 9–13.

Faraone, S. V., Biederman, J., Morley, C. P., & Spencer, T. J. (2008). Effect of stimulants on height and weight: A review of the literature. *Journal of the American Academy of Child and Adolescent Psychiatry, 47*(9), 994–1009.

Faraone, S. V., Biederman, J., Spencer, T., Mick, E., Murray, K., Petty, C., Adamson, J., & Monuteaux, M. C. (2006). Diagnosing adult attention deficit hyperactivity disorder: Are late onset subthreshold diagnoses valid? *American Journal of Psychiatry, 163*(10), 1720–1729.

Faraone, S. V., & Khan, S. A. (2006). Candidate gene studies of attention- deficit/ hyperactivity disorder. *Journal of Clinical Psychiatry, 67*(8),13–20.

Faraone, S. V., Perlis, R. H., Doyle, A. E., Smoller, J. W., Goralnick, J. J., Holmgren, M. A., & Sklar, P. (2005). Molecular genetics of attention-deficit/hyperactivity disorder. *Biological Psychiatry, 57*(11), 1313–1323.

Faraone, S. V., Spencer, T., Aleardi., M, Pagano, C., & Biederman, J. (2004). Meta-analysis of the efficacy of methylphenidate for treating adult attention-deficit/ hyperactivity disorder. *Journal of Clinical Psychopharmacology, 24*(1), 24–29.

Ford, T., Goodman, R., & Meltzer, H. (2004). The relative importance of child, family, school and neighbourhood correlates of childhood psychiatric disorder. *Social Psychiatry and Psychiatric Epidemiology, 39*(6), 487–496.

Hinshaw, S. P., Owens, E. B., Sami, N., & Fargeon, S. (2006). Prospective follow-up of girls with attention-deficit/hyperactivity disorder into adolescence: Evidence for continuing cross-domain impairment. *Journal of Consulting and Clinical Psychology, 74*(3), 489–499.

Jacobvitz, D., Hazen, N., Curran, M., & Hitchens, K. (2004). Observations of early triadic family interactions: Boundary disturbances in the family predict symptoms of depression, anxiety, and attention-deficit/hyperactivity disorder in middle childhood. *Developmental Psychopathology, 16*(3), 577–592.

Jensen, P. S., Arnold, L. E., Swanson, J. M., Vitiello, B., Abikoff, H. B., Greenhill, L. L., Hechtman, L., Hinshaw, S. P., Pelham, W. E., Wells, K. C., Conners, C. K., Elliott, G. R., Epstein, J. N., Hoza, B., March, J. S., Molina, B. S., Newcorn, J. H., Severe, J. B., Wigal, T., Gibbons, R. D., & Hur, K. (2007). 3-year follow up of the NIMH MTA study. *Journal of the American Academy of Child and Adolescent Psychiatry, 46*(8), 989–1002.

Jensen, P., & Hinshaw, S. (2001). ADHD comorbidity findings from the MTA study: comparing comorbid subgroups. *Journal of the American Academy of Child & Adolescent Psychiatry, 40*(2), 147.

Johnson, K. A., Wiersema, J. R., & Kuntsi, J. (2009). What would Carl Popper say? Are current psychological theories of ADHD falsifiable? *Behavioral and Brain Function*, 5(1), 15.

Kahn, R. S., Khoury, J., Nichols, W. C., & Lanphear, B. P. (2003). Role of dopamine transporter genotype and maternal prenatal smoking in childhood hyperactive-impulsive, inattentive, and oppositional behaviors. *Journal of Pediatrics, 143*(1), 104–110.

Kessler, R. C., Adler., L., Ames, M., Barkley, R., Bimbaum, H., Greenberg, P., Johnston, J., Spencer, T., & Ustun, T. B. (2005). The prevalence and effects of adult attention deficit/hyperactivity disorder on work performance in a nationally representative sample of workers. *Journal of Occupational and Environmental Medicine, 47*(6), 565–572.

Kessler, R., Berglund, P., Demler, O., Jin, R., & Walters, E. (2005). Lifetime prevalence and age-of-onset distributions of DSM-IV disorders in the national comorbidity survey replication. *Archives of General Psychiatry, 62*, 593–602.

Knouse, L. E., Bagwell, C. L., Barkley, R. A., & Murphy, K. R. (2005). Accuracy of self-evaluation in adults with ADHD: Evidence from a driving study. *Journal of Attention Disorders, 8*(4), 221–234.

Kreppner, J. M., O'Connor, T. G., Rutter, M., Beckett, C., Castle, J., Croft, C., Dunn, J., & Groothues, C. (2008). Can inattention/overactivity be an institutional deprivation syndrome? *Journal of Abnormal Child Psychology, 29*(6), 513–528.

Langstroem, N. (2002). Child neuropsychiatric disorders: A review of associations with delinquency and substance use. In R. R. Corrado (Ed.), *Multi-problem violent youth: A foundation for comparative research on needs, interventions, and outcomes. Series I: Life and behavioral sciences, volume 324* (pp. 91–104). Amsterdam, Netherlands: IOS Press.

Laucht, M., Skowronek, M. H., Becker, K., Schmidt, M. H., Esser, G., Schulze, T. G., & Rietschel, M. (2007). Interacting effects of the dopamine transporter gene and psychosocial adversity on attention-deficit/hyperactivity disorder symptoms among 15-year-olds from a high risk community sample. *Archives of General Psychiatry, 64*(5), 585–590.

Levy, F., Hay, D. A., & Bennett, K. S. (2006). Genetics of attention deficit hyperactivity disorder: A current review and future prospects. *International Journal of Disability, Development and Education, 53*(1), 5–20.

Linnett, K., Dalsgaard, S., Obel, C., Wisborg, K., Henriksen, T., Rodriquez, A., et al. (2003). Maternal lifestyle factors in pregnancy risk of attention deficit hyperactivity disorder and associated behaviors: A review of the current evidence. *American Journal of Psychiatry, 160*, 1028–1040.

Mannuzza, S., & Klein, R. (1999). Adolescent and adult outcomes in attention- deficit/hyperactivity disorder. In H. Quay & A. Hogan (Eds.), *Handbook of disruptive behavior disorders* (pp. 279–294). New York: Plenum.

Mannuzza, S., Klein, R., & Moulton, J. (2002). Young adult outcome of children with "situational" hyperactivity: A prospective, controlled, follow-up study. *Journal of Abnormal Child Psychology, 30*, 191–198.

Monuteaux, M. C., Faraone, S. V., Gross, L., & Biederman, J. (2007). Predictors, clinical characteristics, and outcome of conduct disorder in girls with attention-deficit/hyperactivity disorder: A longitudinal study. *Psychological Medicine, 37*(12), 1731–1741

The MTA Cooperative Group. (1999). A 14-month randomized clinical trial of treatment strategies for attention-deficit/hyperactivity disorder. *Archives of General Psychiatry, 56*(12), 1073–1086.

National Institutes of Health. (2000). Consensus Development Conference Statement: Diagnosis and treatment of Attention-Deficit/Hyperactivity Disorder (ADHD). *Journal of the American Academy of Child & Adolescent Psychiatry, 39*(2), 182–193.

Newcorn, J. H., Sutton, V. K., Weiss, M. D., & Sumner, C. R. (2009). Clinical responses to atomoxetine in attention-deficit/hyperactivity disorder: The integrated data exploratory analysis (IDEA) study. *Journal of the American Academy of Child and Adolescent Psychiatry, 48*(5), 511–518.

Nigg, J., Nikolas, M., Friderici, K., Park, L., & Zucker, R. A. (2007). Genotype and neuropsychological response inhibition as resilience promoters for attention-deficit/hyperactivity disorder, oppositional defiant disorder, and conduct disorder under conditions of psychosocial adversity. *Developmental Psychopathology, 19*(3), 767–786.

Ohan, J. L., & Johnston, C. (2005). Gender appropriateness of symptom criteria for attention-deficit/hyperactivity disorder, oppositional-defiant disorder, and conduct disorder. *Child Psychiatry and Human Development, 35*(4), 359–381.

Olfson, M., Marcus, S., & Wan, G. (2009). Stimulant dosing for children with ADHD: A medical claims analysis. *Journal of the American Academy of Child and Adolescent Psychiatry, 48*(1), 51–59.

Owens, E. B., Hinshaw, S. P., Kraemer, H. C., Arnold, L. E., Abikoff, H. B., Cantwell, D. P., Conners, C. K., Elliott, G., Greenhill, L. L., Hechtman, L., Hoza, B., Jensen, P. S., March, J. S., Newcorn, J. H., Pelham, W. E., Severe, J. B., Swanson, J. M., Vitiello, B., Wells, K. C., & Wigal, T. (2003). Which treatment for whom for ADHD? Moderators of treatment response in the MTA. *Journal of Consulting and Clinical Psychology, 71*(3), 540–552.

Owens, E. B., Hinshaw, S. P., Lee, S. S., & Lahey, B. B. (2009). Few girls with childhood attention-deficit/hyperactivity disorder show positive adjustment during adolescence. *Journal of Clinical Child and Adolescent Psychology, 38*(1), 132–143.

Patterson, G. R. (1982). *Coercive family process.* Eugene, OR: Castalia.

Patterson, G. R. (1986). Performance models for antisocial boys. *American Psychologist, 1,* 432–444.

Patterson, G. R., DeBaryshe, B. D., & Ramsey, E. (1989). A developmental perspective on antisocial behavior. *American Psychologist, 44,* 329–335.

Pelham, W. E. Jr, & Fabiano, G. A. (2008). Evidence-based psychosocial treatments for attention-deficit/hyperactivity disorder. *Journal of Clinical Child and Adolescent Psychology, 37*(1), 184–214.

Pelham, W. E. Jr, Fabiano, G. A., & Massetti, G. M. (2005). Evidence-based assessment of attention deficit hyperactivity disorder in children and adolescents. *Journal of Clinical Child and Adolescent Psychology, 34*(3), 449–476.

Peterson, K., McDonagh, M. S., & Fu, R. (2008). Comparative benefits and harms of competing medications for adults with attention-deficit hyperactivity disorder: A systematic review and indirect comparison meta-analysis. *Psychopharmacology, 197*(1), 1–11.

Polderman, T. J., Derks, E. M., Hudziak, J. J., Verhulst, F. C., Posthuma, D., & Boomsma, D. I. (2007). Across the continuum of attention skills: A twin study of the SWAN ADHD rating scale. *Journal of Child Psychology and Psychiatry, 48*(11), 1080–1087.

Root, R. W. II, & Resnick, R. J. (2003). An update on the diagnosis and treatment of attention-deficit/hyperactivity disorder in children. *Professional Psychology: Research & Practice, 34*, 34–41.

Rothe, E. M. (2005). Considering cultural diversity in the management of ADHD in Hispanic patients. *Journal of the National Medical Association, 97*(Suppl. 10), 17S–23S.

Rucklidge, J. J., & Tannock, R. (2001). Psychiatric, psychosocial, and cognitive functioning of female adolescents with ADHD. *Journal of the American Academy of Child and Adolescent Psychiatry, 40*(5), 530–540.

Sax, L., & Kautz, K. J. (2003). Who first suggests the diagnosis of attention deficit/ hyperactivity disorders? *Annals of Family Medicine, 1*(3), 171–174.

Schachter, H. M., Pham, B., King, J., Langford, S., & Moher, D. (2001). How efficacious and safe is short-acting methylphenidate for the treatment of attention-deficit disorder in children and adolescents? A meta-analysis. *Canadian Medical Association Journal, 165*(11), 1475–1488.

Shepard, B. A., Carter, A. S., & Cohen, J. E. (2000). Attention-deficit/hyperactivity disorder and the preschool child. In T. E. Brown (Ed.), *Attention-deficit disorders and comorbidities in children, adolescents, and adults* (pp. 407–436). Washington, DC: American Psychiatric Publishing, Inc.

Simon, V., Czobor, P., Bálint, S., Mészáros, Á., & Bitter, I. (2009). Prevalence and correlates of adult attention-deficit hyperactivity disorder: Meta-analysis. *The British Journal of Psychiatry, 194*(3), 204–211.

Sonuga-Burke, E. J., Lasky-Su, J., Neale, B. M., Oades, R., Chen, W., Franke, B., Buitelaar, J., Banaschewski, T., Ebstein, R., Gill, M., Anney, R., Miranda, A., Mulas, F., Roeyers, H., Rothenberger, A., Sergeant, J., Steinhausen, H. C., Thompson, M., Asherson, P., & Faraone, S. V. (2008). Does parental expressed emotion moderate genetic effects in ADHD? An exploration using a genome wide association scan. *American Journal of Medical Genetics Part B: Neuropsychiatric Genetics, 147B*(8), 1359–1368.

Stevens, S. E., Sonuga-Burke, E. J., Kreppner, J. M., Beckett, C., Castle, J., Colvert, E., Groothues, C., Hawkins, A., & Rutter, M. (2008). Inattention/overactivity following early severe institutional deprivation: Presentation and associations in early adolescence. *Journal of Abnormal Child Psychology, 36*(3), 385–398.

Swanson, J., Arnold, L. E., Kraemer, H., Hechtman, L., Molina, B., Hinshaw, S., Vitiello, B., Jensen, P., Steinhoff, K., Lerner, M., Greenhill, L., Abikoff, H., Wells, K., Epstein, J., Elliott, G., Newcorn, J., Hoza, B., & Wigal, T. (2008). Evidence, interpretation, and qualification from multiple reports of long-term outcomes in the Multimodal Treatment study of children with ADHD (MTA): Part I: Executive summary. *Journal of Attention Disorders, 12*(1), 4–14.

Tannock, R., & Brown, T. (2009). ADHD with language and learning disabilities in children and adolescents. In T. Brown (Ed.), *ADHD comorbidities* (pp. 189–232). Washington, DC. American Psychiatric Association.

Tannock, R., & Brown, T. E. (2000). Attention-deficit disorders with learning disorders in children and adolescents. In T. E. Brown (Ed.), *Attention-deficit disorders and comorbidities in children, adolescents, and adults* (pp. 231–295). Washington, DC: American Psychiatric Publishing.

Vedantam, S. (2009). *Debate over drugs for ADHD reignites*. Retrieved on March 27, 2009 from http://www.washingtonpost.com/wp-dyn/content/article/2009/3/26.

Verbeeck, W., Tuinier, S., & Bekkering, G. E. (2009). Antidepressants in the treatment of adult attention-deficit hyperactivity disorder: A systematic review. *Advances in Therapy, 26,* 1–15.

Weiss, G., & Hechtman, L. T. (1993). *Hyperactive children grown up: ADHD in children, adolescents, and adults* (2nd ed.). New York: Guilford Press.

Whalen, C., & Henker, B. (1999). The child with attention-deficit/hyperactivity disorder in family contexts. In H. Quay & A. Hogan (Eds.), *Handbook of disruptive behavior disorders* (pp. 139–155). New York: Kluwer Academic/Plenum.

Wilens, T., Faraone, S., Biederman, J., & Gunawardene, S. (2003). Does stimulant therapy of attention-deficit/hyperactivity disorder beget later substance abuse? A meta-analytic review of the literature. *Pediatrics, 111,* 179–186.

Wolraich, M. L., Bickman, L., Lambert, E. W., Simmons, T., & Doffing, M. A. (2005). Intervening to improve communication between parents, teachers, and primary care providers of children with ADHD or at high risk for ADHD. *Journal of Attention Disorders, 9*(1), 354–368.

Wolraich, M. L., Wibbelsman, C. J., Brown, T. E., Evans, S. W., Gotlieb, E. M., Knight, J. R., Ross, E. C., Shubiner, H. H., Wender, E. H., & Wilens, T. (2005). Attention-deficit/hyperactivity disorder among adolescents: a review of the diagnosis, treatment, and clinical implications. *Pediatrics, 115*(6), 1734–1746.

Wymbs, B. T., Pelham, W. E. Jr, Molina, B. S., Gnagy, E. M., Wilson, T. K., & Greenhouse, J. B. (2008). Rate and predictors of divorce among parents of youths with ADHD. *Journal of Consulting and Clinical Psychology, 76*(5), 735–744.

Appendix: Measures for Attention-Deficit/ Hyperactivity Disorder

Much of this information is drawn from Collett, Ohan, and Myers (2003). Ratings on norms, validity, and reliability are from Hunsley and Mash (2008).

Connors Ratings Scales–Revised (Conners, 1997)

Description
- Revision of popular scale with long history in the evaluation of ADHD to include *DSM-IV* criteria
- Parent (80-item and 27-item versions), teacher (59-item and 28-item versions), and adolescent (87-item and 27-item versions) for youth, ages 3–17
- The full forms of all reporter versions provide comprehensive evaluation, whereas the abbreviated forms aid screening or treatment monitoring.
- Measures cognitive problems/inattention, hyperactivity, oppositional, anxious/shy, perfectionism, social problems, and psychosomatic

Reliability

- Internal consistency is good for parent version and excellent for teacher version.
- Calculated by age and range from moderate to excellent for parent, teacher, and adolescent forms
- Test-retest reliabilities are rated as good.

Validity

- Gender and age difference are consistent with established patterns (i.e., males score higher on externalizing scales and lower on internalizing scales; disruptive behaviors are lower for older age groups).
- Discriminant validity is shown by the scale's ability to differentiate youths with and without ADHD.
- Parents' form demonstrates excellent sensitivity and specificity.
- The comorbidity subscales have poorer psychometric properties.

The Swanson, Nolan, and Pelham-IV Questionnaire (SNAP-IV) (Swanson, 1992; Swanson et al., 2001)

Description

- Parent and teacher versions for children ages 5–11
- Long history in ADHD evaluation, particularly in research; first developed for use with *DSM-III* and updated with each *DSM* revision
- Ninety items (full version, takes 20–30 minutes to complete), 31 items (short version, takes 5–10 minutes)
- Available online

Reliability

- Internal consistency good to excellent
- No information on test-retest reliability
- Interrater agreement between parents and teachers is poor, although this is typical.

ADHD Rating Scale-IV (ADHD RS-IV) (DuPaul, Power, Anastopoulos, & Reid, 1998)

Description

- Updated and directly derived from *DSM-IV* symptom criteria
- Parent (home form) or teacher (school form) for children ages 5–18
- Scale designed for children but can be modified and administered to adults; wording is changed for adults, and "play activities" will be replaced with "leisure activities"
- Eighteen items
- Takes 5–10 minutes to complete
- Spanish translation available

Reliability
- Internal consistency is good.
- Test-retest reliabilities over 4 weeks are at least good for both forms.
- Low interrater agreement between teachers and parents is fairly typical for this type of scale.

Validity
- Age and gender patterns consistent with established trends, indicating more symptoms for males and for younger ages of both genders.
- Construct validity is shown by the scale's basis in *DSM-IV* criteria and is rated as good.
- Convergent validity is evidenced by low to very good correlations with similar measures and direct observations of children's behavior.
- Subscales discriminate between youths with ADHD and both clinical and nonclinical controls.
- Hyperactive/impulsive subscale differentiates children with combined type from inattentive type, with the parent version more useful in this respect than the school form.
- Parent report is better for sensitivity; the teacher report is better for specificity.

Vanderbilt ADHD Parent Rating Scale (VADPRS) (Wolraich, 2003; Wolraich, Feuer, Hannah, Baumgaertel, & Pinnock, 1998)

Description
- Relatively new *DSM-IV*-based scales for ADHD; also assesses oppositional defiant disorder, conduct disorder, anxiety and depression, and parent perceptions of youth school and social functioning
- Forty-three items; parent and teacher versions for children ages 6–12
- Available online
- Takes 10–15 minutes to complete
- Spanish and German translations available

Reliability
- Interrater reliability between parents and teachers is low, as is typical.
- Parent version internal consistency is excellent.

Validity
- Concurrent validity is shown by moderate correlations with the ADHD sections of the Diagnostic Interview Schedule for Children-Version 4-Parent Version
- Both parent and teacher versions have good construct validity.

ADHD Symptoms Rating Scale (ADHD-SRS) (Holland, Gimpel, & Marrell, 2001)

Description
- A recent scale, developed from a review of the literature of descriptors of inattention, hyperactivity, and impulsivity
- Parent and teacher versions for children ages 5–18 years, possibly even preschoolers
- Fifty-six items; takes 15–20 minutes to complete
- Spanish translation available

Reliability
- Excellent internal consistencies and test-retest reliabilities (2 weeks)
- Interrater agreement between parents and teachers is poor, though this is typical.

Validity
- Excellent convergent validity established with similar measures
- Differentiates children with ADHD from nonclinical children

Attention-Deficit Disorder Evaluation Scale–Second Edition (ADDES-2) (McCarney, 2004)

Description
- An updated version of an established scale developed from diagnosticians and educators of students with ADHD to measure inattention and hyperactivity/impulsivity; includes symptoms from *DSM-IV*
- Widely used in clinical settings
- Parent (50 items) and teacher (56 items) versions for children ages 4–18
- Takes 10–15 minutes to complete
- Spanish translation available

Reliability
- Excellent internal consistencies
- Excellent 30-day test-retest reliabilities
- Interrater agreement is good between teachers and between parents, unusual for similar scales
- Adequate test-retest reliability

Validity
- Convergent validity is evidenced by moderate to excellent correlations with comparable scales.
- Discriminant validity between ADHD and nonclinical samples is good.
- Adequate for construct validity

ACTeRS-Second Edition (Ullman, Sleator, & Sprague, 2000)

Description
- Popular in school settings
- Clinicians and parents of ADHD children provided input to development of scale; 11 items assessing inattention and hyperactivity are comparable to *DSM-IV* descriptions.
- Teacher (24 items), Parent (25 items, includes descriptors of preschool behaviors associated with ADHD), Adolescent Self-Report (35 items, includes measure of social functioning) versions for children ages 5–13
- Measures attention, hyperactivity, social skills, oppositional behavior, early childhood problems, impulsivity, and social adjustment
- Takes 5–10 minutes to complete
- Spanish translation available

Reliability
- Internal consistency is excellent, good, and moderate for the teacher, parent, and self-report version, respectively.
- Moderate interrater reliability between teachers

Validity
- Discriminant validity for the parent and self-report version is evidenced by higher ratings for youths who have ADHD than those without.
- Teacher version differentiates children with ADHD from those with learning disabilities.

Brown Attention-Deficit Disorder Scales for Children and Adolescents (BADDS) (Brown, 2001)

Description
- Unlike scales that focus on ADHD symptoms, the BADDS is said to measure deficits in executive functioning underlying ADHD.
- Separate versions for youths 3–7 years, 8–12, and 12–18 are worded to indicate developmentally relevant manifestations of ADHD. For ages 3–7, separate parent and teacher forms are available (44 items). For ages 8–12, separate versions for parent, teacher, and youth self-report (50 items). The

adolescent version can be administered to the adolescent and/or the parent (40 items).

- Scale measures the following: Organizing, Prioritizing, and Activating to Work; Focusing, Sustaining, and Shifting Attention to Tasks; Regulating Alertness, Sustaining Effort and Processing Speed; Managing Frustration and Modulating Emotions; Utilizing Working Memory and Accessing Recall; and Monitoring and Self-Regulating Action (for ages 3–7 and 8–12).
- Takes 10–15 minutes to administer.

Reliability
- Internal consistencies are acceptable for clinical samples and excellent for the normative sample.
- Interrater agreement between parents and teachers is low to moderate for ages 3 to 7 and 8 to 12, somewhat better than other scales. For ages 8 to 12, agreement between the children's self-report and parent-or-teacher self-report is also low to moderate.

Validity
- Convergent validity for the BADDS is evidenced by moderate to excellent correlations with the parent and teacher versions of the CBCL, the BASC, and Conners Ratings Scales.
- Divergent validity is shown by lower correlations between BADDS and internalizing measures.
- Discriminant validity is established by the differences between children with ADHD and the normative samples.

Home Situations Questionnaire (Barkley & Edelbrock, 1987)

Description
- Lists 16 different situations for which parents observe and handle their child's behaviors
- Parents indicate ("yes"/"no") whether problem behaviors occur in these situations; if so, parents rate severity of the problem (1/ "mild" to 9/ "severe").
- Appropriate for children ages 4–11
- Yields two summary scores:

  1. Number of Problem Situations: "an index of the situational diversity of problem behaviors for a given child"
  2. Mean Severity Score: "an index of the severity of problem behaviors across situations"

- Modified versions have been developed to make the scales appropriate for adolescents (Adams, McCarthy, & Kelly, 1995) and specific to problems related to ADHD symptoms (DuPaul & Barkley, 1992).
- Can measure treatment response

Reliability
- Internal consistency is strong.
- Test-retest reliabilities (4 weeks) shown to be moderate for the number of problem situations and moderate to good for problem behavior severity.

Validity
- Number of Problem Situations correlated with the following scales of the Child Behavior Profile: Aggressive (.83); Hyperactive (.73); Delinquent (.48); Depressed (.62); and Social Withdrawal (.62).
- Mean Severity Score correlated with the following scales of the Child Behavior Profile: Aggressive (.69); Hyperactive (.66); Delinquent (.60); Depressed (.46); and Social Withdrawal (.61).
- Number of Problem Situations correlated with the following Child Domain scales of the Parenting Stress Index: Adaptability (.78); Distractibility/Hyperactivity (.76); Mood (.73); and Demanding (.70).
- Mean Severity Score correlated with the following Child Domain scales of the Parenting Stress Index: Adaptability (.63); Distractibility/ Hyperactivity (.75); Mood (.61); and Demanding (.59).
- Summary scales correlated with the Adjustment, Depression, Hyperactivity, Social Skills, and Psychosis scales of the Personality Inventory for Children, ranging from .72 to .81.
- Discriminates between normal children and children diagnosed with attention deficit disorder with hyperactivity and ADHD children and their normal siblings

The Wender Utah Rating Scale (WURS) (Ward, Wender, & Reimherr, 1993)

Description
- Sixty-one-item, self-report measure designed for adults to describe their own childhood behavior
- Purpose in creating scale was to retrospectively establish the childhood diagnosis of ADHD

Reliability
- Split-half reliability correlations comparing odd/even items were satisfactory.
- Satisfactory internal consistency and temporal stability

Validity
A discriminant function analysis correctly classified 64.5%. Among those who did not have ADHD, only 57.5% were correctly classified, compared with 72.1% among those with ADHD. Therefore, the WURS is sensitive in detecting ADHD, but it misclassifies approximately half of those who do not have ADHD.

References for ADHD Measures

Adams, C. D., McCarthy, M., & Kelly, M. L. (1995). Adolescent versions of the Home and School Situations Questionnaires: Initial psychometric properties. *Journal of Clinical Child Psychology, 24*, 377–385.

Barkley, R., & Edelbrock, C. (1987). Assessing situational variation in children's problem behaviors: The Home and School Situations Questionnaires. *Advances in Behavioral Assessment of Children and Families, 3*, 157–176.

Brown, T. E. (2001). *Brown Attention-Deficit Disorder Scales for Children and Adolescents.* San Antonio, TX: Psychological Corporation.

Collett, B. R., Ohan, J. L., & Myers, K. M. (2003). Ten-year review of rating scales. V: Scales assessing attention-deficit/hyperactivity disorder. *Journal of the American Academy of Child and Adolescent Psychiatry, 42*(9), 1015–1023.

Conners, C. (1997). *Conners Rating Scales–Revised technical manual.* North Tonawanda, NY: Multi-Health Systems.

DuPaul, G. J., & Barkley, R. A. (1992). Situational variability of attention problems: Psychometric properties of the Revised Home and School Situations Questionnaires. *Journal of Clinical Child Psychology, 21*, 178–188.

DuPaul, G. J., Power, T. J., Anastopoulos, A. D., & Reid, R. (1998). *ADHD Rating Scale-IV: Checklist, norms, and clinical interpretation.* Eugene, OR: Assessment-Intervention Resources.

Holland, M. I., Gimpel, G. A., & Marrell, K. W. (2001). *ADHD Symptoms Rating Scale manual.* Wilmington, DE: Wide Range.

Hunsley, J., & Mash, E. (2008). A guide to assessments that work. New York: Oxford University Press.

McCarney, S. B. (2004). *The attention deficit disorders evaluation scale, home and school versions: Technical manual.* Columbia, MO: Hawthorne Educational Services.

Swanson, J. (1992). *School based assessments and interventions for ADD students.* Irvine, CA: KC.

Swanson, J., Schuck, S., Mann M., Carlson, C., Hartman, K., Sergeant, J., et al. (2001). Categorical and dimensional definitions and evaluations of symptoms of ADHD: The SNAP and SWAN ratings scales. Retrieved January 9, 2004, from http://www.adhd.net.

Ullman, R. K., Sleator, E. K., & Sprague, R. I. (2000). *ACTeRS teacher and parent forms manual.* Champaign, IL: Metritech.

Ward, M., Wender, P., & Reimherr, F. (1993). The Wender Utah Rating Scale: An aid in the retrospective diagnosis of childhood attention deficit hyperactivity disorder. *American Journal of Psychiatry, 150*(6), 885–890.

Wolraich, M. I. (2003). *Vanderbilt ADHD teacher rating scale (VADTRS) and the Vanderbilt ADHD parent rating scale (VADPRS).* Retrieved January 9, 2004, from http://www.nichq.org.

Wolraich, M. I., Feuer, I. D., Hannah, J. N., Baumgaertel, A., & Pinnock, T. Y. (1998). Obtaining systematic teacher reports of disruptive behavior disorders utilizing DSM-IV. *Journal of Abnormal Psychology, 26*, 141–152.

7 Anxiety Disorders

Anxiety is an unpleasant but normal, functional affect that provides people with warning signs for perceived threats. It includes physiological and psychological symptoms that prepare the individual to confront or avoid the threat (Zvolensky, Lejuez, & Eifert, 2000). The anticipated danger may be internal or external in origin. The symptoms of anxiety include *tension* (trembling, muscle soreness, restlessness, fatigue), *autonomic nervous system hyperactivity* (shortness of breath, feeling smothered, accelerated heart rate, sweating, clammy hands, dry mouth, lightheadedness, abdominal distress, hot flashes or chills, frequent urination, difficulty swallowing, and the feeling of a lump in the throat), and *hypervigilance* (feeling edgy or keyed up, an exaggerated startle response, difficulty concentrating, trouble falling or staying asleep, and irritability) (American Psychiatric Association [APA], 2000).

Anxiety begins as the body's physiological reaction to a threatening stimulus, but the emotions that follow the appraisal of that stimulus can vary. Anxiety becomes problematic when it creates a sense of powerlessness, suggests an impending danger that is unrealistic, produces an exhausting state of vigilance, produces a level of self-absorption that interferes with problem solving, or creates doubt about the nature of reality (Campbell, 2009). The anxiety disorders are characterized by extreme, intense, almost unbearable fear that disrupts social or occupational functioning. These are the most common mental disorders in the United States (Kessler, Chiu, Demler, & Walters, 2005). Overall, the anxiety disorders are estimated to afflict 28.8% of the U.S. population over the life span and 18.1% over any 12-month period (Kessler, Chiu, et al., 2005).

Types of Anxiety Disorders

The *DSM* describes 11 different anxiety disorders, as well as separation anxiety disorder, which is listed under disorders of infancy and childhood. The specific anxiety disorders are defined on the basis of the characteristics of the anxious response or the nature of the feared stimulus. Children can be diagnosed with any of the anxiety disorders with the same criteria used for adults.

Separation anxiety disorder features excessive anxiety about separation from a major attachment figure. Note, however, that anxiety upon separation from a caregiver is normal for babies between the ages of 6 and 18 months. With the disorder, the anxiety at separation may approach a panic level. School refusal is present in the majority of cases. A lifetime prevalence of 4.6% for this disorder has been reported in epidemiological studies (Costello, Egger, & Angold, 2005).

Panic disorders involve unpredictable anxiety attacks. They are coded *with agoraphobia* (the panic attacks arise from anxiety about being in places or circumstances where escape might be difficult or embarrassing), *without agoraphobia* (the attacks are not associated with particular situations but are characterized by fears of losing self-control), or *agoraphobia without a history of panic disorder* (in which panic-like symptoms are experienced in situations from which escape might be difficult). The lifetime rate of panic disorder for adults (4.7%) is higher than the rate of agoraphobia without panic disorder (1.4%) (Kessler, Berglund, et al., 2005). For youth, lifetime rates range from 0.5% to 3.1% (Costello et al., 2005).

A phobia features anxiety that is triggered by a specific object or situation. To qualify as a disorder, the subsequent avoidant behavior must impede the person's functioning or result in considerable distress. Estimates of lifetime prevalence rates for phobias in the community range from 10% to 11.3% (Kessler, Chiu, et al., 2005).

Social phobia involves anxiety related to social situations; fear of negative evaluation from others is the overwhelming worry. For *specific phobia* (anxiety related to a specific stimulus, such as a particular kind of animal) and social phobia, children's symptoms may involve crying, tantrums, paralysis, or clinging. For the diagnosis of social phobia to be made in children, the child must have age-appropriate relationships with familiar people, and the fear of social situations and unfamiliar people must occur with peers as well as adults. Social phobia is one of the most common mental disorders among adults with a community lifetime prevalence rate of 12.1% (Kessler, Berglund, et al., 2005) and a 12-month rate of 6.8% (Kessler, Chiu, et al., 2005). For youth, lifetime rates range from 1.6% to 13.1% (Costello et al., 2005).

Generalized anxiety disorder (GAD) is characterized by persistent, excessive worry that lasts for at least 6 months, occurring more days than not. The anxiety and worry are accompanied by at least three of the following symptoms: restlessness, fatigue, difficulty concentrating, irritability, muscle tension, and disturbed sleep. Children need to show only one such symptom. An 8.6% lifetime prevalence rate has been found for generalized anxiety disorder (Kessler, Berglund, et al., 2005). In youth, lifetime prevalence rates range from 1.6% to 13.1% (Costello et al., 2005).

Obsessive-compulsive disorder (OCD) involves both recurring thoughts that cause marked anxiety and compulsive behaviors that temporarily neutralize anxiety. The obsessions and compulsions are severe enough to be time consuming (greater than 1 hour per day) or cause marked distress or significant impairment. Lifetime prevalence rates are approximately 1.9% in the community overall (Kessler, Berglund, et al., 2005). Prevalence rates for youth range from .7% to 1.7% (Costello et al., 2005).

Posttraumatic stress disorder (*PTSD*) is a type of anxiety disorder involving anxiety symptoms following exposure to an extreme traumatic stressor (APA, 2000). The three major symptom categories include *reexperiencing* (the traumatic events are reexperienced through recurrent or intrusive thoughts or images, nightmares, and flashbacks), *avoidance and numbing* (the person, because of the negative affect and arousal associated with reexperiencing, attempts to protect against these symptoms, and *increased arousal* (the person is in a state of arousal as indicated by hypervigilance, insomnia, inability to concentrate, and an elevated startle response). Intense anxiety symptoms that are experienced immediately after the traumatic event but persist for less than 4 weeks imply a different but related diagnosis: *acute stress disorder* (APA, 2000).

Posttraumatic stress disorder has a lifetime rate in the adult population of 6.8% (Kessler, Berglund, et al., 2005). The lifetime prevalence rate for elderly people is 2.5% (Kessler, Berglund, et al., 2005), although little is known about PTSD in the older adult population (Busuttil, 2004). For youth, lifetime rates of PTSD range between 1.3% and 6.0%. Therefore, it is a relatively rare condition, considering that traumatic events occur in two-thirds of youth (Copeland, Keeler, Angold, & Costello, 2007).

Comorbidity

The anxiety disorders are typically comorbid with each other, as well as with the depressive disorders (APA, 2000). Substance use disorders may also co-occur with anxiety in adults, with both substance use and anxiety serving as risk factors for each other. For example, in a prospective, 7-year study, the presence of an anxiety disorder quadrupled the risk for the onset of alcohol dependence (Kushner, Sher, & Erickson, 1999). At the same time, alcohol dependence increased the risk for an anxiety disorder by three to five times. Longitudinal studies conducted outside the United States also indicate that anxiety disorders may lead to substance use disorders (Goodwin, Fergusson, & Horwood, 2004).

In adults, PTSD is often accompanied by other Axis I psychiatric disorders. In the National Comorbidity Survey, Kessler, Sonnega, Bromet, Hughes, and Nelson (1995) reported that a majority of individuals (88% of men and 79% of women) with PTSD had at least one other lifetime diagnosis. Major depression was the most common comorbid diagnosis, occurring in just under half of men and women with PTSD (Schnurr, Friedman, & Bernardy, 2002).

Along with psychiatric comorbidity, poor physical health is associated with the anxiety disorders, although the direction of causality is unknown (Sareen, Cox, Clara, & Asmundson, 2005). Medical problems may also be a consequence of trauma (Schnurr et al., 2002), even for children and adolescents (Seng, Graham-Bermann, Clark, McCarthy, & Ronis, 2005). Trauma survivors, compared with nontraumatized people, report more medical symptoms, use more medical services, have more medical illnesses confirmed by a physician's examination, and display higher mortality (Foa, Keane, & Friedman, 2000).

Anxiety disorders also increase the risk of suicidality. Having one anxiety disorder increases the odds of suicidal ideation by 7.96 times and the rate of attempts by 5.85 times (Boden, Fergusson, & Horwood, 2007). Risk unfortunately increases with the number of anxiety disorders present. The authors of this longitudinal study suggest that addressing anxiety disorders is an important part of suicide prevention.

Course

Some anxiety disorders, such as the phobias and social anxiety, typically have a childhood onset, while others such as PTSD usually emerge in adulthood (Breslau, Lane, Sampson, & Kessler, 2008). The specific disorders have different prognoses, but most moderate to severe cases are not likely to remit spontaneously. Indeed, the anxiety disorders tend to be chronic, with low rates of recovery and high probabilities of recurrence (Bruce et al., 2005).

Assessment of the Anxiety Disorders

The clinical assessment of anxiety should include the following areas of focus (Bernstein & Shaw, 1997; Gorman et al., 2002):

- History of the onset and development of the anxiety symptoms, including the frequency and nature of a person's symptoms
- Any coexisting psychiatric disorders

- General medical history and a review of a person's medications, including a physical examination to search for a possible physical basis for the anxiety. This is especially critical for older adults without a history of anxiety disorders. If there is a physical basis for the symptoms, the appropriate diagnosis is anxiety disorder due to a general medical condition; for medication or substance-induced anxiety, the appropriate diagnosis is substance-induced anxiety disorder.
- History of substance use disorders
- Response to life transitions and major life events and stressors
- Social, school, occupational, and family history
- Times when the anxiety symptoms are not present or are more manageable

Assessment scales may be useful for evaluating and tracking symptoms over time. (See Appendices I and II for anxiety disorders for youth and adults, respectively, and Appendices III and IV for PTSD for youth and adults, respectively.)

When the client is a child, separate interviews with parents and children are recommended (Velting, Setzer, & Albano, 2004). Frequently, children report fewer symptoms than their parents. Reasons for this discrepancy include the child's desire to answer questions in a socially desirable manner and the child's limited comprehension of the interview questions. Also, children tend to be less reliable than parents in reporting details about the onset and duration of anxiety symptoms. For PTSD, the *DSM* diagnostic criteria have been criticized for lacking validity with children (Scheeringa, Wright, Hunt, & Zeanah, 2006). To assess PTSD, the child's reexperiencing the event can be facilitated through its reenactment with drawings, stories, and play. One should also be aware that children may experience fears of the dark, bad dreams, nightmares, waking up in the middle of the night, separation anxiety, and fears not directly associated with the trauma, such as a fear of monsters (Cohen, 1998). A variety of measurement instruments have been developed for the assessment of PTSD. (See Appendices I and II for a list of measurement tools for children and adults.) Even if the child does not meet criteria for the diagnosis of PTSD, practitioners should offer intervention for any clinically significant symptoms (McHugo et al., 2000).

Risk and Protective Factors

Onset

Determining the risk and protective factors that are specific to any of the anxiety disorders is difficult, as is determining whether the risk factors are specific to anxiety or may apply to a number of other diagnoses (Donovan & Spence, 2000).

Further, the risk factors may be concurrent with the anxiety disorder rather than contributing to its cause. As with other disorders in the *DSM*, the research on protective factors has lagged behind the search for risks. (See Exhibit 7.1 for risk and protective influences for adult anxiety disorders and Exhibit 7.2 for child factors.) Posttraumatic stress disorder in adults is discussed separately in Exhibit 7.3.

Biological Factors

A general predisposition for anxiety, rather than for specific anxiety disorders, is genetically based (Gorman et al., 2002). Results from twin studies suggest that genetic influences are modest, however, ranging between 30% and 40% (Hettema, Neale, & Kendler, 2001).

Risk factors related to an individual's temperament, which is assumed to be biologically based, include *anxiety sensitivity*, *temperamental sensitivity*, and *behavioral inhibition* (Donovan & Spence, 2000). Anxiety sensitivity is the

---

Exhibit 7.1

Risk and Protective Factors for Onset of Anxiety Disorders in Adults

Risk	Protective
Biological	
Estimated heritability across the disorders is modest (30%–40%)	
Cigarette smoking (panic disorder)	
Female gender	
Psychological	
History of separation anxiety disorder (panic disorder)[a]	
Emotional and escape-avoidance coping strategies[b]	Problem-focused coping strategies
Family	
Stressful and/or traumatic life events[c]	
Loss or disruption of relationships or significant life stressor	
Family history of anxiety disorders	
Social	
Lesbian, gay, or bisexual sexual orientation	
Low socioeconomic status	

[a] Hayward, Wilson, Lagle, Killen, and Taylor (2004).
[b] Hino, Takeuchi, and Yamanouchi (2002).
[c] Bandelow et al. (2002).

Risk and Protective Factors for the Onset of Anxiety Disorders in Youth

Risks	Protections
Biological	
Behavioral inhibition	
Temperamental sensitivity toward negativity	
Anxiety sensitivity	
Adolescence[a]	
Psychological	
Emotion-focused or avoidant coping strategies	Problem-focused coping strategies
History of major depression	
Separation anxiety disorder	
Family	
Anxious-resistant attachment developed because of early caregiving experiences[b]	
Parental anxiety	Social support
Traumatic, negative, and stressful life events	
Social	
Low socioeconomic status[c]	

[a] Reardon, Leen-Feldner, and Hayward (2009).
[b] Warren et al. (1997).
[c] Lemstra et al. (2008).
Source: Unless otherwise noted, the information is drawn from Donovan and Spence (2000).

Risk and Protective Factors for Posttraumatic Stress Disorder

Risk	Protective
Biological	
Introversion or behavioral inhibition	Extroversion
Female gender	Male gender
Chronic illness or handicapping condition	Good health
Genetic risk	
Psychological	
Behavioral or psychiatric disorder	No behavioral or psychiatric disorder
Diagnosis of autism spectrum disorder	
Dissociation after trauma	

Social

Family	
Family history of psychiatric illness	No family psychiatric history
Adverse life events and prior child trauma exposure	No prior trauma exposure
Death of a family member	
Immediate social environment	
Lack of social support	Positive support
Broader social factors	
Poverty	Middle to upper socioeconomic
Immigration to the United States because of armed conflict or political repression	status

Features of the Traumatic Experience

Degree of exposure to trauma—intensity, duration, and frequency

Subjective sense of danger

Stressors After the Traumatic Experience

Secondary stressors

Continued experience of adverse events

Type of Traumatic Event

War-related events, criminal victimization, exposure to earthquakes, floods, hurricanes, fires, or serious accidents

Sources: Aciemo, Kilpatrick, and Resnick (1999); Brewin et al. (2000); Debellis (1997); Keane, Weathers, & Foa (2000); McNally (1996); Ozer, Best, Lipsey, and Weiss (2003); Saigh et al. (1999).

tendency to respond fearfully to anxiety symptoms. Temperamental sensitivity is characterized by a range of emotional reactions toward negativity, including fear, sadness, self-dissatisfaction, hostility, and worry. This tendency predisposes people to both anxiety and depression, which often occur together. Behavioral inhibition involves timidity, shyness, emotional restraint, and withdrawal when introduced to unfamiliar situations (Kagan et al., 1988, as cited in Donovan & Spence, 2000). Behavioral inhibition has been associated with elevated physiological indexes of arousal and has been shown to have a strong genetic component.

Psychological Factors

Cognitive theories of PTSD have emerged from Horowitz's (1976) influential information processing model as reviewed by Calhoun and Resick (1993). In the information processing theory of trauma, adjustment to a traumatic event involves incorporation of the experience into cognitive schemas, which are the structures people use to perceive, organize, store, and retrieve experiences and to make meaning of events. In this model, the person may be unable to process exposure to trauma. Instead, the trauma remains in active memory, but outside conscious awareness. The defense mechanisms of denial and numbing are activated to prevent the individual from being overwhelmed. The material stays active and is manifested by flashbacks, nightmares, anxiety, and depression. Cycles of denial and numbing alternate with bouts of intrusive thoughts and intense emotion as the individual attempts to process and integrate the experience into existing cognitive structures.

Social Factors

Social factors, including family influences, the person's learning experiences, and the social cohort to which the individual may belong, can bring about the development of anxiety disorders.

Family Factors

Early caregiving experiences leading to an anxious attachment pattern in an individual may set the stage for later anxiety disorders. Anxious attachment is characterized by an infant's becoming distressed and frantically seeking comfort from the attachment figure through clinging and crying when faced with something he or she fears, such as contact with a stranger (Ainsworth, Blehar, Waters, & Wall, 1978). The subsequent contact with the caregiver, however, does not seem to help the child experience a sense of security or reduce the anxiety. In this attachment pattern, the parent is often withdrawn or uninvolved. In a study that tracked children from infancy to adolescence, youths with an anxious attachment pattern in infancy were more likely to suffer from an anxiety disorder as teenagers than those who were securely attached or showed avoidant attachment (Warren, Huston, Egeland, & Sroufe, 1997).

A number of other interpersonal patterns are seen in families of children with anxiety disorders, such as parental overcontrol, overprotection, and criticism (Donovan & Spence, 2000). In addition to their increased risk from genetically based factors, children of anxious parents may be more likely to observe anxious behavior in their parents and to have fearful behavior reinforced by their parents (Hagopian & Ollendick, 1997). Despite the number of possible family factors involved, these factors only explain about 6% of the variance (McLeod, Wood, & Weisz, 2007).

Living in an adverse family environment predisposes youth with traumatic events to be diagnosed with PTSD. Further, children with parents with PTSD often develop PTSD themselves. This may be due to the following explanations: genetic predisposition; exposure to violence that is directed toward a parent, such as community or domestic violence; or the parents' own PTSD, which hampers their parenting abilities (Linares & Cloitre, 2004). For children of all ages, threat to a caregiver is a risk factor for the development of PTSD (Scheeringa et al., 2006).

Learning Theory

Learning experiences shape anxious behavior. Through the processes of classical (Pavlov, 1932, 1934), operant (Skinner, 1953) and vicarious conditioning (Bandura, 1977), people may learn that certain stimuli are associated with aversive consequences. Fearful and avoidant behaviors may result in certain consequences that are sometimes reinforcing. For instance, if a person once raised a hand to speak in class and was ridiculed, this experience might become conditioned to all classroom experiences. The person might avoid anxiety by never raising a hand in a classroom.

Social Cohort

Social cohort influences were examined by Twenge (2000). She found that child anxiety had significantly increased between the early 1950s and the early 1990s, with social influences explaining about 20% of the variance. She notes that the birth cohort change in anxiety is so large that by the 1980s normal child samples were scoring higher than child psychiatric patients in the 1950s. When looking at the specific social influences that seemed to have contributed to the rise, Twenge (2000) found that it was not economic conditions, but low social connectedness and an increase in environmental threat, such as from crime and the threat of terrorism or war.

Recovery and Adjustment

Little has been studied on risk and protective influences for the recovery of anxiety disorders, but, not surprisingly, those who seek help from the mental health rather than the general health system receive better care (Wang et al., 2005).

Obsessive-compulsive disorder (OCD) has been studied particularly in relation to risk influences. For OCD in adults, high severity of the disorder, the hoarding subtype, presence of a personality disorder, family dysfunction, and accommodation to the disorder were predictors of poor outcome to cognitive-behavioral therapy (CBT; Keeley, Storch, Merlo, & Geffken, 2007). Treatment alliance was a predictor of positive outcome. For OCD in youth, a review of treatment outcome studies indicated that baseline severity of OCD and family problems were linked to a lesser response to CBT, and comorbid tics and externalizing disorders were correlated with a lesser response to medication (Ginsburg, Kingery, Drake, & Grados, 2008).

Intervention

As mentioned, people with anxiety disorders do not often seek treatment from the mental health system. Social workers can inform clients of the empirically based treatments available and the advantages and disadvantages of psycho-social and medication interventions (see Exhibits 7.4 and 7.5). The general consensus for children is that psychosocial treatment should be offered as a first-line treatment. Even the medically oriented American Academy of Child and Adolescent Psychiatry has argued this position, given the safety concerns about medication for youth (i.e., suicidality) and since the effects of medica-tion do not persist beyond its administration (Brown et al., 2007).

Exhibit 7.4

Advantages and Disadvantages of Psychosocial Treatments for Adults

Advantages	Disadvantages
No adverse medication side effects	Limited availability of exposure (the empirically validated intervention)
No danger of developing physiological dependency	Facing fear is often difficult
	Requires discipline, time, and effort in terms of participation, self-monitoring, and homework completion[a]

[a] 10%–30% of clients are unable or unwilling to complete the requirements.
Source: Gorman et al. (2002).

Exhibit 7.5

Advantages and Disadvantages of Medication as Treatment for Anxiety Disorders

Advantages	Disadvantages
Ready availability	Side effects
Less effort required of client	May experience overstimulation[a]
Rapid onset (especially for benzodiazepines)	

[a] In such cases it may be necessary to begin with small dosages and increase gradually.
Source: Gorman et al. (2002).

Psychosocial

In this section, several treatment approaches for anxiety disorders will be discussed, although a major focus will be on CBT since that has been a central research emphasis. Descriptions of interventions for the different anxiety disorders will be followed by their empirical basis, and youth, as well as adult, anxiety treatments will be covered.

Psychodynamic

Both children and adults often receive psychodynamic therapy for anxiety disorders. These therapies encompass a range of techniques and theories, not usually specifically directed toward treating the presenting anxiety disorder. Common elements of these interventions include achieving an understanding of the origins, meanings, and functions of the anxiety; integrating the client's understanding into a larger framework of personality; and developing more adaptive means to achieve the functions served by the symptoms (Gorman et al., 2002). Despite its popularity for people with anxiety disorders, more research is needed to assess the effectiveness of psychodynamic treatment.

Cognitive-Behavioral
Description

Most research has centered on CBT interventions. The purpose of CBT is to adjust the hyperventilation response, the conditioned reactions to physical cues, the fear and avoidance behaviors, and the cognitive aspects of the client's anxiety (Gorman et al., 2002). Twelve-session protocols have been described with both individual and group treatments. Although CBT generally involves a "package"of several techniques, whether all are necessary for a positive outcome is unknown (Gorman et al., 2002). The following components complete the package of cognitive-behavioral techniques:

Psychoeducation provides information to clients and perhaps significant others about anxiety, its self-perpetuating nature, how it can be controlled, and available treatments.

Monitoring anxiety symptoms includes being alert to their frequency, duration, and triggers (internal stimuli such as emotions or external stimuli such as substances and particular contexts).

Cognitive restructuring focuses on correcting the client's misappraisal of bodily sensations as threatening. Specific to panic disorders, cues are generally *interoceptive*; that is, people react with alarm to sensations that take place within the body. For example, becoming overly warm may lead a person to think, "I can't breathe. It's too hot. I'm going to pass out"and so on, working himself or herself into an anxiety state. For children, parents are taught to coach their children in questioning the evidence for their thoughts and arriving at coping solutions, rather than to provide excessive reassurance and answers to their children's anxious thoughts (Velting et al., 2004).

Breathing retraining helps clients by distracting them from anxiety symptoms and providing a sense of control over them.

Progressive muscle relaxation is a skill with which the client learns to reduce tension in anxiety-provoking situations by alternately tightening and relaxing certain muscle groups.

Problem solving is a step-by-step approach for generating a variety of practical solutions to life challenges. It is recommended for children and for those with generalized anxiety disorder (Velting et al., 2004).

Exposure is a process through which the client has to face the feared object until the anxiety dissipates. Exposure can take many forms, such as imaginal (e.g., through guided imagery), symbolic (e.g., through the use of pictures or props), simulated (e.g., through role playing), interoceptive (the client is trained to mimic bodily reactions that arouse panic, such as exercise to speed up the heart rate or spinning in a chair to induce dizziness, and develop tolerance to them), and in vivo (contact with the real situation or stimulus). The in vivo method is preferred and is the ultimate goal of any exposure program (Velting et al., 2004). Exposure is typically conducted in a graduated fashion. The practitioner helps the client construct a hierarchy of feared situations from least to most feared. The typical procedure is to work through the items in that order, conquering smaller fears before going on to tackle bigger ones.

For OCD, cognitive-behavioral intervention features exposure and *response prevention*, in which the client refrains from avoiding the stimulus or engaging in the ritualistic behavior. For example, if a person has an obsession about germs, he is blocked from avoiding what is "germy"or from washing his hands. To help the individual cope during this period, the client is taught anxiety management skills, such as relaxation training, breathing-control training, and cognitive training. A support person is usually enlisted to help the client because the exposure and response prevention processes are difficult to complete otherwise.

The most widely disseminated CBT protocol for childhood anxiety is Philip Kendall's Coping Cat program (Kendall, Kane, Howard, & Siqueland, 1990). This protocol is appropriate for 7- to 16-year-old youths with generalized anxiety disorder, social phobia, or separation anxiety disorder. Individual and group treatment manuals are available for this intervention, with adaptations for greater involvement by family members. Intervention manuals have also been developed for school refusal (Kearney

& Albano, 2000a, 2000b), OCD (March & Mulle, 1998), phobias, separation anxiety disorder, generalized anxiety disorder (Silverman & Kurtines, 1996), and social phobia in children (Beidel & Turner, 1998; Silverman & Kurtines, 1996) and adolescents (Albano, 1995; Hayward et al., 2000).

For child PTSD, trauma-focused CBT has been the focus of research. Although referred to by different names, the common elements include brief treatment (around 12 sessions); psychoeducation; coping skills training; gradual exposure tasks via narratives, drawings, or other imaginal methods; cognitive processing of the abuse experience; and parent management skills training. While some treatments involve only the child, others include parents in individual meetings (Cohen, Deblinger, Mannarino, & Steer, 2004; Cohen & Mannarino, 1996, 1998; Deblinger & Heflin, 1996; Kolko, 1996) or conjoint sessions in addition to individual child and individual parent meetings (Cohen et al., 2004; Deblinger & Heflin, 1996).

Intervention Studies

Adults Since the last edition of this book, many new systematic reviews have been published on CBT treatment outcomes. Some, unfortunately, have not used conventional and updated review methods, which may inflate effect sizes, and these will not be reported here. Instead, we will focus on the methodologically rigorous reviews listed in Exhibit 7.6.

To summarize this research, CBT has been proven effective, although at small effect sizes, over pill or psychological placebo. Hofmann and Smits (2008) examined CBT for the anxiety disorders in adults. Compared to pill or psychological placebo, CBT was effective for anxiety, as well as depression, albeit at small effects. The stronger effect sizes were observed in obsessive-compulsive and acute stress disorder, while weaker effect sizes were found in panic disorder. Another review of psychological treatments for OCD confirmed the effectiveness of CBT for that disorder (Gava et al., 2007). Although OCD has been referred to as chronic and treatment resistant, these results provide encouragement that it can be successfully treated.

Children A Cochrane systematic review was conducted on child and adolescent CBT treatment for social phobia, separation anxiety, panic disorder, and generalized anxiety disorder (excluding PTSD and OCD) (James, Soler, & Weatherall, 2005). (See Exhibit 7.6.) Results of the meta-analysis indicated that remission of the anxiety disorder occurred in 56% of cases versus 28.2% for controls. O'Kearney, Anstey, and von Sanden (2006) also found that CBT was comparable to medication for OCD in youth. For PTSD, CBT has also been shown effective (Wethington et al., 2008) and also for the specific trauma of sexual abuse (Macdonald, Higgins, & Ramchandani, 2006). An implication from these systematic reviews is that CBT can be effective for child anxiety disorders, and social workers should be aware of available treatment manuals for those interventions.

Exhibit 7.6

Summaries of Systematic Reviews and Meta-Analyses

Author/Intervention	Population	Type of Anxiety Disorder	Studies Included	Main Results
Bisson and Andrew (2007) Psychological therapies	Adults	PTSD (at least 3 months in duration)	33	Trauma Focused CBT, EMDR and stress management produce more improvement than other psychotherapies, with individual Trauma Focused CBT and EMDR being more effective than stress management at 2–5 months after treatment
Bridge et al. (2007) SSRIs and other second-generation agents	Children and adolescents	OCD or non-OCD anxiety disorders (excluding PTSD)	Randomized placebo-controlled trials 6 non-OCD anxiety disorders trials of 1136 participants 6 OCD trials of 705 participants	For non-OCD anxiety disorders, the response rate was 69% in antidepressant treated participants and 39% in those receiving placebo; the pooled risk difference was 37%. In the 6 OCD trials pooled rates of response were 52% in SSRI-treated participants and 32% in those receiving placebo; the pooled risk difference was 20%.
Corcoran and Pillai (2008) Parent-involved treatment of child sexual abuse	Children and adolescents	PTSD	5 experimental or quasi-experimental designs	At posttest, the effect of parent-involved treatment on PTSD was .37 and at follow-up was .25.
Gava et al. (2007) Psychological treatment compared to treatment as usual	Adult	OCD	7 randomized, controlled trials of only CBT	Those receiving CBT showed significantly fewer symptoms at posttest (a large effect).
Hofmann and Smits (2008) CBT	Adults	Any anxiety disorder	27 randomized, controlled trials totaling 1496 participants	The effect of CBT on anxiety disorders was large compared to placebo, but was reduced to a small effect when only reporting intent-to-treat clients ($n = 6$ studies).

Study	Population	Focus	Sample	Findings
Hunot et al. (2007) Psychological therapies	Adults	Generalized anxiety disorders	22 randomized and quasi-randomized, controlled trials with a total of 1060 participants	Psychological therapy (CBT) was more effective than treatment as usual or waitlist control in reducing anxiety, worry, and depression at posttest ($n = 13$ studies), but no follow-up studies were available. However, CBT was not more effective than supportive therapy ($n = 6$ studies).
James et al. 2005 Manualized CBT	Children and adolescents	Anxiety disorders (except PTSD and OCD)	13 randomized, controlled studies involved 519 participants	Remission of the anxiety disorder occurred in 56% of cases versus 28.2% of controls.
Kornor et al. (2008) CBT	Adults	Prevention of chronic PTSD when clients had either acute stress disorder or PTSD for a short period	5 randomized trials	CBT was more effective at a statistically significant difference in comparison to supportive counseling at both 3–6 months, but not 9-month and 3–4 year follow-up, although fewer PTSD diagnoses were found for CBT at these follow-up points.
Macdonald, Higgins, and Ramchandani (2006) CBT	Children and adolescents	PTSD and anxiety	Randomized or quasi-randomized controlled trials 10 studies	PTSD symptoms Posttest: .43 effect size (6 studies) Follow-up: .50 effect size (2 studies) Anxiety symptoms Posttest: .21 effect size (5 studies) Follow-up: .28 effect size (2 studies)
O'Kearney, Anstey, and von Sanden (2006) Behavior therapy or CBT, its differential efficacy over medication, and their combination	Children and adolescents	OCD	Randomized or quasi-randomized published and nonpublished studies $n = 4$ studies involving 222 participants	Medication and CBT were equally effective; combined medication and CBT was more effective than medication but not CBT alone.

(continued)

Exhibit 7.6

(Continued)

Author/Intervention	Population	Type of Anxiety Disorder	Studies Included	Main Results
Wethington et al. (2008) CBT, play therapy, art therapy, crisis debriefing, medication	Children and adolescents	PTSD and other anxiety	Experimental and quasi-experimental studies	Individual CBT (n = 11) Significant results for PTSD: −.63 effect size Anxiety: SMD −.31 effect size Group CBT: (n = 10 studies) PTSD: SMD −.56 effect size Anxiety: .37 effect size Play therapy (n = 2) Although studies found benefit, it was difficult to synthesize results. Art therapy (n = 1) Insufficient evidence Psychodynamic (n = 1) Insufficient evidence Medication (n = 2) Insufficient evidence Psychological debriefing: based on a single qualifying study that provided no evidence of beneficial effects

CBT, cognitive-behavioral therapy; OCD, obsessive-compulsive disorder; PTSD, posttraumatic stress disorder; SSRIs, selective serotonin reuptake inhibitors.

EMDR

Another treatment for PTSD is known as eye movement desensitization and reprocessing (EMDR), a controversial approach that uses a client's eye movements to process traumatic memories. Shapiro, its creator, has outlined the method in a book (Shapiro, 2001) and created a training program. In a meta-analysis, 34 studies were examined for the effectiveness of EMDR (Davidson & Parker, 2001). The major finding was that EMDR was not more or less effective than other exposure techniques. This result was also confirmed in a more recent systematic review—that trauma-focused CBT was as effective as EMDR (Bisson & Andrew, 2007). Thus, it is a viable intervention. Indeed, some consider EMDR to be a form of exposure treatment because clients are asked to keep a traumatic memory in their minds as the clinician elicits the eye movements. However, there was no evidence from the meta-analysis that the eye movements were necessary. In addition, there were no significant differences between studies in which the clinicians had participated in approved training and those in which they had not (Davidson & Parker, 2001), contrary to the claims of its proponents that approved EMDR training is essential.

Family

For child anxiety disorders, parent involvement is indicated in the following circumstances (Velting et al., 2004):

- The youth's functioning is seriously compromised by anxiety or comorbidity.
- The child is young in age or developmental level.
- The parents or other family members engage in behavior that accommodates the anxiety.
- A parent has an anxiety disorder or another psychiatric disorder (if so, concurrent individual therapy for the parent is recommended).
- For OCD, there is extensive family involvement in rituals, or there are problems in the family that interfere with the child's individual treatment (King et al., 1998).

Parent–child interventions may include helping parents to encourage the child to face new situations rather than withdraw, to refrain from excessive criticism and intrusiveness, to respond more directly to the child's needs, and to encourage the child to engage in activities despite anxiety. On the other hand, if a teenager presents for treatment but has generally good functioning and no comorbid disorder, less parental involvement is indicated. This helps the teen to address the developmental task of assuming self-responsibility.

Corcoran and Pillai (2008) focused on parent-involved treatment of sexual abuse. Several reasons have been offered as to why nonoffending caregivers should participate in treatment for their child (Corcoran, 1998). Maternal support is a predictor of child adjustment after disclosure, and attending treatment could bolster a parent's level of supportiveness. Mothers may also suffer great distress at learning of their children's sexual abuse, and their negative reactions may impede children's recovery. Intervention may help caregivers cope with stressors associated with their children's sexual victimization, such as separation from a partner, loss of social support, and being involved in legal proceedings. Learning about abuse dynamics can also reduce distress (Deblinger & Heflin, 1996). In addition, treatment can help mothers learn how to identify and handle symptoms in their children and to respond appropriately to their questions and concerns.

In Corcoran and Pillai (2007), the mean effect size for the outcome of PTSD based on five studies was small, yet noteworthy as comparison conditions were often represented by child treatment only. This suggests that the nonoffending caregiver be a focus of treatment for child sexual victimization.

Crisis Debriefing

Crisis debriefing is often used by social workers and other mental health professionals to forestall the development of PTSD when people have undergone trauma. It involves meeting with people either individually but most often in groups, educating them about the nature of trauma and its reactions, and encouraging the exploration of feelings. Unfortunately, crisis debriefing has not yet been found to be helpful for either children or adults and may cause additional distress (Rose, Bisson, Churchill, & Wessely, 2002; Wethington et al., 2008). Thus, social workers should be aware that there is no empirical basis for the use of crisis debriefing. Suggested instead is screening for PTSD symptoms and intervening with those that are at risk with CBT (Kornor et al., 2008) (See Appendices III and IV for screening and assessment measures).

New Technologies

Remote technologies, defined as the telephone, Internet, or videophone, have been studied for their impact on several mental health disorders, including anxiety. These technologies may act to circumvent several possible barriers to services, including having a mental disability such as agoraphobia, having a physical disability, long work hours that inhibit a person's ability to access office-based services, a lack of transportation, or living in a rural area where appropriate services are not available. Only three studies of these technologies have focused on anxiety, totaling 168 participants, but a large effect was found compared to control conditions (Bee et al., 2008). Remote technologies thus offer promise for the delivery of services for people with anxiety, although obviously more study is needed.

Medication and Combined Treatment

A variety of types of medications are available to treat both adults and adolescents with anxiety disorders, and the major classes include the benzodiazepines, azapirones, and selective serotonin reuptake inhibitors (SSRIs) (Bentley & Walsh, 2006). The benzodiazepine drugs were the most popular antianxiety medications through the mid-1990s. They achieve their therapeutic effect by blocking central nervous system stimulation in areas associated with emotion. While still used at times, these medications have an addictive potential and also street value, and thus they have fallen out of favor with physicians, given the newer alternatives. Buspirone is a newer drug classified as an azapirone and balances serotonin levels, which are believed to be anxiolytic in the hippocampus and limbic areas. The most frequently prescribed drugs for anxiety today, however, are the SSRIs, which were originally developed to treat depression. These drugs have an effect on serotonin levels as well as other neurotransmitters; they also demonstrate relatively modest side effects and are safe when taken over time. (See Chapter 10 for a fuller discussion of the SSRIs.)

Adults

A Cochrane Campbell review was conducted on randomized controlled trials of medication for PTSD in adults (Stein, Ipser, & Seedat, 2006). Thirty-five studies were included, totaling 4,597 participants. In studies that could be synthesized because of common outcomes, medication and placebo response occurred in 59.1% and 38.5% of cases, respectively. Medication was superior to placebo in reducing the severity of PTSD symptoms, comorbid depression, and functional disability. Evidence of treatment efficacy was most convincing for the SSRIs. However, as is typical, medication was also associated with more adverse effects than was placebo.

Similarly, the effect of medication, particularly the SSRIs, was better than placebo for the treatment of social anxiety (N = 37 studies), although publication bias may have influenced findings (Stein, Ipser, & Balkom, 2004).

Other than the SSRIs, the azapirones (most commonly Buspirone), which work on the 5-HT1A receptor, have been used to treat generalized anxiety disorder. They appear to be superior to placebo and equivalent to the benzodiazepines (without their addictive potential), but it is unknown whether they are superior to psychotherapy or the antidepressants (Chessick et al., 2006).

Children

In the Bridge et al. (2007) meta-analysis of randomized clinical trials of antidepressant treatment of anxiety disorders, there was a risk difference of 37% between the response of those on medication compared to placebo, but there was also an increased risk of suicidality. The SSRIs were less effective for OCD than for other anxiety disorders, but they still showed a positive effect.

Although physicians often prescribe the SSRIs for children with PTSD, little research has been conducted on them. In the Wethington et al. (2008) meta-analysis, only two studies were found that met inclusion criteria, and the differences in studies and results led to the conclusion that there was "insufficient evidence"for medication for PTSD.

Two multimodal studies examining the differential effectiveness of medication, CBT, and their combination have been conducted for children with anxiety disorders. In the Child–Adolescent Anxiety Multimodal Study, 488 children between the ages of 7 and 17 years who had a primary diagnosis of separation anxiety disorder, generalized anxiety disorder, or social phobia were randomized to the following treatments: CBT (14 sessions); sertraline; a combination of sertraline and CBT; and placebo drug, all for 12 weeks (Walkup et al., 2008). The percentage of children rated as very much or much improved on a clinician-report scale was 80.7% for combination therapy, 59.7% for CBT, and 54.9% for sertraline, and all therapies were found superior to placebo (23.7%). Combination therapy was superior to both monotherapies, but the researchers concluded that parents and providers could choose from any one of the three treatments, depending on preferences and available resources.

Child OCD was the focus of the Pediatric Obsessive-Compulsive Disorder Treatment Study (POTS, 2004). In this study, participants at three academic sites (N = 112) were randomly assigned to receive CBT alone, sertraline alone, combined CBT and sertraline, or pill placebo for 12 weeks. A statistically significant advantage was posed for CBT alone, sertraline alone, and combined treatment compared with placebo. Combined treatment also proved superior to CBT alone and to sertraline alone, which did not differ from each other. In examining this study, the APA Psychological 12 criteria review assigned combination treatment to "probably efficacious"status based on its greater effectiveness compared to sertraline (Barrett, Farrell, Pina, Piacentini, & Peris, 2008). However, the O'Kearney et al. (2006) meta-analysis, in synthesizing the results of two studies for OCD (including POTS), found that combining CBT and medication did not appear to help beyond medication alone. Taking these two reviews together, medication and CBT may be combined for more optimal results, although a single treatment alone can also be chosen.

Social Diversity

SES

Most of the anxiety disorders are more common in those from lower socioeconomic backgrounds (Cronk, Slutske, Madden, Bucholz, & Heath, 2004; Horowitz, McKay, & Marshall, 2005), possibly because of the greater number of stressors affecting those in poverty, as well as greater treatment-seeking behavior, higher education, and higher job levels held by people in higher socioeconomic groups.

Sexual Minorities

Lesbian, gay, and bisexual persons have an increased rate of anxiety disorders that is at least 1.5 times higher than the heterosexual population (King et al., 2008). Stigma and discrimination may partially account for these elevated rates.

Ethnic Minorities

Although African Americans have lower rates of anxiety disorders than Caucasians, their anxiety disorders are more likely to persist (Breslau, Kendler, et al., 2005). This may be partly due to the fact that African Americans tend to seek help from medical rather than mental health settings for anxiety disorders, and they also may complain about somatic rather than emotional or mental symptoms (Gorman et al., 2002). For these reasons, their conditions are sometimes misdiagnosed and thus may not receive appropriate treatment.

Although few treatment outcome studies have been conducted with ethnic minorities, Huey and Polo (2008) found that several CBT studies had been tested with Latino (Asbahr et al., 2005; Ginsburg & Drake, 2002; Silverman et al., 1999) and African American youth (Ginsburg & Drake, 2002; Silverman et al., 1999; Wilson & Rotter, 1986). These treatments were found according to the APA Psychological 12 Task Force Criteria (Chambless & Hollon 1998). to be "possibly efficacious." For "possibly efficacious," at least one study indicates a treatment is superior in the absence of conflicting evidence. This represents a third tier of evidence behind "well-established" and "probably efficacious" interventions. More study clearly needs to be conducted on ethnic minorities.

Critique

Much of the critique involving anxiety disorders will focus specifically on PTSD, which was added to the *DSM* only in 1980. Advocacy by the psychiatric community and Vietnam War veterans who believed themselves to be traumatized on a long-term basis by their war experiences led to PTSD being adopted in the *DSM-III* (Kutchins & Kirk, 1997; McHugh & Treisman, 2006). The process by which this occurred is detailed in Kutchins and Kirk (1997) and is one of their prime examples of how politics can sometimes play a more significant role than scientific evidence in the *DSM* determination of what constitutes a disorder.

Posttraumatic stress disorder is one of the disorders in the *DSM* that is conceptualized in terms of problematic functioning in the person–environment system because a traumatic event, by definition, must have occurred (Bradshaw & Thomlison, 1996). However, PTSD is not a unique outcome of trauma; depression is as common a response, and other anxiety disorders, substance use disorders, and eating disorders may develop (Romano, 2004). In addition, in the majority of cases, PTSD is accompanied by another disorder. Symptom overlap among diagnostic categories helps to explain the high likelihood of lifetime comorbid disorders seen in PTSD. These facts indicate that diagnostic clarity is lacking for PTSD. Indeed, Wakefield, Spitzer, and First (2007) have argued for revisions in the PTSD diagnostic criteria for these reasons. The proposed changes involve the following: tightening the criterion for the traumatic stressor so that it has to be an event that a person either experiences or witnesses; eliminating "acute," "chronic," and "delayed onset" specifiers; and ruling out malingering. Furthermore, symptoms should relate thematically to the trauma and not involve a worsening of a preexisting mood, anxiety, or personality disorder.

We have already outlined some concerns for the diagnosis of PTSD in childhood. In summary, the questionable accuracy of information on childhood symptoms necessary to make the diagnosis, and also the ways that trauma may be experienced differently in children, makes the validity of the diagnosis in childhood questionable.

Case Study

Bob is a single 37-year-old Caucasian male who has come to a social worker employed at a mental health outpatient clinic. Bob looks nervous and is shaking when he enters the social worker's office. When he begins speaking, he blushes. He shows a lack of adequate personal hygiene—his hair is unwashed and looks as if it has been slept on. He smells of unwashed skin, he is unshaven, and his clothes do not match and appear worn.

Bob begins by saying that he gets nervous in public. As he talks to the social worker, he begins to sweat and sounds breathless. His face is red, and the social worker reassures him to take his time and that he is doing fine.

Bob reveals that he lives by himself in a small, rundown trailer with disability benefits as his only income. He reports that his parents live in the area, but he does not speak with them much. He has two siblings and feels that he is the "black sheep of the family," explaining that his siblings are successful in their careers and are married with children. Bob often ridicules himself, making comments such as "I can't do anything right" and "I'm not capable."

Bob talks about having attended every Agoraphobics Building Independent Lives (ABIL) support group in the local area for the last 10 years. As a national network for persons with anxiety disorders, ABIL promotes the use of support groups. Bob occasionally writes articles and poetry for the organization's newsletter. Despite the number of groups he attends, Bob worries for days before he plans to go to a meeting. As he drives to a session, his heart beats rapidly, he gets dizzy and nauseous, and he reports that he sometimes feels like "I'm dying."Bob's biggest fear centers on "embarrassment"and his perception of what others will think of him if he displays such physiological reactions in public. The support group is the only socializing Bob does, aside from occasional visits to his siblings' families, and he reports gaining some comfort from attendance.

He relates that when he goes grocery shopping or to the bank to cash his checks, he often runs out of the place because of anxiety and usually feels better when he gets back into his car. He tries to fight these feelings by going to the mall or the movie rental store, but he just cannot seem to shake them. He denies experiencing any of these anxiety symptoms at home.

Bob says that he has been in and out of therapy since he was a teenager and had frequent thoughts of suicide as an adolescent. Bob does not appear to be suicidal at the present time and has not reported having such feelings since adolescence. His last therapy experience, which he maintained for 6 years, ended 4 years ago. That therapist had suggested his attending the support groups. When he was asked what kind of therapy he had received, Bob could not identify the particular approach but described talking a lot about his childhood and receiving support for his feelings. He said he finally stopped because he got from the groups what he was receiving from the therapist. However, he realizes his life is still very limited and wants to conquer his fears. Throughout the years, he has also tried an array of "alternative therapies,"including hypnosis, which he states have also been ineffective.

Bob has never taken medication for his anxiety disorder because he sees his problem as strictly environmental. He will not give a concrete answer as to why he attributes his problems to environmental causes; however, he often talks about reading self-help books that explain the disorder in this manner.

Bob is reluctant to talk about his past because "that's all the other therapist would talk about"and refers to the approach as abusive. When asked, he said that none of his other relatives, to his knowledge, has an anxiety disorder. He said that there is, however, substance abuse in his family. He said there was not a single event that caused the attacks; its onset seemed insidious. He has now displayed these symptoms for 13 years.

Bob reports himself to be physically healthy and does not smoke, drink, or use narcotics. He enjoys hiking and sometimes camps alone.

Multiaxial Diagnosis

Axis I: 300.23 Social Phobia, Generalized
Axis II: 301.82 Avoidant Personality Disorder (Provisional)
Axis III: V71.09 None
Axis IV: Problems related to the social environment (Bob is isolated and has not formed intimate relationships because of his lack of social interaction)
Occupational problems (Bob has been unemployed for years)
Economic problems (Bob lives on a small supplemental income in a low socioeconomic neighborhood)
GAF: 45

Justification for the Axis I diagnosis of social phobia was based upon Bob's meeting full criteria for the disorder, including the following:

Criterion A: Bob exhibits persistent fear in social situations, demonstrated by blushing, trembling, lack of eye contact, and reports of nausea, dizziness, and feeling like he will die.
Criterion B: Exposure to the feared social situation provokes anxiety, which sometimes takes the form of a panic attack.
Criterion C: Bob recognizes that the fear is excessive and unreasonable.
Criterion D. Bob forces himself to attend support groups but does so with intense anxiety, and he avoids other social contact.
Criterion E. Bob's anxiety interferes significantly with a normal routine (e. g., visiting the grocery store), occupational functioning (he is unable to work), and his social activities and relationships.
Criterion F pertains to youth presentation and therefore is not applicable to this case.
Criterion G: Bob's anxiety is not due to the effects of a substance, a medical condition, or another mental disorder. To rule out panic disorder, Bob reports that he rarely has the unexpected panic attacks that are frequently associated with a diagnosis of panic disorder without agoraphobia. His chief fear is in the social realm; he is deathly afraid of embarrassing or humiliating himself.

The specifier "generalized"has been included because Bob's fears include most social situations.

The *DSM-IV-TR* also suggests consideration of an additional diagnosis of avoidant personality disorder, an Axis II disorder, for individuals with generalized social phobia. Bob has a pervasive pattern, beginning 13 years before, of social inhibition, feelings of inadequacy, and hypersensitivity. He avoids occupational activities because they involve interacting with people (e.g., interviewing, being supervised, and being evaluated). He is unwilling to get involved with people and almost sure that he will not be liked. He has no intimate relationships and is preoccupied with being criticized or rejected in social situations. Bob views himself as socially inept, personally unappealing, and inferior to others, and he is reluctant to take risks or to engage in new activities because they may prove to be embarrassing. Although only four of seven criteria are necessary for the diagnosis, Bob meets all seven. Because the social worker has only had one meeting with Bob, she is making the Axis II provisional at this time.

Bob suffers from certain psychosocial stressors, most of which are consequences of his disorder, as previously described. The social worker assigned Bob a GAF of 45 because Bob suffers such serious impairment in social functioning (the inability to go anywhere there are people) and occupational functioning (inability to hold a job for the past 13 years).

Risk and Protective Factors Assessment

For onset, Bob's risk factors at the psychological level include escape-avoidance coping strategies. At the family level, Bob experienced stressful life events—abuse as a child. For recovery, Bob's low socioeconomic status may prove a risk; however, he has started to attend a clinic that accepts Medicaid payment for services. On the positive side, Bob's physical health is good, and he has never smoked. He exercises by hiking and mountain climbing, which have been shown to improve mood and decrease anxiety. He is intelligent (reading books) and creative and often writes poetry for an organization's newsletter. These strengths are helping Bob to cope with his anxiety on a daily basis.

Treatment Plan

Although Bob's attendance at support groups is a source of comfort for him, a concern is that almost his entire social life revolves around his illness. He has also not been able to maintain the social contacts he makes in the groups, even though he has been attending for 10 years.

The social worker provides Bob with some education about social phobia, most of which he said was already familiar. She explains exposure therapy as the empirically validated approach. His anxiety spikes in reaction to the idea of facing various public situations. The social worker, in response, reassures him that they will work slowly and in a graduated fashion. She says that she will also teach him skills, such as breathing retraining, progressive muscle relaxation, visualization, cognitive restructuring, and self-talk, so that he is able to relax and distract himself during exposure episodes. Finally, she says that while in vivo exposure will be the ultimate goal, they can begin initially with imaginal exposure, in which he simply thinks about the feared situations.

The social worker will also address Bob's social skills, starting with the basics of physical presentation, saying "hello,"and maintaining eye contact. Frequent modeling and rehearsal will take place as he learns these skills.

Medication may be helpful for Bob because he has suffered such severe impairment for such a long duration. Over time, the social worker will work to elicit Bob's perceptions of the advantages and disadvantages of using medication (see Exhibit 7.5) to allow him to make an informed decision. Although Bob reports his physical health as optimal, the social worker will also refer him for a physical examination, as he has not had one in years. If there is any physical basis to his anxiety, this needs to be assessed.

▨ References

Acierno, R., Kilpatrick, D., & Resnick, H. (1999). Posttraumatic stress disorder in adults relative to criminal victimization: Prevalence, risk factors, and comorbidity. In P. Saigh & J. Bermner (Eds.), *Posttraumatic stress disorder: A comprehensive text* (pp. 44–68). Needham Heights, MA: Allyn & Bacon.

Ainsworth, M. D., Blehar, M. C., Waters, E., & Wall, S. (1978). *Patterns of attachment: A psychological study of the strange situation.* Hillsdale, NJ: Erlbaum.

Albano, A. M. (1995). Treatment of social anxiety in adolescents. *Cognitive and Behavioral Practice, 2,* 271–298.

American Psychiatric Association. (2000). *Diagnostic and statistical manual of mental disorders* (4th ed.). Text Revision. Washington, DC: Author.

Asbahr, F. R., Castillo, A. R., Ito, L. M., Latorre, M. D. O., Moreira, M. N., & Lotufo-Neto, F. (2005). Group cognitive-behavioral therapy versus sertraline for the treatment of children and adolescents with obsessive-compulsive disorder. *Journal of the American Academy of Child & Adolescent Psychiatry, 44*(11), 1128–1136.

Bandelow, B., Spaeth, C., Tichauer, A., Broocks, A., Hajak, G., & Ruther, E. (2002). Early traumatic life events, parental attitudes, family history, and birth risk factors in patients with panic disorder. *Comprehensive Psychiatry, 43,* 269–278.

Bandura, A. (1977). *Social learning theory.* Englewood Cliffs, New Jersey: Prentice-Hall.

Barrett, P. M., Farrell, L., Pina, A. A., Piacentini, J., & Peris, T. S. (2008). Evidence-based psychosocial treatments for child and adolescent Obsessive-Compulsive Disorder. *Journal of Clinical Child & Adolescent Psychology, 37,* 131–155.

Bee, P., Bower, P., Lovell, K., Gilbody, S., Richards, D., Gask, L., et al. (2008). Psychotherapy mediated by remote communication technologies: A meta-analytic review. *BMC Psychiatry, 8,* 1–13.

Beidel, D., & Turner, S. (1998). *Shy children, phobic adults: Nature and treatment of social phobia.* Washington, DC: American Psychological Association.

Bentley, K. J. & Walsh, J. (2006). *The social worker and psychotropic medication: Toward effective collaboration with mental health clients, families and providers* (3rd ed.). Monterey, CA: Brooks/Cole-Thomson.

Bernstein, G., & Shaw, K. (1997). Practice parameters for the assessment and treatment of children and adolescents with anxiety disorders. *Journal of the American Academy of Child and Adolescent Psychiatry, 36*(Suppl. 10), 69S–84S.

Bisson, J., & Andrew, M. (2007). Psychological treatment of post-traumatic stress disorder (PTSD). *The Cochrane Database of Systematic Reviews, (3)*, CD003388.

Boden, J. M., Fergusson, D. M., & Horwood, L. J. (2007). Anxiety disorders and suicidal behaviours in adolescence and young adulthood: Findings from a longitudinal study. *Psychological Medicine, 37*(3), 431–440.

Bradshaw, C., & Thomlison, B. (1996). Posttraumatic stress disorder conceptualized as a problem in the person-environment system. In F. Turner (Ed.), *Adult psychopathology: A social work perspective* (pp. 638–660). New York: Free Press.

Breslau, J., Kendler, K., Su, M., Gaxiola-Aguilar, S., & Kessler, R. (2005). Lifetime risk and persistence of psychiatric disorders across ethnic groups in the United States. *Psychological Medicine, 35*(3), 317–327.

Breslau, J., Lane, M., Sampson, N., & Kessler, R. C. (2008). Mental disorders and subsequent educational attainment in a us national sample. *Journal of Psychiatric Research, 42*(9), 708–716.

Brewin, C., & Andrews, B. (2000). Meta-Analysis of Risk Factors for Posttraumatic Stress Disorder in Trauma-Exposed Adults. *Journal of Consulting & Clinical Psychology, 68*(5), 748.

Brewin, C. R, Andrews, B., & Rose, S. (2000). Fear, helplessness, and horror in posttraumatic stress disorder: Investigating DSM-IV criterion A2 in Victims of Violent Crime. *Journal of Traumatic Stress, 13*(3), 499–510.

Bridge, J. A., Iyengar, S., Salary, C. B., Barbe, R. P., Birmaher, B., Pincus, H. A., Ren, L., & Brent, D. A. (2007). Clinical response and risk for reported suicidal ideation and suicide attempts in pediatric antidepressant treatment: A meta-analysis of randomized controlled trials. *Journal of the American Medical Association, 297*(15), 1683–1696.

Brown, R. T., Antonuccio, D. O., DuPaul, G. J., Fristad, M. A., King, C. A., Leslie, L. K., McCormick, G. S., Pelham, W. E. Jr., Piacentini J. C., & Vitiello, B. (2007). *Childhood mental health disorders: Evidence base and contextual factors for psychosocial, psychopharmacological and combined interventions.* Washington, DC: American Psychological Association.

Bruce, S., Yonkers, K., Otto, M., Eisen, J., Weisberg, R., Pagano, M., et al. (2005). Influence of psychiatric comorbidity on recovery and recurrence in generalized anxiety disorder, social phobia, and panic disorder: A 12-Year Prospective Study. *American Journal of Psychiatry, 162*(6), 1179–1187.

Busuttil, W. (2004). Presentations and management of post traumatic stress disorder and the elderly: A need for investigation. *International Journal of Geriatric Psychiatry, 19*(5), 429–439.

Calhoun, K. S., & Resick, P. A. (1993). Post-traumatic stress disorder. In D. H. Barlow (Ed.), *Clinicalhandbook of psychological disorders: A step-by-step treatment manual* (2nd ed., pp. 48–98). New York: Guilford Press.

Campbell, R. J. (2009). *Psychiatric dictionary* (9th ed.). New York: Oxford University Press.

Chambless, D. L., & Hollon, S. (1998). Defining empirically supported therapies. *Journal of Consulting and Clinical Psychology, 66*, 7–18.

Chessick, C. A., Allen, M. H., Thase, M., Batista Miralha da Cunha, A. B., Kapczinski, F. F., de Lima, M. S., et al. (2006). Azapirones for generalized anxiety disorder. *The Cochrane Database of Systematic Reviews, (3)*, CD006115.

Cohen, J. A. (1998). Summary of the practice parameters for the assessment and treatment of children and adolescents with posttraumatic stress disorder. *Journal of the American Academy of Child and Adolescent Psychiatry, 37*(9), 997–1001.

Cohen, J. A., Deblinger, E., Mannarino, A. P., & Steer, R. A. (2004). A multisite, randomized controlled trial for children with sexual abuse-related PTSD symptoms. *Journal of the American Academy of Child & Adolescent Psychiatry, 43*(4), 393–402.

Cohen, J. A., & Mannarino, A. P. (1996). A treatment outcome study for sexually abused preschool children: Initial findings. *Journal of the American Academy of Child and Adolescent Psychiatry, 35*, 42–50.

Cohen, J. A., & Mannarino, A. P. (1998). Factors that mediate treatment outcome of sexually abused preschool children: Six- and 12-month follow up. *Journal of the American Academy of Child Adolescent Psychiatry, 37*(1), 44–51.

Copeland, W. E., Keeler, G., Angold, A., & Costello, E. J. (2007). Traumatic events and posttraumatic stress in childhood. *Archives of General Psychiatry, 64*(5), 557–584.

Corcoran, J. (1998). In defense of mothers of sexual abuse victims. *Families in Society, 49*, 358–369.

Corcoran, J. & Pillai, V. (2007). Effectiveness of secondary pregnancy prevention programs: A meta-analysis. *Research in Social Work Practice, 17*, 5–18.

Corcoran, J., & Pillai, V. (2008). A meta-analysis of parent-involved treatment for child sexual abuse. *Research in Social Work Practice, 18*, 453–464.

Costello, E., Egger, H., & Angold, A. (2005). 10-Year research update review: The epidemiology of child and adolescent psychiatric disorders: I. methods and public health burden. *Journal of the American Academy of Child & Adolescent Psychiatry, 44* (10), 972–986.

Cronk, N., Slutske, W., Madden, P., Bucholz, K., & Heath, A. (2004). Risk for separation anxiety disorder among girls: Paternal absence, socioeconomic disadvantage, and genetic vulnerability. *Journal of Abnormal Psychology, 113*, 237–247.

Davidson, P., & Parker, K. (2001). Eye movement desensitization and reprocessing (EMDR): A meta-analysis. *Journal of Consulting & Clinical Psychology, 69*(2), 305.

Deblinger, E., & Heflin, A.H. (1996). Treating sexually abused children and their nonoffending parents: A cognitive-behavioral approach. Thousand Oaks, CA: Sage.

Donovan, C., & Spence, S. (2000). Prevention of childhood anxiety disorders. *Clinical Psychology Review, 20*, 509–531.

Foa, E. B., Keane, T. M., & Friedman, M. J. (Eds.). (2000). *Effective treatments for PTSD: Practice guidelines from the International Society for Traumatic Stress Studies.* New York: The Guilford Press.

Gava, I., Barbui, C., Aguglia, E., Carlino, D., Churchill, R., De Vanna, M., et al. (2007). Psychological treatments versus treatment as usual for obsessive compulsive disorder (OCD). *Cochrane Database of Systematic Reviews*, (2), CD005333.

Ginsburg, G. S., & Drake, K. L. (2002). School-based treatment for anxious African-American adolescents: A controlled pilot study. *Journal of the American Academy of Child and Adolescent Psychiatry, 41*(7), 768–75.

Ginsburg, G. S., Kingery, J., Drake, K. L., & Grados, M. (2008). Predictors of treatment response in pediatric obsessive-compulsive disorder. *Journal of the American Academy of Child & Adolescent Psychiatry, 47*(8), 868–878.

Goodwin, R., Fergusson, D., & Horwood, L. (2004). Association between anxiety disorders and substance use disorders among young persons: Results of a 21-year longitudinal study. *Journal of Psychiatric Research, 38*(3), 295.

Gorman, J., Shear, K., Cowley, D., Cross, C. D., March, J., Roth, W., et al. (2002). Practice guideline for the treatment of patients with panic disorder. In *American Psychiatric Association practice guidelines for the treatment of psychiatric disorders. Compendium 2002* (pp. 635–696). Washington, DC: American Psychiatric Association.

Hagopian, L., & Ollendick, T. (1997). Anxiety disorders. In R. Ammerman & M. Hersen (Eds.), *Handbook of prevention and treatment with children and adolescents: Intervention in the real world context* (pp. 431–454). New York: Wiley.

Hayward, C., Varady, S., Albano, A. M., Thieneman, M., Henderson, L., & Schatzberg, A. F. (2000). Cognitive behavioral group therapy for female socially phobic adolescents: Results of a pilot study. *Journal of the American Academy of Child and Adolescent Psychiatry, 39*, 721–726.

Hayward, C., Wilson, K. A. Lagle, K., Killen, J. D., & Taylor, C. B. (2004). Parent-reported predictors of adolescent panic attacks. *Journal of the American Academy of Child and Adolescent Psychiatry, 43*, 613–620.

Hettema, J., Neale, M., & Kendler, K. (2001). A Review and Meta-Analysis of the Genetic Epidemiology of Anxiety Disorders. *American Journal of Psychiatry, 158*(10), 1568.

Hino, T., Takeuchi, T., & Yamanouchi, N. (2002). A 1-year follow-up study of coping in patients with panic disorder. *Comprehensive Psychiatry, 43*, 279–284.

Hofmann, S. G., & Smits, J. A. (2008). Cognitive-behavioral therapy for adult anxiety disorders: A meta-analysis of randomized placebo-controlled trials. *Journal of Clinical Psychiatry, 69*(4), 621–632.

Horowitz, M. (1976). *Stress response syndromes*. New York: Aronson.

Horowitz, K., McKay, M., & Marshall, R. (2005). Community violence and urban families: Experiences, effects, and directions for intervention. *American Journal of Orthopsychiatry, 75*(3), 356–368.

Huey, S. J., & Polo, A. J. (2008). Evidence-based psychosocial treatments for ethnic minority youth. *Journal of Clinical Child and Adolescent Psychology, 37*(1), 262–301.

Hunot, V., Churchill, R., Teixeira, V., & de Lima, M. S. (2007). Psychological therapies for generalised anxiety disorder. *The Cochrane database of systematic reviews*, (1), CD001848–CD001848.

James, A., Soler, A., & Weatherall, R. R. W. (2005). Cognitive behavioural therapy for anxiety disorders in children and adolescents. *Cochrane Database of Systematic Reviews*, (4), CD004690.

Keane, T., Weathers, F., & Foa, E., (2000). Diagnosis and assessment. In E. Foa., T. Jeane, & M. Friedman (Eds.), *Effective treatments for PTSD* (pp. 18–36). New York: Guilford.

Kearney, C. A., & Albano, A. M. (2000a). *When children refuse school: A cognitive behavioral therapy approach. Parent workbook*. New York: Psychological Corporation.

Kearney, C. A., & Albano, A. M. (2000b). *When children refuse school: A cognitive behavioral therapy approach. Therapist's manual*. New York: Psychological Corporation.

Keeley, M. L., Storch, E. A., Merlo, L. J., & Geffken, G. R. (2007) Clinical predictors of response to cognitive-behavioral therapy for obsessive-compulsive disorder. *Clinical Psychology Review, 28*(1), 118–130.

Kendall, P., Kane, M., Howard, B., & Siqueland, L. (1990). *Cognitive-behavioral treatment of anxious children: Treatment manual*. Philadelphia, PA: Department of Psychology, Temple University.

Kessler, R., Berglund, O., Demler, O., Jin, R., Merikanas, K., & Walters, E. (2005). Lifetime prevalence and age-of-onset distributions of DSM-IV disorders on the National Comorbidity Survey Replication. *Archives of General Psychiatry, 62,* 593–602.

Kessler, R., Chiu, W., Demler, O., & Walters, E. (2005). Prevalence, severity, and comorbidity of 12-month DSM-IV disorders in the National Comorbidity Survey Replication. *Biological Psychiatry, 58,* 668–676.

Kessler, R., Sonnega, A., Bromet, E., Hughes, M., & Nelson, C. (1995). Lifetime prevalence and ago-of-onset distributions of DSM-IV disorders in the national comorbidity survey replication. *Archives of General Psychiatry, 62,* 593–602.

King, R., Leonard, H., & March, J. (1998). Practice parameters for the assessment and treatment of children and adolescents with obsessive-compulsive disorder. *Journal of the American Academy of Child & Adolescent Psychiatry, 37* (Suppl. 10), 27S–45S.

King, M., Semlyen, J., Tai, S. S., Killapsy, H., Osborn, D., Popelyuk, D., & Nazareth, I. (2008). A systematic review of mental disorder, suicide, and deliberate self harm in lesbian, gay and bisexual people. *BMC Psychiatry, 8,* 70.

Kolko, D. (1996). Individual cognitive behavioral treatment and family. *Child Maltreatment, 1*(4), 323.

Kornor, H., Winje, D., Ekeberg, Ø., Weisæth, L., Kirkehei, I., Johansen, K., et al. (2008). Early trauma-focused cognitive-behavioural therapy to prevent chronicposttraumatic stress disorder and related symptoms: A systematicreview and meta-analysis. *BMC Psychiatry, 81 Downloaded on October* http://www.biomedcentral.com.proxy.library.vcu.edu/1471-244X/8/81

Kushner, M., Sher, K., & Erickson, D. (1999). Prospective analysis of the relation between DSM-III anxiety disorders and alcohol use disorders. *American Journal of Psychiatry, 156* (5), 723.

Kutchins, H., & Kirk, S. A. (1997). *Making us crazy: DSM: The psychiatric bible and the creation of mental disorders*. New York: Free Press.

Lemstra, M., Neudorf, C., D'Arcy, C., Kunst, A., Warren, L. M., & Bennett, N. R. (2008). A systematic review of depressed mood and anxiety by SES in youth aged 10–15 years. *Canadian Journal of Public Health, 99*(2), 125–129.

Linares, L. O., & Cloitre, M. (2004). Intergenerational links between mothers and children with PTSD spectrum illness. In R. P. Silva (Ed.). *Posttraumatic stress disorders in children and adolescents: Handbook* (pp. 177–201). New York: W. W. Norton & Co.

Macdonald, G. M., Higgins, J. P., & Ramchandani, P. (2006). Cognitive-behavioural interventions for children who have been sexually abused. *Cochrane Database Systematic Reviews, 18*(4), CD001930.

March, J. S., & Mulle, K. (1998). *OCD in children and adolescents: A cognitive behavioral therapy manual*. New York: Guilford.

McHugh, P. R., Treisman, G. (2006). PSTD: A problem diagnostic category. *Journal of Anxiety Disorders, 21*(2), 211–222.

McHugo, G., Mooney, D., Racusin, R., Ford, J., & Fleischer, A. (2000). Predicting posttraumatic stress after hospitalization for pediatric injury. *Journal of the American Academy of Child and Adolescent Psychiatry, 39,* 576–583.

McLeod, B. D., Wood, J. J., & Weisz, J. R. (2007). Examining the association between parenting and childhood anxiety: A meta-analysis. *Clinical Psychology Review, 27* (2), 155–172.

McNally, R. J. (1996). More controversies about panic disorder: A reply to Klein. *Behaviour Research and Therapy, 34*(11–12), 855–858.

O'Kearney, R. T., Anstey, K., & von Sanden, C. (2006). Behavioural and cognitive behavioural therapy for obsessive compulsive disorder in children and adolescents. *Cochrane Database of Systematic Reviews,* (4), CD004856.

Ozer, E., Best, S., Lipsey, T., & Weiss, D. (2003). Predictors of posttraumatic stress disorder and symptoms in adults: A meta-analysis. *Psychological Bulletin, 129,* 52–73.

Pavlov, I. (1932). Neuroses in man and animals. *Journal of the American Medical Association, 9,* 1012–1013.

Pavlov, I. (1934). An attempt at a physiological interpretation of obsessional neurosis and paranoia. *Journal of Mental Science, 80,* 187–197.

Pediatric OCD Treatment Study (POTS). (2004). Cognitive-behavior therapy, sertraline, and their combination for children and adolescents with obsessive-compulsive disorder: Randomized controlled trial. *JAMA, 292*(16), 1969–1976.

Reardon, L. E., Leen-Feldner, E. W., & Hayward, C. (2009). A critical review of the empirical literature on the relation between anxiety and puberty. Clinical Psychology Review, 29(1), 1–23.

Romano. C. (2004). Posttraumatic stress disorder—A continuing controversy in neuropsychiatry. *Neuropsychiatry Reviews, 5,* 9–12.

Rose, S. C., Bisson, J., Churchill, R., & Wessely, S. (2002). Psychological debriefing for preventing post traumatic stress disorder (PTSD). *Cochrane Database of Systematic Reviews,* (2), CD000560.

Saigh, P., Yasik, A., Sack, W., & Koplewicz, H. (1999). Child-adolescent posttraumatic stress disorder: Prevalence, risk factors, and comorbidity. In P. Saigh & J. Bremner (Eds.). *Posttraumatic stress disorder: A comprehensive text* (pp. 18–43). Boston: Allyn & Bacon.

Sareen, J., Cox, B., Clara, I., & Asmundson, G. (2005). The relationship between anxiety disorders and physical disorders in the U.S. National Comorbidity Survey. *Depression & Anxiety (1091–4269), 21*(4), 193–202.

Seng, J. S., Graham-Bermann, S. A., Clark, M. K., McCarthy, A. M., & Ronis, D. L. (2005). Posttraumatic stress disorder and physical comorbidity among female children and adolescents: results from service-use data. *Pediatrics, 116*(6), 767–776.

Scheeringa, M., Wright, M., Hunt, J., & Zeanah, C. (2006). Factors affecting the diagnosis and prediction of PTSD symptomatology in children and adolescents. *American Journal of Psychiatry, 163*(4), 644–651.

Schnurr, P., Friedman, M., & Bernardy, N. (2002). Research on posttraumatic stress disorder: Epidemiology, pathophysiology, and assessment. *Journal of Clinical Psychology, 58*(8), 877–889.

Shapiro, F. (2001). *Eye movement desensitization and reprocessing: Basic principles, protocols and procedures* (2nd ed.). New York: Guilford Press.

Silverman, W. K., & Kurtines, W. M. (1996). *Anxiety and phobic disorders: A pragmatic approach.* New York: Plenum.

Silverman, W. K., Kurtines, W. M., Ginsburg, G. S., Weems, C. F., Lumpkin, P. W., & Carmichael, D. H. (1999). Treating anxiety disorders in children with group cognitive-behaviorial therapy: a randomized clinical trial. *Journal of Consulting and Clinical Psychology, 67*(6), 995–1003.

Skinner, B. (1953). *Science and human behavior*. New York: Macmillan.

Stein, D. J., Ipser, J. C., & Balkom, A. J. (2004). Pharmacotherapy for social phobia. *The Cochrane Database of Systematic Reviews,* (4), CD001206.

Stein, D. J., Ipser, J. C., & Seedat, S. (2006). Pharmacotherapy for post traumatic stress disorder (PTSD). *Cochrane Database of Systematic Reviews, 25*(1), CD002795.

Twenge, J. M. (2000). The age of anxiety? The birth cohort change in anxiety and neuroticism, 1952–1993. *Journal of Personality and Social Psychology, 79*(6), 1007–1021.

Velting, O., Setzer, N., & Albano, A. (2004). Update on and advances in assessment and cognitive—Behavioral treatment of anxiety disorders in children and adolescents. *Professional Psychology: Research & Practice, 35*(1), 42–54.

Wakefield, J. C., Spitzer, R. L., & First, M. B. (2007). Saving PTSD from itself in DSM-V. *Journal of Anxiety Disorder, 21*(2), 233–241.

Walkup, J. T., Albano, A. M., Piacentini, J., Birmaher, B., Compton, S. N., Sherrill, J. T., Ginsburg, G. S., Rynn, M. A., McCracken, J., Waslick, B., Iyengar, S., March, J. S., & Kendall, P. C. (2008). Cognitive behavioral therapy, sertraline, or a combination in childhood anxiety. *New England Journal of Medicine, 359*(26), 2753–66.

Wang, P., Berglund, P., Olfson, M., Pincus, H., Wells, K., & Kessler, R. (2005). Failure and delay in initial treatment contact after first onset of mental disorders in the national comorbidity survey replication. *Archives of General Psychiatry, 62*(6), 603–613.

Warren, S., Huston, L., Egeland, B., & Sroufe, L. A. (1997). Child and adolescent anxiety disorders and early attachment. *Journal of the American Academy of Child & Adolescent Psychiatry, 36,* 637–644.

Wethington, H., Hahn, R., Fuqua-Whitley, D., Sipe, T., Crosby, A., Johnson, R. Liberman, A., Moscicki, E., Price, L., Tuma, F., Kalra G., Chattopadhyay, S. (2008). The effectiveness of interventions to reduce psychological harm from traumatic events among children and adolescents: a systematic review. American Journal of Preventative Medicine, 35, 287–313.

Wilson, N. H., & Rotter, J. C. (1986). Anxiety management training and study skills counseling for students on self-esteem and test anxiety and performance. *School Counselor, 34*(1), 18–31.

Zvolensky, M. J., Lejuez, C. W., & Eifert, G. H. (2000) Prediction and control: operational definitions for the experimental analysis of anxiety. *Behaviour Research and Therapy, 38*(7), 653–663.

Appendix I: Anxiety Measures for Children

The information on anxiety measures for children was drawn from Holmbeck et al. (2008).

Beck Anxiety Inventory (BAI) (Beck, Epstein, Brown, & Steer, 1988)

Description
- Twenty-one items in the measure
- Developed to measure anxiety in adolescents and adults (17–80 years)
- Four subscales: subjective, neurophysiological, panic, and autonomic

Reliability
- Internal consistency of .92 with adolescents (.92 to .94 with adults)
- Test-retest reliability of .71 with adolescents at 1 week, .62 at 2 weeks (with adults, .75 at 1 week and 2 weeks)
- Cross-informant reliability of .40 with adolescents using clinician rating and HARS-R

Validity
- Concurrent/predictive validity of .81; adolescents in in-patient settings report more anxiety than adolescents in high schools; able to differentiate anxious from nonanxious groups
- Convergent validity of .58 in adolescents with RCMAS (.51 to.54 in adults with HARS-R & anxiety diaries)

Childhood Anxiety Sensitivity Index (CASI) (Silverman, Fleisig, Rabian, & Peterson, 1991)

Description
- Eighteen items in the measure
- Developed to measure anxiety sensitivity in children (6–17 years)

Reliability
- Internal consistency of .76 to .87 nonclinical, .87 to .88 clinical
- Test-retest reliability of .76 at 2 weeks with nonclinical, .48 at 6 months with nonclinical, and .79 at 1 week with clinical.
- Cross informant reliability not reported.

Validity
- Concurrent/predictive validity: higher anxiety predicted more panic attack symptoms, more anxiety after known triggers, more internal catastrophic attributions about panic symptoms after panic experience. Children with anxiety and panic disorders displayed more sensitivity than those without diagnoses.
- Convergent validity of .50 to .66 general anxiety, .62 to .64 trait anxiety, .74 to .76 fear, .28 to .61 panic attack symptoms, .34 to .43 number of nonclinical panic attack symptoms, .64 general anxiety, .62 to .72 trait anxiety, and .59 fear in clinical.

Fear Survey Schedule for Children Revised (FSSC-R) (Ollendick, 1983; Scherer & Nakamura, 1968)

Description
- Eighty-item measure of fears and fearfulness.
- Target group is children ages 7 to 16 years.

- Five subscales: fear of the unknown, fear of minor injury and small animals, fear of danger and death, medical fear, fear of failure and criticism

Reliability
- Internal consistency of .92 to .94 overall; .57 to .89 for subscales
- Test-retest reliability of .82 at 1 week, .85 at 2 weeks, and .62 at 3 months
- Cross-informant reliability of .21 (child and parent)

Validity
- Concurrent/predictive validity: predicts school absence at 3 months; children fearful of school more fearful overall than control; able to discriminate types of phobias and specific anxiety disorders
- Convergent: .46 to .51 for trait anxiety

Multidimensional Anxiety Scale for Children (MASC) (March, 1998)

Description
- Thirty-nine items in the measure
- Developed to measure anxiety disorders in children and adolescents (8–18 years)
- Four factors: physical symptoms, harm avoidance, social anxiety, and separation anxiety

Reliability
- Internal consistency of .87 to .93 total, .48 to .90 across factors
- Test-retest reliability of .65 to .78 idealized rater at 3 weeks, .87 idealized rater at 3 months, .78 to .88 across raters at 3 weeks, .93 across raters at 3 months
- Cross-informant reliability of .39 for mother and child, .18 for child and father, .15 for father and mother

Validity
- Concurrent/predictive validity not reported.
- Convergent validity of .63 to .76 with RCMAS, .81 with SCARED, .71 with SCAS, with .79 with STAI T- Anxiety, and .63 with FSSC-R.

Revised Children's Manifest Anxiety Scale (RCMAS) (Reynolds & Richmond, 1985)

Description
- Thirty-seven-item measure of generalized, nonspecific, nonsituational anxiety
- Target group: children ages 6 to 19 years

- Four subscales: physiological, worry/oversensitivity, social concerns/concentration, and lie

Reliability
- Internal consistency of .79 to .85 total, .56 to .81 across subscales
- Test-retest reliability of .98 at 3 weeks, .68 at 9 months, and .58 on the lie subscale at 9 months
- Cross-informant reliability was not reported.

Validity
- Concurrent/predictive validity was not reported.
- Convergent validity of .65 to .88 with STAIC, .63 with FSSC-R, .76 with MASC, .85 with SCARED, and .76 with SCAS

Social Anxiety Scale for Children (SASC-R) (La Greca, 1999)

Description
- Twenty-two items in the measure
- Developed to measure feelings of social anxiety in peer relations for children
- Three subscales: fear of negative evaluation from peers, social avoidance and distress specific to new situations or unfamiliar peers, and social avoidance and distress generally around peers

Reliability
- Internal consistency of .60 to .90 across subscales
- Test-retest reliability of .70 total, .51 to .63 across subscales
- Cross-informant reliability not reported

Validity
- Concurrent/predictive validity of –.47 to –.39 across subscales with SPPC social acceptance, –.37 to –.23 with SPPC global self-worth
- Convergent validity of .63 to .81 with SPAI-C, .54 with RCMAS, .54 with CASI, and .52 with TASC

Social Phobia and Anxiety Inventory for Children (SPAI-C) (Beidel, Turner, & Morris, 1995)

Description
- Twenty-six items in the measure
- Developed to measure somatic, cognitive, and behavioral aspects of social phobias and anxiety in children (8–14 years)

Reliability
- Internal consistency of .92 to .95
- Test-retest reliability of .86 at 2 weeks and .63 at 10 months
- Cross-informant reliability of .31 between parent and child

Validity
- Concurrent/predictive validity of .50 for average number of distressing events per day, .41 for distress associated with event
- Convergent validity of .63 to .81 with SASC-R, .50 with STAIC trait, .13 with STAIC state, .53 with FSSC-R failure and criticism, and .45 with CBCI internalizing

State-Trait Anxiety Inventory for Children (STAIC) (Spielberger, 1973)

Description
- Forty-item measure of chronic and acute anxiety
- Target group is children ages 9 to 12 years; has been used with adolescents as well
- Two subscales: T-Anxiety (trait: chronic, pervasive) scale and the S-Anxiety (state: acute-transitory) scale

Reliability
- Internal consistency of .65 to .89 for state anxiety scale, .44 to .94 for trait anxiety scale
- Test-retest reliability of .31 to .71 across the scales at 6 weeks
- Cross-informant reliability was not reported.

Validity
- Concurrent/predictive validity of .58 with somatic complaints
- Convergent validity of .75 with CMAS, .88 with RCMAS, .63 with GASC, .63 with FSSC-R, .79 with MASC, .87 with SCARED, and .79 with SCAS

References for Anxiety Measures for Children

Beck, A. T., Epstein, N., Brown, G., & Steer, R. A. (1988). An inventory for measuring clinical anxiety: Psychometric properties. *Journal of Consulting and Clinical Psychology, 56,* 893–897.

Beidel, D. C., Turner, S. M., & Morris, T. L. (1995). A new inventory to assess childhood social anxiety and phobia: The social phobia and anxiety inventory for children. *Psychological Assessment, 7,* 73–79.

Holmbeck, G. N., Thill, A. W., Bachanas, P., Garber, J., Miller, K. B., Abad, M., Bruno, E. F., Carter, J. S., David-Ferdon, C., Jandasek, B., Mennuti-Washburn, J. E., O'Mahar, K., & Zukerman, J. (2008). Evidence-based assessment in pediatric psychology: Measures of psychosocial adjustment and psychopathology. *Journal of Pediatric Psychology, 33*(9), 958–980.

La Greca, A. M. (1999). *Manual for the social anxiety scales for children and adolescents.* Miami, FL: Author.

March, J. (1998). *Manual for the multidimensional anxiety scale for children (MASC).* Toronto: Multi-Health Symptoms, Inc.

Ollendick, T. H. (1983). Reliability and validity of the revised fear survey schedule for children (FSSC-R). *Behaviour Research and Therapy, 21,* 685–692.

Reynolds, C. R., & Richmond, B. O. (1985). *Revised children's manifest anxiety scale (RCMAS) manual.* Los Angeles: Western Psychological Services.

Scherer, M. W., & Nakamura, C. Y. (1968). A fear survey schedule for children (FSSC-FC): A factor analytic comparison with manifest anxiety (CMAS). *Behaviour Research and Therapy, 6,* 173–182.

Silverman, W. K., Fleisig, W., Rabian, B., & Peterson, R. A. (1991). Childhood anxiety sensitivity index. *Behaviour Research and Therapy, 37,* 903–917.

Spielberger, C. D. (1973). *Manual for the state-trait anxiety inventory for children.* Palo Alto, CA: Consulting Psychologists Press.

Appendix II: Measures for Adult Anxiety Disorders

Specific Phobia and Social Phobia

This information is drawn from Rowa, McCabe, and Antony (2008).

Social Phobia and Anxiety Inventory (SPAI) (Turner, Beidel, Dancu, & Stanley, 1989; Turner, Beidel, & Dancu, 1996)

Description
- Forty-five items
- Measures social phobia symptoms
- Two subscales: social phobia and agoraphobia
- Available in several languages

Reliability
- Strong, especially for the social phobia subscale
- Excellent internal consistency
- Adequate test-retest reliability

Validity
- Strong for the social phobia scale
- Excellent construct validity
- Also validated for adolescents

Social Phobia Inventory (SPIN) (Connor et al., 2000)
Description
- Seventeen items
- Measures social phobia symptoms
- Norms are available for adults and adolescents

Reliability
- Internal consistency is excellent.
- Test-retest reliability is adequate.

Validity
Construct validity is good.

Panic Disorder and Agoraphobia

The following information is drawn from Keller and Craske (2008).

Anxiety Sensitivity Index (ASI) (Reiss et al., 1986)
Description
- Measures fear of physical signs of anxiety
- Sixteen items
- Available in multiple languages

Reliability
- Internal consistency of .84 to .90
- Test-retest reliability of .75 at 2 weeks

Validity
Excellent construct validity, including convergent, criterion, predictive, and discriminate validity

Body Sensations Questionnaire (BSQ) (Chambless et al., 1984)
Description
- Measures level of fear of somatic sensations during an anxious state
- Eighteen items
- Available in a variety of languages

Reliability
- Internal consistency of .84 to .95.
- Test-retest reliability of .67 (over a median of 31 days) to .89 (corrected over a 3-month period)

Validity
Construct validity is good.

Agoraphobic Cognitions Questionnaire (ACQ) (Chambless et al., 1984)
Description
- Measures the frequency of certain thoughts while respondent is in an anxious state
- Fifteen items
- Consists of an overall mean score and mean subscale scores for physical concerns and loss of control
- Available in a variety of languages

Reliability
- Internal consistency of .80 to .87
- Test-retest reliability of .86 to .92, from a nonspecified time period to a 3-month period

Validity
Construct validity is good.

Fear Questionnaire (FQ) (Marks & Matthews, 1979)
Description
- Measures phobic severity and distress, and related symptoms of anxiety and depression
- Agoraphobic subscale consists of five situation items
- Available in a variety of languages

Reliability
- Internal consistency of agoraphobic subscale ranges from .59 to .84
- Test-retest reliability of agoraphobic subscale of .85 to .89 over various time delays of 1 to 16 weeks

Validity
Construct validity is good.

Generalized Anxiety Disorder

The following information is drawn from Gervais and Dugas (2008).

Worry and Anxiety Questionnaire (WAQ) (Dugas et al., 2001)
Description
- Assesses diagnostic criteria for generalized anxiety disorder
- Eleven items

Reliability
Test-retest reliability is .76 at 4 weeks.

Validity

Construct validity is good.

Penn State Worry Questionnaire (PSWQ) (Meyer, Miller, Metzger, & Borkovec, 1990)

Description
- Measures pathological worry
- Sixteen items

Reliability
- Excellent internal consistency
- Good test-retest reliability

Validity

Construct validity is good.

Penn State Worry Questionnaire—Past Week (PSWQ-PW) (Stöber & Bittencourt, 1998)

Description
- Measures worry over the past week
- A reformulation of the PSWQ
- Fifteen items

Reliability
- Internal consistency of .91
- Test-retest reliability of .59

Validity

Construct validity is good.

Intolerance of Uncertainty Scale (IUS) (Original French version: Freeston, Rhéaume, Letarte, Dugas, & Ladouceur, 1994; English translation: Buhr & Dugas, 2002)

Description
- Measures beliefs about uncertainty
- Twenty-seven items
- Available in multiple languages

Reliability
- Internal consistency of .94
- Test-retest reliability of .74 at 5 weeks

Validity

Construct validity is good.

Why-Worry-II (WW-II) (French version: Gosselin et al., 2003; English translation: Holowka, Dugas, Francis, & Laugesen, 2000)

Description

- Measures positive beliefs about worry
- Twenty-five items
- Five subscales

Reliability

- Internal consistency of .93
- Test-retest reliability of .80

Validity

Construct validity is adequate.

Negative Problem Orientation Questionnaire (NPOQ) (Original French version: Gosselin, Ladouceur, & Pelletier, 2005; English translation: Robichaud & Dugas, 2005)

Description

- Measures a dysfunctional cognitive set that negatively influences problem solving
- Twelve items

Reliability

- Internal consistency of .92
- Test-retest reliability of .80 at 5 weeks

Validity

Construct validity is good.

Cognitive Avoidance Questionnaire (CAQ) (Original French version: Gosselin et al., 2002; English translation: Sexton & Dugas, 2008)

Description

- Measures utilization of cognitive avoidance strategies when dealing with threatening intrusive thoughts
- Twenty-five items

Reliability

- Internal consistency of .95
- Test-retest reliability of .85 over a 5-week period

Validity

Construct validity is good.

Obsessive-Compulsive Disorder

The following information is drawn from Abramowitz (2008).

Obsessive Beliefs Questionnaire (OBQ) (Obsessive Compulsive Cognitions Working Group, 2005)
Description
- Assesses dysfunctional beliefs
- Forty-four items
- Three subscales

Reliability
- Internal consistency is excellent.
- Test-retest reliability is good.

Validity

Construct validity is excellent.

Interpretation of Intrusions Inventory (III) (Obsessive Compulsive Cognitions Working Group, 2005)
Description
- Assesses dysfunctional beliefs
- Thirty-one items

Reliability
- Internal consistency is excellent.
- Test-retest reliability is good.

Validity

Construct validity is excellent.

Vancouver Obsessive Compulsive Inventory (VOCI) (Thordarson et al., 2004)
Description
- Assesses a wide range of OCD symptoms
- Fifty-five items
- An update of the Maudsley Obsessional Compulsive Inventory (MOCI)
- Six subscales: contamination, checking, obsessions, hoarding, just right, and indecisiveness

Reliability
- Internal consistency is excellent.
- Test-retest reliability is not applicable.

Validity
Construct validity is adequate.

Revised Obsessive Compulsive Inventory (OCI-R) (Foa et al., 2002)
Description
- Measures OCD symptoms and impulse-control phenomena
- Eighteen items
- Six subscales: washing, checking, ordering, obsessing, hoarding, and neutralizing

Reliability
- Internal consistency is good.
- Test-retest reliability is adequate.

Validity
- Construct validity is good.
- Convergent validity is adequate.
- Divergent validity of some subscales is questionable.

References for Anxiety Measures for Adults

Abramowitz, J. S. (2008). Obsessive-Compulsive Disorder. In J. Hunsley & E. J. Mash (Eds.), A guide to assessments that work (pp. 275–292). New York: Oxford.

Buhr, K., & Dugas, J. J. (2002). The Intolerance of Uncertainty Scale: Psychometric properties of the English version. *Behaviour Research and Therapy, 40*, 931–945.

Chambless, D. L., Caputo, G. C., Bright, P., & Gallagher, R. (1984). Assessment of fear of fear in agoraphobics: The body sensations questionnaire and the agoraphobic cognitions questionnaire. *Journal of Consulting and Clinical Psychology, 52*, 1090–1097.

Connor, K. M., Davidson, J. R. T., Churchill, E., Sherwood, A., Foa, E., & Weisler, R. H. (2000). Psychometric properties of the Social Phobia Inventory (SPIN): New self-rating scale. *British Journal of Psychiatry, 176*, 379–386.

Dugas, J. J., Freeston, M. H., Provencher, M. D., Lachance, S., Ladouceur, R., & Gosselin, P. (2001). Le Questionnaire sur l'inquiétude et l'anxiété: Validation dans des échantillons non cliniques et cliniques. [The Worry and Anxiety Questionnaire: Validation in clinical and non-clinical samples]. *Journal de Thérapie Comportementale et Cognitive, 11*, 31–36.

Foa, E. B., Huppert, J. D., Leiberg, S., Langner, R., Kichic, R., Hajcak, G., et al. (2002). The obsessive-compulsive inventory: Development and validation of a short version. *Psychological Assessment, 14*, 485–496.

Freeston, M. H., Rhéaume, J., Letarte, H., Dugas, M. J., & Ladouceur, R. (1994). Why do people worry? *Personality and Individual Differences, 17*, 791–802.

Gervais, N. J. & Dugas, M. J. (2008). Generalized anxiety disorder. In J. Hunsley & E. J. Mash (Eds.), A guide to assessments that work (pp. 254–274). New York: Oxford.

Gosselin, P., Ladouceur, R., Langlois, F., Freeston, M. H., Dugas, M. J., & Bertrand, J. (2003). Développement et validation d'un nouvel instrument évaluant les croyances erronées à l'égard des inquiétudes [Development and validation of a new instrument evaluating erroneous beliefs about worry]. *European Review of Applied Psychology, 53*, 199–211.

Gosselin, P., Ladouceur, R., & Pelletier, O. (2005). Évaluation de l'attitude d'un individu face aux différents problèmes de vie: Le Questionnaire d'Attitude face aux Problèmes (QAP) [Evaluation of an individual's attitude toward daily life problems: The negative problem orientation questionnaire]. *Journal de Thérapie Comportementale et Cognitive, 15*, 141–153.

Gosselin, P., Langlois, F., Freeston, M. H., Ladouceur, R., Dugas, J. J., & Pelletier, O. (2002). Le Questionnaire d' évitement Cognitif (QEC): Développement et validation auprès d'adultes et d'adolescents. [The Cognitive Avoidance Questionnaire (CAQ): Development and validation among adult and adolescent samples]. *Journal de Thérapie Comportementale et Cognitive, 12*, 24–37.

Holowka, D. W., Dugas, J. J., Francis, K., & Laugesen, N. (2000, November). *Measuring beliefs about worry: A psychometric evaluation of the Why Worry-II Questionnaire.* Poster session presented at the annual convention of the Association for Advancement of Behavior Therapy, New Orleans, LA.

Keller, M. L. & Craske, M. G. (2008). Panic disorder and agoraphobia. In J. Hunsley & E. J. Mash (Eds.), A guide to assessments that work (pp. 229–253). New York: Oxford.

Marks, I. M., & Matthews, A. M. (1979). Brief standard self-rating for phobic patients. *Behaviour Research and Therapy, 17*, 263–267.

Meyer, T. J., Miller, M. L., Metzger, R. L., & Borkovec, T. D. (1990). Development and validation of the Penn State Worry Questionnaire. *Behaviour Research and Therapy, 28*, 487–495.

Obsessive Compulsive Cognitions Working Group. (2005). Psychometric Validation of the Obsessive Belief Questionnaire and Interpretation of Intrusions Inventory: Part 2, Factor Analyses and Testing of a Brief Version. *Behaviour Research and Therapy, 43*, 1527–1542.

Reiss, S., Peterson, R. A., Gursky, D. M., & McNally, R. J. (1986). Anxiety sensitivity, anxiety frequency and the predictions of fearfulness. *Behaviour Research and Therapy, 24*, 1–8.

Robichaud, M., & Dugas, M. J. (2005). Negative problem orientation (part I): Psychometric properties of a new measure. *Behaviour Research and Therapy, 43*, 403–412.

Rowa, K., McCabe, R. E., & Antony, M. M. (2008). Specific phobia and social phobia. In J. Hunsley & E. J. Mash (Eds.), A guide to assessments that work (pp. 207–228). New York: Oxford.

Sexton, K., & Dugas, M. (2008). The Cognitive Avoidance Questionnaire: Validation of the English translation. *Journal of Anxiety Disorders, 22*, 355–370.

Stöber, J., & Bittencourt, J. (1998). Weekly assessment of worry: An adaptation of the Penn State Worry Questionnaire for monitoring changes during treatment. *Behaviour Research and Therapy, 36*, 645–656.

Thordarson, D., Radomsky, A., Rachman, S., Shafran, R., Sawchuck, C., & Hakstain, A. (2004). The Vancouver Obsessional Compulsive Inventory. *Behaviour Research and Therapy, 42*, 1289–1314.

Turner, S. M., Beidel, D. C., & Dancu, C. V. (1996). SPAI-Social Phobia & Anxiety Inventory: Manual. Toronto: Multi-Health Systems.

Turner, S. M., Beidel, D. C., Dancu, C. V., & Stanley, M. A. (1989). An empirically derived inventory to measure social fears and anxiety: The social phobia and anxiety inventory. *Psychological Assessment, 1*, 35–40.

Appendix III: Measures for Child PTSD

Information on PTSD measures was drawn from Fletcher (2007) and Ohan, Myers, and Collett (2002).

Children's PTSD-Reaction Index (CPTS-RI) (Pynoos, 2002)

Description
- Twenty-item, widely used measure of PTSD symptoms for children and adolescents, although training is required
- A clinician-administered scale; can also be a self-report scale with youths older than 8
- Items based on an adult measure of PTSD, derived from the *DSM-III-R*, except, CPTS-RI deviates from *DSM* nomenclature in that it asks about subjective experiences.
- Subscales: reexperiencing/numbing, fear/anxiety, and concentration/sleep
- Takes 20–45 minutes to administer and score

Reliability
- Internal consistency is moderate to good for the reexperiencing/numbing subscale and adequate for the other scales.
- Interrater reliability appears good: kappa of .89 (Nader, Pynoos, Fairbanks, & Frederick, 1990)
- Test-retest reliability is excellent for short term: .93 at 1 week (Nader, Pynoos, Fairbanks, & Frederick, 1990)

Validity

Convergent validity is supported by the excellent agreement of CPTS-RI cutoff scores with PTSD diagnoses; subscales highly correlate with trauma exposure and depression (Carrion, Weems, Ray, & Reiss, 2002; Fletcher, 1996; Foa, Johnson, Feeny, & Treadwell, 2001; Pynoos, Rodriguez, Steinberg, Stuber, & Frederick, 1998).

Trauma Symptom Checklist for Children (Briere, 1996)

Description
- Child version (ages 7–16) of the adult Trauma Symptom Inventory to assess distress and related symptoms after trauma
- Available in 54-item instrument, as well as in shorter forms, 44-item and 40-item version
- Subscales (Anger, Anxiety, Depression, Dissociation, Posttraumatic Stress, and Sexual Concerns) for children 8–15
- Unlike the Children's Impact of Traumatic Events–Revised, this scale does not orient respondents to their abuse experience and is appropriate for children who have not disclosed abuse, as well as those who have. Thus, the scale may be useful with children who have experienced multiple types of abuse.
- Takes 20–39 minutes to administer and score
- Large normative base of ethnically and economically diverse children who do not have a history of trauma
- Also available is the Trauma Symptom Checklist for Young Children for children ages 3–8, to be completed by parents (Briere et al., 2001)

Reliability
Alpha values for normed and clinical samples ranged from .58 to .89 for the subscales (Briere, 1996; Elliot & Briere, 1994).

Validity
- All subscale scores correlated significantly with each other as well as with the youth and parent versions of the Child Behavior Checklist and with instruments conceptually related to the subscales, including the Child Depression Inventory, the Child Dissociative Checklist, the Children's Impact of Traumatic Events–Revised, and the Child Sexual Behavior Inventory.
- Scale scores were higher among those who had experienced sexual penetration during the abuse.

- Scale scores discriminated between children who had disclosed abuse and children who were evaluated for abuse but for whom abuse was not confirmed (Elliott & Briere, 1994).
- Scale scores were highest for those children who disclosed abuse (credible and partially credible), lowest for children who were believed to have been abused but either had not disclosed or had recanted their allegations, and moderate for children who were judged not to have been abused (Elliott & Briere, 1994).

Child PTSD Symptom Scale (CPSS) (Foa, 2002)

Description
- Twenty-six-item, self-report scale specific to the *DSM-IV* concept of PTSD for youths aged 8 to 15 years
- Reexperiencing, Avoidance, and Arousal subscales, with seven items measuring youths' functional impairment as a result of PTSD
- Takes 15 minutes to administer and score

Reliability
- Internal consistency was very good for the total scale (.89) and moderate to good for the subscales (.70–.80).
- Test and retest reliabilities for the total scales were good (.84) and moderate to good for the subscales (.63–.85).

Validity
- CPSS's correlation with a well-established self-report measure of PTSD symptoms supports good convergent validity (Foa, Cashman, Jaycox, & Perry, 1997; Foa, 2002).
- CPSS's low to moderate correlations with measures of depression and anxiety support divergent validity from other internalizing symptoms.

The Children's Impact of Traumatic Events Scale–II (CITES-II) (Wolfe, Gentile, Michienzi, Sas, & Wolfe, 1991)

Description
- A 78-item instrument that measures PTSD symptoms (intrusive thoughts, avoidance, hyperarousal, and sexual anxiety), eroticism, abuse attributions (self-blame and guilt, empowerment, personal vulnerability, and dangerous world), and social reactions (negative reactions by others and social support) in children who have been sexually abused

- Can be used as a self-report measure for children with good reading skills, though it is recommended that it be administered as an interview

Reliability
Internal consistency was varied among the scales: alpha of .89 for the full scale, and .57 to .89 for various subscales (Wolfe et al., 1991).

Validity
Construct validity of the abuse attributions scores was varied. Social support scales were mixed: The Self-Blame and Guilt scale performed very well with negative reactions; however, the Personal Vulnerability and Dangerous World scales performed less adequately but demonstrated convergent validity and symptom prediction.

Child and Adolescent Trauma Survey (CATS) (March, Amaya-Jackson, Terry, & Costanzo, 1997; March, Amaya-Jackson, Murry, & Schulte, 1998)

Description
- Twelve-item self-report measure modeled after the CPTS-RI and the MASC
- Also known as the Kiddie Posttraumatic Syptomatology Scale and Self-Reported Posttraumatic Symptomatology Scale
- Designed to assess PTSD symptomatology; each *DSM-IV* criterion is addressed with at least two questions

Reliability
- Excellent internal and test-retest reliability
- Alphas of .84 one month after qualifying event and .82 three months after qualifying event

Validity
- Sensitive to treatment change
- High CATS scores were correlated with increased exposure to traumatic events.

Children's Revised Impact of Event Scale-13 items (CRIES-13) (Children and War Foundation, 1998)

Description
- Based on IES from Horowitz, Wilner, and Alvarez (1979), one of the earliest measures of PTSD in adults

- Thirteen items
- Designed to assess reexperiencing, avoidance, and overarousal.
- Four-point Likert scale rating on how many times respondent experienced a symptom in the past 7 days
- Available in several languages and in a parent-report format for very young children

Reliability
Alphas were .70 for intrusion subscale, .73 for the avoidance subscale, .60 for the overarousal subscale, and .80 overall (Smith, Perrin, Dyregrov, & Yule, 2003).

Validity
Previous versions (15- and 8-item) were correlated at .76 and .70 with a symptom count of *DSM-IV* PTSD symptoms.

UCLA PTSD Reaction Index for *DSM-IV* (UPRID Child & Parent Report Forms) (Pynoos et al., 1998)

Description
- Forty-nine items derived from the CPTS-RI and refined to more directly assess *DSM-IV* criteria.
- Designed to assess exposure, responses to the exposure, presence of symptoms, and frequency.
- Selected as primary PTSD screen for the National Child Traumatic Stress Network for children ages 7 to 18 years.
- Can be administered self-report, interview, or group administration.
- Takes 20 to 30 minutes to complete

Reliability
- Internal consistency was .87 for the total and ranged from .67 to .82 for subscales.
- Test-retest reliability was high.

Validity
- Correlated with CAPS-CA intensity scale (.82) and K-SADS-PTSD (.70)
- Sensitivity of .82 and specificity of .87

Appendix IV: Measures for Adult PTSD

Information is largely drawn from Keane, Silberbogen, and Weierich (2008) and Saigh and Bremner (1999).

PTSD Symptom Scale-Self Report (PSS-SR) (Foa, Riggs, Dancu, & Rothbaum, 1993)

Description
It is a self-report counterpart to the PTSD Symptom Scale-Interview, a semi-structured interview schedule.

Reliability
Test-retest reliability for total severity over a 1-month interval was .74, and internal consistency was .91.

Validity
- Concurrent validity was supported by the correlation between the PSS-SR and similar measures.
- The scale showed a sensitivity of .62 and an efficiency of .86 for predicting a PTSD diagnosis.

Purdue PTSD Scale–Revised (PPTSD-R) (Lauterbach & Vrana, 1996)

Description
- Seventeen-item measure corresponding to the *DSM III-R* PTSD criteria.
- Items are rated on a 5-point Likert scale, indicating the frequency of symptoms over the past month.

Reliability
- Test-retest reliability for total severity over a 2-week interval was .72.
- Internal consistency was .91.

Validity
- Convergent validity was supported by moderate to strong correlations with similar scales.
- Scores were higher in participants reporting more severe traumatic events and for those seeking treatment for trauma-related difficulties.

Posttraumatic Stress Diagnostic Scale (PDS) (Foa et al., 1993; Foa, 1995)

Description
- Forty-nine items
- Only self-report measure to assess all six criteria for PTSD in the *DSM-IV*

- Four-part self-report measure of PTSD:

  - Part 1. Thirteen-item checklist of potential traumatic events
  - Part 2. Eight items that determine if an event meets the *DSM-IV* definition of Criterion A
  - Part 3. Assesses the frequency over the past month of the 17 PTSD symptoms
  - Part 4. Assesses the impact of symptoms on various aspects of social and occupational functioning

- Tested with combat veterans, accident victims, sexual and nonsexual assault survivors; excellent norms, good clinical utility, highly recommended for diagnosis
- Validated in other languages

Reliability
- Test-retest reliability for symptom severity was .83.
- Interrater reliability was .74.
- Excellent diagnostic rating for internal consistency and good rating for test-retest reliability

Validity
- PDS had a sensitivity of .82, a specificity of .77, and an efficiency of .79.
- Convergent validity was demonstrated through strong correlations with similar measures.
- Good diagnostic rating for content validity; excellent rating for construct validity and validity generalization

Davidson Trauma Scale (DTS) (Davidson, 1996)

Description
- Self-report measure of PTSD, consisting of 17 items corresponding to the *DSM-IV* PTDS symptoms.
- Manual provides a table for converting total DTS scores into a PTSD diagnosis based on the ratio of PTSD cases to noncases at each cutoff score.

Reliability
- Test-retest reliability for total DTS score over a 1-week interval was .86.
- Alpha coefficients for frequency, severity, and total scores were all greater than .90.

Validity
- Good convergent validity, correlating strongly with other trauma measures

- Sensitive to both differences in clinical severity and to improvement in symptoms as a result of treatment

Mississippi Scale for Combat-Related PTSD (Mississippi Scale) (Keane, Caddell, & Taylor, 1988)

Description
- Thirty-five items selected from an initial item pool of 200 items based on the *DSM-III* PTSD criteria and associated features
- Most widely used measure of combat-related PTSD
- A civilian version is also available.
- For diagnosis, norms are rated as excellent; clinical utility is good.

Reliability
- Internal consistency of .94 was reported.
- Test-retest (1 week) reliability of .97 was reported.
- Internal consistency was rated as excellent; interrater reliability was good.

Validity
- Cutoff of 107 had a sensitivity of .93, a specificity of .89, and an efficiency of .90 against a consensus clinical diagnosis of PTSD.
- For diagnosis, content and construct validity were rated as excellent; validity generalization was rated as good.

Penn Inventory for Posttraumatic Stress Disorder (Penn Inventory) (Hammarberg, 1992)

Description
- Twenty-six-item scale based on *DSM-III* and *DSM-III-R* PTSD criteria
- Excellent psychometric properties in three samples, including combat veterans and civilian trauma survivors
- Internal consistency was .94.
- Test-retest reliability was .96.
- A cutoff of 35 yields a sensitivity of .90, a specificity of 1.00, and an efficiency of .94.

Validity
The Penn Inventory correlated strongly with similar measures and the IES and moderately with level of combat exposure.

Impact of Event Scale (Weiss & Marmar, 1997)

Description
- Originally developed by Horowitz, Wilner, and Alvarez in 1979 and redesigned recently to assess *DSM-IV* criteria
- Twenty-two items
- Available in several languages, used with many different trauma populations
- Takes approximately 10 minutes to complete

Reliability
- Internal consistency rated good
- Test-retest reliability is adequate.

Validity
Construct validity is rated as good.

Keane PTSD Scale of the MMPI (PK) (Lyons & Keane, 1992)

Description
- Forty-six true/false items drawn from the MMPI-2; can be administered as part of the MMPI or alone
- Takes 15 minutes to complete

Reliability
- Internal consistency rated excellent
- Test-retest reliability was good.

Validity
Construct validity is excellent.

PTSD Check List (PCL) (Weathers, Litz, Herman, Huska, & Keane, 1993)

Description
- Designed by researchers at the National Center for PTSD and has been revised to assess criteria in the *DSM-IV*
- Seventeen items
- Civilian (PCL-C) and military (PCL-M) versions available; psychometrics tested extensively for both populations
- Takes 5–10 minutes to complete

Reliability
Cook, Elhai, & Arean, 2005; Grubaugh, Elhai, Cusack, Wells, & Frueh, 2006;; Manne, DuHamel, Gallelli, Sorgen, & Redd, 1998; Ruggiero, Del

Ben, Scotti, & Rabalais, 2003; Walker, Newman, Dobie, Ciechanowski, & Katon, 2002)

- Internal consistency is excellent.
- Test-retest reliability was good.

Validity
Construct validity is excellent.

Los Angeles Symptom Checklist (LASC) (King, King, Leskin, & Foy, 1995)

Description
- Originally known as the PTSD Symptom Checklist, which corresponded to the *DSM-III*, now updated for the *DSM-IV*, to diagnose PTSD and assess symptom severity
- Forty-three items
- Originally tested on veterans but has now been tested on several other trauma survivors
- Takes 15 minutes

Reliability
- Internal consistency is excellent.
- Test-retest reliability was good.

Validity
Construct validity is good.

References for PTSD Measures

Briere, J. (1996). *Trauma symptom checklist for children (TSCC), professional manual.* Odessa, FL: Psychological Assessment Resources.

Briere, J., Johnson, K., Bissada, A., Damon, L., Crouch, J., Gil, E., et al. (2001). The trauma symptom checklist for young children (TSCYC): Reliability and association with abuse exposure in a multi-site study. *Child Abuse & Neglect, 25,* 1001–1014.

Carrion, V. G., Weems, C. F., Ray, R. D., & Reiss, A. (2002). Toward an empirical definition of pediatric PTSD: The phenomenology of TSD symptoms in youth. *Journal of the American Academy of Child and Adolescent Psychiatry, 41,* 166–173.

Children and War Foundation (1998). The Children's Impact of Event Scale (13) CRIES-13. Downloaded on October 16, 2009 from http://childrenandwar.org/wp-content/uploads/2009/04/cries-131.doc

Cook, J. M., Elhai, J. D., & Arean, P. A. (2005). Psychometric properties of the PTSD Checklist with older primary care patients. *Journal of Traumatic Stress, 18,* 371–376.

Davidson, J. R. T. (1996). *Davidson trauma scale manual*. Toronto, Canada: Multi-Health Systems.

Elliott, D., & Briere, J. (1994). Forensic sexual abuse evaluations of older children: Disclosures and symptomotalogy. *Behavioural Sciences and the Law, 12*, 261–277.

Fletcher, K. E. (1996). Psychometric review of the When Bad Things Happen Scale. In B. H Stam (Ed.), *Measurement of stress, trauma, and adaptation* (pp. 443–445). Lutherville, MD: Sidran Press.

Fletcher, K. E. (2007). Posttraumatic stress disorder. In E. J. Mash & R. A. Barkley (Eds.), *Assessment of childhood disorders* (pp. 463–483). New York: Guilford.

Foa, E. B. (1995). *Posttraumatic stress diagnostic scale manual*. Minneapolis, MN: National Computer Systems.

Foa, E. B. (2002). *The Child PTSD Symptom Scale (CPSS)*. Philadelphia: Center for the Treatment and Study of Anxiety, University of Pennsylvania, School of Medicine, Department of Psychiatry.

Foa, E. B., Cashman, L., Jaycox, L., & Perry, K. (1997). The validation of a self-report measure of posttraumatic stress disorder: The Posttraumatic Diagnostic Scale. *Psychological Assessment, 9*, 445–451.

Foa, E. B., Johnson, K. M., Feeny, N. C., & Treadwell, K. R. (2001). The Child PTSD Symptom Scale: A preliminary examination of its psychometric properties. *Journal of Clinical Child Psychology, 30*, 376–384.

Foa, E. B., Riggs, D. S., Dancu, C. V., & Rothbaum, B. O. (1993). Reliability and validity of a brief instrument for assessing post-traumatic stress disorder. *Journal of Traumatic Stress, 6*, 459–473.

Grubaugh, A. L., Elhai, J. D., Cusack, K. J., Wells, C., & Frueh, B. C. (2006). Screening for PTSD in public-sector mental health settings: The diagnostic utility of the PTSD Checklist. *Depression and Anxiety, 24*, 124–129.

Hammarberg, M. (1992). Penn inventory for posttraumatic stress disorder: Psychometric properties. *Psychological Assessment, 4*, 67–76.

Horowitz, M. J., Wilner, N., & Alvarez, W. (1979). Impact of event scale: A measure of subjective stress. *Psychosomatic Medicine, 41*, 209–218.

Keane, T. M., Caddell, J. M., & Taylor, K. I. (1988). Mississippi scale for combat-related posttraumatic stress disorder. Three studies in reliability and validity. *Journal of Consulting and Clinical Psychology, 56*, 85–90.

Keane, T. M., Silberbogen, A., & Weierich, M. (2008). Post-traumatic stress disorder. In J. Hunsley & E. Mash (Eds.), *A guide to assessments that work* (pp. 293–317). New York: Oxford University Press.

King, L. A., King, D. W., Leskin, G., & Foy, D. (1995). The Los Angeles Symptom Checklist: A self-report measure of Posttraumatic Stress Disorder, *Assessment, 2*, 1–17.

Lauterbach, D., & Vrana, S. (1996). Three studies on the reliability and validity of a self-report measure of posttraumatic stress disorder. *Assessment, 3*, 17–25.

Lyons, J. A. & Keane, T. M. (1992). Keane PTSD scale: MMPI and MMPI-2 update. *Journal of Traumatic Stress, 5*, 111–117.

Manne, S. L., DuHamel, K., Gallelli, K., Sorgen, K., & Redd, W. H. (1998). Posttraumatic stress disorder among mothers of pediatric cancer survivors: Diagnosis, comorbidity, and utility of the PTSD Checklist as a screening instrument. *Journal of Pediatric Psychology, 23,* 357–366.

March, J. S., Amaya-Jackson, L., Murry, M. C., & Schulte, A. (1998). Cognitive behavioral psychotherapy for children and adolescents with posttraumatic stress disorder after a single-incident stressor. *Journal of the American Academy of Child Psychiatry, 37,* 585–593.

March, J. S., Amaya-Jackson, L., Terry, R., & Costanzo, P. (1997). Posttraumatic symptomatology in children and adolescents after an industrial fire. *Journal of the American Academy of Child Psychiatry, 36,* 1080–1088.

Nader, K., Pynoos, R., Fairbanks, L., & Frederick, C. (1990). Children's PTSD reactions one year after a sniper attack at their school. *American Journal of Psychiatry, 147,* 1526–1530.

Ohan, J. L., Myers, K., & Collett, B. R. (2002). Ten-year review of rating scales, IV: Scales assessing trauma and its effects. *Journal of the American Academy of Child and Adolescent Psychiatry, 41,* 1401–1423.

Pynoos, R. S. (2002). *The child post traumatic stress-reaction index (CPTS-RI).* Los Angeles: UCLA Trauma Psychiatry Service.

Pynoos, R. S., Rodriguez, N., Steinberg, A. M., Stuber, M., & Frederick, C. (1998). *UCLA PTSD index for DSM-IV (Revision I).* Los Angeles: UCLA Trauma Psychiatry Program.

Ruggiero, K. J., Del Ben, K., Scotti, J. R., & Rabalais, A. E. (2003). Psychometric properties of the PTSD Checklist—Civilian Version. *Journal of Traumatic Stress, 16,* 495–502.

Saigh, P., & Bremner, D. (Eds.). (1999). *Posttraumatic stress disorder: A comprehensive text.* Needham Heights, MA: Allyn & Bacon.

Smith, P., Perrin, S., Dyregrov, A., & Yule, W. (2003). Principal components analysis of the impact of event scale with children in war. *Personality and Individual Differences, 34,* 315–322.

Walker, E. A., Newman, E., Dobie, D. J. Ciechanowski, P., & Katon, W. (2002). Validation of the PTSD checklist in an HMO sample of women. *General Hospital Psychiatry, 24,* 375–380.

Weathers, F., Litz, B., Herman, D., Huska, J., & Keane, T. (1993, October). *The PTSD checklist (PCL): Reliability, validity, and diagnostic utility.* Paper presented at the Annual Convention of the International Society for Traumatic Stress Studies, San Antonio, TX.

Weiss, D. & Marmar, C. (1997). The impact of event scale-revised. In J. P. Wilson & T. M. Keane (Eds.), *Assessing psychological trauma and PTSD* (pp. 399–411). New York: Guilford Press.

Wolfe, V., Gentile, C., Michienzi, T., Sas, L., & Wolfe, D. (1991). The children's impact of traumatic events scale: A measure of post-sexual-abuse PTSD symptoms. *Behavioral Assessment, 13,* 359–383.

Disorders With Onset in Adolescence

8 Eating Disorders

The eating disorders are characterized by disturbances in a person's eating behaviors and distorted perceptions of body weight and shape (American Psychiatric Association [APA], 2000). Pathological fears of becoming over-weight lead people with these disorders to engage in drastic, potentially harmful behaviors that are intended to either cause or maintain weight loss (Garfinkel, 1995). *Anorexia nervosa* (AN) and *bulimia nervosa* (BN) are the two primary eating disorders. A third diagnostic category, eating disorder not otherwise specified, is a residual category at present. It is often used to diagnose people who engage in chronic overeating and seek help for that problem. It may become identified in the future as binge eating disorder, but the APA has yet to develop the diagnosis fully. This chapter focuses on the two primary eating disorders.

Anorexia is distinguished by the refusal to sustain a minimal body weight (85% of what is considered normal for body height and age). This is achieved either by restricting or by binge eating and purging, two types of behavior that represent subtypes of the disorder. *Restricting* anorexics main-tain low weight through dieting or excessive exercise. *Binge-eating/purging* types engage in binge eating, purging behaviors, or both. Another criterion for the diagnosis of anorexia is the manifestation of an endocrine problem, manifested primarily by amenorrhea in females, which is the absence of at least three consecutive menstrual cycles (APA, 2000).

In bulimia, a pathological fear of becoming overweight leads to purging behaviors, such as self-induced vomiting and the misuse of laxatives, diuretics, or other medications. Nonpurging clients rely on fasting or excessive exercise to influence their weight. Binge eating and compensatory behaviors must occur about twice weekly for at least 3 months.

Prevalence of the Disorders

In the National Co-Morbidity Survey Replication, bulimia nervosa was found among 1.5% of the U.S. female population, and 0.5% of the male population (Hudson, Hiripi, Pope, & Kessler, 2007). The lifetime prevalence of bulimia nervosa is 1% of the population. The prevalence of anorexia is 0.9% of females and 0.3% of men. The lifetime prevalence of anorexia nervosa is 0.6% of the U.S. population. Bulimia nervosa, in particular, has increased during the second half of the twentieth century (Hudson et al., 2007). Despite the two discrete eating disorders, it must be noted that the majority of treatment-seeking adolescent and adult cases qualify for Eating Disorder Not Otherwise Specified (Eddy, Doyle, Hoste, Herzog, & Le Grange, 2008).

Comorbidity

Most people with eating disorders, especially those with bulimia nervosa, have another psychiatric disorder. Indeed, three or more diagnoses is the most common comorbidity pattern among both anorexia (33.8%) and bulimia (64.4%) (Hudson et al., 2007). The most common comorbid diagnoses are (in order of occurrence) anxiety disorders, impulse control disorders (ODD, CD, ADHD, intermittent explosive disorder), and substance use disorders (Franko et al., 2005; Hudson et al., 2007).

Personality disorders are often present with eating disorders, with estimates ranging from low to 58% of the time (Cassin & von Ranson, 2005). People with bulimia typically suffer from cluster B (borderline) and C personality disorders (avoidant), while cluster C disorders (avoidant and obsessive-compulsive) personality disorders are associated with anorexia.

As well as mental health problems, people with eating disorders may also suffer from serious health complications (see Rome & Ammerman, 2003, for a comprehensive review). In bulimia, purging behaviors may lead to enlarged salivary glands and the erosion of dental enamel. Even more seriously, electrolyte imbalances and chronic dehydration increase the likelihood of both cardiac arrhythmia and renal failure. Specific health risks with anorexia include starvation and malnutrition, which affects many bodily systems. Endocrine problems may include amenorrhea and metabolic abnormalities. Common cardiovascular disturbances include electrolyte imbalances, irregular heart rate, low body temperature, low blood pressure, and heart failure. The client's behaviors may also produce problems in the hematological system (anemia) and the musculocutaneous system (hair covering the body and sensitivity to cold).

Eating disorder symptoms, whether low level (fasting, dieting, using weight loss drink or powder, skipping meals, smoking more cigarettes) or high level (diet pill usage, vomiting, laxative use), are associated with suicidal behavior in adolescents (Crow, Eisenberg, Story, & Neumark-Sztainer, 2008) and physical and mental health problems in adulthood (see Wilson, Grilo, & Vitousek, 2007 for a review). Suicide is the major cause of death for people with AN (Berkman, Lohr, & Bulik, 2007), and suicide rates for those with anorexia are greater than in the normal population (Pompili, Mancinelli, Girardi, Ruberto, & Tatarelli, 2004).

Course

There is wide variation in the course of eating disorders among studies that follow clients over time in terms of weight gain, maintenance of weight gained, establishment of normal eating patterns, and return of regular menses. For bulimia nervosa, a review of 88 studies indicated that 50% of women had recovered at 5- to 10-year follow-up (Keel & Mitchell, 1997). Twenty percent continued to meet full criteria, while 30% showed bulimic symptoms. The risk of relapse abated after 4 years. A meta-analysis of psychotherapy studies showed that about 40% of women with bulimia who complete treatment recover, although this percentage drops to 32.6% when including those who drop out from treatment (Thompson-Brenner, Glass, & Westen, 2003). These statistics indicate that a good outcome is unfortunately not consistent across individuals, although a substantial proportion recover.

A recent 12-year longitudinal study of German women who had been in inpatient facilities for severe eating disorders found that 27.5% had a good outcome, 25.3% an intermediate outcome, 39.6% had a poor outcome, and 7.7% had died (Fichter, Quadflieg, & Hedlund, 2006). One must recognize that an inpatient sample probably represents a severe eating disorder, so numbers may be more encouraging for people with anorexia who are seen as outpatients.

Another finding is that the "crossover" rate between anorexia and bulimia is high. Thirty-six percent of persons with an initial diagnosis of restricting-type anorexia developed bulimia, and 27% of those with an initial diagnosis of bulimia developed anorexia (Tozzi et al., 2005). The majority of the crossover patterns occurred within the first 5 years of the disorder.

Assessment

Screening for the possibility of an eating disorder should routinely be done during the medical assessment of teenage girls and in situations where individuals, particularly adolescent females, have already been diagnosed with another disorder (Lewinsohn, Striegel-Moore, & Seeley, 2000), as both health and mental health professionals (Hudson et al., 2007) often overlook eating disorders. The assessment of a suspected eating disorder optimally includes the following components (Mizes & Palermo, 1997):

- A standard clinical interview
- Client self-monitoring of eating, binging, and purging behavior
- Questionnaire measures of eating disorders, body image, and other psychopathology (see Appendix for a list of measures)
- A medical evaluation that includes a routine checkup, assessment of risk due to weight loss and amenorrhea, laboratory tests of electrolyte imbalances, and, for individuals with bulimia, possible referral to a dentist for problems related to enamel erosion
- Assessment of comorbid disorders
- A developmental history to attend to issues related to temperament and the possibility of psychological, sexual, and physical abuse

Risk and Protective Factors

Onset

Clinical assessment should include an examination of the risk and protective factors associated with the onset of and recovery from eating disorders. Following the lead of White (2000), we consider anorexia and bulimia together, as they share overlapping risk factors, symptoms, and causes. For a complete delineation of risk and protective factors, see Exhibit 8.1. Some of these factors are further described next.

Exhibit 8.1	
Risk and Protective Factors for the Onset of Eating Disorders	
Risk	Protective
Biological	
Heritability	No parental psychopathology
Preterm and obstetrical complications[a]	
Early pubertal maturation	Late pubertal maturation (14 and over)
Adolescent developmental stage	
Obesity (BN)	Lean body build

Dieting	Emphasis on health and fitness rather than weight[c]
Female gender	Male gender
Homosexuality (males)[b]	

Psychological

Comorbid psychiatric disorders, such as depression and anxiety	No comorbid disorders
Traits such as perfectionism, obsessionality, excessive compliance, low self-esteem, and negative affect/attitudes	High self-esteem and strong sense of identity
Body dissatisfaction and distortion	Positive body image
Poor social skills and isolation	Well-developed social and coping skills
Negative emotionality	Positive temperamental disposition

Social

Family	
Interactional problems in the family	Cohesion and positive communication
Attachment problems	Secure attachment
Inadequate parenting	Effective parenting
Transmission of societal emphasis on weight and appearance	Healthy attitudes about weight and shape
Sexual abuse history	No abuse history
Extra-curricular activities: Involvement in sports and dance that emphasize very low body fat	
Social support	
Social isolation, social anxiety, impoverished relationships, public self-consciousness, and failure to seek social support	Social connection, social skills
Socioeconomic status	
Middle and upper SES	
Societal Values	
Emphasis on thinness as female beauty	Participation in cultures or subcultures that
Economic motives to produce body image dissatisfaction to sell products	do not emphasize thinness as an important aspect of female beauty

[a] Favaro, Tenconi, & Santonastaso (2006).
[b] Muise, Stein, and Arbess (2003).
[c] Kelly, Wall, Eisenberg, Story, and Newmark: Sztainer (2005). For those factors that have not been discussed in the text, see Striegel-Moore and Cachelin (1999).
BN, bulimia nervosa.

Biological Factors

Biological factors under consideration for the eating disorders include heritability, early puberty, obesity, picky eating, and dieting. However, any of the biological features associated with the eating disorders may be attributed to the *effects* of starvation rather than their causes. A recent meta-analysis found that AN is moderately heritable and more so than bulimia (Bulik et al., 2006). Other biological influences may be represented by preterm birth and pregnancy complications, which could lead to neurodevelopmental impairment and the development of eating disorders (Favaro, Tenconi, & Santonastaso, 2006).

Adolescence is clearly a developmental stage that makes females vulnerable to eating disorders. The mean age of onset for anorexia nervosa is 18.9 years; for bulimia nervosa, it is 19.7 years (Hudson et al., 2007). In adolescence tension emerges between the cultural ideal of female beauty and the physical reality of the female body after puberty (Striegel-Moore, 1993). Interpersonal relationships are valued more by females than males, and much of the basis of social success has to do with an emphasis on physical attractiveness.

An early onset of puberty (before age 11) has been identified as a particular risk influence, whereas later-onset menarche (age 14 and over) is a protective factor. Girls who mature earlier may be vulnerable for a number of reasons (Mizes & Palmero, 1997; Striegel-Moore, 1993). Early-maturing girls are typically shorter and heavier and therefore further from the current ideal body type for women. They are also a target for teasing and experiences for which they may not be psychologically ready, such as dating and pressures for sexual behavior.

Certain food patterns, some with early onset, present risks for eating disorders. For instance, picky eating in childhood is a risk influence for thin body preoccupation and possibly anorexia (Agras, Bryson, Hammer, & Kraemer, 2007). Childhood obesity poses a risk for bulimia (Stice, 2002), as does dieting (Lowe & Timko, 2004; Patton, Selzer, Coffey, Carlin, & Wolfe, 1999). The restraint and deprivation associated with dieting may leave some persons vulnerable to binging (Lowe, 2002). At the same time, since dieting is fairly normative among adolescent and adult women, it is the more disturbed eating habits and attitudes, along with dieting, that are associated with the development of eating disorders (Fairburn, Cooper, Doll, & Davies, 2005).

Psychological Factors

The high rates of comorbidity for eating disorders with other diagnoses such as depression and anxiety have already been discussed. Psychiatric disorders place an individual at risk for the development of eating disorders (Patton et al., 1999). In addition, the presence of certain personality traits, such as perfectionism, obsessional thinking, excessive compliance, low self-esteem (Fairburn et al., 1999), negative mood, or negative attitudes (Leon, Fulkerson, Perry, Keel, & Klump, 1999), may put an individual at risk. Negative self-evaluation and perfectionism appear to be more common in those with anorexia than in those with bulimia (Fairburn et al., 1999). Body dissatisfaction and, to a lesser extent, body distortion are also predictors of eating disorders (Cash & Deagle, 1997). Protective factors include high self-esteem, positive self-regard, a strong sense of identity, well-developed social and coping skills, and a positive temperament (Striegel-Moore & Cachelin, 1999).

Social Factors

Four aspects of the social context influence the development of risk and protective factors for eating disorders: family factors, social factors in the immediate environment, socioeconomic status, and the influence of the broader social environment.

Family Factors

Family influences on eating disorders have been noted, but whether this is due to genetic mechanisms, childhood experiences, family concerns about weight, family psychopathology, or transaction patterns is unknown (Cooper, 1995; Wilson, Heffernan, & Black, 1996). In addition, specific types of problematic patterns have not been delineated. Sexual abuse, often within the context of the family, occurs with 20%–50% of people with eating disorders (Yager et al., 2002).

Another family process involves the extent to which parents transmit societal values having to do with weight and appearance (Streigel-Moore & Catchelin, 1999). When parents show excessive focus on their own or their children's shape and size, children may feel pressure to lose weight (Kotler, Cohen, Davies, Pine, & Walsh, 2001). In a prospective 11-year study, fathers' own body dissatisfaction was associated with childrens' thin body preoccupation, as was parental overcontrol of child eating and parental teasing about weight and shape (Agras et al., 2007).

Social Factors in the Immediate Environment

A poor social support system evolving from social isolation, social anxiety, and public self-consciousness may increase the risk for eating disorders. Peer teasing about weight may also be detrimental (Agras et al., 2007). Certain extracurricular activities, such as involvement in sports and dance that emphasize very low body fat, put an individual at risk for eating disorders. Activities that emphasize health and fitness protect against the development of eating disorders (Kelly, Wall, Eisenberg, Story, & Neumark-Sztainer, 2004), as well as activities that presumably involve other aspects of the individual aside from appearance and weight.

Societal Factors

The societal overemphasis on thinness for females often results in eating-disordered attitudes and behaviors. Indeed, increased exposure to media, namely magazine and television, was associated with women's body dissatisfaction, the belief that one should attain the thin ideal portrayed, and more anorexic and bulimic symptoms (Grabe, Ward, & Hyde, 2008). Finally, products involving weight and appearance targeted at females are big business, creating strong incentives for corporations to boost markets for products involving weight and appearance that target women's supposed flaws (Mizes & Palmero, 1997).

Unlike many other mental disorders, high socioeconomic status does not confer protection against the development of eating disorders (Striegel-Moore & Cachelin, 1999). Females from middle and upper socioeconomic classes may indeed be more vulnerable due to increased demands in terms of social compliance and perfectionism.

Recovery and Adjustment

Following the onset of an eating disorder, a similar combination of risk and protective mechanisms are thought to maintain the condition, determine whether a person recovers, or predict responses to particular interventions (Gowers & Bryant-Waugh, 2004). Certain risks, described below, have been identified separately for anorexia and bulimia (Gowers & Bryant-Waugh, 2004; Keel, Dorer, Franko, Jackson, & Herzog, 2005). The bulk of these involve psychological risk influences.

Biological
The prognosis for adolescents with anorexia is better than for adults, but this may be confounded by the duration of the illness (see next section). Adolescents typically have had a shorter duration of an eating disorder than adults do.

Psychological
Certain features of the eating disorder itself put an individual at risk for a worsened course. For bulimia, high baseline frequencies of binging and vomiting, and precoccupation and ritualization of eating, are risk influences, whereas a milder form of bulimia is protective for recovery. For anorexia, an initially lower minimum weight bodes poorly for outcome. For both disorders, a more disturbed body image is problematic for adjustment, as is longer duration of the eating disorder. The implication is that eating disorders need to be recognized and treated as soon as possible.

There are certain features of the illness during treatment for bulimia that present risk or protection. An early change in purging frequency bodes well for recovery. However, having only a reduction in bulimic behavior or a short period of abstinence at the conclusion of treatment puts an individual at risk of relapse. The implication is that a lengthy period of abstinence is needed before treatment should be terminated.

Particular patterns of comorbidity are also a concern. For anorexia, sexual problems and a diagnosis of obsessive-compulsive disorder are associated with poor adjustment. For bulimia, a substance use disorder or a personality disorder present risk, as does high initial perfectionism. Impulsivity is a risk influence for the adjustment from both anorexia and bulimia, as is denial of the eating disorder, resistance to treatment, and low motivation to change. Therefore, enhancing the client's motivation before beginning treatment has gained attention recently and been found to positively affect the rapidity of response to intervention. Failure to respond to previous treatment for anorexia additionally has been linked to worse adjustment.

Social

At the social level, disturbed family relationships before the onset of the anorexia is a risk for poor outcome. For both disorders, support and empathic relationships, whether professional or nonprofessional, are keys to recovery (Bell, 2003).

Intervention

In this section, the range of goals for the eating disorders are first discussed. Then treatments for anorexia and bulimia are covered separately in terms of both psychosocial and psychopharmacological interventions. The reader will note that the treatment outcome literature for anorexia is less developed and conclusive than that for bulimia, and literature specifically on adolescents with eating disorders is lacking.

Goals

The goals of intervention with clients who have eating disorders should center, of course, on aspects of their weight and eating behaviors. It is also important, however, to address clients' body image dissatisfaction and distorted attitudes about food, shape, and weight, as these factors are connected to relapse (Mizes & Palmero, 1997). Listed here is the range of appropriate goals for clinical intervention (Yager et al., 2002):

- Restoring healthy weight
- Reduction or elimination of binge-eating and purging behaviors
- Treating physical complications
- Enhancing clients' motivation to participate in treatment and cooperate in the restoration of healthy eating patterns
- Providing education on nutrition and healthy eating patterns, including minimization of food restriction and increasing the variety of foods eaten
- Encouraging healthy but not excessive exercise patterns
- Correcting core maladaptive thoughts, attitudes, and feelings related to the eating disorder
- Treating comorbid disorders
- Addressing themes that may underlie eating disorder behaviors, such as developmental conflicts, identity formation, body image concerns, self-esteem in areas unrelated to weight and shape, sexual and

aggressive difficulties, mood regulation, gender role expectations,
family dysfunction, coping styles, and problem solving
- Enlisting family support and providing family counseling and therapy
where appropriate
- Improving interpersonal and social functioning
- Preventing relapse

Anorexia Nervosa

Outpatient treatment is indicated for most cases of anorexia (National
Institute for Clinical Excellence, 2004). Inpatient hospitalization is necessary
only when the client demonstrates the following characteristics (Foreyt,
Poston, Winebarger, & McGavin, 1998; Golden et al., 2003):

- Serious physical complications, including malnutrition, dehydration,
electrolyte disturbances, cardiac dysrhythmia, and arrested growth
- Extremely low body weight
- Suicide risk
- Lack of response to outpatient treatment
- Lack of available outpatient treatment
- Comorbid disorders that interfere with outpatient treatment (e.g.,
severe depression, obsessive-compulsive disorder)
- A need to be separated from the current living situation

Inpatient services typically take a multidisciplinary approach, involving psychiatry, psychology, nursing, dietetics, occupational therapy, physical therapy,
social services, and general medical services (Foreyt et al., 1998). Behavioral
reinforcement systems often link weight gain to a client's privileges, including
time out of bed or off the unit and permission to exercise or receive visitors
(Yager et al., 2002). Inadequate weight gain often leads to rehospitalization and
worse long-term outcomes (Steinhausen, Grigoroiu-Serbanescu, Boyadjieva,
Neumärker, & Metzke, 2008). Behavioral programs need not be overly strict,
however, such as those in which caloric intake or daily weight is tied to a
schedule of privileges. Instead, programs in which time out of bed is associated
with continued weight gain are generally effective.

Apparently those with inpatient stays benefit from having some control
over the process and pace of intervention (Bell, 2003). Although rapid and
reliable weight gain might occur in inpatient treatment, some limitations have
been noted for both inpatient and residential treatment (Wilson et al., 2007):

- Disrupted continuity of care
- Separation from the natural environment
- Increased identification with the disorder
- Exposure to thinner and more experienced patients may entrench the
disorder.

Despite these guidelines the research literature offers minimal guidance for choosing among inpatient, day treatment, or outpatient care for different subgroups of people with anorexia (Wilson et al., 2007).

Psychosocial Treatment

For AN, a paucity of treatment outcome research exists. A Cochrane Collaboration systematic review of outpatient psychotherapies for AN found only seven studies, and the authors discovered little evidence to support any particular intervention (Hay, Bacaltchuk, & Stefano, 2004). Much attention in the literature has centered on the Maudsley model, a family intervention that has been used with both adolescents and adults. Developed by Dare and Eisler at London's Maudsley Hospital in the 1980s, it has been manualized by Lock, LeGrange, Agras, and Dare (2001). It is influenced by Minuchin's family systems therapy (Minuchin, Rosman, & Baker, 1978), but there are some key differences. In family systems therapy, the family is viewed as the patient and therapy is designed to alter disturbed family processes that gave rise to the problems in the identified patient (i.e., the adolescent with the eating disorder). In the Maudsley model of family therapy, the family is not seen as the source of pathology and instead is incorporated into the treatment team. The main approach is to help parents to unite and stand up to an externalized illness, and refeed their adolescent until a healthy weight is resumed. This family treatment may include therapeutic techniques from traditional family therapy or other schools of psychotherapy.

Although claims have been made by the model's creators and others (e.g., Keel & Haedt, 2008) about its effectiveness, the modality of treatment in each study (family vs. individual) has been confounded with the target of treatment (weight and eating issues vs. no emphasis). As examples, in Robin et al. (1999), psychoanalytically oriented individual therapy was compared to the Maudsley model, and in Russell, Szmukler, Dare, & Eisler (1987), eclectic individual therapy was compared to the model. Therefore, the results of these studies cannot be adequately interpreted or synthesized (Agras et al., 2004; Commission on Adolescent Eating Disorders, 2005).

Subsequent research has focused on examining different formats and levels of intensity of the Maudsley approach (Eisler et al., 2000; Le Grange, Eisler, Dare, & Russell, 1992; Lock, Agras, Bryson, & Kraemer, 2005) rather than testing it against alternative treatment models. For instance, the Maudsley model was designed as a conjoint family treatment (with parents and the child with the eating disorder present), but it has been tested against a condition in which parents were seen separately from the child (Le Grange et al, 1992). The latter condition was actually more effective for those families that were high in expressed emotion (critical comments toward the person with the eating disorder), even at 5-year follow-up (Eisler et al., 2000). This study suggests that conjoint family therapy and "separated" family therapy may be helpful for AN, but the latter is more appropriate for families with high levels of expressed emotion. Additionally, there are some clinical concerns with the Maudsley model, as some families find the process of forcing the child to eat as required too onerous a process and are unable to complete the treatment. The Maudsley model has played an influence on other family interventions for adolescents and young adults (Ball & Mitchell, 2004; Robin, Siegel, Koepke, Moye, & Tice, 1994), but family therapy has not established itself as more helpful than individual therapy.

Although there have been no studies on motivational interviewing with AN, denial and resistance are hallmarks of the disorder, and clients may not be motivated for action-oriented methods. To help build motivation for change, motivational interviewing may pose a viable method for the initial phase of treatment. Motivational interviewing is a collaborative, client-centered, but directive method in which the client's ambivalence to change is explored with the goal of increasing motivation (Miller & Rollnick, 2002). It has been used as a stand-alone contact or delivered over a brief time frame (four sessions). Hopefully, more studies will address motivational interviewing with this disorder.

Medication

A range of medications have been offered for anorexia nervosa, but most typically the selective serotonin reuptake inhibitors (SSRIs). A systematic review of antidepressant medication treatment outcome studies for adult women with AN located few (N = 6) randomized controlled trials (Claudino et al., 2006). In all, medication did little to improve symptoms. Medication may be more appropriate when anxiety or depression is also present, but in general people with anorexia report psychosocial interventions to be more helpful than medication (Bell, 2003). An assessment of the need for antidepressant medications is usually most appropriate following the client's weight gain, when the psychological effects of malnutrition have resolved.

Bulimia Nervosa

Psychosocial Interventions

Bulimia is typically treated on an outpatient basis. Psychosocial treatment outcome studies typically involve cognitive-behavioral therapy (CBT) and interpersonal therapy, although motivational interviewing will also be discussed.

CBT

Cognitive-behavioral treatment is a package of components that includes self-monitoring, social skills training, assertiveness training, problem solving, and cognitive restructuring. The last of these components involves challenging clients' beliefs and distortions, such as: "To be fat is to be a failure, unattractive, and unhappy," "To be thin is to be successful, attractive, and happy," and "To exert self-control is a sign of strength and discipline." Some of these beliefs derive directly from social values, and the client can be helped to identify the extent to which they are dysfunctional and the nonadaptive ways clients have allowed these beliefs to dictate their lives.

Treatment typically has consisted of 16 to 20 sessions of individual therapy over 4–5 months, although it has also been offered as group therapy (Chen et al., 2003; Nevonen & Broberg, 2006). Lock (2005) and Wilson and Sysko (2006) have described adaptations of CBT that take into account the specific developmental features of adolescence, mainly the lack of motivation to change and the need to include family members in treatment. Several systematic reviews and meta-analyses have been conducted on the use of CBT with BN. The focus here will be on those conducted by the Cochrane Collaboration, since they utilize the most rigorous methodology.

The main purpose of the Hay et al. (2004) review was to assess psychotherapies for binging in both bulimia and binge-eating disorder. Cognitive-behavioral therapy held certain advantages: it performed better than wait-list control for bulimic symptoms and depression, and it was more beneficial for binging abstinence compared to other psychotherapies. Group CBT was found to be as effective as individual CBT in the symptoms of bulimia and binge eating. However, CBT was not any better than other psychotherapies for other bulimic symptoms or depression. In other words, it is yet to be established whether CBT is consistently better than other psychotherapies that are also advantageous over control groups.

Interpersonal Therapy

Interpersonal therapy (IPT) has also been used with BN. As discussed in Chapter 9, IPT was originally developed for adults with depression and then used with adolescents for this disorder. When adapted for BN (Fairburn, 1992), IPT focuses exclusively on interpersonal issues, with little or no attention to the modification of binge eating, purging, or overconcern with weight and body shape (Commission on Adolescent Eating Disorders, 2005). Two studies have compared IPT and CBT and both found that IPT does not achieve as many benefits until follow-up (Fairburn, Jones et al., 1991; Fairburn, Norman et al., 1995). Because IPT seems to work more slowly, Shapiro et al. (2007) recommend that CBT be used before IPT, unless the consumer preference is for IPT.

Motivational Interviewing

Although people with BN are generally more motivated than those with AN, they dread the possibility of weight gain. This ambivalence about what getting better means indicates that motivational interviewing may be a useful treatment option. One group design study has been conducted on motivational interviewing with bulimia. Treasure et al. (1999) randomly assigned women with BN to four sessions of CBT or motivational interviewing. Both groups significantly reduced binge eating and purging over the 4-week period, and there were no differences between groups. The results of this study imply that motivational interviewing may perform as well in CBT in reducing BN symptoms, at least initially, although longer-term outcome studies are needed (Kotler, Boudreau, & Devlin, 2003).

Family Therapy

Family therapy (a modified version of the Maudsley model) for BN has been examined in two recent studies (Le Grange, Crosby, Rathouz, & Leventhal, 2007; Schmidt et al., 2007). From these, Keel and Haedt (2008) determined that family therapy was possibly efficacious for younger but not older adolescents.

Medication and Combination Treatment

As noted earlier, psychotropic medications should not be used as the sole or primary treatment of eating disorders, although they may be helpful in many cases as adjunctive interventions (Bacaltchuk, Hay, & Trefiglio, 2001). Some Cochrane systematic reviews have concerned themselves with the use of antidepressants for BN. Bacaltchuk and Hay (2003) examined antidepressants compared to placebo in 19 trials that unfortunately included few adolescents. The authors found that the likelihood of short-term remission from binge episodes was increased with the use of antidepressants (70% reduction) compared to placebo (50% reduction). No statistically significant difference in acceptability of treatment was indicated between antidepressants and placebo. Although they found no conclusive evidence to support significant differences in efficacy among the three classes of antidepressants (SSRIs, tricyclics, or monoamine oxidase inhibitors), the SSRI fluoxetine was the most systematically studied agent and was found to be more acceptable than other medications. Like others (e.g., Shapiro et al., 2007), Bacaltchuk and Hay (2003) noted that effective doses of fluoxetine (Prozac) are often higher (60 mg) than when the drug is used to treat depression (20 mg).

Most medication studies have been conducted with young adults with bulimia and lacking in severe comorbidity. Although improved, the average client remains significantly symptomatic after a course of antidepressant drugs. Many clients with bulimia who respond well to antidepressant treatment continue to do well if they remain on the medication, but there is also a substantial rate of relapse for them. Even clients who improve during long-term medication treatment appear prone to relapse when medication is discontinued.

Bacaltchuk et al. (2001) focused on medication compared to psychotherapy and in combination with it. When medication was compared to psychotherapy, remission rates from eating disorder symptoms were higher for psychotherapy, and dropout rates were much higher for medication. However, there were no statistically significant differences between mean binge frequency and depression between people taking antidepressants and attending psychotherapy. Results of studies lead the authors to conclude that combining medication and psychotherapy produces few consistent gains over psychotherapy alone when considering other outcomes, including depression and binge frequency.

Summary

Eating disorders have been a major focus of research attention for the past 25 years. Still, practice effectiveness research is not extensive. One of the most glaring limitation of the literature is that there are few studies on treatment with adolescents when the eating disorders typically arise. Additionally, the eating disorders not otherwise specified are the most common diagnosis, but they have not been subject to as much research as the other two disorders. Finally, when treatment is procured, providers do not use evidence-based methods (Von Ranson & Robinson, 2006).

Social Diversity

Some epidemiological studies have been done on ethnic factors as they relate to the eating disorders. Although Caucasian women in Western countries do not have higher rates of diagnosable eating disorders than non-Caucasian women, they do have higher rates of body dissatisfaction and general eating disturbances. This latter effect is especially large between Caucasians and African Americans (O'Neill, 2003). Mexican American and African American women are underdiagnosed and undertreated, mainly in terms of binge eating disorder, which will probably attain the status of a *DSM* disorder in the next edition (Cachelin & Striegel-Moore, 2006).

In Western countries, Asians have a similar risk to Caucasians, if not higher (Wildes & Emery, 2001). There is a lack of existing research on eating disorders as they pertain to Hispanic, Native American, East Indian, and Eastern European women (O'Neill, 2003).

Although eating disorders are more prevalent in females, about 25% of cases are represented by males (Hudson et al., 2007). An emerging research finding is that gay males may be at risk for eating disorders (Muise, Stein, & Arbess, 2003).

Critique

A major critique of the diagnosis of eating disorders that is central to the social work perspective is the focus on the internal deficits of those with eating disorders, rather than emphasizing social and cultural attitudes (Pratt &

Woolfenden, 2002). Both anorexia and bulimia have increased throughout recent decades because of cultural standards of thinness (Keel & Klump, 2003). One of the challenges to prevention efforts is changing the dieting and weight preoccupations that are so culturally pervasive (Mizes & Palmero, 1997).

Another class of critiques has to do with the narrowness of the diagnostic criteria for anorexia and bulimia, which results in many persons with serious eating-related problems escaping diagnosis and the possibility of help. Many researchers recommend more relaxed criteria (e.g., Kotler et al., 2001), and several rationales are offered to support such a change (Lewinsohn et al., 2000). First, a considerable proportion of persons seeking treatment for eating disorders are subthreshold cases, meaning that they do not meet enough criteria for formal diagnosis (e.g., Striegel-Moore, Franko, et al., 2005). As a result, "Eating disorder not otherwise specified" is a commonly used diagnosis, given to nearly 50% of clients, particularly adolescents (Yager et al., 2002). In addition, research comparing full-syndrome with subthreshold cases reveals few differences in terms of clinical and psychosocial characteristics, including levels of comorbid depression, suicide attempts, impaired global functioning, and prior treatment. Further, some women who have subthreshold cases may eventually develop a full-blown disorder. For adolescents, even subclinical cases might result in impaired health (Lewinsohn et al., 2000).

Several issues with the existing criteria for bulimia and anorexia are noteworthy; if some of these were to be modified, a significant number of cases from the eating disorder not otherwise specified category would be absorbed. In examining the criteria for bulimia, one problem is with the term "excessive exercise" for inappropriate compensating behavior. "Excessive" implies a large amount of time dedicated to exercise; yet it is not the quantity of physical activity that is salient, but its compulsive quality (Adkins & Keel, 2005). It has been suggested that the word "compulsive" be substituted for "excessive." Another way to define the criteria of excessive is to ask the client whether the postponement of exercise results in intense guilt and whether it is undertaken solely to influence weight or shape (Mond, Hay, Rodgers, & Owen, 2006).

Other critiques for the diagnosis for bulimia involves the duration of binges, the amount of food consumed during binges, and the frequency criterion for bulimia. Although the criterion is that the binge eating happen "in a discrete period of time," no evidence indicates that discrete binges offer any more clinical utility than episodes that occur over an extended period of time (Franko, Wonderlich, Little, & Herzog, 2004). The binge is required to be "an amount that is definitely larger than what most people would eat." However, many women report subjective binge episodes and then feel compelled to purge but perhaps would not meet the criterion because their binges are not sufficiently large (Franko et al., 2004). Better indicators of a binge episode might be the level of mood disturbance involved or the sense of loss of control (Herzog & Delinsky, 2001, as cited in Franko et al., 2004). Finally, the *DSM* requires that the binge and purge episodes must occur at least twice a week for a 3-month period. However, the decision for this minimum frequency was not based on empirical evidence, and bulimic behaviors less frequent than this may still involve a clinically significant problem (Franko et al., 2004).

Issues particular to anorexia involve the validity of including "amenorrhea" as a criterion; some women who are seriously underweight continue to experience menstruation (Striegel-Moore, Franko et al., 2005). Also, the criterion lacks relevance for prepubescent girls and for males (Franko et al., 2004). Another problem with the diagnosis for anorexia is the weight criterion—85% ideal body weight—and it is suggested that it should be replaced with a criterion with more latitude, such as "substantial weight loss" (Anderson, Bowers, & Watson, 2001).

A final critique involves the subtyping of anorexia (whether binge eating and purging or restrincting) and bulimia (purging or nonpurging). Questions have been generated "as to the utility and validity of these subtypes" (Franko et al., 2004, p. 61). For example, anorexia binge eating-purging type may be more like bulimia than restricting anorexia, which may represent a discrete type of eating disorder. Additionally, the bulimia subtypes may not involve a true distinction.

Case Study

Sandra Benitez, age 16, came in with her mother and sister for a session at an outpatient mental health clinic at her school counselor's referral. The school counselor had called Sandra into her office because she had lost 20 pounds, going from 115 to 95. Sandra did not see this as a problem; she said that she looked like she had always wanted to look ever since she had gained weight when she had entered puberty at age 11. She said she had lost the weight by skipping breakfast, eating yogurt for lunch, and then eating reduced portions at dinner. She had also stopped going out with her friends for pizza, fast food, and desserts. She exercised each day, with 20 minutes of jogging. She used to participate in track every year, but ever since she reached puberty, she no longer could run as fast as she used to. She had tried long-distance running, but she "wasn't any good at it," so she quit and now just ran for exercise.

When asked what she did if she ever overate, she said that every once in a while (every 2 weeks or so), she lost control and would eat almost a whole batch of raw cookie dough, for instance. During those times she would atone the next day by eating even less and upping her exercise routine. She admitted to taking laxatives once but said that it was "cheating" and "gross" and that it caused her stomach to hurt too much.

Despite her weight loss, Sandra says that she still does not like her body: Her stomach sticks out, and there is cellulite on her thighs. If she could get the weight off these areas, then she would feel better about herself. She admits to missing one menstrual cycle. She says the worst thing in the world would be if she were fat, and she would kill herself if she got that way. She denies having a problem: "I am not crazy. Everyone wants to be thin."

In heavily accented English, Mrs. Benitez conveyed that her husband could not attend the session because of his work. Mr. Benitez was an architect back in Argentina who, after trying several related jobs in the United States without success, became a real state agent. He spends a lot of time working now, including evenings and weekends. As a result, Mrs. Benitez says that she is the primary disciplinarian, although the girls (Sandra and her 15-year-old sister, Bianca) give her no problems. She says the family is "close."

She agrees that Sandra has a problem with her weight but that there is no need for counseling. Mrs. Benitez says that she is praying for her daughter. (The family practices the Catholic religion.) She says with God's help, the family can handle this by themselves. She says that Sandra is a model child in all other ways.

After a number of probing questions, Mrs. Benitez reluctantly admits that she would make herself throw up when she was a young adult to lose weight, and she had a period of time when she was severely underweight. She is now overweight and admits that she hates her body.

Mrs. Benitez explained that the family came to this country for economic reasons when Sandra was 7 and her younger sister was 5. However, Mrs. Benitez does not like living in the United States, does not like "Americans," and frequently criticizes the culture. She wishes that they could go back home, but she says the economic situation there has become progressively worse, accompanied by an increase in street violence and crime. She says that the only time she worked outside the home was before she was married. She was trained as a teacher in Argentina but says she is not able to do this in the United States because her credentials do not transfer. She adds that she likes being home when the girls come home from school so she can talk over their day with them. She says that neither she nor her husband has friends in this country.

Sandra, in a meeting alone with the therapist, says that her mother is obsessed with eating and her weight. During mealtimes, her mother does not like anyone to talk to her, so she can "enjoy" her food. She often looks at herself in the mirror, saying she is ugly and fat. Sandra admits that she thinks about food and planning her meals and exercise "a lot." She says that it is better than thinking about "guys," though, and that is what it takes to look the way she does.

Sandra says that her parents have a "terrible" marriage: They have not slept in the same room for most of her life, and her father calls her mother "fat" and "crazy." However, Mrs. Benitez says that she has a good marriage: Her husband is a good provider. Sandra says that the idea of having a life like her mother's scares her. She says her mother just watches TV all day and cleans. Sandra and her mother do the cooking for the family. Sandra is obsessed with cookbooks and planning meals for the family. They make traditional Argentinean meals, such as *guisos*, *mondongo*, empanadas, and homemade pasta.

Sandra says that when she was young, she was her daddy's favorite, but since she became a teenager he now seems to prefer her younger sister, Bianca. She says that he did not notice her weight loss until Bianca pointed it out to him. He thinks she is being silly about not eating and should simply "eat up."

Although Bianca is younger than Sandra, she looks older because she is taller and of normal weight. Bianca is dressed in flashy, revealing clothes and wears heavy makeup with styled hair. This is in contrast to Sandra, who is wearing jeans and no makeup. Bianca says, "It'll ruin my life" if Sandra dies from starving herself.

Sandra admits to feelings of depression (sadness, crying, feeling "heavy" and "low," feeling like her life is over and that she cannot go on living). She says that although she has fantasized about throwing herself in front of a moving car, she would not do anything because of her religious belief that suicide is a sin. She says that her feelings of depression began when she was 14, after a boy she liked for a long time "used" her and dumped her. She says that her feelings of depression fluctuate, depending on the attention the boys she likes give her. She has felt better, she says, now that she exercises regularly and has lost weight. She says she sometimes has difficulty sleeping—initially falling asleep, which might take 2 hours. This occurs on average once a week.

When asked about her other coping mechanisms, she says she talks to her friends, her mother, writes in her diary (mainly about the boys she likes, her grades, and how disgusting she is for eating this or that), cooks, restricts her eating, and exercises. She also likes to spend time reading fashion magazines. Sandra spends a lot of time studying. If she does not get an A, she feels terrible about herself. She says that her teachers like her a lot and praise her performance and her good conduct.

Sandra reports no sexual abuse or physical abuse history. She denies using alcohol or any other drugs. She says she is not sexually active, although she thinks her sister might be. Her sister also gets good grades, As and Bs, and is not a discipline problem, although her sister only has one friend.

Sandra has a small circle of friends with whom she hangs around in school, talks on the phone, and goes places on weekends. She has retained her social life, except for eating out with her friends. Two of her friends were so concerned with Sandra's weight loss that they went to their school counselor, which initiated the clinic visit.

Multiaxial Diagnosis

Axis I 307.50 Eating Disorder Not Otherwise Specified 300.4 Dysthmyic
    Disorder
Axis II V71.09 No diagnosis
Axis III None (according to client and parents' report)
Axis IV None
Global Assessment of Functioning: 65

Rationale for Diagnosis

The eating disorder diagnosis is listed because it is the reason clinical
attention was sought. Each of the criteria is listed here with Sandra's
symptoms in italics:

Criterion A: Refusal to maintain body weight at or above a minimally
    normal weight for age and height: Sandra has lost 20 pounds
    when her body weight was already normal.
Criterion B: Intense fear of gaining weight or becoming fat, even though
    underweight: Sandra says that it would be "the worst thing" if she
    were fat and that she would kill herself.
Criterion C: Disturbance in the way in which one's body weight or shape
    is experienced (*although underweight, she still complains about her
    stomach and thighs not being thin enough*), undue influence of body
    weight or shape on self-evaluation (*Sandra feels better about herself now
    that she is underweight; she feels bad about herself if she overeats*), denial of
    the seriousness of the current low body weight (*she does not think she
    has a problem*).
Criterion D: In postmenarcheal females, amenorrhea. Sandra does not
    meet this criterion at this time; she has missed one menstrual cycle
    rather than three consecutive cycles.
Type—Restricting: *Although Sandra admitted to using laxatives, she used
    them only once, and she generally relies on restricting her food intake and
    exercising.*

Because Sandra only meets partial criteria for AN, a diagnosis of eating
disorder not otherwise specified is warranted. Sandra also meets the following criteria for dysthymic disorder:

Criteria A and C: For a 2-year period, Sandra has experienced feelings of
    depression (sadness, crying, feeling "heavy" and "low," feeling like
    her life is over and that she cannot go on living). These feelings have
    persisted most of the day for more days than not during this time
    frame; she has not been without these symptoms for more than a
    couple of days. Although Sandra has had these symptoms for 2

years, for children and adolescents, only a 1-year time period is required.

Criterion B: Of five descriptors listed, Sandra has insomnia, low self-esteem, and feelings of hopelessness (she needs only two).

Sandra has not had a major depressive episode (Criterion D), a manic episode (Criterion E), or a psychotic disorder (Criterion F). She does not use substances; neither does she suffer from a medical condition (Criterion G).

Criterion H: The symptoms cause clinically significant distress.

Early onset: Onset was at age 14.

The rationale for a GAF score of 65 is that although Sandra suffers from depressed mood and occasional suicidal ideation, she functions well academically and socially and has meaningful interpersonal relationships (e.g., her friends, her mother).

Risk and Resilience Assessment and Treatment Plan

A risk and resilience assessment, as well as accompanying goals to reduce risk factors and increase protective factors, is described in Exhibit 8.2. Although Sandra has been diagnosed with a depressive disorder (dysthymia), as well as the eating disorder, the focus of this assessment is on the eating disorder. Sandra has a number of protective factors, but these are outweighed by risk factors for the onset of the eating disorder. Possible goals have been formulated to address risk by different system levels: biological and psychological at the individual level, and family and societal pressures at the environmental level. To gain parental support for these goals, the social worker must take a nonblaming stance and emphasize how the parents can join together and change some of their own behaviors to help Sandra heal from her eating disorder.

Many goals can be enacted at the individual level; however, Sandra seems unmotivated to work on the eating disorder. Although she admits she spends a lot of mental energy on food and restraining her intake, she does not see any other negative consequences at this point. She says that losing weight has helped her feel better about herself. Motivational interviewing techniques, therefore, might be the first line of intervention. She also might be more easily engaged in addressing her depressive feelings, which are painful for her. The occasional suicidal ideation is of concern and should be addressed immediately. Both cognitive-behavioral and interpersonal therapies are used to treat depression, as well as eating disorders.

Overall, given the risk and protective factors contributing to her prognosis, Sandra's potential response to treatment seems favorable. Although she

Exhibit 8.2

Sandra's Risk and Protective Factors Assessment

Risk	Protective	Goals
Biological		
Dieting	No history of obesity	1. Educate Sandra on healthy eating and exercise patterns
Female gender		
Heritablity: *Sandra's mother seems to have some eating-disordered attitudes and behaviors; whether Sandra's problems have been inherited is unknown. The transmission of these attitudes and ways of coping might have been learned.*		2. Weight gain
		3. Refer for physical exam to see if health problems have resulted from her disordered eating.
Early pubertal maturation: *Sandra experienced maturation at age 11.*		
Adolescent developmental stage		
Psychological		
Comorbid psychiatric disorders: *Sandra reports feelings of depression and suicidal thoughts.*	Well-developed social and coping skills: *Some of her coping mechanisms are writing in her diary and talking to her friends and her mother.*	1. Increase coping skills
		2. Correcting core maladaptive thoughts, attitudes, and feelings related to eating disorder
Perfectionism, obsessionality, excessive compliance, low self-esteem, and negative affect/attitudes: *Sandra studies a lot and exercises daily. Her self-esteem depends, in large part, on her weight, boys' approval of her, and grades. Her teachers and her parents say that she has been a model child up until now.*		3. Reducing and hopefully alleviating depressive feelings
		4. Addressing underlying developmental conflicts; idea formation; self-esteem in areas unrelated to weight and shape; sexual and aggressive difficulties; mood regulation; family dysfunction
Body dissatisfaction and distortion: *Despite being underweight at 5 foot 5 inches and 95 pounds, Sandra still feels overweight and is dissatisfied with her body.*		

Social

Family

Interaction problems in the family: *Sandra says that her parents have a "terrible" marriage and that her father calls her mother "fat" and "crazy." However, Mrs. Benitez says that she has a good marriage—her husband is a good provider.*

Inadequate parenting: *Mr. Benitez is often working and Mrs. Benitez shoulders the burden of parenting.*

Transmission or amplification of societal emphasis on weight and appearance: *Mrs. Benitez seems obsessive about food and has evidenced disordered eating.*

Cohesion and positive communication: *Mrs. Benitez reports that the family is close and that she and her daughters have good communication.*

Effective parenting: *Mrs. Benitez says that she has no discipline problems with her daughters; they are compliant.* No abuse history

Social connection: *Sandra has a few close friends with whom she regularly socializes.*

1. Work on strengthening the marital relationship and the ability of partners to work as a team to help Sandra.
2. Increase Mr. Benitez's ability to relate to his daughter as a young woman.
3. Work with Mrs. Benitez on her eating-disordered attitudes and behaviors; as Sandra's mother, she is her model for female functioning.
4. Increase Mrs. Benitez's social support and range of interests, as she may be overinvolved in her daughters' lives to the exclusion of her own.
5. Teach family members communication skills.

Wider Social Environment

Middle and upper SES: *The Benitez family was of middle SES in Argentina, where Mr. Benitez worked as an architect. He now works many hours to maintain their middle-class status.*

Social emphasis on thinness as female beauty: *Both Argentina and U.S. hold these societal values.*

Economic motives to produce body image dissatisfaction to sell products: *Both cultures are saturated with media images of thin women and advertisements related to shape and weight. Sandra avidly reads fashion magazines.*

1. Build Sandra's awareness of societal values and the extent to which she has internalized these.
2. Explore and discuss gender role expectations.
3. Explore and discuss the family's immigration and acculturation process and its possible impact.

SES, socioeconomic status.

has low weight and there seem to be some problems in family functioning, Sandra does not rely upon vomiting, and she is still an adolescent. Problems have yet to become entrenched.

References

Adkins, E. C., & Keel, P. K. (2005). Does "excessive" or "compulsive" best describe exercise as a symptom of bulimia nervosa? *International Journal of Eating Disorders, 38*(1), 24–29.

Agras, W. S., Brandt, H. A., Bulik, C. M., Dolan-Sewell, R., Fairburn, C. G., Halmi, K. A., et al. (2004). Report of National Institutes of Health workshop on overcoming barriers to treatment research in anorexia nervosa. *International Journal of Eating Disorders, 35*(4), 509–521.

Agras, W. S., Bryson, S., Hammer, L. D., & Kraemer, H. C. (2007). Childhood risk factors for thin body preoccupation and social pressure to be thin. *Journal of the American Academy of Child and Adolescent Psychiatry, 46*(2), 171–178.

American Psychiatric Association. (2000). *Diagnostic and statistical manual of mental disorders* (4th ed., Text rev.). Washington, DC: Author.

Anderson, A. E., Bowers, W. A., & Watson, T. (2001). A slimming program for eating disorders not otherwise specified: Reconceptualizing a confusing, residual diagnostic category. *Psychiatric Clinics of North America, 24*(2), 271–280.

Bacaltchuk, J., & Hay, P. (2003). Antidepressants versus placebo for people with bulimia nervosa. *Cochrane Database of Systematic Reviews, 4*, CD003391.

Bacaltchuk, J., Hay, P., & Trefiglio, R. (2001). Antidepressants verses psychological treatments and their combination for bulimia nervosa. *Cochrane Database of Systematic Reviews, 24*, CD003385.

Ball, J., & Mitchell, P. (2004). A randomized controlled study of cognitive behavior theray and behavioral family therapy for anorexia nervosa patients. *Eating. Disorders: The Journal of Treatment & Prevention, 12*(4), 303–314.

Bell, L. (2003). What can we learn from consumer studies and qualitative research in the treatment of eating disorders? *Eat Weight Disorder, 8*(3), 181–187.

Berkman, N. D., Lohr, K. N., & Bulik, C. M. (2007). Outcomes of eating disorders: A systematic review of the literature. *International Journal of Eating Disorders, 40*(4), 293–309.

Bulik, C. M., Sullivan, P. F., Tozzi, F., Furberg, H., Lichtenstein, P., & Pedersen, N. L. (2006). Prevalence, heritability, and prospective risk factors for anorexia nervosa. *Archives of General Psychiatry, 63*(3), 305–312.

Cachelin, F. M., & Striegel-Moore, R. H. (2006). Help seeking and barriers to treatment in a community sample of Mexican American and European American women with eating disorders. *International Journal of Eating Disorders, 39*(2), 154–161.

Cash, T., & Deagle, E. (1997). The nature and extent of body image disturbances in anorexis nervosa and bulimia nervosa. A meta-analysis. *International Journal of Eating Disorders, 22*, 107–126.

Cassin, S., & von Ranson, K. (2005). Personality and eating disorders: A decade in review. *Clinical Psychology Review, 25*(7), 895–916.

Chen, E., Touyz, S. W., Beumont, J. V., Fairburn, C. G., Griffiths, R., Butow, P., et al. (2003). Comparison of group and individual cognitive-behavioral therapy for patients with bulimia nervosa. *International Journal of Eating Disorders, 33*(3), 241–254.

Claudino, A. M., Hay, P., Lima, M. S., Bacaltchuk, J., Schmidt, U., & Treasure, J. (2006). Antidepressants for anorexia nervosa. *Cochrane Database of Systematic Reviews, 25* (1), CD004365.

Commission on Adolescent Eating Disorders. (2005). Treatment of Eating Disorders. In D. L. Evans, E. B. Foa, R. E. Gur, H. Hendin, C. P. O'Brien, M. E. P. Seligman, et al. (Eds.), *Treating and preventing adolescent mental health disorders: What we know and what we don't know* (pp. 283–302). New York: Oxford University Press.

Cooper, Z. (1995). The development and maintenance of eating disorders. In K. D. Brownell & C. G. Fairburn (Eds.), *Eating disorders and obesity: A comprehensive handbook* (pp. 199–206). New York: Guilford.

Crow, S., Eisenberg, M., Story, M., & Neumark-Sztainer, D. (2008). Are body dissatisfaction, eating disturbance, and body mass index predictors of suicidal behavior in adolescents? A longitudinal study. *Journal of Consulting and Clinical Psychology, 76*(5), 887–892.

Eddy, K., Doyle, A., Hoste, R., Herzog, D., & Le Grange, D. (2008). Eating disorder not otherwise specified in adolescents. *Journal of the American Academy of Child and Adolescent Psychiatry, 47*, (2), 156–164.

Eisler, I., Dare, C., Hodes, M., Russell, G., Dodge, E., & Le Grange, D. (2000). Family therapy for adolescent anorexia nervosa: The results of a controlled comparison of two family interventions. *Journal of Child Psychology Psychiatry, 41*(6), 727–736.

Fairburn, C. G. (1992). Interpersonal psychotherapy for bulimia nervosa. In G. L. Klerman & M. W. Weissman (Eds.), *New applications of interpersonal psychotherapy* (pp. 353–378). Washington, DC: American Psychiatric Press.

Fairburn, C., Cooper, Z., Doll, H., & Davies, B. (2005). Identifying dieters who will develop an eating disorder: Aprospective, population-based study. *American Journal of Psychiatry, 162*, 2249–2255.

Fairburn, C. G., Cooper, Z., Doll, H. A., & Welch, S. L. (1999). Risk factors for anorexia nervosa: Three integrated case-control comparisons. *Archives of General Psychiatry, 56*(5), 468–476.

Fairburn, C. G., Jones, R., Peveler, R. C., Carr, S. J., Solomon, R. A., O'Connor, M. E., et al. (1991). Three psychological treatments for bulimia nervosa: A comparative trial. *Archives of General Psychiatry, 48*(5), 463–469.

Fairburn, C. G., Norman, P. A., Welch, S. L., O'Connor, M. E., Doll, H. A., & Peveler, R. C. (1995). A prospective study of outcome in culimia nervosa and long-term effects of three psychological treatment. *Archives of General Psychiatry, 52*(4), 304–312.

Favaro, A., Tenconi, E., & Santonastaso, P. (2006). Perinatal factors and the risk of developing anorexia nervosa and bulimia nervosa. *Archives of General Psychiatry, 63*(1), 82–88.

Fichter, M. M., Quadflieg, N., & Hedlund, S. (2006). Twelve-year course and outcome predictors of anorexia nervosa. *International Journal of Eating Disorders, 39*(2), 87–100.

Foreyt, J., Poston, W., Winebarger, A., & McGavin, J. (1998). Anorexia nervosa and bulimia nervosa. In E. Mash & R. Barkley (Eds.), *Treatment of childhood disorders* (2nd ed., pp. 647–691). New York: Guilford.

Franko, D., Dorer, D., Keel, P., Jackson, S., Manzo, M., & Herzog, D. (2005). How do eating disorders and alcohol use disorder influence each other? *International Journal of Eating Disorders, 38*, (3), 200–207.

Franko, D. L., Wonderlich, S. A., Little, D., & Herzog, D. B. (2004). Diagnosis and classification of eating disorders. In J. K. Thompson (Ed.), *Handbook of Eating Disroders and Obesity*. Hoboken, NJ: John Wiliey & Sons Inc.

Garfinkel, P. (1995). Classification and diagnosis of eating disorders. In K. D. Brownell & C. G. Fairburn (Eds.), *Eating disorders and obesity: A comprehensive handbook* (pp. 125–134). New York: Guilford.

Golden, N. H., Katzman, D. K., Kreipe, R. E., Stevens, S. L., Sawyer, S. M., Rees, J., et al. (2003). Eating disorders in adolescents: Position paper of the Society for Adolescent Medicine. *Journal of Adolescent Health, 33*(6), 496–503.

Gowers, S., & Bryant-Waugh, R. (2004). Management of child and adolescent eating disorders: The current evidence base and future directions. *Journal of Child Psychology and Psychiatry, 45*(1), 63–83.

Grabe, S., Ward, L. M., & Hyde, J. S. (2008). The role of the media in body image concerns among women: A meta-analysis of experimental and correlational studies. *Psychology Bulletin, 134*(3), 460–476.

Hay, P. J., Bacaltchuk, J., & Stefano, S. (2004). Psychotherapy for bulimia nervosa and binging. *Cochrane Database of Systematic Reviews, 3*, CD000562.

Herzog, D. B., & Delinsky, S. S. (2001). Classification of eating disorders. In R. H. Striegel-Moore & L. Smolak (Eds.), *Eating disorders: Innovative directions in research and practice* (pp. 31–50). Washington, DC: American Psychological Association.

Hudson, J. I., Hiripi, E., Pope, H. G., & Kessler, R. (2007). The prevalence and correlates of eating disorders in the national comorbidity survey replication. *Biological Psychiatry, 61*(3), 348–358.

Keel, P. K., Dorer, D. J., Franko, D. L., Jackson, S. C., & Herzog, D. B. (2005). Postremission predictors of relapse in women with eating disorders. *American Journal of Psychiatry, 162*(12), 2263–2268.

Keel, P. K., & Haedt, A. (2008). Evidence-based psychosocial treatments for eating problems and eating disorders. *Journal of Clinical Child Adolescent Psychology, 37*(1), 39–61.

Keel, P. K., & Klump, K. L. (2003). Are eating disorders culture-bound syndromes? Implication for conceptualizing their etiology. *Psychology Bulletin, 129*(5), 747–469.

Keel, P., & Mitchell, J. (1997). Outcome in bulimia nervosa. *American Journal of Psychiatry, 154*, 313–321.

Kelly, A., Wall, M., Eisenberg, M., Story, M., & Neumark-Sztainer, D. (2005). Adolescent girls with high body satisfaction: Who are they and what can they teach us? *Journal of Adolescent Health, 37*(5), 391–396.

Kotler, L. A., Boudreau, G. S., & Devlin, M. J. (2003). Emerging psychotherapies for eating disorders. *Journal Psychiatric Practice, 9*(6), 431–441.

Kotler, L. A., Cohen, P., Davis, M., Pine, D. S., & Walsh, B. T. (2001). Longitudinal. relationships between childhood, adolescent, and adult eating disorders. *Journal of American Academy of Child and Adolescent Psychiatry, 40*(12), 1434–1440.

Le Grange, D., Crosby, R. D., Rathouz, P. J., & Leventhal, B. L. (2007). A randomized controlled comparison of family-based treatment and supportive psychotherapy for adolescent bulimia nervosa. *Archives of General Psychiatry, 64*(9), 1049–1056.

Le Grange, D., Eisler, I., Dare, C., & Russell, G. F. M. (1992). Evaluation of family treatments in adolescent anorexia nervosa: A pilot study. *International Journal of Eating Disorders, 12*, 347–357.

Leon, G. R., Fulkerson, J. A., Perry, C. L., Keel, P. K., & Klump, K. L. (1999). Three to four year prospective evaluation of personality and behavioral risk factors for later disordered eating in adolescent girls and boys. *Journal of Youth and Adolescence, 28*, 181.

Lewinsohn, P. M., Striegel-Moore, R. H., & Seeley, J. R. (2000). Epidemiology and natural course of eating disorders in young women from adolescence to young adulthood. *Journal of American Academy of Child and Adolescent Psychiatry, 39*(10), 1284–1292.

Lock, J. (2005). Adjusting cognitive behavior therapy for adolescents with bulimia nervosa: Results of case series. *American Journal of Psychotherapy, 59*(3), 267–281.

Lock, J., Agras, W. S., Bryson, S., & Kraemer, H. C. (2005). A comparison of short- and long-term family therapy for adolescent anorexia nervosa. *Journal of the American Academy of Child and Adolescent Psychiatry, 44*(7), 632–639.

Lock, J., Le Grange, D., Agras, W. S., Dare, D., & Agras, W. (2001). *Treatment manual for anorexia nervosa: A family based approach.* New York: Guilford.

Lowe, M. R. (2002). Dietary restraint and overeating. In K. D. Brownell (Ed.), *Eating disorders and obesity* (pp. 88–92). New York: Guildford.

Lowe, M., & Timko, C. (2004). What a difference a diet makes: Towards an understanding of differences between restrained dieters and restrained nondieters. *Eating Behaviors, 5*, 199–208.

Miller, W., & Rollnick, S. (2002). *Motivational interviewing* (2nd ed.). New York: Guilford.

Minuchin, S., Rosman, B. L., & Baker, L. (1978). *Psychosomatic families: Anorexia in context.* Cambridge, MA: Harvard University Press.

Mizes, J. S., & Palmero, T. M. (1997). Eating disorders. In R. T. Ammerman & M. Hersen (Eds.), *Handbook of prevention and treatment with children and adolescents: Intervention in the real world context* (pp. 238–258). New York: Wiley.

Mond, J., Hay, P., Rodgers, B., & Owen, C. (2006). Self-recognition of disordered eating among women with bulimic-type eating disorders: A community-based study. *International Journal of Eating Disorders, 38*(8), 747–753.

Muise, A., Stein, D., & Arbess, G. (2003). Eating disorders in adolescent boys: A review of adolescent and young adult literature. *Journal of Adolescent Health, 33*, 427–435.

National Institute for Clinical Excellence. (2004). Eating disorders: Core interventions in the treatment and management of anorexia nervosa, bulimia nervosa, and related eating disorders. Retrieved July 17, 2009, from http://www.nice.org.uk/nicemedia/pdf/cg009niceguidance.pdf

Nevonen, L., & Broberg, A. G. (2006). A comparison of sequenced individual and group psychotherapy for patients with bulimia nervosa. *International Journal of Eating Disorders, 39*(2), 117–127.

O'Neill, S. (2003). African American women and eating disturbances: A meta-analysis. *Journal of Black Psychology, 29*, 3–16.

Patton, G. C., Selzer, R., Coffey, C., Carlin, J. B. & Wolfe, R. (1999). Onset of adolescent eating disorders: Population based cohort study over 3 years. *British Medical Journal, 318*, 765–768.

Pompili, M., Mancinelli, I., Girardi, P., Ruberto, A., & Tatarelli, R. (2004). Suicide in anorexia nervosa: A meta-analysis. *International Journal of Eating Disorders, 36*(1), 99–103.

Pratt, B., & Woolfenden, S. (2002). Interventions for preventing eating disorders in children and adolescents. *The Cochrane Database of Systematic Reviews,* (2), CD002891.

Robin, A. L., Siegel, P. T., Koepke, T., Moye, A. W., & Tice, S. (1994). Family therapy versus individual therapy for adolescent females with anorexia nervosa. *Journal of Developmental and Behavioral Pediatrics, 15*(2), 111–116.

Robin, A. L., Seigel, P. T., Moye, A. W., Gilroy, M., Barker, D. A., & Sikand, A., (1999). A controlled comparison of family versus individual therapy for adolescents with anorexia nervosa. *Journal of American Academy of Child and Adolescent Psychiatry, 38,* 1482–1489.

Rome, E. S., & Ammerman, S. (2003). Medical complications of eating disorders: An update. *Journal of Adolescent Health, 33*(6), 418–426.

Russell, G. F., Szmukler, G. I., Dare, C., & Eisler, I. (1987). An evaluation of family therapy in anorexia nervosa and bulimia nervosa. *Archives of General Psychiatry, 44* (12), 1047–1056.

Schmidt, U., Lee, S., Beecham, J., Perkins, S., Treasure, J., Yi, I., et al. (2007). A randomized controlled trial of family therapy and cognitive behavior therapy guided self-care for adolescents with bulimia nervosa and related disorders. *American Journal of Psychiatry, 164*(4), 591–598.

Shapiro, J. R., Berkman, N. D., Brownley, K. A., Sedway, J. A., Lohr, K. N., & Bulik, C. M. (2007). Bulimia nervosa treatment: A systematic review of randomized controlled trials. *International Journal of Eating Disorders, 40,* 321–336.

Steinhausen, H. C., Grigoroiu-Serbanescu, M., Boyadjieva, S., Neumärker, K. J., & Metzke, C. W. (2008). Course and predictors of rehospitalization in adolescent anorexia nervosa in a multisite study. *International Journal of Eating Disorders, 41*(1), 29–36.

Stice, E. (2002). Risk and maintenance factors for eating pathology: A meta-analytic review. *Psychological Bulletin, 128*(5), 825–848.

Striegel-Moore, R. H. (1993). Etiology of binge eating: A developmental perspective. *International Journal of Social Psychiatry, 32,* 383–387.

Striegel-Moore, R. H., & Cachelin, F. M. (1999). Body image concerns and disordered eating in adolescent girls: Risk and protective factors. In N. G. Johnson, M. C. Roberts, & J. Worell (Eds.), *Beyond appearance: A new look at adolescent girls* (pp. 85–108). Washington, DC: American Psychological Association.

Striegel-Moore, R. H., Franko, D. L., Thompson, D., Barton, B., Schreiber, G. B., & Daniels, S. R. (2005). An empirical study of the typology of bulimia nervosa and its spectrum variants. *Psychological Medicine, 35*(11), 1563–1572.

Thompson-Brenner, H., Glass, S., & Westen, D. (2003). A multidimensional meta-analysis of psychotherapy for bulimia nervosa. *Clinical Psychology: Science and Practice, 10,* 269–287.

Tozzi, F., Thornton, L. M., Klump, K. L., Fichter, M. M., Halmi, K. A., Kaplan, A. S., et al. (2005). Symptom fluctuation in eating disorders: Correlates of diagnostic crossover. *American Journal of Psychiatry, 162*(4), 732–740.

Treasure, J., Katzman, M., Schmidt, U., Troop, N., Todd, G., & de Silva, P. (1999). Engagement and outcome in treatment of bulimia nervosa: First phase of a sequential design comparing motivation enhancement therapy and cognitive behavioural therapy. *Behaviour Research and Therapy, 37,* 405–418.

Von Ranson, K. M., & Robinson, K. E. (2006). Who is providing what type of psychotherapy to eating disorder client? A survey. *International Journal of Eating Disorders, 39*(1), 27–34.

White, J. (2000). The prevention of eating disorders: A review of the research on risk factors with implications for practice. *Journal of Child and Adolescent Psychiatric Nursing, 13*, 76–88.

Wildes, A. J., & Emery, R. E. (2001). The roles of ethnicity and culture in the development of eating disturbance and body dissatisfaction: A meta-analytic review. *Clinical Psychology Review, 21*(4), 521–551.

Wilson, G. T., Grilo, C. M., & Vitousek, K. M. (2007). Psychological treatment of eating disorders. *American Psychology, 62*(3), 199–216.

Wilson, G., Heffernan, K., & Black, C. (1996). Eating disorders. In E. Mash & R. Barkley (Eds.), *Child psychopathology* (pp. 541–571). New York: Guilford.

Wilson, G. T., & Sysko, R. (2006). Cognitive-behavioural therapy for adolescents with bulimis nervosa. *European Eating Disorders Review, 14*(1), 8–16.

Yager, J., Anderson, A., Devlin, M., Egger, H., Herzog, D., Mitchell, J., et al. (2002). Practice guidelines for the treatment of patients with eating disorders. APA Steering Committee on Practice Guidelines (Eds.). In *American Psychiatric Association practice guidelines for the treatment of psychiatric disorders: Compendium 2002* (2nd ed., pp. 697–766). Washington, DC: American Psychiatric Association.

Appendix: Measures for Eating Disorders

The revision for this edition was drawn from Sysko (2008).

The Eating Attitudes Test (Garner & Garfinkel, 1979)

Description
- Most commonly used self-report inventory for assessing eating disorders
- Forty-item version with 7 factors: food preoccupation, body image for thinness, vomiting and laxative abuse, dieting, slow eating, clandestine eating, and perceived social pressure to gain weight 26-item version with three factors (Garner, Olmsted, Bohr, & Garfinkel, 1982):

  1. Dieting (an avoidance of high-calorie food and a preoccupation with thinness)
  2. Bulimia and food preoccupation (bulimic thoughts and thoughts about food)
  3. Oral control (self-control of eating and perceived pressure from others to gain weight)

- Yields a total score and may be best used as a screening device or as a rough index of treatment progress (Anderson & Williamson, 2002)
- Versions available for children and the non-English-speaking

Reliability
- Overall alpha coefficient = .94
- Alpha coefficients range from .83 to .92 for both the 26-item and 40-item versions (Garner et al., 1982)

Validity
- Although not significantly related to measures of dieting, weight fluctuation, or neuroticism, indicating discriminant validity, scores discriminated between female patients with AN and normal university students.
- Normal-weight females and obese females scored lower than did anorexic patients.
- Twenty-six-item version correlates with 40-item version ($r = .98$) (Garner et al., 1982).

Eating Disorders Examination-Questionnaire Version (Fairburn & Beglin, 1994)

Description
- Thirty-eight-item self-report inventory developed from the Eating Disorders Examination, a semistructured interview
- Takes 15 minutes to complete
- Four subscales: *(a)* restraint, *(b)* shape concern, *(c)* weight concerns, and *(d)* eating concerns

Reliability
- Internal consistency rated good
- Test-retest reliability is rated less than adequate (Black & Wilson, 1996; Wolk, Loeb, & Walsh, 2005).

Validity
- Concurrent validity is strong between Eating Disorders Examination and the Questionnaire Version on purging, but not for binge eating, and higher levels of disturbance are found on the questionnaire version.
- Construct validity data are unavailable (Black & Wilson, 1996; Wolk et al., 2005).

Eating Disorder Diagnostic Scale (EDDS) (Stice, Telch, & Rizvi, 2000)

Description
- Designed to assess AN, BN, binge eating disorder, and an overall score for symptoms of eating disorder
- Twenty-two items

Reliability
- Internal consistency rated good
- Test-retest reliability was adequate (Peterson & Mitchell, 2005; Stice, Fisher, & Martinez, 2004; Stice, Orjada, & Tristan, 2006; Stice & Ragan, 2002; Stice et al, 2000).

Validity
Construct validity was rated as adequate (Peterson & Mitchell, 2005; Stice et al., 2004; Stice et al., 2006; Stice & Ragan, 2002; Stice et al, 2000).

References for Eating Disorder Measures

Anderson, D., & Williamson, D. (2002). Outcome measurement in eating disorders. In W. IsHak, T. Burt, & L. Sederer (Eds.), *Outcome measurement in psychiatry: A critical review* (pp. 289–301). Washington, DC: American Psychiatric Publishing.

Black, C. M., & Wilson, G. T. (1996). Assessment of eating disorders: Interview versus questionnaire. *International Journal of Eating Disorders, 20,* 43–50.

Fairburn, C., & Beglin, S. (1994). Assessment of eating disorders: Interview or self-report questionnaire? *International Journal of Eating Disorders, 16,* 363–370.

Garner, D. M., & Garfinkel, P. E. (1979). *The eating attitude test: An index of the symptoms of anorexia nervosa* (9th ed.). Cambridge, England: Cambridge University Press.

Garner, D. M., Olmsted, M. P., Bohr, Y., & Garfinkel, P. E. (1982). The eating attitudes test: Psychometric features and clinical correlates. *Psychological Medicine, 12,* 871–878.

Peterson, C. B., & Mitchell, J. E. (2005). Self-report measures. In J. E. Mitchell & C. B. Peterson (Eds.), *Assessment of eating disorders* (pp. 98–119). New York: Guilford Press.

Stice, E., Fisher, M., & Martinez, E. (2004). Eating disorder diagnostic scale: Additional evidence of reliability and validity. *Psychological Assessment, 16,* 60–71.

Stice, E., Orjada, K., & Tristan, J. (2006). Trial of a psychoeducational eating disturbance intervention for college women: A replication and extension. *International Journal of Eating Disorders, 39,* 233–239.

Stice, E., & Ragan, J. (2002). A preliminary controlled evaluation of an eating disturbance psychoeducational intervention for college students. *International Journal of Eating Disorders, 31,* 159–171.

Stice, E., Telch, C. F., & Rizvi, S. L. (2000). Development and validation of the eating disorder diagnostic scale: A brief self-report measure of anorexia, bulimia, and binge-eating disorder. *Psychological Assessment, 12,* 123–131.

Sysko, R. (2008). Eating disorders. In J. Hunsley & E. Mash (Eds.), *A guide to assessments that work* (pp. 515–534). New York: Oxford University Press.

Wolk, S. L., Loeb, K. L., & Walsh, B. T. (2005). Assessment of patients with anorxia nervosa: Interview versus self-report. *International Journal of Eating Disorders, 37*, 92–99.

9   Depression

The mood disorders, along with bipolar disorder, are made up of the depressive disorders, which involve two separate disorders, major depressive disorder and dysthymic disorder. *Major depressive* disorder is defined as a period of at least 2 weeks during which a person experiences a depressed mood or loss of interest in nearly all life activities. Symptoms occur in the following domains:

- Affective, including sadness, anxiety, anger, irritability, emptiness, and emotional numbness
- Behavioral, including agitation, crying, flatness of expression, and a slowness of physical movement and speech
- Attitudes toward the self, including guilt, shame, low self-esteem, helplessness, pessimism, hopelessness, and thoughts of death and suicide
- Cognitive, including decreased ability to think and concentrate
- Physiological, including an inability to experience pleasure; changes in appetite, weight, and sleep patterns; a loss of energy; feelings of fatigue; decreased sex drive; and somatic complaints

Dysthymic disorder represents a general personality style featuring symptoms that are similar to, but less intense than, those of major depression. Many people with major depression experience this disorder when in remission from the major episode, but it occurs more often by itself. This diagnosis requires 2 years of a continuously depressed mood. It generally has an early age of onset (childhood through early adulthood) and produces impairments in school, work, and social life.

Prevalence

Depression is the most prevalent lifetime disorder, and it is experienced by 16.6% of the U.S. population (Kessler, Berglund, Demler, Jin, & Walters, 2005). In 2004, major depressive disorder was reported by 6.7%, and dysthmic disorder was present in 1.5%, of the population (Kessler, Chiu, Demler, & Walters, 2005). For older adults, *DSM-IV* diagnosable depression rates range from 0.8% to 8% (Kraaij, Arensman, & Spinhoven, 2002). The prevalence of depressive disorders is 2.8% in children and 5.7% in adolescents (Costello, Erkanli, & Angold, 2006).

Comorbidity

Nearly three-fourths (72.1%) of adults with major depressive disorder experience other disorders in their lifetimes (Kessler, Berglund, et al., 2005). The most common comorbid disorders by far are the anxiety disorders (59.2%), followed by impulse control disorders and substance use disorders. For adolescents in the Treatment for Adolescents with Depression Study (TADS Team, 2007), the most common concurrent diagnoses were anxiety disorders, especially generalized anxiety disorder (15.3%) and social phobia (10.7%), attention-deficit/hyperactivity disorder (13.7%), oppositional defiant disorder (13.2%), and dysthymia (10.5%).

Course

The course of the depressive disorders is variable. Some people have only one episode of major depression, whereas others have recurrent episodes. Some people have episodes separated by many years of normal functioning, others have clusters of episodes, and still others have increasingly frequent episodes as they grow older (Karasu, Gelenberg, Merriam, & Wang, 2002). Some cases are chronic; a large, longitudinal study of primary care patients from clinics around the world found that depression was continuously sustained for a 12-month period for a significant portion (33.5%) of the sample (Barkow et al., 2003). In 20% to 35% of cases, residual symptoms and social or occupational impairment continue between episodes (Karasu et al., 2002).

Untreated major depression typically persists for at least a 4-month period (Eaton et al., 2008; Karasu et al., 2002). Perhaps 50% of people will suffer another episode, at which time criteria for recurrent major depressive disorder are met (Eaton et al., 2008).

Assessment

Information and guidelines follow on the assessment of depression in adolescence and the elderly, as well as how to assess for suicide risk. Assessment tools that might be helpful for screening and measuring treatment progress are provided in Appendix I (children and adolescents) and Appendix II (adults and the elderly). As discussed in Chapter 1, making a least restrictive diagnosis may mean assigning a diagnosis of adjustment disorder with depressed mood when a stressor is associated with the onset of symptoms within 3 months. This diagnosis is commonly assigned in many practice settings, especially outpatient clinics, instead of a more serious mood disorder.

Adolescence

The criteria for diagnosing depression in children and adolescents are similar to those used for adults, with several differences (Waslick, Kandel, & Kakouros, 2002). First, *irritable mood* is a criterion for youths but not for adults, although adults often (about 50%) experience irritability. The *weight loss* criterion is *not* used with children, because children and adolescents are continuing to develop physically and are subject to weight fluctuations regardless of mental status. The *DSM* specifies, however, that youths can meet the appetite and weight disturbance criteria by not sustaining normal standards of growth and weight. For dysthymia, only a 1-year duration is required for adolescents as compared with the 2-year criterion for adults (American Psychiatric Association [APA], 2000).

For conducting a diagnostic assessment with children and adolescents, a greater reliance on collateral reports from parents and teachers may be necessary (Waslick et al., 2002). Current research practice involves counting a symptom as present if *either* the parent or the child reports its existence (Waslick et al., 2002).

Older Adults

The elderly do not typically complain of feeling sad, anxious, or hopeless; they may speak instead of physical ailments (Agency for Health Care Policy and Research [AHCPR], 1993; Bird & Parslow, 2002). Indeed, the elderly tend to show more physical signs, such as weight loss, insomnia, and fatigue, as well as cognitive disturbances, such as memory impairment and difficulty concentrating. However, these symptoms are also common to medical conditions that often affect the elderly, such as diabetes, heart disease, Parkinson disease, and Alzheimer disease. In addition, such symptoms can be brought on by medication the elderly person takes for physical disorders. Moreover, knowledge about depression is scant among the elderly; many do not believe it is a health problem that can be treated. They may see depression instead as stigmatizing—a character weakness or a sign of being "crazy" (American Association for Geriatric Psychiatry [AAGP], 2002). Further, the majority of the elderly view depression as a normal event in older age (Laidlaw, Thompson, Gallagher-Thompson, & Dick-Siskin, 2003). Depression in older adults can thus be difficult to diagnose, and as a result, many cases go undetected. The Geriatric Depression Scale can be helpful in this regard as a screening tool for the elderly, even among those with cognitive disorders (see Appendix II).

Assessment of Suicidal Risk

Once it has been determined that a person suffers from a depressive disorder, it is critical to assess for the risk of suicide, which is associated with the presence of the following (Borges et al., 2006; Fawcett, 2006):

- Suicidal or homicidal ideation with intent or plans
- History and seriousness of previous attempts (a key factor)
- Access to means for suicide and the lethality of those means
- Psychotic symptoms
- Severe anxiety
- Substance use
- Conduct problems
- Family history of, or recent exposure to, suicide

Some social factors involved with suicide attempts include young age, low socioeconomic status, divorce (Borges et al., 2006), and cultural and religious beliefs that promote suicide. For example, suicide may be perceived as a noble way to handle difficulties (Department of Health and Human Services, 2001).

Considering these risk factors, the social worker, in consultation with others involved with the person's care, must determine the least restrictive alternative that will promote client safety (see Exhibit 9.1). A key preventive measure, when people have firearms in their household, is to ask them to remove these items from their home and give them to others for safekeeping. However, one study indicated that even when parents are warned about having firearms, they often do not remove them (Brent, Baugher, Birmaher, Kolko, & Bridge, 2000). Therefore, it is important that social workers discuss with parents and suicidal adults the risk of possessing firearms in the home and monitor their behavior around this issue.

Exhibit 9.1

Options for Care Considering Suicidal Risk

Inpatient	Outpatient	If Outpatient
• Psychosis is present. • Suicidal or homicidal ideation is preset, with significant substance abuse, severe hopelessness, strong impulses to act on the ideas, or specific suicide plans. • Inadequate social support for effective outpatient treatment • Complicating psychiatric or general medical conditions make outpatient medication treatment unsafe.	• Psychosis is absent. • Substance abuse is not a problem • Person indicates control over suicidal thoughts	• Provide education about symptoms of depression and the effectiveness of treatment. • Develop a "no harm" contract." • Advise abstinence from substances, which may increase depressive symptoms and impulsive behaviors. • See clients weekly to monitor suicidal ideation, hopelessness, and substance abuse. • Explain to family members how to respond to suicidal ideas. • Remove firearms from the house.

Source: Agency for Health Care Policy and Research (1993).

Risk and Protective Factors

Onset

A variety of risk and protective factors for the onset of depression have been identified in adolescents (see Exhibit 9.2), adults (see Exhibit 9.3), and the elderly (see Exhibit 9.4). Some of these will be detailed below.

Genetics   *Nature or Nuture or both?*

Major depression tends to run in families, which supports, at least in part, a process of genetic transmission. Based on a meta-analysis of five twin studies, the variance explaining the heritability for major depression is significant, in the range of 31% to 42% (Sullivan, Neale, & Kendler, 2000). (However, this also means that the majority of the variance is environmental in nature.) No specific genetic marker for major depression has been found. Still, certain variations in genes, called *polymorphisms*, may increase one's risk for depression.

Exhibit 9.2

Risk and Protective Factors for the Onset of Adolescent Depression

Risk	Protective
Biological	
Genetic influence	
Female gender	Male gender
Cognitive	
Formal operations stage	
Psychological	
Negative attributional style	Active problem-solving skills
Ruminative thinking style	
Social	
Family	
Weak parent-child attachment	
Maternal disengagement[a]	
Parental criticism and hostility	
Ineffective parenting	
Enmeshed family relationships	
Parental psychopathology, particularly depression	
Child maltreatment	
Other stressful life events	
Peer	
Peer rejection	Peer support and acceptance[b]
Interpersonal stress	
Socioeconomic	
Low socioeconomic status[c]	Mid-to-high socioeconomic status
Neighborhood risk[d]	Cohesive neighborhood

[a] Dietz et al. (2008)
[b] Gutman and Sameroff (2004).
[c] Lemstra et al. (2008).
[d] Gutman and Sameroff (2004).

Genes can predispose individuals to major depressive disorder in various ways. They help control the metabolism of neurotransmitters, the numbers of particular types of neurons and their connections, the intracellular transmission of neuron signals, and the speed with which all of these activities take place in response to environmental stressors. The serotonin transporter gene is the most studied in major depressive disorder. It is known to slow down the

Risk and Protective Factors for Onset of Depression in Adults

Risk	Protective
Biological	
Genetics: a history of depression in first-degree relative	No first-degree relative history
Female	Male
Medical problems[a]	Good health
Psychological	
Negative cognitive style	Active coping mechanisms
Insecure attachment style	
Social	
Family	
Marital problems,[b]	Supportive, intimate relationships
Poor intimate relationships	
Low social support and interaction	Social support and connections
Stressful life events,[c] especially those involving loss[d]	

[a] Ciesla and Roberts (2001); Karasu et al. (2002).
[b] Uebelacker and Whisman (2006).
[c] Kraaij, Arensman, and Spinhoven (2002).
[d] De Beurs et al. (2001).

Risk and Protective Factors for the Onset of Depression in the Elderly

Risk	Protective
Biological	
Sleep problems	
Female gender	Male gender
Medical problems (e.g., Alzheimer disease, stroke, Parkinson disease, heart disease, cancer, and arthritis)	
Psychological	
• Previous depression	
• Bereavement	
Social	
Peer	
Socioeconomic	

Sources: Cole and Dendukuri (2003); Alexopoulos et al. (2001); Shanmugham, Karp, Drayer, Reynolds, and Alexopoulos (2005).

synthesis of the serotonin transporter, which reduces the speed at which serotonin neurons can adapt to changes in environmental stimulation. Given that an acute stressor increases serotonin release, the polymorphism may influence a person's sensitivity to stress (aan het Rot, Mathew, & Charney, 2009).

Stressful life events such as child maltreatment are thought to play a role in adult depression, particularly chronic depression, because of its influence on the serotonin polymorphism (Brown & Harris, 2008). That is, child abuse and trauma alter one's internal stress response, which suggests that a gene–environment interaction may be important in the development of depression. Further, stressful life events may increase the reactivity of the hypothalamic-pituitary-adrenal axis and the release of cortisone, which, over time, may lead to structural changes in the brain (aan het Rot et al., 2009). In contrast, it was observed in two studies that other polymorphisms (known as CRHR1) appear to moderate the effect of child abuse on the risk for adult depressive symptoms (Bradley et al., 2008).

In sum, the biology of depression involves a complex and reciprocal process of the interrelated systems of the brain, about which much remains unknown. This explains why treatment with antidepressant medication, which targets only certain neurotransmitters, often does not lead to symptom improvement.

Cognitive Factors

Increased vulnerability for depression may occur in adolescence because it is a time of life when the capacity for personal reflection, abstract reasoning, and formal operational thought develop. At this stage, youth can first consider *causality* for the events in their lives, and they may develop a *depressive attributional style* (Abramson, Seligman, & Teasdale, 1978). This style attributes negative events to internal, stable, and global attributions ("I failed the test because I was stupid"), while positive outcomes are ascribed to external, transient, and specific reasons ("I passed the test because it was easy"). Adolescence is also a time in development when a *future orientation* develops; with this ability, the adolescent may experience hopelessness about the future (Abela, Brozina, & Haigh, 2002).

Depression is related to significant cognitive distortions, such as Beck's conceptualization of the "cognitive triad" of depression: thoughts about the self as worthless, the world as unfair, and the future as hopeless (Beck, Rush, Shaw, & Emery, 1979). Another aspect of negative thinking patterns involves what has been identified as the "depressive attributional style"

Family Factors

Family factors can present risks for the development, maintenance, and relapse of depression in youths (Diamond, Reis, Diamond, Siqueland, & Isaacs, 2002). Sander and McCarty (2005) conducted a review of family factors and their association with youth depression and concluded that a lack of parental warmth and availability was a consistent risk factor for youth depression. Stress, depression, marital conflict, and social support, in turn, influenced parental warmth and availability. A recent meta-analysis of 45 studies looked at the link between specific parenting behaviors and youth depression and found a moderate relationship (r = .28) (McLeod, Weisz, & Wood, 2007). Hostility from parents correlated in particular with child depression. The direction of causality is, of course, at question since child depression may elicit negative parental reactions or hostility that can give rise to depression in children. A number of studies have indicated a significant relationship between depression and childhood physical and sexual abuse that arises within families (Penza, Heim, & Nemeroff, 2006). Of all types of maltreatment, sexual abuse poses the greatest risk for depression and suicide attempts (Fergusson, Boden, & Horwood, 2008).

Depression in mothers is a particular risk factor for youth depression, for many possible reasons. First, genetic factors may be involved (Goodman, 2007). Other biological factors may include the abnormal neuroendocrine functioning that has been found in women who are depressed during pregnancy. As a result, the fetus may be exposed to increased cortisol levels and experience a reduced blood flow, leading to slower growth and less movement. Psychosocial explanations have also been posited (Goodman, 2007). Maternal needs for nurturing and care can interfere with a mother's ability to meet children's emotional and social needs. Mothers may be emotionally unavailable and feel a sense of helplessness in the midst of parenting challenges. Parents may model depressive affect, thinking patterns, and behaviors for their children and then reinforce their children's depressive behaviors. Depressed parents also tend to see their children's behavior in a negative light, using low rates of reward and high rates of punishment or responding indiscriminately to the child's behavior.

Of course, research over the past five decades has tended to "blame" mothers for a variety of mental, emotional, and behavioral problems in children, so social workers need to be careful not to accept the findings just described as support for that tradition. Social workers should use this knowledge instead to help identify possible depression in parents and apply appropriate services. Evidence is also accumulating that fathers play an important role in families with depressed mothers, either by exacerbating the risk of psychopathology in the child or by protecting the child from the adverse effects of maternal depression (Goodman, 2007).

Recovery and Adjustment

Although a population-based study found few predictors of recovery from, or recurrence of, depression (Eaton et al., 2008), other studies have found some risk and protective factors that influence outcomes (Friedman et al., 2009; Klein, Shankman, & Rose, 2008), including nonresponse to treatment (McGrath et al., 2008). (See Exhibit 9.5.)

Exhibit 9.5

**Risk and Protective Influences for Adult Depression Recovery
and Adjustment**

Risk	Protective
Biological	
Childhood onset[a]	
Familial loading of chronic depression	
Medical problems	
Psychological	
Personality disorders[b]	Absence of personality disorders
Drug abuse	
Comorbid Axis I, including PTSD and anxiety	
Frequency of depressive episodes in adolescence[c]	
Hypochondriasis	
Melancholic subtype	
Social	
Family	
Poor childhood maternal relationship	
Sexual abuse history	
Socioeconomic	
Less than college education	

[a] Crum et al. (2008); Korczak and Goldstein (2009).
[b] Newton-Howes, Tyrer, and Johnson (2006).
[c] Fergusson, Boden, and Horwood (2007).
PTSD, posttraumatic stress disorder.
Sources: Friedman et al. (2009); McGrath et al. (2008).

Intervention

Adults with depression tend to seek help for their disorder about 6 to 8 years
after its onset (Wang et al., 2005). This is seen as a decrease in time to treatment
from the past and is most likely due to national public awareness campaigns,
the marketing of medications directly to consumers, and expanded insurance
coverage. There are several options for treatment of depression that present
certain advantages and disadvantages. These options, discussed in Exhibit
9.7, include psychotherapy, bibliotherapy, and medication. We will also discuss some alternative treatments (see Exhibit 9.6), meaning those that do not
involve professionals, as a significant proportion of people seem to prefer
these (Druss et al., 2007).

Psychosocial Interventions

Compared to antidepressants, the use of psychotherapy to treat depression has decreased since 1996 to 2005 (Olfson & Marcus, 2009). The psychotherapies explored here include cognitive-behavioral therapy (CBT), interpersonal therapy, and family therapy. Alternative therapies are also discussed as many consumers find these appealing. Then we will turn to examining the latest research on treating depression in the adolescent, adult, and elderly age groups.

Types of Treatment
Cognitive-Behavioral Therapy

Intervention research has tended to focus on cognitive-behavioral models. *Behavioral* models focus on the development of coping skills, especially in the domain of social skills and choosing pleasant daily activities, so that youths receive more positive reinforcement from their environments. *Cognitive* models include assessing and changing the distorted thinking that people with depression exhibit, in which they cast everyday experiences in a negative light. Interventions based on cognitive-behavioral models include the following components:

- The identification and restructuring of depressive thinking
- Social skills training (how to make and maintain friendships)
- Communication and social problem solving (how to share feelings and resolve conflicts without alienating others)
- Developing aptitudes pertaining to self-esteem (establishing performance goals)
- Progressive relaxation training to ease the stress and tension that can undercut enjoyment of activities
- Structuring mood-boosting activities into daily life

Interventions involve modeling by the social worker, behavioral rehearsal in the session, and the assignment of homework to practice skills.

Klein, Jacobs, and Reinecke (2007) conducted a meta-analysis of CBT for adolescents with a diagnosis of depression. An overall effect size of .53 was found at posttest for the 11 randomized, controlled trials. At 9 months, the mean weighted effect size was 0.59. Note that the focus on only published studies might have inflated the size of the effect over those found with the reviews above.

Interpersonal Therapy

Interpersonal therapy (IPT) is a psychodynamic intervention but is characterized by its brief nature (approximately 12 sessions). Interpersonal therapy focuses on how current interpersonal relationships have contributed to depression, and the goal of the social worker is to help the client repair and resolve these conflicts (Weissman, Markowitz, & Klerman, 2000). The intervention plan focuses on significant role transitions, grief processes, and interpersonal disputes or deficits. This intervention has been adapted for use with adolescents (Mufson, Dorta, Moreau, & Weissman, 2005).

Interpersonal therapy has been used with Puerto Rican youth in studies. Rossello and Bernal (1999) found that both culturally adapted CBT and IPT produced reductions in depressive symptoms and increases in self-esteem compared to the waitlist control group. Significantly, 82% of the participants in IPT, and 59% of those in CBT, were in the functional range at posttest. In their subsequent study, CBT produced an even greater percentage of improvements (Rossello, Bernal, and Rivera-Medina, 2008).

For adults, CBT is considered equivalent to IPT in effectiveness (Elkin et al., 1995). A recent study comparing the two therapies indicated that persons high in attachment avoidance were more likely to remit from depression if they received CBT (McBride, Atkinson, Quilty, & Bagby, 2006). In future studies it will thus be important to establish which type of treatment is best suited to the characteristics of clients. It is interesting to note in the Cuijpers, van Straten, Andersson, and van Oppen (2008) meta-analysis that IPT was more effective than the other therapies, and these results need replication. Unfortunately, training opportunities for IPT are less available than for CBT.

Family Intervention

Despite the known links between family factors and depression in youth, few studies have explored family-based interventions. In several studies, a parenting component was added to cognitive-behavioral group intervention for adolescents with depression, but no particular benefits were gained by doing so (Clarke, Rohde, Lewinsohn, Hops, & Seeley, 1999; Lewinsohn, Clarke, Hops, & Andrews, 1990).

A systematic review was conducted of studies on family therapy for both children and adult with depression, but the heterogeneous nature of the studies made their synthesis difficult (Henken, Huibers, Churchill, Restifo, & Roelofs, 2007). The researchers' conclusion was that family therapy appears more effective than no treatment or waitlist control, but it is unknown whether it is as effective as other interventions.

Alternative Treatments

As noted, many people prefer alternative treatments for mental health problems (Druss et al., 2007). This is related to a lack of client mobility (disability, lack of transportation, lack of child care), the fact that office visits are only available when work or child care schedules prohibit attendance, region of residence (rural areas where provision of evidence-based treatment is scant and trained providers are lacking), lack of financial resources, or the desire for privacy. Bibliotherapy may also be included as an alternative treatment; it is discussed in Exhibit 9.7, and the others are detailed in Exhibit 9.6.

Exhibit 9.6

Alternative Biological Treatments

Description of Intervention and Its Proposed Action	Research Basis	Implications
St. John's Wort (hypericum extract), an herbal preparation: Although antidepressive mechanism is unknown, may inhibit the uptake of serotonin, norepinephrine, and dopamine.	St. John's Wort is shown to be advantageous to placebo in treating people with major depression and comparable to antidepressants with fewer side effects.[a]	St. John's Wort may be effective with mild depression, yet people should be aware of varying quality across brands.
S-Adenosylmethionine (SAMe), an herbal preparation, is a compound manufactured in the body. SAMe's impact on depression is unknown, but may relate to synthesis of serotonin, dopamine, and norepinephrine.	Regardless of doses, method of intake (oral, intramuscular, intravenous) and comparison or control treatments, SAMe was shown to be equally or more effective than antidepressants and placebo.[b]	SAMe may be effective for depressive disorders with adults. Further trials are needed to determine SAMe effectiveness with children.
Exercise, both aerobic (cardiovascular) and anaerobic (muscle-building), may involve physiological mechanisms, like sleep regulation or creation of endorphins, or psychological mechanisms, like breaking a pattern of negative thoughts and working against the inactivity and withdrawal that characterize depression.	Exercise is shown to be more effective than control conditions and comparable to cognitive therapy in treating clinical depression.[c] For adults who have depressive symptoms, but not clinical depression, exercise had more mixed results.[d]	Exercise may be an effective tool for treating adults and older adults with depressive disorders.

(continued)

Exhibit 9.6

(Continued)

Description of Intervention and Its Proposed Action	Research Basis	Implications
Light therapy, emitted from a box or lamp, exposes the eyes to bright light for a set duration, often in the morning.	Light therapy compared favorably to placebo in treating seasonal affective disorder (SAD) in adults.[e] However, evidence of its effectiveness with nonseasonal depression for both children and adults is mixed.[f, g]	Light therapy appears to be effective with SAD but has uncertain effectiveness for other forms of depression.

[a] Linde, Mulrow, Berner, and Egger (2005).
[b] Jorm et al. (2002).
[c] Mead et al. (2008).
[d] Jorm et al. (2002).
[e] Golden et al. (2005).
[f] Tuunainen, Kripke, and Endo (2004).
[g] Jorm et al. (2006).
Source: Morgan and Jorm (2008).

Age Groups and Treatment
Adolescent

The Weisz, McCarty, and Valeri (2006) meta-analysis targeted psychotherapy of child and adolescent depression and included doctoral dissertations along with the published research. Weisz et al. (2006) located 35 studies and found an overall effect size of .34 with regard to improvement of depression. The authors note that this effect is less than that obtained for the treatment of other child problems. At follow-up, the effects diminished still further. However, the benefits of the interventions held up across variations in their characteristics. That is, for both group and individual modalities, the treatments that focused on CBT (cognitive restructuring and so forth) versus noncognitive treatment, and treatments of varying lengths of time, performed equally well.

Another systematic review was recently published on child and adolescent psychotherapy treatment for depression (Watanabe, Hunot, Omori, Churchill, & Furukawa, 2007). These researchers also required that their studies center on manualized treatment. A particular theoretical framework was not specified, although family therapy was excluded because it did not include a specific focus on decreasing depressive symptoms. Twenty-seven studies were included in this study, and psychotherapy was found to be significantly superior to waitlist or attention-placebo, but not to treatment as usual (nonmanualized interventions).

These reviews offer an important quantitative overview of psychosocial treatment of depression in children and adolescents. Overall, treatment appears to result in a small positive effect on depression symptoms, although these gains appear to dissipate over time.

Adults

Different psychotherapies for depression in adults were compared in a meta-analysis, as follows (Cuijpers et al., 2008):

- Interpersonal therapy (described below)
- Psychodynamic therapy
- Nondirective supportive treatment, defined as any unstructured therapy without specific techniques such as offering empathy and helping people to ventilate their experiences and emotions
- CBT (detailed in the next section)
- Behavioral activation treatment, a type of CBT centering on activity scheduling and increasing pleasant activities
- Problem-solving therapy, which focuses on behaviorally defining specific problems, brainstorming ideas to solve them, and deciding upon and implementing solutions.

The authors found that none of the treatments were appreciably more efficacious than others, except for interpersonal therapy (which was superior to others at a small effect size) and nondirective, supportive therapy (which was less effective than the others at a very small effect). The authors hypothesized that the high dropout rate found for CBT might have been due to the difficulty people find in working on cognitive processes and the requirement of homework. The dropout rate was statistically lower for problem-solving therapy. The authors believed this may have been due to the fact that problem-solving directly addressed clients' presenting concerns. Behavioral activation treatment and problem solving are relatively simpler treatments than the full CBT package and may be just as effective (Cuijpers, van Straten, & Warmerdam, 2007a, 2007b). One limitation of the Cuijpers et al. (2008) meta-analysis, although the findings are interesting, is that effect sizes calculated were nonindependent, which means that comparison groups were sometimes counted more than once. This may render the results less valid.

Older Adults

Little methodologically strong research has been undertaken on psychotherapy with older adults. In one recent systematic review, only seven small trials were found, totaling 153 participants (Wilson, Mottram, & Vassilas, 2008). In the five studies that compared CBT to controls, CBT was more effective, but when compared to active controls, differences were less clear. In the three trials that compared CBT and psychodynamic interventions, no differences were found. Although the results are encouraging for CBT and psychodynamic interventions, further research will have to determine whether these psychotherapies can outperform active control conditions.

In a review of the qualitative literature on depression in the elderly, the importance of social support was the most frequently cited means of coping with depression, preventing it, and curing it once it had begun (Corcoran, 2009). Older people also saw a lack of social support either because of death of loved ones or because of neglect or conflict with family members as the reason for depression. Social workers, therefore, may help older clients with depression link to social supports (particularly informal social support) and repair family conflicts. Older people also saw activity as a way to dispel depression. Therefore, a behavioral activation approach may be an initial way to approach intervention before trying a more complicated intervention. Religion and spirituality were further mentioned as ways to alleviate depression. These coping mechanisms included prayer, meditation, or speaking with a spiritual leader. An implication is that a social worker can inquire about the potential benefits of religion or spiritual practices in helping a depressed older adult.

Medication

The use of antidepressants has increased drastically in recent years from 5.84% in 1996 to 10.12% in the United States in 2005 (Olfson & Marcus, 2009). At the same time, the use of antipsychotics to treat depression has also increased. Most medications are prescribed by general practitioners rather than psychiatrists.

The tricyclic antidepressants, so named because of their chemical structure, were the most commonly prescribed antidepressants through the 1980s. They work by blocking the reuptake of norepinephrine and serotonin and, to a lesser extent, dopamine (Bentley & Walsh, 2006). The newer antidepressants are characterized by their actions on serotonin. The selective serotonin reuptake inhibitor (SSRI) drugs block serotonin but in general do not interfere with the normal actions of norepinephrine. The dual serotonin and norepinephrine reuptake inhibitors (SNRIs) do not interfere with other chemicals that are affected by the cyclic antidepressants to cause adverse effects.

Youth

Although the tricyclic medications have been studied in relation to depression, the available evidence is that they are not effective for children and show little benefit for adolescents (see Brown et al., 2007 for a review). Despite the rise in popularity in the SSRIs, a recent downturn has occurred in prescribing rates due to concerns about increased suicidal risk in youth taking antidepressants. Indeed, the United Kingdom has now banned the SSRIs for youth 18 and younger, and in 2004, The Food and Drug Advisory Administration (2004) issued a "black box" warning label on SSRIs about this risk. As a result of these concerns, recent reviews on the SSRIs not only concentrate on outcome but also suicide risk.

The Hetrick, Merry, McKenzie, Sindahl, and Proctor (2007) and Bridge et al. (2007) meta-analyses will be a focus here because of their comprehensiveness in inclusion of studies and otherwise strong methodologies. In examining the SSRI treatment outcome studies in youth overall, Hetrick et al. found significant improvement in depression compared to placebo but also 80% greater risk of a suicide event, which was defined as suicidal ideation or an attempt. Interestingly, the reason for increased risk is unknown and does not seem related to the effectiveness of the medication (Bridge et al., 2007).

Separate results for the different SSRIs have been aggregated, when data were available from the primary studies. Prozac (fluoxetine) and Zoloft (sertraline) have shown sufficient efficacy for adolescents, but only Prozac has received sufficient support for children (Bridge et al., 2007; Usala, Clavenna, Zuddas, & Bonati, 2008; Whittington, Kendall, Fonagy, Cottrell, & Cotgrove, 2004). The reason why depressed children respond better to fluoxetine compared with other agents is unclear but could be due to study quality, location, or properties of the medication itself, such as its long half-life (Bridge et al., 2007).

From the findings of these meta-analyses, practitioners should educate youth and their families about the potential benefits and risks of SSRIs and help them consider various options for treatment. The risk of suicide should be assessed and, if medication is used, it should be closely monitored. The FDA recommends that teens be seen more frequently in the first 3 months after a new prescription is issued (Leslie, Newman, Chesney, & Perrin, 2005). However, Richardson, Lewis, Casey-Goldstein, McCauley, and Katon (2007) cite evidence that this recommendation is only met in about 30% of cases, and a greater proportion of teens (40%) are not seen even once during this time. The Richardon et al. (2007) focus group study with pediatric providers found that few were aware of the FDA recommendation; they were also concerned that youth and families would not come to additional appointments because they were already irregular in attending scheduled appointments.

Several large-scale studies have recently been conducted testing the differential effects of medication and CBT and their combination (Melvin et al., 2006; TADS Team, 2007). Their findings have been mixed as to whether combined treatment is superior to monotherapy (either medication or CBT). Adolescents who were nonresponsive to an initial trial of treatment were the focus of additional studies (Brent et al., 2008; Goodyer et al., 2008), but again findings were not conclusive across studies. In Brent et al. (2008), the most advantageous condition was a switch to another SSRI with the addition of CBT, but in the British ADAPT trial (Goodyer et al., 2008), an SSRI was sufficient in treating depressed teens who had not initially responded to a brief psychosocial intervention. Based on these studies, definitive conclusions are not possible as to whether teens with depression are best served through CBT, medication, or their combination.

Exhibit 9.7

Type of Treatments, Benefits, Costs, Indications, and Contraindications

Type of Treatment	Benefits	Limitations	Indications and Contraindications
Medication	1. Ease of administration 2. Effective for all severity levels of depression (mild, moderate, and severe) 3. Rapid response is possible (4-6 weeks)	1. Need for monitoring for response 2. Side effects 3. Can be used for suicide attempts 4. Nonadherence is high 5. Not effective in all cases 6. Often takes a process of trial and error to find the appropriate medication and dosage.	1. History of prior positive response 2. History of first-degree relatives' positive response 3. For severe depression 4. For melancholic depression 5. If there is adherence to medication regime 6. Client preference 7. Experience of doctor with the medication 8. Medical illnesses or other medications that make antidepressant use risky 9. Cost considerations
Psychotherapy	1. Lack of physiological side effects 2. Individual learns to cope with or avoid factors that precipitate episodes	1. Not recommended as sole treatment for severe depression 2. Many fail to complete course of treatment 3. Need high-quality treatment; availability of well-trained practitioners 4. Sessions time-consuming	1. Because of cost-effectiveness, cognitive-behavioral therapy recommended as a first-line treatment (Antonuccio, Thomas, & Danton, 1997). 2. For mild, moderate, or chronic depression 3. When psychosocial stress, difficulty coping, and interpersonal problems are present 4. Client preference 5. In cases of pregnancy, lactation, or the desire to become pregnant

Combined medication and psychotherapy treatment (Arnow & Constantino, 2003)	Same as above	Same as above	1. For severe depression 2. Recommended if psychotherapy alone has not been successful (Antonuccio et al., 1997) 3. A history of psychosocial problems, with and without depression 4. History of problems with treatment adherence
Bibliotherapy	1. For mild to moderate depression 2. Found more effective than no treatment (Gregory, Canning, Lee, & Wise, 2004) 3. Client can work at own pace at home 4. Client can receive services if geographical or transportation barriers are an issue. 5. Cost-effective for those unable to afford medication or psychotherapy 6. Provides skills for coping after treatment has ended	1. Not appropriate for severe depression 2. Not appropriate for those who are unmotivated, have low reading ability or cognitive impairments, or have not responded to individual therapy	*Feeling Good* (Burns, 1999) and *Control Your Depression* (Lewinsohn, Munoz, Youngren, & Zeiss, 1986) have been empirically validated, but many other self-help books available have not been researched.

Sources: Karasu et al. (2002); AHCPR (1993).

Adults

Through the 1980s the tricylic antidepressants were usually prescribed for the treatment of depression. Today, however, it is commonly believed that the SSRIs are more effective. Still, a meta-analysis of 102 randomized controlled trials (10,706 patients) found no overall difference in efficacy between the SSRIs and tricyclics, although the tricyclics appear more effective in inpatient settings (Anderson, 2000). At the same time, the SSRIs are better tolerated, with significantly lower rates of treatment discontinuation overall. The same pattern of results—similar efficacy but more adverse effects with the tricyclics—were found in a systematic review of medication for older people with depression (Mottram, Wilson, & Strobl, 2006).

In general, it is difficult to predict how a certain individual will react to a particular medication. The process of finding an appropriate medication and dosage is one of trial and error (Healy, 2002). One interesting finding from a meta-analysis of 96 studies that compared antidepressant medication and placebo is that the placebo effect accounted for 68% of improvement from depression, while medication effects accounted for the smaller proportion (Rief et al., 2009). Therefore, it seems that the major influence of antidepressants may be due to placebo or people's expectation that they will get better.

Recent evidence suggests that an early treatment response to antidepressants (within the first 2 weeks) might predict whether a person ends up doing well on a particular medication (Szegedi et al., 2009). The authors of this meta-analysis concluded that a lack of improvement during the first 2 weeks on a drug may indicate that changes in depression management should be considered.

In terms of particular medications that may confer advantages, at least in grouped data, a recent systematic review compared the efficacy of different SSRIs and other new antidepressants for the treatment of depression (Cipriani et al., 2009). Mirtazapine (Remeron), escitalopram (Lexapro), venlafaxine (Effexor), and setraline (Zoloft) showed statistically significant improvements on depression compared to duloextenine (Cymbalta), fluoxetine (Prozac), fluvoxamine (Luvox), paroxetine (Paxil), and reboxetine (Edronax, Vestra). The latter medication showed a lesser effect compared to the others. Lexapro and Zoloft were more acceptable to consumers, leading to less discontinuation than some of the others.

Although, as mentioned, concerns have been raised about the use of medication with youth because of the risk of suicidality, a recent systematic review indicated that for adults (after young adulthood) and the elderly, the SSRIs reduce rather than increase risk of suicide (Barbui, Esposito, & Cipriani, 2009).

Many people in clinical settings are offered both medication and psychosocial intervention, but it is unknown if there is an additive effect. A meta-analysis was conducted comparing psychotherapy to combined psychotherapy and medication, including 19 studies and 1,838 participants

(Cuijpers, van Straten, Warmerdam, & Andersson, 2009). A limitation of this review is that there was some nonindependence (i.e., some study comparison groups were counted more than once). Still, this meta-analysis is discussed here to provide some illumination into the issue of the potential benefit of combined treatments over single treatment. A small effect size (SMD = 0.35) was found at posttest, indicating an advantage of combined treatments, but at follow-up any benefit had disappeared when CBT was used as the psychotherapy condition. Therefore, according to the results of this study, if CBT is used to treat depression, then there is little advantage of also offering medication.

Older Adults

Another meta-analysis was undertaken on the efficacy of second-generation antidepressants, which included the SSRIs and newer agents (i.e., buproprion, mirtazapine, venlafaxine, and duloxetine) (Nelson, Delucchi, & Schneider, 2008). When pooling the 10 studies that met inclusion criteria, a 10% improvement on depression was found over placebo, but many people had to discontinue drug treatment because of adverse side effects. Therefore, a careful weighing of the risks and benefits is needed to determine whether these agents will be helpful with a depressed older person's treatment.

Social Diversity

As we have already discussed youth and older adults with depression, here we will explore treatment and its relevance to females, sexual minorities and diverse cultural groups.

Gender

In epidemiological, community, and clinical youth samples, depression is consistently found to be much more prevalent (about twice the rate) in females than in males (Kovacs, 2001). This gender gap, which emerges by age 14, is found internationally—across Canada, Great Britain, and the United States (Wade, Cairney, & Pevalin, 2002)—and persists across the life span (Kessler, 2003) into old age (Barry, Allore, Guo, Bruce, & Gill, 2008). It does not appear to be related to either reporting bias or help-seeking behaviors (Kessler, 2003).

Various biological and psychosocial reasons have been postulated for the gender gap in depression. Biological theories consider the hormonal shifts females experience during premenses, pregnancy, postpartum, and menopause (Desai & Jann, 2000). One set of researchers studied the pubertal development of 100 Caucasian girls between age 10 and 14 and found that early puberty predicted higher levels of emotional arousal, which in turn predicted increased depressive affect (Graber, Brooks-Gunn, & Warren, 2006). In this sample, negative life events and attention difficulties appeared to stimulate the production of certain biochemicals associated with depression and aggression.

Regarding adulthood, almost one-fifth of women (19.2%) have a major depressive episode during the first 3 months postpartum (Gavin et al., 2005). The specific mechanisms by which hormones exert their influence have not been delineated, although it is thought to be related to the increase of gonadal hormones, such as estrogen, which control the coding of serotonin (Steiner, Dunn, & Born, 2003). It may be instead that hormonal changes interact with genetic vulnerabilities and psychosocial influences. For example, depression may result in a genetically vulnerable person undergoing role changes involved with reproductive events in societies that devalue women's roles.

Psychosocial explanations for the gender gap in depression highlight the stressful life events that females experience, such as sexual abuse and family violence. Other stressors come in the form of financial hardship, neighborhood disadvantages, women's work being less highly regarded and paid than men's work, and role overload, as women often assume primary responsibility for taking care of children and the home, even when they are employed outside the home (Le et al., 2003).

For teen girls, interpersonal stress may contribute to the onset of depression. Adolescent females invest more in relationships than boys do. They tend to exhibit a heightened concern about what others think of them and a greater dependence on the approval of others for their sense of self-worth (Girgus & Nolen-Hoeksema, 2006). These tendencies lead to greater sensitivity and reactivity to interpersonal stress (Rudolph, 2002). Thus, the emotional distress girls may experience seems to put them at risk for further problems in relationships, creating a cycle of distress that may result in depressive symptoms.

Females have also been found to use negative coping mechanisms, such as rumination, which is defined as the tendency to focus on the symptoms of a poor mood, mulling over the reasons for its occurrence in incessantly, passive ways rather than in an active, problem-solving manner (Nolen-Hoeksema, 2002).

Environmental Factors?

Sexual Minorities

Lesbian, gay, and bisexual people have an increased rate of depressive disorder, at least 1.5 times higher than the heterosexual population (King et al., 2008). For gay and bisexual men, in particular, lifetime prevalence rates of suicide attempts are higher when compared to heterosexual men. Stigma and discrimination may partially account for these higher rates.

Ethnicity

In terms of prevalence rates among people of different ethnicities, there appear to be few differential rates. While Latinos report more symptoms than Caucasians, the difference is small and not clinically meaningful (Menselson, Rehkopf, & Kubzansky, 2008). However, Latino youth had elevated scores on the Children's Depression Inventory compared to either Caucasian or African American samples. According to the Centers for Disease Control and Prevention (2008), rates of suicide attempts and plans among adolescent Latinas are significantly higher than their Caucasian and African American counterparts. Unfortunately, there are few treatment outcome studies focusing on Latino youth, with the exception of Rosselló and Bernal studies with Puerto Rican youth (discussed previously).

Very little is known about the treatment of depression in ethnic minorities in general. For example, only 37% of the 35 treatment outcome studies on youth depression reviewed by Weisz et al. (2006) even reported information on ethnicity. Of note, is the lack of studies on American Indians and Alaskan Natives, who have the highest rate of suicide in the 15–24 age group (CDC, 2004 as cited in David-Ferdon & Kaslow, 2008).

For adults, African American and Latinos' use of antidepressants lags behind that of Caucasians, with the rate for African Americans particularly low (Olfson & Marcus, 2009). African Americans may find medication less preferable than counseling, may lack knowledge about antidepressants, may have less trust in treatment service providers, and may suffer from reduced access to care. Of note is that in the Olfson and Marcus (2009) study people with no insurance were less likely to be treated with medication than those who were either publicly or privately insured.

Critique

As with many of the other disorders, the internal nature of dysfunction assumption integral to the *DSM* approach can be critiqued. The social worker should be aware that although biological susceptibility may play a significant role in the development of depression (explaining perhaps 30% of the variance), the majority of contributing factors are psychosocial in nature. Additionally, the interactional effect of genetics and the environment is highlighted in recent studies, and this is significant both in terms of risk and protection.

Summary

Since major depression is the single most common mental health disorder in the United States, social workers will likely be involved with this population. No matter the setting of intervention, social workers can identify people who are depressed and refer them to appropriate treatment. They can also administer treatment themselves, using one of the tested interventions discussed in this chapter. When resources are limited, social workers can let clients with depression know about some low-cost and easy-to-implement alternatives, such as exercise, bibliotherapy (specifically the manuals *Feeling Good* and *Controlling Your Depression*), and St. John's Wort. Although results of studies require replication, it is also possible that relaxation training, behavior activation (helping people structure their days with activities, particularly ones that are enjoyable to them), and problem-solving therapies may be helpful for lifting depression, and they are relatively easier and quicker to implement than the packages of CBT of which they are often a part.

Case Study

Joseph, a 54-year-old, Caucasian male immigrant from the Czech Republic, was admitted to a psychiatric hospital following a suicide attempt. Admitting records showed that his landlady had found him in his rented room in a disoriented state, almost catatonic, unable to function, and with cuts on his left wrist. He had recently lost his job. The landlady was concerned and called authorities. Upon assessment at a community mental health facility, it was determined he was a potential threat to himself and was committed to a psychiatric hospital.

The day after his admission, Joseph met with the treatment team: a psychiatrist, psychologist, occupational therapist, nurse, and social worker. Joseph entered the room walking slowly, with a fatigued and visibly drawn countenance. When questioned as to why he was there, he said he did not know and started to cry. He was unable to provide much information at that meeting except to say his name and where he lived.

Two days later, Joseph was more talkative during a more in-depth assessment conducted by the social worker. The client has been in the United States for 20 years. He has one sister who lives in the area. He attended college in the Czech Republic, and his parents still live there. He has been employed most of his life and recently worked at a tile company driving a truck. However, he lost that job 3 weeks prior to admission to the hospital. He lives alone in a rented room of a house shared with three other men. He has no insurance.

Joseph said he has never previously been hospitalized, and there is no history of mental illness in the family. He has no faith preference now but was raised Catholic. He denies any history of substance abuse or physical or sexual abuse.

Four years ago, Joseph was separated from his wife and later divorced. He had two previous marriages and has a 31-year-old son living in the Czech Republic from his first wife. He has two sons, 12 and 15 years old, by the third wife, who lives in the area. He said his divorce decreed that he is not allowed to see these children. He was not able to provide further details on the reasons behind the court decision.

Joseph said his youngest son has attention-deficit/hyperactivity disorder, and this caused marital tension because his wife thought he was too firm with the son. His sister also thought so, and she sided with his wife in seeking a divorce. He has to pay $1000 a month in child support, and because he has lost his job, he feels overwhelmed with his situation.

Joseph credits his severe depression to intense grief over the divorce, which he says he did not want. He kept saying that it was all his fault. When pressed, he said one night 3 years ago, he and his wife got into an argument when he had been drinking. She called the police, and he was subsequently charged with a domestic assault. After he attended anger management classes, the charge was dismissed. His wife obtained a restraining order, but he violated it once. He was consequently jailed for 1 day. He has not seen his children in 3 years.

He said the intense loneliness he feels and his remorse over not seeing his children have caused him to feel sad and depressed. Missing his son's birthday a month before was the breaking point. He was in so much emotional pain that he found it difficult to get out of bed and go to work. As a result of absenteeism, he was fired. He despaired about his life and made a half-hearted attempt to slit his wrists.

Despite his obvious despair, Joseph did say he wanted to figure out a way to end his depression and get on with his life. He said he used to have interests in music and played a flute. In addition, he said he likes to garden and wanted to get back into that as well. He said he feels his greatest strength is the ability to pick himself up and keep going, which is what he has done in the past. He also said he wants to eventually be able to see his sons.

Additional Information Needed

The social worker would have liked more information about the circumstances of Joseph's divorce, the restraining order his former wife obtained, and the alleged decree that he is not allowed to see his children. She had attempted to gain more information from Joseph, but he was not forthcoming with details. In addition, the social worker wanted to know the reasons for his other two failed marriages. Finally, the social worker was curious about the extent of Joseph's drinking. He denied alcohol abuse but said alcohol was involved in his domestic fights with his wife.

Diagnosis

Axis I: 296.2 Major Depressive Disorder, Single episode, Severe.
Axis II: V71.09 No diagnosis
Axis III: None
Axis IV: Problems in primary support group. Divorced.
Problems in social environment. Lives alone, lack of friends and family in area. Occupational problems. Unemployed. Economic problems. Inadequate finances to meet expenses, lack of insurance.
Axis V: GAF 50

Rationale

According to Joseph's self-report, he met seven of the nine symptoms from Criterion A for a major depressive episode (a minimum of five symptoms are needed to make the diagnosis). He experienced the following symptoms for most of the day, nearly every day for the previous 3 weeks (a minimum of 2 weeks is required for the diagnosis): *(a)* depressed mood, *(b)* markedly diminished interest or pleasure in almost all activities, *(c)* hypersomnia, *(d)* fatigue or loss of energy nearly every day, *(e)* feelings of worthlessness or excessive or inappropriate guilt, *(f)* diminished ability to think or concentrate, and *(g)* suicide attempt. Further, Criteria B (there was no evidence of a mixed episode), C (the symptoms caused clinically significant distress and impairment in his occupational area of functioning), D (the symptoms were not due to the physiological effects of a substance or a medical condition), and E (the symptoms are not better accounted for by bereavement) were met. He was diagnosed with major depressive disorder, severe because of the number of symptoms and the presence of a suicide attempt. The social worker gave him a GAF of 50 (serious), again because of the suicide attempt that warranted his hospitalization and also his job loss as a result of the depression.

Risk and Protective Factors Assessment and Treatment Formulation

The social worker completed a risk and protective factors assessment for the onset of Joseph's depression and for his recovery. (See Exhibit 9.8 for a list of onset factors.) Related to his potential for recovery, on the positive side, Joseph had not suffered previous episodes, and he has no co-occurring psychiatric or medical condition. On the negative side, he had severe depression on admittance to the hospital, and he is divorced.

Case Study of Joseph: Risk and Protective Factors Assessment for Onset of Depression

Risk	Protective
Biological	
	No first-degree relative history
	Good health
Psychological	
Negative cognitive style	Had coping skills before current episode
Social	
Marital problems, divorce	Has job skills, previous employment
Low social support and interaction	History
Stressful life events, especially those involving loss (job, family, country of origin)	
Low socioeconomic status	

Intervention

Treatment goals included reduction of depressive symptoms, the development of increased social support and coping skills, some resolution of his feelings about his recent marriage, renewed contact with his children, and employment. Interpersonal therapy was the treatment of choice because Joseph's depression seemed tied to loss of relationships and interpersonal problems.

References

aan het Rot, M., Mathew, S. J., & Charney, D. S. (2009). Neurobiological mechanisms in major depressive disorder. *Canadian Medical Association Journal, 180*(3), 305–313.

Abela, J. R. Z., Brozina, K., & Haigh, E. P. (2002). An examination of the response styles theory of depression in third-and seventh-grade children: A short-term longitudinal study. *Journal of Abnormal Child Psychology, 30*(5), 515–527.

Abramson, L. Y., Seligman, M. E., & Teasdale, J. D. (1978). Learned helplessness in humans: Critique and reformulation. *Journal of Abnormal Psychology, 87*, 49–74.

Anderson, I. (2000). Selective serotonin reuptake inhibitors versus tricyclic antidepressants: a meta-analysis of efficacy and tolerability. *Journal of Affective Disorders, 58*, 19–36.

Agency for Health Care Policy and Research. (1993). *Depression in primary care: Vol. 1. Detection and diagnosis clinical practice Guideline*. Retrieved April 9, 2004, from http://www.mentalhealth.com/bookah/p44-d1.html

Alexopoulos, G. S., Katz, I. R., Reynolds, C. F., Carpenter, D., Docherty, J. P., & Ross, R. W. (2001). Pharmacotherapy of depression in older patients: A summary of the expert consensus guidelines. *Journal of Psychiatric Practice, 7*(6), 361–376.

American Association for Geriatric Psychiatry (AAGP). (2002). *Depression in late life: Not a natural part of aging*. Retrieved August 16, 2003, from http://www.aagpgpa.org/p_c/depression2.asp

American Psychiatric Association. (2000). *Diagnostic and statistical manual of mental disorders* (4th ed., text rev.). Washington, DC: Author.

Antonuccio, D., Thomas, M., & Danton, W. (1997). A cost-effectiveness analysis of cognitive behavior therapy and fluoxetine (Prozac) in the treatment of depression. *Behavior Therapy, 28*, 187–210.

Arnow, B. A., & Constantino, M. J. (2003). Effectiveness of psychotherapy and combination treatment for chronic depression. *Journal of Clinical Psychology, 59*(8), 893–905.

Barbui, C., Esposito, E., & Cipriani, A. (2009). Selective serotonin reuptake inhibitors and risk of suicide: A systematic review of observational studies. *Canadian Medical Association Journal, 180*, 291–297.

Barkow, K., Maier, W., Ustun, T. B., Gansicke, M., Wittchen, H. U., & Heun, R. (2003). Risk factors for depression at 12-month follow-up in adult primary health care patients with major depression: An international prospective study. *Journal of Affective Disorders, 76*, 157–169.

Barry, L. C., Allore, H. G., Guo, Z., Bruce, M. L., & Gill, T. M. (2008). Higher burden of depression among older women: The effect of onset, persistence, and mortality over time. *Archives of General Psychiatry, 65*(2), 172–178.

Beck, A., Rush, A., Shaw, B., & Emery, G. (1979). *Cognitive therapy of depression*. New York: Guilford.

Bentley, K. J., & Walsh, J. (2006). *The social worker and psychotropic medication: Toward effective collaboration with mental health clients, families and providers* (3rd ed.). Monterey, CA: Brooks/Cole-Thomson.

Bird, M., & Parslow, R. (2002). Potential for community programs to prevent depression in older people. *Medical Journal of Australia, 7*, 107–110.

Borges, G., Angst, J., Nock, M., Ruscio, A. M., Walters, E., & Kessler, R. (2006). A risk index for 12-month suicide attempts in the National Comorbidity Survey Replication (NCR-S). *Psychological Medicine, 36*, 1747–1757.

Bradley, R. G., Binder, E. B., Epstein, M. P., Tang, Y., Nair, H. P., Liu, W., et al. (2008). Influence of child abuse on adult depression: Moderation by the corticotropin-releasing hormone receptor gene. *Archives of General Psychiatry, 65*(2), 190–200.

Brent, D. A., Baugher, M., Birmaher, B., Kolko, D. J., & Bridge, J. (2000). Compliance with recommendations to remove firearms in families participating in a clinical trial for adolescent depression. *Journal of the American Academy of Child and Adolescent Psychiatry, 39*, 1220–1226.

Brent, D., Emslie, G., Clarke, G., Wagner, K. D., Asarnow, J. R., Keller, M., et al. (2008). Switching to another SSRI or to Venlafaxine with or without cognitive behavioral therapy for adolescents with SSRI- resistant depression: The TORDIA randomized controlled trial. *Journal of the American Medical Association, 299*(8), 901–913.

Bridge, J. A., Iyengar, S., Salary, C. B., Barbe, R. P., Birmaher, B., Pincus, H. A., et al. (2007). Clinical response and risk for reported suicidal ideation and suicide attempts in pediatric antidepressant treatment: A meta-analysis of randomized controlled trials. *The Journal of the American Medical Association, 297*, 1683–1696.

Brown, G. W., & Harris, T. O. (2008). Depression and the serotonin transporter 5-HTTLPR polymorphism: A review and a hypothesis concerning gene-environment interaction. *Journal of Affective Disorders 111*, 1–12.

Brown, R. T., Antonuccio, D. O., Dupaul, G. J., Fristad, M. A., King, C. A., Leslie, L. K., et al. (2007). Childhood mental health disorders: Evidence-base and contextual factors for psychosocial, psychopharmacological, and combined interventions. Washington, DC: American Psychological Association.

Burns, D. (1999). *Feeling good: The new mood therapy* (Rev. ed.). New York: Avon.

Centers for Disease Control and Prevention. (2008). *Youth risk behavior surveillance system (YRBS) survey. Health behaviors by race/ethnicity. National YRBS 2007.* Retrieved on January 2, 2009, from http://www.cdc.gov/HealthyYouth/yrbs/pdf/yrbs07_us_disparity_race.pdf

Ciesla, J. A., & Roberts, J. E. (2001). Meta-analysis of the relationship between HIV infection and risk for depressive disorders. *American Journal of Psychiatry, 158*(5), 725–730.

Cipriani, A., Furukawa, T. A., Salanti, G., Geddes, J. R., Higgins, J. P., Churchill, R., et al. (2009). Comparative efficacy and acceptability of 12 new-generation antidepressants: A multiple-treatments meta-analysis. *The Lancet, 373*(9665), 746–758.

Clarke, G., Rohde, P., Lewinsohn, P., Hops, H., & Seeley, J. (1999). Cognitive-behavioral treatment of adolescent depression: Efficacy of acute group treatment and booster sessions. *Journal of the American Academy of Child and AdolescentPsychiatry, 38*, , 272–279.

Cole, M., & Dendukuri, N. (2003). Risk factors for depression among elderly community studies: A systematic review and meta-analysis. *American Journal of Psychiatry, 160*, 1147–1156.

Corcoran, J. (2009). *The elderly and depression: A meta-synthesis.* Manuscript in preparation.

Costello, E., Erkanli, A., & Angold, A. (2006). Is there an epidemic of child or adolescent depression?. *Journal of Child Psychology & Psychiatry, 47*(12), 1263-1271.

Crum, R. M., Green, K. M., Storr, C. L, Chan, Y-F., Ialongo, N., Stuart, E., et al. (2008). Depressed mood in childhood and subsequent alcohol use through adolescence and young adulthood. *Archives of General Psychiatry, 65*(6), 702–712.

Cuijpers, P., van Straten, A., Andersson, G., & van Oppen, P. (2008). Psychotherapy for depression in adults: A meta-analysis of comparative outcome studies. *Journal of Consulting and Clinical Psychology, 76*(6), 909–922.

Cuijpers, P., van Straten, A., & Warmerdam, L. (2007a). Problem solving therapies for depression: A meta analysis. *European Psychiatry*, (1), 9–15.

Cuijpers, P., van Straten, A., & Warmerdam, L. (2007b). Behavioral activation treatments of depression: A meta-analysis. *Clinical Psychology Review, 27*(3), 318–326.

Cuijpers, P., van Straten, A., Warmerdam, L., & Andersson, G. (2009). Psychotherapy versus the combination of psychotherapy and pharmacotherapy in the treatment of depression: A meta-analysis. *Depression and Anxiety, 26*(3), 279–288.

David-Ferdon, C., & Kaslow, N. J. (2008). Evidence-based psychosocial treatments for child and adolescent depression. *Journal of Clinical Child and Adolescent Psychology, 37*(1), 62–104.

De Beurs, E., Beekman, A., Geerlings, S., Deeg, D., Van Dyck, R., & Van Tilburg, W. (2001). On becoming depressed or anxious in late life: Similar vulnerability factors but different effects of stressful life events. *British Journal of Psychiatry, 179*(5), 426–431.

Department of Health and Human Services. (2001). *Mental health: Culture, race, ethnicity. Supplement to mental health: Report of the Surgeon General.* Retrieved on June 8, 2009, from http://mentalhealth.samhsa.gov/cre/default.asp

Desai, H., & Jann, M. (2000). Major depression in women: A review of the literature. *Journal of the American Pharmaceutical Association, 40,* 525–537.

Diamond, G. S., Reis, B. F., Diamond, G. M., Siqueland, L., & Isaacs, L. (2002). Attachment-based family therapy for depressed adolescents: A treatment development study. *Journal of the American Academy of Child and Adolescent Psychiatry, 41*(10), 1190–1197.

Dietz, L. J., Birmaher, B., Williamson, D. E., Silk, J. S., Dahl, R. E., Axelson, D. A., et al. (2008). Mother-child interactions in depressed children and children at high risk and low risk for future depression. *Journal of the American Academy of Child and Adolescent Psychiatry, 47*(5), 574–582.

Druss, B. G., Wang, P. S., Sampson, N. A., Olfson, M., Pincus, H. A., Wells, K. B., et al. (2007). Understanding mental health treatment in persons without mental diagnoses: Results from the National Comorbidity Survey Replication. *Archives of General Psychiatry, 64*(10), 1196–1203.

Eaton, W. W., Shao, H., Nestadt, G., Hochang, B., Bienvenu, J., & Zandi, P. (2008). Population-based study of first onset and chronicity in major depressive disorder. *Archives of General Psychiatry, 65*(5), 513–520.

Elkin, I., Gibbons, R. D., Shea, M. T., Sotsky, S. M., Watkins, J. T., Pilkonis, P. A., et al. (1995). Initial severity and differential treatment outcome in the National Institute of Mental Health Treatment of Depression Collaborative Research Program. *Journal of Consulting and Clinical Psychology, 63,* , 841–847.

Fawcett, J. (2006). Depressive disorders. In R. L. Simon & R. E. Hales (Eds.), *The American Psychiatric Publishing textbook of suicide assessment and management* (1st ed., pp. 255–275). Washington, DC: American Psychiatric Publishing.

Fergusson, D. M., Boden, J. M., & Horwood, L. J. (2007). Recurrence of major depression in adolescence and early adulthood, and later mental health, educational and economic outcomes. *British Journal of Psychiatry, 191,* , 335–342.

Fergusson, D. M., Boden, J. M., & Horwood, L. J. (2008). Exposure to childhood sexual and physical abuse and adjustment in early adulthood. *Child Abuse and Neglect, 32*(6), 607–619.

Food and Drug Administration. (2004). *FDA public health advisory. Suicidality in children and adolescents being treated with antidepressant medications.* Rockville, MD: Author.

Friedman, E. S., Wisniewski, S. R., Gilmer, W., Nierenberg, A. A., Rush, A. J., Fava, et al. (2009). Sociodemographic, clinical, and treatment characteristics associated with worsened depression during treatment with citalopram: Results of the NIMH Star (*)D trial [Electronic Version]. *Depression and Anxiety, 26*(7), 612–621.

Gavin, N. I., Gaynes, B. N., Lohr, K. N., Meltzer-Brody, S., Gartlehner, G., & Swinson, T. (2005). Perinatal depression: A systematic review of prevalence and incidence. *Obstetrics and Gynecology, 106*(5 Pt 1), 1071–1083.

Girgus, J., & Nolen-Hoeksema, S. (2006). Cognition and depression. In C. L. Keyes & S. H. Goodman (Eds.), *Women and depression: A handbook for the social, behavioral, and biomedical sciences* (pp. 147–175). New York: Cambridge University Press.

Golden, R. N., Gaynes, B. N., Ekstrom, R. D., Hamer, R. M., Jacobsen, F. M., Suppes, T., et al. (2005). The efficacy of light therapy in the treatment of mood disorders: A review and meta-analysis of the evidence.*American Journal of Psychiatry, 162*, 656–662.

Goodman, S. H. (2007). Depression in mothers. *Annual Review of Clinical Psychology, 3*, 107–135.

Goodyer, I. M., Dubicka, B., Wilkinson, P., Kelvin, R., Roberts, C., Byford, S., et al. (2008). A randomised controlled trial of cognitive behaviour therapy in adolescents with major depression treated by selective serotonin reuptake inhibitors. The ADAPT trail. *Health Technology Assessment, 12*(14), iii–iv, ix–60.

Graber, J. A., Brooks-Gunn, J., & Warren, M. E. (2006). Pubertal effects on adjustment in girls: Moving from demonstrating effects to identifying pathways. *Journal of Youth and Adolescence, 35*(3), 413–423.

Gregory, R. J., Canning, S. S., Lee, T. W., & Wise, J. C. (2004). Cognitive bibliotherapy for depression: A meta-analysis. *Professional Psychology: Research and Practice, 35*, 275–280.

Gutman, L. M., & Sameroff, A. J. (2004). Continuities in depression from adolescence to young adulthood: Contrasting ecological influences. *Development and Psychopathology, 16*, 967–984.

Healy, D. (2002). *The creation of psychopharmacology*. Cambridge, MA: Harvard University Press.

Henken, T., Huibers, M., Churchill, R., Restifo, K., & Roelofs, J. (2007). Family therapy for depression. *Cochrane Database of Systematic Reviews, 3*, , Art. No.: CD006728. DOI: 10.1002/14651858.CD006728.

Hetrick, S. E., Merry, S., McKenzie, J., Sindahl, P., & Proctor, M. (2007). Selective serotonin reuptake inhibitors (SSRIs) for depressive disorders in children and adolescents. *Cochrane Database of Systematic Reviews, 3*, Art. No.: CD004851.

Jorm, A. F., Christensen, H., Griffiths, K. M., & Rodgers, B. (2002). Effectiveness of complementary and self-help treatments for depression. *Medical Journal of Australia, 176*(Suppl. 10), S84–S95.

Karasu, T. B., Gelenberg, A., Merriam, A., & Wang, P. (2002). Practice guidelines for the treatment of patients with major depressive disorder. In APA Steering Committee on Practice Guidelines (Ed.), *American Psychiatric Association practice guidelines for the treatment of psychiatric disorder: Compendium 2002* (2nd ed., pp. 463–545). Washington, DC: American Psychiatric Association.

Kessler, R., Berglund, P., Demler, O., Jin, R., & Walters, E. (2005). Lifetime prevalence and age-of-onset distributions of DSM-IV disorders in the National Comorbidity Survey Replication. *Archives of General Psychiatry, 62*, 593–602.

Kessler, R. C. (2003). Epidemiology of women and depression. *Journal of Affective Disorders, 74*(1), 5–13.

Kessler, R., Chiu, W. T., Demler, O., & Walters, E. (2005). Prevalence, severity, and comorbidity of 12-month DSM-IV disorders in the National Comorbidity Survey Replication. *Archives of General Psychiatry, 62*, 617–627.

King, M., Semlyen, J., Tai, S. S., Killapsy, H., Osborn, D., Popelyuk, D., et al. (2008). A systematic review of mental disorder, suicide, and deliberate self harm in lesbian, gay and bisexual people. *BMC Psychiatry, 8*, 70.

Klein, J. B., Jacobs, R. H., & Reinecke, M. A. (2007). Cognitive-behavioral therapy for adolescent depression: A meta-analytic investigation of changes in effect-size estimates. *Journal of the American Academy of Child and Adolescent Psychiatry, 46*(11), 1403–1413.

Klein, D. N., Shankman, S. A., & Rose, S. (2008). Dysthymic disorder and double depression: Prediction of 10-year course trajectories and outcomes. *Journal of Psychiatric Research, 42*(5), 408–415.

Korczak, D. J., & Goldstein, B. I. (2009). Childhood onset major depressive disorder: Course of illness and psychiatric comorbidity in a community sample [Electronic Version]. *The Journal of Pediatrics, 155*(1), 118–123.

Kovacs, M. (2001). Gender and the course of major depressive disorder through adolescence in clinically referred youngsters. *Journal of the American Academy of Child and Adolescent Psychiatry, 40*, 1079–1085.

Kraaij, V., Arensman, E., & Spinhoven, P. (2002). Negative life events and depression in elderly persons: A meta-analysis. *Journals of Gerontology Series B-Psychological Sciences & Social Sciences, 57B*(1), 87–94.

Laidlaw, K., Thompson, L., Gallagher-Thompson, D., & Dick-Siskin, L. (2003). *Cognitive behaviour therapy with older people*. Chichester, England: John Wiley.

Le, H. N., Munoz, R., Ippen, C. G., & Stoddard, J. (2003). Treatment is not enough: We must prevent major depression in women. *Prevention and Treatment*. Retrieved on December 31, 2003, from http://80-gateway1.ovid.com.proxy.library.vcu.edu/ovidweb.cgi.

Lemstra, M., Neudorf, C., D'Arcy, C., Kunst, A., Warren, L. M., & Bennett, N. R. (2008). A systematic review of depressed mood and anxiety by SES in youth aged 10–15 years. *Canadian Journal of Public Health, 99*(2), 125–129.

Leslie, L. K., Newman, T. B., Chesney, P. J., & Perrin, J. (2005). The Food and Drug Administration. *Pediatrics, 116*(1), 195–204.

Lewinsohn, P. M., Clarke, G. N., Hops, H., & Andrews, J. (1990). Cognitive-behavioral treatment for depressed adolescents. *Behavior Therapy, 21*, , 385–401.

Lewinsohn, P. M., Munoz, R. F., Youngren, M. A., & Zeiss, A. M. (1986). *Control your depression* (2nd ed.). Englewood Cliffs, NJ: Prentice-Hall.

Linde, K., Mulrow, C. D., Berner, M., & Egger, M. (2005). St John's wort for depression. *Cochrane Database of Systematic Reviews, 2*, , Art. No.: CD000448.

McBride, C., Atkinson, L., Quilty, L. C., & Bagby, R. M. (2006). Attachment as moderator of treatment outcome in major depression: A randomized control trial of interpersonal psychotherapy versus cognitive behavior therapy. *Journal of Consulting and Clinical Psychology, 74*(6), 1041–1054.

McGrath, P. J., Khan, A. Y., Trivedi, M. H., Stewart J. W., Morris D. W., Wisniewski S. R., et al. (2008). Response to a selective serotonin reuptake inhibitor (citalopram) in major depressive disorder with melancholic features: A star*d report. *The Journal of Clinical Psychiatry, 69*(12), 1847–1855.

McLeod, B. D., Weisz, J. R., & Wood, J. J. (2007). Examining the association between parenting and childhood depression: A meta-analysis. *Clinical Psychology Review, 27*(8), 986–1003.

Mead, G., Morley, W., & Campbell, P., Greig, C., McMurdo, M., & Lawlor, D. (2008). Exercise for depression. *Cochrane Database of Systematic Reviews, 4,* , Art. No.: CD004366. DOI: 10.1002/14651858.CD004366.pub3.

Melvin, G. A., Tonge, B. J., King, N. J., Heyne, D., Gordon, M. S., & Klimkeit, E. (2006). A comparison of cognitive-behavioral therapy, sertraline, and their combination for adolescent depression. *Journal of the American Academy of Child and Adolescent Psychiatry, 45,* 1151–1161.

Menselson, T., Rehkopf, D. H., & Kubzansky, L. D. (2008). Depression among Latinos in the United States: A meta-analytic review. *Journal of Consulting and Clinical Psychology, 76*(3), 355–366.

Morgan, A. J., & Jorm, A. (2008). Self-help interventions for depressive disorders and depressive symptoms: A systematic review. *Annals of General Psychiatry, 7,* 13. Doi:10.1186/1744-859X-7-13

Mottram, P., Wilson, K., & Strobl, J. (2006). Antidepressants for depressed elderly. *The Cochrane Database of Systematic Reviews, 1,* , Art. No.: CD003491.

Mufson, L., Dorta, K. P., Moreau, D., & Weissman, M. M. (2005). Efficacy to effectiveness: Adaptations of interpersonal psychotherapy for adolescent depression. In E. Hibbs & P. Jensen (Eds.), *Psychosocial treatments for child and adolescent disorders: Empirically based strategies for clinical practice* (2nd ed., pp. 165–186) Washington, DC: American Psychological Association.

Nelson, J. C, Delucchi, K., & Schneider, L. S. (2008). Efficacy of second generation antidepressants in late-life depression: A meta-analysis of the evidence. *The American Journal of Geriatric Psychiatry, 16*(7), 558–567.

Newton-Howes, G., Tyrer, P., & Johnson, T. (2006). Personality disorder and the outcome of depression: Meta-analysis of published studies. *The British Journal of Psychiatry, 188,* 13–20.

Nolen-Hoeksema, S. (2002). Gender differences in depression. In I. H. Gotlib & C. Hammen (Eds.), *Handbook of depression* (pp. 492–509). New York: Guilford.

Olfson, M., & Marcus, S. (2009). National patterns in antidepressant medication treatment. *Archives of General Psychiatry, 66,* 848–856.

Penza, K., Heim, C., & Nemeroff, C. (2006). Trauma and depression. In C. L. M. Keyes & S. H. Goodman (Eds.), *Women and depression, handbook for the social, behavioral, and biomedical sciences* (pp. 360–381). New York: Cambridge University Press.

Rief, W., Nestoriuc, Y., Weiss, S., Welzel, E., Barsky, A. J., & Hofmann, S. G. (2009). Meta-analysis of the placebo response in antidepressant trials. *Journal of Affective Disorders, 118*(1–3), 1–8. Doi:10.1016/j.jad.2009.01.029.

Richardson, L. P., Lewis, C. W., Casey-Goldstein, M., McCauley E., & Katon, W. (2007). Pediatric primary care providers and adolescent depression: A qualitative study of barriers to treatment and the effect of the black box warning. *Journal of Adolescent Health, 40*(5), 433–439.

Rossello, J., & Bernal, G. (1999). The efficacy of cognitive-behavioral and interpersonal treatments for depression in Puerto Rican adolescents. *Journal of Consulting and Clinical Psychology, 67,* 734–745.

Rossello, J., Bernal, G., & Rivera-Medina, C. (2008). Individual and group CBT and IPT for Puerto Rican adolescents with depressive symptoms. *Cultural Diversity and Ethnic Minority Psychology, 14*(3), 234–245.

Rudolph, K. (2002). Gender differences in emotional responses to interpersonal stress during adolescence. *Journal of Adolescent Health, 30*, 3–13.

Sander, J. B., & McCarty, C. A. (2005). Youth depression in the family context: Familial risk factors and models of treatment. *Clinical Child and Family Psychology Review, 8*(3), 203–219.

Shanmugham, B., Karp, J., Drayer, R., Reynolds, C. F. 3rd, & Alexopoulos, G. (2005). Evidence-based pharmacologic interventions for geriatric depression. *Psychiatric Clinics of North America, 28*(4), 821–835.

Steiner, M., Dunn, E., & Born, L. (2003). Hormones and mood: From menarche to menopause and beyond. *Journal of Affective Disorders, 74*(1), 67–83.

Sullivan, P. F., Neale, M. C., & Kendler, K. S. (2000). Genetic epidemiology of major depression: Review and meta-analysis. *American Journal of Psychiatry, 157*(10), 1552–1562.

Szegedi, A., Jansen, W. T., van Willigenburg, A. P., van der Meulen, E., Stassen, H. H., & Thase, M. E. (2009). Early improvement in the first 2 weeks as a predictor of treatment outcome in patients with major depressive disorder: A meta-analysis including 6562 patients. *Journal of Clinical Psychiatry, 70*(3), 344–353.

The TADS Team. (2007). The treatment for adolescents with depression study (TADS): Long-term effectiveness and safety outcomes. *Archives of General Psychiatry, 64* (10), 1132–1144.

Tuunainen, A., Kripke, D. F., Endo, T. (2004). Light therapy for non-seasonal depression. *Cochrane Database of Systematic Reviews, 2*, Art. No.: CD004050.

Uebelacker, L. A., & Whisman, M. A. (2006). Moderators of the association between relationship discord and major depression in a national population-based sample. *Journal of Family Psychology, 20*, 40–46.

Usala, T., Clavenna, A., Zuddas, A., & Bonati, M. (2008). Randomised controlled trials of selective serotonin reuptake inhibitors in treating depression in children and adolescents: A systematic review and meta-analysis. *European Neuropsychopharmacology, 18*, (1), 62–73.

Wade, T. J., Cairney, J., & Pevalin, D. J. (2002). Emergence of gender differences in depression during adolescence: National panel results from three countries. *Journal of the American Academy of Child and Adolescent Psychiatry, 41*, , 190–199.

Wang, P. S., Berglund, P., Olfson, M., Pincus, H. A., Wells, K. B., & Kessler, R. C. (2005). Failure and delay in initial treatment contact after first onset of mental disorders in the National Comorbidity Survey Replication. *Archives of General Psychiatry, 62*(6), 603–613.

Waslick, B. D., Kandel, B. A., & Kakouros, B. S. (2002). Depression in children and adolescents: An overview. In D. Shaffer & B. D. Waslick (Eds.), *The many faces of depression in children and adolescents* (pp. 1–36). Washington, DC: American Psychiatric Publishing.

Watanabe, N., Hunot, V., Omori, I. M., Churchill, R., & Furukawa, T. A. (2007). Psychotherapy for depression among children and adolescents: A systematic review. *Acta Psychiatrica Scandinavica, 116*(2), 84–95.

Weissman, M. M., Markowitz, J. C., & Klerman, G. L. (2000). *Comprehensive Guide to Interpersonal Psychotherapy*. New York: Basic Books.

Weisz, J. R., McCarty, C. A., & Valeri, S. M. (2006). Effects of psychotherapy for depression in children and adolescents: A meta-analysis. *Psychological Bulletin, 132*, 132–149.

Whittington, C., Kendall, T., Fonagy, P., Cottrell, D., & Cotgrove, A. (2004). Use of selective serotonin reuptake inhibitors in childhood depression. *Lancet, 364* (9435), 661.

Wilson, K., Mottram, P. G., & Vassilas, C. (2008). Psychotherapeutic treatments for older depressed people. *Cochrane Database of Systematic Reviews, 1,* , Art. No.: CD004853. DOI: 10.1002/14651858.CD004853.pub2.

Appendix I: Measures for Childhood and Adolescent Depression

This review was largely drawn from Myers and Winters (2002) and Dougherty, Klein, Olino, and Laptook (2008).

Children's Depression Inventory (Kovacs, 1992)

Description
- Twenty-seven-item, self-report inventory for children from ages 8 to 13
- Measuring severity ("0" to "2") of overt symptoms of depression, such as sadness, sleep and eating disturbances, anhedonia, and suicidal ideation
- Modified from the Beck Depression Inventory for adults
- Translated into several languages
- For prognostic purposes, norms are rated as excellent, clinical utility is adequate, and the instrument is highly recommended.

Reliability
- Internal consistency has been rated good
- Test-retest reliability adequate

Validity
- Possesses predictive validity for future functioning
- Shows variable sensitivity to changes during therapy
- Clinician's ratings of depression from a psychiatric interview correlated with Children's Depression Inventory ($r = .55$)
- Discriminated between psychiatric sample and nonclinic group and between child guidance and pediatric samples, though with a high false-negative rate

- Construct validity rated good
- Children who scored high on depression for Children's Depression Inventory made more internal-stable-global attributions for failure and more external-unstable-specific attributions for success as measured by the Attributional Style Questionnaire ($r = .52$) (Kaslow, Rehm, & Siegel, 1984).
- Children's Depression Inventory was negatively correlated with the Coopersmith Self-Esteem Inventory ($r = -.72$) (Kaslow et al., 1984).
- Teachers reported depressed children as more internalizing than nondepressed children but not more externalizing (Kaslow et al., 1984).

Reynolds Adolescent Depression Scale (RADS) (Reynolds, 1987, 2002)

Description
- Measures *DSM-III* criteria for depression over the past 2 weeks
- Has primarily been developed and used with school samples
- Recommended for screening, rather than outcome
- For prognosis, norms rated as excellent, clinical utility adequate, and the instrument is highly recommended.
- There is also the Reynolds Child Depression Scale (RCDS), which has similar psychometric properties.

Reliability
- Excellent internal reliability
- Very good stability with samples of diverse youth from multiple nationalities, and both clinical and community samples
- For prognosis, internal consistency rated excellent and test-retest reliability was good.

Validity
- Rooted in *DSM-III* diagnostic criteria ensures construct validity
- Correlates highly with other depression measures, as well as with measures of related constructs (e.g., anxiety and self-esteem) and has been used as a validation standard for other measures
- Inversely correlated with youth competence

Center for Epidemiologic Studies-Depression for Children and Adolescents (Weissman, Orvaschel, & Padian, 1980)

Description
- Comprises items empirically derived from other adult depression scales
- Assesses symptoms over the past 2 weeks
- Widely employed with adolescents

- Internal reliability is moderate to good.
- Moderate to good correlations stability for adolescents, though not children

Validity
- Moderate correlations with conduct disorder
- Fails to differentiate youth with depression from psychiatric controls

Beck Depression Inventory II (Beck, Steer, Ball, & Ranieri, 1996)

Note that the BDI is included in both Appendixes I and II because the target audience includes both adolescents and adults.

Description
- Self-report measure with 21 items, each having four answer options
- Targeted audience includes depressed adults, adolescents, elderly individuals, inpatients, outpatients, primary care patients, and patients with medical conditions
- Works well with a wide range of ages and cultures, as well as both males and females

Reliability
- Internal consistency of this measure was .93 for college students and .92 for outpatients.
- Test-retest reliability rated excellent

Validity
Construct validity of this scale was shown in its .76 correlation to the depression subscale Symptom Checklist 90-Rev and its .60 correlation with the Minnesota Multiphasic Personality Inventory.

Mood and Feelings Questionnaire (MFQ) (Angold, Costello, Messer, & Pickles, 1995)

Description
- Thirteen items on the shorter scale (SMFQ); 32 on the longer version
- Designed to assess depression within the past 2 weeks
- Ages 8 to 18 years
- Takes 10 minutes to complete

Reliability
- Internal consistency rated good
- Test-retest reliability was adequate.

Validity

Construct validity was rated good.

Appendix II: Measures for Adult Depression

This review draws from Burt and Ishak (2002), Persons and Fresco (2008), and Fiske and O'Riley (2008).

Zung Self-Rating Depression Scale (Zung, 1965)

Description
- Self-report measure with 20 items, each having four answer options
- Targeted audience is depressed adults, adolescents, elderly individuals, inpatients, outpatients, primary care patients, and patients with medical conditions.

Reliability

Internal consistency rated adequate

Validity (Biggs, Wylie, & Ziegler, 1978)
- Correlates highly with other depression measures.
- Sensitivity was found to be adequate.
- Construct validity rated adequate

Beck Depression Inventory II (Beck et al., 1996)

Description
- Self-report measure with 21 items, each having four answer options.
- Targeted audience includes depressed adults, adolescents, elderly individuals, inpatients, outpatients, primary care patients, and patients with medical conditions.
- Works well with a wide range of ages and cultures, as well as both males and females.

Reliability
- Internal consistency of this measure was .93 for college students and .92 for outpatients.
- Variability in test-retest reliabilities
- Internal consistency rated excellent
- Test-retest reliability rated excellent

Validity

Construct validity of this scale was shown in its .76 correlation to the depression subscale Symptom Checklist 90-Rev and its .60 correlation with the Minnesota Multiphasic Personality Inventory.

Center for Epidemiologic Studies Depression Scale (Radloff, 1977)

Description
- Self-report measure with 20 items, all items scored on a 0–3 scale
- Purpose is to measure frequency and duration (but not intensity) of depression in individuals
- Targeted population is the general public
- No cost to use
- Takes 5–10 minutes to complete

Reliability
- Internal consistency was .85 in the general population and .90 in the psychiatric population.
- Test-retest reliability rated good

Validity
Correlation with the Hamilton Rating Scale for Depression ranged from .49 to .85. Correlation with the Zung scale was .69, and the correlation to the Symptom Checklist-90 ranged from .73 to .89.

Geriatric Depression Scale (Yesavage et al., 1982–1983)

Description
- Screens for depression in the elderly
- Can also be used with the cognitively impaired (Burke, Nitcher, Roccaforte, & Wengel, 1992; Feher, Larrabee, & Crook, 1992)
- Can be self-administered or administered by an interviewer in 5–10 minutes
- Available in a 30-item long form or 15-, 10-, 4-, and 1-item short forms
- Items answered either "yes" or "no"
- Available in different languages (Chinese, German, French)

Reliability
- Fifteen-item version has a high internal consistency (Cronbach's alpha = .80) (D'Ath, Katona, Mullan, Evans, & Katona, 1994).
- Cronbach's alpha was .72 for the 10-item form and .55 for the 4-item form.
- Agreement between short scales and the 15-item scales was 95% (10-item), 91% (4-item), and 79% (1-item), respectively.
- Test-retest reliability rated good

Validity
- A single item, "Do you feel that your life is empty?" identified 84% of cases of depression (D'Ath et al., 1994).
- Sensitivity of 10-item version was 87% and specificity was 77% (using a cutoff of 3–4); sensitivity of 4-item version was 89% and specificity was 65% (cutoff of 1); sensitivity of 1-item version was 59% and specificity was 75%.
- Has good concurrent validity with the Melancholia scale of the Hamilton Rating Scale for Depression ($r = .77$) (Salamero & Marcos, 1992).
- Construct validity rated adequate

Quick Inventory of Depressive Symptomatology–Self-Rated (QIDS-SR) (Rush et al., 2003)

Description
- This is a shorter version of the Inventory of Depressive Symptomatology (IDS-SR), which also assesses anxiety. Both were adapted from clinician-administered instruments.
- Sixteen items
- Designed to assess severity of depressive symptoms, measures all the symptom domains in the *DSM-IV*
- Available in 13 languages
- The scales and related information are available at http://www.ids-qids.org.

Reliability
- Internal consistency rated excellent
- Test-retest reliability rated excellent

Validity
Construct validity rated excellent

References for Depression Measures

Angold, A., Costello, E. J., Messer, S. C., & Pickles, A. (1995). Development of a short questionnaire for use in epidemiological studies of depression in children and adolescents. *International Journal of Methods in Psychiatric Research, 5*, 237–249.

Beck, A., Steer, R., Ball, R., & Ranieri, W. (1996). Comparison of Beck Depression Inventories I-A and II in psychiatric outpatients. *Journal of Personality Assessment, 67*, 588–597.

Biggs, J., Wylie, L., & Ziegler, V. (1978). Validity of the Zung Self-Rating Depression Scale. *British Journal of Psychiatry, 132*, 381–385.

Burke, W., Nitcher, R., Roccaforte, W., & Wengel, S. (1992). A prospective evaluation of the Geriatric Depression Scale in an outpatient geriatric assessment center. *Journal of the American Geriatrics Society, 40,* 1227–1230.

Burt, T., & Ishak, W. (2002). Outcome measurement in mood disorders. In T. Burt, L. Sederer, & W. Ishak (Eds.), *Outcome measurement in psychiatry: Critical review* (pp. 155–190). Washington, DC: American Psychiatric Publishing.

D'Ath, P., Katona, P., Mullan, E., Evans, S., & Katona, C. (1994). Screening, detection and management of depression in elderly primary care attenders. I. The acceptability and performance of the 15 item Geriatric Depression Scale (GDS-15) and the development of short versions, *Family Practice, 11,* 260–266.

Dougherty, L., Klein, D., Olino, T., & Laptook, R. (2008). Depression in children and adolescents. In J. Hunsley & E. Mash (Eds.), *A guide to assessments that work* (pps. 69–95). New York: Oxford University Press.

Feher, E., Larrabee, G., & Crook, T. (1992). Factors attenuating the validity of the Geriatric Depression Scale in a dementia population. *Journal of the American Geriatrics Society, 40,* 906–909.

Fiske, A., & O'Riley, A. (2008). In J. Hunsley & E. Mash (Eds.), *A guide to assessments that work* (pp. 138–157). New York: Oxford University Press.

Kaslow, N., Rehm, L., & Siegel, A. (1984). Social-cognitive and cognitive correlates of depression in children. *Journal of Abnormal Child Psychology, 12,* 605–620.

Kovacs, M. (1992). *Children's Depression Inventory manual.* North Tonawanda, NY: Multi-Health Systems.

Myers, K., & Winters, N. C. (2002). Ten-year review of rating scales II: Scales for internalizing disorders. *Journal of the American Academy of Child and Adolescent Psychiatry, 41,* 634–660.

Persons, J., & Fresco, D. (2008). Adult depression. In J. Hunsley & E. Mash (Eds.), *A guide to assessments that work* (pp. 96–120). New York: Oxford University Press.

Radloff, L. (1977). The CES-D Scale: A self-report depression scale for research in the general population. *Applied Psychological Measurement, 1, ,* 385–401.

Reynolds, W. (1987). *Reynolds Adolescent Depression Scale (RADS).* Odessa, FL: Psychological Assessment Resources.

Reynolds, W. (2002). *Reynolds Adolescent Depression Scale – 2nd Edition. Professional manual.* Psychological Assessment Resources (Lutz FLA.).

Rush, A. J., Trivedi, M. H., Ibrahim, H. M., Carmody, T. J., Arrow, B., Klein, D. N., et al. (2003). The 16-item Quick Inventory of Depressive Symptomatology (QIDS), Clinician Rating (QIDS-C), and Self-Report (QIDS-SR): A psychometric evaluation in patients with chronic major depression. *Biological Psychiatry, 54,* 585.

Salamero, M., & Marcos, T. (1992). Factor study of the Geriatric Depression Scale. *Acta Psychiatrica Scandinavica, 86,* 283–286.

Weissman, M., Orvaschel, H., & Padian, N. (1980). Children's symptom and social functioning self-report scales: Comparison of mothers' and children's reports. *Journal of Nervous and Mental Disorders, 168,* 736–740.

Yesavage, J. A., Brink, T. L., Owen, R., Lum, O., Huang, V., Adey, M., et al. (1982–1983). Development and validation of a geriatric depression scale: A preliminary report. *Journal of Psychiatric Research, 17,* 37–49.

Zung, W. W. (1965) A self-rating depression scale. *Archives of General Psychiatry, 12,* 63–70.

10 Substance Use Disorders

The *DSM* provides diagnostic information for 11 classes of substances, including alcohol, amphetamines, caffeine, cannabis, cocaine, hallucinogens, inhalants, nicotine, opioids, phencyclidine, and sedatives/hypnotics/anxiolytics (American Psychiatric Association [APA], 2000). The manual also includes general criteria for *substance abuse* and *substance dependence*, the two types of *substance-related disorders*, rather than separate criteria for each class. The defining characteristic of *abuse* is the negative consequences of use, while *dependence* refers to compulsive use despite serious consequences, and is often accompanied by tolerance and withdrawal. The *DSM* also describes *substance-induced disorders*, which include intoxication, withdrawal, dementia, amnesia, psychosis, mood, anxiety, sexual dysfunction, and sleep.

Alcohol-related disorders in adolescence and adulthood are the primary focus of this chapter, and the other substances are discussed less extensively.

████████ **Prevalence**

Substance use and abuse disorders are highly prevalent in the United States. The National Epidemiologic Survey on Alcohol and Related Conditioned reported a 17.8% lifetime prevalence of alcohol abuse and a 4.7% prevalence during the past year (Hasin, Stinson, Ogburn, & Grant, 2007). The lifetime prevalence for alcohol dependence was 12.5% and past year dependence was 3.8%. The lifetime and 12-month prevalence of drug abuse was 1.4% and 7.7%, respectively, and for drug dependence was 0.6% and 2.6%, respectively (Compton, Thomas, Stinson, & Grant, 2007). The risk for dependence was greater for males.

Males are more likely to experience an alcohol use disorder, at a rate of 5:1, but this ratio depends on the age sampled (i.e., young adult samples might have closer gaps between men and women). Men are overrepresented among the amphetamine, cannabis, cocaine, hallucinogen, inhalant, opioid, and phency-clidine-related disorders. Women may be at an equal or even higher risk for prescription drug abuse of sedatives, hypnotics, and antianxiety drugs.

Comorbidity

A majority of adolescents (60%) have at least one psychiatric disorder along with a substance use disorder (Armstrong & Costello, 2002). The disruptive disorders—conduct disorder, oppositional defiant disorder, and attention-deficit/hyperactivity disorder (ADHD)—are most common, followed by depression (Armstrong & Costello, 2002). Adults are often similarly afflicted with comorbid disorders. Twenty percent of people with a substance use disorder also have a mood disorder (Grant et al., 2004). Almost as frequent are concurrent anxiety disorders, which occur in the last 12 months in 18% of those with substance use disorders in the United States. The co-occurrence of substance use and personality disorders is 39% for those with alcohol dependence and 69% of those with drug dependence (Jané-Llopis & Matytsina, 2006). Antisocial personality disorder is particularly common in men who abuse substances.

Because of high comorbidity rates between substance abuse/dependence and other disorders, individuals with other disorders should be routinely questioned about their substance use patterns. The social worker needs to establish the chronology of symptom patterns and assess whether the other disorder was present before the substance use, what the symptoms were like for the client during periods of abstinence, and how the chemical use affected the other disorder. Some authors recommend a period of 3 to 4 weeks after the person has stopped using before diagnosing the presence of another disorder or prescribing medication for that disorder (Miller & Fine, 1993). This recommendation implies that comorbidity prevalence rates may be artificially elevated by the practice of assigning diagnoses before some symptoms related to the substance use have abated. On the other hand, social workers should monitor clients in the early stages of abstinence for the emergence of symptoms, such as those of posttraumatic stress disorder (PTSD), which may have been masked by the use of substances (Petrakis, Gonzalez, Rosenheck, & Krystal, 2002).

Course of the Disorders

The typical onset for a substance use disorder begins in late adolescence or early adulthood. Having an adolescent substance use disorder puts the individual at risk for continuation into adulthood (Brook, Brook, Zhang, Cohen, & Whiteman, 2002; Rohde, Lewinsohn, Kahler, Seeley, & Brown, 2001). Despite the severe consequences to health and well-being, only a minority of those afflicted with drug and alcohol disorders seeks treatment (Compton et al., 2007; Hasin, Stinson, Ogburn, & Grant, 2007). For drug use disorders, lifetime help-seeking behavior is uncommon (8.1% for abuse and 37.9% for dependence) (Compton et al., 2007). Only 24.1% of those with alcohol dependence ever receive treatment (Hasin et al., 2007). For adolescents, only 10% of those that have substance use disorders receive treatment (Kraft, Schubert, Pond, & Aguirre-Molina, 2006).

The course of substance disorders is variable (Mirin et al., 2002). Some people have chronic, lifelong problems, others have periods of remittance followed by relapse, and still others are able to quit or reduce use to acceptable levels. Related to chronic use, medical problems related to drinking include gastrointestinal problems (gastritis, ulcers, and, in about 15% of heavy users, cirrhosis of the liver and pancreatitis) and cardiovascular conditions (hypertension and high levels of cholesterol, which increase the risk of heart disease) (Corrao, Bagnardi, Zambon, & Arico, 1999; Mirin et al., 2002). While low levels of drinking, defined as one to two drinks per day for women and two to four drinks for men, may be protective against mortality, excessive drinking is associated with higher mortality (Di Castelnuovo et al., 2006).

Problems related to cocaine use include weight loss and malnutrition, myocardial infarction, and stroke. Selling cocaine is associated with traumatic injuries from violent attacks. For heroin (opioid) use, transmission of HIV infection from needle use, tuberculosis, malnutrition, and head trauma are prevalent. The death rate is high among those who do not receive treatment—about 10 per 1000 annually (Mirin et al., 2002). Death typically results from injuries sustained while buying or selling drugs. HIV infection is another cause of death.

Assessment

During clinical assessment, the social worker should focus on the following factors (Bukstein et al., 1997; Riggs & Whitmore, 1999):

- Onset, progression, patterns, context, and frequency of use of all substances
- Tolerance or withdrawal symptoms
- Major life events

- Other disorders, including the relationship between the onset and progression of the symptoms and substance use
- "Triggers" and context of use
- Perceived advantages and disadvantages of use
- Motivations and goals for treatment
- Number of times the individual has quit and the strategies that were used
- Financial and legal status
- Education and employment status
- Condition of health (a physical examination may be warranted)
- Social support networks
- Coping skills

Also see Appendices I and II for descriptions of self-report measurement tools that can be used with adolescents and adults, respectively.

Adolescents should receive a confidential individual interview and also a parent interview (Riggs & Whitmore, 1999). The social worker, in addition to asking questions about the child, should address the extent of parental substance use, parents' attitudes toward their child's use, the amount of monitoring and supervision the youth receives, and the level of attachment and cohesion in the family (Bukstein et al., 2005).

For older adults, ageist attitudes of health care providers may present obstacles to assessment (Vinton & Wambach, 2005). Providers may not bring up substance abuse; they also may not believe elders can benefit from intervention or that their quality of life would improve as a result. The reliability of elder self-report may also be suspect. Denial, sense of stigma, social desirability effects, and memory loss can affect the accurate recollection or admission of alcohol problems. It is sometimes difficult to tell whether physical and cognitive problems found in older adults are due to the process of aging or the effects of consumption. Screening for alcohol abuse among the elderly includes *(a)* the quantity and frequency of alcohol consumption, *(b)* alcohol-related social and legal problems (e.g., housing problems, falls or accidents, poor nutrition, inadequate self-and home care, lack of exercise, and social isolation), *(c)* alcohol-related health problems, *(d)* symptoms of drunkenness and dependence, and *(e)* self-recognition of alcohol-related problems (Vinton & Wambach, 2005).

Risk and Protective Factors

Risk and protective factors for the onset of adolescent substance use are described in Exhibit 10.1. For adolescents, certain influences present at the completion of treatment, including participation in after care and Alchoholics Anonymous (AA) meetings, a lack of substance-using peers, involvement in a variety of non-substance-related activities, use of coping strategies learned in

Exhibit 10.1

Risk and Protective Factors for Adolescent Substance Use

System Level	Risk	Protective
Biological	Male	
	Genetics	
Psychological	Impulsivity and ADHD symptoms	Goal direction
	Early onset of experimentation	
	Aggression and under-controlled behavior in childhood	
	Sensation-seeking behavior	
	Low feelings of guilt	
	Conduct problems and delinquency	
Peers	Social impairment	
	Affiliation with deviant peers	
	Peer substance abuse	Having abstinent friends
School	Low achievement and academic failure	
	Truancy	
	Suspension	
	Low motivation, negative attitude toward school	Positive connection to school
Family	Parental substance abuse	
	Sibling substance abuse	
	Permissive parental values about teen alcohol and drug use	Parental warnings about alcohol use
	Harsh, inconsistent, and ineffective discipline strategies	
	Lack of monitoring and supervision	Parental control and supervision
	Child abuse and other trauma	
	Poor relationships with parents and siblings, low bonding	Being close to parents
		Low level of family conflict
		A warm and supportive family environment
	Unemployment, poor education of mother	
	Teens running away from home	
Community	Availability	Clear community prohibitions, such as higher taxes on liquor
Race	Caucasian (alcohol)	
	Hispanic (drug use)	
Sexual identity	Lesbian, gay, and bisexual youth	Heterosexual

ADHD, attention-deficit/hyperactivity disorder.

Sources: Farrell and White (1998); French, Finkbiner, and Duhamel (2002); Hawkins, Catalano, and Miller (1992); Jessor, Van Den Bos, Vanderryn, Costa, and Turbin (1995); Kaplow, Curran, and Dodge (2002); Kilpatrick et al. (2000); Latimer, Newcomb, Winters, and Stinchfield (2000); Loeber, Farrington, Stouthamer-Loeber, and Van Kammen (1998); Marshal et al., 2008; Martin et al. (2002); National Institute on Drug Abuse (1997).

treatment, and motivation to continue sobriety, are associated with recovery (Chung & Maisto, 2006). Risk influences for substance use problems after treatment involve high levels of internalizing and externalizing disorders in youth (Babor, Webb, Burleson, & Kaminer, 2002).

Risk and protective factors for the onset and recovery of adult substance use disorders are delineated in Exhibit 10.2 and 10.3, respectively.

Exhibit 10.2

Risk and Protective Factors for Onset of Adult Substance Use Disorders

Risks	Protective Factors
Biology	
Genetics[a]	No family history
Male	Female
	Asian origin (a deficiency of an enzyme that breaks down alcohol after its ingestion is present in 50% of Japanese, Chinese, and Korean people[b])
Psychological	
Childhood depression[c]	No prior mental disorder
Antisocial personality disorder (male)	
Social	
Family	
Sexual abuse (particularly for females)	No history of sexual abuse
Being unmarried	Being married
Peer	
Substance-using peers	Friends who do not support substance use
Culture	
Native American	
Neighborhood	
Availability of drugs	Lack of availability

[a] The influence of genetics is low overall, but stronger for males (Walters, 2002).
[b] Luczak, Glatt, and Wall (2006).
[c] Crum et al. (2008).

Exhibit 10.3

Risk and Protective Factors for Course of Substance Use Disorders

Risks	Protective Factors
Features of Use	
The year after treatment is high risk for relapse	Two years of abstinence
High levels of pretreatment use[a]	
Substance use during treatment	
Biological	
Female	
Life Events	
Physical and/or sexual victimization[b]	
Psychological	
Concurrent disorders, especially personality disorders (borderline and antisocial)	Lack of concurrent disorders
	Motivation
Social	
Family	
Lack of family support	Family support for sobriety
Social Support	
Substance-using peers	Non-substance-using peers
	AA attendance (or at least contact with one member from AA)[c]
	Ability to develop new relationships
Culture	
Ethnic minority	Intervention that integrates culturally relevant beliefs and healing practices
SES	
Low SES	

[a] Karageorge and Wisdom (2001).
[b] Orwin, Maranda, and Brady (2001).
[c] Bond, Kaskutas, and Weisner (2003).
AA, Alcoholics Anonymous; SES, socioeconomic status.

Intervention

Goals

For people with substance abuse problems, common intervention goals include reducing or eliminating the substance use and reducing the physical harm associated with such use. Other goals involve improving psychological and social functioning (mending disrupted relationships, reducing impulsivity, building social and vocational skills, and maintaining employment) and relapse prevention. For adolescents, intervention should also include family involvement and prioritize the improvement of communication among family members (Bukstein et al., 2005). Parents should be helped to consistently provide proper guidance and set limits for the child. Any addiction patterns in the parents must be recognized and, if possible, treated. Intervention should also help adolescents and their families to develop an alcohol- and drug-free lifestyle, including recreational activities with non-substance-using peers. Indeed, treatment plans that include a comprehensive array of services, including life skills, recreational sessions, and vocational and educational skills training, have been associated with improved outcomes for adolescents (Orwin & Ellis, 2001).

Reducing and Ameliorating Substance Use

For adolescents, abstinence is always recommended, but as the person matures into adulthood, controlled alcohol use may be a possibility (Bukstein et al., 2005). However, controversy surrounds the goal of controlled drinking (Mirin et al., 2002). For some users, controlled drinking might be an intermediate goal with a long-term goal of abstinence. Controlled use might be unrealistic for others, however, as any further use may pose too high a risk. Those who attain total abstinence show the best prognosis over time because any use may entail disinhibition, increased cravings for other drugs, poor judgment, and an increased risk of relapse.

The following guidelines cited by Mirin et al. (2002) help to determine who might be appropriate candidates for controlled drinking. Such candidates should be:

- In the early stages of alcohol abuse
- Realistically confident that they can control their drinking
- Able to demonstrate improved occupational and psychological functioning as a result of reduced use

Behavioral self-control training has been developed to help people control their drinking. This includes spacing out drinks, prolonging the duration of drinks, and switching to lower-proof drinks. Identifying high-risk situations and self-monitoring are other key components of the process. Walters (2002) conducted a meta-analysis of 17 studies on behavioral self-control training and found that they showed comparative effectiveness with abstinence-based programs. As a result, Walters maintains that individuals in treatment should be offered a choice of goals.

Harm Reduction

Behavioral self-control training falls under the rubric of harm reduction. On a direct practice level, harm reduction means working with clients to reduce the harmful consequences of the behavior, such as reducing the use of substances and encouraging the use of condoms and clean needles (Van Wormer & Davis, 2008). On a policy level, it means refraining from administering certain legal consequences and punishments for the use of illegal behaviors such as drug use. Punishment is seen as having the potential to drive risk behavior underground for fear of consequences, and thus at times actually encouraging the use of unsafe practices. Alternative interventions such as methadone treatment instead of illegal heroin use and the provision of clean needles and condoms are promoted instead.

Treatment Settings

Commonly available treatment settings for substance abusers include hospitals, residential treatment facilities, partial hospital care, and outpatient programs (see Exhibit 10.4). In the United States, inpatient treatment was the modality of choice until recently, when the typical length of stay decreased substantially; now the vast majority of those with substance use problems are treated on an outpatient basis.

Client characteristics that influence decisions about the treatment setting include the potential harm of withdrawal and the extent of environmental support for sobriety. Symptoms of alcohol withdrawal typically begin within 4 to 12 hours after cessation or reduction of alcohol use. They peak in intensity during the second day of abstinence and generally resolve within 4 or 5 days. Serious complications may include seizures, hallucinations, and delirium, although these are now rare. In the past, mortality rates for alcohol withdrawal delirium were as high as 20% but currently are closer to 1% because of improvements in diagnosis and medical intervention. Still, withdrawal can be life threatening for elderly people who have significant physical dependence (U.S. Department of Health and Human Services, 2001).

The social environment plays a role in attitudes about use and in what circumstances, as well as choice of substances and one's motivation and ability to comply with interventions. Peer and family support are critical factors for recovery. Conversely, significant others who enable use and drug availability bode poorly for outcome. Such risks need to be addressed in treatment with either a high degree of community support or temporary removal from these circumstances through residential treatment. For further guidance on appropriate placement, social workers should be aware of the Patient Placement Criteria for the Treatment of Substance-Related Disorders

Exhibit 10.4

Treatment Settings

Setting	Indications
Hospitalization	Severe withdrawal or a documented history of heavy alcohol use and high tolerance
	People who repeatedly fail to cooperate with or benefit from outpatient detoxification
	Following a drug overdose that cannot be safely treated in an outpatient or emergency room setting
	Severe or medically complicated syndromes
	Comorbid general medical conditions that make ambulatory detoxification unsafe
	A history of not engaging in or benefiting from treatment in a less intensive setting
	Psychiatric comorbidity that markedly impairs the person's ability to participate in or benefit from treatment, or the comorbid disorder itself requires hospital care (e.g., depression with suicidal thoughts or acute psychosis)
	Lack of response to less intensive treatment, or when substance use poses an ongoing threat to physical or mental health
Residential (at least 3 months)	People who do not meet criteria for hospitalization but whose lives have come to focus predominantly on substance use and who lack sufficient living skills and social supports to maintain abstinence in an outpatient setting
	Severe withdrawal or a history of heavy alcohol use and high tolerance, placing the person at risk for withdrawal
	People who repeatedly fail to cooperate with or benefit from outpatient detoxification
	Some programs are specifically designed for adolescents, pregnant or postpartum women, and women with young children
	Includes therapeutic communities in which the community itself is seen as the method of change (De Leon, 2008)
Partial hospital care	People who require intensive care but have a reasonable probability of refraining from substance use outside a restricted setting
	People leaving hospitals or residential settings who remain at high risk for relapse (insufficient motivation, severe psychiatric comorbidity, or a history of immediate relapse)
	People returning to high-risk environments who have limited psychosocial supports for remaining drug free
	People who respond poorly to intensive outpatient treatment
Outpatient treatment	People whose clinical condition or environmental circumstances do not require a more intensive level of care
	People who are cocaine dependent (but this is applied intensively; more than once a week)

Source: Mirin et al. (2002).

of the American Society of Addiction Medicine (Mee-Lee, Shulman, Fishman, Gastfriend, & Griffith, 2001).

Adolescents who access care for substance abuse are often in other intervention systems, such as child welfare, juvenile justice, and mental health. The needs of each young person may consequently be managed by multiple agencies, and providing quality treatment often requires the social worker's navigation across these systems (Kraft et al., 2006).

Psychosocial Treatments

One means of conceptualizing intervention for people with substance use disorders is the *transtheoretical stages of change model*. Six stages of change are formulated in this model, based on the individual's readiness to change. Intervention techniques from different theoretical orientations are used to match the relevant stage of change, with a primary focus on building clients' motivation to take action toward their goals. This intervention model is delineated in Exhibit 10.5.

Exhibit 10.5

The Stages of Change and Strategies at Each Stage

Stage of Change	Characteristics	Change Strategies
Precontemplation	Unwilling to do anything about the problem	Link the client with self-help groups for education
	Sees the problem behavior as possessing more advantages than disadvantages	Motivational interviewing
		Behavioral training for partners
	Usually coerced or pressured to seek help by others	
Contemplation	Client begins to consider there is a problem and the feasibility and costs of changing the behavior	Provide education about the disorder and the recovery process
	Wants to understand the behavior and frequently feels distress over it	Bolster the advantages of changing and problem-solve about how to lessen the disadvantages
	Thinks about making change in the next 6 months	Identify social support systems
		Couples therapy
		Cognitive-behavioral: Self-monitoring; functional analysis; consider alternative reinforcers for the problem behaviors

Preparation (Determination)	Person is poised to change in the next month	Couples therapy Cognitive-behavioral: Set goals; develop a change plan; develop coping skills
Action	Client has started to modify the problem behavior or the environment in an effort to promote change in the past 6 months	Couples therapy Cognitive-behavioral: Appraise high-risk situations and coping strategies to overcome these; apply alternative reinforcers to problem behaviors Assess social support systems so others are a resource for change rather than a hindrance
Maintenance	Sustained change has occurred for at least 6 months	Help the individual find alternative sources of satisfaction and continue to support lifestyle changes Cognitive-behavioral: Assist the client in practicing and applying coping strategies; remain vigilant for cognitive distortions that might be associated with the problem and ways to counteract them; maintain environmental control
Relapse	The problem behavior has resumed; another cycle has begun, and the client reenters either the precontemplation or the contemplation stage	Cognitive-behavioral: Develop a greater awareness of high-risk situations and coping strategies needed to address these challenges

Source: Adapted from Connors, Donovan, and DiClemente (2001).

Originators of the stages of change model claim that it is empirically derived and has garnered much research support (e.g., Prochaska, DiClemente, & Norcross, 1994; Velicer, Hughes, Fava, Prochaska, & DiClemente, 1995). According to a comprehensive review, however, there is as yet no firm evidence that people progress systematically through each stage of change (Littell & Girvin, 2002). At the same time, a meta-analysis of 47 studies did reveal that cognitive-affective processes were more indicative of the stages of contemplation or preparation and that behavioral processes were more common in the action stage (Rosen, 2000), which generally supports the hypothesized movement of change from a cognitive to a behavioral process as clients become ready to take action toward change.

The treatment models discussed in this chapter—motivational interviewing, AA-based approaches, family therapy, and cognitive-behavioral therapy (CBT)—are organized according to the stages of change model in Exhibit 10.5. In this way, the social worker can decide when a particular treatment approach can be introduced at an optimal time.

Systematic reviews using Cochrane Collaboration standards of methodology are lacking in the alcohol disorders treatment field for adults and for substance use disorders, in general, for adolescents and adults. However, other reviews (Imel, Wampold, Miller, & Fleming, 2008) and large-scale studies suggest few differences in terms of improvement for the different treatment models that have been tested for adult drinking (Project MATCH, 1997) and adolescent cannabis misuse (Titus & Dennis, 2006).

Motivational Interviewing

Motivational interviewing is "a client-centered, directive method for enhancing intrinsic motivation to change by exploring and resolving ambivalence" (Miller & Rollnick, 2002, p. 25). Originally developed for the treatment of substance abuse, it has been used both as a stand-alone treatment and as a way to engage people in other interventions (Walitzer, Dermen, & Conners, 1999). In terms of the stages of change model, motivational interviewing is helpful for those in either the precontemplation (denying the need for change) or contemplation (considering change) stages.

Several guiding principles for the practitioner underlie the techniques of motivational interviewing:

- Listening and expressing empathy
- Developing discrepancies between problem behavior and the client's goals and values
- "Rolling" with resistance, which means avoiding power struggles and instead making statements that help clients argue for change
- Supporting self-efficacy, or the client's sense of confidence that he or she can change
- Developing a change plan

A meta-analysis of randomized, controlled trials was conducted of studies on motivational interviewing (Vasilaki, Hosier, & Cox, 2006). When motivational interviewing was compared to no treatment, the overall effect size was small. Interestingly, when motivational interviewing was compared to other treatments, it performed better—at a small to moderate effect. The average duration in these studies of motivational interviewing was only 53 minutes, which was much shorter than the comparison treatments. Therefore, it appears that for such a brief time investment, motivational interviewing may produce a potentially high impact.

The social worker should consider learning the principles and techniques of motivational interviewing because they often work with people—both adolescents and adults—who are mandated to treatment settings. The other benefit of motivational interviewing is that it can be implemented in a brief fashion and can be potentially effective with clients who exhibit high levels of anger (Longabaugh, Wirtz, Zweben, & Stout, 1998; Project MATCH, 1997).

Cognitive-Behavioral Interventions

There are many interventions based on the cognitive-behavioral theoretical perspective, most of which integrate strategies founded on classical conditioning, operant conditioning, and social learning perspectives. The CBT perspective considers substance use to be a result of learned behaviors that begin and are maintained in the context of a person's unique interpersonal and social environment. Different interventions focus on certain aspects of the substance use behavior, and these can be combined into a comprehensive CBT approach that includes self-monitoring, the avoidance of certain stimulus cues, changing reinforcement patterns, and developing coping skills to manage and resist urges to use. Other skills that can be incorporated into the intervention may include substance refusal skills, communication skills, problem-solving skills, assertiveness, relaxation training, anger management, modifying cognitive distortions, and relapse prevention (Kaminer & Waldron, 2006). See Exhibit 10.6 for a description of CBT models in use for substance use disorders.

Exhibit 10.6

Cognitive-Behavioral Interventions

Theoretical Basis	Interventions
Classical conditioning: acquisition of preferences and aversions for alcohol and drugs, tolerance, and urges and craving	Identifying stimulus cues (triggers), including setting, time, and place; and learning strategies (either avoidance or techniques from different learning perspectives, such as self-control and reinforcers for competing behaviors)
Operant theory: views alcohol and drug use as due to specific antecedents and consequences. Reinforcement arises from the physiological effects of substances, the reduction of tension, attenuation of negative affect, or enhancement of social interactions.	Contingency management approaches: identifying alternative reinforcers, such as vouchers for drug-free urine tests that can be exchanged for rewards such as movie tickets (Higgins & Silverman, 2008) Community reinforcement approaches: family members or peers reinforce substance-free behaviors (Miller, Meyers, & Hiller-Sturmhofel, 1999)
Social learning model: substance is used due to modeling from others (peers, adults) in combination with individual's cognitive-processes (i.e., stress-coping model)	Coping skills training

Source: Kaminer and Waldron (2006).

Family Interventions

When possible, family participation is helpful for intervening with a person who has a substance abuse problem. A substantial burden is imposed on families when a member has a substance use disorder. Families also have a tremendous potential impact on perpetuating or ameliorating these problems. Families can clearly affect the abuser's motivation and ability to comply with intervention (Mirin et al., 2002).

A traditional approach for family members of those with substance use problems is Al-Anon. The 12 steps are used to facilitate family member well-being and to cultivate detachment from the afflicted individual's addiction. Al-Anon has not typically been studied except in comparison to some of the interventions described later in this chapter.

Another widely known but little studied approach is the Johnson Institute intervention in which confrontation to the addict is provided by family members with the goal of engagement in treatment (Johnson, 1986). When family members undergo the training, only a proportion end up going through the confrontation procedure (about 30%), but for those who do, there is a high rate of treatment engagement (see review by Miller, Meyers, & Tonigan, 1999).

Another class of family interventions essentially trains family members in behavioral techniques to exert influence on the "drinker" so that the person may develop motivation to change. This approach emphasizes that the family member is not responsible for the alcoholic person's behavior. Rather, the family member removes conditions in the environment supportive of drinking, reinforces appropriate behavior of the addict, gives feedback about inappropriate behavior while drinking, and provides consequences if behavior exceeds agreed-upon limits. This intervention is given various names, including *unilateral therapy* (Thomas, Santa, Bronson, & Oyserman, 1987), *reinforcement training* (Sisson & Azrin, 1986), the *pressures to change* model (Barber & Gilbertson, 1996), and more recently, CRAFT (*community reinforcement as a family training approach* (Meyers, Miller, Hill, & Tonigan, 1999; Miller, Meyers, & Tonigan, 1999). For adolescents, *family behavior therapy* (Donohue & Azrin, 2001) falls under a similar rubric. In the few studies that have been conducted, these models have resulted in greater treatment entry rates than the comparison conditions, including Al-Anon (Thomas & Corcoran, 2001). While one review indicated that the well-being of partners did not improve as a result of intervention, Miller, Meyers, and Tonigan (1999) reported increased adjustment for family members using CRAFT that were equivalent to the other conditions. These differing results may be that the CRAFT study included parents as well as partners, whereas the previous studies concentrated on only partners, and family members tended to have more success in engaging their loved one in treatment (Miller et al., 1999).

Behavioral couples therapy is another research-focused approach for use when there is both a substance use problem (either alcohol or drug use) and a conflict issue within the couple. The main objective of couples therapy is to alter patterns of interaction that maintain chemical abuse and build a relationship that more effectively supports sobriety (O'Farrell & Fals-Stewart, 2006). These interventions are cognitive-behavioral in nature, entailing building communication skills, planning family activities, initiating caring behaviors, and expressing feelings. Intervention is generally brief (10–15 sessions) and is delivered in either individual or couples' group modalities. A meta-analysis on behavioral couples therapy involved 12 randomized controlled studies (Powers, Vedel, & Emmelkamp, 2008). Behavioral couples therapy was superior to control conditions (usually individual treatment) at posttest on relationship satisfaction, but it was not until the follow-up period when substance use outcomes were superior to control conditions. The authors believed that the increase in relationship satisfaction over time led to the reductions in substance use at follow-up. Therefore, couples treatment might be indicated when there is severe marital conflict as well as substance abuse, and both partners are motivated to participate in this modality. However, the research in this area has mainly focused on marital partners, rather than partners in any other kind of relationship.

Family therapy approaches have received the most attention for adolescent substance abuse disorders (Bukstein et al., 2005). Because of the multidimensional nature of substance use problems in adolescence, most family therapy approaches to treatment are models that integrate several theoretical frameworks. For instance, *brief strategic family therapy* (Szapocznik & Williams, 2000) incorporates both structural and strategic techniques. *Functional family therapy* possesses elements of structural and strategic family systems approaches, as well as behavioral family therapy, with a particular emphasis on the functions of symptoms (Alexander & Parsons, 1982). Both *multidimensional family therapy* (Liddle, 1999) and *multisystemic therapy* (Henggeler, Schoenwald, Borduin, Rowland, & Cunningham, 1998) are presented as "ecologically integrative approaches" (Mirin et al., 2002), because they go beyond family therapy to modify multiple domains of functioning affecting the youth's behavior, including other key supports and systems in the youth's life. Waldron and Turner (2008) claim that multidimensional family therapy, multisystemic therapy, and functional family therapy are empirically supported treatments. Given some of the concerns about multisystemic therapy with juvenile offenders after subjecting the treatment to stringent systematic review procedures (Littell, Popa, & Forsythe, 2005), these findings should be viewed with caution (see Chapter 5). Further systematic review using updated and conventional methods for each of these treatments is therefore warranted.

Alcoholics Anonymous Approaches

Alcoholics Anonymous self-help groups and treatment-based approaches (the Minnesota model) have tended to predominate in the substance abuse treatment field (Fuller & Hiller-Sturmhofel, 1999; Kelly, Myers, & Brown, 2002; Sheehan & Owen, 1999). We consider these approaches separately here. First, AA self-help groups offer a number of potential advantages for alcohol users[1] (Mirin et al., 2002):

- Referral is appropriate at all stages of the treatment process, even for those who may still actively abuse substances.
- Individuals who attend AA or Narcotics Anonymous regularly receive group support, including reminders of the disastrous consequences of substance use and the benefits of abstinence and sobriety.
- Participants receive straightforward advice and encouragement about avoiding relapse.
- The process of working through the 12 steps with a sponsor provides a structured opportunity for the person to assess the role of past life experiences and personal identity in the development and maintenance of the substance use disorder. A sponsor who is compatible with the individual can provide important guidance and support during the recovery process, particularly during periods of emotional distress and increased craving.
- Opportunities for substance-free social events and interactions are available.
- Members can attend meetings on a self-determined or prescribed schedule—every day if necessary. Periods associated with high risk for relapse, such as weekends, holidays, and evenings are particularly appropriate for attendance.
- Self-help groups based on the 12-step model are also available for family members and friends (such as Al-Anon, Alateen, and Nar-Anon). Such groups provide support and education about the illness and help to reduce maladaptive enabling behavior in family and friends.

The research on AA self-help groups is scant and methodologically limited, and, to our knowledge, there have not been any updated systematic reviews or meta-analyses conducted since the last edition of this volume. In one meta-analysis, Tonigan, Toscova, and Miller (1996) examined the relationship between AA attendance and drinking. Although attendance was linked to reduced drinking, the relationship was small. In another meta-analysis, Kownacki and Shadish (1999) indicated that those who voluntarily attended AA did better than those who chose not to utilize AA, and that individuals coerced into attending 12-step groups did not reduce their drinking. Regarding AA as part of an inpatient treatment model, few randomized studies have been conducted, and these provide mild support for its helpfulness (Kownacki & Shadish, 1999).

Other studies show support for AA as a treatment model. For adolescents, abstinence rates for small-scale evaluations of 12-step-based interventions are reported in the range of 50% to 60% (Winters, Stinchfield, Opland, Weller, & Latimer, 2000). In the Project MATCH study described earlier, the 12-step facilitation intervention (a formal treatment approach that guides the individual through the first five steps of AA and encourages AA participation) was as effective as CBT and motivational interviewing. Indeed, individuals in after care treatment who were initially severely dependent, and individuals in outpatient treatment whose social networks supported drinking, had better results with the AA-based treatment than with the cognitive-behavioral and motivational interviewing conditions at 3-year follow-up (Longabaugh, Wirtz, Zweben, & Stout, 1998; Project MATCH, 1997). In another study, 133 adults were randomly assigned to either a cognitive-behavioral or an AA relapse prevention approach. The latter intervention produced the most favorable substance use outcomes, particularly for those with high initial psychological distress (Brown, Seraganian, Tremblay, & Annis, 2002).

Social Diversity

Sexual Minorities

Gay men and lesbian women are at increased risk for substance abuse for a number of reasons (Beatty et al., 1999). Gay bars, where alcohol is a main feature, are still one of the few legitimate places in most cities for gays and lesbians to meet and socialize. A second risk factor for substance abuse among gays and lesbians is that they are not able to fully partake in societal institutions that tend to attenuate substance use among heterosexuals, such as marriage and family life. Third, many gay and lesbian people do not have the array of support from family, friends, and acquaintances. The loss of peers and acquaintances in the gay network is another burden to which the gay community is susceptible, which might lead to alcohol and drug use for coping with grief.

Fourth, "sexual minority status may entail personal confrontation with prejudicial attitudes, discriminatory behaviors, unfairness and unequal power, hatred, and verbal, emotional, or physical abuse" (Beatty et al., 1999, pp. 545–546). The stress from discrimination may lead some people to cope through the use of alcohol or drugs. Along with the other risks substances pose, use by gay males might lower inhibitions and decrease safe sexual practices, which, in turn, might lead to the possibility of HIV infection.

Specialized programming for gays and lesbians is available, though very few programs exist and empirical support for their effectiveness is lacking (Beatty et al., 1999). Social workers should be aware that there are AA groups for gay men and lesbians (LAMBDA) in most larger communities.

Ethnic minorities are at risk for a lack of engagement in services (Mirin et al., 2002). Although it is recommended that intervention should integrate culturally relevant beliefs and healing practices, taking into account the level of the client's acculturation and the particular group's values (Castro,

Proescholdbell, Abeita, & Rodriquez, 1999), guidelines tend to be general and not subject to empirical testing. Future research should ensure that treatment outcome is assessed in terms of ethnicity to examine whether tested interventions have a differential impact on people from different ethnic groups.

Women

Women are susceptible to the "telescoping effect," a rapid onset of addiction and health problems once they begin drinking (Brady & Back, 2008). This progression may be partly due to physiological factors, although psychosocial influences may enter into the process. Because women have a higher ratio of fat and a lower ratio of water in their bodies, alcohol and drugs enter the system at greater concentrations and thus with more potency. The female body's inability to metabolize alcohol means the alcohol is absorbed directly through the protective barrier of the stomach, leading to an increased risk of liver problems, and then a higher rate of medical problems and death.

Children born to addicted mothers are also at risk for health problems (Finnegan & Kandall, 2008). Short-term risks include fetal alcohol syndrome, low birth weight (which puts a child at risk for other disorders), the complications of postnatal withdrawal, and HIV infection. These potential short-term effects may also have long-term consequences for children, such as cognitive and motor development problems.

Women tend to be underrepresented in treatment. Financial barriers, such as lack of money and health insurance, child care, and transportation prevent many women from seeking treatment. Other explanations for women's underutilization of services include their greater perceptions of the social stigma associated with drug and alcohol abuse. Once they are in treatment, women are found to have a higher prevalence than men of primary comorbid depressive and anxiety disorders that require specific intervention. Many women with substance use disorders have a history of physical or sexual abuse (both as children and adults), which may influence their treatment participation and outcomes (Orwin, Maranda, & Brady, 2001).

Another pattern of women is that they often develop substance use problems in the context of relationships (Ashley, Marsden, & Brady, 2003). Many women have become involved with drugs or alcohol through a partner. Female clients also tend to have more family responsibilities and need more help with family-related problems.

A review of 38 studies on the effect of women-specific substance abuse treatment programming found a consistently positive effect on alcohol and drug use reduction, employment, mental health outcomes, and decreased criminality, among other measures (Ashley et al., 2003). The following components were related to the effectiveness of such programs: child care provision; prenatal care; women-only admissions; supplemental services that addressed female topics, such as sexuality, parenting, and relationships;

mental health programming; and comprehensive services, such as vocational and employment services. These components may not only reduce barriers to treatment entry and retention but also improve outcomes because they address the salient needs of women who abuse substances. In a meta-analysis on 33 studies of women's treatment, more specific results were found (Orwin, Francisco, & Bernichon, 2001). Pregnancy and personal adjustment were the outcomes most affected by women's programming, rather than substance use itself.

Co-occurring Psychiatric and Substance Use Disorders

As discussed, people with substance use disorders have high rates of comorbid disorders. In the chapters on schizophrenia, the affective disorders (bipolar disorder and depression), the anxiety disorders, ADHD, eating disorders, and personality disorders, the elevated risk of substance use is reported. The social worker should be aware that treatment of comorbid disorders will not spontaneously resolve the substance use disorder. Over time, it often takes on a life of its own (Mirin et al., 2002). Therefore, both the substance use and the mental health disorder need to be addressed. Medications are often prescribed for co-occurring psychiatric disorders, although they typically do not affect the substance use (Petrakis et al., 2002).

For those with schizophrenia, the immediate goal might be stabilization of the psychiatric illness, followed by motivational interviewing. Confrontation, a commonly used technique in many substance abuse treatment settings, may not be effective for those who are potentially psychotic or suicidal (Petrakis et al., 2002); a supportive approach might be indicated instead. As always, the social worker must attend not only to the psychotherapeutic needs of the individual but also to concrete needs, such as homelessness and physical health. Ongoing case management might be necessary to help navigate the client through the necessary mental health, addiction, health, housing, and welfare services. Indeed, in a meta-analysis of intervention for co-occurring disorders, while effect sizes overall were low, intensive case management had the highest effect (Dumaine, 2003).

The social worker should know about several treatment manuals that have been developed for people with co-occurring schizophrenia and substance use disorders (Ziedonis et al., 2005). The approaches include dual recovery therapy, modified CBT and motivational enhancement therapy, and the Substance Abuse Management Module. All of these approaches include components of motivational interviewing, relapse prevention, and social skills training as well as encourage participation in 12-step mutual help programs. The manuals were developed to take into account the various special needs of persons with psychotic disorders such as low motivation and cognitive impairment (Ross, 2008).

A Cochrane systematic review was conducted on treatments applied to people with both substance use and serious mental illness (Cleary, Hunt, Matheson, & Walter, 2009). Although integrated treatment—treating both the substance use problem and the mental disorder in the same system of care—has been touted (New Freedom Commission on Mental Health, 2003), neither it nor any other treatment showed benefits over treatment as usual in Cleary et al. (2009). However, methodological problems of the primary studies hampered any firm conclusions about the research.

For persons with depression, anxiety (Petrakis et al., 2002; Ross, 2008), and eating disorders (Sysko & Hildebrandt, 2009), CBT might be indicated because the techniques can address both the psychiatric and substance use concerns. Bipolar disorder concurrent with substance abuse disorders has also been tested with cognitive behavioral models (Schmitz et al., 2002; Weiss et al., 2000). Of the various anxiety disorders, PTSD has garnered the most research for CBT in treating comorbid substance use disorders (Ross, 2008). A treatment manual, Seeking Safety, has been developed and reduces both PTSD and substance use in women with these comorbid disorders (Hien, Cohen, Miele, Litt, & Capstick, 2004; Najavits, Weiss, & Liese, 1996).

For clients with personality disorders, two manual-based interventions have been developed. Dialectical behavioral therapy is used for persons with co-occurring borderline personality disorder and substance use disorders (Dimeff, Comtois, & Linehan, 2003), and an intervention known as dual-focus schema therapy also addresses the symptoms of both personality disorders and substance abuse (Ball, 1998). Of the two, dialectical behavior therapy has demonstrated greater efficacy for improving symptoms related to both disorders (Dimeff et al., 2003; Ross, 2008).

A systematic review of the published literature examined the advantages of integrated treatment for anxiety and depression when it occurred with substance use disorders (Hesse, 2009). The four studies that used an integrated approach for both depression and substance use disorders indicated that it offered benefits for reducing substance use. However, for anxiety, only substance use treatment was better for reducing substance use. More research for treatment of co-occurring disorders is clearly needed given the conflicting findings and methodological problems for anxiety and depression comorbid with substance use.

Pharmacological Interventions

Two types of medications are currently used in substance abuse treatment: aversive medications, designed to deter client drinking, and anticraving medications, which purport to reduce one's desire to use substances (Fuller & Hiller-Sturmhofel, 1999). The primary aversive drug, disulfiram (Antabuse), inhibits the activity of aldehyde dehydrogenase, the enzyme that metabolizes acetaldehyde, the first metabolic breakdown product of alcohol. In the presence of disulfiram, alcohol use results in an accumulation of toxic levels of acetaldehyde, which is accompanied by a variety of unpleasant and potentially dangerous (but rarely lethal) symptoms (Mirin et al., 2002). Compliance with this medication is often difficult to secure, however, and physicians may be reluctant to prescribe because of people's adverse reactions to the medication (McLellan, 2008).

Medications to prevent relapse are called antidipsotropics. Naltrexone, a drug that is being increasingly used in the United States, is one of these. Naltrexone is an opioid receptor antagonist, a substance that blocks opioid receptors in the brain, so that the individual fails to experience positive effects from opiate use (but it is also used for alcohol). Acamprosate has been more recently approved by the FDA; it is thought to stabilize a chemical balance in the brain that is otherwise disrupted by alcohol abuse, possibly by blocking glutamine receptors while activating gamma-aminobutyric acid (Williams, 2005). A meta-analysis of naltrexone and acamprosate for alcohol dependence showed that acamprosate was better at preventing a relapse, and naltrexone was better at preventing a "lapse" from becoming a relapse (that is, it prevented heavy drinking) (Rösner, Leucht, Lehert, & Soyka, 2008).

For opioid addiction specifically, methadone and buprenorphine (the latter can be prescribed on an outpatient basis) can be used as substitution therapy with goals being the prevention of withdrawal, the elimination of cravings, and the blockage of euphoric effects obtained by illegal opiate use (Bukstein & Cornelius, 2006).

Summary of Treatment

Social workers are probably familiar with AA (12 steps), as this has been the long-standing approach to treatment for addiction. However, social workers should also be familiar with other available treatments that have shown some evidence basis for their use in the different settings in which social work may be involved. In order to assist the social worker in program planning and practice with substance use, adolescent treatment manuals can be found at http://www.chestnut.org/li/bookstore/ and adult manuals can be located at http://www.drugabuse.gov/drugpages/treatment.html (under Other NIDA Resources on Treatment Research) and http://www.commed.uchc.edu/match/pubs/monograph.htm

Critique

Major critiques of the substance-related diagnoses include their questionable applicability to older adults and adolescents. For the elderly, *DSM-IV* criteria include increased tolerance to the effects of the substance, which results in increased consumption over time. Yet changes related to physiology and reactions to prescription drugs may alter their drug tolerance as well (U.S. Department of Health and Human Services, 2001). Decreased tolerance to alcohol among older persons may lead to decreased consumption of alcohol with no apparent reduction in intoxication. Further, diagnostic criteria that relate to the impact of drug use on the typical tasks of young and middle adulthood, such as school or work performance or child rearing, may be largely irrelevant to older adults, who often live alone and are retired. For these reasons, abuse and dependence among older adults may be underestimated.

For adolescents, the symptoms required for psychological dependence, such as impairment of control, craving, and preoccupation with use, have not been examined (Bukstein & Kaminer, 1994; Winters, 2006). In addition, *DSM* substance abuse criteria largely rest on the negative consequences of use. This criterion may be problematic when applied to adolescents. Rather than substance use leading to negative consequences, often preexisting factors, such as family problems, or concurrent factors, such as another disorder, are responsible for the symptom pattern.

Despite the popularity of a primary disease model of addiction, problematic substance use in adolescents may be better conceptualized as a symptom of a more inclusive pattern of deviant behavior (Jessor & Jessor, 1977). Bukstein and Kaminer (1994) suggest that the substance use disorders should either have criteria specific to adolescents or substance use patterns should be covered in the criteria for conduct disorder in adolescents.

Case Study

Andrew is a 40-year-old Caucasian homosexual male. He was diagnosed HIV-positive 12 years ago as a result of a blood transfusion and is legally blind because of retinal detachments that occurred 4 years before that. His CD4 counts are such that he does not have an AIDS diagnosis. He receives services at a comprehensive HIV health clinic, where he sees a psychiatrist, a medical doctor, a nurse, and a social worker, who has been his case manager for 5 years.

Andrew's current medications include protease inhibitors and antiretrovirals for the HIV, Ritalin for the ADHD with which he was diagnosed as a child, the antidepressant Zoloft for dysthymia (diagnosed by the health center's psychiatrist 3 years previously), and Ambien, a sedative for sleep.

Andrew is unemployed, receiving full disability benefits from the Social Security Administration. He resides in a studio apartment in a working-class neighborhood. Andrew's immediate family consists of his mother and a younger brother. His father is presumably still alive but abandoned the family when Andrew was 9 years old, and no communication exists between them. Andrew's mother, whom Andrew refers to as "an active alcoholic," remarried five more times and is currently single. Andrew and his mother, who lives in another state, speak weekly by telephone, but no visits have occurred in the past 2 years. Andrew's brother is incarcerated on drug charges.

Andrew's local support system is made up of the other residents in his apartment building and two friends who live locally and visit regularly. He is currently not involved in any church or social organizations. He has terminated his church attendance and no longer performs voluntary public speaking on HIV prevention for the health clinic, saying, "What's the point in doing any of these things?" He has begun to spend more and more time alone.

The most significant relationship in Andrew's adult life was his 10-year romantic partnership with Shane, who died of complications of AIDS 5 years ago. Andrew has lost numerous friends to AIDS, as well as his partner. His goal is to meet someone with whom he can engage in a close relationship. He has placed ads in newspapers and on the Web and has frequented clubs known for sex parties.

After canceling several consecutive appointments, Andrew met with the social worker and confessed to thoughts of death. As for other depressive symptoms, he said he found it difficult to sleep at night but then slept late into the day. Andrew has discontinued taking his HIV medications, no longer wishing to "prolong the inevitable"—that he will die. He said he sees no point to his existence. Other than not taking his medications, Andrew does not admit to having a plan to commit suicide.

Andrew admitted to frequent abuse of his Ritalin and Ambien (three times per week for each) and occasional use of illegal street drugs, such as Ecstasy and cocaine (once weekly), in combination with increased alcohol consumption (almost every day, with an average of a six-pack of beer). Andrew had denied substance use during past visits, when his social worker and psychiatrist questioned why he had been getting his prescriptions refilled before they were due. The only reason he had agreed to see the social worker that day was because his visit with the psychiatrist required making contact with his case manager.

Andrew said he had not told the social worker about his substance use because he knows that services depend on his being "clean." (A routine part of the informed consent at the clinic is that the individual will partake in a recovery program if drug and alcohol abuse is present.) Andrew reported that his escalating use in the past year was due to feelings of depression: "[If I] didn't feel so depressed, then I wouldn't be doing this. Sometimes the pain is unbearable."

Multiaxial Diagnosis

The following multiaxial diagnosis was given to Andrew after this visit:

Axis I 304.80 Polysubstance Dependence
      296.23 Major Depressive Disorder, Single Episode, Severe Without Psychotic Features
      296.23 Dysthymic Disorder V15.81 Noncompliance With Treatment (HIV)
      314.01 Attention-Deficit/Hyperactivity Disorder, Combined Type

Axis II V71.09 No Diagnosis
Axis III Human Immunodeficiency Virus (HIV)
   Retinal detachment
Axis IV Housing Problems—disagreements with neighbors,
      dissatisfaction with housing arrangement
   Problems Related to the Social Environment—social isolation; limited
      support system
Axis V GAF = 30

The polysubstance dependence diagnosis was made because Andrew has repeatedly used five groups of substances (alcohol, sedatives, cocaine, amphetamines, and hallucinogens) during the last 12-month period. "Further, during this period, the dependence criteria were met for substances as a group but not for any specific substance" (APA, 2000, p. 93). Andrew understands the dangers of mixing his medicines with alcohol or other drugs and taking more medicine than prescribed. He also chose to ignore the risk of losing his psychiatric care if he continued to misuse his medicines.

Andrew had been diagnosed previously with dysthymia, but his depression seems to have worsened in that he has now discontinued his HIV medicines and no longer cares whether he dies. He admits to feelings of worthlessness, he has problems with sleep, and he has markedly diminished interest in activities, such as going to church and partaking in speaking engagements. He said that his depression is so painful and ever-present that he uses substances to cope with it. He thus now meets five of nine symptoms for a major depressive episode. Andrew said that although he has always been a bit depressed throughout his life (dysmthia), he has never felt this kind of excruciating emotional pain. In that case, single episode is coded rather than a recurrent pattern of major depressive episodes. Given the fact that he is threatening his life by not taking his HIV medications, the severe nature of the depression seems important to note.

With this kind of pattern, it is difficult to ascertain whether his alcohol and drug abuse have contributed to the depression. A period of withdrawal from these substances will be necessary to gain a more accurate understanding of his depression. The polysubstance dependence diagnosis was placed first because it has to be treated in order to successfully treat his depression. Noncompliance with treatment is offered as a V-code, and the diagnosis of ADHD was made when Andrew was a child. The psychiatrist will need to reassess this diagnosis and its applicability at this stage of his life. Andrew's depression and substance abuse have also clouded the diagnostic picture.

A risk and resilience assessment on Andrew's substance abuse is provided in Exhibit 10.7. On balance, it can be seen that Andrew's patterns of risk outweigh any protective factors. Therefore, an intervention plan urgently needs to reduce risk and bolster protection.

Exhibit 10.7

Andrew's Risk and Protective Factors Assessment

Risks	Protective Factors
Biology	
Genetics: Andrew might have a genetic predisposition toward substance use; his mother and relatives are heavy alcohol users. Andrew has a brother who is currently incarcerated for drug charges.	
Andrew does not have much information about his father.	
Andrew is male, and males tend to have higher rates of alcohol disorders, as well as most other substance use disorders.	
Psychological	
Depression: Andrew suffers from depression and was diagnosed with attention-deficit/ hyperactivity disorder as a child.	Andrew has shown personal resilience in surviving a difficult childhood and living through deaths of his partner and many friends.
Social	
Family	
Although Andrew was not sexually abused as a child, he was physically abused by two different stepfathers. His mother modeled alcohol abuse and subjected Andrew and his brother to unstable relationships.	
Peer	
People he knows from his apartment complex and neighborhood are involved with drugs and alcohol, and alcohol and drugs are readily available.	Andrew's two close friends are not substance using.
Andrew has suffered a number of losses from his friends and partner dying of AIDS	
Gay bars, where alcohol is available, are a "major social institution in the gay community." [a]	
Neighborhood	
Availability of drugs	
Services	Andrew has access to a comprehensive array of services at the HIV health clinic.

[a] Beatty et al. (1999), p. 545.

The treatment plan involved first a "no harm" contract, which Andrew agreed to sign. He reluctantly agreed to attend the clinic's substance abuse group and also AA groups for gay men and lesbian women in the community. These groups would have the additional potential benefit of bolstering his support system in favor of non-substance-abusing peers.

Although the sedatives and Ritalin were no longer to be prescribed, the prescription of Andrew's psychotropic medications (Zoloft) would be dependent on his abstinence or harm reduction from alcohol. Antidepressants are typically not subject to abuse but do not work therapeutically if they are mixed with alcohol or other drugs. A consideration is for the psychiatrist to change the antidepressant medication to Effexor, once Andrew has had several weeks of sobriety. Effexor has the advantage of potentially treating both depression and ADHD symptoms in adults.

Motivational interviewing would be used for a dual purpose: both to induce treatment compliance with HIV medications and to shift Andrew's motivation for change of his substance use patterns. His motivation to stop abusing substances is initially low. When he has gained sufficient motivation, CBT will be the treatment of choice because it can address the substance use and depression, as well as the insomnia Andrew complains about. In addition, many of the triggers for substance use are related to his depression. His feelings of grief and loss and how to manage these painful feelings will be an important aspect of his coping plan.

Conclusion

Even if they are not employed in substance abuse treatment settings, social workers will find themselves working with clients who have substance-related problems. The high comorbidity between substance-related disorders and other disorders means that there is a large amount of overlap between other mental/emotional disorders and substance use. The social worker should know how to assess for the presence of substance use disorders, as well as have knowledge of the full range of treatment approaches available.

Note

1. Although AA might have certain advantages, not everyone will respond to the approach. The social worker should be aware that other self-help groups for addictions exist. Examples include S.M.A.R.T. Recovery (based on Albert Ellis's cognitive-behavioral approach, http://www.smartrecovery.org/)

and Women for Sobriety (a self-help group developed specifically for women, http://www.womenforsobriety.org/). A comprehensive review of self-help programs is offered by Nowinski (1999).

References

Alexander, J., & Parsons, B. V. (1982). *Functional family therapy*. Monterey, CA: Brooks/Cole.

American Psychiatric Association. (2000). *Diagnostic and statistical manual of mental disorders* (4th ed., text rev.). Washington, DC: Author.

Armstrong, T., & Costello, J. (2002). Community studies on adolescent substance use, abuse, or dependence and psychiatric comorbidity. *Journal of Consulting and Clinical Psychology, 70*, 1224–1239.

Ashley, O., Marsden, M. E., & Brady, T. (2003). Effectiveness of substance abuse treatment programming for women: A review. *American Journal of Drug and Alcohol Abuse, 29*, 19–54.

Babor, T., Webb, C., Burleson, J., & Kaminer, Y. (2002). Subtypes for classifying adolescents with marijuana use disorders: Construct validity and clinical implications. *Addiction, 97*(Suppl. 1), 58–69.

Ball, S. (1998). Manualized treatment for substance abusers with personality disorders: Dual focus schema therapy. *Addiction Behavior, 23*, 883–891.

Barber, J. G., & Gilbertson, R. (1996). An experimental study of brief unilateral intervention for the partners of heavy drinkers. *Research on Social Work Practice, 6*, 325–336.

Beatty, R., Geckle, M., Huggins, J., Kapner, C., Lewis, K., & Sandstrom, D. (1999). Gay men, lesbians, and bisexuals. In B. McCrady & E. Epstein (Eds.), *Addictions: A comprehensive guidebook* (pp. 542–551). New York: Oxford University Press.

Bond, J., Kaskutas, L. A., & Weisner, C. (2003). The persistent influence of social networks and Alcoholics Anonymous on abstinence. *Quarterly Journal of Studies on Alcohol, 64*, 579–588.

Brady, K. & Back, S. (2008). Women and addiction. In M. Galanter & H. Kleber (Eds.), *The American Psychiatric Publishing textbook of substance abuse treatment* (pp. 555–564). Arlington, VA: American Psychiatric Publishing.

Brook, D., Brook, J., Zhang, C., Cohen, P., & Whiteman, M. (2002). Drug use and the risk of major depressive disorder, alcohol dependence, and substance use disorders. *Archives of General Psychiatry, 59*, 1039–1044.

Brown, T., Seraganian, P., Tremblay, J., & Annis, H. (2002). Process and outcome changes with relapse prevention versus 12-step aftercare programs for substance abusers. *Addiction, 97*, 677–689.

Bukstein, O., Dunne, J., Ayres, W., Arnold, V., Benedek, E., Bensenn, R., et al. (1997). Practice parameters for the assessment and treatment of children and adolescents with substance use disorders. *Journal of the American Academy of Child and Adolescent Psychiatry, 36*, 140–157.

Bukstein, O. G., Bernet, W., Arnold, V., Beitchman, J., Shaw, J., Benson, R. S., Kinlan, J., McClellan, J., Stock, S., & Ptakowski, K. K. (2005). Practice parameter for the assessment and treatment of children and adolescents with substance use disorders: Work Group on Quality Issues. *Journal of the American Academy of Child and Adolescent Psychiatry, 44*(6), 609–621.

Bukstein, O. G., & Cornelius, J. (2006). Psychopharmacology of adolescents with substance use disorders: Using diagnostic-specific treatments. In H. Liddle & C. Rowe (Eds.), *Adolescents substance abuse: Research and clinical advances* (pp. 241–263). New York: Cambridge University Press.

Bukstein, O., & Kaminer, Y. (1994). The nosology of adolescent substance abuse. *American Journal on Addictions, 3*, 1–13.

Castro, F., Proescholdbell, R. J., Abeita, L., & Rodriquez, D. (1999). Ethnic and cultural minority groups. In B. McCrady & E. Epstein (Eds.), *Addictions: A comprehensive guidebook* (pp. 499–526). New York: Oxford University Press.

Chung, T., & Maisto, S. A. (2006). Relapse to alcohol and other drug use in treated adolescents: Review and reconsideration of relapse as a change point in clinical course. *Clinical Psychology Review, 26*(2), 149–161.

Cleary, M., Hunt, G. E., Matheson, S., & Walter, G. (2009). Psychosocial treatments for people with co-occurring severe mental illness and substance misuse: Systematic review. *Journal of Advanced Nursing, 65*(2), 238–258.

Compton, W. M., Thomas, Y. F., Stinson, F. S., & Grant, B. F. (2007). Prevalence, correlates, disability, and comorbidity of DSM-IV drug abuse and dependence in the United States: results from the national epidemiologic survey on alcohol and related conditions. *Archives of General Psychiatry, 64*(5), 566–576.

Connors, G., Donovan, D., & DiClemente, C. (2001). *Substance abuse treatment and the stages of change: Selecting and planning interventions.* New York: Guilford Press.

Corrao, G., Bagnardi, V., Zambon, A., & Arico, S. (1999). Exploring the dose-response relationship between alcohol consumption and the risk of several alcohol-related conditions: A meta-analysis. *Addiction, 94*, , 1551–1573.

Crum, R. M., Green, K. M., Storr, C. L., Chan, Y-F., Ialongo, N., Stuart, E. A., & Anthony, J. C. (2008). Depressed mood in childhood and subsequent alcohol use through adolescence and young adulthood. *Archives of General Psychiatry, 65*(6), 702–712.

De Leon, G. (2008). Therapeutic communities. In M. Galanter & H. Kleber (Eds.), *The American Psychiatric Publishing textbook of substance abuse treatment* (pp. 459–475). Arlington, VA: American Psychiatric Publishing.

Di Castelnuovo, A., Costanzo, S., Bagnardi, V., Donatti, M. B., Iacoviella, L., & de Gaetano, G. (2006). Alcohol dosing and total mortality in men and women: An updated meta-analysis of 34 prospective studies. *Archives of Internal Medicine, 166*(22), 2437–2445.

Dimeff, L., Comtois, K., & Linehan, M. (2003). Co-occurring addictive and borderline personality disorders. In A. Graham, T. Schulz, M. Mayo-Smith et al. (Eds.), *Principles of addiction medicine* (3rd ed., pp. 1359–1370). Chevy Chase, MD: American Society of Addiction Medicine.

Donohue, B., & Azrin, N. (2001). Family behavior therapy. In E. F. Wagner, & H. B. Waldron (Eds.), *Innovations in adolescent substance abuse interventions* (pp. 205–227). Amsterdam, Netherlands: Pergamon/Elsevier Science.

Dumaine, M. (2003). Meta-analysis of interventions with co-occurring disorders of severe mental illness and substance abuse: Implications for social work practice. *Research on Social Work Practice, 13*, 142–165.

Farrell, A., & White, K. (1998). Peer influences and drug use among urban adolescents: Family structure and parent-adolescent relationship as protective factors. *Journal of Consulting and Clinical Psychology, 66*, 248–258.

Finnegan, L., & Kandall, S. (2008). Perinatal substance abuse: Drug dependence, motherhood, and the newborn. In M. Galanter & H. Kleber (Eds.), *The American Psychiatric Publishing textbook of substance abuse treatment* (pp. 565–580). Arlington, VA: American Psychiatric Publishing.

French, K., Finkbiner, R., & Duhamel, L. (2002). *Patterns of substance use among minority youth and adults in the United States: An overview and synthesis of national survey findings.* Fairfax, VA: Caliber Associates.

Fuller, R., & Hiller-Sturmhofel, S. (1999). Alocholism treatment in the United States: An overview. *Alcohol Research and Health, 23*, 69–77.

Grant, B. F., Stinson, F. S., Dawson, D. A., Chou, S. P., Ruan, W. J., & Pickering, R. P. (2004). Co-occurrence of 12-month alcohol and drug use disorders and personality disorders in the United States: Results from the national epidemiologic survey on alcohol and related conditions. *Archives of General Psychiatry, 61*(4), 361–368.

Hasin, D. S., Stinson, F. S., Ogburn, E., & Grant, B. F. (2007). Prevalence, correlates, disability, and comorbidity of DSM-IV alcohol abuse and dependence in the united states: Results from the national epidemiologic survey on alcohol and related conditions. *Archives of General Psychiatry, 64*(7), 830–842.

Hawkins, J. D., Catalano, R., & Miller, J. (1992). Risk and protective factors for alcohol and other drug problems in adolescence and early adulthood: Implications for substance abuse prevention. *Psychological Bulletin, 112*, 64–105.

Henggeler, S. W., Schoenwald, S. K., Borduin, C., Rowland, M., & Cunningham, P. B. (1998). *Multisystemic treatment of antisocial behavior in children and adolescents.* New York: Guilford.

Hesse, M. (2009). Integrated psychological treatment for substance use and co-morbid anxiety or depression vs. treatment for substance use alone: A systematic review of the published literature. *BMC Psychiatry, 9*(1), 6.

Hien, D., Cohen, L., Miele, G., Litt, L. C., & Capstick, C. (2004). Promising treatments for women with comorbid PTSD and substance use disorders. *Americal Journal of Psychiatry, 161*, 1426–1432.

Higgins, S., & Silverman, K. (2008). Contingency management. In M. Galanter & H. Kleber (Eds.), *The American Psychiatric Publishing textbook of substance abuse treatment* (pp. 387–399). Arlington, VA: American Psychiatric Publishing.

Imel, Z. E., Wampold, B. E., Miller, S. D., & Fleming, R. R. (2008). Distinctions without a difference: Direct comparisons of psychotherapies for alcohol use disorders. *Psychology of Addictive Behaviors, 22*(4), 533–543.

Jané-Llopis, E., & Matytsina, I. (2006). Mental health and alcohol, drugs and tobacco: A review of the comorbidity between mental disorders and the use of alcohol, tobacco and illicit drugs. *Drug and Alcohol Review, 25*(6), 515–536.

Jessor, R., & Jessor, S. L. (1977). *Problem behavior and psychosocial development: A longitudinal study of youth.* New York: Academic Press.

Jessor, R., Van Den Bos, J., Vanderryn, J., Costa, F., & Turbin, M. (1995). Protective factors in adolescent problem behavior: Moderator effects and developmental change. *Developmental Psychology, 31*, 923–933.

Johnson, V. E. (1986). *Intervention: How to help those who don't want help.* Minneapolis, MN: Johnson Institute.

Kaminer, Y., & Waldron, H B. (2006). Evidence-based cognitive–behavioral therapies for adolescent substance use disorders: applications and challenges.

In H. Liddle & C. Rowe (Eds.), *Adolescent substance abuse: Research and clinical advances* (pp. 396–420). New York: Cambridge University Press.

Kaplow, J., Curran, P., & Dodge, K. (2002). Conduct problems prevention research group. Child, parent, and peer predictors of early-onset substance use: A multisite longitudinal study. *Journal of Abnormal Child Psychology, 30,* 199–216.

Karageorge, K., & Wisdom, G. (2001). *Physically and sexually abused women in substance abuse treatment: Treatment services and outcomes.* Fairfax, VA: Caliber Associates.

Kelly, J., Myers, M., & Brown, S. (2002). Do adolescents affiliate with 12-step groups? A multivariate process model of effects. *Journal of Studies on Alcohol, 63,* 293–305.

Kilpatrick, D. G., Acierno, R., Saunders, B., Resnick, H., Best, C. L., & Schnurr, P. P. (2000). Risk factors for adolescent substance abuse and dependence: Data from a national sample. *Journal of Consulting and Clinical Psychology, 68,* 19–30.

Kownacki, R., & Shadish, W. (1999). Does Alcoholics Anonymous work? The results from a meta-analysis of controlled experiments. *Substance Use and Misuse, 34,* 1897–1916.

Kraft, M. K., Schubert, K., Pond, A., & Aguirre-Molina, M. (2006). Adolescent treatment services: The context of care. In H. Liddle & C. Rowe (Eds.), *Adolescent substance abuse: Research and clinical advances* (pp. 174–188). New York: Cambridge University Press.

Latimer, W., Newcomb, M., Winters, K., & Stinchfield, R. (2000). Adolescent substance abuse treatment outcome: The role of substance abuse problem severity, psychosocial, and treatment factors. *Journal of Consulting and Clinical Psychology, 68,* 684–696.

Liddle, H. (1999). Theory development in a family-based therapy for adolescent drug abuse. *Journal of Clinical Child Psychology, 28,* 521–532.

Littell, J., & Girvin, H. (2002). Stages of change: A critique. *Behavior Modification, 26,* 223–273.

Littell, J. H., Popa, M., & Forsythe, B. (2005). Multisystemic therapy for social, emotional, and behavioral problems in youth aged 10–17 (Cochrane Review). In: *The Cochrane Library,* Issue 3, 2005. Chichester, England: John Wiley and Sons.

Loeber, R., Farrington, D., Stouthamer-Loeber, M., & Van Kammen, W. B. (1998). *Antisocial behavior and mental health problems: Explanatory factors in childhood and adolescence.* Mahwah, NJ: Erlbaum.

Longabaugh, R., Wirtz, P., Zweben, A., & Stout, R. (1998). Network support for drinking: Alcoholics Anonymous and long term matching effects. *Addiction, 93,* 1313–1333.

Luczak, S. E., Glatt, S. J., & Wall, T. L. (2006). Meta-analyses of aldh2 and adh1b with alcohol dependence in Asians. *Psychological Bulletin, 132*(4), 607–621.

Marshal, M. P., Friedman, M. S., Stall, R., King, K., Miles, J., Gold, M., Bukstein, O., & Morse, J. (2008). Sexual orientation and adolescent substance use: A meta-analysis and methodological review. *Addiction, 103*(4), 546–556.

Martin, C., Kelly, T., Rayens, M. K., Brogli, B. R., Brenzel, A., Smith, W. J., et al. (2002). Sensation seeking, puberty and nicotine, alcohol and marijuana use in adolescence. *Journal of the American Academy of Child and Adolescent Psychiatry, 41,* 1495–1502.

McLellan, A. T. (2008). Evolution in addiction treatment concepts and methods. In M. Galanter & H. Kleber (Eds.), *The American Psychiatric Publishing textbook of substance abuse treatment* (pp. 93–108). Arlington, VA: American Psychiatric Publishing.

Mee-Lee, D., Shulman, G., Fishman, M., Gastfriend, D. R., & Griffith, J. H. (2001). *ASAM Patient Placement Criteria for the treatment of substance-related disorders* (2nd ed., rev.). Chevy Chase, MD: American Society of Addiction Medicine.

Meyers, R., Miller, W., Hill, D., & Tonigan, J. (1999). Community Reinforcement and Family Training (CRAFT): Engaging unmotivated drug users in treatment. *Journal of Substance Abuse, 10,* 118.

Miller, N. S., & Fine, J. (1993). Current epidemiology of comorbidity of psychiatric and addictive disorders. *Psychiatric Clinics of North America, 16,* 1–10.

Miller, W., Meyers, R., & Hiller-Sturmhofel, S. (1999). The community-reinforcement approach. *Alcohol Research and Health, 23,* 116–121.

Miller, W., Meyers, R., & Tonigan, J. (1999). Engaging the unmotivated in treatment for alcohol problems: A comparison of three strategies for intervention through family members. *Journal of Consulting and Clinical Psychology, 67,* 688–697.

Miller, W., & Rollnick, S. (2002). *Motivational interviewing: Preparing people to change addictive behavior* (2nd ed.). New York: Guilford.

Mirin, S., Batki, S., Bukstein, O., Isbell, P., Kleber, H., Schottenfeld, R., et al. (2002). Practice guideline for the treatment of patients with substance use disorders: Alcohol, cocaine, opioids. *American Psychiatric Association practice guidelines for the treatment of psychiatric disorders: Compendium 2002* (pp. 249–348). Washington, DC: American Psychiatric Association.

Najavits, L., Weiss, R., & Liese, B. (1996). Group cognitive behavioral therapy for women with PTSD and substance use disorder. *Journal of Substance Abuse Treatment, 13,* 13–22.

National Institute on Drug Abuse. (1997). *Preventing drug use among children and adolescents* [Booklet]. Washington, DC: Author.

New Freedom Commission on Mental Health. (2003). Achieving the promise: Transforming Mental Health Care in America./Final Report/. DHHS Pub. No. SMA-03-3832. Rockville, MD.

Nowinski, J. (1999). Self-help groups for addictions. In B. McCrady & E. Epstein (Eds.), *Addictions: A comprehensive guidebook* (pp. 328–346). New York: Oxford University Press.

O'Farrell, T. J., & Fals-Stewart, W. (2006). *Behavioral couples therapy for alcoholism and drug abuse.* New York: Guilford.

Orwin, R., & Ellis, B. (2001). *The effectiveness of treatment components in reducing drug use in adolescents and young adults: A Re-analysis of the Job Corps Drug Treatment Enrichment Project.* Fairfax, VA: Caliber Associates.

Orwin, R., Francisco, L., & Bernichon, T. (2001). *Effectiveness of women's substance abuse treatment programs: A meta-analysis.* Fairfax, VA: Caliber Associates.

Orwin, R., Maranda, M., & Brady, T. (2001). *Impact of prior physical and sexual victimization on substance abuse treatment outcomes.* Fairfax, VA: Caliber Associates.

Petrakis, I., Gonzalez, G., Rosenheck, R., & Krystal, J. (2002). Comorbidity of alcoholism and psychiatric disorders: An overview. *Alcohol Research and Health, 26,* 81–90.

Powers, M. B., Vedel, E., & Emmelkamp, P. M. (2008). Behavioral couples therapy (BCT) for alcohol and drug use disorders: A meta-analysis. Clinical Psychology Review, 28(6), 952–962.

Prochaska, J., DiClemente, C., & Norcross, J. (1994). *Changing for good.* New York: Avon.

Project MATCH Research Group. (1997). Matching alcoholism treatments to client heterogeneity: Project MATCH posttreatment drinking outcomes. *Journal of Studies on Alcohol, 58,* 7–29.

Riggs, P., & Whitmore, E. (1999). Substance use disorders and disruptive behavior disorders. In R. Hendren (Ed.), *Disruptive behavior disorders in children and adolescents, Vol. 18, No. 2. Review of psychiatry series* (pp. 133–173). Washington, DC: American Psychiatric Association.

Rohde, P., Lewinsohn, P., Kahler, C., Seeley, J., & Brown, R. (2001). Natural course of alcohol use disorders from adolescence to young adulthood. *Journal of the American Academy of Child and Adolescent Psychiatry, 40*, 83–90.

Rosen, C. (2000). Is the sequencing of change processes by stage consistent across health problems: A meta-analysis. *Health Psychology, 19*, 593–604.

Rösner, S., Leucht, S., Lehert, P., & Soyka, M. (2008). Acamprosate supports abstinence, naltrexone prevents excessive drinking: Evidence from a meta-analysis with unreported outcomes. *Journal of Psychopharmacology, 22*(1), 11–23.

Ross, S. (2008). The mentally ill substance abuser. In M. Galanter & H. Kleber (Eds.), *The American Psychiatric Publishing textbook of substance abuse treatment* (pp. 537–564). Arlington, VA: American Psychiatric Publishing.

Schmitz, J., Averill, P., Sayre, S., McLeary, P., Moeller, F. G., & Swann, A. (2002). Cognitive-behavioral treatment of bipolar disorder and substance abuse: A preliminary randomized study. *Addictive Disorders and Their Treatment, 1*, 17–24.

Sheehan, T., & Owen, P. (1999). The disease model. In B. McCrady & E. Epstein (Eds.), *Addictions: A comprehensive guidebook* (pp. 268–286). New York: Oxford University Press.

Sisson, R. W., & Azrin, N. H. (1986). Family-member involvement to initiate and promote treatment of problem drinkers. *Journal of Behavioral Therapy and Experiential Psychiatry, 17*, 15–21.

Sysko, R., & Hildebrandt, T. (2009). Cognitive-behavioural therapy for individuals with bulimia nervosa and a co-occurring substance use disorder. *European Eating Disorders Review, 17*(2), 89–100.

Szapocznik, J., & Williams, R. A. (2000). Brief strategic family therapy: Twenty-five years of interplay among theory, research and practice in adolescent behavior problems and drug abuse. *Clinical Child and Family Psychology Review, 3*, 117–135.

Thomas, C., & Corcoran, J. (2001). Empirically-based marital and family interventions for alcohol abuse: A review. *Research on Social Work Practice, 11*, 549–575.

Thomas, E. J., Santa, C., Bronson, D., & Oyserman, D. (1987). Unilateral family therapy with the spouses of alcoholics. *Journal of Social Service Research, 10*, 145–162.

Titus, J., & Dennis, M. (2006). Cannabis youth treatment intervention: Preliminary findings and implications. In H. Liddle & C. Rowe (Eds.), *Adolescent substance abuse: Research and clinical advances* (pp. 104–126). New York: Cambridge University Press.

Tonigan, J., Toscova, R., & Miller, W. (1996). Meta-analysis of the literature on Alcoholics Anonymous: Sample and study characteristics moderate findings. *Journal of Studies on Alcohol, 57*, 65–72.

U.S. Department of Health and Human Services. (2001). *Mental health: A report of the Surgeon General.* Retrieved 2009, from http://www.surgeongeneral.gov/library/mentalhealth/home.html

Van Wormer, K. & Davis, D. R. (2008). Addiction treatment: A strengths perspective (2nd ed.). Belmont, CA: Cengage.

Vasilaki, E. I., Hosier, S. G., & Cox, W. M. (2006). The efficacy of motivational interviewing as a brief intervention for excessive drinking: A meta-analytic review. *Alcohol and Alcoholism, 41*(3), 328–335.

Velicer, W., Hughes, S., Fava, J., Prochaska, J., & DiClemente, C. (1995). An empirical typology of subjects within stage of change. *Addictive Behaviors, 20*, 299–320.

Vinton, L., & Wambach, K. (2005). Alcohol and drug use among elderly people. In C. A. McNeese & D. DiNitto (Eds.), *Chemical dependency: A systems approach* (pp. 484–502). Boston: Pearson.

Waldron, H. B., & Turner, C. W. (2008). Evidence based psychosocial treatments for adolescent substance abuse. *Journal of Clinical Child and Adolescent Psychology, 37*(1), 238–261.

Walitzer, K., Dermen, K., & Conners, G. (1999). Strategies for preparing clients for treatment: A review. *Behavior Modification, 23*, 129–151.

Walters, G. (2002). The heritability of alcohol abuse and dependence: A meta-analysis of behavior genetic research. *American Journal of Drug and Alcohol Abuse, 28*, 557–584.

Weiss, R., Griffin, M., Greenfield, S., Najavits, L. M., Wyner, D., Soto, J. A., & Hennen, J. A. (2000). Group therapy for patients with bipolar disorder and substance dependence: Results of a pilot study. *Journal of Clinical Psychiatry, 61*, 361–367.

Williams, S. H. (2005). Medications for treating alcohol dependence. *American Family Physician 72*(9), 1775-1780.

Winters, K. (2006). Clinical perspectives on the assessment of adolescent drug abuse. In H. Liddle & C. Rowe (Eds.), *Adolescent substance abuse: Research and clinical advances* (pp. 223–240). New York: Cambridge University Press.

Winters, K., Stinchfield, R., Opland, E., Weller, C., & Latimer, W. (2000). The effectiveness of the Minnesota Model approach in the treatment of adolescent drug abusers. *Addiction, 95*, 601–612.

Ziedonis, D. M., Smelson, D., Rosenthal, R. N., Batki, S. L., Green, A. I., Henry, R. J., Montoya, I., Parks, J., & Weiss, R. D. (2005). Improving the care of individuals with schizophrenia and substance use disorders: Consensus recommendations. *Journal of Psychiatric Practice, 11*(5), 315–339.

▰ Appendix I: Measures for Adolescent Substance Use Disorders

Information on adolescent measures was drawn from Allen and Columbus (1995), Hunsley and Mash (2008), Jensen (2004), Rahdert (1991), and Winters and Stinchfield (1995). The National Institute on Drug Abuse (http://www.drugabuse.gov) also has other assessment protocols for adolescents available.

Adolescent Obsessive-Compulsive Drinking Scale (A-OCDS) (Deas, Roberts, Randall, & Anton, 2001)

Description

For case conceptualization and treatment planning, norms were rated good, and clinical utility rated adequate.

Reliability

For case conceptualization and treatment planning, internal consistency rated good, and test-retest reliability was unavailable.

Validity

For case conceptualization and treatment planning, content validity and construct validity were rated good, and validity generalization was rated adequate.

Adolescent Relapse Coping Questionnaire (ARCQ) (Myers & Brown, 1990)

Description
- For case conceptualization and treatment planning, norms were rated adequate, and clinical utility was rated adequate.
- Designed to measure coping skills

Reliability

For case conceptualization and treatment planning, internal consistency rated adequate, and test-retest reliability was unavailable.

Validity

For case conceptualization and treatment planning, content validity and construct validity were rated adequate, and validity generalization was rated less than adequate.

Personal Experience Screening Questionnaire (Winters, 1992)

Description
- Eighteen-item self-report with 4-point response option (never/once or twice/sometimes/often) screens for adolescent alcohol and drug problems
- The test is scored for problem severity, drug use history, and psychological problems. The total score for problem severity gets either a green or a red flag. The red flag score suggests the need for further assessment.

Reliability

High internal consistency (.90–.91)

Validity
- Differentiates between drug clinic (highest scores), juvenile offender (next highest scores), and normal school groups
- A discriminant function analysis correctly classified 87% of the school clinic group.
- Eighty-seven percent correct classification of those who need a comprehensive drug abuse assessment

Personal Experience Inventory (Winters & Henly, 1989; Winters, Latimer, Stinchfield, & Henly, 1999; Winters, Stinchfield, & Henly, 1993)

Description
- Self-report inventory for age 12–18, written at a sixth-grade level
- Thirty-three scales in two major sections: *(a)* chemical use problem severity, including negative and positive consequences of use, and *(b)* personal and environmental risk factors
- A parent version has also been created.
- Forty-five minutes required
- Widely used in clinical settings for assessment of adolescent chemical dependency and psychosocial risk

Reliability
All scales demonstrated reliability (internal consistency and test-retest).

Validity
All scales demonstrated construct validity (clinical diagnoses, treatment referral decisions, group status, and other measures of problem severity and risk).

Adolescent Alcohol Involvement Scale (Mayer & Filstead, 1979)

Description
- Fourteen-item, self-report
- Takes 15 minutes to complete
- Assesses type/frequency of drinking, reasons for onset of drinking, the context of drinking, short- and long-term consequences of drinking, the adolescent's perception about drinking, and other people's perceptions
- Score reveals severity of problems.

Reliability
Internal consistency ranges from .55 to .76.

Validity
Scores correlate to diagnosis and ratings from other measures.

Adolescent Drug Involvement Scale (Moberg & Hahn, 1991)

Description
- Modification of the Adolescent Alcohol Involvement Scale
- Twelve-item scale measuring level of drug involvement (defined in terms of consequences, motivations, and sense of control) in adolescents (but has not been tested on minority or inner-city youth)

Reliability
Internal consistency is alpha coefficient of .85.

Validity
High correlations with self-reported levels of drug use (.72), teens' perceptions of drug use severity (.79), and clinical assessments (.75)

References for Adolescent Substance Use Disorders Measures

Allen, J., & Columbus, M. (1995). *Assessing alcohol problems: A guide for clinicians and researchers*. Bethesda, MD: National Institute on Alcohol Abuse and Alcoholism.

Deas, D., Roberts, J., Randall, C., & Anton, R. (2001). Adolescent obsessive-compulsive drinking scale: An assessment tool for problem drinking. *Journal of the National Medical Association*, 93, 92–103.

Hunsley, J., & Mash, E. (2008). *A guide to assessments that work*. New York: Oxford University Press.

Jenson, J. (2004). Risk and protective factors for alcohol and other drug use in childhood and adolescence. In M. Fraser (Ed.), *Risk and resilience in childhood: An ecological perspective* (2nd ed., pp. 183–208). Washington, DC: National Association of Social Workers Press.

Mayer, J., & Filstead, W. (1979). The adolescent alcohol involvement scale: An instrument for measuring adolescent use and misuse of alcohol. *Journal of Alcohol Studies*, 4, 291–300.

Moberg, D. P., & Hahn, L. (1991). The adolescent drug involvement scale. *Journal of Adolescent Chemical Dependency*, 2, 75–88.

Myers, M. G. & Brown, S. A. (1990). Coping and appraisal in potential relapse situations among adolescent substance abusers following treatment. *Journal of Adolescent Chemical Dependency*, 1, 95–115.

Rahdert, E. (1991). *The adolescent assessment/referral system manual*. Rockville, MD: U.S. Department of Health and Human Services.

Winters, K. C. (1992). Development of an adolescent alcohol and other drug abuse screening scale: Personal experience screening questionnaire. *Addictive Behaviors*, 17, 479–490.

Winters, K., & Henly, G. (1989). *Personal Experience Inventory (PEI) test and manual*. Los Angeles: Western Psychological Services.

Winters, K., Latimer, W., Stinchfield, R., & Henly, G. (1999). Assessing adolescent drug use with the Personal Experience Inventory. In M. E. Maruish (Ed.), *The use of psychological testing for treatment planning and outcomes assessment* (2nd ed., pp. 599–630). Mahwah, NJ: Erlbaum.

Winters, K., & Stinchfield, R. (1995). Current issues and future needs in the assessment of adolescent drug abuse. In E. Radhert & D. Czechowicz (Eds.), *Adolescent drug abuse: Clinical assessment and therapeutic intervention* (NIDA monograph 156, pp. 146–170). Rockville, MD: National Institute on Drug Abuse.

Winters, K., Stinchfield, R., & Henly, G. (1993). Further validation of new scales measuring adolescent alcohol and other drug abuse. *Journal of Studies on Alcohol*, 54, 534–541.

Appendix II: Measures for Adult Substance Use Disorders

Information for this appendix was drawn from Allen and Columbus (1995) and Hunsley and Mash (2008).

Michigan Alcoholism Screening Test (Selzer, 1971)

Description
- A 25-item index of severity of alcohol misuse, response format 0–1
- Screens for alcoholism with a variety of populations
- Useful in assessing extent of lifetime alcohol-related consequences
- Briefer versions have been developed: the 10-item Brief MAST (Pokorny, Miller, & Kaplan, 1972); the 13-item Short MAST (Selzer, Vinokur, & Van Rooijen, 1975); a geriatric version, MAST-G (Blow et al., 1992); a version for general medical populations, Self-Administered Alcoholism Screening Test (Swensen & Morse, 1975); and a version that determines between lifetime and current problems with alcohol, Veterans Alcoholism Screening Test (Magruder-Habib, Harris, & Fraker, 1982).
- For case identification and diagnosis, norms were rated excellent, clinical utility rated adequate, and the instrument was highly recommended.
- Takes 8 minutes to complete

Reliability
- A meta-analysis of 470 measurement instruments showed that internal consistency was about .80 and was less reliable with females and non clinical populations (Shields, Howell, Potter, & Weiss, 2007).
- For case identification and diagnosis, internal consistency rated good and test-retest reliability was adequate.

Validity
- Factor analysis yielded five factors, along with a strong unidimensional component (Skinner, 1979):

  o Recognition of alcohol problem by self and others
  o Legal, work, and social problems
  o Help seeking
  o Marital-family difficulties
  o Liver pathology

- Correlations with the following Personality Research Form constructs: Impulsivity (.24), Affiliation (–.24), Hypochondriasis (.25), Depression (.29), Anxiety (.24), Thinking Disorder (.20), Social Introversion (.24), Self-Depreciation (.32), and Deviation (.26) (Skinner, 1979)

- Scores correlated with lifetime daily average consumption (.58) (Skinner, 1979).
- For case identification and diagnosis, content validity was rated adequate, construct validity was rated good, and validity generalization was rated excellent.

Drug Abuse Screening Test (Skinner, 1982)

Description
- Twenty-eight items ("yes"/"no") tapping various consequences of drug use
- Parallels items on Michigan Alcoholism Screening Test
- Ten-item short form also available. Both focus on negative consequences of drug use, rather than specifics of use (frequency, quantity).
- Five factors: early psychosocial complications with problem recognition, late onset of serious social consequences, treatment/help seeking, illegal activities, and inability to control drug use. Psychometrics for the factors are not available, so the scale must be used as a whole (Staley & El-Guebaly, 1990).
- Screening tool to determine whether someone might have a substance use disorder and need further treatment
- For screening and diagnosis, clinical utility rated adequate.

Reliability
- Internal consistency = .92
- For diagnosis, internal consistency rated excellent, and test-retest reliability was unavailable (Skinner, 1982; Gavin, Ross, & Skinner, 1989).

Validity
- Factor analysis indicates a single dimension.
- High scores correlated with stable accommodation, work record, and family contact.
- High scores correlated with more frequent use of cannabis, barbiturates, and opiates other than heroin.
- High scores correlated with Impulse Expression and Social Deviation of Basic Personality Inventory.
- For diagnosis, content validity and construct validity were rated adequate, and validity generalization was rated excellent (Gavin et al., 1989; Skinner, 1982).

Inventory of Drug Use Consequences (Tonigan & Miller, 2002)

Description
- Fifty-item self-administered measure of consequences of alcohol and drug use
- Parallel to the Drinker Inventory of Consequences

- Focus on consequences related to *(a)* Impulse Control, *(b)* Social Responsibility, and *(c)* Physical, *(d)* Interpersonal, and *(e)* Intrapersonal domains (same for Drinker Inventory of Consequences)
- InDUC is available in versions that capture lifetime problems related to drug use and a Likert-scaled frequency estimate of recent problems (last 90 days).
- Useful for assessment, as well as change over time
- Takes approximately 10 to 15 minutes to complete
- For case conceptualization and treatment planning, clinical utility rated adequate, and the measure is highly recommended. For treatment monitoring and outcome evaluation, clinical utility rated adequate, and the measure is highly recommended (Tonigan & Miller, 2002).

Reliability
- Four of five scales good to excellent stability; intrapersonal consequences reliability poor
- For case conceptualization and treatment planning, internal consistency is excellent, and test-retest reliability is good. For treatment monitoring and outcome evaluation, internal consistency rated excellent, and test-retest reliability rated good (Tonigan & Miller, 2002).

Validity
- A confirmatory factor analysis showed that the four scales (Impulse Control, Social Responsibility, Physical, and Interpersonal) conveyed were the larger construct of adverse consequences.
- Sensitive to treatment change
- For case conceptualization and treatment, content validity is good, and construct validity and validity generalization are adequate. For treatment monitoring and outcome evaluation, content validity rated good, and construct validity and validity generalization rated adequate (Tonigan & Miller, 2002).

University of Rhode Island Change Assessment Scale (URICA) (McConnaughy, DiClemente, Prochaska, & Velicer, 1989; McConnaughy, Prochaska, & Velicer, 1983)

Description
- Thirty-two-item scale assesses attitudes toward changing behaviors based on the stages of change model.
- Four 8-item subscales correspond to the four stages of change: pre-contemplation, contemplation, action, and maintenance.
- Rated on a 5-point Likert scale of 1 (not at all) to 5 (extremely) in response to how important this statement is to them

- Target group is outpatient and inpatient substance use disorders treatment and adult populations.
- Self-administered test that takes 5–10 minutes to complete
- For case conceptualization and treatment planning, norms were rated excellent and clinical utility rated adequate. For treatment monitoring and outcome evaluation, norms rated excellent and clinical utility rated adequate (DiClemente & Hughes, 1990).

Reliability
Dozois, Westra, Collins, Fung, and Garry (2004)
For different samples (outpatient alcohol treatment, self-identified anxious undergraduates, and individuals presenting for the treatment of panic disorder) internal consistency coefficients were found to be good for the subscales: Precontemplation ranged from .69 to 77, Contemplation ranged from .75 to .80, Action ranged from .82 to .90, and Maintenance ranged from .81 to .90.

DiClemente and Hughes (1990)
For case conceptualization and treatment planning, internal consistency rated good. For treatment monitoring and outcome evaluation, internal consistency rated good.

Validity
Dozois et al. (2004)
- Precontemplation, Contemplation, and Maintenance subscales were associated in expected directions with a number of indexes of symptomatology, self-esteem, hopelessness, perceived costs and benefits of worrying, and actual help-seeking behavior, therefore demonstrating adequate convergent and divergent validity.
- Factor analysis support has been mixed. The factor structure provided a moderate fit to four subscales in the subclinical sample and was a poor fit to these scales in the clinical sample.
- Moderate predictive validity in relation to treatment retention and outcome

DiClemente and Hughes (1990)
For case conceptualization and treatment planning, construct validity rated good, and validity generalization rated excellent. For treatment monitoring and outcome evaluation, construct validity rated good, and validity generalization rated excellent.

CAGE Questionnaire for Alcohol Misuse (Ewing, 1968)

Description
- Four-item screen for alcoholism.

  o Cut: Have you ever felt that you ought to cut down on your drinking?
  o Annoyed: Have people annoyed you by criticizing your drinking?

- o Guilty: Have you ever felt bad or guilty about your drinking?
- o Eye-opener: Have you ever had a drink first thing in the morning to steady your nerves or to get rid of a hangover?

- Scored 0 for no responses and 1 for yes.
- Easily memorized and administered as an interview in about 30 seconds.

Reliability
Dhalla and Kopec (2007)
- High test-retest reliability: .80 to .95
- Adequate correlations to other alcoholism screening instruments (AUDIT & SMAST): .48 to .70.

Validity
Dhalla and Kopec (2007)
- Sensitivity: 0.71
- Specificity: 0.90
- Not as effective in some populations: White women, prenatal women, college students
- Not as effective for less severe forms of drinking

References for Adult Substance Use Disorders Measures

Allen, J., & Columbus, M. (1995). *Assessing alcohol problems: A guide for clinicians and researchers.* Bethesda, MD: National Institute on Alcohol Abuse and Alcoholism.

Blow, F. C., Brower, K. J., Schulenberg, J. E., Demo-Dananberg, L. M., Young, J. P., & Beresford, T. P. (1992). The Michigan Alcoholism Screening Test–Geriatric Version (MAST-G): A new elderly-specific screening instrument. *Alcoholism: Clinical and Experimental Research, 16,* 372.

DiClemente, C. C., & Hughes, S. O. (1990). Stages of change profiles in outpatient alcoholism treatment. *Journal of Substance Abuse, 2,* 217–235.

Dhalla, S., & Kopec, J. A. (2007). The CAGE questionnaire for alcohol misuse: A review of reliability and validity studies. *Clinical Investigative Medicine, 30*(1), 33–41.

Dozois, D., Westra, H., Collins, K., Fung, T., & Garry, J. (2004). Stages of change in anxiety: Psychometric properties of the University of Rhode Island Change Assessment (URICA) scale. *Behaviour Research and Therapy, 42,* 711–729.

Ewing, J. A. (1968). Detecting alcoholism: The Cage questionnaire. *Journal of the American Medical Association, 252,* 1905–1907.

Gavin, D. R., Ross, H. E., & Skinner, H. A. (1989). Diagnostic validity of the Drug Abuse Screening Test in the assessment of DSM-III drug disorders. *British Journal of Addiction, 84,* 301–307.

Hunsley, J., & Mash, E. (2008). *A guide to assessments that work*. New York: Oxford University Press.

Magruder-Habib, K., Harris, K., & Fraker, G. (1982). Validation of the Veterans Alcoholism Screening Test. *Journal of Studies on Alcohol, 43*, , 910–926.

McConnaughy, E., DiClemente, C., Prochaska, J., & Velicer, W. (1989). Stages of change in psychotherapy: A follow-up report. *Psychotherapy: Theory, Research, Practice, Training, 26*, 494–503.

McConnaughy, E. A., Prochaska, J. O., & Velicer, W. F. (1983). Stages of change in psychotherapy: Measurement and sample profiles. *Psychotherapy: Theory, Research and Practice, 20*, 368–375.

Pokorny, A. D., Miller, B. A., & Kaplan, H. B. (1972). The brief MAST: A shortened version of the Michigan Alcoholism Screening Test. *American Journal of Psychiatry, 129*, 342–345.

Selzer, M. (1971). The Michigan Alcoholism Screening Test: The quest for a new diagnostic instrument. *American Journal of Psychiatry, 127*, 1653–1658.

Selzer, M., Vinokur, A., & Van Rooijen, L. (1975). A self-administered short Michigan alcoholism screening test (SMAST). *Journal of Studies on Alcohol, 36*, 117–126.

Shields, A., Howell, R., Potter, J., & Weiss, R. (2007). The Michigan Alcoholism Screening Test and its shortened form: A meta-analytic inquiry into score reliability. *Substance Use and Misuse, 42*, 1783–1800.

Skinner, H. (1979). A multivariate evaluation of the MAST. *Journal of Studies on Alcohol, 40*, 831–843.

Skinner, H. (1982). The drug abuse screening test. *Addictive Behavior, 7*, 363–371.

Staley, D. & El-Guebaly, N. (1990). Psychometric properties of the Drug Abuse Screening Test in a psychiatric patient population. *Addictive Behaviours, 15*, 257–264.

Swenson, W., & Morse, R. (1975). The use of a self-administered alcoholism screening test (SAAST) in a medical center. *Mayo Clinic Proceedings, 50*, 204–208.

Tonigan, J. S., & Miller, W. R. (2002). The Inventory of Drug Use Consequences (InDUC): Test-retest stability and sensitivity to detect change. *Psychology of Addictive Behaviors, 16*, 165–168.

11   Sexual Disorders: Pedophilia

People engage in a wide variety of sexual practices for purposes of procreation, expressing love, satisfying their sex drives, and for pleasure. Attempts to categorize sexual behavior as *normal* or *deviant* are often controversial because the process may be characterized by moral biases. In its chapter on sexual and gender identity disorders, the *DSM-IV-TR* includes material on *sexual function* disorders, *gender identity* disorders, and the *paraphilias*. These disorders are included as such because the behaviors cause considerable distress to the person or to other people who may be victimized by the behavior.

After briefly reviewing all the paraphilias, we will focus on pedophilia. We will also briefly consider the validity of the "gender identity disorder" diagnosis, which has become controversial in the human service professions. Pedophilia is characterized by repeated intense sexual desires, fantasies, or behaviors concerning sexual activity with a sexually immature child (American Psychiatric Association [APA], 2000). It is the most common paraphilia that involves physical contact a(Fagan, Wise, Schmidt, & Berlin, 2002). It is almost universally condemned as inappropriate and criminal sexual behavior.

The Paraphilias

This set of disorders is characterized by recurrent and intense sexual urges, fantasies, or behaviors that involve unusual objects, activities, or situations

(APA, 2000). Of all the sexual disorders, it is the clients with paraphilias who most often come to the attention of social workers. The list of specific paraphilias includes pedophilia, which will be described in the next section, as well as the following:

- Exhibitionism: exposure of one's genitals to others
- Fetishism: use of nonliving objects in sexual activity
- Frotteurism: touching or rubbing one's genitals against a nonconsenting person
- Masochism: voluntarily receiving humiliation or suffering during a sexual act
- Sadism: inflicting humiliation or suffering on others (who may be consenting) during a sexual act
- Transvestic fetishism: cross-dressing
- Voyeurism: observing sexual activity by others (who are usually not consenting)

The paraphilias tend to be long term, and in fact the diagnostic criteria mandate that the symptoms are present for at least 6 months. People with any paraphilia tend to engage in several different paraphilias during a lifetime (Manley & Koehler, 2001). Interestingly, these disorders are almost never diagnosed in females. The only major exception is sexual masochism, and even that is estimated to occur at a 20:1 ratio of men to women (APA, 2000).

Persons with paraphilias are careful to conceal their urges or acts (Craig, Browne, Beech, & Stringer, 2006). The associated fantasies tend to be always present, but the person may or may not act on them, depending on the strength of the urge and the person's efforts to resist it. Symptomatic behaviors may increase in response to psychosocial stressors when accompanied by increased opportunities to engage in the behavior. The deviant behaviors usually disrupt these individuals' potential for long-term bonding with sexual partners. Many people with paraphilias report that their behaviors do not cause them distress; their condition is problematic only because it leads to social limitations due to the reactions of others. Some persons with the disorders, however, do report shame, guilt, and depression regarding the symptoms.

The paraphilias are probably much more prevalent than the frequency of clinical diagnosis suggests, given the large worldwide market in paraphilic pornography and related paraphenalia (O'Grady, 2001). The most common diagnoses in clinics specializing in the treatment of these disorders are pedophilia, voyeurism, and exhibitionism. Sadism and masochism are far less frequently reported.

Pedophilia

The term *pedophilia* ironically derives from a Greek word meaning "love of children" (Fagan et al., 2002). As described earlier, pedophilia is characterized by a person's repeated and intense sexual desires, fantasies, or behaviors concerning activity with a sexually immature child. To merit the diagnosis, the person must either act on these desires or be so distressed by them that he experiences significant impairments in work, social, or personal functioning (O'Grady, 2001). People diagnosed with pedophilia must meet the following *DSM-IV-TR* criteria (APA, 2000):

- Over a period of at least 6 months, the person must experience recurrent, intense, sexually arousing fantasies, sexual urges, or behaviors involving sexual activity with a prepubescent child or children (generally age 13 or younger).
- The person has acted on these sexual urges, or the sexual urges or fantasies cause marked distress or interpersonal difficulty.
- The person is at least 16 years old and at least 5 years older than the target child or children.

The diagnosis should include a specifier indicating whether the client is attracted only to children (exclusive type) or is sometimes attracted to adults (nonexclusive type). The practitioner should also note when the pedophilia is limited to incest.

Knowledge about the nature and scope of pedophilia is limited because almost all data comes from studies of convicted offenders. Still, from their reviews of the literature, Ward and Sigert (2002) and Murray (2000) have developed a general psychological profile of pedophiles and other child molesters. Personality tests consistently reveal that pedophiles are emotionally immature, have a fear of being unable to function adequately in adult sexual relationships, and are socially introverted. They lack social skills and tend to avoid contact with other adults. They demonstrate inappropriate forms of sexual arousal, usually showing an enduring sexual interest in children. Pedophilia is associated with a lack of sexual and emotional gratification, leading the person to choose children as an outlet for these feelings. Sexual offenders often report taking solace in sexual thoughts and behaviors when confronted with stressful life events. The association of alcohol use with pedophilia supports the idea that some people with urges to abuse children can contain those urges until coming under the influence of an intoxicant. Pedophiles often justify their inappropriate sexual behaviors by rationalizing that the behaviors are "educational" for the child or that the victim had initiated or readily consented to, and received pleasure from, the acts. The vast majority of pedophiles are male, and such women tend to offend with "older" children.

There are different types of pedophiles. Some only look, and others want to touch or undress the child, but most pedophilic acts involve oral sex or the touching of either the child's or the perpetrator's genitals (Fagan et al., 2002). In most cases, pedophiles are familiar to the child that they attack; they may be a relative, friend, or neighbor (Nordland, 2001). Less than 3% of all reported sexual abuse cases are perpetrated by strangers who kidnap and then sexually assault the child (Rosenberg, 2002).

People with pedophilia generally express an attraction to children of a certain age range (Murray, 2000). Some prefer males, some prefer females, and some do not have a clear preference. Pedophiles attracted to females usually prefer 8–10 year olds, and those attracted to males usually prefer slightly older children. Pedophilia among females is reported more often, although it may not occur more often. Some pedophiles threaten the target children, and others go to extremes to gain access to desired children and develop elaborate strategies for gaining their trust and compliance. The seduction process may be quite lengthy, and the perpetrator may be attentive to the child's needs in order to gain his or her affection and loyalty. The pedophile usually does not experience distress following his actions.

Prevalence

The prevalence of pedophilia is difficult to estimate because it is a disorder a person would tend to deny unless assessed in a clinical setting. Further, not all researchers use the same definition of the disorder. Bromberg and Johnson (2001) suggest a 4% prevalence of pedophilia but add that, because 27% of adult females and 16% of adult males report sexual victimization as a child, the prevalence may be higher. Despite the difficulties inherent in estimating its prevalence, Seto (2004) describes a series of university studies indicating that 9% of male respondents had fantasized about having sex with a young child, 5% had masturbated to such a fantasy, and 7% would engage in such a sexual relationship if there was no possibility of punishment. Five percent of the respondents actually had an active interest in developing such a relationship with a child. Interestingly, female college students reported similar frequencies of these ideas.

Most studies of pedophilia are limited to North American, Western European, and Australian populations, where the taboo against such behavior is strong. Some cultures exist where adult–child sexual interaction are permissible, although usually only in ritual celebrations, as in Samba and some areas of Micronesia (Seto, 2004).

Comorbidity

People with pedophilia often display additional problem behaviors and *DSM* diagnoses. A meta-analysis by Whitaker et al. (2008) identified specific disorders that are comorbid with pedophilia among adults. Fifty percent to 60% experience anxiety disorders and 60%–80% have mood disorders at some time in their lives. Further, 70%–80% have personality disorders, with 43% having

Cluster C disorders (avoidant, dependent, obsessive-compulsive), 33% having Cluster B disorders (antisocial, borderline, histrionic, and narcissistic), and 18% having Cluster A disorders (paranoid, schizoid, or schizotypal).

Adolescent sex offenders experience greater overall psychopathology than nonoffenders, including conduct disorder and the borderline and narcissistic personality disorders (Caldwell, 2002). Their lives are also characterized by delinquency offenses, unstable family situations, poor social skills, and more school problems than nonoffending adolescents.

Course

A meta-analysis indicates that the recidivism rate for sexual offenses is 13.4% (Hanson & Bussiere, 1998). The authors emphasize that these rates should be considered underestimates, in that many postintervention offenses probably remain undetected. According to the U.S. National Institute of Justice on Child Sexual Molestation, the rate of childhood sexual *and* nonsexual reoffenses by men previously charged and convicted is over 50% at 25 years (Rosler & Witztum, 2000).

Assessment

Not all unusual sexual behavior is evidence of a paraphilia. These behaviors may also result from a loss of judgment that is symptomatic of other disorders, such as mental retardation, dementia, personality changes due to a medical condition, substance intoxication, a manic episode, and schizophrenia (Laws & O'Donohue, 2008). Such behaviors may also occur in antisocial youth, whose offending behavior represents one aspect of their exploitative behaviors, and in people with neurological disorders that interfere with their ability to regulate aggressive and sexual drives (Righthand & Welch, 2004). These other disorders can be distinguished from a paraphilia by the fact that the behavior occurs exclusively during the course of the disorder and does not represent the person's preferred sexual pattern.

The American Academy of Child and Adolescent Psychiatry (2000) has developed practice parameters for clinicians who work with sexually abusive children and adolescents, based on its reviews of the literature. These assessment guidelines are also applicable to adults. The academy asserts that practitioners needs to understand the many biological and psychosocial factors that determine a child's sexual development, gender role, sexual orientation, patterns of sexual arousal, sexual cognitions, sexual socialization, and how sexual and aggressive patterns of behavior may become interrelated for some people. Toward this end, practitioners need to gather the following information about the client:

- Sexual history, including thought patterns and behaviors regarding sexual activity and its relationship to any aggressive acts
- Developmental and social history
- Legal history
- Medical and psychiatric history
- School and academic history, including intellectual capacities and any learning disabilities that are common to sexual offenders
- Mental status examination, including personality style, coping style, substance use, and inclinations toward self-harm

Most verbally based assessments of pedophiles may have limited validity because of the individual's tendency to deny deviant thoughts, feelings, and behaviors. Formal measures of deviant sexual behavior may be used in the process (see the Appendix at the end of this chapter for a sample of these). Risk assessments of sexual offenders should consider separately, however, the offender's risk for sexual and nonsexual recidivism, because most recidivists engage in nonsexual crimes following program discharge (Seto, 2008).

A *phallometric* assessment is often conducted with sexual offenders. This is a process whereby the person's penile tumescence, or volume change, is measured in response to erotic stimuli. Formally known as a *penile plethysmo-graph* (PPG), this is the most commonly used means of determining male preferences for sex partners of different ages (Seto, 2008). Following the client's consent, in a comfortable office setting, a strain gauge is placed around the penis to measure its changing circumference in response to various sexual stimuli. The client is then presented with stimuli such as slides, movies, audiotapes of sexual activity, and videotapes of behavioral interactions between men and children. With each presentation, the client is asked to rate his level of arousal on a scale of 0 to 100 while his physiological arousal is measured. Following the assessment, comparisons are made between the client's arousal responses to normal and aberrant materials. Results are immediately shared with the client, because this may be the first time he is made aware of these differential arousal patterns.

Risk and Protective Influences

Onset

Biological Mechanisms
Relatively little research has been done on possible biological risk mechanisms for pedophilia. Many of the studies that have been done include small sample sizes so their results must be considered tentative. There is a consensus among researchers that biological causes may contribute to its etiology, but the relevant factors remain unclear. As noted earlier, almost all pedophiles are men, which suggests hormonal risk factors but could also

reflect socialization differences between the sexes. One group of researchers in a small study considered a possible association between sexual offending, antisocial personality, and testosterone levels. For the sexual offenders, an antisocial personality index was positively correlated with mean saliva testosterone. Intensity of sexual activity in general was also significantly related to testosterone in both rapists and child molesters but not in the control males (Aromaki, Lindman, & Eriksson, 2002). Another small study tested the hypothesis that certain deficits in serotonin transmission exist in persons with pedophilia (Maes et al., 2001). The results supported the hypothesis, but the researchers recommended that future studies on this topic should focus on serotonin's postsynaptic receptor up-regulation and lowered presynaptic activity.

Other studies have examined less specific neurodevelopmental abnormalities in persons with pedophilia. Researchers at the Quinsy Institute for Sex and Reproduction found (with a sample size of 600) that pedophiles had elevated levels of non-right-handedness (NRH), although the effect size was small (Bogaert, 2001). Most cerebral researchers argue that elevated NRH in clinical groups can result from developmental or central nervous system (CNS) disorders. This finding suggests that pedophiles' behavior is more directly related to CNS developmental abnormalities than to the NRH factor. Further, no relationship was found in this study between the pedophile's educational background and NRH, an association that is sometimes found in general criminal populations. In further consideration of the role of neurodevelopmental characteristics in determining sexual preferences, some researchers propose that early childhood sexual abuse, especially that which occurs prior to age 6, may cause some relevant CNS abnormalities (Blanchard et al., 2002; Cohen et al., 2002). These researchers also suggest that pedophiles may be influenced by genetic factors originating in mothers who have psychiatric problems.

Some promising research is underway on structural nervous system differences between pedophiles and nonoffenders using magnetic resonance imaging (Seto, 2008). Specific areas of interest include the frontal lobes (which play a role in the inhibition of sexual responses) and the temporal-limbic area (where sexual behavior is regulated).

Psychological Mechanisms

A growing literature is developing around the cognitive distortions experienced by pedophiles. Several studies have found support for five implicit beliefs held by child abusers that account for most of their thought distortions (Marziano, Ward, Beech, & Paattison, 2006). These include, in order of prevalence, the child as a sexual being (the child wants to engage in sexual activity with adults), uncontrollability (the abuser's actions are outside his control), the dangerous world theory (other adults are abusive and rejecting, and thus the pedophile must rescue and control the child), the nature of harm (sexual activity does not cause harm and may be beneficial to the child), and entitlement theory (the abuser is superior to, or more important than, others). Each of these core beliefs contributes to the pedophile's acting out.

It has also been reported that men with arousal patterns to children tend to be of lower intelligence and socioeconomic status (Laws & O'Donohue, 2008). It is hypothesized that both of these characteristics are negatively correlated with mainstream or socially acceptable attitudes and behaviors about sex.

Social Influences

Adverse family backgrounds can contribute to a person's later development of inappropriate sexual conduct. Pedophiles generally come from families with marital breakups, parental mental illness, harsh or inconsistent parenting, substance abuse, criminality, and high rates of physical abuse and neglect (Lee, Jackson, Pattison, & Ward, 2002; Whitaker et al., 2008). Various types of emotional and physical abuse are also risk influences for the disorder. Most of the studies that examine these factors must be interpreted with caution, however, because of the general lack of reliability of client and family self-reports and the failure of some researchers to investigate a range of adverse childhood conditions. Most of these risk influences, when taken in isolation, are not specific to the development of sexual disorders.

A history of sexual abuse is more prevalent in sexual abusers than in the general population and in nonsexual abusers. Reports of sexual victimization in the history of adolescent sex offenders vary from 19% to 82% (Fortune & Lambie, 2005). Young victims of abuse may internalize the aggressive and erotic facets of their experiences into patterns of deviant sexual gratification through social learning, imitation, and modeling (Lee et. al., 2002). Adolescents who have been sexually victimized, for example, manifest more deviant erectile responses to sexual stimuli than adolescents who have not been so abused. One study of 64 sex offenders and 33 nonsex, nondrug, and nonviolent property offenders yielded interesting data on this point (Lee et. al., 2002). The researchers hypothesized that childhood sexual abuse, physical abuse, emotional abuse, behavior problems, and family dysfunction are general developmental risk factors for a variety of paraphilias. They also hypothesized that childhood sexual abuse would be a specific risk factor for pedophilia. Both hypotheses were supported.

Early caregiving is acknowledged as a foundation on which children build their later relationships (Seto, 2008). The child who does not receive affection and a sense of interpersonal security from primary caregivers is at risk for a variety of problems in later relationships outside the family. More specifically, research suggests that insecure attachment is a developmental risk factor for pedophilia (Sawle & Kear-Colwell, 2001). According to attachment theory, infants develop the cognitive schemas (internal perspectives about the environment) of their caregivers and others in the immediate environment, relying on them to predict caregiver behavior and regulate their own behavior. In this way, the "healthy" infant achieves a feeling of security and ultimately internalizes positive attachment experiences (Bowlby, 1979). Children who experience high levels of separation or rejection when distressed become less empathetic toward others. The cyclic relationship between parenting styles and attachment appears to contribute to the risk of pedophilia (Hall & Hall, 2007).

Combining the risk influences of poor attachment and sexual abuse, it has been hypothesized that people are at risk to sexually abuse children when they cannot get their emotional needs met, regulate their emotional well-being, respond empathetically to others, and seek assistance to manage their abusive inclinations (Hall & Hall, 2007). An adult who has not developed a secure attachment system may construe early abusive sexual experiences as enticing because they represent a form of intimacy, regardless of their deviant nature.

Several other family risk influences for pedophilia have been investigated, though with less empirical support. One set of researchers found that the number of older brothers (but not sisters) in a family could lead to sexual deviance, specifically a preference for children or for coercive sex (Seto, 2008). The proposed reason for this is that later-born male children tend to lack same-sex siblings close in age who might provide appropriate social modeling.

Cultural and social attitudes and practices may have some influence on the potential pedophile's development, although there is little evidence to support this assertion. Although no mainstream organizations support pedophilia, marginal organizations promote sexual behavior between children and adults as positive. One of these is the North America Man/Boy Love Association (NAMBLA, 2009). Exposure to these groups may provide the learning and modeling needed to support pedophilic behaviors. It has already been noted that pedophiles tend to be socially isolated, so cultures and social environments that reinforce personal isolation may be considered risk factors.

The risk and protective influences for pedophilia are described next and shown in Exhibit 11.1

Recovery and Adjustment

A meta-analysis of 61 follow-up studies (with an average of 4–5 years) identified the factors most strongly related to recidivism among sexual offenders (Hanson & Bussiere, 1998). On average, the sexual offense recidivism rate

Exhibit 11.1

Risk and Protective Influences for the Onset of Pedophilia

Risk Influences	Protective Influences
Biological	
Being male	Being female
Elevated plasma epinephrine and norepinephrine levels	
Frontal or temporal lobe abnormalities	
Head injury before age 13	
Increased sympathetic nervous system activity	Normal neurotransmitter activity in nervous systems
Low levels of serotonin	
Non-right-handedness (may signify developmental abnormalities)	Right-handedness
Low intelligence	Average to high intelligence
Psychological	
Childhood behavioral problems	
Aggression/hostility	
Depression	
Anxiety	
Low self-esteem	
External locus of control	Internal locus of control
Lack of empathy	Capacity for empathy
Lack of problem-solving ability	
Problems with self-regulation (impulse control)	Self-regulation capability
Comorbid substance abuse disorder	No history of psychiatric or substance abuse disorder
Social	
Later birth order	Earlier birth order
Harsh or inconsistent parenting	
Sexual abuse as a child	Absence of abuse as a child
Disorganized family	
Mother has undergone psychiatric treatment	Presence of nonblaming and emotionally supportive caregivers
Poor attachment style	Secure attachment to parents
Exposure to deviant sexual subcultures	
Living alone or with a parent as an adult	
Difficulties forming adult relationships, including intimate relationships with adult partners	The ability to form and maintain adult relationships, including those with intimacy
Lack of, or erratic, employment	Stable employment

was 13.4% (with 23,393 cases studied). Some subgroups of the sample, however, reoffended at higher rates. Recidivism rates were 18.9% for rapists (N = 1839), 12.7% for child molesters (N = 9603), and 12.2% for nonsexual violent offenders (N = 7155). The recidivism rate for pedophiles involving a preference for males was roughly twice that for those who preferred females.

The strongest predictors of sexual recidivism were factors related to sexual deviance. Other factors associated with general criminal behavior, such as younger age, prior violent offenses, and juvenile delinquency, were predictive to a much lesser extent. The risk for sexual offense recidivism was increased for those whose deviance was characterized by prior sexual offenses, the victimization of strangers or other people outside the family, the onset of sexual offending at an early age, the selection of male victims, or engagement in diverse sexual crimes. Neither the degree of sexual contact, the type of force used, nor injuries to the victims were significant predictors of sexual offense recidivism. Sex offenders who failed to complete treatment were at a higher risk for reoffending than those who completed treatment. The offenders were more likely to experience general criminal recidivism (crimes not related to sexual offenses) if they ended treatment prematurely, denied their sexual offense, or showed low motivation for treatment.

The major factors related to the offender's recovery included a willingness to accept responsibility for his offenses as evidenced by admission of the offense, acceptance of the behavior as a problem, motivation to stop offending, and a willingness to participate in treatment (Drapeau, Korner, Granger, & Brunet, 2005). For a compilation of risk and protective factors for the potential recovery from pedophilia, see Exhibit 11.2.

Exhibit 11.2

Risk and Protective Influences for the Course of Pedophilia

Risk	Protection
Biological	
Earlier age of onset	Later age of onset
Psychological	
Type of criminal behavior (at younger age, violent offenses, more sexual offenses)	No prior offenses
General criminal behavior	
Greater frequency of acts	
Threats in the commission of the crime	Lesser frequency of acts
Existence of preceding offenses	Absence of threats in the commission of the crime
Deviant sexual interests	
Inability to experience conventional sex	Ability to experience conventional sex
Male victims	

(continued)

Exhibit 11.2

(Continued)

Risk	Protection
Choosing strangers as victims (rather than boys known to the perpetrator)	Choosing boys that the perpetrator knows
	Motivation for change
Lack of motivation for change	Refusal to blame the victim
Blaming of victim	No substance abuse
Presence of substance abuse	Absence of a personality disorder
Having a diagnosed personality disorder	Ability to complete intervention
Failure to complete treatment	

Social

History of abuse	No history of abuse

Sources: Aromaki, Lindman, and Eriksson (2002); Blanchard et al. (2002); Bogaert (2001); Cohen et al. (2002); Connolly and Woolans (2008); Fortune and Lambie (2005); Hall and Hall (2007); Laws and O'Donohue (2008); Lee, Jackson, Pattison, and Ward (2002); Maes et al. (2001); Marziano, Ward, Beech, and Pattison (2006); Sawle and Kear-Colwell (2001); Seto (2008); Whitaker et al. (2008).

Intervention

Psychosocial

Goals

Deviant sexual arousal and offending, while a serious presenting problem, is only one aspect of the pedophile's total being. For long-term success, intervention should address a range of dimensions of the client's life, including maladaptive thought processes, low self-esteem, depression, socialization difficulties, and the need for skills in the areas of problem solving, communication, anger management, impulse control, and intimacy (Rosenberg, 2002). Intervention goals should be focused on the following (Bradford, 2001; Efta-Breibach & Freeman, 2004; Hall & Hall, 2008):

- Confronting the person's denial
- Decreasing deviant sexual arousal
- Facilitating the development of nondeviant sexual interests
- Promoting victim empathy
- Enhancing social and interpersonal skills
- Assisting with values clarification
- Clarifying cognitive distortions

Family intervention is essential in cases of incest (Federoff, 2008). Educational intervention modules can provide offenders and families with information about normal sexuality, sexual deviancy, cognitive distortions, appropriate interpersonal behavior, strategies for coping with sexual impulses, victim awareness and empathy, anger management, assertiveness training, social skills training, stress reduction, and relaxation management.

The Therapeutic Relationship

Practitioner/client relationship factors related to the successful engagement of pedophiles have been identified. One pair of researchers rejects confrontational intervention models, arguing that because of the difficulties that pedophiles have with relationships, a more empathic and supportive approach is needed (Kear-Colwell & Boer, 2000). Pedophiles generally come into treatment unwilling to disclose their problems, because their abusive backgrounds and attachment problems prevent them from bonding with adults. Pedophiles tend to be socially isolated, and a significant number of them have negative views about interacting with adults. They describe their need for contact with children as emotionally and socially important, as well as sexually important. Any adult relationship that demands a degree of intimacy, including those found in intervention programs, can be highly anxiety provoking. Some research supports the idea that empathic practitioner style is associated with positive outcomes for pedophiles, perhaps more so than therapeutic technique (Drapeau, et al., 2005). The development of trust, a consistent relationship, and a therapeutic alliance may help these clients move toward the idea that change is possible.

Cognitive-Behavioral Therapy

Cognitive-behavioral approaches are considered to be the most effective intervention methods for pedophiles (Losel & Schmucker, 2005; Saunders, Berliner, & Hanson, 2004). Interventions that address the specific elements of the offender's beliefs and feelings that lead to sexual offending, and include an individualized relapse prevention component, are considered most likely to prevent new sexual offenses. Treatment tends to be 1 to 2 years in length, with weekly sessions. Specific techniques include the following:

- *Covert sensitization*: The practitioner guides the client through a process of learning to associate *unpleasant* thoughts and feelings with sexually stimulating deviant imagery, thus extinguishing previously pleasant associations. For example, a client may be shown pornographic images of young children and helped to associate these images with such negative thoughts as imprisonment and family rejection. The practitioner must repeatedly walk the client through this process before it becomes ingrained in the client's mind. While artificial, covert sensitization helps the client anticipate and manage the anxiety that he will experience when in actual stimulating situations.

- *Assisted covert sensitization*: This is similar to the previous process except that the client is provided with external aversive stimuli, such as noxious odors, to associate with the deviant imagery.
- *Imaginal sensitization*: Teaching relaxation techniques such as deep breathing to interrupt sexually stimulating imagery. If the client can learn to relax, he may be able to interrupt the rise in anxiety associated with deviant imagery.
- *Satiation techniques*: Prescribing frequent masturbation to the client as a means of lowering his sex drive. Men experience a reduction in sexual tension following ejaculation.
- *Sexual arousal reconditioning*: Pairing the client's feelings of sexual arousal with appropriate nondeviant sexual stimulation—in other words, finding appropriate outlets for it. This may involve sexual contact with an adult partner or masturbation.
- *Relapse prevention through the client's clear awareness of each phase of the sexual assault cycle and its implications.*

A final component of intervention is an extended after care period, with the practitioner's close monitoring of behavior and the promotion of natural social supports. Recently, the courts have been mandating longer probationary periods and parole sanctions to sexual offenders in general (Fagan et al., 2002).

Group Interventions

Group intervention is preferred to individual treatment for sex offenders because the abuser is less able to minimize, deny, and rationalize problem behaviors. Marshall (1999) provides a model of how group interventions challenge the pedophile's problem cognitions and behaviors:

- Denial or minimization: Each offender is required to give full disclosure of his offenses, including his thoughts and feelings at the time. The other members of the group challenge the person's tendency to minimize the seriousness of the offense.
- Distorted perceptions: Group members challenge a person's self-serving perceptions of his behavior and distorted beliefs about the feelings of the victim at the time of the offense.
- Victim empathy: This is a lengthy process, facilitated by role plays, of the client's becoming able to recognize the nature of emotions in others and to adopt the other person's perspective during an offense. During these role plays, the client replicates the victim's emotions and takes action to reduce the victim's distress.
- Pro-offending attitudes include negative views of women and children and procrime beliefs. These are challenged as they arise at any time in group discussion.

- Attachment style: Each offender describes his most recent relationship and, if possible, at least one previous relationship, so that his attachment (or relationship) style can be inferred. The group discusses the disadvantages of those ways of relating to significant others. The benefits of appropriate intimacy and appropriate sexual relations are reviewed. The nature of jealousy and how it can be exaggerated is also reviewed. The client is helped to develop social skills to promote a greater potential for intimacy.
- Deviant fantasies (related to the offense): Offenders are required to identify and list their sexual and aggressive fantasies and then monitor their frequency and strength. They must indicate whether and how they attempt to resist the fantasies. Group discussion follows around the meaning of the person's fantasies and the role they play in the offending behavior.
- Relapse prevention: This includes an identification of the client's typical offense cycle, a specification of the factors that increase risk, a delineation of coping skills that may reduce risk, and the establishment of a series of plans to avoid risk. Each offender is required to list and share two warning signs: one that only he can observe (such as fantasies) and another that his parole supervisor or family and friends can observe. The client and designated others actively monitor the potential for relapse by using these warning signs.

Adolescent Programs

Adolescent sex offender treatment is most often carried out in specialized programs and usually includes a variety of cognitive-behavioral techniques designed to change clients' offense-supportive beliefs and attributions, improve their handling of negative emotions, teach behavioral risk management, and promote prosocial behaviors (Saunders et al., 2004). There is no clear scientific evidence that favors a particular approach or demonstrates conclusively that an intervention is effective. Still, short-to moderate-term sexual recidivism rates are not high (less than 10%) after any type of treatment. One point for emphasis is that adolescents tend not to present the same degree of sexual deviancy and psychopathic behavior as adults. Most outcome studies note that nonsexual recidivism is higher than sexual recidivism, which underscores the importance of broad behavioral goals in these interventions.

Adolescent sex offender treatment programs generally include 30 to 75 outpatient sessions (Saunders et al., 2004). Treatment components usually target awareness of the consequences of abusive behavior, increasing victim empathy, identifying personal risk factors, promoting healthy sexual attitudes and beliefs, social skills training, sex education, anger management, and relapse prevention. The personal history of the offender's sexual victimization must always be addressed, and behavioral techniques or medications should be used to modify deviant sexual arousal. Intervention components for parents should include providing support for behavior change, encouraging supervision and monitoring, teaching recognition of risk signs, and promoting guidance and support to the adolescent.

Treatment Outcome Studies

A meta-analysis was conducted on treatment outcome studies for sexual offender treatment and included both adults and adolescents (Losel & Schmucker, 2005). In all, treatment helped reduce sexual recidivism by 37%, which is a small effect. Cognitive-behavioral approaches were most effective, while nonbehavioral treatments did not produce a statistically significant effect. Not surprisingly, those who dropped out were less successful than those who completed treatment. An interesting finding was that organic treatments, involving castration and hormonal medication, were more effective than psychosocial interventions. However, there are adverse effects and ethical considerations in using these types of treatments.

Saunders et. al (2004) stress that, of the 24 types of intervention they reviewed, none met the highest standard of being "well-supported and efficacious" and only one met the criterion for the second highest standard, "supported and probably efficacious" (adult child molester therapy). Most were classified as "supported and acceptable." The interventions with empirical support tend to share characteristics of being goal directed and structured, with an emphasis on skill building to manage emotional distress and behavioral disturbances. A repetitive practice of skills is evident in the more effective programs.

Medication

Some advances in psychotropic medications have been made during the past 20 years to assist with lowering libido and decreasing the incidence of deviant sexual thoughts and actions among pedophiles (Hughes, 2007). For example, the selective serotonin reuptake inhibiting antidepressant drugs (SSRIs) all share the common effect of decreasing libido. Although this is an undesired effect for many consumers, it can in higher doses decrease libido in the pedophile to the extent that he may be better able to resist sexual fantasy. The effectiveness of the SSRIs for this purpose is modest, however.

A class of medications known as antiandrogen agents is often used to treat pedophilia and the other paraphilias (Bradford, 2001; Hughes, 2007). Androgens are male hormones (including testosterone) that are naturally produced in the body and are necessary for normal male sexual development. Androgen drugs are sometimes used to replace the hormones when the body is unable to produce enough on its own. With pedophiles, antiandrogen drugs are prescribed to reduce these hormones and thus reduce the client's sex drive, even while the symptomatic thoughts continue. These drugs have had only modest success, however, in part because of their adverse effects (nausea, diarrhea, breast enlargement, anemia, and erection problems). Furthermore, it is difficult to monitor the client's adherence to such a regimen.

A relatively new class of long-term injectible antiandrogen medications, known as gonadotropin-releasing hormone agonists, is being tested, thus far with modest positive results (Birken, Hill, & Berner, 2003). At best, then, the use of medications can only serve as adjuncts to the psychosocial interventions.

Finally, surgical castration (which is usually involuntary) is permissible in several states as a treatment for repeat sexual offenders (Weinberger, Sreenivasan, Garrick, & Osran, 2005). This procedure involves removal of the male testes, which lowers the level of testosterone in the body and diminishes one's sex drive. Surgical castration does not completely eliminate the sex drive, and ingesting testosterone can reverse its effects. Adverse effects of the process include emotional lability and depression. Still, a worldwide review of studies on the procedure, while limited in scope and methodologically flawed, indicates that castrated sexual reoffenders are only 3% likely to commit new sexual offenses, compared to 46% of noncastrated reoffenders.

Critique of the Diagnosis

Disorders with clear or probable biological components, such as schizophrenia, autism, bipolar disorder, the dementias, and major depression, tend to have credibility among the general public as valid mental disorders. Few biological markers have been identified or even speculated as causal for pedophilia. Even so, many people consider it to be a mental disorder on the basis of the grossly deviant sexual thoughts and behaviors that are central to the condition. Pedophile behavior is so harmful to the child victims, so contrary to the values of American society, and so disruptive to the life of the person who has the disorder that the public at large treats it at least in part as a mental disorder.

Pedophilia behaviors are also criminal conditions, however, and those who are convicted are usually sentenced to prisons rather than treatment facilities. In fact, there seems to be a public fear that conceptualizing pedophilia too strongly as a mental disorder may provide perpetrators with a basis to claim innocence of their associated crimes. Because pedophilia is a chronic condition, citizens are reluctant to give convicted sexual offenders a free rein in the social mainstream after they have served their sentences or completed their intervention programs (Shanahan & Donato, 2001). It may be concluded, then, that pedophilia is accepted by professionals and the public alike as a mental disorder; although unlike almost all other *DSM* diagnoses (and along with some of the other paraphilias), it holds equal status as a criminal condition.

Although we focus on a limited number of diagnoses in this chapter, it is important to mention that some researchers have proposed adjustments in the organization of the *DSM* "Sexual Disorders" chapter. Manley and Koehler (2001) believe that a new category of "sexual behavior disorders" should include all sexually problematic activities that are either excessive or restrictive,. Additionally, Kafka (2001) proposes a new classification of "paraphilia-related disorders" to include all sexual behaviors that are obsessive but do not involve the presence of another person (masturbation, phone sex, cybersex, pornography, promiscuity, sexual desire incompatibility.) It is not yet known what changes, if any, will appear in *DSM-V*.

One of the three major diagnostic categories in the *DSM* sexual disorders chapter is gender identity disorder. This is highly controversial among many social workers (and others) as an example of how social and cultural norms may drive decisions about mental illness. We describe the controversy here as an example of how social workers may take a critical position with regard to the psychiatric profession's process of determining disorders and their scientific validity.

Gender identity disorder (GID) is characterized by a strong and persistent cross-gender identification and a persistent discomfort with one's assigned biological sex. The disorder is considered to be rare, although it is believed to be more prevalent in men by a ratio of 3:1 to 6:1 (Coolidge, Thede, & Young, 2002). Fewer than half of persons with GID desire sexual reassignment surgery (Sohn & Bosinki, 2007). A majority of persons who meet the diagnostic criteria aspire to live in their current bodies but without constraints related to socially constructed sex roles. Such persons generally experience great distress and some problems in social functioning due to the stigma and marginalization they experience from others. For those who do seek surgery, the process must be preceded by 12 months of real-life experience living as a member of the desired sex, and at least 6 months of continuous hormonal treatments (Sohn & Bosinski, 2007).

The "disorder" of GID has been criticized on several grounds, as follows (Langer & Martin, 2004):

- *It represents a bias that supports current Western sex-role stereotyping as valid.* There is a lack of consensus on gender appropriateness across the world, and some societies are far more tolerant of ambiguities in this regard than ours. Proponents of GID assume that adherence to gender stereotypes is healthy.
- *The diagnosis provides a means of keeping homosexuality in the* DSM. Although homosexuality was removed from the *DSM* in 1973, GID appeared in the very next version, and it was seen by some as a way to identify children (boys only) with the potential to become homosexual and to "treat" them with reorientation procedures (Gottschalk, 2003). The association between GID in childhood and later homosexuality is unclear;

there is evidence to suggest that boys who do not enjoy gender-typed roles and activities are more likely to become homosexual, but the same "logic" does not hold true for women.

- *The diagnostic category of GID demonstrates poor validity and reliability in the APA's own tests* (Langer & Martin, 2004).
- *The behaviors associated with GID are statistically deviant, but there is no evidence that they represent a dysfunction.* The disorder is associated with depression, but this is likely due to feelings of rejection and stigma similar to those experienced by persons who are gay, lesbian, and bisexual.
- *The* DSM-IV-TR *cautions that the GID diagnosis should not be made if the person is a nonconformist regarding stereotypical sex-role behavior* (p. 580). This caveat is vague and open to broad interpretation. When does nonconformity spill over into dysfunction, and is the dysfunction a side effect of marginalization or evidence of some internal disturbance?

Proponents of GID treatment programs enumerate three objectives: minimization of social ostracism, treatment of underlying psychopathology, and prevention against the development of adult transsexualism (Haldeman, 2000). The first outcome is important, but the other two include assumptions about the appropriateness of sex-role behavior and, as indicated earlier, a minority of persons with the diagnosis seeks reassignment surgery anyway.

Considering the limited literature supporting the diagnosis and treatment of GID, one may wonder whose problem it is. Negative reactions to gender-atypical persons in a society are a matter of fact, but the social work code of ethics suggests that these might be corrected by adjusting social attitudes rather than obliging some children to modify their own behavior.

Case Study

Norman is a 62-year-old Caucasian male referred for a psychosexual evaluation and follow-up sex offense treatment through The Division of Probation and Parole. He had been convicted of sexually assaulting a 7-year-old female and was recently released from jail after serving a 6-month period of incarceration with suspended time from his sentence. Norman had allegedly set out to "comfort" the young girl (a stranger) who was upset about losing money in a park, and the girl's mother a(who came upon the scene) had seen him stroking her genital area beneath her shorts. At present Norman expresses high motivation to enter into treatment, feeling frustrated by the erratic course of his interpersonal life.

Norman grew up in a small rural community. He lived in that area until his mid-twenties when he relocated to another state for employment. Norman relates that he was the oldest of five children born of his parents. He has one brother who is 18 years his junior, a female sibling who died shortly after birth, and a set of female twins, now 48. His mother died when he was 4 years old during childbirth.

Norman describes an adverse and abusive childhood. Norman's father could not handle four young children and placed them (along with Norman) with a maternal grandaunt. Norman fondly recalls time spent with his father during his childhood but acknowledges he saw him rarely and missed having him involved in his life.

Norman had no prior relationship with his grandaunt and viewed her as a stranger to him and his siblings. She then became physically abusive to all the children. Since his female twin siblings were infants, the grandaunt bonded with them in a manner that she did not replicate for Norman and his brother, which Norman found difficult to understand and accept.

The home was also incestuous, with a variety of sexual relationships going on. Norman reports he was sexually abused by an older cousin, the daughter of his grandaunt, who was 5 years his senior. He remembers her getting into bed with him as a preschooler, but only "snapshots" of her sexually assaulting him. He remembers another incident shortly afterward where he and his cousin were in the backseat of a car and she aggressively attempted to have sex with him. He believes this continued for several years. Norman said another one of his cousins was sexually offending a sister, who became pregnant and delivered a disabled child who subsequently died due to birth defects. Norman was accused of abusing the cousin and fathering the child, which resulted in him being further ostracized within the household. Norman recalls generally poor sexual boundaries and a great deal of inappropriate touching among family members. He acknowledges that by age 5 or 6, he was touching his younger sisters and viewed himself as becoming a sex offender at that age.

Norman's father remarried when he was 10 years old; after that he began staying with his father off and on until the age of 16. At that age he moved from his grandaunt's home and never returned. Norman had quit school after the ninth grade, believing he was "smarter than his teachers." He was frequently in trouble at school for oppositional behavior, fighting, and petty theft, and he viewed himself as a "lazy student." Norman joined the army at age 17 and remained in active service for 13 months. He reports that he received a general discharge under honorable conditions after being placed in a stockade due to fighting with his commander. When released from the army, he worked a series of manual labor jobs and was described as a competent employee.

Norman had no significant criminal history prior to the sexual offense other than some misdemeanor charges from early adulthood related to drinking in public and a driving under the influence (DUI) charge, received 6 years ago. Norman began drinking at 4 years of age, recalling that he finished off the remains of moonshine in adult glasses. He continued drinking in this manner and recalls that by age 12 he was drinking too much and too frequently. He drank heavily during his teens and early twenties, but despite receiving the single DUI citation states that he has not consumed alcohol of any significance for the last several decades.

He reports a life of relatively appropriate choices, including two marriages and one child. He was only able to engage sexually with his wives during the courtship period of their relationships. Although he remained married for a significant number of years to each wife, he describes their relationships as becoming that of "brother and sister" rather than a romantic involvement between adult lovers. Eventually, in both marriages, this became a problem for his wives and played a significant role in the relationships ending.

Norman's adult sexual history indicates that he spent his teens and early twenties engaged in sexual contact with a variety of individuals that he knew only casually. He reports his first consensual sexual relationship occurred when he was 20 years of age. Most of his sexual encounters involved alcohol and were "one-night stands." Currently, Norman has difficulty performing sexually due to having type II diabetes.

Norman reluctantly admitted to a pervasive arousal to children. He acknowledged that he has always been aroused by children and states that it is something he has lived with "since day one." He reported that he has attempted to stay away from children and avoid his arousal patterns because he knew it was wrong. He acknowledges reluctantly that he continues to masturbate to fantasies of sexual contact with children. By his report, his fantasies are constant and intrusive. He said he has never been able to control them and describes them as compulsive in nature.

Norman and his second wife became foster parents and provided care for 10 to 15 children in their household. Although he denied it initially, he later acknowledged a history of fondling the breasts and genitals of various female foster children, as well as other girls outside the home (about 50 victims in all). He maintains that his arousal to children is exclusive to females of elementary school age and when a child reaches her teenage years, he is no longer sexually interested. Despite the number of victims, Norman states that he despises his sexual arousal to children and has worked on not acting on his sexual urges.

Norman states that he has "never caused physical harm to a child." This has been his primary cognitive distortion that he used to keep his offending behavior in place. He has convinced himself that his decision to never penetrate a child vaginally keeps his actions from being harmful to the child. Norman was later able to acknowledge that he caused significant emotional and mental harm that damaged his victims over the years.

Norman has engaged in other paraphilias throughout his life. He admits to a history of voyeurism beginning as a juvenile and continuing through his twenties with victims numbering in the hundreds. He continues to fantasize about peeping on unsuspecting individuals.

He also has a history of public masturbation and exhibitionism that began as a juvenile and continues to the present time. He says this behavior, which has occurred in the "dozens of times," occurs when he has sexual fantasies about children and is trying not to act on them by sexually offending a child.

Norman has been honest with his daughter and ex-wife about his attraction to children and admitted to his offense. He receives emotional support from both of them. He continues to feel financially responsible for his ex-wife since their marriage ended with his criminal conviction, and he recognizes the emotional and financial losses she experienced because of his actions. He was going through foreclosure on his home at the time he was referred for evaluation. He recognizes significant financial stressors but appears to be addressing them adequately and realistically.

Penile plethysmograph testing verified Norman's disclosure of his current inability to achieve an erection. He demonstrated no penile response to the stimuli, but galvanic skin response and respiration data indicated his approach to the test was honest without evidence of attempts to manipulate data through controlling breathing or responses.

Diagnosis

Axis I:
302.2 Pedophilia, Sexually Attracted to Females, Nonexclusive Type
302.4 Exhibitionism
302.82 Voyeurism

Axis II: 799.9 Deferred

Axis III Type II Diabetes, by history

Axis IV Problems with Legal System
Problems with finances
Problems with primary support system (recent divorce)
Other psychosocial problems (estrangement from family of origin).

Axis V 65

Justification for Diagnosis

Axis I
Pedophilia, Sexual Attraction to Females, Nonexclusive Type

- Criterion A: At 62 years of age, client admits to a lifetime of sexual interest and arousal with elementary school–age females.
- Criteria B and C: has sexual offended children after the age of 16 more than 5 years his junior

- Sexually Attracted to Females: maintains he has never been aroused by male children
- Nonexclusive Type: has had sexual intercourse with adult females but is unable to sustain sexual performance after initial courtship period

Exhibitionism

- Criterion A: acknowledges sexually arousing fantasies involving exposing himself and masturbating in public since his teenage years.
- Criterion B: Although his frequency of engaging in the behavior has decreased over the years, he has disclosed victims numbering in the dozens and current fantasies of masturbating in public.

Voyeurism

- Criterion A: Norman acknowledges sexually arousing fantasies involving peeping on individuals without their knowledge while they are engaged in sexual behaviors or naked.
- Criterion B: Although his frequency of engaging in the behavior has decreased over the years, he has disclosed victims numbering in the hundreds and current fantasies of peeping on unsuspecting individuals.

Axis II
The presented symptomatology does not constitute a personality disorder and Norman's level of functioning refutes the possibility of mental retardation.

Axis III
Norman has a diagnosis of type II diabetes and is currently under the care of a physician for the condition.

Axis IV
Norman is currently dealing with reintegration into the community after a 6-month period of incarceration. As a result of his conviction and incarceration, he has limited financial resources, is losing his house in foreclosure, will be looking for housing, and continues to help his ex-wife with her bills and obligations

Axis V
A GAF score of 65 was assigned because Norman appears to be addressing the stressors in his life adequately. He is functioning fairly well and maintains relationships with his daughter and ex-wife.

Risk and Protective Influences

Norman demonstrated a variety of risk influences for the onset of pedophilia. He is male, was sexually abused as a youth, and came from a disorganized family that featured poor attachments and inconsistent parenting. Norman also demonstrated impulse control problems and subsequent behavior problems, including oppositional behavior, fighting, and theft. He developed a substance use disorder at a very young age.

Norman's disclosure of pervasive and enduring sexual attraction to female, elementary school–age children coupled with lack of arousal and sexual performance with adult females, places him at risk for reoffense. His long history of offending and high number of victims increases this risk. His variety of sexually offending behaviors increases his overall risk. Norman admits active fantasies involving children, voyeurism, and exhibitionism. He describes these thoughts as compulsive and pervasive. The only mitigating factors are his advancing age, decreased sexual activity (by client's report), recent insight into his actions, the ongoing support of his ex-wife (although he has no other active supports), and his expressed desire to address his problem through treatment and community interventions.

Treatment Plan

Given Norman's significant family history with regard to incest and sexual abuse, it is recommended he complete a full disclosure sexual history. The primary focus would be his offending behaviors with a secondary focus on his own victimization. The honesty of his report should be assessed through use of a full disclosure sexual history polygraph. Norman should participate in sex offense specific counseling with a treatment provider who specializes in sex offender treatment. Compliance with community safety issues should be monitored through maintenance polygraphs and client should utilize a probation and treatment-approved chaperone for all contact with minor children.

Norman's intervention will include an educational component to inform the client about the patterns of his deviant behavior. This may allow him to control urges and cope with sexual triggers. Desensitization to potential triggers will be included to gradually increase his tolerance of external stimulants. The implementation of cognitive restructuring will be useful to combat Norman's cognitive distortions related to his offensive behavior. Relaxation techniques may also aid in the process. Treatment will also focus on building empathy for the victim, and anger management components will be included to further control for the antecedents of his sexually offensive behavior.

References

American Academy of Child & Adolescent Psychiatry (2000). Summary of the practice parameters for the assessment and treatment of children and adolescents who are sexually abusive of others. *Journal of the American Academy of Child and Adolescent Psychiatry*, 39(1), 127–130.

American Psychiatric Association. (2000). *Diagnostic and statistical manual of mental disorders* (4th ed., rev.). Washington, DC: Author.

Aromaki, A. S., Lindman, R. E., & Eriksson, C. J. P. (2002). Testosterone, sexuality and antisocial personality in rapists and child molesters: A pilot study. *Psychiatry Research, 110*(3), 239–247.

Birken, P., Hill, A., & Bemer, W. (2003). Pharmacotherapy of paraphilias with long-acting agonists of luteinizing hormone-releasing hormone: A systematic review. *Journal of Clinical Psychiatry, 64*(8), 890–897.

Blanchard, R., Christensen, B., Strong, S., Cantor, J., Kuban, M., Klassen, P., et al. (2002). Retrospective self-reports of childhood accidents causing unconsciousness in phallometrically diagnosed pedophiles. *Archives of Sexual Behavior, 31*(6), 511–516.

Bogaert, A. F. (2001). Handedness, criminality, and sexual offending. *Neuropsychologia, 39*(5), 465–469.

Bowlby, J. (1979). *The making and breaking of affectional bonds*. London: Tavistock.

Bradford, J. M. W. (2001). The neurobiology, neuropharmacology, and pharmacological treatment of the paraphilias and compulsive sexual behavior. *Canadian Journal of Psychiatry, 46*(1), 26–33.

Bromberg, D. S., & Johnson, B. T. (2001). Sexual interest in children, child sexual abuse, and psychological sequelae for children. *Psychology in the Schools, 38*(4), 343–355.

Caldwell, M. F. (2002. What we do not know about juvenile sexual reoffence risk. *Child Maltreatment, 7*, 291–302.

Cohen, L. J., Mikiforov, K., Gans, G., Poznansky, O., McGeoch, P., Weaver, C., et al. (2002). Heterosexual male perpetrators of childhood sexual abuse: A preliminary neurospychiatric model. *Psychiatric Quarterly, 73*(4), 313–336.

Connolly, M., & Woollons, R. (2008). Childhood sexual experiences and adult offending: An exploratory comparison of three criminal groups. *Child Abuse Review, 17*, 119–132.

Coolidge, F. L., Thede, L. L., & Young, S. E. (2002). The heritability of gender identity disorder in a child and adolescent twin sample. *Behavior Genetics, 32*(4), 251–258.

Craig, L. A., Browne, K. D., Beech, A., & Stringer, I. (2006). Psychosexual characteristics of sexual offenders and the relationship to sexual reconviction. *Psychology, Crime, and Law 12*(3), 231–243.

Drapeau, M., Korner, A. C., Granger, L., & Brunet, L. (2005). What sex abusers say about their treatment: Results from a qualitative study on pedophiles in treatment at a Canadian Penitentiary Clinic. *Journal of Child Sexual Abuse, 14*(1), 91–114.

Efta-Breitbach, J., & Freeman, K. A. (2004). Treatment of juveniles who sexually offend: An overview. *Journal of Child Sexual Abuse, 13*(3/4), 125–137.

Fagan, P., Wise, T., Schmidt, C., & Berlin, F. (2002). Pedophilia. *The Journal of the American Medical Association, 288*(19), 2458–2466.

Federoff, J. P. (2008). Treatment of paraphilic sexual disorders. In D. L. Rowland & L. Incrocci (Eds.), *Handbook of sexual and gender identity disorders* (pp. 563–586). Hoboken, NJ: Wiley.

Fortune, C. A., & Lambie, I. (2005). Sexually abusive youth: A review of recidivism studies and methodological issues for future research. *Clinical Psychology Review, 26*, 1078–1095.

Gottschalk, L. (2003). Same-sex sexuality and childhood gender non-conformity: A spurious connection. *Journal of Gender Studies, 12*(1), 35–49.

Haldeman, D. C. (2000). Gender atypical youth: Clinical and social issues. *School Psychology Review, 29*(2), 192–200.

Hall, R. C., & Hall, R. C. (2007). A profile of pedophilia: Definition, characteristics of offenders, recidivism, treatment outcomes, and forensic issues. Retrieved July 29, 2009, from the Mayo Foundation for Medical Education and Research Web site: http://www.mayoclinicproceedings.com

Hanson, R. K., & Bussière, M. T. (1998). Predicting relapse: A meta-analysis of sexual offender recidivism studies. *Journal of Consulting and Clinical Psychology, 66*(2), 348–362.

Hughes, J. R. (2007). Review of medical reports on pedophilia. *Clinical Pediatrics, 46*(8), 667–682.

Kafka, M. P. (2001). The paraphilia-related disorders: A proposal for a unified classification of nonparaphilic hypersexuality disorders. *Sexual Addiction and Compulsivity, 8*, 227–239.

Kear-Colwell, J., & Boer, D. P. (2000). The treatment of pedophiles: Clinical experience and the implications of recent research. *International Journal of Offender Therapy and Comparative Criminology, 44*(5), 593–605.

Langer, S. J., & Martin, J. I. (2004). How dresses can make you mentally ill: Examining gender identity disorder in children. *Child and Adolescent Social Work Journal, 21*(1), 5–20.

Laws, Dr. R. & O'Donohue, W. (2008). *Sexual deviance: Theory, assessment, and treatment* (2nd ed.). New York: Guilford.

Lee, J. K. P., Jackson, H. J., Pattison, P., & Ward, T. (2002). Developmental risk factors for sexual offending. *Child Abuse and Neglect, 26*(1), 73–92.

Lösel, F., & Schmucker, M. (2005). The effectiveness of treatment for sexual offenders: A comprehensive meta-analysis. *Journal of Experimental Criminology, 1*(1), 117–146.

Maes, M., van West, D., De Vos, N., Westenberg, H., Van Hunsel, F., Hendriks, D., et al. (2001). Lower baseline plasma cortisol and prolactin together with increased body temperature and higher mCPP-induced cortisol responses in men with pedophilia. *Neuropsychopharmacology, 24*(1), 37–46.

Manley, G., & Koehler, J. (2001). Sexual behavior disorders: Proposed new classification in the DSM-V. *Sexual Addiction and Compulsivity, 8*, 253–265.

Marshall, W. L. (1999). Current status of North American assessment and treatment programs for sexual offenders. *Journal of Interpersonal Violence, 14*(3), 221–239.

Marziano, V., Ward, T., Beech, A. R., & Pattison, P. (2006). Identification of five fundamental implicit theories underlying cognitive distortions in child abusers: A preliminary study. *Psychology, Crime, and Law, 12*(1), 97–105.

Murray, J. B. (2000). Psychological profile of pedophiles and child molesters. *The Journal of Psychology, 134*(2), a311–324.

North American Man/Boy Love Association. (2009). Retrieved July 25, 2009, from http://www.nambla1.org

O'Grady, R. (2001). Eradicating pedophilia: Toward the humanization of society. *Journal of International Affairs, 55*(1), 123–140.

Righthand, S., & Welch, C. (2004). Youth who sexually offend: Theoretical issues. *Journal of Child Sexual Abuse, 13*(3/4), 15–32.

Rosler, A., & Witztum, E. (2000). Pharmacotherapy of paraphilias in the next millennium. *Behavioral Sciences and the Law, 18*, 43–56.

Rosenberg, M. (2002). Treatment considerations for pedophilia: Recent headlines aside, this disorder has long confronted the behavioral healthcare community with difficult challenges. *Behavioral Health Management, 22*(4), 38–42.

Saunders, B. E., Berliner, L., & Hanson, R. F. (Eds.). (2004). *Child physical and sexual abuse: Guidelines for treatment (Revised report: April 26, 2004).* Charleston, SC: National Crime Victims Research and Treatment Center.

Sawle, G. A., & Kear-Colwell, J. (2001). Adult attachment style and pedophilia: A developmental perspective. *International Journal of Offender Therapy and Comparative Criminology, 45*(1), 32–50.

Seto, M. C. (2008). Assessment methods. In M. C. Seto (Ed.), *Pedophilia and sexual offending against children: Theory, assessment, and intervention* (pp. 23–45). Washington, DC: American Psychological Association.

Seto, M. C., (2004). Pedophilia and sexual offenses against children. *Annual Review of Sex Research, 15,* 321–361.

Seto, M. C., Abramowitz, C. S., & Barbaree, H. E. (2008). Paraphilias. In J. Hunsley & E. Mash (Eds.), *A guide to assessments that work* (pp. 488–513). New York: Oxford University Press.

Shanahan, M., & Donato, D. (2001). Counting the cost: Estimating the economic benefit of pedophile treatment programs. *Child Abuse and Neglect, 25*(4), 541–555.

Sohn, M., & Bosinki, H. A. G. (2007). Gender identity disorders: Diagnostic and surgical aspects. *Journal of Sexuality and Medicine, 4,* 1193–1208.

Ward, T., & Seigert, R. J. (2002). Toward a comprehensive theory of child sexual abuse: A theory knitting perspective. *Psychology, Crime, and Law, 8,* 319–351.

Weinberger, L. E., Sreenivasan, S., Garrick, T., & Osran, H. (2005). The impact of surgical castration on sexual recidivism risk among sexually violent predatory offenders. *Journal of the American Academy of Psychiatry and the Law, 33*(1), 16–36.

Whitaker, D. J., Le, B., Hanson, R. K., Baker, C. K., McMahon, P. M., Ryan, G., Klein, A., & Rice, D. D. (2008). Risk factors for the perpetration of child sexual abuse: A review and meta-analysis. *Child Abuse and Neglect, 32,* 529–548.

Appendix: Instruments Used to Assess Pedophilia and Other Sexual Offenders

The revision for this edition was drawn from Seto, Abramowitz, and Barbaree (2008).

The Multiphasic Sex Inventory (MSI) (Kalichman, Henderson, Shealy, & Dwyer, 1992; original authors: Nichols & Molinder, 1984)

Description
- A 200-item true/false self-report inventory designed to assist in the comprehensive assessment of sex offenders

- Reflects a conceptual framework of sex offender motivational and behavioral characteristics; includes scales for deviant acts, cognitive processes, behavioral aspects of offenses, and deceptive styles
- Includes three sexual deviance scales, five atypical sexual outlet scales, a sexual dysfunction scale (comprised of four subscales), six validity scales, and a scale measuring sex knowledge
- For diagnosis, norms were rated good, clinical utility was rated excellent, and the instrument was highly recommended (Day, Miner, Sturgeon, & Murphy, 1989; Kalichman et al., 1992; Nichols & Molinder, 1984).

Reliability
- Internal consistencies ranged from .53 to .90; scales with heterogeneous content demonstrated lower comparative reliability.
- For diagnosis, internal consistency was rated good and test-retest reliability was excellent (Day et al., 1989; Kalichman et al., 1992; Nichols & Molinder, 1984).

Validity
- Response patterns reflected what was predicted by the researchers based on theoretical and clinical descriptions of sex offenders.
- A negative correlation was found between victim ages and Child Molestation scores.
- Substantial positive correlations were found between distress-related MSI subscales and MMPI distress scales, MSI and MMPI validity scales, and MSI scales and measures of personality type.
- For diagnosis, content validity was rated adequate, and construct validity and validity generalization were rated excellent (Baldwin & Roys, 1998; Barnard, Robbins, Tingle, Shaw, & Newman, 1987; Craig, Browne, Beech, & Stringer, 2006; Day et al., 1989; Kalichman et al., 1992; Nichols & Molinder, 1984).

Sexual Interest Cardsort Questionnaire (SICQ) (Holland, Zolondek, Abel, Jordan, & Becker, 2000)

Description
- For diagnosis, norms were rated adequate, and clinical utility rated good (Holland et al., 2000).
- Seventy-five descriptions of explicit sexual acts that relate to different paraphilia diagnoses, respondent scores interest on a 7-point scale. Newer version contains 45 items

Reliability

For diagnosis, internal consistency rated excellent (Holland et al., 2000).

Validity

For diagnosis, content validity was rated good, construct validity was rated excellent, and validity generalization was rated good (Holland et al., 2000; Laws, Hanson, Osborn, & Greenbaum, 2000).

Multidimensional Assessment of Sex Aggression (MASA) (Knight, Prentky, & Cerce, 1994)

Description

- For diagnosis, norms were rated adequate, and clinical utility rated good (Knight et al., 1994).
- Assesses domains, including antisocial behavior, aggression, social competence, paraphilias, sexual preoccupation, offense planning, sexual attitudes, and pornography use
- Designed to assess adult male offenders, but it has recently also been tested with adolescent male offenders
- Sadism and paraphilias scales have good internal consistencies and test-retest reliabilities.

Reliability

For diagnosis, internal consistency and test-retest reliability rated good (Knight et al., 1994).

Validity

For diagnosis, content validity, construct validity, and validity generalization rated good (Daversa, 2005; Knight et al., 1994).

The Static-99 Sex Offender Risk Assessment (Austin, Peyton, & Johnson, 2003; Hanson & Thornton, 2000)

Description

- A 10-item sex offender recidivism risk assessment instrument that is completed through an offender's file review
- Items assess prior sex offenses (charges and convictions), prior sentencing dates, convictions for noncontact sex offenses, index of nonsexual violence, prior nonsexual violence, unrelated victims, stranger victims, male victims, offender age, and offender marital status. These are conceptualized as static risk, and they are historical variables that either cannot be changed or are highly stable and unlikely to change.
- Offenders are scored with a yes/no response or a structured scale ranging in value from 0 to 3.

- Scores between 0 and 1 are considered "low" risk, 2 to 3 are "medium-low" risk, 4 to 5 are "medium-high" risk, and 6 to 10 are "high" risk.
- For case conceptualization and treatment planning, norms were rated excellent, clinical utility was rated good, and the instrument was highly recommended (Barbaree, Seto, Langton, & Peacock, 2001; Hanson & Thornton, 2000).

Reliability
- Two hundred twenty offenders were independently rated by two researchers with 81.4%–98.6% agreement across items, 40.9% agreement on total score, and 73.2% agreement on risk level.
- For case conceptualization and treatment planning, interrater reliability was excellent (Barbaree et al., 2001; Hanson & Thornton, 2000).

Validity
- Predictive validity was assessed by comparing risk levels of 78 respondents with actual recidivism over a 12-month period; distinct differences in rates were observed among the risk categories.
- For case conceptualization and treatment planning, content validity was rated adequate, construct validity was rated excellent, and validity generalization was rated good (Barbaree et al., 2001; Hanson & Thornton, 2000).

References for Instruments Used to Assess Pedophillia and Other Sexual Offenders

Austin, J., Peyton, J., & Johnson, K. D. (2003). *Reliability and validity study of Static-99/RRASOR sex offender risk assessment instruments.* Final report submitted to the Pennsylvania Board of Probation and Parole. Institute on Crime, Justice, and Corrections, George Washington University, Washington, DC.

Baldwin, K., & Roys, D. T. (1998). Factors associated with denial in a sample of alleged adult sexual offenders. *Behavioral Science, 10,* 211–226.

Barbaree, H. E., Seto, M. C., Langton, C. M., & Peacock, E. J. (2001). Evaluating the predictive accuracy of six risk assessment instruments for adult sex offenders. *Criminal Justice and Behavior, 28,* 490–521.

Barnard, G. W., Robbins, L., Tingle, D., Shaw, T., & Newman, G. (1987). Development of a computerized sexual assessment laboratory. *Bulletin of the American Academy of Psychiatry and Law, 15,* 339–347.

Craig, L. A., Browne, K. D., Beech, A., & Stringer, I. (2006). Psychosexual characteristics of sexual offenders and the relationship to sexual reconviction. *Psychology, Crime, and Law, 12,* 231–243.

Daversa, M. (2005). Early caregiver instability and maltreatment experiences in the prediction of age of victims of adolescent sexual offenders. *Dissertation Abstracts International, 65*(08-B), 4319.

Day, D. M., Miner, M. H., Sturgeon, V. H., & Murphy, J. (1989). Assessment of sexual arousal by means of physiological and self-report measures. In D. R. Laws (Ed.), *Relapse prevention with sex offenders* (pp. 115–123). New York: Guilford.

Hanson, R. K., & Thornton, D. (2000). Improving risk assessments for sex offenders: A comparison of three actuarial studies. *Law and Human Behavior, 24*(1), 119–136.

Holland, L. A., Zolondek, S. C., Abel, G. G., Jordan, A. D., & Becker, J. V. (2000). Psychometric analysis of the Sexual Interest Cardsort Questionnaire. *Sexual Abuse: A Journal of Research and Treatment, 12,* 107–122.

Kalichman, S. C., Henderson, M. C., Shealy, L. S., & Dwyer, M. (1992). Psychometric properties of the multiphasic sex inventory in assessing sex offenders. *Criminal Justice and Behavior, 19*(4), 384–396.

Knight, R. A., Prentky, R. A., & Cerce, D. D. (1994). The development, reliability, and validity of an inventory for the Multidimensional Assessment of Sex and Aggression. *Criminal Justice and Behavior, 21,* 72–94.

Laws, D. R., Hanson, R. K., Osborn, C. A., & Greenbaum, P. E. (2000). Classification of child molesters by plethysmographic assessment of sexual arousal and a self-report measure of sexual preference. *Journal of Interpersonal Violence, 15,* 1297–1312.

Nichols, H. R., & Molinder, I. (1984). *Multiphasic Sex Inventory manual.* Tacoma, WA: Nichols & Molinder Assessments.

PART III

Disorders With Onset in Adulthood

12 Bipolar Disorder

Bipolar disorder is a disorder of *mood* in which, over time, a person experiences one or more *manic episodes* that are usually accompanied by one or more *major depressive episodes* (APA, 2000). Medication is always a major, and sometimes the only, intervention for this disorder because of its effectiveness with so many clients. Nonetheless, the medicalization of bipolar disorder has tended to obscure the fact that it has an uncertain etiology. Bipolar disorder features both manic and depressive episodes (APA, 2000). A *manic episode* is a distinct period in which a person's predominant mood is elevated, expansive, or irritable to a degree that there is serious impairment in occupational and social functioning. Manic episodes may be characterized by any of the following symptoms (at least three must be present): unrealistically inflated self-esteem, a decreased need for sleep, pressured speech, racing thoughts, distractibility, an increase in unrealistic goal-directed activity, and involvement in activities that have a potential for painful consequences. Manic episodes are rapid in onset and may persist for a few days up to several months.

A *major depressive episode* is a period of at least two weeks during which a person experiences a depressed mood or loss of interest in nearly all common life activities. Symptoms may include (five or more must be present) depressed mood, diminished interest or pleasure in most activities, significant and unintentional weight loss *or* gain, insomnia *or* hypersomnia, feelings of physical agitation *or* retardation, loss of energy, feelings of worthlessness or excessive guilt, a diminished ability to think or concentrate, and persistent thoughts of death or suicide.

Another feature of bipolar disorder, one that often disrupts the continuity of intervention, is the *hypomanic* episode (APA, 2000). This refers to the person's gradual escalation over a period of several days to several weeks from a stable mood to a manic state. It is a mild form of mania that may be pleasurable for the client. He or she experiences higher self-esteem, a decreased need for sleep, a higher energy level, an increase in overall productivity, and more intensive involvement in pleasurable activities. Its related behaviors are often socially acceptable and consequently the hypomanic person may receive positive reinforcement from friends and employers. At these times, however, the client's decreased insight may lead him or her to believe that the bipolar disorder has permanently remitted and there is no need to continue with medication or other interventions. The potential for a full manic episode thus becomes greater. In fact, poor insight, or the lack of awareness of having a mental illness, is a prominent characteristic in the active phases of bipolar disorder.

There are two types of bipolar disorder (APA, 2000). *Bipolar I* disorder is characterized by one or more manic episodes, usually accompanied by a major depressive episode. *Bipolar II* disorder is characterized by one or more major depressive episodes accompanied by at least one hypomanic episode. In other words, bipolar I disorder features a mix of mood episodes, whereas in bipolar II disorder depressive episodes predominate. These subtypes were first introduced in *DSM-IV*. Prior to that time, while it was recognized that persons could have varying courses of mood episodes, the disorder was considered to represent a single phenomenology.

Bipolar II disorder, which is more common than bipolar I disorder, resembles a milder form of classic manic-depressive disorder with regard to symptom intensity. Yet it is characterized by a higher incidence of comorbidity, suicidal behavior, and rapid cycling (Vieta & Suppes, 2008). Such persons experience fewer hospitalizations and psychotic features but more interpersonal conflicts, marital problems, and episodes of family breakdown. Many persons with bipolar II disorder are initially misdiagnosed with major depression, and the occurrence of antidepressant-induced mania often leads to their rediagnosis (Chun & Dunner, 2004).

The diagnosis of Bipolar Disorder Not Otherwise Specified is sometimes given to children and adolescents who do not meet the formal *DSM* criteria for bipolar I or II disorder, but who exhibit a symptom profile believed to be unique to that age group (see "Assessment" section). Often, persons who are given this diagnosis experience manic episodes less than 7 days in duration.

There are six subtypes of bipolar disorder, intended to reflect the severity of the most recent mood episode and its aftermath. These include *mild* (meeting minimum symptom criteria), *moderate*, *severe* (the client requires almost continuous supervision) *without psychotic features, severe with psychotic features, in partial remission,* and *in full remission.* There are also four specifiers that may be used to more clearly describe the nature of most recent mood episode. These include *catatonic* (featuring a pronounced psychomotor disturbance), *melancholic* (referring to the client's presentation during a major depressive episode), *atypical,* and *postpartum* (occurring within 4 weeks of delivery of the child). Bipolar disorder may also be present *with* or *without full interepisode recovery, with seasonal pattern,* and *with rapid cycling* (defined as four mood episodes in a 12-month period). The most recent major depressive episode may be *chronic* (meeting full criteria for 2 years or more).

Prevalence

Worldwide estimates of the prevalence of bipolar disorder range from 0.5% to 5% (Matza, Rajagopalan, Thompson, & Lissovoy, 2005). The estimated prevalence in the National Comorbidity Replication Survey was 3.9% with a 12-month prevalence of 2.6% (Kessler et al., 2005). The lifetime prevalence of bipolar I disorder is equal in men and women (close to 1%). Bipolar II disorder is slightly more prevalent overall (1.1%) and is more common among women (up to 5%) (Barnes & Mitchell, 2005). In men the number of manic episodes equals or exceeds the number of depressive episodes, while in women depressive episodes predominate.

Between 1994 and 2003 there was a 40-fold increase in child and adolescent diagnoses of the disorder (now estimated as having a 1%–5% prevalence), with only a two-fold increase among adults (Moreno et al., 2007). This increase may be due to changing diagnostic criteria (perhaps informally), a greater practitioner sensitivity to the symptoms of the disorder, or a true increase in the disorder's prevalence. There are far lower prevalence rates of childhood bipolar disorder in Europe (Holtman, Bolte, & Poustka, 2008).

Comorbidity

Bipolar I disorder is often comorbid with the substance use, anxiety, and personality disorders (Grant et al., 2005). The highest rates of comorbidity are 71% for anxiety, 56% for a substance use disorder, 49% for alcohol abuse, 47% for social phobia, and 36% for a personality disorder (Marangell, Kupfer, Sachs, & Swann, 2006). Bipolar disorder is modestly associated with medical illnesses in adulthood, including cardiovascular, cerebrovascular, and respiratory diseases (Carney & Jones, 2006).

The most common comorbidites identified in youths diagnosed with bipolar disorder were found in a meta-analysis to include attention-deficit/hyperactivity disorder, oppositional defiant disorder, conduct disorder, and the anxiety disorders (Kowatch, Youngstrom, Danielyan, & Findling, 2005).

Course

Bipolar disorder is recurrent and chronic and is the sixth leading cause of disability for persons aged 15 to 44 years (Woods, 2000). The typical age of onset of a manic episode is late adolescence into the mid-twenties, but bipolar disorder may begin at any time from childhood through midlife (Hirschfeld, Lewis, & Vornick, 2003). It has recently been suggested that its onset may occur before age 16 (Post et al., 2006). Twenty percent to 30% of adults with bipolar disorder report that they experienced their first episode before age 20. Approximately 30%–35% of persons experience their first episode of bipolar disorder between the ages of 20 and 30, and 25% report the first episode between ages 40 and 50 years. A first manic episode after the age of 40 is unusual and may be due to a medical condition or to substance abuse.

Bipolar I disorder is highly recurrent, with 90% of persons who have a manic episode developing future episodes (Sierra, Livianos, Arques, & Castello, 2007). The number of episodes tends to average four in 10 years (APA, 2000). Fifty percent of persons with bipolar disorder move through alternating manic and depressed cycles (Tyrer, 2006). Ten percent experience rapid cycling (APA, 2000), which implies a poorer long-term outcome, since such persons are at a higher risk for both relapse and suicidal ideation (75% have contemplated suicide) (Mackinnon, Potash, McMahon, & Simpson, 2005). Forty percent have a "mixed" type of the disorder, in which a prolonged depressive episode features short bursts of mania. A majority of persons (70%–90%) return to a stable mood and functioning capacity between episodes.

A recent systematic review concluded that between 5% and 15% of persons with bipolar II disorder develop a manic episode within 5 years, which means that their diagnosis must be changed to bipolar I disorder (Vieta & Suppes, 2008). Clients with bipolar II disorder tend to have a greater total number of hypomanic and depressive episodes than bipolar I clients, and they may also have a shorter duration of episodes and more persistent depression. For both types of bipolar disorder the duration between episodes (the *interepisode* period) tends to be longer after the initial episode, decreasing as further cycles occur (Geller, Tillman, Bolhofner, & Zimmerman, 2008).

Despite manic and hypomanic episodes being the hallmarks of the bipolar disorders, depressive episodes are experienced for a greater length of time. Studies of the natural course of bipolar disorder over one decade indicate that persons with bipolar I disorder experience depression for 30.6% of weeks, compared with 9.8% of weeks for hypomanic or manic symptoms (Michalak, Murray, Young, & Lam, 2008). Persons with bipolar II disorder experience depression for 51.9% of weeks, compared to 1.4% of weeks for hypomanic symptoms. Clearly it is the depressive symptoms that dominate either type of the disorder. Furthermore, persons with the disorder attempt suicide at a similar rate to those with major depression (Oquendo & Mann, 2006).

Although bipolar disorder is cyclic, some persons do not experience complete remission after a first (or subsequent) episode. In one study 40% of persons with the disorder continued to experience lingering symptoms of anxiety and depression for a full year after the first episode (Conus et al., 2006). Further, over 60% did not return to their previous level of functioning after 1 year. Another literature review concluded that over the course of bipolar disorder a person may develop chronic mild to moderate problems with attention, learning, memory, and executive function (Burdick, Braca, Goldberg, & Malhotra, 2007).

The bipolar client may experience additional emotional problems related to fears of the recurrence of mood swings and dealing with the loss of relationships and his or her former sense of self. In a qualitative study it was found that clients tended to develop "contradictory identities" depending on their mood state (Inder et al., 2008). They are unable to differentiate their selves from the illness and to decide which is "real." The stigma of their interpersonal experiences further shapes their confused self-definition, and as a result they fail to experience coherence and consistency in their identities. An adolescent who develops bipolar disorder may experience a particularly severe arrest in psychological development, acquiring self-efficacy and dependency problems that endure into adulthood.

It should not be surprising that persons with bipolar disorder tend to experience serious social functioning problems. The person's mood swings and erratic behavior may be a source of ongoing turmoil in family, peer, and professional relationships, testing the limits of those relationships until others are exhausted and drained of empathy (Miklowitz, 2007). Married persons with bipolar disorder are at a high risk for family conflicts, sexual difficulties, and divorce (Lam, Donaldson, Brown, & Malliaris, 2005). The "well" spouse's self-esteem can diminish while being blamed for the family's problems, acting as a buffer between the client and community, and making concessions to the client in an effort to maintain family stability. If the marriage continues, other problems may include the well spouse's guilt feelings Conflicts with partners are most intense during manic periods.

The same interpersonal patterns described above contribute to the bipolar client's occupational problems. One study indicated a stable working capacity in only 45% of clients, and 28% experienced a steady decline in job status and performance (Hirschfeld, Lewis, & Vornik, 2003). Thirty percent to 60% fail to regain full occupational and social function between mood episodes. Missed work, poor work quality, and conflicts with coworkers all contribute to the downward trend for clients who cannot maintain mood stability.

Assessment

Because of its biological influences, social workers need to participate in a multidisciplinary assessment of persons with possible bipolar disorder along with medical professionals. General assessment guidelines are as follows:

- Assess family history for the presence of bipolar disorder, other mood disorders, or substance use disorders.
- Assess the client's social history for evidence of any significant mood problems.
- Facilitate a medical examination to rule out any medical conditions that may be responsible for the symptoms.
- Make sure the symptoms are not the result of the direct physiological effects of substance abuse.
- Rule out major depression, which would be the diagnosis in the absence of any manic or hypomanic episodes.
- Rule out cyclothymic disorder, which is characterized by the presence of hypomanic episodes and episodes of depression that do not meet criteria for that disorder.
- Rule out psychotic disorders, which are characterized by psychotic symptoms in the absence of a mood disorders (Sands & Harrow, 2000).
- Assess for suicidal ideation.
- Assess the quality of the client's social supports.
- Evaluate the client's insight into the disorder.

It is also important to differentiate bipolar disorder from borderline personality disorder (Zanarini, Frankenburg, Hennen, & Silk, 2004). There is much symptom overlap between them, as both types of clients may experience dramatic mood swings, alternating periods of depression and elation, and transient psychotic symptoms, but the mood changes with the personality disorder are related to interpersonal influences and chronic feelings of insecurity, while bipolar disorder features more biologically patterned mood changes (Stone, 2006).

While bipolar disorder can occur in childhood and adolescence, its diagnosis, treatment, and increasing prevalence among those persons are controversial issues among human service professionals. The validity of childhood bipolar disorder and its diagnostic criteria are hotly debated (Smith, 2007). The National Institute of Mental Health recommends not diagnosing children less than 6 years of age with bipolar disorder (Cahill et al., 2007). It also identifies two different types of the disorder in children. Those with a "narrow phenotype" (fewer observable symptoms) have the classic symptoms of mania and depression, although many of these children experience rapid cycling and fail to meet the 4–7 day *DSM* criterion for mania. Children with the "broad phenotype" (said to be far more common) present with irritability, mood lability, temper outbursts, hyperactivity, and poor concentration.

Several sets of diagnostic criteria for childhood and adolescent bipolar disorder have been suggested. As an example, we present the criteria developed by Birmaher et al. (2006). Their diagnosis of bipolar disorder not otherwise specified (BPD-NOS) for children and adolescents requires the following:

- The "core positive" symptom, which is the presence of distinct period of abnormally elevated, expansive, or irritable mood
- A minimum of two "B" criteria symptoms (related to mania and/or depression) if mood is mostly elated, or three other "B" criteria if the person is irritable
- A clear change from the person's typical functioning (consistent with *DSM* guidelines for hypomania)
- Four or more hours of mood (hypomanic, manic, or depressed) within a 24-hour period to be counted as an index day of the disturbance
- Four or more days at a minimum over the course of a lifetime; nonconsecutive days are acceptable.

Keeping in mind that criteria such as these are still being refined, we now turn to a discussion of the risk and protective influences for bipolar disorder.

Risk and Protective Influences

Onset

During the past three decades, bipolar disorder has been considered primarily a disorder of brain functioning, although the exact etiology is uncertain. There may be psychological and social, as well as biological, components to the onset and course of the disorder (Leahy, 2007).

The risk and protective influences for the onset of bipolar disorder are summarized in Exhibit 12.1.

Genetic Mechanisms

Children of a bipolar parent are at an increased risk for developing mental disorders in general, and their chances of developing bipolar disorder are between 2% and 10% (Youngstrom, Findling, Youngstrom, & Calabrese, 2005). Persons who have a first-degree relative with a mood disorder are more likely to have an earlier age of onset than persons without a familial pattern. Twin studies are even more compelling. A study of identical and fraternal twins in which one member of the pair had bipolar disorder showed a concordance rate of 85% (McGuffin et al., 2003).

Exhibit 12.1

Risk and Protective Influences for the Onset of Bipolar Disorder

Risk Influences	Protective Influences
Genetic/Biological	
First-degree relative with bipolar disorder	Absence of mood disorders among first-degree relatives
Endocrine system imbalances	Asian race
Neurotransmitter imbalances	
Irregular circadian rhythms	
Obstetrical complications	
Giving birth (postpartum hormone changes)	
Psychological	
Poor sleep hygiene	Effective communication and problem-solving skills
Irregular daily living routines	Structured daily living routines
Traumatic experiences during childhood	Sense of self-direction, internal rewards
Hypersensitivity	
Self-criticism, low self-esteem	Positive self-esteem
Exaggerated use of denial	
Substance abuse disorders	Absence of substance abuse
Mood lability	
Transient psychotic episodes	
Social	
Ongoing conflict with family members	Positive family relationships

Sources: Berk et al. (2007); Ryan et al. (2006); Newman (2006); Youngstrom, Findling, Youngstrom, and Calabrese (2005); Post, Leverich, King, and Weiss (2001); Scott, McNeil, and Cavenaugh (2006); Swann (2006).

Several decades ago, researchers speculated that the potential for bipolar disorder emanated from a single gene, but this theory has lost support and studies are now focusing on polygenic models of transmission (Ryan et al., 2006). While genetic research remains promising, the "core" of bipolar disorder remains elusive. The likelihood of genetic mechanisms is complicated by indications that bipolar disorder with late-life onset (after 40 years) has no apparent association with family history.

Brain Functioning

The limbic system and its associated regions in the brain are thought to serve as the primary site of dysfunction for all the mood disorders. Four areas under review in the biological study of bipolar disorder include the role of neuro-transmitters, the endocrine system, physical biorhythms, and birth complications (Swann, 2006).

The amount and activity of norepinephrine, serotonin, gamma-aminobu-tyric acid (GABA), and perhaps other central nervous system nerve tract messengers are clearly abnormal in persons with bipolar disorder (Miklowitz, 2007). Still, it is unknown what causes these imbalances to occur. One theory proposes that bipolar disorder results from a "kindling" process in limbic system neuron tracts (Schatzberg & Nemeroff, 2004). That is, persons with the disorder may experience a chronic, low-grade repetitive firing of electrical impulses in certain cell tracts that occasionally "erupt" into a manic state.

[handwritten margin note: Tests to check these levels?]

Other theories focus on the actions of the thyroid and other endocrine glands to account for nervous system changes that contribute to manic and depressive episodes (Newman, 2006). Biorhythms, or the body's natural sleep and wake cycles, are erratic in some bipolar clients and may account for, or result from, chemical imbalances which trigger manic episodes.

Damage to the limbic system, basal ganglia, and hypothalamus, which are centers of emotional activity in the brain, may contribute to episodes of the disorder. Most researchers agree that these biological processes are significant in the onset and course of bipolar disorder, but there are no brain imaging techniques that might provide details about them. Finally, a few studies have associated obstetrical complications with early-onset and severe bipolar disorder, which is seen as an association with damage to these systems (Scott, McNeil, & Cavenaugh, 2006).

Psychosocial Influences

Stressful life events play an activating role in early episodes of bipolar disorder, with subsequent episodes arising more in the absence of clear external precipitants (Newman, 2006). Many of these life events are associated with subsequent social rhythm disruptions (sleep, wake, and activity cycles) (Berk et al., 2007). Persons with bipolar disorder who have a history of extreme early-life adversity (such as physical or sexual abuse in childhood or adolescence) show an earlier age of onset, faster and more frequent cycling, increased suicidality, and more comorbid conditions, including alcohol and substance abuse (Post, Leverich, King, & Weiss, 2001). The extent to which these behaviors are related to psychosocial or biological mechanisms is not known, however.

Recovery and Adjustment

Several factors have to do with an improved adjustment. These involve insight into the disorder, stress, and family factors, which will be elaborated upon further. The risk and protective influences are listed in Exhibit 12.2.

Exhibit 12.2

Risk and Protective Influences for the Course of Bipolar Disorder

Risk Influence	Protective Influence
Biological	
Childhood onset	Adolescent or adult onset
Antidepressant drugs (for bipolar I type)	
No. of previous episodes	
Persistence of affective symptoms	Absence of interepisode mood symptoms
	Medication adherence
Substance use	
Psychological	
Irregular social rhythms	Regular social rhythms, sleep cycle
Introversion/obsessiveness	
History of anxiety	Knowledge about the disorder
Exaggerated use of denial	Willingness to assume responsibility for the disorder
Social	
Low levels of social support	Identification and use of social and community resources
	Participation in support groups
Absence of professional intervention	Ongoing positive alliance with family, mental health professionals
Marital conflicts	
Work-related difficulties	
High family expressed emotion	

Sources: Miklowitz (2007); Sachs, Printz, Kahn, Carpenter, and Docherty (2000); Schenkel, West, Harral, Patel, and Pavuluri (2008); Tyrer (2006).

Insight

The client's denial or lack of insight into bipolar disorder poses a major challenge to recovery (Miklowitz, 2007). When manic, the client may be reluctant to accept the need for medication and other interventions. Episodes of mania and depression tend to be brief in comparison to the duration of normal mood activity, and the client may decide after a period of stability that there is no longer a need for precautionary interventions. This is a concern because it is recommended that most bipolar clients take medication during the active phases of the disorder *and* during periods of stability (Sachs, Printz, Kahn, Carpenter, & Docherty, 2000).

Stress

Clients who experience high levels of life stress in general *after* the onset of bipolar disorder are four times more likely to have a relapse than clients with low levels of life stress (Tyrer, 2006). Events that can cause these episodes include disruptions in daily routines or sleep–wake cycles, such as air travel and changes in work schedules. Relapse risk is also related to negative interactions with close relatives (Miklowitz, 2007).

Family Factors

As discussed, the person's mood swings and erratic behavior may be a source of ongoing turmoil in family relationships (Miklowitz, 2007). Significant others become confused by perceived changes in the client's personality. In one large longitudinal study 89%, 52%, and 61% of caregivers, respectively, reported moderate or high burden in relation to client problem behaviors, role dysfunction, and disruption in household routines (Perlick et al., 2007).

High-burden caregivers report more physical health problems, depressive symptoms, health risk behavior, and health service use, and less social support than less-burdened caregivers. These patterns also hold true for children and adolescents with bipolar disorder. Such parent–child relationships are characterized by less warmth, affection, and intimacy, and more quarreling, which increases the risk for relapse (Schenkel, West, Harral, Patel, & Pavuluri, 2008). Persons from families that are high in expressed emotion are likely to suffer a relapse during a 9-month follow-up period, while higher social support is associated with a more rapid recovery from a bipolar episode (Schenkel et al., 2008). Persons who are more distressed by their relatives' criticisms exhibit more severe and manic symptoms than persons who are less distressed (Miklowitz, Wisniewski, Otto, & Sachs, 2005).

Interventions

Medication is a primary intervention for bipolar disorder, but psychosocial interventions are also helpful for controlling the course of the disorder. Typically, service providers concentrate first on stabilizing the client's mental status and then introduce psychosocial interventions (Fava, Ruini, & Rafanelli, 2005). Both types of intervention are reviewed here.

Medication

The medications discussed here (summarized in Exhibit 12.3) are used to treat both types of bipolar disorder. The primary medications used to stabilize a client with bipolar disorder are lithium, the antiepilepsy medications, and the antipsychotic medications (the latter during manic episodes). Most physicians

Exhibit 12.3

Medication for Bipolar Disorder

Medication	Effectiveness	Disadvantages
Lithium	Stabilizes both manic and depressive episodes[f] Prevents relapses for at least a year but is most effective in preventing manic relapses[g] Not as effective at long-term follow-up (5 years)[h]	Not as effective for mixed or rapid-cycling episodes With sudden discontinuation can precipitate a rebound mood episode Common side effects: confusion, mild diarrhea, mild fatigue, hand tremor, increased thirst, increased urination, muscle weakness, mild nausea, weight gain
Anticonvulsants	Stabilizes faster than lithium (2–5 days compared to 14 days)	*Carbamazepine* Common side effects: confusion, memory disturbance, dizziness, lowered white blood cell count (benign), nausea, sedation, skin rash, tremor *Lamotrigine* Common side effects: dizziness, nausea, constipation, blurred vision, drowsiness, diarrhea, headache, weakness, weight loss *Valproic acid* Common side effects: hair loss, nausea, sedation
Antipsychotics	Superior to placebo in treating mania and may be effective for depression, with no significant differences in effectiveness among them[i]	Common Adverse Effects of Antipsychotic Medications Aripriprazole: hypotension, cognitive confusion, sedation Olanzapine: weight gain, hypotension

		Quetiapene: sedation, hypotension, dry mouth, constipation, weight gain
		Risperidone: weight gain, sedation, hypotension, reduced sex drive
		Ziprasidone: sedation, nausea, constipation, dizziness, restlessness
Antidepressants	Not generally used for the treatment of bipolar I disorder as it may induce mania; there is also a risk for manic episodes for bipolar II disorder [i]	Common: anxiety and restlessness, constipation, dry mouth, headache, nausea and vomiting, sedation

[f] Burgess et al. (2001).
[g] Geddes, Burgess, Hawton, Jamison, and Goodwin (2004).
[h] Scott et al. (2007).
[i] Perlis, Welge, Vornik, Hirschfield, and Keck (2006).
[j] Bond, Noronha, Kauer-Sant'Anna, Lam, and Yatham (2008); Vieta and Suppes (2008).

recommend that clients take medications even when their mood stabilizes, to reduce the risk of recurrence of another mood episode. When a client is in a manic state, physicians want a quick positive response to a mood stabilizer. If there is no such response within a week, another medication will likely be used. A third drug may be used if a partial response seems to plateau after 2 weeks. Generally, a single mood-stabilizing drug is not effective over time, and a combination of medications (sometimes including an antipsychotic drug) is more often used (Hamrin & Pachler, 2007).

It should be emphasized that the quality of the relationship between the physician and client is a significant predictor of outcome in pharmacology intervention (Gaudiano & Miller, 2006). Specifically, the variables of client expectancy and the perception of an alliance with the physician are most consistently predictive of the number of months the client stays in treatment.

The likelihood that clients with bipolar disorder will eventually experience a relapse reflects the nature of the disorder and the limitations of current medication regimens. Clients should be informed that one of the most common reasons for relapse is the discontinuation of an effective medication regimen against medical advice. Many clients, however, do not adhere to their regimens at least occasionally during the course of their treatment. One study found that 81% of clients were intentionally nonadherent at least once during their course of medication therapy (Clatworthy, Bowskill, Rank, Parham, &

Horne, 2007). Reasons for this behavior included the experience of current adverse effects, concerns about future adverse effects, and doubts about the ongoing need for medication. The waxing and waning course of bipolar disorder may discourage medication adherence more so than some other disorders.

Lithium

Lithium is the best studied of the mood stabilizing drugs. Its mechanism of action is not clearly understood, but it is believed to affect the flow of sodium, which affects excitation, through nerve and muscle cells in the body (Huang, Lei, & El-Mallach, 2007). Like other drugs, lithium is only effective as long as a steady blood level of the drug is maintained. Because the amount of the drug in the client's blood is equal to that in the nervous system, lithium levels are easily monitored. People who take lithium must get their blood drawn regularly. The difference between therapeutic and toxic levels is not great, so monitoring blood levels is particularly important. Routine monitoring of lithium levels may be performed monthly for the first 4 to 6 months. For the remainder of the first year, these measures can be obtained every 2 to 4 months, and every 6 months thereafter. At low levels the medication has no effect, and high levels indicate possible toxicity, which can be physically dangerous.

Anticonvulsant Medications

Three other medications, formally classified as anticonvulsants, are FDA-approved for the treatment of bipolar disorder—valproate, carbamazepine, and lamotrigine (Melvin et al., 2008). Newer anticonvulsant drugs are also available but have not been as widely used as mood stabilizers. These drugs appear to increase the prevalence of the GABA neurotransmitter, which has antimanic properties, in the nervous system. Valproate is the most thoroughly tested of these drugs, and it has become a first-line choice for this purpose along with lithium. Carbamazepine is a leading alternative to lithium and valproate. The third anticonvulsant drug, lamotrigine, is newer and has been used less often.

Like lithium, all of these drugs need to be taken more than once daily to maintain a therapeutic level. Their prescription does not require frequent blood tests, however, since they do not share lithium's characteristic of being evenly distributed throughout the circulatory and nervous systems. At the same time, studies indicate that the side-effect profiles of these drugs are similar to lithium in terms of the consumer's subjective discomfort (Melvin et al., 2008). The anticonvulsant drugs are also used in the treatment of children with bipolar disorder, but few studies have been done to establish their long-term safety (McIntosh & Trotter, 2006).

Antidepressants

Antidepressant medications are not generally used for the treatment of bipolar I disorder. They have in fact been shown to induce mania in as many as one-third of all such clients, and one-fourth of consumers experience the activation of a rapid-cycling course (Vieta & Suppess, 2008). A recent meta-analysis concluded that antidepressant medications are not superior to mood-stabilizing drugs in controlling either type of bipolar disorder over the long term (Ghaemi, Wingo, Filkowski, & Baldessarini, 2008). The medications are generally used only after nonresponse to mood stabilizers (Goldberg, 2000).

In bipolar II disorder, however, antidepressants are often used along with an antimania drug for mood stabilization (Cipriani et al., 2006). The SSRI drugs are used most often because of their relatively mild adverse effects. After a first episode of bipolar depression, antidepressant therapy should be tapered in 2–6 months, a much shorter continuation period than is advised for nonbipolar depression.

Antipsychotic Medications

It was noted earlier that a variety of antipsychotic medications are used with mood stabilizing medications to control mania until the primary medications take effect. Approximately one-third of persons with bipolar disorder use these during the maintenance phase of treatment as well because they tend to experience periods of intense agitation (Faravelli, Rosi, & Scarpato, 2006). Among the newer antipsychotic medications, aripriprazole, olanzapine, risperidone, quietapine, and ziprasidone have been tested as treatment adjuncts for bipolar disorder. It is hypothesized that, due to their dopamine and serotonin antagonist activity, these drugs may have an impact on mania and depression as well as psychosis. Olanzapine was the first atypical antipsychotic drug to be approved by the Food and Drug Administration for the treatment of acute mania.

Electroconvulsive Therapy

Electroconvulsive therapy is a somatic intervention during which brief electrical shocks are given to the client, usually in a series over a period of several weeks. This intervention is usually reserved for use with inpatients or persons who do not respond well to the available medications. While this form of treatment seems overly invasive to some professionals, it is a demonstrated safe and effective method of stabilizing a client's mood (Rush, Sackeim, & Marangell, 2005). Still, its adverse effects include impairments in verbal learning and memory capacity, and for those reasons it is never a first choice for intervention (MacQueen, Parkin, Marriott, Begin, & Hasley, 2007).

Psychosocial Interventions

A systematic review concluded that, while symptoms recovery from acute episodes of mania or bipolar depression is achieved in as many as 90% of persons, full symptomatic recovery is achieved slowly, and residual symptoms of fluctuating severity are common (Huxley & Baldessarini, 2007). As few as one-third of clients achieve full social and occupational functional recovery to premorbid levels, which supports the importance of psychosocial interventions. Psychoeducation, family-focused interventions, cognitive-behavioral therapy, and interpersonal therapy have all been subject to testing. Because these interventions are all supported by at least one randomized trial, the National Institute of Mental Health has initiated a Systematic Treatment Enhancement Program to further examine the efficacy of these approaches (Miklowitz & Otto, 2006). These models share commonalities: to increase awareness and understanding of the disorder and its treatment, as well as the importance of compliance, to promote the stability of the social and sleep rhythms, to reduce substance misuse, and to help the individual prevent relapse (Scott, Colom, & Vieta, 2007). Although psychosocial interventions may prevent relapse (Scott, Colom, & Vieta, 2007), the relative efficacy of interventions has not been established, which may be because of the similarities between them (Beynon, Soares-Weiser, Woolacott, Duffy, & Geddes, 2008). In this section we will review each of these interventions, and they may prevent relapse.

Psychoeducation

Because bipolar disorder is confusing to the client and those close to him or her in the best of circumstances, the social worker should always include didactic education as part of an intervention program (Justo, Soares, & Calil, 2007). The goals of psychoeducation are to support medication adherence among clients, enhance social and occupational functioning, recruit family and spouse support as appropriate, and identify psychosocial stresses that may trigger mood episodes. Further, psychoeducation can help people with bipolar disorder develop a regular schedule of daily living activities (regular times for sleep, meals, exercise, and work), which in turn can prevent disrupted rhythms or stressful life events from triggering a bipolar episode. Because bipolar disorder shares many of the same clinical characteristics as schizophrenia, including a relapse-remission course, significant psychosocial impairment, the need for ongoing medication compliance, and the negative impact of family stress on clinical outcomes, some psychoeducational approaches developed for schizophrenia have been adapted for use with these persons (Rea et al., 2003).

Family Interventions

There is much evidence that expressed emotion (EE), defined as excessive amounts of face-to-face contact and hostile and critical comments between persons and their relatives, is associated with poorer outcomes in bipolar disorder (Miklowitz et al., 2005). While the bipolar person's ratings of family member criticisms do not themselves predict mood symptoms, those persons who are more distressed by relatives' criticisms have more severe manic and depressive symptoms, and proportionately fewer "well" days. Again, these data do not suggest that family members merit blame; however, they underscore the disruptive impact of bipolar disorder and show that changing family interactions through psychoeducation can be beneficial to all persons involved.

Miklowitz and colleagues have formulated and tested a specific intervention for families called family focused treatment (FFT) (Miklowitz & Taylor, 2006). The components of FFT include family education (about the nature, symptoms, prognosis, and etiology of bipolar disorder), communication skills development (active listening, delivering positive and negative verbal feedback, and requesting changes in the behavior of others), and problem solving (identifying and defining problems, generating and evaluating solutions, and implementing solutions). A similar FFT group was developed for families with adolescent client members (Miklowitz et al., 2004). Program modifications include addressing the developmental issues common to adolescents and the unique clinical presentations of bipolar adolescents.

A systematic review of family interventions for bipolar disorder, which included seven randomized, controlled studies, found that studies were too different to quantitatively synthesize (Justo et al., 2007). Future research in this area is called for, as well as evaluating family interventions other than psychoeducation.

Interpersonal Therapy

Interpersonal therapy (IPT) is based on the assumption that interpersonal conflicts are a major source of depression for clients, including those with bipolar disorder (Frank, 2007). It also assumes that circadian (sleep–wake cycle) and social rhythms influence the course of affective disorders. That is, life events can alter the stability of one's social rhythms. Significant changes in biological rhythms can create somatic symptoms that lead to manic and depressive episodes. Interpersonal therapy focuses on strategies for addressing any of four specific problem areas in the client's life: unresolved grief, interpersonal disputes, interpersonal deficits, or role transitions.

Two large studies have supported the efficacy of IPT in combination with medication compared to other forms of intensive clinical management, which focus on medications and symptoms management (Miklowitz & Otto, 2006).

Cognitive-Behavioral Therapy

Cognitive-behavioral interventions challenge a client's cognitions that may activate episodes of mania or depression, and they can also target cognitions related to medication compliance. This range of interventions, which can be implemented for different lengths of time, emphasizes collaborative goal setting, skills development in medication adherence, stress management skills, cognitive restructuring techniques for depression and mania, problem-solving techniques, and methods to enhance interpersonal communication (Zaretsky, Lancee, Miller, Harris, & Parikh, 2008). Persons receiving cognitive-behavioral interventions are also taught self-monitoring of symptoms and sleep patterns, behavioral activation strategies for depression, and stimulus control strategies for hypomania.

The Recovery Model of Mental Illness

This discussion of interventions for people with bipolar disorder must include an overview of the recent client-initiated recovery model of mental illness. The recovery model for disorders such as bipolar disorder emphasizes an individual's personal journey to recovery that involves developing hope, a secure base and sense of self, supportive relationships, empowerment, social inclusion, coping skills, and life meaning (Stotland, Mattson, & Bergeson, 2008). This concept has gained impetus from the perceived failure by service providers and the wider society to adequately support social inclusion for people with mental illnesses.

Most research on mental illness in the United States is based on a medical model. As more people have become involved in advocacy efforts for persons with disabilities, the recovery model of disability has incorporated the central belief that that the experiences of people with the disability, not the expertise of professionals, should be the critical factor in making decisions about intervention and also social policy. This approach emphasizes self-advocacy and a resolve that the world should be altered to accommodate persons with disabilities, rather than altering people who have chronic disabilities.

Recovery involves clients accepting and owning their illnesses and making decisions about the types of services they wish to receive. Clients assume the role of active consumers of services, with health care professionals acting as their partners in assessment, goal setting, and choosing intervention modalities. With this perspective the focus of treatment for bipolar disorder has broadened to incorporate the long-term goals of recovery, which encompass functional improvement and improved quality of life. With care focused on a comprehensive recovery model, people with bipolar disorder do not perceive themselves as "clients" of human service professionals so much as persons who can lead productive and gratifying lives with only a partial reliance on those professionals who represent the "medical" model of mental illness.

Special Populations

Bipolar disorder presents differently, or is assessed differently, in certain populations. For example, there are gender differences in the presentation of bipolar I disorder (Ingram & Smith, 2008). Its overall prevalence is the same among men and women, but the first mood episode in males is more likely to be manic. In men the number of manic episodes equals or exceeds the number of depressive episodes, while in women depressive episodes predominate. Rapid cycling bipolar disorder is more common in women. Women have an increased risk of developing subsequent episodes of bipolar I disorder in the postpartum period, and some women have their first episode at that time. Bipolar II disorder has an overall greater prevalence among women.

Bipolar women are 2.7 times more likely than men to have a comorbid disorder, being at risk for metabolic changes that increase their risk of diabetes (possibly related to medication use) and vascular disease (Taylor & MacQueen, 2006). Persons with bipolar disorder have a shorter than average life expectancy. A woman who develops bipolar disorder at the age of 25 may lose up to 9 years in life expectancy due to cardiovascular and other medical problems (Michalak et al., 2008).

Regarding racial differences, one cross-national study found that the prevalence of bipolar disorder is roughly equal among Caucasian, Latino, and African American populations, but less common among persons of Asian background (Zhang & Snowden, 1999). Still, among children and adolescents who present with similar symptoms, bipolar disorder is more often diagnosed among Caucasians, while African American children are more likely to receive a disruptive behavior disorder diagnosis (Muroff, Edelsohn, Joe, & Ford, 2008).

Lithium, carbamazepine, valproate, and lamotrigine are all used in the treatment of children with bipolar disorder, although none of these has been subject to randomized, controlled trials. The prospects of chronic weight problems and long-term effects on kidney function in children for all of these medications need to be considered (Findling, 2009).

Lithium seems to have an anti-aggression effect on children and adolescents, which is a positive benefit (Hamrin & Patcher, 2007). It is not advised for children under age 8, however, as its effects have not been adequately studied in that population. When used by older children and adolescents, whose systems tend to clear medications quickly, a higher dose may be required to achieve a therapeutic effect. Adolescents appear to tolerate long-term lithium treatment well, but there are concerns about its effects on thyroid and kidney function.

Other concerns about mood stabilizing drugs have arisen with special populations. Their decreased kidney clearance rates put older adults at a higher risk for toxic blood levels when using lithium (Schatzberg & Nemeroff, 2004). They may be prescribed a smaller dose because they metabolize drugs more slowly. Lithium should not be prescribed for women during pregnancy, as it is associated with fetal heart problems (Bowden, 2000). It is excreted in breast milk and thus should also not be used by women while breastfeeding. It has also been noted that African American persons with bipolar disorder tend to be prescribed more antipsychotic medications than other racial groups, and they are not followed as closely in the community by case managers (Kupfer, Frank, Grochocinski, Houck, & Brown, 2005). The same considerations about lithium for pregnant women, children, and older adults apply to the anticonvulsant medications.

Critique of the Diagnosis

The onset of bipolar disorder appears to result from a complex set of biological, psychological, and to a lesser extent, social factors. Prior to the publication of *DSM-III*, when it was known as manic depression or manic-depressive illness, many clinical theorists and practitioners conceptualized this disorder as a primarily psychological strategy for dealing with internal and environmental stress. Today, however, research overwhelmingly suggests that biological factors are predominant, and other factors may account more for the timing and course of the disorder rather than its onset. While much remains to be learned about the causes of bipolar disorder, its onset appears to require certain biological processes that occur independently of external factors. For this reason it has legitimacy within the social work value system as a mental disorder. Its combinations of manic and depressive episodes and cycles are also rather unique among disorders in the *DSM*.

Still, there are several controversial aspects to the diagnosis of bipolar disorder. The society at large seems to maintain a sense of uncertainty and ambivalence about the role of psychological and social factors in the disorder, as family members and others struggle with how to respond to the disruptive behaviors of clients, particularly when in a manic state (Post et al., 2001) Secondly, the disorder has been diagnosed more often in children and adolescents in the past 20 years. There is much disagreement about the symptom profile in this age group, raising issues of its validity. Another issue, also related to diagnostic validity, is the relationship of bipolar I and bipolar II disorder, and bipolar II disorder and major depression. These distinctions were only established with the publication of *DSM-IV* in 1994, and the differences between these sets of disorders remains somewhat unclear.

Case Study

Donna was a single, 23-year-old college student in her final undergraduate semester. She was referred to the community mental health center following a 1-month hospitalization for an initial manic episode. She had been psychotic with paranoid delusions during this episode, which was also characterized by sleeplessness, hyperactivity, racing thoughts, hypersexuality, and alcohol abuse. Donna, who had never lived away from her parents, was well-stabilized on lithium and thiothixene at the time of her agency intake. She was still quite anxious, frightened by what had happened, and reluctant to resume her normal activities for fear of precipitating another manic episode. She also reported having two periods of depression during the past year. She lost all of her energy, stayed home in her room, took naps, felt tired, and often cried about her inability to force herself to be more active. Donna had not been suicidal. Her parents worried during her depressive phases that Donna was upset about her lack of a clear career path and having few friends.

Donna was the second oldest of six children in a family that experienced much internal tension. Her father was a laborer in a concrete manufacturing company. Still bitter about an early-career bankruptcy, he was a long-term alcohol abuser (an indicator of a possible affective disorder) and was physically abusive of his wife. Most of the children were attractive, socially sophisticated, and outwardly successful, but there was a shared family denial of the father's problem behaviors. Donna stated that she had "no direction" in life. She was by all accounts the child most dependent on her parents, and for that reason the scapegoat for the family problems. Her father often said, "If only Donna would grow up, we could all accomplish so much more." Donna became anxious whenever they were out of town and in fact had experienced her manic episode while they were on a vacation.

With only two semesters remaining in her college curriculum, Donna had begun failing or dropping essential courses, apparently postponing graduation and the onset of adulthood. These milestones, viewed by many young adults as exciting accomplishments, symbolized for Donna a troubling end to her adolescence. She had always felt fearful of independent living and liked to rely on her parents for financial and emotional support. She felt personally inadequate and wished to continue living with her parents. Her sleep patterns became fitful; she was often awake and wandered about the house at night. The fact that Donna's bipolar symptoms emerged along with her family's rising expectations of her self-sufficiency seemed significant.

Donna felt badly about herself as she recovered from the manic episode, but she was a willing participant in the agency's services. Her parents seemed supportive of her getting rehabilitation help, even though they had difficulty comprehending what had happened to their daughter.

In summary, Donna's personal and family circumstances included various risk factors for bipolar disorder as well as risk and protective factors for its course. Regarding risks, Donna's father was a long-time alcohol abuser, which may have masked an affective disorder. There were longstanding interpersonal conflicts among all family members, creating an unsettled domestic situation. Most of the children felt alienated from their father, and they seemed to be in competition for their mother's favor, which created an atmosphere of distrust. Donna was extremely dependent on her parents for meeting her basic needs and was afraid of moving away from home. She had few available extended family, as her father had passively allowed those relationships to dissolve over the years. Most people outside the family perceived Donna as friendly, but she had few close relationships with peers and never any boyfriends, so her social skills were not well developed. Finally, she admitted to an irregular sleep–wake cycle when stressed, characterized by bouts of insomnia (3–5 hours of sleep per night) for several weeks at a time.

In speculating about the course of the disorder, Donna had access to several important protective factors. She was a voluntary participant in treatment, including a willingness to take prescribed medications. Her social worker had informational access to a variety of support resources in the community that she could utilize. Donna's parents were interested in her welfare. Some risks were also present, however, including ongoing family conflict, her parents' ambivalence about participating in a psychoeducational group, and Donna's persistently dependent attitudes toward her caregivers.

Diagnosis

Axis I: Bipolar I disorder, most recent episode mixed, severe with psychotic features, in partial remission. Donna has recently experienced both depressive and manic episodes. She had two major depressive episodes in the past year that lasted approximately 3 weeks each. At those times she had felt extremely sad, became withdrawn, and avoided all activities outside the family. She took regular naps and complained of chronic fatigue. She felt worthless and had occasional crying spells. Her more recent manic episode, the abnormal, elevated mood, lasted for 2 full weeks including the hospitalization. She reported, and hospital records confirmed, that she experienced grandiose self-esteem, got very little sleep, was continuously talkative, had racing thoughts, and was sexually promiscuous. She had delusional ideas about her future as a businesswoman and had been fearful of encountering the Devil, whom she thought was pursuing her in human form. Donna's mania had remitted within 1 week of her hospitalization and the introduction of medications.

Axis II: Dependent Personality Features. While this is not a chapter on personality disorders, the social worker was struck by Donna's high level of dependence on others, especially her parents, and believed that these issues would be significant in her counseling. These characteristics included Donna's difficulty making decisions, needing her parents to assume responsibility for her life, an inability to disagree with others, and difficulty initiating and sustaining any personal projects because of her lack of confidence. He did not want to diagnose a personality disorder, but by highlighting the presence of features of this disorder, he could make them a part of the focus of the intervention.

Axis III: None. There were no physical causes or contributors to her Axis I or II disorders.

Axis IV: Problems with primary support group and problems related to the social environment. Donna was having difficulty with life transition issues, most prominently her move into adulthood (she was adult by age and with her college degree would be recognized as an adult by her society). She was also aware that her parents, in spite of their support, might begin to have different occupational expectations of her following her college graduation.

Axis V: Current GAF = 60 (moderate symptoms of her disorder, moderate difficulty in social and school functioning); highest GAF during the past year = 70 (no symptoms of bipolar disorder, only slight problems with school and social functioning).

Intervention Plan

Goal: Donna will avoid severe mood swings through the regular use of appropriate medications.

Objective: Monthly visits with the agency psychiatrist for the prescription and monitoring of lithium and thiothixene

Objective: Weekly visits with agency clinical social worker for review of mental status and to monitor effectiveness of medications, including any adverse effects

Goal: Donna will reduce the nature of her life stresses that might contribute to bipolar mood episodes.

Objective: Weekly visits with the agency social worker to explore the nature of predictable life stresses and develop skills for coping with them

Goal: Donna will establish personal goals and begin working toward them.

Objective: Weekly meetings with the social worker in which the client will (a) be permitted to think about and set her own goals regarding schooling, work, social life, family participation, and work, and (b) develop beginning plans for achieving these goals

Goal: Donna and her family will share a supportive family environment.

Objective: Parents will attend the agency education and support group for relatives of persons with bipolar disorder.

Objective: Monthly meetings between the social worker, client, and parents to help set mutually agreeable expectations for the client's participation in family and social activities

Goal: Donna will promote her ongoing mood stability through a structuring of her activities of daily living life.

Objective: Daily completion of the Social Rhythm Scale (see Appendix), which will be reviewed in weekly session with the social worker.

Summary

Bipolar disorder is a disorder of mood in which, over time, a person experiences one or more manic episodes that are usually accompanied by one or more major depressive episodes. The disorder is associated with chemical imbalances in the nervous system. Social workers are active in the assessment, intervention, and mental status monitoring of persons with bipolar disorder, because it is a long-term mental illness that can result in a variety of problems in social functioning. Social workers need to be aware of the actions of the mood stabilizing medications, both positive and negative, since they frequently spend more time providing interventions for clients than the prescribing physicians. Practitioners also need to be aware of the serious impact of bipolar disorder on a client's sense of self so that they can provide psychosocial interventions to help clients organize and maintain productive lives with minimal symptom recurrence.

References

American Psychiatric Association. (2000). *Diagnostic and statistical manual of mental disorders* (4th ed., rev.). Washington, DC: Author.

Barnes, C., & Mitchell, P. (2005). Considerations in the management of bipolar disorder in women. *Australian and New Zealand Journal of Psychiatry, 39*(8), 662–673.

Berk, M., Conus, P., Lucas, N., Hallam, K., Malhi, G. S., Dodd, S., et al. (2007). Setting the stage: from prodrome to treatment resistance in bipolar disorder. *Bipolar Disorders, 9*, 671–678.

Beynon, S., Soares-Weiser, K., Woolacott, N., Duffy, S., & Geddes, J. R. (2008). Psychosocial interventions for the prevention of relapse in bipolar disorder: Systematic review of controlled trials. *British Journal of Psychiatry, 192*, 5–11.

Birmaher, B., Axelson, D., Strober, M., Gill, M. K., Valeri, S., Chiappetta, L., Ryan, N., Leonard, H., Hunt, J., Iyengar, S., & Keller, M. (2006). Clinical course of children and adolescents with bipolar spectrum disorders. *Archives of General Psychiatry, 63*(2), 175–183.

Bond, D. J., Noronha, M. M., Kauer-Sant'Anna, M., Lam, R. W., & Yatham, L. N. (2008). Antidepressant-associated mood elevations in bipolar II disorder compared with bipolar I disorder and major depressive disorder: A systematic review and meta-analysis. *Journal of Clinical Psychiatry, 69*(10), 1589–1601.

Bowden, C. L. (2000). Efficacy of lithium in mania and maintenance therapy of bipolar depression. *Journal of Clinical Psychiatry, 61*(Suppl. 9), 35–40.

Burdick, K. E., Braca, R. J., Goldberg, J. F., & Malhotra, A. K. (2007). Cognitive dysfunction in bipolar disorder: Future place of Pharmaco therapy. *CNS Drugs, 21*(12), 971–981.

Burgess, S., Geddes, J., Hawton, K., Townsend, E., Jamison, K., & Goodwin, G. (2001). Lithium for maintenance treatment of mood disorders. *Cochrane Database of Systematic Reviews*, Issue 3. CD003013. DOI: 10.1002/14651858.CD003013.

Cahill, C. M., Hanstock, T., Jairam, R., Hazell, P., Walter, G., & Malhi, G. S. (2007). Comparison of guidelines for juvenile bipolar disorder. *Australian and New Zealand Journal of Psychiatry, 41*(6), 479–484.

Carney, C. P., & Jones, L. E. (2006). Medical comorbidity in women and men with bipolar disorders: A population-based controlled study. *Psychosomatic Medicine, 68*(5), 684–691.

Chun, B. J. D. H., & Dunner, D. L. (2004). A review of antidepressant-induced hypomania in major depression: Suggestions for DSM-V. *Bipolar Disorders, 6,* 32–42.

Cipriani, A., Smith, K., Burgess, S., Carney, S., Goodwin, G., & Geddes, J. (2006). Lithium versus antidepressants in the long-term treatment of unipolar affective disorder. *Cochrane Database of Systematic Reviews,* Issue 4, CD003492. DOI: 10.1002/14651858.CD003492.pub2.

Clatworthy, J., Bowskill, R., Rank, T., Parham, R., & Horne, R. (2007). Adherence to medication in bipolar disorder: A qualitative study exploring the role of patients' beliefs about the condition and its treatment. *Bipolar Disorder, 9,* 656–664.

Conus, P., Cotton, S., Abdel-Baki, A., Lambert, M., Berk, M., & McGorry, P. D. (2006). Symptomatic and functional outcome 12 months after a ?rst episode of psychotic mania: barriers to recovery in a catchment area sample. *Bipolar Disorders, 8,* 221–231.

Faravelli, C., Rosi, S., & Scarpato, M. A. (2006). Threshold and subthreshold bipolar disorders in the Sesto Fiorentino Study. *Journal of Affective Disorders, 94*(1–3),111–119.

Fava, G. A., Ruini, C., & Rafanelli, C., (2005). Sequential treatment of mood and anxiety disorders. *Journal of Clinical Psychiatry, 66*(11), 1392–1400.

Findling, R. L. (2009). Treatment of childhood-onset bipolar disorder. In C. A. Zarate & H. K. Manji (Eds.), *Bipolar depression: Molecular neurobiology, clinical diagnosis and pharmacotherapy* (pp. 241–252). Cambridge, MA: BirkhÄuser.

Frank, E. (2007). Interpersonal and social rhythm therapy: A means of improving depression and preventing relapse in bipolar disorder. *Journal of Clinical Psychology: In Session, 63*(5), 463–473.

Gaudiano, B. A., & Miller, I. W. (2006). Patients' expectancies, the alliance in pharmacotherapy, and treatment outcomes in bipolar disorder. *Journal of Counseling and Clinical Psychology, 74*(4), 671–676.

Geddes, J. R., Burgess, S., Hawton, K., Jamison, K., & Goodwin, G. M. (2004). Long-term lithium therapy for bipolar disorder: Systematic review and meta-analysis of randomized controlled trials. *American Journal of Psychiatry, 161*(2), 217–222.

Geller, B., Tillman, R., Bolhofner, K., & Zimerman, B. (2008). Child bipolar I disorder: Prospective continuity with adult bipolar I disorder; characteristics of second and third episodes; predictors of 8-year outcome. *Archives of General Psychiatry, 65*(10), 1125–1133.

Ghaemi, S. N., Wingo, A. P., Filkowski, M. A., & Baldessarini, R. J. (2008). Long-term antidepressant treatment in bipolar disorder: Meta-analysis of benefits and risks. *Acta Psychiatrica Scandinavia, 118*(5), 347–356.

Goldberg, J. F. (2000). Treatment guidelines: Current and future management of bipolar disorder. *Journal of Clinical Psychiatry, 61*(Suppl. 13), 12–18.

Grant, B. F., Stinson, F. S., Hasin, D. S., Dawson, D. A., Chou, S. P., Ruan, W. J., et al. (2005). Prevalence, correlates, and comorbidity of bipolar I disorder and Axis I and II disorders: Results from the national epidemiologic survey on alcohol and related conditions. *Journal of Clinical Psychiatry, 66*, 1205–1215.

Hamrin, V., & Pachler, M. (2007). Pediatric bipolar disorder: Evidence-based psychopharmalogical treatments. *Journal of Child and Adolescent Psychiatric Nursing, 20*(1), 40–58.

Hirschfeld, R. M. A., Lewis, L., & Vornik, L. A. (2003). Perceptions and impact of bipolar disorder: How far have we come? Results of the National Depressive and Manic Depressive Association's 2000 survey of individuals with bipolar disorder. *Journal of Clinical Psychiatry, 64*(2), 161–174.

Holtmann, M., Bolte, S., & Poustka, F. (2008). Rapid increase in rates of bipolar disorder in youth: "True" bipolarity or misdiagnosed severe disruptive behavior disorders? *Archives of General Psychiatry, 65*(4), 477.

Huang, X., Lei, Z., & El-Mallach, R. S. (2007). Lithium normalizes elevated intracellular sodium. *Bipolar Disorder, 9*(3), 298–300.

Huxley, N., & Balessarini, R. J. (2007). Disability and its treatment in bipolar disorder patients. *Bipolar Disorders, 9*, 183–196.

Inder, M. L., Crowe, M. T., Moor, S., Luty, S. E., Carter, J. D., & Joyce, P. R. (2008). "I actually don't know who I am": The impact of bipolar disorder on the sense of self. *Psychiatry, 71*(2), 123–133.

Ingram, R., & Smith, L. T. (2008). Mood disorders. In J. E. Maddux & B. A. Winstead (Eds.), *Psychopathology: Foundations for a contemporary understanding* (2nd ed., pp.171–197). New York: Routledge/Taylor & Francis Group.

Johnson, S. L., Miller, C., & Eisner, L. (2008). Bipolar disorder. In J. Hunsley & E. J. Mash (Eds.), *A guide to assessments that work* (pp. 121–137). New York: Oxford University Press.

Justo, L. P., Soares, B. G. O., & Calil, H. M. (2007). Family intervention in bipolar disorder. *Cochrane Database of Systematic Reviews*, Issue 4. CD005617. DOI: 10.1002/14651858.CD005167.

Kessler, R. C., Berglund, P., Demler, O., Jin, R., Merikangas, K. R., & Walters, E. E. (2005). Replication. *Archives of General Psychiatry, 62*(6), 593–602.

Kowatch, R. A., Youngstrom, E. A., Danielyan, A., & Findling, R. L. (2005). Review and meta-analysis of the phenomenology and clinical characteristics of mania in children and adolescents. *Bipolar Disorders, 7*, 483–496.

Kupfer, D. J., Frank, E. J., Grochocinski, V., Houck, P. R., & Brown, C. (2005). African-American participants in a bipolar disorder registry: Clinical and treatment characteristics. *Bipolar Disorders, 7*(1), 82–88.

Lam, D., Donaldson, C., Brown, Y., & Malliaris, Y. (2005). Burden and marital and sexual satisfaction in the partners of bipolar patients. *Bipolar Disorders, 7*, 431–440.

Leahy, R. L. (2007). Bipolar disorder: Causes, contexts, and treatments. *Journal of Clinical Psychology, 63*(5), 417–424.

Mackinnon, D., Potash, J., McMahon, F. & Simpson, S. (2005). Rapid mood switching and suicidality in familial bipolar disorder. *Bipolar Disorders: An International Journal of Psychiatry and Neurosciences, 7*(5), 441.

MacQueen, G., Parkin, C., Marriott, M., Begin, H., & Hasey, G. (2007). The long-term impact of treatment with electroconvulsive therapy on discrete memory systems in patients with bipolar disorder. *Journal of Psychiatry and Neuroscience, 32*(4), 241–249.

Marangell, L. B., Kupfer, D. J., Sachs, G. S., & Swann, A. C. (2006). Emerging therapies for bipolar depression. *Journal of Clinical Psychiatry, 67*(7), 1140–1151.

Matza, L. S., Rajagopalan, K. S., Thompson, C. L., & Lissovoy, G. (2005). Misdiagnosed patients with bipolar disorder: Comorbidities, treatment patterns, and direct treatment costs. *Journal of Clinical Psychiatry, 66*(11), 1432–1440.

McGuffin, P., Rijsdijk, F., Andrew, M., Sham, P., Katz, R., & Cardino, A. (2003). The heritability of bipolar affective disorder and the genetic relationship to unipolar depression. *Archives of General Psychiatry, 60*, 497–502.

McIntosh, D. E., & Trotter, J. S. (2006). Early onset bipolar spectrum disorder: Psychopharmacological, psychological, and educational management. *Psychology in the Schools, 43*(4), 451–460.

Melvin, C. L., Carey, T. S., Goodman, F., Oldham, J. M., Williams, J. W., & Ranney, L. H. (2008). Effectiveness of antiepileptic drugs for the treatment of bipolar disorder: Findings from a systematic review. *Journal of Psychiatric Practice, 14*(1), 9–14.

Michalak, E. E., Murray, G., Young, A. H., & Lam, R. W. (2008). Burden of bipolar depression: Impact of disorder and medications on quality of life. *CNS Drugs, 22*(5), 389–404.

Miklowitz, D. J. (2007). The role of the family in the course and treatment of bipolar disorder. *Current Directions in Psychological Science, 16*(4), 192–196.

Miklowitz, D. J., George, E. L., Axelson, D. A., Kim, E. Y., Birmhauer, B., Schenk, C., et al. (2004). Family focused treatment for adolescents with bipolar disorder. *Journal of Affective Disorders, 82*(Suppl. 1), s113–s128.

Miklowitz, D. J., & Otto, M. W. (2006). New psychosocial interventions for bipolar disorder: A review of the literature and introduction of the Systematic Treatment Enhancement Program. *Journal of Cognitive Psychotherapy: An International Quarterly, 20* (1), 215–227.

Miklowitz, D. J., & Taylor, D. O. (2006). Family-focused treatment of the suicidal bipolar patient. *Bipolar Disorders, 8*, 640–651.

Miklowitz, D. J., Wisniewski, S. M., Otto, M. W., & Sachs, G. S. (2005). Perceived criticism from family members as a predictor of the one-year course of bipolar disorder. *Psychiatry Research, 136*(2–3), 101–111.

Moreno, C., Laje, G., Blanco, C., Jiung, H., Schmidt, A. B., & Olfson, M. (2007). National trends in the outpatient diagnosis and treatment of bipolar disorder in youth. *Archives of General Psychiatry, 64*(9), 1032–1038.

Muroff, J., Edelsohn, G. A., Joe, S., & Ford, B. C. (2008). The role of race in diagnostic and disposition decision making in a pediatric psychiatric emergency service. *General Hospital Psychiatry, 30*(3), 269–276.

Newman, C. F. (2006). Bipolar disorder. In F. Andrasik (Ed.), *Comprehensive handbook of personality and psychopathology. Vol. 2: Adult Psychopathology* (pp. 244–261). Hoboken, NJ: Wiley.

Oquendo, M. A., & Mann, J. J. (2006). Suicidal behavior in bipolar disorder: State of the biological, clinical and interventions evidence. *Bipolar Disorders, 8*, 523–525.

Perlick, D. A., Rosenheck, R. A., Miklowitz, D. J., Chessick, C., Wolff, N., Kaczynski, R., et al. (2007). Prevalence and correlates of burden among caregivers of patients with bipolar disorder enrolled in the Systematic Treatment Enhancement Program for bipolar disorder. *Bipolar Disorders, 9*, 262–273.

Perlis, R. H., Welge, J. A., Vornik, M. S., Hirschfield, R. M. A., & Keck, P. E. (2006). Atypical antipsychotics in the treatment of mania: A meta-analysis of randomized, placebo-controlled trials. *Journal of Clinical Psychiatry, 67*(4), 509–516.

Post, R. M., Leverich, G. B., King, Q., & Weiss, S. R. (2001). Developmental vulnerabilities to the onset and course of bipolar disorder. *Development and Psychopathology, 13*(1), 581–598.

Post, R. M., Leveritch, G. B., Luckenbaugh, D., Altshuler, L., Frye, M. A., & Suppes, T. (2006, April). *An excess of childhood-onset bipolar disorder in the United States compared with Europe.* Paper presented at the National Institute of Mental Health Pediatric Bipolar Disorder Conference, Chicago, IL.

Rea, M. M., Tompson, M. C., Miklowitz, D. J., Goldstein, M. J., Hwang, S. & Mintz, J. (2003). *Journal of Consulting and Clinical Psychology, 71*(3), 482–492.

Rush, A. J., Sackeim, H. A., & Marangell, L. B. (2005). Effects of 12 months of vagus nerve stimulation in treatment-resistant depression: A naturalistic study. *Biological Psychiatry, 58*(5), 355–363.

Ryan, M. M., Lockstone, H. E., Huffaker, S. J., Wayland, M. T., Webster, M. J., & Bahn, S. (2006). Gene expression analysis of bipolar disorder reveals downregulation of the ubiquitin cycle and alterations in synaptic genes. *Molecular Psychiatry, 11*(10), 965–978.

Sachs, G. S., Printz, D. J., Kahn, D. A., Carpenter, D., & Docherty, J. P. (2000). *Medication treatment of bipolar disorder.* New York: McGraw-Hill.

Sands, J. R., & Harrow, M. (2000). Bipolar disorder: Psychopathology, biology, and diagnosis. In M. Hersen & A. S. Bellack (Eds.), *Psychopathology in adulthood* (2nd ed., pp. 326–347). Needham Heights, MA: Allyn & Bacon.

Schatzberg, A. F. & Nemeroff, C. B. (Eds.). (2004). *Essentials of clinical psychopharmacology* (3rd ed.). Washington, DC: American Psychiatric Press.

Schenkel, L. S., West, A. E., Harral, E. M., Patel, N. B., & Pavuluri, M. N. (2008). Parent-child interactions in pediatric bipolar disorder. *Journal of Clinical Psychology, 64*(4), 422–437.

Scott, J., Colom, F., & Vieta, E. (2007). A meta-analysis of relapse rates with adjunctive psychological therapies compared to usual psychiatric treatment for bipolar disorders. *International Journal of Neuropsychopharmacology, 10*(1), 123–129.

Scott, J., McNeill, Y., & Cavanaugh, J. (2006). Exposure to obstetric complications and subsequent development of bipolar disorder: Systematic review. *British Journal of Psychiatry, 189*, 3–11.

Sierra, P., Livianos, L., Arques, S., Castello, J., & Rojo, L. (2007). Prodromal symptoms to relapse in Bipolar disorder. *Australian and New Zealand Journal of Psychiatry, 41*, 385–391.

Smith, D. H. (2007). Controversies in childhood bipolar disorders. *Canadian Journal of Psychiatry, 52*(7), 407–408.

Stone, M. H. (2006). Relationship of borderline personality disorder and bipolar disorder. *American Journal of Psychiatry, 163*(7), 1126–1128.

Stotland, N. L., Mattson, M. G., & Bergeson, S. (2008). The recovery concept: Clinician and consumer perspectives. *Journal of Psychiatric Practice, 14*(Suppl. 2), 45–54.

Swann, A. C. (2006). Neurobiology of bipolar depression. In R. S. El Mallakh & N. S. Ghaemi (Eds.), *Bipolar depression: A comprehensive guide* (pp. 37–68). Washington, DC: American Psychiatric Publishing.

Taylor, V., & MacQueen, G. (2006). Associations between bipolar disorder and metabolic syndrome: A review. *Journal of Clinical Psychiatry, 67*, 1034–1041.

Tyrer, S. (2006). What does history teach us about factors associated with relapse in bipolar affective disorder? *Journal of Psychopharmacology, 20*(Suppl. 2), 4–11.

Vieta, E., & Suppes, T. (2008). Bipolar II disorder: Arguments for and against a distinct diagnostic entity. *Bipolar Disorders, 10*, 163–178.

Woods, S. W. (2000). The economic burden of bipolar disease. *Journal of Clinical Psychiatry, 61*(Suppl. 13), 38–41.

Youngstrom, E. A., Findling, R. L., Youngstrom, J. K., & Calabrese, J. R. (2005). Toward an evidence-based assessment of pediatric bipolar disorder. *Journal of Clinical Child and Adolescent Psychology, 34*(3), 433–448.

Zanarini, M. C., Frankenburg, F. R., Hennen, J., & Silk, K. R. (2004). Mental health service utilization by borderline personality disorder patients and Axis II comparison subjects followed prospectively for six years. *Journal of Clinical Psychiatry, 65*(1), 28–36.

Zaretsky, A., Lancee, W., Miller, C., Harris, A., & Parikh, S. V. (2008). Is cognitive-behavioural therapy more effective than psychoeducation in bipolar disorder? *The Canadian Journal of Psychiatry, 53*(7), 441–448.

Zhang, A. Y., & Snowden, L. R. (1999). Ethnic characteristics of mental disorders in five U.S. communities. *Cultural Diversity and Ethnic Minority Psychology, 5*(2), 134–146.

Appendix: Instruments Used to Assess Bipolar Disorder

Revisions for this edition are drawn from Johnson, Miller, and Eisner (2008).

Altman Self-Rating Mania Scale (Altman, Hedeker, Peterson, & Davis, 1997)

Description
- A five-item, self-administered multiple choice scale to measure manic symptoms
- Each item is rated on a continuum of 0 to 4.
- Includes subscales for mania, psychosis, irritability
- For treatment monitoring and outcome evaluation, norms were rated as adequate and clinical utility was rated as good (Altman, Hedeker, Peterson, & Davis, 2001; Altman et al., 1997).

Reliability
- Test-retest reliability of .86 to .89 (with 1- to 7-day intervals for inpatient clients)

- For treatment monitoring and outcome evaluation, internal consistency and test-retest reliability were rated as adequate (Altman et al., 1997, 2001).

Validity
- Cronbach's alpha = .79 for the mania subscale, .65 for the psychosis and irritability subscales; correlations of .72 and .77 with the Mania Rating Scale and the Clinician-administered Altman Scale for Mania.
- For treatment monitoring and outcome evaluation, content validity and validity generalization were rated as adequate, and construct validity was rated as good.

General Behavior Inventory (Adapted) (Youngstrom, Findling, Danielson, & Calabrese, 2001)

Description
- Versions exist with between 52 and 73 items, though the original contained 69 items. This variety in versions makes obtaining good psychometrics a challenge.
- Each item rates behavior on a scale of 0 to 3, with higher scored indicating more severe symptoms.

Reliability
- Cronbach's alpha = .97 for the depression subscale, .96 for the hypomania subscale.
- For diagnosis, internal consistency was rated excellent and test-retest reliability was adequate (Depue & Klein, 1988; Depue, Krauss, Spoont, & Arbisi, 1989; Klein, Dickstein, Taylor, & Harding, 1989; Mallon, Klein, Bornstein, & Slater, 1986).

Validity
- Discriminant function analysis indicated accuracy of placement of respondents into diagnostic groups.
- For diagnosis, content validity was rated adequate and construct validity was rated as good (Depue & Klein, 1988; Depue et al., 1989; Klein et al, 1989; Mallon et al., 1986).

Young Mania Rating Scale (Young, Biggs, Ziegler, & Meyer, 1978)

Description
- An 11-item scale that measures symptoms of mania. The scale measures manic state rather than manic traits and is not intended to be diagnostic.

- Each item is scored along a continuum from 0 (absent) to 4 (extreme). Four items are given twice the weight as the other seven items to compensate for poor cooperation from severely ill respondents. Scores may range from 0 to 60.
- Should be administered in the context of a 15- to 30-minute clinical interview based on the client's report of his or her condition during the previous 48 hours and the practitioner's behavioral observations, with an emphasis on the latter
- For treatment monitoring and outcome evaluation, norms and clinical utility were both rated as adequate (Fristad, Weller, & Weller, 1992, 1995; Young, Biggs, Ziegler, & Meyer, 1978).

Reliability
- Interrater reliability = .93 for total scores, .66–.92 for individual items
- For treatment monitoring and outcome evaluation, internal consistency and interrater reliability were excellent (Fristad et al., 1992, 1995; Young, Biggs, Ziegler, & Meyer, 1978).

Validity
- Positive correlations were found with the Beigel-Murphy Scale (.71) and the Petterson Rating Scale (.89).
- For treatment monitoring and outcome evaluation, content validity and validity generalization were rated as adequate and construct validity was rated as good (Fristad et al., 1992, 1995; Young, Biggs, Ziegler, & Meyer, 1978).

References for Assessment Instruments for Bipolar Disorder

Altman, E. G., Hedeker, D. R., Peterson, J. L., & Davis, J. M. (1997). The Altman self-rating mania scale. *Biological Psychiatry, 42*(10), 948–955.

Altman, E. G., Hedeker, D., Peterson, J. L., & Davis, J. M. (2001). A comparative evaluation of three self-rating scales for acute mania. *Biological Psychiatry, 50,* 468–471.

Axelson, D., Birmaher, B. J., Brent, D., Wassic, S., Hoover, C., Bridge, J., et al. (2003). A preliminary study of the kiddie schedule for affective disorders and schizophrenia for school-age children mania rating scale for children and adolescents. *Journal of Child and Adolescent Psychopharmacology, 13,* 463–470.

Depue, R. A., & Klein, D. N. (1988). Identification of unipolar and bipolar affective conditions in nonclinical and clinical populations by the General Behavior Inventory. In D. L. Dunner, E. S. Gershon, & J. E. Barrett (Eds.), *Relatives at risk for mental disorder,* (pp. 179–204). New York: Raven Press, Ltd.

Depue, R. A., Krauss, S., Spoont, M. R., & Arbisi, P. (1989). General behavior inventory identification of unipolar and bipolar affective conditions in a non-clinical university population. *Journal of Abnormal Psychology, 98,* 117–126.

Fristad, M. A., Weller, E. B., & Weller, R. A. (1992). The Mania Rating Scale: Can it be used in children. *Journal of American Academy of Child and Adolescent Psychiatry, 31,* 252–257.

Fristad, M. A., Weller, E. B., & Weller, R. A. (1995). The Mania Rating Scale (MRS): Further reliability and validity studies with children. *Annals of Clinical Psychiatry, 7,* 127–132.

Geller, B., Zimmerman, B., Williams, M., Bolhofner, K., Craney, J. L., DelBello, M. P., et al. (2001). Reliability of the Washington University in St Louis Kiddie Schedule for Affective Disorders and Schizophrenia (WASH-U-KSADS) mania and rapid cycling sections. *Journal of Academy of Child and Adolescent Psychiatry, 40,* 450–455.

Kaufman, J., Birmaher, B., Brent, D., Rao, U., Flynn, C., Moeci, P., et al. (1997). Schedule for Affective Disorders and Schizophrenia for School-Age Children—Present and Lifetime Version (K-SADS-PL): Initial reliability and validity data. *Journal of the American Academy of Child & Adolescent Psychiatry, 36,* 980–988.

Klein, D. N., Dickstein, S., Taylor, E. B., & Harding, K. (1989). Identifying chronic affective disorders in outpatients: Validation of the general behavior inventory. *Journal of Consulting and Clinical Psychology, 57,* 106–111.

Mallon, J. C., Klein, D. N., Bornstein, R. F., & Slater, J. F. (1986). Discriminant validity of the general behavior inventory: An outpatient study. *Journal of Personality Assessment, 50,* 568–577.

Young, R. C., Biggs, J. T., Ziegler, V. E., & Meyer, D. A. (1978). A rating scale for mania: Reliability, validity, and sensitivity. *British Journal of Psychiatry, 133,* 429–435.

Youngstrom, E. A., Findling, R. L., Danielson, C. K., & Calabrese, J. R. (2001). Discriminative validity of hypomanic and depressive symptoms on the General Behavior Inventory. *Psychological Assessment, 13*(2), 267–276.

13 Personality Disorders

The *DSM-IV* category of personality disorders represents an attempt by human service practitioners to identify and help those clients whose chronic problems in social functioning are related to ingrained and persistent patterns of thinking, behaving, and feeling. While few professionals question the existence of clients with such persistent problems, the idea of a personality as *disordered* is controversial in the social work profession (and others). Some believe that it represents negative labeling and disregards the profession's transactional, person-in-environment perspective on human functioning. In this chapter we will consider the concept of personality disorder, its rationale for inclusion in the *DSM-IV*, and some alternative ways that it might be operationalized. We will also discuss in detail the nature of one personality disorder that is often encountered by clinical social workers: the borderline type.

Can a Personality Be Disordered?

Personality is an extremely difficult concept to define. One noted theorist defines personality as a stable set of tendencies and characteristics that determine commonalties and differences in people; thoughts, beliefs, and actions that have continuity over time and may not be easily understood as the sole result of the social and biological pressures of a moment (Maddi, 2007). This definition illustrates the complexity of the concept. Theorists and researchers have developed many models of personality over the years that include different core features, developmental processes, and peripheral characteristics.

There is still no consensus, however, on what a personality is. A problem with the concept of a personality *disorder*, then, is that the primary concept on which it is based is vague (Hogan, 2005). The ambiguity of the concept is partly related to the fact that it emerged out of psychodynamic theory, which often relies on mental constructs that are difficult to operationalize. Furthermore, social workers should be concerned about using these diagnoses because they appear to describe the *total person*, rather than particular aspects of the person, and they are often used in pejorative terms. Even Millon and Grossman (2006), arguing in favor of the concept, admit that the notion of a personality disorder as an "entity within a person" is not accurate. They feel more comfortable focusing on personality *patterns*; repetitive behaviors and feelings that are problematic. As we proceed through this chapter the reader should keep in mind that social and environmental factors always have a significant influence on the thoughts, feelings, and behaviors of clients who exhibit rigid responses to life stress.

Characteristics of Personality Disorders

According to *DSM-IV* the personality disorders are categorized by enduring cognitions and behaviors that:

- Are deviant from cultural standards
- Are pervasive and rigid
- Have an onset in adolescence or early adulthood
- Are stable over time
- Lead to unhappiness and impairment
- Include maladaptive behavior in at least two of the following areas: *affect* (range and intensity of emotions), *cognition* (how the self and others are perceived), *impulse control*, and *interpersonal functioning*.

Many theorists have attempted to summarize the core features of personality disorders. Millon (1996) asserts three behavioral characteristics that distinguish pathological from normal personalities. First is *tenuous stability*; the person is fragile and lacks resilience under stress. Second is *adaptive inflexibility*, as the person has few strategies for coping with stress. Finally are *vicious cycles*, in that the person's maladaptive behavior patterns seem not only to leave current problems unsolved but also generate new problems. Watson, Clark, and Chmielewski (2008) write that people with personality disorders tend to be *irresponsible* (unable to acknowledge their part in things going wrong), *lacking in empathy* (being too driven by their own needs), *deficient in problem-solving skills*, have an *external locus of control* (seeing control and power as existing outside of themselves), and *generate distress in others* (rather than themselves).

The 10 personality disorders are defined in Exhibit 13.1. The *DSM* classifies these personality disorders into three *clusters*, based on shared core characteristics (Lindsay, Dana, Dosen, Gabriel, & Young, 2007). Cluster A includes the *paranoid, schizoid,* and *schizotypal* disorders. These persons are considered by others to be odd and eccentric. These disorders are believed to have a strong genetic base and are more common in the biological relatives of people with schizophrenia. Still, the great majority of persons with these disorders never develop an Axis I disorder. The Cluster B disorders (*antisocial, borderline, histrionic,* and *narcissistic*) are characterized by dramatic, emotional, and erratic presentations. These disorders may have a partial genetic base in that they have associations with other *DSM* Axis I disorders (such as antisocial personality with substance abuse, borderline personality with mood disorders, and histrionic personality with somatic disorders). The Cluster C disorders (*avoidant, dependent,* and *obsessive-compulsive*) feature anxious or fearful presentations. They are associated with the anxiety disorders.

With this introduction we now move into a discussion of borderline personality disorder. Persons with this disorder are frequently encountered in clinical settings and have historically been difficult for practitioners to effectively treat. Many of the principles of assessment and intervention described here are also relevant to clients with other personality disorders.

Exhibit 13.1	
The *DSM-IV-TR* Personality Disorders and Their Core Features	
Paranoid	Distrust and suspiciousness
Schizoid	Detachment from social relationships
Schizotypal	Acute discomfort in close relationships, cognitive or perceptual distortions, and eccentric behavior
Antisocial	Distrust of other and violations of their rights
Borderline	Instability in interpersonal relationships, self-image, affect, and impulse control
Histrionic	Excessive emotionality and attention-seeking
Narcissistic	Grandiosity, a need for admiration, and a lack of empathy
Avoidant	Social inhibition, feelings of inadequacy, and hypersensitivity to negative evaluation
Dependent	Submissive and clinging behavior related to an excessive need to be taken care of
Obsessive-compulsive	Preoccupation with orderliness, perfectionism, and control

Borderline Personality Disorder

Borderline personality disorder (BPD) is characterized by a pattern of instability in interpersonal relationships and self-image, and a capacity for frequent and intense negative emotions. While there is disagreement about the core features of the disorder, most observers agree on the two characteristics of *highly variable mood* and *impulsive behavior*; these were borne out in a large research study by Trull (2001).

Persons with BPD are usually dramatic, energetic, and lively, and they may be personable and charming at times. They become self-disclosive to people they like very early in those relationships. When upset, however, their presentation changes abruptly, and they become extremely angry, negative, depressed, and self-destructive in various ways. This is due to their characteristic defense (or coping) mechanism of splitting, meaning that they cannot maintain an idea of another person as having both positive and negative qualities. People are judged as being either all good or all bad. For the person with BPD, a significant other may be seen as all good and treated as such, but when he behaves in a way that is perceived as disappointing that person becomes all bad and may be completely rejected, temporarily or permanently. One study found that persons with BPD have a stronger tendency to view others negatively than persons with any other personality disorders (Arntz & Veen, 2001).

It is paradoxical that while persons with BPD have difficulty maintaining relationships, they are extremely social and cannot tolerate being alone. Their behaviors involve frantic efforts to avoid abandonment, the possibility of which creates overwhelming anxiety. They experience frequent emotional turmoil and are often in crisis due to their intense feelings of anger, emptiness, and hopelessness that occur when stressed. The person with BPD experiences severe depression when feeling abandoned or mistreated by others, even though they often distort the motives of others.

Other common features of BPD include anxiety, transient psychotic symptoms, suicidal or self-mutilating behaviors, and substance abuse. Up to 55% of inpatients with BPD have histories of suicide attempts, although the actual suicide rate is 5%–10%, similar to that for persons with schizophrenia and major affective disorder (APA, 2000). Up to 80% have committed acts of self-mutilation (such as cutting the forearms or face). Studies have shown that nonsuicidal acts of self-mutilation are intended to express anger, punish oneself, generate normal feelings when experiencing numbness or depersonalization, or distract oneself from painful feelings, while suicide attempts are intended to permanently relieve negative emotions (e. g., Brown, Comtois, & Linehan, 2002).

The diagnostic term *borderline* is misleading. When it was first developed for *DSM-III* in the late 1970s, BPD was believed to characterize clients who were on the "border" between psychotic and neurotic disorders. This vague distinction is no longer conceptually useful but the term has persisted. Suggestions for alternative nomenclature have included "cycloid" and "emotionally unstable" personality disorder (Millon, 1996). The "borderline" term is also misleading in that it tends to be misattributed to nonpsychotic clients who are especially difficult for clinical practitioners to engage in a steady, crisis-free intervention, and thus it may be overused.

The personality disorders are always recorded on Axis II. If the social worker plans to focus intervention on the personality disorder, the term *principal diagnosis* should be included in parentheses. The Cluster A disorders may be specified as *premorbid* if they were present before the symptoms of the Axis I diagnosis (if an Axis I diagnosis will be the primary focus of intervention). This provision reflects the thinking that the Cluster A disorders may be precursors to certain psychotic disorders.

Prevalence

Borderline personality disorder is a significant mental health problem that is present in cultures around the world (APA, 2000). A recent national study found that it can be diagnosed in 5.9% of adults, and it is the most common personality disorder found in clinical settings (Grant et al., 2008). Due to their interpersonally chaotic lifestyles, these individuals may be found among multiproblem clients in a variety of social service settings.

Comorbidity

Many other disorders are often comorbid with BPD, partly because its diagnostic criteria include strong indicators for other disorders. The most commonly seen Axis I disorders include the mood, anxiety, and substance abuse disorders, with 29.4%, 21.5%, and 14.1% 1-year comorbidity rates, respectively (Grant, et al., 2008). Bipolar disorder, panic disorder, and any substance dependence diagnosis are the most common of these. There is overlap among the symptoms of the personality disorders as well, and BPD most often co-occurs with the antisocial, avoidant, and narcissistic types (Grilo, Sanislow, & McGlashan, 2002). It is sometimes difficult to decide when Axis I symptoms are distinctive enough that a separate disorder should be diagnosed; for that reason the practitioner should be cautious in making such a determination. When the practitioner combines an Axis I disorder and BPD, intervention should focus on both disorders. The presence of BPD is a risk influence for recovery from an Axis I disorder.

The presence of substance use has major implications for treatment, since clients with BPD who abuse substances generally have a poor outcome and are at a higher risk for suicide and also death or injury from accidents (Kolla, Eisneberg, & Links, 2008). To the extent that clients may use various substances to mask depression, anxiety, and other related symptoms, their willingness to take appropriate prescription medications may help to alleviate the underlying symptoms and thus reduce their temptation to use alcohol or drugs. Men with BPD are more likely than women to present with comorbid substance abuse disorders, however, while women more often present with PTSD and eating disorders (Skodol, 2005).

Course

The social cost for clients with BPD and their families is substantial. Recent data indicate that clients with BPD show greater lifetime utilization of most major categories of medication, and of most types of psychotherapy, than clients with schizotypal, avoidant, obsessive-compulsive personality disorder, or major depressive disorder (Zanarini, Frankenburg, Hennen, & Silk, 2004).

Long-term follow-up studies of treated clients with BPD indicate that its course is variable. One study of 351 young adults found that BPD predicted negative outcomes in the areas of academic achievement and social maladjustment over the subsequent 2 years, regardless of the presence of any other pathology (Bagge et al., 2004).

Longitudinal studies indicate that about one-third of clients with BPD appear to recover 10 years after initial diagnosis, solidifying their identity during the intervening years and replacing their self-damaging acts, inordinate anger, and stormy relationships with more mature and modulated behavior patterns (Paris, 2003). After 10 years of intervention, 50% of clients no longer meet the full criteria for the disorder. Longitudinal studies of hospitalized clients with BPD indicate that even though they may gradually attain functional roles 10–15 years after admission to psychiatric facilities, only about one-half of the women and one-quarter of the men will have attained enduring success in intimacy (as indicated by marriage or long-term sexual partnership). One-half to three-quarters of clients will have achieved stable full-time employment. A limitation of these studies is that they concentrated on clients with BPD from middle class or upper middle class families. Clients with the disorder from backgrounds of poverty may have substantially lower success rates in the spheres of intimacy and work.

One measure of improvement over time for persons with BPD is reduction in suicidal and self-mutilation actions. One 10-year study found a dramatic decline in these acts, even though their prevalence remained higher than among a comparison group of clients with other personality disorders (Zanarini et al., 2008).

Assessment

The practitioner must always be cautious about diagnosing a personality disorder, partly because he or she will be making judgments about personality functioning in the context of the client's ethnic, cultural, and social background. Some cultures, for example, value interpersonal dependency more than others do (Whaley, 2001).

Personality disorders should rarely be diagnosed in children and adolescents. Personality patterns are evolving during those years and are not considered to reach a state of constancy until late adolescence or young adulthood. Borderline personality disorder especially lacks validity in young people because many of its symptoms have been shown to occur in the course of normal adolescence (Chabrol et al., 2004).

Because personality disorders represent ingrained patterns of interaction with significant others, social workers should always look beyond the presenting problem issue to the client's interpersonal history. The social worker should investigate the quality of the client's overall relationship patterns with family, friends, and associates, and how these either help or hinder social and occupational functioning. Included below are the types of questions that the social worker should address during the assessment of BPD (Walsh, 2010):

- What recent stressors account for the client's symptoms? Does this appear to be an isolated situation or part of a general pattern?
- Is the client's presenting problem an outcome of conflicted interactions with significant others? If so, is this an isolated situation, or part of a general pattern?
- Does the client maintain positive relationships with some significant others (such as friends, family, and coworkers), or are most relationships conflicted?
- Does the client appear to be replicating old relationships in the present, for example, those with parents or early caregivers?
- Do the client's problem behaviors represent efforts to master old traumas by repeating them with people in the present?
- Has the client's personality changed as the result of a medical condition?
- Is the client under the influence of any substances that might account for the symptoms of anxiety and depression?
- Is there evidence of a history of hypomanic or manic episodes? Of depressive episodes?
- If the client is an older adolescent or young adult, are identity concerns related to a developmental phase?
- If the client displays manipulative behaviors toward others, including the social worker, are they related to a desire to elicit nurturance or for power or personal gain?

- What cultural conditions may be affecting the client's relationship-seeking behavior?
- What environmental conditions may be affecting the client's relationship-seeking behavior?

The practitioner must also be aware that any personality disorder implies long-term patterns of problematic functioning; therefore, one should be reluctant to apply the diagnosis when there is little evidence about the duration of the client's difficulties.

Risk and Protective Influences

Onset

Borderline personality disorder most likely results from a combination of biological and environmental influences (see Exhibit 13.2). One theorist writes that BPD is what happens when the child with a difficult temperament meets an invalidating environment (Linehan, 1993). A recent large-scale study of the genetic and environmental risk mechanisms among twins found that BPD is the result of approximately 37.1% genetic and 62.9% environmental influences (Kendler et al., 2008). These persons seem to have a predisposition to affective instability and a childhood history of neglect, abuse, loss, or lack of

Exhibit 13.2		
Risks and Protective Influences for the Onset of Borderline Personality Disorder		
Risks	Protective	
Biological		
Genetic heritability	No affective disorders or mental illness in immediate or extended family	
Psychological		
A difficult or sensitive temperament	Easy temperament	
Social		
Absence of parent figures	Adequate presence of parent figures	
Chaotic, adverse family life	Stable family life	
Sexual abuse	No sexual abuse or trauma	

Sources: Grant et al. (2008), Gurvits, Holm, and Severinsson (2008), Koenigsberg and Siever (2000), Kendler et al. (2008), MacKinnon and Pies (2006), Skodol et al. (2002), Weston and Riolo (2007).

validation. Borderline personality disorder is approximately five times more common among first-degree biological relatives of those with the disorder than in the general population (APA, 2000). There is also a greater familial risk with BPD for substance abuse disorders, antisocial personality disorder, and mood disorders. Still, these risks may be related to environment conditions as well as personal constitution.

Biological Influences

The biological causes of BPD are speculative (Johnson, 1999). Certain of the "cardinal" symptoms, including impulsivity, irritability, hypersensitivity to stimulation, and emotional lability, reactivity, and intensity, are often associated with a biological foundation. In particular, researchers have studied the link between BPD and two neurotransmitters: serotonin (which is diminished) and norepinephrine (which is overactive) (Gurvits, Koenigsberg, & Siever, 2000). Serotonin has been linked to impulsive behavior and both external and self-directed aggression.

A relationship between the personality and the affective disorders has long been argued, which supports a shared biological component (Mackinnon & Pies, 2006). Persons with BPD are said to have a cyclothymic temperament, or mood swings that resemble bipolar disorder (the interpersonal conflicts are a differentiating factor). Biological contributors to this process may include elevations of the person's catecholamines (neurotransmitters that mediate mood states and aggression) and dysfunctions in the locus caeruleus (used for information processing and memory), the amygdala in the limbic system (that manages fear and anxiety), and the hippocampus (a center of emotional experience) (Skodol et al., 2002).

Psychological Influences

While there is limited evidence to support their validity, psychoanalytic theorists have produced a rich literature regarding persons with BPD (Weston & Riolo, 2007). These clients are said to have failed to negotiate successfully the delicate task of separating from primary caregivers while maintaining an internalized sense of being cared for. During their infancy they either were, or believed themselves to be, abandoned. According to Kernberg (1985), these individuals are fixated at a separation-individuation phase of development whereby they cannot clearly distinguish between the self and other people. They feel that when a parent or other close attachment figure is not physically present or immediately available, he or she is gone forever. The person often experiences intense separation anxiety as a result and thus tends to be dependent and "clingy."

Social Influences

Most empirical research shows a marked relationship between childhood trauma and borderline symptoms. Such trauma includes loss, sexual and physical violence, neglect, abuse, witnessing domestic violence, and parental substance abuse or criminality. In a meta-analysis by Holm and Severinsson

(2008), three themes emerged from the literature on the relationship between trauma and personality development, including emotional abuse and neglect, a tendency toward self-injury, and interpersonal problems related to difficulties regulating emotions. A high prevalence of reported childhood abuse was revealed, and in fact ongoing sexual abuse in childhood was the best predictor of the severity of borderline syndromes. One study of 290 persons with BPD found a positive association between the severity of childhood sexual abuse and the severity of functional impairment (Zanarini et al., 2002). Dissociative symptoms (in which there is a temporary loss of some aspect of consciousness or identity) were positively associated with inconsistent treatment by a caregiver, sexual abuse by a caregiver, witnessing sexual violence as a child, and an adult rape history (Zanarini, Ruser, Frankenberg, Hennen, & Gunderson, 2000).

In considering general interpersonal factors in the family, Benjamin (1996) lists four features in the development of the borderline personality. First is family chaos, which contributes to a sense of drama and unpredictability in the family. Second is traumatic abandonment. The third factor is the family's belief that a member's independence is a negative characteristic, resulting in punishment of children who take initiatives in that direction. Finally, the client is only positively reinforced (cared for) when he or she is in crisis.

Another risk influence for BPD is the structure of Western society, in which the upbringing of most children is limited to one or two primary caregivers, without additional consistent parent figures available to "fill in" when these caregivers prove to be inadequate. This is in contrast to some cultural groups where extended family may routinely provide major parenting roles. Borderline personality disorder is thus less prevalent among Hispanic persons and Asian women, while interestingly it is more prevalent among Native Americans (Grant, et al., 2008). Western society's reliance on the nuclear family fails to provide opportunities for children to have "second chances" to develop healthy attachments when these might be developmentally beneficial.

Recovery and Adjustment

Borderline personality disorder, as an Axis II diagnosis, is assumed to be stable and long-term compared to most Axis I diagnoses, although recent research (described earlier) indicates that it has an unpredictable course (Ruocco, 2005). What follows is a discussion of mechanisms that are associated with its persistence and remission (also see Exhibit 13.3 below).

Biological/Psychological

The biological mechanisms associated with the onset of BPD are also associated with its persistence, although some other client characteristics influence a person's potential for recovery (Ruocco, 2005). It is difficult to separate the biological and psychological mechanisms that are operative over time, so

Exhibit 13.3

Risk and Protective Influences for the Course of Borderline Personality Disorder

Risk Influences	Protective Influences
Biological	
Lower IQ	Higher IQ
Psychological	
High levels of affective instability and impulsivity	Low affective instability and impulsivity
Self-harm behaviors	Does not engage in self-harm behaviors
Comorbid Axis I or II disorders	Absence of comorbid disorders
	Psychological maturation
Social	
Engagement in intense relationships	Absence of intense relationships
Stressful life events	Lack of personal crises, negative life events
Lack of participation in intervention	Participation in professional intervention

Sources: Pagano et al. (2004), Paris (2002), Rocco (2005), Shea et al., (2004), Soloff and Fabelo (2008).

these are combined in this section. First, relatively low levels of the symptoms of affective instability and impulsivity act as protective mechanisms (Paris, 2002). Intelligence is another protective mechanism, as it relates to the client's ability to learn from experience or adjust behaviors in response to negative outcomes. This also includes the person's ability to develop coping strategies that do not involve self-harm. In a study of over 500 persons with BPD from the Collaborative Longitudinal Personality Disorders Study, physical health and the absence of comorbid Axis I or II disorders (especially substance abuse, major depression, posttraumatic stress disorder, and panic disorder) were associated with positive outcomes (Shea et al., 2004).

Social Influences

A study of more than 600 other persons from the Collaborative Longitudinal Study identified several social influences on recovery for persons with BPD (Pagano et al., 2004). These included integrating oneself into a validating social environment and avoiding involvement in criminal and legal matters. Marriage or partnership with a person who fills a "caregiver" role promotes positive functioning; any type of stable interpersonal environment serves the same purpose. On the other hand, it was found in a 15-year multisite follow-up study of persons with BPD that engaging in relationships characterized by intensity was a risk influence (Paris, 2002). This researcher added that any negative life events as identified by the client tend to worsen adaptive outcomes. Another 5-year longitudinal study concluded that positive changes over time were due to any form of intervention and a nonspecific psychological maturation (Soloff & Fablo, 2008).

Interventions

Psychosocial

Standard Components of Treatment

Clients with BPD are challenging for practitioners to engage in a sustained process of intervention. It is estimated that 40%–60% of these clients drop out of intervention prematurely (Marziali, 2002). Standard components of intervention include the practitioner's establishing and maintaining a therapeutic framework and alliance, monitoring the client's safety, providing education about the disorder, consistent supportive or insight-oriented therapy, and coordinating intervention by other providers (such as physicians and rehabilitation counselors). Many practitioners create a hierarchy of intervention goals, usually focusing first on promoting physical safety and eliminating self-destructive behavior (Johnson, 1999).

Because of clients' labile moods, changing motivation, and self-harm tendencies, the social worker should establish at the outset a clear and explicit agreement, or contract, about how the intervention will proceed (Levy et al., 2006). This contract should address when, where, and with what frequency sessions will be held; a plan for crises management; and expectations about such miscellaneous issues as scheduling, attendance, and payment. Because of the client's potential for impulsive behavior, practitioners must be comfortable with setting limits on self-destructive behaviors. That is, social workers need to lay out what they see as the necessary conditions to make intervention viable with the understanding that it will depend on the client's adherence to certain minimal conditions.

While validating clients' suffering, practitioners must also help them make appropriate responsibility for their actions. Effective intervention helps clients realize that while they were not responsible for the neglect and abuse, they are responsible for controlling and preventing self-destructive patterns in the present and future (Ryle, 2004). Interpretations of here and now behavior as it links to events in the past are useful for helping clients learn about their tendencies toward repetition of maladaptive behavior patterns. As previously noted, splitting is a major defense mechanism of clients with BPD. The self and others are often regarded as "all good" or "all bad." Intervention must be geared toward helping the client begin to experience the shades of gray between these extremes and integrate the positive and negative aspects of the self and others.

Treatment Settings and Modalities

When possible, group interventions are preferable for persons with BPD because they provide a mutually supportive environment with opportunities for members to provide and receive empathic feedback, dilute the intensity of client projections onto the practitioner, provide more opportunities for learning and experimenting with new patterns of behavior, and provide more feedback about self-destructive tendencies (Marziali, 2002). Some clients with BPD may need to be seen in protective environments, usually for short periods of time. Indications for partial or brief inpatient hospitalization include dangerous, impulsive behavior that cannot be managed in an out-patient setting; nonadherence with outpatient intervention and a deterior-ating clinical picture, complex comorbidity that requires intensive clinical assessment of response to intervention, and transient psychotic episodes associated with loss of impulse control or impaired judgment (APA, 2000).

Specific Interventions

There are empirical data supporting particular types of intervention. All randomized controlled trials involving psychological interventions for people with BPD were considered in a literature review by Binks et al. (2006). Seven studies were identified in their review, involving 262 clients. The authors found empirical support for dialectical behavior therapy (DBT) and one type of psychoanalytic-orientated intervention (described below as "mentalization-based"). In the remainder of this section we will elaborate on these interventions and also discuss other interventions that have been tested with this population, including cognitive/schema therapy, interpersonal therapy, and integrated therapy.

Dialectical Behavior Therapy

Dialectical behavior therapy (DBT) is an intensive intervention based on cognitive-behavioral and social learning theories that combines weekly indi-vidual sessions with group work (Linehan, 1993; Robins & Chatman, 2002). The term *dialectical* refers to the challenge of balancing one's needs for both self-acceptance and change, as well as the premise that BPD is a product of biological and environmental influences. The goal of treatment is to help the client engage in functional, life-enhancing behavior even when intense emo-tions are present.

Practitioners of DBT view client behaviors as natural reactions to envir-onmental reinforcers. In the case of BPD, one of the most frequent dialectical tensions is that a behavior such as self-injury is both functional (short-term stress reduction) and dysfunctional (negative effects on health and interper-sonal functioning in the long term.) This tension is resolved by finding a synthesis—validating the client's need to relieve stress while helping him or her utilize skills to reduce stress in the long run. Intervention focuses on shaping and reinforcing more adaptive behaviors while also providing clients with a validating environment. Practitioners pay attention to the factors that maintain dysfunctional behaviors such as reinforcers of self-injurious behaviors and aversive consequences of more effective behavior. A challenge of this approach is to balance these efforts to change with acceptance and validation.

Unique features of DBT include its five purposes, as follows:

- Enhancing client motivation to change, and rehearsing cognitive and behavioral skills that can help clients regulate emotions, in 1-hour individual sessions
- Enhancing mindfulness, interpersonal skills, emotion regulation, and distress tolerance, in 2-hour weekly skills groups
- Ensuring the generalization of skills to activities of daily living with as-needed phone consultations
- Enhancing therapist effectiveness with 1-hour consultation team meetings
- Structuring the environment to support both the client and practitioner's capabilities

The four stages of therapy include *(1)* eliminating the client's most severely disabling and dangerous behaviors (this is the focus of most empirical research on the modality thus far), *(2)* helping clients experience emotions rather than avoid or inhibit them, *(3)* addressing problems in living, including Axis I disorders, career problems, and marital problems, and *(4)* helping clients develop the capacity for freedom and joy.

Dialectical behavior therapy has "well-established" empirical support based on seven randomized controlled trials across four research teams (Lynch, Trost, Salsman, & Linehan, 2007). In these studies the DBT must have included individual therapy, a formal skills-training group, a therapist consultation team, some form of coaching (usually by telephone), and a treatment length of at least 6 months for outpatient clients and 2 months for inpatient clients. A subsequent study has shown that an abbreviated form of DBT (provided over 6 months instead of 1 year) is effective in reducing self-injurious and suicidal behavior (Stanley, Brodsky, Nelson, & Dulit, 2007).

Psychodynamic Intervention

Psychodynamic intervention involves careful attention to the therapist–client relationship with thoughtfully timed interpretations of transference and resistance. It draws from three major theoretical perspectives: ego psychology, object relations, and self-psychology. Psychodynamic intervention is usually conceptualized as operating on an exploratory–supportive continuum of interventions (Berzoff, 2007). On the supportive end of the continuum, goals involve the strengthening of defenses, development of self-esteem, validation of feelings, internalization of the therapeutic relationship, and creation of a greater capacity to cope with disturbing feelings. At the exploratory end of the continuum, the goals are to make unconscious patterns more consciously available, increase affect tolerance, build a capacity to delay impulsive action, provide insight into relationship problems, and develop reflective functioning toward a greater appreciation of internal motivation in the self and others.

In transference-focused psychotherapy (TFP), BPD is assumed to involve an abundance of negative affect in relation to positive affect. The mechanisms of change at the level of the client in TFP involve the integration of polarized representations of the self and others (Levy et al, 2006). That is, the client should experience the practitioner as a safe haven to express the self in the context of a working contract that spells out the limits and scope of the intervention. The practitioner must work from a theoretically coherent approach involving some type of treatment contract, hierarchy of problems addressed, and the use of clarification, confrontation (honest inquiry about disparate information), and transference interpretations of the relationship. The TFP therapist provides the client with the opportunity to integrate cognitions and affects that were previously disorganized. Through these actions, the practitioner helps the client to increase reflective ability, integrate feelings with thoughts, gain greater control over emotions, and further place his or her new learning into various life contexts.

A model of psychodynamic intervention known as mentalization-based treatment (MBT) consists of 18 months of individual and group therapy within a structured program provided by a supervised team (Bateman & Fonagy, 2008). Expressive therapy using art and writing groups is included. Crises are managed within the team and a psychiatrist working within the program prescribed medication. The client and practitioner collaboratively generate alternative perspectives of the client's experience of himself or herself and others by moving from validating and supportive interventions to exploring the relationship itself as it suggests alternative understanding. This manualized psychodynamic therapy is recognized to overlap with transference-focused psychotherapy.

Interpersonal Therapy

Interpersonal therapy (IPT), also described in Chapter 9, is a manual-based intervention that addresses the nature of a client's interpersonal problems as they contribute to an emotional disorder (Weissman, 2006). Interpersonal therapy focuses on a client's use of defenses, the underlying thought patterns that influence one's evaluation of the self and others, and the client–practitioner relationship as a model for other relationships. The goals of the intervention are to enhance clients' mastery of current social roles and adaptation to interpersonal situations. The intervention focuses on any of the following four areas: bereavement, struggles regarding interpersonal relationships, disturbing life events, and social isolation. Interpersonal therapy is usually provided in 12–16 one-hour sessions in individual and group formats.

A form of interpersonal therapy has been adapted for use with persons who have BPD (Markowitz, Bleiberg, Pessin, & Skodol, 2007). The protocol includes a two-stage treatment. In the first phase, individual clients participate in eighteen 50-minute IPT sessions over 16 weeks, with the goals of establishing a therapeutic alliance, limiting self-destructive behaviors, and experiencing symptomatic relief. The second stage includes 16 more weekly sessions with the "typical" IPT goals of building on initial gains, developing more adaptive interpersonal skills, and maintaining a strong therapeutic alliance. Clients are also offered a 10-minute telephone contact once weekly, as needed, to handle crises and maintain therapeutic continuity. This variation on the basic IPT model is currently being tested for effectiveness (Markowitz et al, 2007).

Cognitive/Schema Therapy

According to cognitive therapy, persons with BPD are characterized by dysfunctional core belief systems (schemas) that are enduring and inflexible and lead to cognitive distortions such as dichotomous thinking (Wenzel, Chapman, Newman, Back, & Brown, 2006). When these beliefs are activated, they lead to extreme emotional and behavioral reactions that provide additional confirmation for their beliefs. It is hypothesized that a change in dysfunctional beliefs is the primary mechanism of change associated with cognitive therapy. This is done through cognitive restructuring, behavioral experiments, and the use of imagery. Clients are taught new coping skills to manage mood and suicidal ideation, increase social and relaxation skills, and improve rational problem-solving strategies.

Schema therapy is a cognitive approach that also draws on emotion-focused interventions (Kellogg & Young, 2006). Schemas are entrenched belief systems typically developed during trouble childhoods in which the basic needs of the child were not met, and the child embraced maladaptive coping styles. Clients with BPD are conceptualized as being under the sway of five aspects of the self, including the abandoned or abused child, the angry and impulsive child, the detached protector, the punitive parent, and the healthy adult. Four mechanisms of change in schema therapy include limited reparenting (the practitioner tries to compensate for these deficits), emotion-focused work (imagery and dialogues), cognitive restructuring and education, and behavior pattern breaking. Intervention is divided into the three stages of bonding and emotional regulation, schema mode change, and the development of autonomy. Through blending these strategies for change, the client develops a healthier adult mode, which leads to a greater ability to attain emotional stability, goal-directed behavior, mutually affirming relationships, and general well-being. Both of these therapies have limited empirical support but are currently under investigation in efforts to demonstrate their efficacy (van Genderen, Arntz, Drost, Sendt, & Baumgarten-Kuster, 2009).

Integrated Therapy

As described earlier, several interventions are associated with significant change in persons who have personality disorders. The evidence also suggests, however, that outcomes may be domain specific, with some interventions being more effective in treating some behaviors than others (Piper & Joyce, 2001). For example, DBT interventions are useful in building skills for managing self-harm and regulating emotions, whereas transference focused therapy targets interpersonal relationships and places less importance on skill building. Livesley (2007) thus argues the merits of an "integrated" approach to intervention. Rather than selecting among treatments that are limited in terms of range and scope of problems addressed, he offers a model in which the practitioner selects effective interventions from different treatments for each domain of client need. Because using multiple methods could lead to disorganized treatment, he proposes two intervention steps that can be used to avoid this potential problem.

First, the practitioner uses generic methods of change common to all effective treatments (Beutler, 1991). These common factors have a relational and supportive component based on the therapeutic relationship and a technical component that provides new learning experiences and opportunities to apply new skills. The second stage of specific interventions draws from different models that are tailored to the needs of individual clients and the issues that are the focus of attention at any given moment. This stage includes five hierarchical phases of change, including client safety, the containment of dangerous behaviors, control and regulation of affect, exploration and change, and integration and synthesis (Livesley, 2003). This interesting approach to intervention selects elements from a variety of therapies, but because it is not highly structured it has not been tested for effectiveness.

Medications

Clients with BPD often receive medications to help manage some of their symptoms, including depression, suicidal ideation, angry outbursts, impulsive behavior, and transient psychotic ideation. Prescribing effective medications is difficult, however, because of challenges presented by the disorder's symptom heterogeneity and the frequent presence of comorbid disorders. All of the authors cited in this section emphasize that medication interventions alone are not sufficient to help persons with BPD achieve significant and lasting mental status improvements.

In a Cochrane review, Binks et al. (2006b) reported on the results of 10 (total N = 554) randomized, controlled studies. The studies comparing antidepressants with placebo demonstrated small positive effects with fluoxetine offering greater reductions in anger than the other antidepressants. The antipsychotic haloperidol appears to be better than antidepressants for symptoms of hostility and psychotic ideation. There were few differences between MAO inhibitors (the first class of antidepressants, rarely used today) and placebo except that people given the MAOI drugs were less hostile. Comparison of MAOIs with antipsychotic drugs did not show convincing differences. There is modest evidence that antipsychotic drugs and mood stabilizers such as divalporex positively affect some symptoms more effectively than placebo. In summary, some of the antipsychotic and antidepressant medications are helpful in controlling some symptoms of BPD, but not with great effect.

Other recent pharmacological and neurological research adds detail to the above findings. One author suggests that BPD encompasses three clusters of target symptoms: affective instability, impulsive aggression, and transient psychotic phenomenon (Sperry, 2006). It appears that affective instability is related to brain abnormalities in adrenergic and cholinergic systems, and agents like lithium carbonate and anticonvulsants such as carbamazepine can be effective in modulating affects. Abnormalities in central nervous system serotonin function resulting in impulsivity seem to respond to SSRI agents like fluoxetine, a drug that is also effective in treating symptoms related to depressed mood and impulsive aggression. Finally, abnormalities in dopamine systems may account for transient psychotic symptoms, and low-dose antipsychotic drugs have been shown to be effective with this symptom cluster. Kolla, Eisenberg, and Links (2008) reviewed the literature on BPD and found that suicidal ideation has been reduced with the use of SSRI drugs, the newer antipsychotic medications (such as clozapine and olanza-pine), and the anticonvulsant drugs used to treat mood instability.

Social Diversity

Borderline personality disorder is diagnosed predominantly in women, with an estimated gender ratio of 3:1, although it is equally prevalent among men and women in the general population (Lenzenweger, Lane, Loranger, & Kessler, 2007). It is more prevalent among Native American men, younger and single adults, and persons with lower incomes and education. It is less prevalent among Hispanic persons and Asian women. People with BPD are at a higher than average risk for unemployment, which is associated with low socioeconomic status.

It is interesting to note from the earlier discussion on treatment that all of the interventions for persons with BPD leave room for the social worker to individualize his or her strategies and pace (Livesley, 2007). For example, with men who tend to exhibit substance abuse problems along with the primary diagnosis the social worker will probably choose to focus on containing those behaviors. For women, who are more likely to have a history of sexual abuse, the social worker will probably focus on the behaviors that stem from reactions to that abuse, including being cautious about stirring up related emotional content too quickly. Finally, because

BPD is often seen in persons from low socioeconomic status, shorter-term interventions may need to be adapted in consideration of their financial and time constraints.

Critique of the Diagnosis

Borderline personality disorder is a highly problematic diagnostic category. The reasons for this were articulated early in the chapter but will be summarized here. First, like the other personality disorders, it is based on a concept (personality) that is itself difficult to capture. Second, BPD has shown to be an invalid and unreliable diagnosis in some research studies (Paris, 2005). Clients with the diagnosis may have quite different symptom clusters and as a result present very differently to practitioners. Problems with validity and reliability have rendered progress slow for determining what kinds of intervention might be helpful for clients. Finally, because one's *personality* is synonymous with the *person*, the BPD diagnosis (like the others) seems to present practitioners with an ethical dilemma in reinforcing a strong deficits perspective. In spite of these concerns, all clients with symptoms of BPD have very real, ongoing problems, and practitioners should remain committed to working with them so that they can achieve their goals of improved relationships and social integration.

A growing number of theorists and researchers are asserting that the *DSM* categorical approach, in which the disorders are considered to be discrete entities, is flawed (Widiger, 2007). Issues of concern include diagnostic unreliability, excessive comorbidity among the disorders, high functional variability among persons with the same diagnosis, and a limited research base for some of the categories. Perhaps the simplest way to address some of these concerns is to add severity criteria to the disorders, based on the number of qualifying symptoms. More comprehensively, as briefly described in Chapter 2, attempts have been made to identify the most fundamental *dimensions* that underlie the domain of normal and abnormal personality functioning, and to assess clients on a continuum of normalcy and pathology with respect to those dimensions. Clients would be assessed as to their position on each of these dimensions and given a set of scores rather than a categorical diagnosis.

Case Study

Shannon was a 19-year-old, Caucasian, single, working female, referred to the mental health clinic from a psychiatric hospital following a 2-week stay in the crisis unit. She had experienced more than a dozen hospitalizations in the 18 months since her high school graduation. All of her hospitalizations were due to depression and suicidal ideation. There was no history of any intervention prior to her high school graduation, however, and no sustained outpatient intervention since then. The client was still taking antidepressant medications as prescribed by the hospital psychiatrist but reported no perceived benefits from them.

The practitioner learned that Shannon was the fourth and youngest girl born to a Roman Catholic couple. The family was middle class but upwardly mobile. Her parents had a rural background but had moved to a suburban area when Shannon was 5 years old. Shannon did not recall many details of her past but described a childhood of neglect, stating that her parents left all cooking, cleaning, laundering, and other household routines to the children. She said that her mother was always cold and emotionally withholding. Shannon remembered her father coming into her room at night, sitting by her bedside, and quietly stroking her hair, which made her extremely uncomfortable. Shannon later stated that she did not get along with any of her siblings and was frequently made the scapegoat for family conflicts. As a teenager she took long walks through her neighborhood each night to escape her parents' arguing and her sibling's teasing. She spoke fondly of a neighborhood policeman whom she often saw on her walks and several aunts and uncles who lived a few miles away.

On the day after her graduation Shannon moved into the home of an older male friend, his two adolescent children, and two other female acquaintances. She had become acquainted with them while working as an emergency medical technician at the local volunteer fire department. Shannon had developed an early interest in nursing and by age 18 was handling herself skillfully on rescue squad runs. Her work life represented a major strength. Shannon was at best cordial with her own family, however. Her parents refused to attend a joint session at the mental health center. When speaking to the practitioner on the phone, her mother said, "Don't let that loser try to blame us for anything."

Shannon's personality style was characterized by superficial pleasantness but a refusal (or inability) to discuss personal information. She had few acquaintances and spent all of her free time with her housemates. Young men showed interest in her at times, but Shannon was anxious about this and avoided getting involved with them. When pressed for detail about these and other personal matters, Shannon became anxious, quiet, and withdrawn. She appeared to dissociate at times as evidenced by her staring blankly and becoming unresponsive for several minutes. She denied feeling angry about anything, but the practitioner believed that she was keeping these feelings out of her awareness. He believed that keeping her anger inside contributed to her depression. She was often passive-aggressive toward the practitioner through her tendencies to miss appointments or come late. Shannon engaged in one serious form of self-mutilation: she would sometimes slam her right fist against a wall or table (always when alone), often breaking bones and tearing tendons.

The practitioner perceived Shannon as a suicide risk because she was so isolated, depressed, and with little evident hope for betterment. When she did talk she quietly spoke of herself as an evil, worthless, and stupid person. What was most striking to the social worker was her lack of connection to others even though she experienced alarming anxiety when alone. These episodes often occurred during her chronically sleepless nights when she would lie in bed for hours and experience escalating terror about losing control of herself.

After her fourth visit to the agency, Shannon gave a letter to the practitioner and asked that he wait until she left to read it. In the letter she detailed her history of sexual abuse by her father that spanned the ages of 5 through 17. She recalled few details of the incidents and had not discussed them with anyone else. Shannon added that the incest was her own fault, proof that she was a disgusting human being. There was to be no salvation for her, and it meant that she could never become close to anyone.

When they met a few days later, Shannon wept throughout the hour. The practitioner acknowledged reading the letter and expressed his shocked reaction to her revelations. He asked why she had written the letter. Shannon said she never trusted anyone and assumed that anyone who knew her secret would reject her. She admitted to feeling confused by the practitioner's persistent interest in her. She wondered what he had wanted from her and suspected that the motives were sexual. It was only after their first several weeks of work that she considered he might be interested in her welfare. Still, she continued to demonstrate ambivalence in her relationship with him.

Diagnostic Formulation

The practitioner diagnosed Shannon on Axis I with major depression. She met most of the criteria with the following symptoms: feelings of sadness, anxiety, anger, irritability, and emotional numbness; a flatness of expression; feelings of guilt, shame, low self-esteem, helplessness, pessimism, hopelessness; thoughts of death and suicide; impairment in her ability to think and concentrate; the inability to experience pleasure; and poor sleep patterns. The depression was severe. The agency physician supported this diagnosis because he was treating the client with antidepressant medicine.

Shannon was diagnosed with borderline personality disorder on Axis II, and the practitioner considered this as the principal diagnosis. She met criteria, including frantic efforts to avoid abandonment; a pattern of unstable interpersonal relationships; a persistent unstable self-image and sense of self, impulsive behavior (engaging in reckless physical activity), recurrent suicidal and self-mutilating behavior, mood instability, chronic feelings of emptiness, and intense anger that was generally suppressed.

There was no diagnosis on Axis III, given the client's good physical health.

Shannon was noted on Axis IV as having problems with her primary support group and the social environment. She experienced severe and long-term discord with her parents and some siblings, had no close friends, and tended to view others as evil. Furthermore, while she had a job, a place to stay, and some friends, none of these were secure resources. She functioned well as an emergency medical technician but otherwise had a poor work record.

Shannon's current GAF was set at 50. She did not have problems in occupational functioning, but her suicidal ideation was chronic, as were her interpersonal problems.

Summary of the Differential Diagnosis

Axis I: Major depression, recurrent, severe, without psychotic features, without full interepisode recovery.
Axis II: Borderline Personality Disorder (principal diagnosis)
Axis III: None
Axis IV: Primary support group (parents, siblings, peers) and social environment (work and social life)
Axis V: Current GAF = 50; highest GAF past year = 50

Intervention Plan

Shannon made a tentative connection with the social worker as evidenced by her keeping almost all scheduled appointments with him, following several weeks of intermittent no-shows or cancellations. The social worker kept reminding her that, while he would be available, she needed to assume responsibility for her treatment. The social worker did not have access to group interventions (and thus dialectical behavior therapy), so he decided to utilize interpersonal therapy with the client, drawing on some exercises adapted from dialectical behavior therapy. He described to Shannon the structured process of first becoming able to manage her self-injurious behaviors and then examining her relationship patterns in some depth over a 3- to 4-month period, and she agreed. It must be emphasized that the client's commitment to the intervention was not continuous; she changed her mind about participating with the social worker depending on her mood.

The social worker needed to develop their working relationship carefully in light of the client's tendency to engage in splitting behaviors (seeing others as "all bad" when disappointed in them). He was careful to balance his support and demand behaviors, always insisting that the client was responsible for her actions, as they worked toward Shannon's goals of a more stable temperament, the elimination of her self-harm tendencies, better social skills and interpersonal awareness, and her desire to attend nursing school. To plan ahead for probable crisis situations, the social worker helped Shannon articulate existing support systems on which she could rely, and he also informed the nearby emergency services unit of Shannon's clinical situation so that she could call or drive there when feeling self-destructive. The social worker also needed to clarify with the client his policy regarding phone calls. Because they had agreed to meet for weekly sessions on Tuesdays, he would available for one phone call per week on Friday afternoon, for additional support. He stated clearly that he would not respond to other phone calls, and that these should be directed to the emergency services unit.

During the first several months of their work together, the social worker provided Shannon with behavioral strategies for improving her coping and assertiveness skills. Toward this end the social worker referred to a dialectical behavior therapy treatment manual for material in teaching Shannon skills in the areas of mood regulation, tolerating distress, interpersonal effectiveness, and correcting maladaptive cognitions. Shannon's ability to engage in these practices was occasionally interrupted by periods of depression, and the social worker needed to spend some of their time helping her recover from perceived crisis episodes related to conflicts with friends and family. Still, the social worker was able to demonstrate consistent empathy for the client and managed to maintain (or at times, win back) her trust. Shannon "quit" therapy on two occasions, complaining that the social worker's limits on contact were "unreasonable," but she returned within a few weeks. The focus of their work gradually moved from behavioral management into new interpersonal skill development.

Shannon did not appear to respond well to the prescribed antidepressant medication, but the physician encouraged her to continue taking it, thinking that it may be helping to reduce her anxiety.

When the interpersonal therapy ends, her social worker may agree to provide Shannon with occasional supportive counseling and then refer her to an incest survivors group as a means of addressing her issues in a supportive environment. Family intervention was not considered in the intervention plan because the client was alienated from her family and did not wish to work toward reunification.

Appendix: Instruments Used to Assess DSM-IV Personality Disorders

Revisions for this edition are drawn from Widiger (2008).

Dimensional Assessment of Personality Pathology Basic Questionnaire (DAPP-BQ) (Livesley, Jackson, & Schroeder, 1989)

Description
- Questionnaire containing 290 items
- Measures 18 personality dimensions derived from an analysis of prototypical features of personality disorders

- Items measured on a 5-point Likert scale
- Used in cross-sectional research such as twin studies of the genetics of personality traits
- For treatment monitoring and outcome evaluation, norms were rated good, clinical utility rated excellent, and the instrument was highly recommended (Clark & Livesley, 2002; Livesley, 2001, 2003).

Reliability
- Internal consistency for the clinical sample was high (.84–.94).
- Test-retest reliability ranged from .81 to .93.
- For treatment monitoring and outcome evaluation, internal consistency rated excellent and test-retest reliability was good (Clark & Livesley, 2002; Livesley, 2001, 2003).

Validity
- Correlation with similar scales on the Schedule for Nonadaptive Personality was .53 (range: .01–.78)
- For treatment monitoring and outcome evaluation, content validity, construct validity, and validity generalization were rated excellent (Clark & Livesley, 2002; Livesley, 2001, 2003).

Millon Clinical Multiaxial Inventory (Millon, Davis, & Millon, 1997)

Description
- Used to assess all *DSM* personality types (from the text and appendix)
- One hundred seventy-five items in true-false format, administered by the client or a clinician
- Divided into 13 personality disorder scales and 9 symptom scales accessing anxiety, depression, thought disorder, etc.
- Requires 20–25 minutes for completion
- For diagnosis, norms were rated excellent, and clinical utility was rated less than adequate (Millon, Davis, & Millon, 1997).

Reliability
- Reliability for the dimension of total personality disorder features was .77 after 1 year and .70 after 3 years,
- For diagnosis, internal consistency rated good and test-retest reliability was less than adequate (Millon, Davis, & Millon, 1997).

Validity
- Comparison with other instruments yielded low correlation (criterion validity).

- For diagnosis, content validity and construct validity were rated adequate, and validity generalization was rated less than adequate (Millon, Davis, & Millon, 1997).

NEO Personality Inventory-Revised (Costa & McRae, 1992)

Description
- Questionnaire (240 items) that yields scores on each domain of the five-factor model of personality (neuroticism, extraversion, openness, agreeableness, and conscientiousness) and 30 facets of each domain
- Each facet is assessed by eight nonoverlapping items with a 5-point scale.
- Two forms are available: one for self-report and the other for peer, spouse, or expert report
- Requires 35–40 minutes to complete
- A short form is available (60 items) that assesses only the five domains; this requires 10–15 minutes to complete
- Results are interpreted by comparing domain and facet scores with an appropriate normative group
- For case conceptualization and treatment planning, norms were rated excellent and the instrument was highly recommended (Allik, 2005; Costa & McRae, 1992).

Reliability
- Alpha coefficients for both long forms ranged from .86 to .95 for domain scores and .56 to .78 for facet scores.
- Test-retest reliability was .51–.91 for the five domains and .51–.92 for the facets.
- Internal consistency for the short form ranged from .68 to .86; test-retest reliability was .75–.83.
- For case conceptualization and treatment planning, internal consistency and test-retest reliability were excellent (Allik, 2005; Costa & McRae, 1992).

Validity
- Scale scores correlated well (.60–.69) with a variety of other five-factor measures.
- The various domains and facets of the NEO have correlated moderately well with similar subscales from other instruments.
- For case conceptualization and treatment planning, content validity, construct validity, and validity generalization were rated excellent (Allik, 2005; Costa & McRae, 1992).

Personality Assessment Inventory (Morey, 1991)

Description
- Questionnaire containing 344 items
- Items scored on a 4-point Likert type scale (false to very true)
- Used as a general diagnostic aid and measure of psychopathology
- Includes 22 scales, 11 assessing major symptoms, 2 assessing interpersonal phenomena, 5 assessing data useful for treatment consideration, and 4 assessing test validity
- Takes 40–50 minutes to complete
- For diagnosis, norms were rated excellent, clinical utility rated less than adequate (Morey & Boggs, 2004).

Reliability
- Median internal consistency of the full scales and subscales is good (.82 and .66).
- Short-term stability ranged from .73 to .85 for full scales, .77 to .88 for subscales, and .60 to .90 for the personality scales.
- For diagnosis, internal consistency rated good and test-retest reliability was adequate (Morey & Boggs, 2004).

Validity
- Good discriminant validity between borderline features and antisocial features scales in clinical samples
- Convergent validity has been demonstrated in comparisons with several other personality measures.
- Data not yet reported regarding long-term change in treated samples, including state versus trait change characteristics.
- For diagnosis, content validity was rated less than adequate and construct validity was rated adequate (Morey & Boggs, 2004).

Personality Diagnostic Questionnaire for DSM-IV (Hyler, 1994)

Description
- Assesses the 10 personality disorders in the body of the *DSM-IV* and two types in the appendix
- One hundred true-false items
- Available in many languages
- For diagnosis, norms were rated less than adequate, and clinical utility was rated good (Bagby & Farvolden, 2004).

Reliability
- Good internal consistency (.64) for the Italian version
- Stability correlation for the number of borderline personality was $r = .54$; scores were lower after 2 years.

- For diagnosis, internal consistency and test-retest reliability were adequate (Bagby & Farvolden, 2004).

Validity
- Criterion validity is reported as low (but not specifically stated).
- Clinical Significance Scale was designed to minimize false diagnoses; more research is needed to establish this characteristic.
- For diagnosis, content validity was rated good, construct validity was rated less than adequate, and validity generalization was rated adequate (Bagby & Farvolden, 2004).

Schedule for Nonadaptive and Adaptive Personality (Clark, 1993)

Description
- A self-report test comprised of 375 true-false items designed to assess trait dimensions in the domain of personality disorders
- Assesses 12 clinical traits and three temperament scales, derived from clinically identified personality disorder criteria
- Used in cross-sectional research
- For diagnosis, norms were rated adequate, clinical utility rated good (Clark, Simms, Wu, & Casillas, in press).

Reliability
- Internal consistency = .81, with a range of .71 to .92
- Test-retest reliability = .79
- Interscale correlations are low.
- For diagnosis, internal consistency rated good and test-retest reliability was adequate (Clark, Simms, Wu, & Casillas, in press).

Validity
- Convergent validity is good (.53).
- Its utility as a change measure has not yet been reported.
- For diagnosis, content validity and construct validity were rated adequate (Clark, Simms, Wu, & Casillas, in press).

Wisconsin Personality Inventory (WISPI) (Klein et al., 1993)

Description
- Self-report questionnaire consisting of 214 items
- Subjects are asked to rate themselves over the past 5 years on a 10-point scale (never or not at all true to always or extremely true)

- Eleven scales represent personality disorder types that are based on themes in the *DSM-III-R*, but formulated according to Benjamin's theory of the structural analysis of social behavior.
- For diagnosis, norms were rated adequate, clinical utility was rated good (Klein et al., 1993).

Reliability and Validity
- Cronbach's alphas for the 11 personality disorders range from .81 to .95.
- High 2-week retest reliability with median .88
- Stability are scores lower at the 3–4 months (.75)
- For diagnosis, internal consistency rated good and test-retest reliability was adequate (Klein et al., 1993).
- For diagnosis, content validity and construct validity rated adequate (Klein et al., 1993).

References

American Psychiatric Association. (2000). *Diagnostic and statistical manual of mental disorders* (4th ed., rev.). Washington, DC: Author.

Arntz, A., & Veen, G. (2001). Evaluations of others by borderline patients. *Journal of Nervous and Mental Disease, 189*(8), 513–521.

Bagge, C., Nickell, A., Stepp, S., Durrett, C., Jackson, K., & Trull, T. J. (2004). Borderline personality disorder features predict negative outcomes 2 years later. *Journal of Abnormal Psychology, 113*(2), 279–288.

Bateman, A., & Fonagy, P. (2008). 8-year follow-up of patients treated for borderline personality disorder: Mentalization-based treatment versus treatment as usual. *American Journal of Psychiatry, 165*, 631–638.

Benjamin, L. S. (1996). An interpersonal theory of personality disorders. In J. F. Clarkin & M. F. Lenzenweger (Eds.), *Major theories of personality disorder* (pp. 141–220). New York: Guilford Press.

Berzoff, J. (2007). *Inside out and outside in: Psychodynamic clinical theory and practice in contemporary multicultural contexts.* Lanham, MD: Jason Aronson.

Beutler, L. E. (1991). Selective treatment matching: Systematic eclectic psychotherapy. *Psychotherapy: Theory, Research, Practice, Training, 28*(3) 457–462.

Binks C. A., Fenton, M., McCarthy, L., Lee, T., Adams, C. E., & Duggan, C. (2006b). Pharmacological interventions for people with borderline personality disorder. *Cochrane Database of Systematic Reviews* 2006, Issue 1. Art. No.: CD005653. DOI: 10.1002/14651858.CD005653.

Binks, C. A., Fenton, M., McCarthy, L., Lee T., Adams, C. E., & Duggan, C. (2006a) Psychological therapies for people with borderline personality disorder. *Cochrane Database of Systematic Reviews* 2006, Issue 1. Art. No.: CD005652. DOI: 10.1002/14651858.CD005652.

Brown, M. Z., Comtois, K. A., & Linehan, M. M. (2002). Reasons for suicide attempts and nonsuicidal self-injury in women with borderline personality disorder. *Journal of Abnormal Psychology, 111*(1), 198–202.

Chabrol, H., Montovany, A., Duconge, E., Kallmeyer, A., Mullet, E., & Leichsenring, M. (2004). Factor structure of the borderline personality inventory in adolescents. *European Journal of Psychological Assessment*, *20*(1), 9–65.

Grant, B. F., Chou, S. P., Goldstein, R. B., Huang, B., Stinson, F. S., Saha, T. D., Smith, S. M., Dawson, D. A., Pulay, A. J., Pickering, R. P., & Ruan, W. J. (2008). Prevalence, correlates, and comorbidity of DSM-IV borderline personality disorder: Results from the wave 2 national epidemiologic survey on alcohol and related conditions. *Journal of Clinical Psychiatry*, *69*(4), 533–545.

Grilo, C. M., Sanislow, C. A., & McGlashan, T. H. (2002). Co-occurrence of *DSM-IV* personality disorders with borderline personality disorder. *Journal of Nervous and Mental Disease*, *190*(8), 552–553.

Gurvits, I. G., Koenigsberg, H. W., & Siever, L. J. (2000). Neurotransmitter dysfunction in patients with borderline personality disorder. *Psychiatric Clinics of North America*, *23*(1), 27–40.

Hogan, R. (2005). In defense of personality measurement: New wine for old whiners. *Human Performance*, *18*(4), 331–341.

Holm, A. L., & Severinsson, E. (2008). The emotional pain and distress of borderline personality disorder: A review of the literature. *International Journal of Mental Health Nursing*, *17*(1), 27–35.

Johnson, H. C. (1999). Borderline personality disorder. In F. J. Turner (Ed.), *Adult psychopathology: A social work perspective* (pp. 430–456). New York: Free Press.

Kellogg, S. H., & Young, J. E. (2006). Schema therapy for borderline personality disorder. *Journal of Clinical Psychology*, *62*(4), 445–458.

Kendler, K. S., Aggen, S. H., Czajkowski, N., Raysamb, E., Tambs, K., Torgersen, S., Neale, M. C., & Reichborn-Kjennerud, T. (2008). The structure of genetic and environmental risk factors for DSM-IV personality disorders. *Archives of General Psychiatry*, *65*(12), 1438–1446,

Kernberg, O. (1985). *Borderline conditions and pathological narcissism*. New York: Jason Aronson.

Kolla, N. J., Eisenberg, H., & Links, P. S. (2008). Epidemiology, risk factors, and psychopharmacological management of suicide behavior n borderline personality disorder. *Archives of Suicide Research*, *12*, 1–19.

Lenzenweger, M. F., Lane, M. C., Loranger, A. W., & Kessler, R. C. (2007) DSM-IV Personality Disorders in the National Comorbidity Survey Replication. *Biological Psychiatry*, *62*(6), 553–564.

Levy, K. M., Clarkin, J. F., Yeoman, F. E., Scott, L. N., Wasserman, R. H., & Kernberg, O. F. (2006). The mechanisms of change in the treatment of borderline personality disorder with transference focused psychotherapy. *Journal of Clinical Psychology*, *62*(4), 481–501.

Lindsay, W R., Dana, L. A., Dosen, A., Gabriel, S. R., & Young, S. (2007). Personality disorders. In R. Fletcher, E. Loschen, C. Chrissoula, & M. First (Eds.), *Diagnostic manual–intellectual disability: A textbook of diagnosis of mental disorders in persons with intellectual disability* (pp. 511–532). Kingston, NY: National Association for the Dually Diagnosed.

Linehan, M. M. (1993). *Cognitive behavioral treatment of borderline clients*. New York: Guilford.

Livesley, W. J. (2007). The relevance of an integrated approach to the treatment of personality disordered offenders. *Psychology, Crime, & Law*, *13*(1), 27–46.

Lynch, T. R., Trost, W. T., Salsman, N., & Linehan, M. M. (2007). Dislectical behavior therapy for borderline personality disorder. *Annual Review of Clinical Psychology, 3,* 181–205.

Lynam D. R., & Widiger, T. A. (2007). Using a general model of personality to understand sex differences in the personality disorders. *Journal of Personality Disorders, 21*(6), 583–602.

MacKinnon, D. F., & Pies, R. (2006). Affective instability as rapid cycling: Theoretical and clinical implications for borderline personality and bipolar spectrum disorders. *Bipolar Disorders, 8,* 1–14.

Maddi, S. R., (2007); Personality theories facilitate integrating the five principles and deducing hypotheses for testing. *American Psychologist, 62*(1), 58–59.

Markowitz, , J. C., Bleiberg, K., Pessin, H., & Skodol, A. E. (2007). Adapting interpersonal therapy for borderline personality disorder. *Journal of Mental Health, 16*(1), 103–116.

Marziali, E. (2002). Borderline personality disorders. In A. R. Roberts & G. J. Greene (Eds.), *Social workers' desk reference* (pp. 360–364). New York: Oxford University Press.

Millon, T. (1996). *Personality disorders: DSM-IV and beyond.* New York: Wiley.

Millon, T., & Grossman, S. D. (2006). Goals of a theory of personality. In J. C. Thomas, D. L. Segal, & M. Hersen (Eds.), *Comprehensive handbook of personality and psychopathology, Vol. 1: Personality and everyday functioning* (pp. 3–222). Hoboken, NJ: John Wiley & Sons.

Pagano, M. E., Skodol, A. E., Stout, R. L., Shea, M. T., Yen, S., Grilo, C. M., Sanislow, C. A., Bender, D. S., McGlashan, T. H., Zanarini, M. C., & Gunderson, J. G. (2004). Stressful life events as predictors of functioning: findings from the Collaborative Longitudinal Personality Disorders Study. *Acta Psychiatrica Scandanavia, 110*: 421–429.

Paris, J. (2005). The diagnosis of borderline personality disorder: Problematic but better than the alternatives. *Annals of Clinical Psychiatry, 17*(1), 41–46.

Paris, J. (2003). *Personality disorders over time: Precursors, course, and outcome.* Washington, DC: American Psychiatric Publishing.

Paris, J. (2002). Implications of long-term outcome research for the management of patients with borderline personality disorder. *Harvard Review of Psychiatry, 10,* 315–323.

Piper, W. E., & Joyce, A. S. (2001). Psychosocial treatment outcome. In J. W. Livesley (Ed.), *Handbook of personality disorders: Theory, research, and treatment* (pp. 323–343). New York: Guilford Press.

Robins, C. J., & Chapman, A. L. (2004). Dialectical behavior therapy: Current status, recent developments, and future directions. *Journal of Personality Disorders, 18*(1), 73–89.

Ruocco, A. C. (2005). Reevaluating the distinction between Axis I and Axis II disorders: The case of borderline personality disorder. *Journal of Clinical Psychology, 61*(12), 1509–1523.

Ryle, A. (2004). The contribution of cognitive analytic therapy to the treatment of borderline personality disorder. *Journal of Personality Disorders, 18*(1), 3–35.

Shea, T. M., Stout, R. L., Yesn, S., Pagano, M. E., Skodol, A. E., Morey, L. C., Gunderson, J. G., McGlashan, T. H., Grilo, C. M., Sanislow, C. A., Bender, D. S., & Zanarini, M. C. (2004). Associations in the course of personality disorders and Axis I Disorders over time. *Journal of Abnormal Psychology, 113*(4), 499–508.

Skodol, A. E. (2005). The borderline diagnosis: Concepts, criteria, and controversies. In J. G. Gunderson, P. D. Hoffman (Eds.), *Understanding and treating borderline personality disorder: A guide for professionals and families* (pp. 3–19). Arlington, VA: American Psychiatric Publishing, Inc.

Skodol, A. E., Siever, L. J., Livesley, W. J., Gunderson, J. G., Pfohl, B, & Widiger, T. A. (2002). The borderline diagnosis II: Biology, genetics, and clinical course. *Biological Psychiatry, 51*(12), 951–963.

Soloff, P. H., & Fablo, A. (2008). Prospective predictors of suicide attempts in borderline personality disorder and one, two, and two-to-five-year follow up. *Journal of Personality Disorders, 22*(2), 123–134.

Sperry, L. (2006). Psychopharmacology as an adjunct to psychotherapy in the treatment of personality disorders. Journal of Individual Psychology, 62(3), 324–337.

Stanley, B., Brodsky, B., Nelson, J. D., & Dulit, R. (2007). Brief dialectical behavior therapy (DBT-B) for suicidal behavior and non-suicidal self injury. *Archives of Suicide Research, 11*, 337–371.

Trull, T. J. (2001). Structural relations between borderline personality disorder features and putative etiological correlates. *Journal of Abnormal Psychology, 110*(3), 471–481.

Van Genderen, H., Arntz, A., Drost, J., Sendt, K., & Baumgarten-Kuster, S. (2009). *Schema therapy for borderline personality disorder.* New York: Wiley-Blackwell.

Walsh, J. (2010). *Theories for direct social work practice (2nd ed).* Pacific Grove, CA: Brooks/Cole.

Watson, D., Clark, L. A., & Chmielewski, M. (2008). Structures of personality and their relevance to psychopathology: II. Further articulation of a comprehensive unified trait structure. *Journal of Personality, 76*(6), 1545–1586.

Weissman, M. M. (2006). A brief history of interpersonal psychotherapy. *Psychiatric Annals, 36*(8), 553–557.

Wenzel, A., Chapman, J. E., Newman, C. F., Beck, A. T., & Brown, G. K. (2006). Hypothesized mechanisms of change in cognitive therapy for borderline personality disorder. *Journal of Clinical Psychology, 62*(4), 503–516.

Weston, C. G., & Riolo, S. A. (2007). Childhood and adolescent precursors to adult personality disorders. *Psychiatric Annals, 37*(2), 114–120.

Whaley, A. L. (2001). Cultural mistrust: An important psychological construct for diagnosis and treatment of African Americans. *Professional Psychology: Theory and Practice, 32*(6), 555–562.

Widiger, T. A. (2007). Current controversies in nosology and diagnosis of personality disorders. *Psychiatric Annals, 37*(2), 93–99.

Zanarini, M. C., Frankenburg, F. R., Hennen, J., & Silk, K. R. (2004). Mental health service utilization by borderline personality disorder patients and Axis II comparison subjects followed prospectively for six years. *Journal of Clinical Psychiatry, 65*(1), 28–36.

Zanarini, M. C., Ruser, T. F., Frankenberg, F. R., Hennen, J., & Gunderson, J. G. (2000). Risk factors associated with the dissociative experiences of borderline patients. *Journal of Nervous and Mental Disease, 188*(1), 26–30.

Zanarini, M. C., Yong, L., Frankenberg, F. R., Hennen, J., Reich, D. B., Marino, M. F., et al. (2002). Severity of reported childhood sexual abuse and its relationship to severity of borderline psychopathology and psychosocial impairment among borderline inpatients. *Journal of Nervous and Mental Disease, 190*(6), 381–387.

References for *DSM-IV* Personality Disorders Instruments

Allik, J. (2005). Personality dimensions across cultures. *Journal of Personality Disorders, 19,* 212–232.

Bagby, R. M., & Farvolden, P. (2004). The Personality Diagnostic Questionnaire-4 (PDQ-4). In M. J. Hilsenroth, D. L. Segal, & M. Hersen (Eds.), *Comprehensive handbook of psychological assessment, Vol. 2. Personality assessment* (pp. 122–133). New York: Wiley.

Clark, L. (1993). *Manual for the schedule for nonadaptive and adaptive personality.* Minneapolis: University of Minnesota Press.

Clark, L. A., & Livesley, W. J. (2002). Two approaches to identifying the dimensions of personality disorder: Convergence on the five-factor model. In P. T. Costa & T. A. Widiger (Eds.), *Personality disorders and the five-factor model of personality* (2nd ed., pp. 161–176). Washington, DC: American Psychological Association.

Clark, L. A., Simms, L. J., Wu, K. D., & Casillas, A. (in press). *Manual for the Schedule for Nonadaptive and Adaptive Personality (SNAP-2).* Minneapolis: University of Minnesota Press.

Costa, P. T., & McRae, R. R. (1992). *NEO-PI-R professional manual.* Odessa, FL: Psychological Assessment Resources.

Hyler, S. (1994). *Personality diagnostic questionnaire.* New York: New York State Psychiatric Institute.

Livesley, W. J. (2001). Conceptual and taxonomic issues. In W. J. Livesley (Ed.), *Handbook of personality disorders. Theory, research, and treatment* (pp. 3–38). New York: Guilford.

Livesley, W. J. (2003). Diagnostic dilemmas in classifying personality disorder. In K. A. Phillips, M. B. First, & H. A. Pincus (Eds.), *Advancing DSM. Dilemmas in psychiatric diagnosis* (pp. 153–190). Washington, DC: American Psychiatric Association.

Livesley, W., Jackson, D., & Schroeder, M. (1989). A study of the factorial structure of personality pathology. *Journal of Personality Disorders, 3,* 292–306.

Millon, T., Davis, R., & Millon, C. (1997). Millon Clinical Multiaxial Inventory: I and II. *Journal of Counseling and Development, 70,* 421–426.

Morey, L. (1991). *Personality assessment inventory: Professional manual.* Odessa, FL: Psychological Assessment Resources.

Morey, L. C. & Boggs, C. (2004). The personality assessment inventory (PAI). In M. J. Hilsenroth, D. L. Segal, & M. Hersen (Eds.), *Comprehensive handbook of psychological assessment, Vol. 2. Personality assessment* (pp. 15–29). New York: Wiley.

Widiger, T. (2008). Personality disorders. In J. Hunsley & E. Mash (Eds.), *A guide to assessments that work.* New York: Oxford University Press.

14 Schizophrenia and Other Psychotic Disorders

Schizophrenia is a mental disorder characterized by a person's abnormal patterns of thought and perception, as inferred from his or her language and behavior. The fact that it is primarily a disorder of *thought* distinguishes it from severe disorders of *mood* such as bipolar disorder. Schizophrenia includes two types of symptoms (APA, 2000). *Positive* symptoms represent exaggerations of normal behavior. These include hallucinations, delusions, disorganized thought processes, and tendencies toward agitation. *Hallucinations* are sense perceptions of external objects when those objects are not present. These may be *auditory, visual, gustatory* (the perception of taste), *tactile* (feeling an object), *somatic* (an unreal experience within the body), and *olfactory* (a false sense of smell). *Delusions* are false beliefs that a person maintains even though overwhelmingly contradicted by social reality. They include *persecutory* (people or forces are attempting to bring one harm), *erotomanic* (another person is in love with the individual), *somatic* (pertaining to body functioning), and *grandiose* (an exaggerated sense of power, knowledge, or identity) beliefs, *thought broadcasting* (one's thoughts are overheard by others), *thought insertion* or *withdrawal* (others are putting thoughts into, or taking thoughts out of, one's head), delusions of *being controlled* (thoughts, feelings, or actions are imposed by an external force), and delusions of *reference* (neutral events have special significance for the person). The *negative* symptoms of schizophrenia represent the diminution of what would be considered normal behavior. These include flat or blunted affect (the absence of expression), social withdrawal, noncommunication, anhedonia (blandness) or passivity, and ambivalence in decision making.

Schizophrenia is characterized by at least 6 months of continuous symptoms (APA, 2000). The person must display two or more of the *active* or positive symptoms for at least 1 month. The remainder of the 6 months may feature positive or negative symptoms, and there must also be a decline in the person's social functioning skills. Signs of the disturbance may be limited to negative symptoms during the premorbid (prior to the active phase) or residual (after stabilization from an active phase) periods.

There are five subtypes of schizophrenia (APA, 2000), as follows:

- *Paranoid* schizophrenia features a preoccupation with delusions or auditory hallucinations but a preservation of cognitive functioning and range of mood.
- *Disorganized* schizophrenia is characterized by disorganized speech, behavior, and flat or inappropriate (exaggerated) affect.
- *Catatonic* schizophrenia features disturbances of immobility or excessive mobility, mutism (not speaking), odd gestures, echolalia (repeating the words of others), or echopraxia (repeating the movements of others).
- *Undifferentiated* schizophrenia describes persons who exhibit a range of symptoms but do not meet the criteria for the above three subtypes.
- *Residual* schizophrenia describes persons who display only negative symptoms after an active episode. This may be transient or persist for many years.

The *DSM* also provides six course specifiers for further detailing the client's unique experience with the disorder: *continuous, episodic* with (or with no) interepisode residual symptoms, *single episode* in partial (or full) remission, or *unspecified*. The reader is referred to the *DSM* for the details of these specifiers.

Prevalence

Schizophrenia has an approximate 1% worldwide prevalence (Murray & Jones, 2003). Despite data collection and diagnostic differences, there is remarkable consistency in prevalence among most nations of the world. In some areas the prevalence is very low (the southwest Pacific region) and very high (western Ireland and Croatia, Yugoslavia). Data from the NIMH-sponsored Epidemiological Catchment Area research project noted the lifetime prevalence of schizophrenia to be 1.3% of the United States population (Kessler et al., 2005). The incidence (new cases each year) was estimated at 0.025%–0.05% of the population.

The prevalence of schizophrenia is twice as high in lower as compared to higher socioeconomic classes (Mulvany, O'Callaghan, Takei, Byrne, & Fearon, 2001). The "downward drift" hypothesis holds that many persons who develop schizophrenia lose their occupational and social skills and fall into the lower classes, while others with premorbid personality traits never develop adequate skills to establish themselves in stable social roles. Prevalence differences may also be related to the increased stressors found among persons in lower socioeconomic groups.

Comorbidity

A national comorbidity study found that 79.4% of persons with lifetime nonaffective psychosis (most often schizophrenia) meet the criteria for one or more other disorders (Kessler et al., 2005). These include a mood disorder (most often major depression) (52.6%), anxiety disorders (especially the phobias, posttraumatic stress disorder, and panic disorder) (62.9%), and substance abuse (26.8%). A meta-analysis found that persons with schizophrenia who abuse substances experience fewer negative symptoms than those who are abstinent (Potvin, Sepehry, & Stip, 2006). This suggests either that substance abuse relieves negative symptoms or that persons with fewer negative symptoms are more prone to substance use. Finally, schizophrenia is often comorbid with the schizotypal, schizoid, and paranoid personality disorders (Newton-Howes, Tyrer, North, & Yang, 2007).

Course

Many individuals who develop schizophrenia display what is called *premorbid*, or "early warning" signs. These include a slow, gradual development of symptoms, a loss of interest in life activities, deterioration in self-care, and particularly, social withdrawal (Bechdolf et al., 2006; Tarbox & Pogue-Geile, 2008).These behaviors are often difficult for families and other loved ones to understand. The signs can exist for many years, but when present they do *not* guarantee the eventual onset of schizophrenia. The person may develop instead a *schizoid* or *schizotypal* personality disorder (see Chapter 13), or perhaps no diagnosis.

The age of onset of schizophrenia is between 15 and 40 years. Approximately 10% of persons with schizophrenia experience its initial onset during late childhood and adolescence (Conus, Cotton, Schimmelmann, McCurry, & Lambert, 2007). The disorder is rare before the ages of 11 or 12. Men tend to have their first episodes between the ages of 18 to 26, while this occurs for females between the ages of 26 to 40 years (Seeman, 2003). There is an equal prevalence for males and females, however, and a fairly equal geographical distribution throughout the world. Women tend to have higher levels of premorbid (prepsychotic) functioning, and more positive symptoms, than men do. Women also have a better prognosis with regard to their response to intervention and social functioning potential. Persons with an early age of onset tend to have a poorer premorbid adjustment, more prominent negative symptoms, and more evidence of cognitive impairment (Byrne, Agerbo, & Mortensen, 2002). The duration of schizophrenia is the same regardless of age of onset, although there is a negative correlation between age of onset and chances for a positive outcome.

Persons with schizophrenia are far less likely to marry, both in the years preceding and the years after their first psychotic break (Agerboo, Byrne, Eaton, & Mortensen, 2004). Suicide is the number one cause of premature death in schizophrenia, as 20%–40% of persons attempt suicide at some point in their lives and 5%–10% succeed (Johnson, Gooding, & Tarrier, 2008). The average life span of persons with schizophrenia is approximately 10 years shorter than the national average in the United States, although this is due to lifestyle factors such as diet, physical health, and risks related to poverty rather than neurological features of the disorder (Dixon, Messias, & Wohlheiter, 2006).

Assessment

The assessment of schizophrenia is done though client interviews, interviews with significant others, and history gathering, all of which should cover the following areas:

- Observations or reports of any two of the following symptoms, with at least 1 month's duration: delusions, hallucinations, disorganized speech, grossly disorganized or catatonic behavior, and negative symptoms.
- The duration of active symptoms, to rule out brief reactive psychosis or schizophreniform disorder
- A medical evaluation referral, to rule out any medical conditions that may be contributing to symptom development
- The possibility of major affective, pervasive developmental, obsessive-compulsive, and substance use disorders must be evaluated and ruled out.
- Substance use or abuse, which may be causing or contributing to symptoms
- Psychosocial stressors, which may be contributing to symptom development
- Biological influences will be supported if there are any psychotic or mood disorders among relatives.
- Family system stresses might precipitate an onset of psychotic symptoms.

- The presence of mood swings now or in the client's history might indicate a schizoaffective, major depressive, or bipolar disorder.
- Quality of premorbid functioning may support the presence of a possible schizoptypal, schizoid, or paranoid personality disorder, which raises the risk for schizophrenia.

Schizophrenia must be differentiated from *schizophreniform disorder,* which is similar except for the criterion of duration. That is, if a client has the symptoms of schizophrenia, and the active and residual phases have persisted for more than 1 month but less than 6 months, he or she should receive the latter diagnosis. It may turn out that the client does indeed have schizophrenia, but this cannot be concluded in the absence of the duration criterion. A person with schizophreniform disorder should be given one of two specifiers. The first, *with good prognostic features,* is appropriate if the onset of psychotic symptoms is within 4 weeks of the first noticeable change in the person's behavior, he or she had good prior functioning, and he or she maintains a normal range of mood. Otherwise the *without good prognostic features* specifier is used, and the client is more likely to have schizophrenia.

Schizophrenia must also be differentiated from a similar disorder known as *schizoaffective disorder.* A person with that disorder experiences a continuous period of mental illness featuring symptoms that meet "Criterion A" for schizophrenia that are *concurrent* at some time with either a manic, major depressive, or mixed mood episode (see Chapter 12 for a description of these). Further, the person's delusions or hallucinations must persist for at least 2 weeks in the absence of prominent mood symptoms, and the symptoms of the mood episodes must be present for a substantial portion of the total duration of the illness. In its presentation schizoaffective disorder is in some ways "halfway" between schizophrenia and bipolar disorder (although many theorists place it more closely to the thought disorder). Another way to conceptualize schizoaffective disorder is that it resembles a bipolar disorder that never quite stabilizes.

Risk and Protective Influences for Schizophrenia

Onset

The specific causes of schizophrenia are not known. Most research at present is focused in the genetic and biological areas, but psychological influences cannot be ruled out, particularly with regard to the course of the disorder. The *stress/ diathesis theory* holds that schizophrenia results from a mix of constitutional mechanisms (perhaps 70% due to heritability and biology) and environmental and stress factors (approximately 30%) (Cardno & Murray, 2003). Those external influences, however, are not specific to schizophrenia. They may include insults to the brain, threatening physical environments, emotionally intrusive or demanding experiences, emotional deprivation, and disruptions to cognitive processes. A summary of risk and protective influences for the initial onset of schizophrenia is included in Exhibit 14.1 below.

Biological Influences
Central Nervous System

Biological theories of schizophrenia implicate the brain's limbic system, frontal cortex, and basal ganglia as primary sites of malfunction (Conklin & Iacono, 2003). Whether symptoms result from abnormal development or deterioration of function is not clear. The genetic transmission of schizophrenia is supported by the higher than average risk mechanisms among family members of persons

---

Exhibit 14.1

Risk and Protective Influences for the Onset of Schizophrenia

Risk Influences

Biological

Genetic vulnerability (first-degree relative with a schizophrenia spectrum disorder)
Dopamine hyperactivity
"Small" limbic system in the forebrain
Abnormal brain development during prenatal months
Enlarged ventricles, decreased brain size
Premature birth or maternal bleeding
Age 18–25 for men, 26–40 for women
Maternal exposure to death or other severe stress during first trimester
Premature birth or excess maternal bleeding
Traumatic brain injury
Experience of trauma or victimization
Low socioeconomic status
Family dysfunction, poor parenting

Psychological

Substance use disorder in adolescence
Significant decline in mental status or functioning in adolescence
Suicide attempts
Brief intermittent psychotic symptoms

Environmental

Winter or early spring birth
Maternal virus during first trimester

Psychological

Absence of substance use disorder
Stable mental status and functioning in adolescence
Stable mood
Absence of any psychotic symptoms

Protective Factors

Biological

Normal dopamine activity
No family history of schizophrenia spectrum disorders
Normal-size central nervous system components
Normal prenatal development

Environmental

Summer, fall, late spring season of birth
Healthy maternal pregnancy
Absence of major stressors or traumatic events

---

with the disorder (Cardno & Murray, 2003). A *monozygotic* (identical) twin of a person with schizophrenia has a 47% chance to develop the disorder. A *dyzygotic* (nonidentical) twin has only a 12% likelihood, which is the same probability as a child with one parent with schizophrenia. A non-twin sibling has an 8% chance of developing the disorder. Other risk influences include a maternal history of schizophrenia and affective disorder (Byrne, Agerbo, & Mortensen, 2002).

The age of onset for a child tends to be earlier when the mother has schizophrenia. Further, negative symptoms are frequently seen among nonpsychotic first-degree relatives of people with schizophrenia. In genetically predisposed subjects, the change from vulnerability to developing psychosis may be marked by a reduced size and impaired function of the temporal lobe (Johnstone, Cosway, & Lawrie, 2002). Traumatic brain injury, often cited as a contributing cause of the disorder, increases the chances of schizophrenia in families, but only when there is already a genetic loading (Malapsina et al., 2001).

There is growing evidence for deficiencies in neurological development as causal in schizophrenia. Neuropsychological deficits in attention, verbal memory, and the executive functions of planning, organizing, problem solving, and abstracting are prominent in its etiology (Fatjó-Vilas et al., 2008). Weinberger introduced the neurodevelopment hypothesis of schizophrenia in 1987, using imaging techniques to observe structural brain changes at the onset of the disorder. He believed that a *lesion* (injury), perhaps involving several brain regions, was activated by an unspecified external factor to trigger its onset. Brain imaging techniques have since revealed enlarged ventricles in many persons with schizophrenia that may be a contributing cause through the consequent reduction in brain tissue (Wood et al., 2008).

A variety of other neurodevelopmental phenomena have been hypothesized to account for the onset of schizophrenia (Meinecke, 2001). These include mechanisms of central nervous system development, the quality of neural connections, the manner in which sensory-driven and internal neural activities influence the formation of circuits that underlie brain functions, and the maturation of the prefrontal cortex dopamine system. The dopamine hypothesis, established in the 1960s, asserted that schizophrenia results from an excess of that neurotransmitter in the nervous system (van Os, Rutten, Bart, & Poulton, 2008). More recently, causal roles of other neurotransmitters, including serotonin and norepinephrine, have been proposed. A "two-hit" hypothesis holds that genetic or environmental mechanisms may disrupt early central nervous system development, and these conditions are affected again during neurological changes later in life to produce a "second hit" (Maynard, Siklich, Lieberman, & LaMantia, 2001).

In Utero and Birth Complications
Both brain trauma from birth complications and prenatal viral exposure have also been postulated as causal influences for schizophrenia. A review of

studies that investigated links between obstetrical complications and family history of schizophrenia, age at onset, and gender revealed an association between age of onset and obstetrical complications (Mittal, Ellman, & Cannon, 2008). Persons with an onset before age 22 were 2.7 times more likely to have had a history of obstetrical complications than those with a later age onset, and 10 times more likely to have had a Caesarian birth. There was no association found between obstetric complications and family history of schizophrenia or gender.

The risk of schizophrenia is higher in children whose mothers are exposed to the death of a relative, or to certain other major psychological stresses, during the first trimester of pregnancy (Khashan et al., 2008). Furthermore, there are higher than expected frequencies of prenatal exposure to viruses in individuals who later develop schizophrenia (Kirkpatrick, Herrera Catanedo, & Vazquez-Barquero, 2002). People with schizophrenia tend to be born in winter or early spring, which implies that their mothers were pregnant during a time of year when certain viruses are more prevalent. Postmortem studies show brain abnormalities indicative of developmental problems in the second or third trimester of pregnancy such as altered cell migration in the hippocampus and prefrontal cortex. There is some evidence that persons with schizophrenia who were born in summer months have more negative than positive symptoms (Kirkpatrick et al., 2002).

Psychological Influences

Various psychological theories have been postulated as significant to the development of schizophrenia. Some of these have largely been discredited but are presented here because they remain a strong part of the legacy of the disorder. Freud (1966) placed neurosis and psychosis on a continuum as resulting from similar psychological mechanisms. He wavered, however, between a defense and deficit theory of schizophrenia. The defense theory conceptualized psychotic symptoms as a means of adapting to internal conflict. Deficit theory implied a nonspecific organic defect resulting in one's inability to sustain attachments to others, and instead becoming preoccupied with internal experience.

Developmental theorists assert that mental disorders result from the inability to progress successfully through critical life stages. For example, problems with normal separation from the primary caregiver during the first few years of life may result in schizophrenia if developmental arrests result in an inability to psychologically distinguish the self from others (Mahler, Pine, & Bergman, 1975). The failure to make the transition from adolescence to young adulthood, with its challenges of forming peer relationships, patterning sexual behavior, revising personal values, and developing independent living skills, has also been suggested as producing a regression that may result in schizophrenia (Walker, McMillan, & Mittal, 2007).

Social Influences

Several social risk influences for schizophrenia have been identified in recent studies, although they all assume the presence of an underlying biological vulnerability. The eventual onset of schizophrenia has been linked to childhood trauma and victimization, which produces psychotic symptoms in some young persons as they make the transition to adolescence (De Loore et al., 2007). An epidemiological study found that childhood and adolescent trauma, substance abuse, and suicidal ideation put a person at risk for later schizophrenia (Conus et al., 2007).

Recovery and Adjustment

Complete and permanent remission in schizophrenia is relatively uncommon (van Os et al., 2006), and its course is variable depending on a confluence of risk and protective influences (see Exhibit 14.2). A person with the disorder may experience a chronic course, with symptoms being more or less florid but never really disappearing (the course specifier of "continuous" would be appropriate here), or one in which periods of psychosis are interspersed with periods of remission (full or partial). As with many physical and mental disorders, an accurate prediction of any individual's course is impossible.

Exhibit 14.2

Risk and Protective Influences for the Course of Schizophrenia

Risk Influences	Protective Influences
Poor premorbid adjustment	Later age of onset
Gradual onset (no precipitating events)	Brief duration of active phase
Poor insight about the disorder	Good interepisode functioning (minimal residual symptoms
Prominent negative symptoms	Insight
Delay of intervention	Absence of brain structure abnormalities
Live in large urban area	Family history of mood disorder
Repeated relapses	Early intervention
Medication absence or noncompliance	Active support system
Absence of a support system	Family participation in interventions
Noncompliance with, or absence of, psychosocial interventions	Participation in a range of psychosocial interventions
	Interest in independent living, assistance with activities of daily living

Family Influences

When a person has schizophrenia, a chronic state of emotional burden develops that is shared by all family members (McFarlane, 2002). Common reactions include stress, anxiety, resentment of the impaired member, grief, and depression. Spouses tend to blame each other for family turmoil, and siblings tend to blame parents. There is little time available for family leisure activities and one adult, usually the mother, becomes the primary caretaker of the impaired member. Siblings have some reactions unique from the parents, including emotional constriction in personality development, isolation from peers, and jealousy about the attention given to the impaired member (Smith & Greenberg, 2008).

For the above reasons, the concept of family (or caregiver) expressed emotion (EE) has been prominent in the schizophrenia literature for the past 35 years. It has been operationalized to include ratings of family member hostility toward the ill relative, emotional overinvolvement with the relative, and the degree of warmth with which the relative refers to the client; it also includes frequency counts of critical and positive comments about the client (Kymalainen & Weisman de Mamani, 2008). Low EE family environments are associated with fewer symptom relapses and rehospitalizations than high EE environments are.

As a research measure EE provides one means for determining the kinds of family environments that put the person with schizophrenia at risk of, or keep him or her protected from, symptom relapses. We should add that many family advocacy groups have objected to the EE measure as blaming them for their family member's illness (Mohr, Lafuze,& Mohr, 2000).

Other Social Support

Regarding protective influences, several components of social support have been identified with a better adjustment. Persons with schizophrenia tend to function best with a moderate amount of face-to-face interaction with significant others (Davidson, Harding, & Spaniol, 2005). They respond favorably to attitudes of acceptance, reasonable expectations, opportunities to develop social and vocational skills, and a relatively small number, but broad range, of social supports. These may include family members, friends, neighbors, work peers, school peers, informal community relations, and perhaps members of shared religious groups and organizations (Lenoir, Dingemans, Schene, Hart, & Linszen, 2002).

Social Stigma

For many people, coping with schizophrenia is made more difficult by the stigma they experience caused by other people's negative attitudes and behavior. This social rejection can lead to their social marginalization and low quality of life. The effects of stigma were borne out in a 27-nation study that investigated the nature, direction, and severity of anticipated and experienced discrimination reported by people with schizophrenia (Thornicroft, Brohan,

Rose, Sartorius, & Leese, 2009). The authors reported that negative discrimination was experienced by 47% of the study participants in making or keeping friends, by 43% from family members, by 29% in finding a job, by 29% in keeping a job, and by 27% when pursuing intimate relationships. Anticipated discrimination affected 64% of respondents in applying for work, training, or education, and by 55% who were seeking close relationships. Almost three-quarters (72%) of respondents felt the need to conceal their diagnosis. Finally, a third of participants anticipated discrimination for job seeking and close personal relationships when no discrimination was experienced.

Interventions

Social workers provide services to people with schizophrenia in hospitals, day treatment centers, community mental health centers, private clinics, residential centers, group homes, rehabilitation centers, psychosocial club-houses, and drop-in centers. There is a consensus that the treatment of schizophrenia should always be multimodal and include interventions targeted at specific symptoms as well as the social and educational needs of the client and family. For children as well as adults, intervention should consist of the practitioner's recognition of the phase of the illness (prodromal, acute, recovery, residual, or chronic), medications, and psychosocial interventions (McClellan & Werry, 2000).

Medication

Psychotropic medication is the primary intervention modality for persons with schizophrenia. There is approximately a 66% chance that a person with schizophrenia will respond positively to treatment with an antipsychotic medication (Schatzberg & Nemeroff, 2006). While almost all physicians recommend antipsychotic medication for persons with schizophrenia, there is debate about the effectiveness, long-term adverse effects, and the relative risks and benefits of their use with regard to the consumer's physical and emotional well-being. The major critic of medication practices in the field of social work is David Cohen (2002), who argues that many psychotropic medication studies are methodologically flawed. He concludes that claims of effectiveness are exaggerated and the development of significant adverse effects is underreported. It must be recognized that a majority of people with schizophrenia have difficulty adhering when this has been assessed over a 4-year period (Valenstein, et al., 2006).

The First-Generation Drugs
The first generation of antipsychotic drugs, most popular between the 1950s and 1980s, act primarily by binding to dopamine receptors and blocking its

transmission. The antipsychotic medications differ in their side effect profiles and milligram amounts required in equivalent doses. The first-generation medications are more effective at reducing the positive than the negative symptoms of schizophrenia.

These medications act on all dopamine sites in the brain, but only those in the forebrain produce the symptoms of schizophrenia. Systematic reviews have indicated that the first-generation medications, such as halo-peridol (Joy, Adams, & Lawrie, 2006), are effective, although they have harsh side effect profiles. The effects of dopamine sites in other parts of the brain extend from the midbrain to the basal ganglia, which governs motor activity. A reduction in dopamine in these areas causes adverse effects of *akathisia* (restlessness and agitation), *dystonia* (muscle spasms), *parkinsonism* (muscle stiffness and tremor), and *tardive dyskinesia* (involuntary smooth muscle movements of the face and limbs). *Anticholinergic* medications are often prescribed to combat these effects, even though they have their own adverse effects of blurred vision, dry mouth, and constipation. Adverse effects are a particular concern for older adults who take these medications, as they tend to experience them more acutely (Marriott, Neil, & Waddingham, 2006).

The Second-Generation Drugs

The second-generation antipsychotic medications, available in the United States since the late 1980s, act differently than those developed earlier (Julien, 2001). Clozapine, the first of these, differentially affects the dopamine receptors, as well as having an impact on serotonin and other receptors (Faron-Górecka, Górecki, Kusmider, Wasylewski, & Dziedzicka-Wasylewska, 2008). Clozapine's sites of action are the limbic forebrain and the frontal cortex; thus, it does not carry the risk of adverse effects for the muscular system. In blocking receptors for ser-otonin, it suggests that this neurotransmitter has a role in the production of symptoms. This medication has been limited in use because it carries the possibility of a rare but serious adverse effect of white blood cell depletion (agranulocytosis).

Other new drugs soon followed. Risperidone, introduced in 1994, may have fewer adverse effects than the first-generation drugs (Stahl, 2000). It has an affinity for both dopamine and serotonin receptors, and it supports the hypothesis that the serotonin antagonists diminish many of the adverse effects noted above. Olanzapine is an antagonist of all dopamine receptors, some serotonin receptors, and several other receptors. Sertindole is even more specifically targeted, interacting predominantly with one type of dopamine receptor, but it does not attach to receptors that produce sedative and anticholinergic effects such as dry mouth, blurred vision, and constipa-tion. The actions of the newer drugs (also including aripiprazole, amisul-pride, ziprasidone, and quietapine) cast doubt that any single effect is responsible for their clinical activity (Schatzberg & Nemeroff, 2004).

Further, their somewhat better alleviation of negative symptoms suggests that serotonin antagonist activity is significant in this regard. Systematic literature reviews indicate that the newer medications may provide marginally significant benefits for consumers in terms of clinical improvement over the first-generation antipsychotics (Hunter, Joy, Kennedy, Gilbody, & Song, 2003), and the atypical antipsychotics tend to be equivalent to each other (Gilbody, Bagnall, Duggan, & Tuunainen, 2000). Unfortunately, there may be a small increased risk for diabetes among the second-generation antipsychotics (Smith et al., 2009).

Social Work Roles

Bentley and Walsh (2006) have outlined six roles for social workers with regard to clients using psychotropic medications. In the role of *physician's assistant*, the social worker supports the recommendations of the client's physician regarding medication use. The *consultant/collaborator* performs preliminary screenings to determine clients' possible needs for medication, makes referrals to physicians, and regularly consults with the physician and client. The *advocate* supports the client's expressed wishes regarding medication and presents them to others in the service milieu. The social worker may also *monitor* the positive and negative effects of medication. The *educator* provides clients and significant others with information about issues relevant to medication use, including actions, benefits, and risks. Finally, the *researcher* uses case reports and other research designs to study how medications affect the lives of clients and families and how they interact with other interventions.

Electroconvulsive Therapy

Electroconvulsive therapy (ECT), in which an electric shock is delivered to the client via electrodes applied to the scalp, remains an effective intervention for some persons with schizophrenia. In a systematic review of 26 studies, Tharyan and Adams (2005) found that ECT in combination with antipsychotic drugs is beneficial to people with schizophrenia when rapid global improvement and symptom reduction are desired or the client shows limited response to medication alone. These positive effects are most evident in the short term.

Psychosocial

Despite advances in the pharmacological treatment of schizophrenia, psychosocial interventions are also used in practice and have been tested. These include psychodynamic (Malmberg & Fenton, 2001), supportive therapies (Buckley, Pettit, & Adams, 2007), and life skills programs (Tungpunkom & Nicol, 2008), which unfortunately have not been indicated as helpful in Cochrane

Collaboration reviews. Cognitive and behavioral interventions are based on the premise that current beliefs and attitudes largely mediate a person's affect and behavior (Berlin, 2002). Clients are helped to modify their dysfunctional assumptions about the self, the world, and the future; improve their coping responses to stressful events and life challenges; relabel some psychotic experiences as symptoms rather than external reality; and improve their social skills (Jones, Cormac, Silveira da Mota Neto, & Campbell, 2004). A systematic review of cognitive-behavioral therapy (CBT) studies concluded that while there may be benefits of CBT for the positive symptoms of schizophrenia in the short term, evidence does not support it being advantageous over supportive counseling or standard care (Jones et al., 2004).

Social skills training (SST) is a type of cognitive/behavioral intervention that addresses deficits in interpersonal relating that are frequently found among persons with schizophrenia. A meta-analysis of randomized, control group research studies on this topic was recently conducted by Kurtz and Mueser (2008). Reviewing 22 studies, they concluded that such training was effective, with certain caveats. Clients seem to perform best on tests of the content of the training intervention, but somewhat less well on their transfer of training skills to their activities of daily living. Social skills training also seems to have a mild positive effect on general measures of pathology, although it also must be recognized that because the way the meta-analysis was conducted, effect sizes might have been inflated.

Psychoeducation

The purpose of psychoeducation is to increase the person's knowledge of schizophrenia and its treatment with the goal of enhancing compliance and coping. The intervention can be provided in individual or group formats. In a systematic review of 10 randomized controlled trials, it was found that psychoeducation resulted in greater medication compliance and significantly decreased relapse or readmission rates for participants at 9–18 months follow-up, compared with standard care (Pekkala & Merinder, 2002). The authors emphasize that psychoeducation should comprise only one part of a comprehensive intervention program. Family psychoeducation will be discussed next.

Family Interventions

Family psychoeducation describes interventions that are focused on educating participants about the ill relative's schizophrenia, helping them develop social and resource supports in managing the disorder, and developing coping skills to deal with the related challenge (Griffiths, 2006). Psychoeducation can be provided to single families or to multiple families in groups, and it usually includes the following topics (Dixon et al., 2001; Kopelowicz, Liberman, & Zarate, 2002; SAMHSA, 2009):

- Empathic engagement will all members
- Education about the nature of schizophrenia and how to cope with it
- Family assistance with utilizing available treatments and community resources
- Mutual support provision within the family or group
- Social network enhancement outside the family
- The teaching of stress management techniques
- The teaching of communication and problem-solving skills
- Family member encouragement to pursue their own well-being

When the client is an adult, families tend to be interested in family relationship issues and the client's denial, noncompliance with intervention, and positive symptoms. When the client is an adolescent, families tend to be more concerned about mood and problem behaviors (Polio, North, Reid, Eyrich, & McClendon, 2006). Older adult caregivers in groups want help in permanency planning for their child (Lukens & McFarlane, 2004).

Some family program developers emphasize that the potentially supportive roles of religion and spirituality should be addressed or at least welcomed (Phillips, Larkin, & Paragement, 2002). That is, participants should be encouraged to express their spiritual beliefs and how these affect, or perhaps have been affected by, the presence of chronic mental illness. Further, the issue of leaders being able to appreciate the cultural contexts of families' lives has recently been highlighted as an important component of psychoeducation. Such cultural sensitivity enables the leader to explore member needs and biases and establish a sense of mutuality in goals (Shin, 2004).

Pharoah, Mari, Rathbone, and Wong (2006) conducted a systematic review of the randomized studies done on family intervention in schizophrenia. They concluded that while family interventions may reduce the risk of relapse and improve compliance with medications, differences between family intervention and standard care are modest.

Case Management

Case management is a term used to describe a variety of community-based intervention modalities that attempt to help clients receive a full range of support and rehabilitation services in a timely, appropriate fashion (Rubin, 1992). While practice activities may differ somewhat depending on the setting, they usually include assessment of client needs, strengths, and limitations; planning for appropriate service acquisition; linkage with service providers from various systems; advocacy on behalf of clients with other providers; monitoring of overall service quality; and evaluation (Kanter, 1995). Case management interventions are usually carried out in the context of large community-based programs. It might come as a surprise to learn that case management, however, in a Cochrane Campbell review, did not produce improvement over standard care (Marshall, Gray, Lockwood, & Green, 2000). The authors concluded: "case management is an intervention of questionable value, to the extent that it is doubtful whether it should be offered by community psychiatric services" (Marshall et al., 2000, Abstract).

A specific type of case management, assertive community treatment (ACT), was developed by Stein and Test (1980) in Wisconsin and has since been replicated in many other sites around the world. By 1996 there were 397 such programs in the United States (Mueser, Bond, Drake, & Resnick, 1998). The core characteristics of the ACT model of service delivery are assertive engagement, "in vivo" delivery of services, a multidisciplinary team approach, staff continuity over time, low staff-to-client ratios, and frequent client contacts. Services are provided in the client's home, at shopping malls, places of work, or wherever the client feels comfortable, and services focus on everyday needs. Frequency of contact is variable depending on assessed client need. Staff-to-client ratios are approximately one-to-ten. Other kinds of intensive case management programs share some, but not all, characteristics of the ACT model.

In a systematic review of randomized, controlled studies, ACT reduced hospital readmittance rates, length of time in hospital, and improved housing and employment outcomes over standard community care, although no differences between these types of intervention were found for mental state or social functioning (Marshall & Lockwood, 2000). The studies on case management indicate that while case management itself does not have supportive evidence, ACT as a specific model does. Therefore, social workers responsible for programming for people with severe mental illness should recognize that ACT most likely is the case management program to be promoted.

Crisis Management

Crisis management is based on crisis theory, and it usually involves a multidisciplinary team offering intensive services often on a 24-hour basis. The purpose of crisis intervention is to prevent hospitalization, prevent worsening of symptoms, and help lessen the stress of family members and other caregivers involved in the crisis (Joy, Adams, & Rice, 2006). In a Cochrane Collaboration review of randomized, controlled studies although almost half (45%) of the crisis/home care group were hospitalized and no statistical difference was found between crisis care and hospitalization, repeat admission was avoided and family burden was reduced through crisis care. Furthermore, patients and their families found crisis care more satisfactory.

Vocational Rehabilitation

Vocational rehabilitation is defined as work-related activity that provides clients with pay and the experience of participating in productive social activity. The goals of vocational programs may be full-time competitive employment, any paid or volunteer job, the development of job-related skills, and job satisfaction. There are a couple of different approaches to vocational employment. The first kind is prevocational training, which involves preparation of people before they enter the workforce. The second type, supported employment, involves placing people in employment without such preparation, and in studies supported employment resulted in greater employment at 12 months (34% of people employed compared to 12% of those in prevocational training (Marshall et al., 2003). People of those in supported employment also worked more hours and were paid more per month. Social workers should be aware of these findings and implement supported employment in their settings.

A recent systematic review further suggests that ACT intervention models produce vocational outcomes that are superior to usual treatment (Kirsh & Cockburn, 2007). Of seven randomized controlled trials carried out on this topic, six favored ACT in terms of employment outcomes. The data indicate that one-third to one-half of all clients were working at some time. The authors emphasize that ACT teams who designated a vocational specialist were most successful in this regard. A plateau effect may be associated with this intervention, however, as 64% of clients who participated in ACT for longer than 1 year were employed at some time, while the average rate of employment over a 10-year period was 33%.

Summary

To summarize, schizophrenia is a chronic mental disorder that is not readily responsive to interventions that are based on a desire to return clients to a previous level of social and vocational functioning. The various interventions described here can certainly help clients to experience fewer symptoms and enjoy a higher quality of life, but they remain limited in the scope of their impact. It appears that almost all clients with schizophrenia require long-term intervention to maximize their potential.

Social Diversity

Ethnicity

Schizophrenia tends to be diagnosed among African American persons more frequently than Caucasians. Research suggests, however, that this diagnostic difference results from practitioners attributing and weighing particular observations differently for clients of different races (Trierweiler et al., 2006). That is, clinicians tend to interpret the suspicious attitudes of African American persons as symptomatic of schizophrenia, representing delusions or negative symptoms, rather than learned attitudes for managing uncomfortable situations.

Critique of the Diagnosis

Schizophrenia remains an enigma. While it is among the most disabling of all mental disorders, researchers and clinical practitioners are not able to describe exactly what it is, how it is caused, or how it can be effectively prevented or treated. There is a consensus, however, that its primary causes are biological or hereditary (although there remains some debate about the extent of those influences), and that family and social environments are more significant to its course than its onset. There is also a greater worldwide agreement on its basic symptom profile. Schizophrenia thus appears to be recognized as a "valid" mental disorder, although a more clear differentiation from similar conditions such as schizoaffective disorder and schizotypal personality disorder will further clarify its nature. As more information about its neurobiology is developed, professionals may become able to articulate its core features.

There is some disagreement about the nature of schizophrenia—whether the symptoms represent a single disorder or several disorders. Some theorists write about the *schizophrenia spectrum* disorders, hypothesized to include a range of disorders that may represent different "degrees" of schizophrenia. There include schizoaffective disorder and the schizotypal, paranoid, and schizoid personality disorders (Keefe & Fenton, 2007). A person with the genetic potential for schizophrenia may develop one of these related disorders if environmental conditions are protective. Furthermore, some theorists have called for a reformulation of the diagnosis of schizophrenia along a continuum of characteristics that derive in different ways from a "core" deficit called *schizotaxia*, which is still an unspecified biological condition (Tsuang, Stone, & Faraone, 2000). The current *DSM* formulation, however, while not valid beyond dispute, represents an increase in worldwide reliability over the past 50 years as it corresponds more closely to the *ICD* description.

While it is unlikely that the criteria for schizophrenia will significantly change in *DSM-V*, some theorists and researchers advocate for adjustments. For example, because of the symptomatic overlap between schizophrenia and other disorders that feature psychotic symptoms, some argue for a dimensional diagnostic system that would rate symptom scores and their psychosocial development impact along a continuum (Dutta et al., 2007). Others assert that the diagnostic specificity of the disorder would be enhanced if the presence of cognitive impairment was required in all cases (Keefe & Fenton, 2007).

Case Study

Rachel was a Caucasian 29-year-old, single, unemployed female, living alone, who was referred to the community mental health center following a short-term hospitalization that was prompted by an exacerbation of psychotic symptoms. Rachel had experienced mental illness for 3 years by this time.

Her symptoms included auditory hallucinations, many of which tormented her. She heard the voices of family members (none of whom lived nearby) degrading her as a worthless person doomed to a life of failure. She also heard the voices of angels each night, sometimes being awakened by them as they whispered kindly that she would survive her suffering. Rachel often cried and sometimes screamed for relief when she heard these voices.

Rachel also experienced grandiose and persecutory delusions. She was Jewish and believed herself to be a direct descendant of the Biblical Rachel, which accounted for special status in the eyes of God. She believed that God had appointed her to be the spiritual caretaker of her parents, especially her father, to whom she felt particularly attached. In fact, Rachel's stated purpose in life was to sit quietly and concentrate on their well-being for several hours per day. She believed that this would insure their safety and happiness. Rachel also believed in reincarnation and that she had been repeatedly tortured in previous lives. Most recently she had been put to death in a gas chamber by Nazis during World War II. She often talked about having vivid flashbacks to these events. Interestingly, while Rachel had some negative symptoms of schizophrenia, these were not prominent. She had a full range of emotional expression.

Rachel had not been able to work or maintain social relationships since the onset of her disorder. Her symptoms were continuous and she had no insight into them. The symptoms were not *all* present in her thinking *all* the time, but during the course of each day she experienced some of them. During most of her conversations with other people, even those she did not know well, Rachel shared her preoccupations, believing that they would be readily affirmed. Her anxiety required that she spend much of her time alone, away from the sensory stimulation presented by sounds, colors, and people that tended to overwhelm her. Finally, with her lack of insight, Rachel demonstrated poor judgment in her limited social interactions. She liked men, for example, and would openly seduce them while sharing her bizarre thoughts. This led to their rejection of her, although they sometimes exploited her sexually.

Regarding her history, Rachel had been an energetic, personable child; the second of four children born to a physician and his wife. She was a high academic achiever but also unusually moody, given to temper tantrums and frequent interpersonal conflicts. Despite her wishes to the contrary, Rachel had not maintained any long-term relationships with males as an adolescent or young adult, and she often fought with her best girl friends. Her friends considered her to be demanding and rigid. During adolescence she developed and was treated for anorexia for several years. Rachel later could not recall any causes for that disorder, saying only that she was a "sad and mixed-up kid." Throughout her life she had been on fair terms with her family. She idolized her father but did not get along as well with her mother—they argued often, which was her pattern with most people. She had comfortable, but not close, relationships with her siblings. One sister (who was the only family member living nearby—about 75 miles away) described her as an intelligent, temperamental young woman who could be charming but was often "flaky" and had trouble getting along with most people.

Rachel's psychotic symptoms developed when she was about 25, living away from home at a university where she was trying to complete a bachelor's degree in English. She was working long hours on her thesis when she began hearing voices, at first only at night. These terrified her but she told no one about them. They became worse, occupying her mind to the point that she could no longer concentrate on her schoolwork. Eventually Rachel became so frightened of what was happening that she went to her friends and family and begged them for help. At that point she experienced the first of her three hospitalizations, and she never returned to school or to independent living. At the time of her community mental health center referral she was living on limited funds derived from dwindling family savings and a social security account. A younger brother was helping her manage her money.

Diagnosis

Axis I: Schizophrenia, paranoid type, continuous. (Rachel experiences continuous auditory hallucinations. She also has delusional beliefs about being a descendant of key Biblical figures. These symptoms have been present every day for the past 3 years. She meets the criteria for paranoid type because she has a preoccupation with delusions, some of which are tormenting, while her cognitive functioning and range of mood are relatively intact. Rachel's quality of social functioning has deteriorated significantly from the onset of her active symptoms. She comes from a prominent family but at present is living in a small apartment with little ready cash. Rachel's anorexia is not included on Axis I because it was an adolescent disorder from which she recovered.)

Axis II: None. (Some persons who develop schizophrenia have a premorbid history that suggests a paranoid, schizoid, or schizotypal personality disorder, but this is not true of Rachel.)

Axis III: Agranulocytosis by history. (Rachel had taken the drug clozaril at one time but needed to be switched to another medication because she experienced a depleted white blood cell count.)

Avis IV: Problems related to the social environment. (Rachel is living alone but experiences regular interpersonal stress when she tries to interact with others.)

Axis V: Current GAF = 30; Highest GAF past year = 40. (Her two global assessments of functioning on Axis V reflect Rachel's serious and continuous problems with social, occupational, and leisure functioning but also indicate that she is capable of functioning at a higher level than she is at present. The score of 25 indicates that her behavior is considerably influenced by delusions and hallucinations, she experiences serious impairment in her judgment, and she has difficulties functioning in most areas of her life. At times during the past year the severity of her symptoms was less pronounced, and her level of functioning somewhat higher as a result.)

The Intervention Plan

The following intervention plan was constructed collaboratively by Rachel and her social worker. This accounts for both the client-centered nature of the goals and objectives and the absence of professional terminology. This was an initial plan that would be updated every 3 months, and thus not all of the goals are considered to be long term in nature.

Goal 1: Rachel will develop a comfortable working relationship with the agency social worker.

Objective: Biweekly home visits by the social worker to discuss issues pertinent to Rachel's activities of daily living, including solving problems of concern to the client.

Goal 2: To minimize the distress Rachel experiences when hearing the voices of God and her family.

Objectives:

(a) Monthly meetings with the agency physician for the prescription and monitoring of appropriate medications (Rachel was prescribed the second-generation drug risperidone)

(b) Biweekly monitoring of the effects of the medication as reported by the client and observed by the social worker, including positive effects and any adverse physical effects

(c) Biweekly consultation of the social worker with the physician to keep the physician updated about the medication's effects

Goal 3: For Rachel's parents and siblings to interact with her in ways that are helpful to her recovery and will preserve positive family relationships.

Objectives:

(a) Beginning immediately the social worker will maintain phone contact with parents and other siblings as requested and approved by Rachel to provide them with information about mental illness and its treatment.

(b) To inform all family members within 2 weeks of the county chapters of the National Alliance for the Mentally Ill and the Mental Health Association

(c) To invite Rachel's sister living nearby to attend the agency's regularly scheduled family education and support group, now or at any time while Rachel is a client.

Goal 4: To increase Rachel's level of comfort with social activity
Objectives:

(a) Biweekly meetings with the social worker to discuss and monitor Rachel's social goals and options for meeting people. The social worker will help Rachel select appropriate informal social activities
(b) Referral to formal services such as the agency clubhouse and drop-in center as requested by the client.

Goal 5: To expand the range of Rachel's social network supports
Objectives:

(a) Within 2 weeks the social worker will educate Rachel about the county's Center for Vocational Alternatives and refer her there for vocational assessment if desired.
(b) Rachel will be educated about the county's Schizophrenics Anonymous self-help group within 1 month and be referred for participation if desired.
(c) The social worker will provide Rachel with information about volunteer opportunities in the county as requested.

References

Agerbo, E., Byrne, M., & Eaton, W. W., & Mortensen, P. B. (2004). Marital and labor market status in the long run in schizophrenia. *Archives of General Psychiatry, 61*, 28–33.

American Psychiatric Association. (2000). *Diagnostic and statistical manual of mental disorders* (4th ed., text rev.). Washington, DC: Author.

Bechdolf, A., Phillips, L. J., Francey, S. M., Leicester, S., Morrison, A. P., Veith, V., Klosterkotter, J., & McGorry, P. D. (2006). Recent approaches to psychological interventions for people at risk of psychosis. *European Archives of Psychiatry and Clinical Neuroscience, 256*, 159–173.

Bentley, K. J., & Walsh, J. (2006). *The social worker and psychotropic medication* (3rd ed.). Pacific Grove, CA: Brooks/Cole.

Berlin, S. B. (2002). *Clinical social work practice: A cognitive-integrative perspective.* New York: Oxford.

Byrne, M., Agerbo, E., & Mortensen, P. B. (2002). Family history of psychiatric disorders and age at first contact in schizophrenia: An epidemiological study. *The British Journal of Psychiatry, 181*(43), 19–25.

Cardno, A., & Murray, R. M. (2003). The "classic" genetic epidemiology of schizophrenia.In R. M. Murray & P. B. Jones (Eds.), *The epidemiology of schizophrenia*(pp. 195–219). New York: Cambridge University Press.

Cohen, D. (2002). Research on the drug treatment of schizophrenia: A critical reappraisal and implications for social work education. *Journal of Social Work Education*, *38*(2), 217–239.

Conklin, H. M., & Iacono, W. G. (2003). At issue: Assessment of schizophrenia: Getting closer to the cause. *Schizophrenia Bulletin*, *29*(3), 409–412.

Conus, P., Cotton, S., Schimmelmann, B. G., McGorry, P. D., & Lambert, M. (2007). The first-episode psychosis outcome study: Premorbid and baseline characteristics of an epidemiological cohort of 661 first-episode psychosis patients. *Early Intervention in Psychiatry*, *1*, 191–200.

Davidson, L., Harding, C., & Spaniol, L. (2005). *Recovery from severe mental illnesses: Research evidence and implications for practice, Vol. 1.* Boston: Center for Psychiatric Rehabilitation.

De Loore, E., Drukker, M., Gunther, N., Feron, F., Deboutte, D., Sabbe, B., Mengelers, R., van Os, J., & Myin-Germeys, I. (2007). Childhood negative experiences and subclinical psychosis in adolescence: A longitudinal general population study. *Early Intervention in Psychiatry*, *1*, 201–207.

Dixon, L., McFarlane, W. R., Lefley, H., Lucksted, A., Cohen, M., Falloon, I., Mueser, K., Milkwort, D., Solomon, P., & Sondheim, D. (2001). Evidence-based practices for services to families of people with psychiatric disabilities. *Psychiatric Services*, *52*(7), 903–910.

Dixon, L., Messius, E., & Wohlheiter, K. (2006). Nonpsychiatric comorbid disorders. In J. A. Lieberman, T. S. Stroup, & D. O. Perkins (Eds.), *The American Psychiatric Publishing textbook of schizophrenia* (pp. 383–393). Arlington, VA: American Psychiatric Publishing.

Dutta, R., Greene, T., Addington, J., McKenzie, K., Phillips, M., & Murray, R. M., (2007). Biological, life course, and cross-cultural studies all point toward the value of dimensional and developmental ratings in the classification of psychosis. *Schizophrenia Bulletin*, *33*(4), 868–876.

Faron-Górecka, A., Górecki, A., Kusmider, M., Wasylewski, Z., & Dziedzicka-Wasylewska, M. (2008) The role of D-sub-1-D-sub-2 receptor hetero-dimerization in the mechanism of action of clozapine. *European Neuropsychopharmacology*, *18*(9), 682–691.

Fatjó-Vilas, M., Gourion, D., Campanera, S., Mouaffak, F., Levy-Rueff, M., Navarro, M. E., Chayet, M., Miret, S., Krebs, M. O., & Fañanás, L. (2008). New evidences of gene and environment interactions affecting prenatal neurodevelopment in schizophrenia-spectrum disorders: A family dermatoglyphic study. *Schizophrenia Research*, *103*(1–3), 209–217.

Freud, S. (1966). *Introductory lectures on psychoanalysis.* New York: W. W. Norton.

Gilbody, S. M., Bagnall, A. M., Duggan, L., & Tuunainen, A. (2000). Risperidone versus other atypical antipsychotic medication for schizophrenia. *Cochrane Database of Systematic Reviews*, *3*, Art. No.: CD002306. DOI: 10.1002/14651858.CD002306.

Griffiths, C. A. (2006). The theories, mechanisms, benefits, and practical delivery of psychosocial educational interventions for people with mental health disorders. *International Journal of Psychosocial Rehabilitation*, *11*(1), 21–28.

Hunter, R. H., Joy, C. B., Kennedy, E., Gilbody, S. M., & Song, F. (2003). Risperidone versus typical antipsychotic medication for schizophrenia. *Cochrane Database of Systematic Reviews*, *2*, Art. No.: CD000440. DOI: 10.1002/14651858.CD000440.

Johnson, J., Gooding, P., & Tarrier, N. (2008). Suicide risk in schizophrenia: Explanatory models and clinical implications, the Schematic Appraisal Model of Suicide (SAMS). *Psychology and Psychotherapy: Theory, Research and Practice, 81*(1), 55–77.

Johnstone, E. C., Cosway, R., & Lawrie, S. M. (2002). Distinguishing characteristics of subjects with good and poor early outcome in the Edinburgh high-risk study. *The British Journal of Psychiatry, 181*(43), s26–s29.

Jones, C., Cormac, I., Silveira da Mota Neto, J. I., & Campbell, C. (2004). Cognitive behaviour therapy for schizophrenia. *Cochrane Database of Systematic Reviews, 4*, Art. No.: CD000524. DOI: 10.1002/14651858.CD002305.

Joy, C., Adams, C., & Rice, K. (2006). Crisis intervention for people with severe mental illnesses. *Cochrane Database of Systematic Reviews, 4*, CD001087.

Joy, C. B., Adams, C. E., & Lawrie, S. (2006). Haloperidol versus placebo for schizophrenia. *Cochrane Database of Systematic Reviews, 4*, Art. No.: CD003082. DOI: 10.1002/14651858.CD000524.

Julien, R. M. (2001). *A primer of drug action: A concise, nontechnical guide to the actions, uses, and side effects of psychoactive drugs* (9th ed.). New York: W. H. Freeman.

Kanter, J. (1995). Case management with long term patients: A comprehensive approach. In S. Soreff (Ed.), *Handbook for the treatment of the seriously mentally ill* (pp. 169–189). Seattle, WA: Hogrefe and Humber.

Keefe, R. S., & Fenton, W. S. (2007). How should DSM-V criteria for schizophrenia include cognitive impairment? *Schizophrenia Bulletin, 33*(4), 912–920.

Kessler, R. C., Birnbaun, H., Demler, O., Falloon, I. R., Gagnon, E., Guyer, M., Howes, J., Kendler, K. S., Shi, L., Walters, E., & Wu, E. Q. (2005). The prevalence and correlates of nonaffective psychosis in the national comorbidity survey replication. *Biological Psychiatry, 58*(8), 668–676.

Khashan, A. S., Abel, K. M., McNamee, R., Pedersen, M. G., Webb, R. T., Baker, P. N., Kenny, L. C., & Mortensen, P. B. (2008). High risk of offspring schizophrenia following antenatal maternal exposure to severe adverse life events. *Archives of General Psychiatry, 65*(2), 146–152.

Kirkpatrick, B., Herrera Catanedo, S., & Vazquez-Barquero, J. (2002). Summer birth and deficit schizophrenia: Cantabria, Spain. *Journal of Nervous and Mental Disease, 190*(8), 526–532.

Kirsh, B., & Cockburn, L. (2007). Employment outcomes associated with ACT: A review of ACT literature. *American Journal of Psychiatric Rehabilitation, 10*(1), 31–51.

Kopelowicz, A., Liberman, R. P., & Zarate, R. (2002). Psychosocial treatments for schizophrenia. In P. E. Nathan & J. M. Gorman (Eds.), *A guide to treatments that work* (pp. 201–226). New York: Oxford.

Kurtz, M. M., & Mueser, K. T. (2008). A meta-analysis of controlled research on social skills training for schizophrenia. *Journal of Consulting and Clinical Psychology, 76*(3), 491–504.

Kymalainen, J. A., & Weisman de Mamani, A. G. (2008) Expressed emotion, communication deviance, and culture in families of patients with schizophrenia: A review of the literature. *Cultural Diversity and Ethnic Minority Psychology, 14*(2), 85–91.

Lenoir, M. E., Dingemans, P., Schene, A. H., Hart, A. A., & Linszen, D. H. (2002). The course of parental expressed emotion and psychotic episodes after family intervention in recent-onset schizophrenia: A longitudinal study. *Social Psychiatry and Psychiatric Epidemiology, 39*(2), 69–75.

Lukens, E. P., & McFarlane, W. R. (2006). Psychoeducation as evidence-based practice: Considerations for practice, research, and policy. In A. R. Roberts & K. R. Yeager (Eds.), *Foundations of evidence-based social work practice* (pp. 291–313). New York: Oxford.

Mahler, M. S., Pine, F., & Bergman, A. (1975). *The psychological birth of the human infant.* New York: Basic Books.

Malaspina, D., Goetz, R. R., Friedman, J. H., Kaufmann, C. A., Faraone, S. V., Tsuang, M., et al. (2001). Traumatic brain injury and schizophrenia in members of schizophrenia and bipolar disorder pedigrees. *The American Journal of Psychiatry, 158*(3), 440–446.

Malmberg, L., & Fenton, M. (2001). Individual psychodynamic psychotherapy and psychoanalysis for schizophrenia and severe mental illness. *Cochrane Database of Systematic Reviews, 3,* Art. No.: CD001360. DOI: 10.1002/14651858.CD001360.

Marriott, R. G., Neil, W., & Waddingham, S. (2006). Antipsychotic medication for elderly people with schizophrenia, *Cochrane Database of Systematic Reviews, 1,* Art. No.: CD005580. DOI: 10.1002/14651858.CD005580.

Marshall, M., Crowther, R., Almaraz-Serrano, A. M., Creed, F., Sledge, W. H., Kluiter, H., Roberts, C., Hill, E,. & Wiersma, D. (2003). Day hospital versus admission for acute psychiatric disorders. *Cochrane Database of Systematic Reviews* 2003, Issue 1. Art. No.: CD004026. DOI: 10.1002/14651858.CD004026.

Marshall, M., Gray, A., Lockwood, A., & Green, R. (2000). Case management for people with severe mental disorders. *Cochrane Database of Systematic Review, 2,* CD000050.

Marshall, M. & Lockwood, A. (2000). Assertive community treatment for people with severe mental disorders. *Cochrane Database of Systematic Review, 2,* CD001089.

Maynard, T. M., Siklich, L., Lieberman, J. A., & La Mantia, A. S. (2001). Neural development, cell-cell signaling, and the "two-hit" hypothesis of schizophrenia. *Schizophrenia Bulletin, 27*(3), 457–476.

McClellan, J., & Werry, J. (2000). Summary of the practice parameters for the assessment and treatment of children and adolescents with schizophrenia. *Journal of the American Academy of Child and Adolescent Psychiatry, 39*(12), 1580–1582.

McFarlane, W. R., (2002). *Multifamily groups in the treatment of severe psychiatric disorders.* New York: Guilford.

Meinecke, D. L. (2001). Editor's introduction: The developmental etiology of schizophrenia hypothesis: What is the evidence? *Schizophrenia Bulletin, 27*(3), 335–336.

Mittal, V. A., Ellman, L. M., & Cannon, T. D. (2008) Gene-environment interaction and covariation in schizophrenia: The role of obstetric complications. *Schizophrenia Bulletin, 34*(6), 1083–1094.

Mohr, W. K., Lafuze, J. E., & Mohr, B. D. (2000). Opening caregiver minds: National Alliance for the Mentally Ill's (NAMI) Provider Education Program. *Archives of Psychiatric Nursing, 14*(5), 235–243.

Mueser, K. T., Bond, G. R., Drake, R. E., & Resnick, S. G. (1998). Models of community care for severe mental illness: A review of research on case management. *Schizophrenia Bulletin, 24,* 37–74.

Mulvany, F., O'Callaghan, E., Takei, N., Byrne, M., & Fearon, P. (2001). Effects of social class at birth on risk and presentation of schizophrenia: Case-control study. *British Medical Journal, 323*(7326), 1398–1401.

Murray, R. M., & Jones, P. B. (Eds.). (2003). *The epidemiology of schizophrenia*. New York: Cambridge University Press.

Newton-Howes, G., Tyrer, P., North, B., & Yang, M. (2008). The prevalence of personality disorder in schizophrenia and psychotic disorders: systematic review of rates and explanatory modeling. *Psychological Medicine, 38*, 1075–1082.

Pekkala, E. & Merinder, L., (2002). Psychoeducation for schizophrenia. *Cochrane Database of Systematic Reviews, 2*, Art. No.: CD002831. DOI: 10.1002/14651858. CD002831.

Pharoah, F., Mari, J., Rathbone, J., & Wong, W. (2006). Family intervention for schizophrenia. *Cochrane Database of Systematic Reviews, 4*, Art. No.: CD000088. DOI: 10.1002/14651858.CD000088.

Pollio, D. E., North, C. S., & Reid, D. L., Eyrich, K. M., & McClendon, J. R. (2006). Differences in problems faced by families with a child coping with a serious emotional disorder or an adult member coping with mental illness. *Journal of Social Service Research, 32*(4), 83–98.

Potvin, S., Sepehry, A. A., & Stip, E. (2006). A meta-analysis of negative symptoms in dual diagnosis schizophrenia. *Psychological Medicine, 36*(4), 431–440.

Rubin, A. (1992). Case management. In S. M. Rose (Ed.), *Case management and social work practice* (pp. 5–24). New York: Longman.

Schatzberg, A. F., & Nemeroff, C. B. (Eds.). (2006). *Essentials of clinical psychopharmacology (2nd ed.).* Washington, DC: American Psychiatric Press.

Seeman, M. V. (2003). Gender differences in schizophrenia across the life span. In C. I. Cohen (Ed.), *Schizophrenia into later life: Treatment, research, and policy* (pp. 141–154). Washington, DC: American Psychiatric Publishing.

Smith, M., Hopkins, D., Peveler, R., Holt, R., Woodward, M., & Ismail, K. (2009). First- v. second-generation antipsychotics and risk for diabetes in schizophrenia: Systematic review and meta-analysis. *British Journal of Psychiatry, 192*, 406–411.

Smith, M. J., & Greenberg, J. S. (2008) Factors contributing to the quality of sibling relationships for adults with schizophrenia. *Psychiatric Services, 59*(1), 57–62.

Stahl, S. M. (2000). *Essential psychopharmacology: Neuroscientific basis and practical applications* (2nd ed.). New York: Cambridge University Press.

Substance Abuse and Mental Health Services Administration. (2009). *Evidence-based practices: Shaping mental health services toward recovery.* Retrieved April 1, 2009, from http://www.innovations.ahrq.gov/content.aspx?id=313

Stein, L. I., & Test, M. A. (1980). Alternative mental hospital treatment: I. Conceptual model, treatment program, and clinical evaluation. *Archives of General Psychiatry, 37*, 392–397.

Tarbox, S. I., & Pogue-Giele, M. F. (2008). Development of social functioning in preschizophrenic children and adolescents: A systematic review. *Psychological Bulletin, 34*(4), 561–583.

Tharyan, P. & Adams, C. E. (2005). Electroconvulsive therapy for schizophrenia. *Cochrane Database of Systematic Reviews, 2*, Art. No.: CD000076. DOI: 10.1002/ 14651858.CD000076.

Thornicroft, G., Brohan, E., Rose, D., Sartorius, N., & Leese, M. (2009) Global pattern of experienced and anticipated discrimination against people with schizophrenia: A cross-sectional survey. *The Lancet, 373*(9661), 408–415.

Trierweiler, S. J., Neighbors, H. W., Munday, C., Thompson, E. E., Jackson, J. S., & Binion, V. J. (2006). Differences in patterns of symptom attribution in diagnosing schizophrenia between African American and non-African American clinicians. *American Journal of Orthopsychiatry, 76*(2), 154–160.

Tsuang, M. T., Stone, W. S., & Faraone, S. (2000). Toward reformulating the diagnosis of schizophrenia. *American Journal of Psychiatry, 157*(7), 1041–1050.

Tungpunkom, P. & Nicol, M. (2008). Life skills programmes for chronic mental illness. *Cochrane Database of Systematic Reviews, 2,* Art. No.: CD000381. DOI: 10.1002/14651858.CD000381.

Valenstein, M., Ganoczy, D., McCarthy, J. F., Kim, H., Lee, T. A., & Blow, F. C. (2006). Antipsychotic adherence over time among patients receiving treatment for schizophrenia: a retrospective review. *Journal of Clinical Psychiatry, 67,* 1542–1550.

Van Os, J., Burns, T., Cavallaro, R., Leucht, S., Peuskens, J., Helldin, L., Bernardo, M., Arango, C., Fleischhacker, W., Lachaux, B., & Kane, J. M. (2006). Standar-dized remission criteria in schizophrenia. *Acta Psychiatrica Scandinavica, 113*(2), 91–95.

Van Os, J., Rutten, Bart, P. F., & Poulton, R. (2008). Gene-environmental interactions in schizophrenia: Review of epidemiological findings and future directions. *Schizophrenia Bulletin, 34*(6), 1066–1082.

Walker, E. F., McMillan, A., & Mittal, V. (2007) Neurohormones, neurodevelopment, and the prodrome of psychosis in adolescence. In D. Romer & E. F. Walker (Eds.), *Adolescent psychopathology and the developing brain: Integrating brain and prevention science* (pp. 264–283). New York: Oxford University Press.

Wood, S. J., Pantelis, C., Velakoulis, D., Yücel, M., Fornito, A., & McGorry, P. D. (2008). Progressive changes in the development toward schizophrenia: Studies in subjects at increased symptomatic risk. *Schizophrenia Bulletin, 34*(2), 322–329.

Appendix: Measures for Schizophrenia

Ratings on norms, validity, and reliability are from Hunsley and Mash (2008).

The Brief Psychiatric Rating Scale (BPRS) (Andersen et al., 1989; Overall & Gorman, 1962)

Description
- Measures symptom changes in persons with schizophrenia
- Not a diagnostic tool but provides a clinical profile at a single point in time.
- Several versions exist; the best known includes 18 items, each rated on a 7-point scale.
- Includes 12 items specific to schizophrenia and six for depression

- Constructed for measuring symptoms of schizophrenia, but along with the depression items may also be considered a schizoaffective scale
- Scores may be obtained for the four domains of thinking disturbance, withdrawal/retardation, hostility/suspicion, and anxiety/depression.
- Includes recommended cut-off scores for evaluating the severity of symptoms.
- The practitioner assesses most client symptoms at the time of the interview, but six items may be scored on the basis of conditions during the prior 3 days.
- Requires 30 minutes to administer; it does not include a standard interview protocol
- For case conceptualization and treatment planning, norms and clinical utility rated adequate, and the instrument was highly recommended (Hafkenscheid, 1993; Hedlund & Vieweg, 1980; Lukoff, Nuechterlein, & Ventura, 1986; Overall & Gorham, 1962).

Reliability
- Spearman intraclass coefficients of seven raters was .74 to .83.
- For case conceptualization and treatment planning, internal consistency rated good, interrater reliability rated excellent, and test-retest reliability was adequate (Hafkenscheid, 1993; Hedlund & Vieweg, 1980; Lukoff et al., 1986; Overall & Gorham, 1962).

Validity
- Concurrent validity with one other rating scale (475 respondents) was .93.
- For case conceptualization and treatment planning, content validity was rated adequate, construct validity was rated good, and validity generalization was rated excellent (Hafkenscheid, 1993; Hedlund & Vieweg, 1980; Lukoff et al., 1986; Overall & Gorham, 1962).

The Positive and Negative Syndrome Scale for Schizophrenia (Kay, Fiszbein, & Opler, 1987)

Description
- Practitioner-administered 30-item scale measures positive and negative symptoms of schizophrenia and general psychopathology
- Includes 18 items adapted from the BPRS and 12 additional items
- Each item includes a definition and anchoring criteria for the 7-point ratings.
- Ratings are based on information specific to a time period, usually the previous week. The practitioner derives information primarily from

the clinical interview but may utilize input from other professionals and family members.

- The 30–40 minute semiformal interview consists of four prescribed phases: rapport development; probes of pathology; questions about mood, anxiety, orientation, and reasoning; and probes for areas where the client seems ambivalent.
- For case conceptualization and treatment planning, norms were rated adequate, clinical utility rated adequate, and the instrument was highly recommended (Kay et al., 1987).

Reliability

- Cronbach's alphas = .73 for the positive symptom subscale, .83 for the negative symptom subscale, and .79 for the general psychopathology subscale.
- For case conceptualization and treatment planning, internal consistency rated good, interrater reliability was excellent, and test-retest reliability was adequate (Kay et al., 1987).

Validity

- Construct validity was supported by the inverse correlation of the positive and negative subscale scores.
- Criterion validity was supported by the relationship of the scale to a variety of external client variables, including history of pathology, family history, cognitive functioning, affective functioning, and subscale scores from the Brief Psychiatric Rating Scale.
- For case conceptualization and treatment planning, content validity was rated adequate, and construct validity and validity generalization rated excellent (Kay et al., 1987).

The Scale for the Assessment of Negative Symptoms (SANS) and the Scale for the Assessment of Positive Symptoms (SAPS) (Andreasen, 1982; Andreasen & Olsen, 1982)

Description

- The SANS is a 25-item instrument rated along a 6-point scale with five subscales for affect, poverty of speech, apathy, anhedonia, and impairment of attention.
- The SAPS is a 35-item instrument with four subscales that measure hallucinations, delusions, bizarreness, and positive thought disorder, and one global measure of affect.
- Subscales for both instruments include a global rating index.
- Symptom ratings are to be considered within a time frame of 1 month.

- The SANS and SAPS are designed to be used by a practitioner in conjunction with client interviews, clinical observations, family member observations, reports from professionals, and client self-report.
- For case conceptualization and treatment planning, SANS norms were rated adequate and clinical utility rated adequate (Andreasen, 1981, 1984; Mueser, Sayers, Schooler, Mance, & Haas, 1994; Vadhan, Serper, Harvey, Chou, & Cancro, 2001).

Reliability
- Internal consistency for total scores was .90 for the SANS and .86 for the SAPS.
- Intraclass correlations produced reliability scores averaging .83 to .92 for the global summary and total scores for both instruments.
- Internal consistency for the global summary scores was .47 for the SANS and .58 for the SAPS.
- Test-retest reliability over a 2-year period ranged between .40 and .50.

Validity
- For case conceptualization and treatment planning, SANS internal consistency rated good, interrater reliability rated excellent, and test-retest reliability was adequate (Andreasen, 1981, 1984; Mueser et al., 1994; Vadhan et al., 2001).
- Factor analysis indicated that the two instruments measure fairly independent dimensions of symptomatology.
- Criterion validity was supported by the fact that outpatient subjects had less severe positive and negative symptomatology than inpatients did, and persons without schizophrenia had fewer symptoms than either group.
- For case conceptualization and treatment planning, SANS content validity was rated adequate and construct validity and validity generalization rated excellent (Andreasen, 1981, 1984; Mueser et al., 1994; Vadhan et al., 2001).

Quality of Life Scale (QLS) (Heinrichs, Hanlon, & Carpenter, 1984)

Description
- Twenty-one items
- Designed to assess the deficit syndrome concept in individuals with schizophrenia
- Includes four domains: interpersonal functioning, instrumental role functioning, intrapsychic factors, and possession of common objects/participation in common activities.

- Designed as a research interview
- For diagnosis, norms and clinical utility rated adequate (Heinrichs et al., 1984).

Reliability
For diagnosis, internal consistency rated good, interrater reliability was excellent and test-retest reliability was adequate (Glynn et al., 2002; Heinrichs et al., 1984).

Validity
For diagnosis, content validity was rated adequate, construct validity was rated good, and validity generalization was rated excellent (Glynn et al., 2002; Heinrichs et al., 1984).

References for Assessment Instruments for Schizophrenia

Andersen, J., Larsen, J. K., Schultz, V., Nielsen, B. M., Korner, A., Behnke, K., et al. (1989). The brief psychiatric rating scale: Dimension of schizophrenia—reliability and construct validity. *Psychopathology, 22*, 168–176.

Andreasen, N. C. (1981). *Scale for the Assessment of Negative Symptoms (SANS)*. Iowa City: University of Iowa.

Andreasen, N. C. (1982). Negative symptoms of schizophrenia: Definition and reliability. *Archives of General Psychiatry, 39*, 784–788.

Andreasen, N. C. (1984). *Modified Scale for the Assessment of Negative Symptoms.* Bethesda, MD: US Department of Health and Human Services.

Andreasen, N. C., & Olsen, S. (1982). Negative vs. positive schizophrenia: Definition and validation. *Archives of General Psychiatry, 39*, 789–794.

Glynn, S. M., Marder, S. R., Liberman, R. P., Blair, K., Wirshing, W. C., Wirshing, D. A., et al. (2002). Supplementing clinic-based skills training with manual-based community support sessions: Effects on social adjustment of patients with schizophrenia. *American Journal of Psychiatry, 159*, 829–837.

Hafkenscheid, A. (1993). Reliability of a standardized and expanded Brief Psychiatric Rating Scale: A replication study. *Acta Psychiatrica Scandinavica, 88*, 305–310.

Hedlund, J. L. & Vieweg, B. W. (1980). The Brief Psychiatric Rating Scale (BPRS): A comprehensive review. *Journal of Operational Psychiatry, 11*(1), 48–65.

Heinrichs, D. W., Hanlon, T. E., & Carpenter, W. T. (1984). The Quality of Life Scale: An instrument for rating the schizophrenia deficit syndrome. *Schizophrenia Bulletin, 10*, 388–396.

Hunsley, J., & Marsh, E. J. (Eds.) (2008). *A guide to assessments that work.* New York: Oxford University Press.

Kay, S. R., Fiszbein, A., & Opler, L. A. (1987). The positive and negative syndrome scale for schizophrenia. *Schizophrenia Bulletin, 13*(2), 261–275.

Lukoff, D., Nuechterlein, K. H., & Ventura, J. (1986). Manual for the expanded Brief Psychiatric Rating Scale (BPRS). *Schizophrenia Bulletin, 12*, 594–602.

Mueser, K. T., Sayers, S. L., Schooler, N. R., Mance, R. M., & Haas, G. L. (1994). A multisite investigation of the reliability of the Scale for the Assessment of Negative Symptoms. *American Journal of Psychiatry, 151*, 1453–1462.

Overall, J. E., & Gorman, D. R. (1962). The Brief Psychiatric Rating Scale. *Psychological Reports, 10*, 799–812.

Vadhan, N. P., Serper, M. R., Harvey, P. D., Chou, J. C., & Cancro, R. (2001). Convergent validity and neuropsychological correlates of the Schedule for the Assessment of Negative Symptoms (SANS) attention subscale. *Journal of Nervous and Mental Disease, 189*, 637–641.

PART IV

Disorders With Onset in the Elderly

15 Cognitive Disorders

Cognition can be defined as conscious thinking processes—mental activities of which people are aware. Cognitive *processes* include a person's taking in relevant information from the environment, synthesizing that information, and formulating a plan of action based on that synthesis (Tucker-Drob, Johnson, & Jones, 2009). Cognitive *disorders* are characterized by deficits in a person's thought processes or memory that are due to brain dysfunction and represent a significant decline from the previous level of functioning (American Psychiatric Association, 2000). This chapter focuses on two highly debilitating cognitive disorders classified as *dementias* that are experienced mostly by older adults: Alzheimer's disease (AD) and vascular dementia (VaD). Both are *degenerative* disorders, meaning they involve a progressive decline in the number of functioning neurons in the person's central nervous system. These disorders are *not* a normal part of the aging process. Before considering AD and VaD in detail, we will review the concept of dementia in general and briefly describe the other *DSM* cognitive disorders.

Dementia

Besides AD and VaD, there are many other types of dementias that stem from identifiable medical conditions (APA, 2000). These include dementias from long-term substance abuse and HIV disease, head trauma, Parkinsons disease (affecting movement), Huntington's disease (affecting cognition, emotion, and movement), Pick's disease (affecting personality, language, social skills, emotions, and behavior), and Creutzfeldt-Jacob's disease (a "slow virus" that produces the symptoms of dementia).

Memory impairment is *always* required to make a diagnosis of dementia. Other prominent symptoms may include (APA, 2000) the following:

- Aphasia: loss of the ability to use words appropriately
- Apraxia: loss of the ability to use common objects correctly
- Agnosia: loss of the ability to understand sound and visual input
- Loss of executive functioning: an inability to plan, organize, follow sequences, and think abstractly

Old age is often falsely stereotyped as a stage of life that includes high rates of dementia. In fact, only 5% of people between the ages of 65 and 80 have severe dementia, with another 15% having a mild form of the condition (Ruitenberg, Ott, van Swieten, Hofman, & Breteler, 2001). Twenty percent of people over 80 have severe dementia, and its highest prevalence occurs above the age of 85. Dementia is rare among children and adolescents, but it can occur at any age as the result of certain medical conditions (APA, 2000). A diagnosis of dementia does not imply an unremitting downward course. There are a variety of reversible dementias, such as those due to pernicious anemia, brain tumors, hypothyroidism, infections, and nutritional deficiencies.

A *DSM* diagnosis of dementia can be coded as *uncomplicated* (without delusions, delirium, or depression), *with delusions, with depression,* or *with delirium*. Approximately 30% to 40% have delusions (often persecutory), 20% to 30% experience hallucinations (primarily with AD) and 40% to 50% of people with dementia experience symptoms of anxiety and depression, with 10% to 20% qualifying for a major depressive disorder (Altman, 2001).

The onset of dementia presents a person with profound challenges related to quality of life. Research on early-stage dementia is mainly in the domain of biological etiology, but in one meta-synthesis of qualitative research the experience of living with dementia was investigated (Steeman, Decasterle, Godderis, & Grypdonck, 2006). Studies show that memory loss often immediately threatens one's perceptions of security, autonomy, and being a meaningful member of society. At early stages of memory loss, individuals use self-protecting strategies such as denial and overestimating their cognitive abilities to deal with perceived changes. The memory impairment itself may make it difficult for an individual to deal with these changes, however, which causes frustration, uncertainty, and fear. Most people regard their difficulties as part of normal ageing, and one-third view their condition as stable or improving (Clare, Goater, & Woods, 2006). Almost all persons described some positive coping strategies, but participants who believed that nothing could be done to help were more likely to experience significant depression or anxiety.

Behavior problems are the leading reason family members seek medical intervention on behalf of a person with dementia (Finkel, 2001). The following is a list of behaviors that may be evidenced by such persons. Not all people exhibit all of these behaviors, and they occur with varying degrees of severity:

- Perceptual disturbances, including delusions (false beliefs), hallucinations (false sense perceptions), and the misidentification of people
- Mood disturbances (depression and apathy)
- Wandering and other dangerous or careless behavior
- Agitation or rage (including restlessness, hostile behavior, or screaming)
- Sleep disturbances (insomnia or disruptions in sleep rhythm)
- Distressing repetitive behavior
- Inappropriate sexual behavior (fondling, touching, masturbation, verbal remarks)
- Incontinence
- Refusal to eat

Other Cognitive Disorders

The *DSM-IV-TR* includes two types of cognitive disorders in addition to the dementias. *Delirium* is the most common cognitive disorder and the least debilitating. It is defined as any disturbance in a person's consciousness and cognitive ability that develops and persists during a short time period (just hours or days) (APA, 2000). A person with delirium experiences impairment in his or her awareness of the environment and a reduced ability to focus, sustain, or shift attention. The disorder may be characterized by impairments in orientation, the capacity to discriminate sensory input, and the ability to integrate present with past experiences, as well as rambling or incoherent speech and unwarranted expressions of fear. Delirium has a brief, fluctuating course and resolves rapidly when its cause is identified and treated. The symptoms generally recede in 3 to 7 days, although sometimes the process can take up to 2 weeks.

Unlike dementia, delirium originates outside the central nervous system. Its possible causes include metabolic and cardiovascular illnesses, electrolyte imbalances, the physical stress of surgery and postoperative pain, fever (children with high fevers commonly develop short-term delusions), infection, blood loss, insomnia, side effects or toxicity from some medications, intoxication, and alcohol withdrawal. Risk influences for the disorder include older age, preexisting brain damage or sensory impairment, alcohol dependence, diabetes, malnutrition, and a history of delirium (Schofield, 2008).

The *amnestic disorders* feature impairments of memory that do not include any other type of cognitive difficulty (Isenberg, 2005). They are relatively uncommon and are associated with the effects of substance abuse and various medical conditions. Unlike delirium, the amnestic disorders may result in temporary or permanent memory impairment, depending on the cause. Some people with the disorder develop a tendency to confabulate; that is, they attempt to fill in their memory gaps by making up information that they hope is true.

Transient forms of the amnestic disorders, with full recovery, can develop from epilepsy, the side effects of electroconvulsive therapy and some medications, thiamine deficiency, and hypoxia (temporary oxygen loss) (Vinters, 2006). Permanent amnesia may result from head trauma, carbon monoxide poisoning, cerebral infarction (cell death in certain areas of the brain due to an obstruction of blood flow), hemorrhage (internal bleeding), and brain swelling related to herpes simplex.

Some symptoms of dementia and delirium are similar, but the two types of disorders can be differentiated by their course (Wells & Whitehouse, 2000). The symptoms of delirium fluctuate and are short term, whereas the symptoms of dementia are relatively stable or deteriorating. Amnestic disorder is characterized by memory impairment only, without any other significant cognitive difficulty.

Alzheimer's Disease

Alzheimer's disease, the most common form of dementia, is characterized by the development of cognitive deficits resulting from a diffuse atrophy (wasting away) of tissue in several areas of the brain (Cummings & Cole, 2002). Fifty percent to 60% of people with dementia have AD, the most common form of dementia worldwide (Suh & Shah, 2001). It is named after a nineteenth-century German physician, Alois Alzheimer, who first formally described the disease in a published case study.

Prevalence

Prevalence estimates for AD range from 1.4% to 1.6% for people age 65 to 69 years, rising to 16% to 25% for those over 85 years old (APA, 2000). Approximately 5 million Americans were diagnosed with AD in 2001, and the number may rise to 15 million (34 million worldwide) by 2050 if effective forms of prevention and treatment are not found. The average age of diagnosis is 80 years, and the symptom of memory loss affects nearly 50% of people over the age of 85 with various levels of severity (Boise, Neal, & Kaye, 2004). More than half of persons with AD receive care in their homes.

Comorbidity

The most common observable symptoms of AD are apathy (found in 72% of persons), agitation and aggression (60%), anxiety (48%), and depression (48%)

(Waldemer et al., 2007). Ten percent to 20% qualify for a diagnosis of major depressive disorder. Depression in AD presents somewhat differently than "typical" depression, however, featuring the symptoms of poor motivation, delusions, anxiety, and agitation, but not featuring suicidal ideas, guilt, and low self-esteem (Rosenberg et al., 2005). Furthermore, persons with AD and depression are twice as likely to develop delusions (Bassiony et al., 2002). The presence of delusions is associated with lower educational levels, African American race, severity of the dementia, and the use of anti-anxiety medications (Bassiony et al., 2000). Hallucinations are associated with older age, depression, aggression, poor health, and use of antihypertensive medications.

Course

Alzheimer's disease has a gradual onset and progresses with a slow, steady decline in the person's cognitive functioning (Steeman et al., 2006). The duration of its course ranges from 3 to 20 years, although 5 to 10 years is more common. Its causes are not yet known and there is no cure, although emerging medical treatments may slow its course.

Assessment

Social workers who are involved with clients who have dementia are likely to function as members of interdisciplinary health care teams. They can provide comprehensive psychosocial assessments of client and family functioning, but physicians and nurses must conduct medical evaluations. Social workers can provide a variety of psychosocial therapies (described later) that may be beneficial to clients' quality of life, and they may be particularly helpful in providing supportive services to family members and other caregivers.

Alzheimer's disease is unfortunately a "rule-out" diagnosis. Rather than being positively identified by medical examination and tests, it is ruled "in" if other possible conditions cannot account for the symptoms (Altman, 2001). This is also true, of course, of many *DSM* diagnoses that are based on observable behavior only. A physician is required to diagnose this disorder. Formally termed *dementia of the Alzheimer's type*, the disorder requires that the client demonstrate a gradual and progressive worsening of short-term memory and at least one of the other brain function impairments listed earlier (APA, 2000). The deficits must account for significant impairment in social and occupational functioning. Identifiable medical conditions that may cause the symptoms need to be ruled out. Alzheimer's disease may be recorded as *with early onset* (before age 65) or *with late onset*. A minority of AD patients develop the disorder in their 40s and 50s, and an earlier onset implies a more rapid course. This form of AD often runs in families and is most likely to have a purely genetic cause (McMurtray, Ringman, & Chao, 2006). The following symptoms of AD are listed in the order in which they develop:

- Loss of recent memory
- Loss of judgment
- Problems with abstract thinking
- Loss of higher order functions (planning)
- Personality changes (exaggerations of normal traits)

Some people with AD experience a phenomenon called *sundowning*—an increase in level of confusion during the late afternoon and evening hours.

Risk and Protective Mechanisms

Onset

Biological Risk Mechanisms

The risk and protective biological, psychological, and social mechanisms for the onset of AD are summarized in Exhibit 15.1, but the role of genetics and biology is universally accepted as critical in the etiology and course of AD, although specific information about these processes is lacking. An analysis of the Swedish Twin Registry reported a 58%–79% biological heritablility for AD for both men and women (Gatz et al., 2006). Age of onset is more similar for monozygotic than dizygotic twin pairs, however, which suggests an important role for environmental influences.

A healthy brain contains about 140 billion neurons, all of which generate electrical signals through neurotransmitter activity to help people think, remember, feel, and move. In people with AD, these neurons slowly die. As they die, lower levels of essential neurotransmitters are produced, creating signaling problems among cells. There is, for example, a reduction in the neurotransmitters acetylcholine and norepinephrine and an undesired increase in glutamate.

Autopsies of people with AD show that brain cells in the cortex and hippocampus, areas that are responsible for learning, reasoning, and memory, have become clogged with two abnormal structures. *Neurofibrillary tangles* are twisted masses of protein fibers inside cells or neurons, and *plaques* are deposits of a sticky protein called amyloid that is surrounded by debris from deteriorating neurons (Meeks, Ropacki, & Jeste, 2006). Alterations in the composition of blood vessels are also apparent. Although there is no agreement about the primary causes of AD, many agree that its symptoms begin with a protein called amyloid beta (Ziabreva, Perry, & Perry, 2006). All people produce this protein, which is harmless in small amounts. It is part of a larger molecule known as the amyloid-precursor protein (APP), a normal protein that extends from a neuron's outer membrane. While performing its normal

Exhibit 15.1

Risk and Protective Mechanisms for the Onset of Alzheimer's Disease

Risk	Protective
Genetic/Biological	
Advanced age (65 and over)	
Family history	No family history of Alzheimer's disease
Genetic (chromosome 1, 14 19, 21)	Genetics (APOE e2 allele)
Down syndrome	
History of head trauma	
Female gender	Male gender
Small strokes or cerebrovascular disease	No history of stroke or cardiovascular disease, low cholesterol
Diabetes	
African American or Hispanic	European American
Lack of exercise	Long-term exercise
Diet (fatty foods, low blood levels of folic acid and vitamin B_{12}, elevated plasma and homocysteine level)	Low-fat diet, high in folic acid and vitamin B_{12}, high fish diet
Environmental toxins (water pollutants, aluminum)	No ingestion of toxic metals and chemicals
Smoking cigarettes	No history of smoking
	Moderate wine consumption
	Use of nonsteroidal anti-inflammatory drugs
	Hormonal treatment
	Antihypertensive agents
Psychological	
Depression	Stable mood
Stress	Lower levels of stress
	Early detection and intervention
Social	
Low educational status	Higher educational status
Low occupational status	Higher occupational status
	Activities that require cognitive functions

Sources: Gatz et al. (2006); Jedrziewski, Lee, and Trojanowski (2005); McMurtray, Ringman, and Chao (2006): Nowotny, Smemo, and Goate (2005), Ownby, Crocco, Avecedo, John, and Loewenstein (2006), Ruitenberg, Ott, van Swieten, Hofman, and Breteler (2001); Ziabreva, Perry, and Perry (2006).

functions, APP gets "chopped up" by enzymes, leaving residue to dissolve in the brain's watery recesses (the glial cells). Occasionally, and for unknown reasons, a pair of enzymes (beta and gamma secretase) cleaves APP in the wrong places, leaving behind an insoluble amyloid fragment. Some people produce these "junk" neurons faster than others do, but after 70 or 80 years, all brains carry at least a modest amyloid burden.

Some amyloid molecules lose their natural spiral shape and flatten out. They become prone to bind to one another, forming fibrils, like woven carpet fibers, to create larger masses. Amyloid fibrils also bind with proteins like secretase, which makes them less soluble and still harder for the body to clear. Fibrils bind with each other to grow into plaques (thin, hard substances). When these substances reach a certain threshold, the brain can no longer function efficiently.

Alzheimer's disease may be transmitted genetically, and mutations in any of four genes (located on chromosomes 1, 14, 19, and 21) are associated with its development (Nowotny, Smemo, & Goate, 2005). Researchers speculate that the protein made by the apolipoprotein-4 (APOE-4) gene promotes the accumulation of amyloid in the brain or interferes with its removal. The APOE-2 and 3 proteins appear to protect against AD by strengthening structures vital to nerve cell functioning. Findings for APOE genes have been more consistent for Caucasians than for others. This indicates that APOE may not be the culprit itself but rather may be located near the "culprit" factor or that members of other groups possess other genes that blunt the effect of the genetic risk factors. Another example of this process is found in people with Down syndrome, which is related to an extra copy of chromosome 21. These persons also have an increased risk of AD, and mothers who deliver such children prior to age 35 also have an increased risk because they may carry the marker gene (Gatz et al., 2006)

Some biological risk influences for AD are associated with gender and race. There is a gender difference in AD, but not significantly until the age of 90, after which it is higher among women (Ruitenberg et al., 2001). One study of thousands of persons with AD and healthy volunteers revealed that the APOE-4 gene appears to increase the risk of AD for persons in many ethnic groups, but perhaps more consistently for Caucasians. It must be emphasized that AD is a genetically heterogenous disorder, and advances in the knowledge of the human genome may contribute to more accurate profiles of the development and course of the disorder (Papassotiropoulos, Fountoulakis, Dunckley, Stephan, & Reiman, 2006). Early-onset AD often runs in families and is most likely to have a purely genetic cause (McMurtray et al., 2006).

Several biological protective influences have been identified with AD (Jedrziewski, Lee, & Trojanowski, 2005). These include regular exercise, the maintenance of low cholesterol, the use of statins (medications that work to lower cholesterol) and the absence of head trauma. Dietary habits that include the ingestion of vegetables, fruits, cereals, saturated fats, omega-3 fatty acids, antioxidants, and the ginkgo herb are considered to be protective mechanisms, while unsaturated fats and high intake of meats are risk influences (Asada, 2007). Diabetes, which features poor glucose metabolism, is another biological risk influence.

Psychological Risk Influences

There are no known psychological causes of AD. When people begin to experience the symptoms, however, depression and anxiety are common. People may exhibit mood swings, become distrustful of others, and show increased stubbornness. Those emotional states and behaviors may be in response to frustration and changes in self-image, but biological reasons have also been offered to explain why depression is often present with AD (Ownby, Crocco, Acevedo, John, & Loewenstein, 2006). There is an association between late-onset depression and AD, in that such persons have a twofold risk of developing dementia (van Reekum et al., 2005). Higher rates of depression are found among first- and second-degree relatives of people with AD that includes depression in comparison with relatives of people who experience AD without additional cognitive or affective symptoms. This may be because the characteristic neurofibrillary tangles are higher in cerebral areas, where the pathogenesis of depression takes place, and thus the two disorders may share a biological association.

Social Risk Influences

Lifestyle factors may contribute to negative health conditions that put some people at greater risk for the disorder, although the role of these factors is somewhat speculative (Lyketsos et al., 2000). The prevalence of various possible contributing factors, including infections, nutritional deficiencies, brain injury, endocrine conditions, cerebrovascular diseases, seizure disorders, substance abuse, and brain tumors, varies across cultural groups. People with higher risks of these types may have relatively modest educational backgrounds and occupational status. Their lifestyles may include poor exercise habits, a greater likelihood of smoking cigarettes, and the ingestion of environmental toxins such as water pollutants and aluminum.

Protective risk influences for Alzheimer's disease are summarized in Exhibit 15.1.

Recovery and Adjustment

As noted earlier, AD features an unremitting downward course, but the quality of the person's life is often determined by the quality of health care and family support provided him or her. In this section we focus on the characteristics of caregivers that influence the person's adjustment.

Only one-third of people with dementia in the United States live in nursing homes (Boise et al., 2004), which means that families are the primary caregivers for these individuals. Although the symptoms of AD are distressing for the affected person, the situation may be equally or more stressful for the caregivers, particularly as the disease progresses (Phillipe, Lalloue, & Preux, 2006). The primary caregiver, usually a member of the client's family, is often required to take the lead in organizing interventions. This often creates an uncomfortable power shift in the relationship. The caregiver is challenged to monitor the client's changing levels of dependence and independence as the disease progresses. He or she must care for the loved one, preserve the client's dignity, and balance his or her own limits on time, energy, and patience. The stress to family member caretakers may be heightened by their fears of loss, guilt over not being an adequate caregiver, ambivalence about the caregiver role, competitiveness with each other, and fears about their own mortality.

It should be noted that there are activities enjoyed by persons with dementia and their family caregivers, although this is a seldom-researched topic. One study of 46 persons with dementia and their caregivers found that the following activities were listed as enjoyable by all parties involved: looking at photographs, sharing expressions of love, sharing meals, being outdoors, listening to music, laughing, reading or listening to the news, recalling past events, being with friends, and watching television (Searson, Hendry, Ramachandrian, Burns, & Purandare, 2008).

Positive associations have consistently been found between caregiver coping and patient quality of life (McClendon, Smyth, & Neundorfer, 2004). Caregivers with proactive problem-solving strategies are less stressed than those with avoidance coping strategies (Cooper, Katona, Orrell, & Livingston, 2008). One study of persons with AD living in the community found a positive association between caregiver coping and patient survival time (McClendon et al., 2004). Conversely, the caregiver's internalizing (vs. shared) coping style was correlated with shorter recipient survival time. The authors speculate that the more withdrawn-internal caregivers are less psychologically available to the person with dementia and may provide less person-centered care. Another study of caregivers, representing all stages of the disease, found that the availability of emotional support for the caregiver has a mediating effect on depression, somatic complaints, and life satisfaction (Cooper et al., 2004).

There are some differences among caregivers of older adults (not limited to AD) from different ethnic groups with regard to stress, resource availability, and psychological outcomes. Minority caregivers are younger, less likely to be a spouse, and more likely to receive informal support from persons outside the family (Pinquant & Sorensen, 2006). They provide more care than Caucasian caregivers and feel stronger obligations to do so. Asian American caregivers use less formal support than Caucasian caregivers, and are more depressed than their Caucasian counterparts. Asian American families are slower to seek professional interventions than

Western families, being more likely to rely on cultural traditions of family caregiving (Jones, Chow, & Getz, 2005).

Other differences among ethnic groups have been noted. Hispanic caregivers experience less depression, lower levels of role captivity (being constrained from managing other life roles), and higher amounts of self-acceptance than non-Hispanic caregivers (Morano & Sanders, 2005). Further, for Hispanic caregivers the subjective sense of burden mediates the effects of stress on somatic complaints and depression (Morano, 2003). African American caregivers experienced lower levels of caregiver burden than Caucasian caregivers. All ethnic minority caregivers reported worse physical health than Caucasian caregivers, however.

Vascular Dementia

Vascular dementia (VaD) is a progressive, irreversible cognitive disorder caused by blocked blood vessels to the brain due to cerebral infarction or hemorrhage. (The word *vascular* refers to blood vessels.) It accounts for 10% to 15% of all types of dementia (Waldemar et al., 2007). Vascular dementia was once known as *multi-infarct* dementia because it typically results from a person's experiencing several strokes (episodes of sudden paralysis due to breaking blood vessels in the brain). The physiological disturbances affect small and medium-size cerebral brain vessels, which undergo disruption and produce permanent areas of injury. The onset of VaD is usually abrupt and features a fluctuating course that includes periods of stability followed by periods of rapid decline in functioning (in contrast to the slower progression of AD). The diagnostic criteria for VaD include the following:

- Memory impairment
- One or more of the cognitive disturbances (aphasia, apraxia, and agnosia)
- Disturbances in executive functioning
- The presence of specific neurological signs and symptoms or evidence of cerebrovascular disease that is judged to be etiologically related to the disturbance

The *DSM-IV* diagnosis may include the specifiers with *delirium*, *delusions*, *depressed mood*, or *uncomplicated*. The specifier *with behavioral disturbance* may also be used. Prior to diagnosis, several medical conditions must first be ruled out, including delirium from underlying physical illness, adverse drug reactions, infections, and reactions to sensory disturbances and environmental stresses. Unlike AD, the central nervous system damage can be assessed with computerized tomography and magnetic resonance imaging. White matter lesions, for example, are significantly more prevalent and observable in magnetic resonance examinations of persons with VaD (Hentschel, Damina, Krumm, & Froelich, 2007).

Thus, people with AD are otherwise healthier than people with VaD. The latter disease is more clearly the result of preexisting cardiovascular health problems. Depression is also more common (up to eight times more so) in VaD than in AD (Newman, 1998). Persons with VaD also experience more diminished bone mineral density during the course of the disorder (Suzuki et al., 2007).

Prevalence

Vascular dementia affects between 12.2% and 31.8% of stroke victims within 3 months to 1 year after the stroke (Mackowiak-Cordoliani, Bombois, Memin, Henon, & Pasquier, 2005). It is approximately one-third as prevalent as AD among persons aged 65 years (affecting 1.5%) and half as prevalent as AD among persons aged 80, affecting approximately 10% of that population (Dartigues, 2004; Fitspatrick et al., 2004). Prevalence rates are slightly higher among African American persons.

Comorbidity

Depression is a relatively frequent complication of VaD, more so than with AD (Bonavita et al., 2001). Approximately 27% of people with VaD experience major depression. Psychological factors play an important role, but there may be organic reasons for the association because the severity of VaD is correlated with the proximity of lesions to the left frontal pole in the brain. People with the dementia also tend to have other health problems, which can be expected because the disorder is an outcome of cardiovascular conditions.

Course

Particularly high rates of dementia are observed following clinical stroke, with a nine-fold increase in risk over the first year, followed by a two-fold annual risk each year afterward (Wells & Whitehouse, 2000). The pattern of deficits in VaD is variable, depending on which regions of the brain are damaged. Severity of the disorder can range from minor to excessive symptom presentations (Waldemar et al., 2007).

Assessment

The symptomatic heterogeneity of VaD often hinders accurate diagnosis (Dib, 2001). In fact, the symptoms often overlap with those of AD (10%–15% of patients have both types of dementia). Furthermore, some researchers specify subtypes of VaD (small-vessel, large-vessel, and a combined small-vessel/Alzheimer's type), which makes the condition difficult to distinguish from other dementias (Andin, Gustafson, Brun, & Passant, 2006). While the number of neuropsychiatric symptoms is similar in both AD and VaD, the types of symptoms differ (Fernandez-Martinez et al., 2008). Specifically, sleep disturbances, appetite changes, and aberrant motor behaviors are less prevalent in VaD.

Researchers disagree about the appropriate means of diagnosing VaD. The *DSM* criteria are questioned because they allow a high degree of subjective judgment and require evidence of multiple cognitive deficits. These are serious concerns because dementia is most treatable in its early stages; thus, clients can benefit greatly from early diagnosis.

Researchers debate the level of cerebral vascular pathology that must be present to permit a valid diagnosis (Stewart, 2002). The initial stages of dementia are characterized by fatigue, difficulty in sustaining mental performance, and the tendency to fail in novel or complex tasks. Early diagnosis in high-risk people is difficult, and its accuracy will require the development of advanced imaging markers and global diagnostic tools. Some researchers have proposed subtypes of VaD. One such classification might include Type 1, for major diseases such as strokes, Type 2 for smaller lesions, and Type 3 for damage to certain areas of white brain matter.

Risk and Protective Mechanisms

Onset

Biological Risk Mechanisms

As already described, biological processes are responsible for damage to the nervous system that results in the onset of VaD. Although the precise health factors that put a person at risk for VaD are unknown, the health history often includes long-standing hypertension and vascular disease processes (Stewart, 2002). Other risk influences for VaD include hypertension, smoking, diabetes, cardiac rhythm disorders, excess body fat, high cholesterol, and an imbalance in antioxidant activity (Exhibit 15.2). Vascular dementia is more common in men, who are likelier to develop hypertension and other cardiovascular diseases (Ruitenberg et al., 2001).

There are conflicting reports about the status of diabetes as a risk mechanism for dementia. A 5-year study of 5574 subjects, initially without cognitive impairment, in the Canadian Study on Health and Aging revealed no association between diabetes and the incidence of AD, although such an association was found with VaD (MacKnight, Rockwood, Await, & McDowell, 2002). Evidence of the role of vascular factors in the onset of AD was also found, supporting the idea that vascular health factors may play a role

Exhibit 15.2	
Risk and Protective Factors for the Onset of Vascular Dementia	
Risk Factors	Protective Factors
Biological	
Genetic vulnerability (APOE)	No genetic loading for APOE
High blood pressure	Normal blood pressure
High fat levels	Normal fat levels
Diabetes	
Glucose intolerance	Normal insulin processing, glucose tolerance
Lifestyle factors (no smoking, exercise)	Lifestyle factors (smoking, lack of
CNS inflammation	Absence of CNS disease activity
Cerebral perfusion	
Neuroendocrine dysfunction	
Oxidative stress	
Excitotoxicity	
Vascular (blood vessel) disease	
Stroke	
Ischemia	
Amyloid deposits	
Psychological	
Stress experiences that affect blood pressure and general health	Stress management skills
Depression	Stable mood
Social	
Lower educational level	Higher educational level
Inadequate social support	Functional social support
Poor access to health care	Access to health care
Lower socioeconomic status	Higher socioeconomic status
CNS, central nervous system.	

in the onset of both disorders. More recent literature reviews also support the causal link between diabetes and VaD (Misciagna, Masullo, Giordano, & Silveri, 2005).

Psychological and Social Risk Influences

No psychological mechanisms are associated with the onset of VaD or a worsening of symptoms. As with AD, however, it is likely that lifestyle factors influence a person's physical health in ways that may be protective of, or put the person at risk for, the dementia. Regarding psychological factors, stress has been shown to have a negative influence on cardiovascular functioning and could be a factor in sustaining a person's high blood pressure (Boston, Dennis, & Jagger, 1999). Regarding social influences, low educational and socioeconomic status is associated with exercise, smoking, and diet practices that may be significant contributors to the onset of VaD (Atchley, 2000).

Intervention

Medications

No known medical treatment exists at the present time to cure AD or stop the progression of the disease. Tacrine, the first drug approved by the Food and Drug Administration (FDA), has been the most extensively studied thus far, with only modest success. However, many people cannot tolerate the drug because of side effects, and only 30% of consumers experience its intended benefits, so it has been used infrequently in recent years (Qizilbash et al., 1998).

The FDA has approved four other drugs since 1994 that are intended to have a mild to moderate effect on its presentation: tacrine (Cognex), done-pezil, rivastigmine (Exelon), and galantamine (Reminyl) (Kalb & Rosenberg, 2004). Like tacrine, these are all classified as *cholinesterase inhibitors*, which work by inhibiting the breakdown of a key brain chemical, acetylcholine. The medications may at best slow the process and temporarily stabilize some of the symptoms. A systematic review reveals that these medications may improve cognitive function and global level of functioning in mild to moderate AD, but no solid evidence exists yet for their positive impact in severe dementia (Birks, 2006).

The ideal remedy for AD would slow the production of amyloid by disabling the enzymes that fabricate it (Altman, 2001; Atchley, 2000). Current drug research is focused on the development of *beta secretase*, since the earlier *gamma blockers* seemed to interfere with normal brain function. Other drugs being targeted prevent the binding of amyloid fragments to form fibrils (Chen, Zhang, Li, & Le, 2007). Still other drugs may bolster the immune system to ward off development of amyloid or control the distribution of glutamate in the brain, which occurs when a person's amyloid burden rises and, when chronically elevated, destroys neurons (Schulte-Herbruggen, Jockers-Scherubl, & Hellweg, 2008). New drugs under investigation may mimic the protective actions of enzymes known as APOE-2 or 3, or block the effects of another relevant enzyme, APP-4. Drug therapy (and perhaps diet) may be able to decrease blood levels of certain enzymes, remove excess amyloid, and support growth factors that keep brains healthy (Lavretsky, Nguyen, & Goldstein, 2006). Although the role of the APOE enzyme in the production of AD is questionable, several insurance companies have investigated the possibility of requiring APOE blood tests for subscribers prior to granting them health coverage, a highly controversial move.

Other types of medications may be effective for treating the symptoms of psychosis, agitation, and depression in persons with AD and VaD (Raicu & Workman, 2000). These are only briefly mentioned here because they are described more fully in other chapters of this book. In general, all psychotropic medications are prescribed in lower doses for elderly clients than for other age groups because of their slower metabolism and rates of clearance through the kidneys (Bentley & Walsh, 2006). The effectiveness of these medications may also be compromised by interactions with other medications the person might be taking. Older adults tend to be more sensitive than younger age groups to the adverse physical effects of all medications. Although it is the physician's responsibility to titrate medications appropriately, the social worker should participate in the process by monitoring their positive and negative effects through observation and discussion with the client and family.

The only effective medications for reducing or eliminating symptoms of psychosis and agitation are the antipsychotic drugs (Ballard, Waite, & Birks, 2006). No differences in effectiveness have been found between the older ("conventional") and newer ("atypical") medications. The choice of a drug often depends on the side-effect profile. Some antipsychotic drugs tend to be sedating, and others are more likely to induce muscle stiffness, among other possible adverse effects.

Antidepressant drugs are used for the symptoms of depression and agitation often experienced by dementia clients. One systematic review of controlled studies found weak support for the contention that antidepressants are an effective intervention for persons with depression and dementia (Bains, Birks, & Dening, 2002). Another review of randomized trials found that antidepressant drugs improved depression but did not reduce agitation (Sink, Holden, & Yaffe, 2005). The newer selective serotonin reuptake inhibitors are generally the first choice of physicians because of their relatively mild side-effect profiles. The antianxiety benzodiazepine drugs and the anticonvulsant drugs may also be helpful in reducing agitation among people with dementia (Stahl, 2008).

Psychosocial Interventions

Because of the inevitable progression of both of these dementias, nonmedical interventions are focused on promoting the client's safety, comfort, and productivity for as long as possible, and helping the family or other caregivers be more capable of managing the stress that often accompanies their role (Phillipe et al., 2006). Unfortunately, it was not until the 1980s that health care professionals demonstrated a commitment to working with clients who have dementia, as evidenced by staffing and resources, and began developing formal intervention protocols (Cohen, 2001). Many psychosocial interventions are widely accepted by professional caregivers as effective, but there is not yet extensive research supporting these assumptions. Before we discuss some of these interventions, practice guidelines regarding the range of interventions that social workers and other professionals might apply with clients follow (Rabins et al., 2002).

Establish and maintain an alliance with the client and family. Useful principles for developing a positive worker–client relationship with people who have dementia include maintaining a calm, reassuring demeanor with the client, using simple language, asking one question at a time, speaking slowly, always referring to the client by name, being alert to certain words to which the client consistently responds, trying to interact with the client when he or she is calm, being alert to nonverbal communications, and moving slowly in the client's presence.

Arrange and participate in a diagnostic evaluation, and link the client with resources for any needed medical care. Although the social worker cannot directly engage in medical testing, he or she can provide appropriate case management activities (referral, linkage, follow-up, and advocacy) to make sure that a thorough evaluation is conducted.

Assess and monitor the client's noncognitive (emotional and behavioral) mental status. This includes being alert to the possibility of the client's developing problems with depression and anxiety.

Monitor provisions for the client's safety and intervene when appropriate. Some standard guidelines for family members who have a client living at home are providing the client with a safe, structured, predictable routine; minimizing the intrusion of environmental stimuli that may be overwhelming; minimizing the demands to which the client must respond; and distracting the client from confusing or agitating situations (Epple, 2002; Finkel, 2001).

Intervene to decrease the hazards of the client's wandering behavior (if applicable). Families may be helped to minimize the potential dangers of this behavior by locking doors, putting small "gates" at the top of staircases, or simply becoming alert to signs of the client's tendency to wander.

Advise the client and family concerning driving and other client activities that put people at risk. Family members often feel guilty or cannot agree on when to set limits on some of these activities, and the practitioner's "objective" point of view may be useful in resolving dilemmas.

Educate the client and family about the illness and available interventions. Families may have no knowledge of the process of cognitive decline or the many services available in (some) communities to manage it.

Advise the family regarding sources of care and support. Psychoeducational interventions with family members and caregivers are essential, and their positive outcomes are supported by the literature. Families need to be educated about how to interact with the client, modify the client's environment, provide appropriate types of support, and manage their own sense of burden. Respite care should ideally begin during the early phase of the disorder so that the client comes to accept it as a standard part of the routine. As dementia progresses, the client may resist any such changes.

Assess and refer the family for assistance with any related financial and legal issues. The stresses related to long-range money management and decisions about conservatorship require professional consultation if available.

One issue that often arises in working with impaired older adults is that professionals, like family members and other caregivers, are inclined to become controlling of the behavior and choices of clients. A study of 80 social workers in three northeastern states indicated that less support is held for the autonomy of people with AD than for people with VaD (Healy, 1999). That is, the practitioners tended to become authoritarian and directive in working with these clients. Social workers were most controlling if they had concerns about client safety and caregiver burden. These professional behaviors may be appropriate, but when working with these clients, social workers should be careful to uphold the value of self-determination to the extent possible.

Interventions for people with dementia are described in Exhibit 15.3. In a review of studies according to a ranking formulated by the Oxford Centre for Evidence-Based Medicine, only behavioral management, staff training on behavioral management, and cognitive stimulation earned a grade of "B" based on evidence of benefit in studies (in an A through D ranking system) (Livingston, Johnston, Katona, Paton, & Lyketsos, 2005). Other reviews have centered on these interventions. Although reminiscence therapy did not receive a good recommendation in Livingston et al. (2005), a Cochrane Center systematic review of reminiscence therapy involving four randomized controlled trials indicated improvements from reminiscence therapy on the person's cognitive capacity and mood, as well as functional ability (Woods, Spector, Jones, Orrell, & Davies, 2005). Reminiscence therapy also reduced strain for caregivers. Another Cochrane review was done on validation therapy, but methodologically strong studies were lacking on which to base conclusions (Neal & Wright, 2003).

Behavioral interventions can be effective in reducing or abolishing certain problem behaviors characteristic of clients with dementia, including aggression, screaming, poor hygiene, and incontinence (Logsdon, McCurry, & Teri, 2007). Behavioral conditioning becomes less effective as one's dementia progresses, due to the decreased responsiveness to external stimuli, and thus it is more indicated in the early stages of the disorder (Spira & Edelstein, 2007). There is little evidence that such interventions are effective in reducing wandering behavior, however (Robinson et al., 2006). As an aside, there have been no randomized, controlled trials focusing on wandering, which is a major behavioral concern among those with dementia (Hermans, Htay, & McShane, 2007).

Interventions

Intervention	Description
Behavioral interventions	Using the principles of operant therapy, involves the following steps: (1) Clarify the target behavior, breaking it into steps if necessary. (2) Identify the relevant antecedent cues and consequent reinforcers of target behavior. (3) Enlist assistance of caregivers in developing new environmental conditions (antecedents) that will increase likelihood of desired behavior. (4) Teach caregivers how to reinforce client's performance of desired behaviors (with praise, hugs, or a special "reward" activity).
Reminiscence therapy	Stimulate client's memory and mood in the context of systematically discussing events in his or her life history
Validation therapy	Accepting the reality and personal truth of of the person with dementia's experiences without argument, which is is believed to help by facilitating freeemotional expression and also potentially resolving old conflicts (Feil & De Klerk-Rubin, 2002; Neal & Wright, 2003)
Reality orientation	Providing factual information (day, date, weather, time, names) to orient client to current circumstances
Cognitive stimulation therapy	Uses information processing rather than facts to orient the client
Sensory enhancement	Includes music therapy, hand massage, and the like
Art therapy	Focus on the person's self-expression through visual and musical means, which may help tapinto memories (Abraham, 2005)

A meta-analysis of interventions for older adults with cognitive (and other) disorders provides empirical support for several of the strategies described in this section (Bharani & Snowden, 2005). Further, memory and cognitive retraining interventions and support groups for caregivers are classified as "probably efficacious." That is, they have been validated by at least two experiments with waitlist control groups, one or more group experiments by a single investigator, or less than three single-case experiments that used comparison groups.

Interventions for Caregivers

As discussed, family burden is significant when an elderly parent has dementia. Psychoeducational interventions are used with groups of families or individual families with programs ranging from four to 20 sessions

(Corcoran & Gleason-Wynn, 2003). The intervention helps caregivers understand the process of dementia and to cope with their mixed emotional reactions (Gallagher-Thompson et al., 2003). Caregivers can benefit from planned respite care, information about dementia, services, benefits, and recognition for their hard work. In addition, they need help in recognizing and dealing with caregiver stress. Only group psychoeducational interventions appear to positively affect depression in caregivers, however (Thompson et al., 2007). Such support groups for caregivers are classified as "probably efficacious" (Bharani & Snowden, 2005).

Brodaty, Green, and Koshers (2003) conducted a meta-analysis of 30 studies to review outcomes of caregiver interventions, most of which were psychoeducational. The studies included predominantly female spouses. Overall the interventions were found to significantly reduce caregiver depression and improve knowledge, coping skills, and social support. However, caregiver burden was not lessened. Including the care receiver was found to be important to the success of a program.

Social Diversity

With regard to VaD and (to a lesser extent) AD, persons of low socioeconomic status appear to be at higher risk because of their consumption of high-fat foods, vitamin deficiencies, poor exercise habits, and ingestion of environmental toxins (Patterson, Feightner, Garcia, & MacKnight, 2007). The existence of protective mechanisms related to diet and lifestyle suggest that the social worker must make special efforts to reach members of these groups and provide education about self-care issues related to lifestyle and diet even before they develop any symptoms of dementia.

The dementias overwhelmingly affect the special population of older adults, which mandates that caregivers (often younger family members) be involved in the intervention process when possible. In order to secure appropriate supportive services for all members of the family, social workers need to be adept at assessing diverse family forms with their unique strengths and limitations. For example, some families are inclusive of extended relatives, while others are small with rigid boundaries. Hispanic caregivers experience less depression and higher amounts of self-acceptance than other caregivers, African American caregivers experience lower levels of caregiver stress than Caucasian caregivers, and Asian American caregivers tend to me more depressed than Caucasian caregivers and also less engaged with formal support services (Morano & Saunders, 2005). Professionals must be prepared to engage in more outreach with Asian American families.

Critique of the Diagnosis of Dementia

Research on AD and VaD overwhelmingly concludes that both disorders result from degenerative biological processes in the brain. There appear to be no significant psychological or social factors that directly affect their onset, although their ultimate course (particularly with VaD) may be either exacerbated or slowed in response to some emotional and social factors. For these reasons, the dementias are universally accepted as medical disorders. Disorders that have strong biological components such as these do not generate much debate within the social work profession about negative labeling, stigma, subjectivity, and the effects of values on diagnosis. Alzheimer's disease and VaD are among the more easily accepted *DSM* disorders by social workers.

Case Study

Mary Louise Hollman was an 80-year-old married mother of three grown children, two of whom lived nearby. She and her retired husband, John, also had nine grandchildren. Since her husband retired 15 years ago, they had led moderately active lives, including daily walks and frequent visits with their children and friends. Having emigrated from Germany in early childhood, the couple had never been sociable with their more "Americanized" neighbors. Mary Louise was in generally good physical condition, but John had a history of heart problems and was now using a pacemaker. His activities were restricted because he needed to be careful about his level of exertion. They had limited financial resources and were living in a trailer park.

Mary Louise had been complaining of forgetfulness for the past 5 years. She had trouble remembering where she put such items as her keys, money, books, grocery store items, and other small personal items. Occasionally her memory slips were dangerous, such as when she forgot to turn off the stove after cooking. Mary Louise usually laughed about these oversights, making jokes about the trials of the aging process. Her children were only mildly concerned about her cognitive functioning. They assumed that forgetfulness was typical of most people in their mid-70s and beyond. Indeed, they were all over 40 years old and had begun to notice that their own memory skills were not as sharp as they once were. Mary Louise's own mother, however, had experienced AD for the last 7 years of her life, so Mary Louise and her family members carried a quiet concern about her welfare. One afternoon when her daughter Kathleen was visiting, Mary Louise asked where the bathroom was. This startled Kathleen and convinced her that Mary Louise's memory problem had become serious.

Assessment and Diagnosis

Kathleen persuaded her reluctant father to schedule an appointment for Mary Louise with the family physician. After John described the presenting problems, Dr. Hinson suspected dementia, considering Mary Louise's age and reported course of memory decline. The doctor first conducted a mental status examination of Mary Louise's sense of time and place and her ability to remember, understand, communicate, and compute simple math problems. In assessing the family history, Dr. Hinson learned that Mary Louise's mother had experienced similar signs of memory loss at about the same age. The patient's mother had in fact lived with the Hollman family during the last 5 years of her life. This established a genetic link to AD.

Dr. Hinson completed a comprehensive physical exam to more systematically investigate the possibility of dementia. He wanted to rule out any physical conditions that might be causing Mary Louise's worsening memory, such as hypothyroidism, vitamin B12 or folic acid deficiency, niacin deficiency, neurosyphilis, and infections. Blood and urine tests yielded no support for these factors. Mary Louise had suffered no head trauma, so it was unlikely she had suffered a subdural hematoma (brain swelling). John confirmed that Mary Louise had never been much of a drinker and had never used nonprescription drugs.

Following his tests, Dr. Hinson concluded that no physical or medication-related conditions were contributing to Mary Louise's memory loss and confusion. Prior to diagnosis, however, he referred Mary Louise for a neurological exam, cognitive screening exam, and brain scan (magnetic resonance image) to further assess possible medical causes of her condition. He also recommended a full psychiatric examination to rule out mood factors (especially major depression) that might be contributing to the symptoms. These tests confirmed significant deficits in Mary Louise's memory, vision-motor coordination, and language skills but yielded no signs of strokes, tumors, or other medical problems. The psychological testing revealed that Mary Louise was experiencing moderate anxiety and depression, but these symptoms appeared to center around an awareness of her memory loss.

With all of this information, the following diagnosis was made for Mary Louise:

Axis I: Dementia of the Alzheimer's Type, With Late Onset, Uncomplicated (Mary Louise displayed no significant symptoms of delusions or delirium, and her depression appeared to be only moderate. It is possible that over time her condition might change, and one of these specifiers would be added.)

Axis II: No diagnosis

Axis III: Alzheimer's disease (Because it is a medical condition, AD is recorded on this axis even though it may seem redundant with the Axis I diagnosis.)

Axis IV: None. Although the Hollman family had limited material resources, they were accustomed to living within their means and had experienced no stress related to this issue.

Axis V: Current GAF = 40 (serious impairment in reality testing), Highest in Past Year = 55 (moderate symptoms)

Goal Formulation and Treatment Planning

After reviewing the full medical report, Dr. Hinson prescribed donepezil (Aricept) for Mary Louise, one of the four FDA-approved drugs for the treatment of AD. The medications do not stop the onset or progression of the disorder, but it was hoped that the drug would slow the process and temporarily stabilize some of the symptoms. He also referred Mary Louise and her husband to a comprehensive senior citizens service center in her community. A social worker there helped the couple develop an intervention plan. The goals included the following:

- To maintain Mary Louise's current levels of cognitive and physical functioning as long as possible
- For Mary Louise to function as a contributing member of her family and community
- To reduce Mary Louise's feelings of sadness and anxiety
- For Mary Louise's family members to become more knowledgeable about dementia, including an awareness of all community support services

The first two goals would be addressed by Mary Louise's participation in three formal group activities provided at the community center. *Reminiscence* group therapy, a process of sharing memories of major events and transitions in one's life, was appropriate because older memories are more durable than newer ones in persons with AD (Tadaka & Kanagawa, 2007). The purposes of the group are to reduce apathy, alleviate depression, and increase social interaction, life satisfaction, morale, self-esteem, and the client's sense of control. The *remotivation* group is a structured discussion program that includes the goals of stimulating and revitalizing individuals who have lost interest in the present or the future (Metiteri et al., 2001). It serves to resocialize members to events in their social worlds and encourage their pursuit of interests to the extent possible. Each session revolves around a common topic like pets, gardening, art, hobbies, holidays, and vacations. All of the group sessions were 30 minutes in duration, which is considered appropriate for older adults with mental and physical limitations. For people with AD, however, reality orientation efforts should be constant and involve every staff member at the center throughout the day.

Mary Louise's third goal would be addressed through her participation in exercise groups and other activities with her family and friends, such as walking, housekeeping, gardening, and maintaining contact with her friends in the neighborhood. Mary Louise was in good physical condition, but to sustain her activity routine she would need to be regularly encouraged and directed or she may begin to forget about these activities. Mary Louise's final goal would be addressed through the family's modulating her environment and reducing stimuli when she becomes anxious. Soothing music and designated quiet areas often help with this. Surrounding her with mementos from her children and friends might promote a positive attitude, by keeping alive memories of her loved ones. Helping her family members learn to offer reassurance when she is anxious or sad would also be important. Mary Louise can be helped to learn and practice relaxation exercises to manage her anxiety.

The final goal would be addressed by the social worker meeting with Mary Louise's husband, John, and their two children who lived in town on a weekly basis for 4 weeks to provide them with a structured family education series about AD and the typical challenges experienced by caregivers. The family would be encouraged to share responsibility for Mary Louise's supervision and monitoring and to take advantage of respite opportunities, particularly as the disease progresses. They would also be encouraged to participate in the senior center's monthly support group for the relatives of dementia patients.

None of the health care professionals who worked with Mary Louise could predict the course of deterioration of her cognitive functioning. All of them agreed, however, that while the medication might provide some benefit, the group and family interventions were most critical for maximizing her potential for ongoing quality of life. They were advised by the social worker to frequently encourage the client and family's participation because, as noted earlier, they did not have a history of extensive social integration.

Summary

All of the cognitive disorders have primarily biological origins. Not all of them are degenerative, although this chapter has focused on two types of dementia that are. It is fortunate that delirium, the most common cognitive disorder, is always temporary (it can also be a symptom of many other *DSM* disorders) and that the amnestic disorders are reversible in many cases. Furthermore, the mental status of clients with several of the dementias related to specific health problems may also be stabilized and improved. Social workers who intervene with any of these clients are likely to do so as members of interdisciplinary health care teams. They can provide a variety of psychosocial therapies that may be beneficial to clients' functioning levels and quality of life, and they may be particularly helpful in providing supportive services to family members and other caregivers. Despite the biological causes of the dementias, attention to all aspects of the client's functioning is significant to their course.

References

Abraham, R. (2005). *When words have lost their meaning: Alzheimer's patients communicate through art.* Westport, CT: Praeger Publishers/Greenwood Publishing Group

Altman, L. J. (2001). *Alzheimer's disease.* San Diego, CA: Lucent.

American Psychiatric Association. (2000). *Diagnostic and statistical manual of mental disorders* (4th ed., text rev.). Washington, DC: Author.

Andin, U., Gustafson, L., Brun, A., & Passant, U. (2006). Clinical manifestations in neuropathologically defined subgroups of vascular dementia. *International Journal of Geriatric Psychiatry, 21,* 688–697.

Asada, T. (2007). Prevention of Alzheimer's disease: Putative nutritive factors. *Psychogeriatrics, 7*(3), 125–131.

Atchley, R. (2000). *Social forces and aging: An introduction to social gerontology.* Belmont, CA: Wadsworth.

Bains, J., Birks, J., & Dening, T. (2002). Antidepressants for treating depression in dementia. *Cochrane Database of Systematic Reviews, 4,* CD003944.

Ballard, C. G., Waite, J., & Birks, J. (2006). Atypical antipsychotics for aggression and psychosis in Alzheimer's disease. *Cochrane Database of Systematic Reviews,* Issue 1. Art. No.: CD003476. DOI: 10.1002/14651858.CD003476.pub2.

Bassiony, M. M., Warren, A., Rosenblatt, A., Baker, A., Steinberg, M., Steele, C. D., Sheppard, J. E., & Lyketsos, C. G. (2002). The relationship between delusions and depression in Alzheimer's disease. *International Journal of Geriatric Psychiatry, 17,* 549–556.

Bentley, K. J., & Walsh, J. (2006). *The social worker and psychotropic medication* (3rd ed.). Pacific Grove, CA: Brooks/Cole.

Bharani, N., & Snowden, M. (2005). Evidence-based interventions for nursing home residents with dementia-related behavioral symptoms. *Psychiatric Clinics of North America, 28,* 985–1005.

Birks, J. (2006). Cholinesterase inhibitors for Alzheimer's disease. *Cochrane Database of Systematic Reviews, 1,* Art. No.: CD005593. DOI: 10.1002/14651858.CD005593.

Boise, L., Neal, M. B., & Kaye, J. (2004). Dementia assessment in primary care: Results from a study in three managed care systems. *The Journals of Gerontology Series A: Biological Sciences and Medical Sciences, 59,* M621–M626.

Bonavita, V., Iavarone, A., & Sorrentino, G. (2001). Depression in neurological diseases: A review. *Archives of General Psychiatry, suppl.7,* 49–66.

Boston, P. F., Dennis, M. S., & Jagger, C. (1999). Factors associated with vascular dementia in an elderly community population. *International Journal of Geriatric Psychiatry, 14,* 761–766.

Brodaty, H., Green, A., & Koshera, A. (2003). Meta-analysis of psychosocial interventions for caregivers of people with dementia. *Journal of the American Geriatrics Society, 51*(5), 657–664.

Chen, S., Zhang, X. J., Li, L., & Le, W. (2007). Current experimental therapy for Alzheimer's disease. *Current Neuropharmacology, 5*(2), 127–134.

Clare, L., Goater, T., & Woods, B. (2006). Illness representations in early-stage dementia: A preliminary investigation. *International Journal of Geriatric Psychiatry, 21*(8), 761–767.

Cohen, G. D. (2001). Criteria for success in interventions for Alzheimer's disease. *American Journal of Geriatric Psychiatry, 9*(2), 95–98.

Cooper, C., Katone, C., Orrell, M., & Livingston, G. (2004). Coping strategies and anxiety in caregivers of people with Alzheimer's disease: The LASER-AD study. *Journal of Affective Disorders, 90*(1), 15–20.

Corcoran, J., & Gleason-Wynn, P. (2003). Psychoeducation with Caregivers of Older Adults. In J. Corcoran, *Clinical applications of evidence-based family interventions* (pp. 297–320). New York: Oxford.

Cummings, L. J., & Cole, G. (2002). Alzheimer's disease. *Journal of the American Medical Association, 287,* 2335–2339.

Dartigues, J. F. (2004). Epidemiology and prevalence of Alzheimer's disease and risk factors. *Psychogeriatrics, 4*(4), 120–123.

Epple, D. M. (2002). Senile dementia of the Alzheimer's type. *Clinical Social Work Journal, 30,* 95–110.

Feil, N., & De Klerk-Rubin, V. (2002). *The validation breakthrough: Simple techniques for communicating with people with "Alzheimer's-Type Dementia"* (2nd ed.). Baltimore: Health Professions Press.

Fernandez-Martinez, M., Castro, J., Molano, A., Zarranz, J. J., Rodrigo, R. M., & Ortega, R. (2008). Prevalence of neuropsychiatric symptoms in Alzheimer's disease and vascular dementia. *Current Alzheimer's Research, 5*(1), 61–69.

Finkel, S. I. (2001). Behavioral and psychological symptoms of dementia: A current focus for clinicians, researchers, and caregivers. *Journal of Clinical Psychiatry, 62* (Suppl. 21), 3–6.

Fitspatrick, A. L., Kuller, L. H., Ives, D. G., Lopez, O., Jagust, W., Breitner, J. C. S., Jones, B., Lyketsos, C., & Dulberg, C. (2004). Incidence and prevalence of dementia in the cardiovascular health study. *Journal of the American Geriatrics Society, 52*(2), 195–204.

Gallagher-Thompson, D., Haley, W., Guy, D., Rupert, M., Argüelles, T., Zeiss, L. M., Long, C., Tennstedt, S., & Ory, M. (2003). Tailoring psychological interventions for ethnically diverse dementia caregivers. *Clinical Psychology: Science and Practice, 10*(4), 423–438.

Gatz, M., Reynolds, C. A., Fratiglioni, L., Johansson, B., Mortimer, J. A., Berg, S., Fishe, A., & Pedersen, N. L. (2006). Role of genetics and environments for explaining Alzheimer's disease. *The Archives of General Psychiatry, 63,* 168–174.

Grassel, E., Wiltfang, J., & Kornhuber, J. (2003). Non-drug therapies for dementia: An overview of the current situation with regard to proof of effectiveness. *Dementia and Geriatric Cognitive Disorders, 15*(3), 115–125.

Healy, T. C. (1999). Community-dwelling cognitively impaired frail elders: An analysis of social workers' decisions concerning support for autonomy. *Social Work in Health Care, 30,* 27–47.

Hentschel, F., Damina, M., Krumm, B., & Froelich, L. (2007). White matter lesions – Age-adjusted values for cognitively healthy and demented subjects. *Acta Neurologica Scandinavica, 115*(3), 174–180.

Hermans, D., Htay, U., & McShane, R. (2007). Non-pharmacological interventions for wandering of people with dementia in the domestic setting. *Cochrane Database Systematic Review, 1,* CD005994.

Isenberg, K. E. (2005). Cognitive disorders: Delirium and amnestic disorder. In E. H. Rubin, C. F. Zorumski, & C. F. Madden (Eds.), *Adult psychiatry* (2nd ed., pp. 154–181). Malden, MA: Blackwell.

Jedrziewski, M. K., Lee, V. M., & Trojanowski, J. Q. (2007) Physical activity and cognitive health. *Alzheimers Dementia, 3*(2), 98–108.

Jones, R. S., Chow, T. W., & Getz, M. (2005). Asian Americans and Alzheimer's disease: Assimilation, culture, and beliefs. *Journal of Aging Studies, 20*(1), 11–25.

Kalb, C., & Rosenberg, D. (2004). Nancy's next campaign. *Newsweek, 143*(25), 39–44.

Kong, E. H., Evans, L., & Guevara, J. (2009). Nonpharmacological intervention for agitation in dementia: A systematic review and meta-analysis. *Aging and Mental Health, 13*, 512–520.

Lavretsky, H., Nguyen, L. H., & Goldstein, M. Z. (2006). Diagnosis and treatment of neuropsychiatric symptoms in Alzheimer's disease. *Psychiatric Services, 57*(5), 617–619.

Livingston, G., Johnston, K., Katona C., Paton, J., & Lyketsos, C. G. (2005). Systematic review of psychological approaches to the management of neuropsychiatric symptoms of dementia. *American Journal of Psychiatry, 162*, 1996–2021.

Logsdon, R. G., McCurry, S. M., & Teri, L. (2007). Evidence-based psychological treatments for disruptive behaviors in individuals with dementia. *Psychology and Aging, 22*(1), 28–36.

Lyketsos, C. G., Steinberg, M., Tschanz, J. T., Norton, M. C., Steffens, D. C., & Breitner, J. C. S. (2000). Mental and behavioral disturbances in dementia: Findings from the Cache County study on memory in aging. *American Journal of Psychiatry, 157*, 708–714.

MacKnight, C., Rockwood, K., Await, E., & McDowell, I. (2002). Diabetes mellitus and the risk of dementia, Alzheimer's disease and vascular cognitive impairment in the Canadian study of health and aging. *Dementia and Geriatric Cognitive Disorders, 14*, 77–83.

Mackowiak-Cordoliani, M. A., Bombois, S., Memin, A., Henon, H., & Pasquier, F., (2005). Poststroke dementia in the elderly. *Drugs and Aging, 22*(6), 483–493.

McClendon, M. J., Smyth, K. A., & Neundorfer, M. M. (2004). Survival of persons with Alzheimer's disease: Caregiver coping matters. *The Gerontologist, 44*(4), 508–519.

McMurtray, A. M., Ringman, J., & Chao, S. Z. (2006). Family history of dementia in early-onset versus very late-onset Alzheimer's disease. *International Journal of Geriatric Psychiatry, 21*(6), 597–598.

Meeks, T. W., Ropacki, S. A., & Jeste, D. V. (2006). The neurobiology of neuropsychiatric syndromes in dementia. *Current Opinion in Psychiatry, 19*(6), 581–586.

Metiteri, T., Zanetti, O., Geroldi, C., Frisoni, G. B., DeLeo, D., Dello Buono, M., Bianchetti, A., & Trabucchi, M. (2001). Reality orientation therapy to delay outcomes of progression in patients with dementia: A retrospective study. *Clinical Rehabilitation, 15*(5), 471–478.

Misciagna, S., Masullo, C., Giordano, A., & Silveri, M. C. (2005). Vascular dementia and Alzheimer's disease: The unsolved problem of clinical and neuropsycholgical differential diagnosis. *International Journal of Neuroscience, 115*, 1657–1667.

Mizrahi, R., & Starkstein, S. E., (2007). Epidemiology and management of apathy in patients with Alzheimer's disease. *Drugs and Aging, 24*(7), 547–554.

Morano, C. L. (2003). Appraisal and coping: Moderators or mediators of stress in Alzheimer's disease caregivers. *Social Work Research, 27*(2), 116–128.

Morano, C. L., & Sanders, S. (2005). Exploring differences in depression, role captivity, and self-acceptance in Hispanic and non-Hispanic adult children caregivers. *Journal of Ethnic and Cultural Diversity in Social Work, 14*(1-2), 27–46.

Neal, M., & Wright, P. B. (2003). Validation therapy for dementia. *Cochrane Database of Systematic Reviews*, 3, Art. No.: CD001394. DOI: 10.1002/14651858.CD001394.

Newman, S. C. (1998). The prevalence of depression in Alzheimer's disease and vascular dementia in a population sample. *Journal of Affective Disorders*, 52(169–176).

Nomura, T. (2002). Evaluative research on reminiscence groups for people with dementia. In J. D. Webster & B. K. Haight (Eds.), *Critical advances in reminiscence work: From theory to application* (pp. 289–299). New York: Springer.

Nowotny, P., Smemo, S., & Goate, A. M.. (2005). Genetic risk factors for late-onset Alzheimer's disease. In C. F. Zorumski & E. H. Rubin (Eds.), *Psychopathology in the genome and neuroscience era* (pp. 51–62). Washington, DC: American Psychiatric Publishing.

Ownby, R. L., Crocco, E., Avecedo, A., John, V., & Loewenstein, D. (2006). Depression and risk for Alzheimer's disease. *Archives of General Psychiatry*, 63, 530–538.

Papassotriopoulos, A., Fountoulakis, M., Dunckley, T., Stephan, D. A., & Reiman, E. M. (2006). Genetics, transcriptomics, and proteomics of Alzheimer's disease. *The Journal of Clinical Psychiatry*, 67(4), 652–670.

Patterson, C., Feightner, J., Garcia, A., & MacKnight, C. (2007). Primary prevention of dementia. *Alzheimers and Dementia*, 3(4), 348–354.

Phillipe, T., Lalloue, F., & Preux, P. (2006). Dementia patients' caregivers' quality of life: The PIXEL study. *International Journal of Geriatric Psychiatry*, 21(1), 50–56.

Pinquant, M., & Sorensen, S. (2006). Ethnic differences in stressors, resources, and psychological outcomes of family caregiving: A meta-analysis. *The Gerontologist*, 45, 90–106.

Qizilbash, N., Whitehead, A., Higgins, J., Wilcock, G., Schneider, L., & Farlow, M. (1998). Cholinesterase inhibition for Alzheimer's disease: A meta-analysis of the tacrine trials. *Journal of the American Medical Association*, 280(20), 1777–1782.

Rabins, P., Bland, W., Bright-Long, L., Cohen, E., Katz, I., Rovner, B., et al. (2002). Practice guidelines for the treatment of patients with Alzheimer's disease and other dementias of late life. In American Psychiatric Association (Ed.), *Practice guidelines for the treatment of psychiatric disorders* (pp. 67–135). Washington, DC: American Psychiatric Association.

Raicu, R. G., & Workman, R. H. (2000). Management of psychotic and depressive features in patients with vascular dementia. *Topics in Stroke Rehabilitation*, 7(3), 11–19.

Robinson, L., Hutchings, D., Corner, L., Beyer, F., Dickinson, H., & Vanoli, A. (2006). A systematic literature review of the effectiveness of non-pharmacological interventions to prevent wandering in dementia and evaluation of the ethical implications and acceptability of their use. *Health Technology Assessment*, 10(26).

Rosenberg, P. B., Onyikel, C. U., Katz, I. R., Porsteinsson, A. P., Mintzer, J. E., Schneider, L. S., Rabins, P. V., Meinerto, C. L., Martin, B. K., & Lyketsol, C. G. (2005). Clinical application of operationalized criteria for "Depression of Alzheimer's Disease." *International Journal of Geriatric Psychiatry*, 20, 119–127.

Ruitenberg, A., Ott, A., van Swieten, J. C., Hofman, A., & Breteler, M. M. B. (2001). Incidence of dementia: Does gender make a difference? *Neurobiology of Aging*, 22, 575–580.

Schofield, I. (2008). Delirium: Challenges for clinical governance. *Journal of Nursing Management*, 16(2), 127–133.

Schulte-Herbrüggen, O., Jockers-Scherübl, M. C., & Hellweg, R. (2008). Neurotrophins–from pathophysiology to treatment in Alzheimer's disease. *Current Alzheimer's Research*, 5(1), 38–44.

Searson, R., Hendry, A. M., Ramachandran, R., Burns, A., & Purandare, N. (2008). Activities enjoyed by patients with dementia together with their spouses and psychological morbidity in carers. *Aging & Mental Health, 12*(2), 276–282.

Sink, K. M., Holden, K. F., & Yaffe, K. (2005). Drugs minimally effective for neuropsychiatric symptoms of dementia. *The Journal of Family Practice, 54*(5), 407.

Spira, A. P., & Edelstein, B. A. (2007). Operant conditioning in older adults with Alzheimer's disease. *The Psychological Record, 57*, 409–427.

Stahl, S. M. (2008). *Stahl's essential psychopharmacology: Neuroscientific basis and practical applications.* New York: Cambridge University Press.

Steeman, E., Decasterle, B. D., Godderis, J., & Grypdonck, M. (2006). Living with early-stage dementia: a review of qualitative studies. *Journal of Advanced Nursing, 54*(6), 722–738.

Stewart, R. (2002). Vascular dementia: A diagnosis running out of time? *British Journal of Psychiatry, 180*, 152–156.

Suh, G. H., & Shah, A. (2001). A review of the epidemiological transition in dementia: Cross-national comparisons of the indices related to Alzheimer's disease and vascular dementia. *Acta Psychiatrica Scandinavia, 104*, 4–11.

Suzuki, A., Fukuo, K., Yasuda, O., Taniguchi, K., Kitano, S., & Ogihara, T. (2007). Different changes of bone mineral density and nutritional status after hospitalization between vascular dementia and Alzheimer's disease in elderly female patients. *Geriatrics and Gerontology International, 7*(4), 363–370.

Tadaka, E., & Kanagawa, K. (2007). Effects of reminiscence group in elderly people with Alzheimer's disease and vascular dementia in a community setting. *Geriatrics & Gerontology International, 7*(2), 167–173.

Thompson, C. A., Spilsbury, K., Hall, J., Birks, Y., Barnes, C., & Adamson, J. (2007). Systematic review of information and support interventions for caregivers of people with dementia. *BMC Geriatrics, 7*, 18.

Tucker-Drob, E. M., Johnson, K. E., & Jones, R. N. (2009). The cognitive reserve hypothesis: A longitudinal examination of age-associated declines in reasoning and processing speed. *Developmental Psychology, 45*(2), 431–446.

Van Reekum, R., Binns, M., Clarke, D., Chayer, C., Conn, D., Hermrmann, H. S., Mayberg, H. S., Rewilak, D., Simard, M., & Stuss, D. T. (2005). Is late-life depression a predictor of Alzheimer's disease? Results from a historical cohort study. *International Journal of Geriatric Psychiatry, 20*, 80–82.

Vinters, H. V. (2006). Neuropathology of amnestic mild cognitive impairment. *Archives of Neurology, 63*(5), 645–646.

Waldemar, G., Dubois, B., Emre, M., Georges, J., McKeith, G., Rossor, M., Schultens, P., Tariska, P., & Winblad, B. (2007). Recommendations for the diagnosis and management of Alzheimer's disease and other disorders associated with dementia: EFNS guidelines. *European Journal of Neurology, 14*, 1–26.

Wells, C. E., & Whitehouse, P. J. (2000). Dementia. In B. S. Fogel, R. B. Schiffer, & S. M. Rao (Eds.), *Synopsis of neuropsychiatry* (pp. 425–435). Philadelphia: Lippincott Williams & Wilkins.

Woods, B., Spector, A. E., Jones, C. A., Orrell, M., & Davies, S. P. (2005). Reminiscence therapy for dementia. *Cochrane Database of Systematic Reviews, 2*, Art. No.: CD001120. DOI: 10.1002/14651858.CD001120.

Ziabreva, I., Perry, E., & Perry, R. (2006). Altered neurogenesis in Alzheimer's disease. *Journal of Psychosomatic Research, 61*(3), 311–316.

Appendix: Instruments Used to Assess Dementia

The Mini-Mental Status Examination (Folstein, Folstein, & McHugh, 1975)

Description

- Assesses a client's orientation, recall, attention, ability to perform basic calculations, and language comprehension
- Tracks changes in a client's cognitive state over time
- A client responds to questions, makes calculations, is asked to complete several tasks, and copies a design.
- A person can score between 0 and 30 points; a score below 23 suggests significant impairment, and a score below 20 indicates definite impairment.

Reliability

- Tested with 206 respondents diagnosed with dementia, psychotic disorders, and personality disorders, and 63 controls.
- Twenty-four-hour test-retest reliability was .89 with the same examiner, and .83 with multiple examiners.
- Clinically stable respondents had a .98 score correlation over 28 days.

Validity

- Test scores accurately separated the clinical sample into those with dementia, depression, and depression with cognitive impairment.
- Concurrent validity was demonstrated by correlating MMSE scores with WAIS scores; resulting Pearson's Rs were .78 for verbal IQ and .66 for performance IQ.

The Clinical Dementia Rating Scale (Hughes, Berg, Danziger, Cohen, & Martin, 1982; Marin et al., 2001)

Description

- Measures levels of cognitive and functional impairment in persons with dementia, utilizing the six domains of memory, orientation, judgment and problem solving, home and hobbies, community affairs, and personal care
- Each domain is rated according to five levels of impairment (none to severe)
- A global score (0–3) reflects overall performance in the six domains.
- May be administered by any human services provider to a client or significant other

Reliability
Interrater reliability was measured between .95 and .98 for the six domains, and .99 for the global score.

Validity

The CDR was validated against the Mini-Mental Status Examination using a one-way analysis of variance with a test for linearity.

The Pocket Smell Test (Duff, McCaffrey, & Solomon, 2002)

Description

- Olfactory dysfunction has been noted in AD and other neuropsychiatric conditions. This test is a three-item "scratch and sniff" measure used to discriminate elderly people with AD from those with VaD or major depression.
- On each item, the examiner releases an odor by scratching the odor patch with a pencil. The client smells the odor and chooses one of four response alternatives. These may be read to clients, and they are encouraged to guess if they are not sure of a response. Correct responses are lemon, lilac, and smoke.
- Two or more errors are highly suggestive of AD.

Reliability

Reliability was not reported.

Validity

Among clients previously diagnosed with AD, VaD, and major depression (N = 60), classification accuracy was 95%, sensitivity was 100%, and specificity was 92.5%.

The Ten-Point Clock Test (Moretti, Torre, Antonello, Cassato, & Bava, 2002)

Description

- Assesses cognitive impairment and is helpful in distinguishing disease processes from normal aging. Also helps to distinguish AD from VaD.
- An 11.4 cm diameter circle is traced with a template. The client is asked to put the numbers on the face of the clock and then make the clock read 10 minutes after 11. A 10-point scoring system is used to quantify the accuracy of the spatial arrangement of the numbers and setting of the hands.

Reliability

Reliability is not reported.

Validity

Significant correlations were reported with client scores on a variety of other measures (Mini-Mental Status Examination, a proverb test, tests of language fluency and visual-spatial skills). Scores of clients with AD and VaD also correlated significantly with different measures.

The Quality of Life-Alzheimer's Disease (QOL-AD) Scale (Thorgrimsen et al., 2003)

Description

- A dementia-specific 13-item self-report scale covering the areas of physical energy, energy, mood, living situation, memory, family, marriage, friends, chores, fun, money, self, and life as a whole
- Persons with mild to moderate dementia can accurately complete the scale.
- Scored on a four-point Likert scale, yielding a single score
- Can also be completed by caregivers

Reliability

- Cronbach's alpha = .82
- Interrater reliability exceeded .70.

Validity

- Instrument established content validity.
- Construct validity was good with the principal component analysis showing all 13 items of the scale loading on the QOL factor.

References for Assessment Instruments for Dementia

Duff, K., McCaffrey, R. J., & Solomon, G. S. (2002). The pocket smell test: Successfully discriminating probable Alzheimer's dementia from vascular dementia and major depression. *Journal of Clinical Neuropsychiatry, 14*(2), 197–201.

Folstein, M. F., Folstein, S., & McHugh, P. R. (1975). Mini-mental state: A practical method for grading the cognitive state of patients for the clinician. *Journal of Psychiatric Residency, 12,* 189–198.

Hughes, C. P., Berg, L., Danziger, W. L., Cohen, L. A., & Martin, R. L. (1982). A new clinical scale for the staging of dementia. *British Journal of Psychiatry, 140,* 566–572.

Marin, D. B., Flynn, S., Mare, M., Lantz, M., Hsu, M. A., Laurans, M., Paredes, M., Shreve, T., Zaklad, G. R., & Mohs, R. C. (2001). Reliability and validity of a chronic care facility adaptation of the Clinical Dementia Rating Scale. *International Journal of Geriatric Psychiatry, 16,* 745–750.

Moretti, R., Torre, P., Antonello, R. M., Cassato, G., & Bava, A. (2002). Ten-point clock test: A correlation analysis with other neuropsychological test in dementia. *International Journal of Geriatric Psychiatry, 17,* 347–353.

Thorgrimsen, L., Selwood, A., Spector, A., Royan, L., de Madariaga, M., Woods, R. T., & Orrell, M. (2003). Whose quality of life is it anyway? The validity and reliability of the Quality of Life-Alzheimer's Disease (QOL-AD) scale. *Alzheimer's Disease and Associated Disorders, 17*(4), 201–208.

adult(s)
   disorders of. *See* adult disorders
   older. *See* older adults
adult disorders, 369–466. *See also specific*
         disorders
   bipolar disorder, 371–402
   depression, 253–93. *See also* depression,
         in adults
   interventions for, medications, 381–85,
         382t–83t
   personality disorders, 403–34
   schizophrenia, 435–66
Agoraphobic Cognitions Questionnaire
         (ACQ), 200
Agoraphobics Building Independent
         Lives (ABIL) support group, 184
akathisia, 446
Alcoholics Anonymous (AA), 297
   in substance use disorders
         management, 309–11
alpha-2 agonists, for ODD and CD,
         110–11
alternative treatments, for depression,
         264, 265t–66t
Altman Self-Rating Mania Scale,
         399–400
Alzheimer's disease (AD), 472–79, 475t
   assessment of, 473–74
   biological factors, 474–77, 475t
   case study, 489–92
   comorbidity of, 472–73
   course of, 473
   described, 472
   measures for, 498–500
   prevalence of, 472
   psychological factors, 475t, 477
   recovery and adjustment, 477–79
   risk and protective factors,
         474–77, 475t
   social factors, 475t, 477
American Academy of Child and
         Adolescent Psychiatry, 171
   on pedophilia, 341
American Association for Intellectual and
         Developmental Disabilities
         (AAIDD), 37–38, 53
American Association on Mental
         Retardation, 37–38

American Medico-Psychological
         Association, 13
American Psychiatric Association (APA)
   criticisms of *DSM* of, 22–23
   in *DSM* evolution, 14–21
   mental disorders defined by, 12
   mental disorders recognized by, 4, 13
American Society of Addiction
         Medicine, Patient Placement
         Criteria for the Treatment of
         Substance-Related Disorders of,
         302, 304
amnestic disorders, 471–72
anorexia nervosa
   assessment of, 224
   behavior types in, 221
   biological factors, 224t–25t, 225–26
   comorbidity of, 222–23
   course of, 223
   described, 221–22
   interventions for, 230–32
         Maudsley model, 231–32
         medications, 232
         psychosocial, 231–32
   prevalence of, 222
   psychological factors, 225t, 226–27
   recovery and adjustment, 228–29
   risk and protective factors, 224–28,
         224t–25t
   social diversity in, 235
   social factors, 225t, 227–28
   suicidal behavior and, 223
anticholinergic(s), in schizophrenia
         management, 446
anticonvulsant(s), for bipolar disorder,
         382t, 384
antidepressant(s)
   for bipolar disorder, 383t, 385
   for VaD, 484
antipsychotic(s)
   for bipolar disorder, 382t–83t, 385
   for ODD and CD, 110
   for VaD, 484
anxiety
   defined, 161
   described, 161–62
   symptoms of, 161–62
      monitoring of, 172

Behavioral and Emotional Rating Scale
(BERS), 61–62
behavioral disorders, classification of,
13–14
behavioral interventions
for PDDs, 77–78
for VaD, 486, 487t
benzodiazepine(s), for anxiety disorders,
180
beta secretase, 483
biological factors
in AD, 474–77, 475t
in borderline personality disorder,
410t, 411, 413t
in eating disorders, 224t–25t, 225–26
in ODD and CD, 98t, 99–100
in pedophilia, 342–43, 346t, 347t
in schizophrenia, 440–42, 440t
in VaD, 481–82, 482t
bipolar disorder, 371–402
assessment of, 376–77
instruments in, 399–401
brain functioning in, 378–79
case study, 390–93
comorbidity of, 373–74
course of, 374–76
risk and protective factors in, 380t
described, 371
diagnosis of, critique of, 390
family factors in, 381
features of, 371–72
genetics in, 377–78, 378t
insight into, 380
interventions for, 381–90, 382t–83t
anticonvulsants, 382t, 384
antipsychotics, 382t–83t, 385
CBT, 387–88
ECT, 385
family interventions, 386–87
FTT, 387
IPT, 387
lithium, 382t, 384
psychoeducation, 386
psychosocial, 386–88
prevalence of, 373
psychosocial factors, 378t, 379
recovery and adjustment, 379–81
recovery model of, 388–90

risk and protective factors, 377–79,
378t, 380t
stress and, 381
subtypes of, 372–73
types of, 372
bipolar disorder not otherwise specified,
372
diagnosis of, 377
bipolar I disorder
comorbidity of, 373
course of, 374
described, 372
prevalence of, 373
bipolar II disorder
course of, 374
described, 372
prevalence of, 373
birth complications, schizophrenia
related to, 440t, 441–42
Body Sensations Questionnaire (BSQ), 199
borderline personality disorder, 405t,
406–425, 410t, 413t
assessment of, 409–10
biological factors, 410t, 411, 413t
case study, 421–25
comorbidity of, 407–8
course of, 408
described, 406–7
diagnosis of, critique of, 421
interventions for
cognitive/schema therapy, 418
DBT, 415–16
integrated therapy, 419
IPT, 417–18
MBT, 417
medications, 419–20
psychodynamic, 416–17
psychosocial, 414–19
TFP, 417
prevalence of, 407
psychological factors, 410t, 411, 413t
recovery and adjustment, 412–14
risk and protective factors, 410–12,
410t, 413t
social diversity in, 420
social factors, 410t, 411–12, 413t
brain functioning, in bipolar disorder,
378–79

schizophrenia (*Continued*)
    social support, 444
    social work roles, 447
    SST, 448
    vocational rehabilitation, 450–51
  measures for, 461–65
  paranoid, 436
  prevalence of, 436–37
  psychological factors, 440t, 442
  recovery and adjustment, 443–45
  residual, 436
  risk and protective factors, 439–43,
    440t, 443t
  social diversity in, 451
  social factors, 440t, 443
  social stigma of, 444–45
  stress/diathesis theory for, 439–40
  subtypes of, 436
  symptoms of, 435–36
  undifferentiated, 436
  in utero complications and, 440t,
    441–42
school interventions, for ADHD,
    137–39
selective norepinephrine reuptake
    inhibitors (SNRIs), for ODD and
    CD, 109–10
selective serotonin reuptake inhibitors
    (SSRIs), for anxiety disorders, 180
sensitization
  covert, in pedophilia management,
    349–50
  imaginal, in pedophilia management,
    350
separation anxiety disorder, described,
    162
sertindole, in schizophrenia
    management, 446
sexual arousal reconditioning, in
    pedophilia management, 350
sexual disorders, 337–67. *See also*
    pedophilia
  measures for, 363–66
  paraphilias, 337–38
  pedophilia, 337–67
Sexual Interest Cardsort Questionnaire
    (SICQ), 364–65
sexual minorities

anxiety disorders and, 182
depression and, 274
substance use disorders and, 311–12
SMD. *See* standardized mean difference
    (SMD)
SNRIs. *See* selective norepinephrine
    reuptake inhibitors (SNRIs)
Social Anxiety Scale for Children
    (SASC-R), 196
social diversity
  in anxiety disorders, 181–82
  in borderline personality disorder, 420
  in depression, 273–75
  in eating disorders, 235
  in schizophrenia, 451
  in substance use disorders, 311–14
    and LAMBDA, 311
  in VaD, 488
social factors
  in AD, 475t, 477
  in borderline personality disorder,
    410t, 411–12, 413t
  in eating disorders, 225t, 227–28
  in ODD and CD, 98t–99t, 101–2
  in pedophilia, 344–45, 346t, 348t
  in schizophrenia, 440t, 443
  in VaD, 482–483, 482t
social phobia, described, 162–63
Social Phobia and Anxiety Inventory
    (SPAI), 198
Social Phobia and Anxiety Inventory for
    Children (SPAI-C), 196–97
Social Phobia Inventory (SPIN), 199
social skills training (SST)
  for PDDs, 79
  in schizophrenia management, 448
social stigma, schizophrenia and, 444–45
social support, in schizophrenia
    management, 444
social work
  characteristics of, 12
  DSM and, 11–33
social work interventions
  focus of, 12
  in schizophrenia management, 447
societal factors, in eating disorders, 225t,
    227–28
socioeconomic status